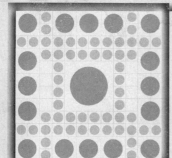

Economics
A Tool for Critically Understanding Society

Ninth Edition

Tom Riddell
Smith College

Jean Shackelford
Bucknell University

Geoffrey Schneider
Bucknell University

Steve Stamos
Bucknell University

Addison-Wesley

Boston   Columbus   Indianapolis   New York   San Francisco   Upper Saddle River
Amsterdam   Cape Town   Dubai   London   Madrid   Milan   Munich   Paris   Montreal   Toronto
Delhi   Mexico City   Sao Paulo   Sydney   Hong Kong   Seoul   Singapore   Taipei   Tokyo

THE PEARSON SERIES IN ECONOMICS

*denotes myeconlab titles

Log onto www.myeconlab.com to learn more

Editorial Director: Sally Yagan
Editor in Chief: Donna Battista
Acquisitions Editor: Noel Kamm Seibert
Editorial Assistant: Carolyn Terbush
Director of Marketing: Kate Valentine
Executive Marketing Manager: Lori DeShazo
Marketing Assistant: Justin Jacob
Senior Manufacturing Buyer: Carol Melville
Managing Editor: Nancy H. Fenton
Senior Production Project Manager: Nancy Freihofer
Permissions Project Supervisor: Michael Joyce
Cover Designer: Elena Sidorova
Cover Art: © Murat Taner/Corbis
Supplements Editor: Alison Eusden
Production Coordination, Text Design, and Composition: Elm Street Publishing Services
 and Integra Software Services Pvt. Ltd.
Printer/Binder: Courier Stoughton
Cover Printer: Courier Stoughton
Text Font: Janson

Credits and acknowledgments borrowed from other sources and reproduced, with permission, in this textbook appear on appropriate page within text or on page 605.

Library of Congress Cataloging-in-Publication Data

Economics: a tool for critically understanding society/Tom Riddell ... [et al.]; with contributions
 by Bill Cooper.—9th ed.
 p. cm.
 Includes bibliographical references and index.
 ISBN 0-13-136849-4 (alk. paper)
 1. Economics. I. Riddell, Tom, 1944–
HB171.5.R43 2009
330—dc22

                    2009041845

10 9 8 7 6 5 4 3

Addison-Wesley
is an imprint of

www.pearsonhighered.com

ISBN 10:   0-13-136849-4
ISBN 13: 978-0-13-136849-1

Brief Contents

Contents

PART 1

Economic Methodology, History, and the Development of Modern Economic Thought   1

CHAPTER 3   Adam Smith, Classical Liberalism, and the Division of Labor   33

CHAPTER 4   Karl Marx and the Socialist Critique of Capitalism   48

CHAPTER 5   The Rise and Fall of Laissez-Faire in the U.S. Economy   64

PART 2

Microeconomics 89

CHAPTER 9   Noncompetitive Markets and Inefficiency   164

CHAPTER 10   Resource Markets and the Distribution of Income   193

CHAPTER 11   Corporations and Labor Unions   220

CHAPTER 12   The Economic Role of Government   244

PART 3

Macroeconomics   285

CHAPTER 13   Macroeconomics: Issues and Problems   287

CHAPTER 14   Macroeconomic Theory: Classical and Keynesian Models   313

CHAPTER 15   Fiscal Policy: Government Spending and Taxation   349

CHAPTER 16   Financial Markets, Money, and Monetary Policy   375

CHAPTER 22   Modern Economic Systems   550

Foreword

Economics: A Tool for Critically Understanding Society is basically a one-semester text, although it may be appropriate for use in some full-year introductory economics courses. The scope of the book is less than that of most full-year texts. It does not try to cover everything. We emphasize the fundamentals of economics and focus on relevant applications of those concepts. In our experience, too much information, too much qualification, and too much supplementary material can get in the way of a solid foundation in the essential and relatively simple concepts. Furthermore, adequate examples from contemporary economic events are reported in the press every day to complement and enrich textbook economics.

Our objective through each edition has been to retain simplicity while at the same time adequately covering the basic micro- and macroeconomic concepts.

NEW TO THE NINTH EDITION

In the ninth edition of *Economics: A Tool for Critically Understanding Society* we have updated economic data and commentary on policy and critical issues. We have continued reorganizing the first section of the book by integrating economic history, history of economic thought, and methodology into Part 1. Other topics such as the global economy have been moved to later sections of book. Substantial revisions include the following:

❖ Reorganization of the introductory chapters integrating economic methodology, economic history, and the history of economic thought.

❖ Aspects of the former Chapter 2 exploring issues of the global economy are now integrated throughout the text in Parts 2–4.

❖ Extensive coverage of the 2007–2009 financial crisis, including integrating current events with economic theory.

❖ Coverage of the 2007–2009 Great Recession in the United States and aspects of government programs to prevent depression.

❖ A new section on the liberal market economies and coordinated market economies that comprise modern economic systems.

❖ Additional box features highlighting current issues.

❖ Companion Website updates that include new material as well as examples transferred from earlier editions of the text.

❖ Significantly revised and updated "Thinking Critically" sections.

Throughout the text, we have continued to supplement the development of basic economic concepts with cartoons and articles. We have reduced the number of reproduced articles based on the conclusion that a multitude of examples is available from following current economic events and requiring (or encouraging) students to read a newspaper. To emphasize the development of critical thinking and the controversial nature of economics, each part of the text ends with a "Thinking Critically" section with different views of important issues. In addition, the chapters contain questions for students to answer as they read through and review the text. We introduced this concept in the fifth edition, and we are delighted to see that it has been adopted by other economic principles texts. We feel it continues to provide a strong pedagogical contribution.

Consequently, we are convinced (both in theory and in practice) that this text is suitable for use in either one-semester or full-year courses. The Preface to the Instructor contains suggested outlines for one-semester and two-semester courses. Obviously, in a full-year course, there is more time to use supplementary material on issues or themes in modern economics.

The remarkable economic downturn and financial collapse experienced in the United States and throughout the world in 2008 and 2009 saw growth subside and unemployment soar. The first year of the Obama administration dealt with rising jobless rates, home foreclosures, and a financial system unable to perform its primary functions. An array of government programs was implemented to rescue the economy from a repeat of the Great Depression of the 1930s. These two years are in stark contrast to the preceding decade, when the U.S. economy found itself in excellent shape following a period of record-setting economic growth that featured both low unemployment and low inflation that began in 1995. Increases in worker productivity (worker output per hour) and budget surpluses produced the longest recorded period of economic growth in U.S. history. However, following the September 2001 terrorist attacks on the United States and the continuing wars in Iraq and Afganistan, budget deficits returned and political, economic, and foreign policy agendas turned toward domestic policies centered around military expenditures and homeland security.

In early 2001, a series of economic scandals were uncovered involving large-scale corporate fraud in major U.S. companies. And an "overbought" technology sector—hyped by misleading reporting—plummeted, wiping out billions of dollars of corporate and personal wealth and depleting the retirement funds of others. A decade earlier the banking system went through a similar period of turmoil. In the late 1980s, hundreds of savings banks around the country failed; in the 1990s and in 2003, bank mergers literally changed the face of the industry. Increased international competition and one-stop banking increased. Today, financial fraud scandals and loose regulation of financial institutions and markets have once again wiped out not only retirement funds but many banks and financial institutions as fallout from a housing bubble continues.

Even before the Great Recession of 2007–2009 caused unemployment rates to soar, workers were finding relatively fewer high-paying jobs and more low-wage jobs. Families continued to rely on multiple wage earners to make adequate family incomes. Despite some reforms, discrimination against women and minorities continued to deprive many of the chance for full economic advancement. As the population and labor force become increasingly diverse, job and wage discrimination will be an even greater challenge.

On the international scene, the United States continues to run persistent trade deficits and to face sharp competition in domestic and international markets from other advanced nations and from some of the newly industrializing countries. International debt problems pose potential threats to the stability of the international financial system. Extensive poverty and hunger throughout the world assault our sensitivities and responsibilities. Environmental problems such as climate change, the disposal of toxic wastes, deforestation, and the depletion of the ozone layer require truly global solutions. In the post–Cold War period, we have seen events that challenge peace and lead to uncertainty, including the dramatic changes sweeping Eastern Europe, the rise of nationalism in many areas of the world, continuing regional conflicts including those in the Middle East, along with a worldwide terrorist threat.

This list of problems is not all-inclusive, but it is suggestive. It highlights the economic importance of the U.S. and global economies at the start of the twenty-first century. This combination of strengths and weaknesses provides fertile ground for politicians, the media, and the public at large, as economists try to understand what is going on. What accounts for economic successes and failures? How can we address these economic problems and restore economic growth and stability? How can we utilize the resources at our disposal to respond to human needs? How do students now make their way in this world and find gainful employment?

The recent experiences of the U.S. economy and its historical roots have produced ferment in the field of economics. There are many competing explanations for U.S. successes and failures. Economists even disagree about what to call a problem. Conservative economists have their explanations about what is wrong with the economy and how their policies will correct it. Those further to the right chime in with their own theories and suggestions. Keynesian and neo-Keynesian economists focus on the limitations inherent in these approaches and offer their solutions. Further to the left, based on their own assumptions and economic perspectives, other economists argue for industrial policy, public ownership, democratic economic planning, and increased attention to economic equity.

These debates are not sterile. They are a part of the public dialogue in this country—in the media, in political campaigns, in communities—about important problems and what to do about them. An informed position—indeed, being an informed citizen in a liberal democracy—requires following events, paying attention to the discussion, and developing an understanding of how the economy works. In this context, the study of economics can contribute to our efforts to develop a critical understanding of our society and to work actively toward improving its performance in the future.

This introductory economics textbook is dedicated to promoting that effort. It attempts to develop fundamental economic tools of analysis in clear, simple, and understandable terms. It is designed to encourage the application of those tools to analyzing the most important economic issues facing the country, the world, and its people. And it emphasizes the variety of theories and ideas that economists and others have developed to explain U.S. and world economic events. We believe that the approach of this text helps students develop their critical ability to understand and analyze economic problems. It is readable, emphasizes relevant concerns, and does not avoid controversy. It is "user friendly."

ACKNOWLEDGMENTS

Once again, we appreciate the contributions of numerous staff members at Pearson, Noel Seibert, Nancy Fenton, Nancy Freihofer, Carolyn Terbush, Alison Eusden, and Angela Lee. They have been supportive in their assistance, advice, and cooperation in this edition of *Economics: A Tool for Critically Understanding Society*. We appreciate their contributions. We are particularly indebted to Denise Clinton for her encouragement and perseverance. Bucknell University has continued to provide support for our work.

Colleagues who offered helpful criticisms and suggestions for improving the text include Dean Baker, Adrienne Birecree, Greg Krohn, John Pool, Charles Sackrey, Frank Slavik, and David Wells. For past editions of the text, we appreciate the work of Teresa Amott, David Black, Jeffrey Blais, Victor Brajer, Paul Briggs, Fikret Ceyhun, Kace Chalmers, Norris Clement, James Cobbe, Thomas Cook, E. R. Dietrich, Anthony Dukes, Robert Drago, Cynthia Foreman, Gary E. Francis, Lorenzo Garbo, John R. Garrett, Heather Grob, John A. Hansen, Richard B. Hansen, John S. Heywood, Steve Hickerson, Mariam Khawar, Christine B. Lloyd, Stewart Long, Tom Maddox, Claron Nelson, Ned C. Pearlstein, Charlotte A. Price, Bruce Richard, Bruce Roberts, Edward A. Sayre, Philip Schuchman, Harry George Shaffer, Larry Simmons, Robert Sonora, Donald C. Tetmeyer, Mariano Torras, Dale Warnke, Stephen L. Widener, Edward Young, and Michael Zweig. For the ninth edition, we are grateful to Clare Battista, William Doyle, Robin Koenigsberg, Gary McDonnell, Orgul Ozturk, and Valerie Voorheis for their comments. Over the course of nine editions, we have received valuable research and preparation assistance from Brian Brinkman, Bob Brown, Chad Brown, Elizabeth Buchanan, Diane Collins, Dan Dillon, Lauren Ewald, Seth Foreman, Beverly Griffith, Karen Guarino, Patricia Hohl, Tony John, Jenae Johnson, Sharon Killian, Susan Lehman, Stephanie Metz, James O'Connor, Pam Paaso, Jill Pompeii, Stephanie Quinn, Christie Rowe, Kaitlin Shepard, Letitia Sloan, Michell Walborn, Meagan Willits, and Ruth Wynkoop. We would also like to acknowledge the continuing contribution of Alice VanBuskirk.

Dedication

We would like to dedicate this edition to our families.

T.R., J.S., G.S., S.S.
Lewisburg, Pensylvania

Preface

To the Instructor

Throughout the past several decades, teachers of introductory economics have expressed a good bit of dissatisfaction with the available textbooks. Not surprisingly, this discontent has led to the continual development of new textbooks for both one-semester and two-semester courses. Many of the new books, but not all, have attempted to cut down on the encyclopedic nature of the prototypical Samuelson text, and many have introduced readings and problems that are up-to-date and relevant to the current population of introductory economics students. This book is in that tradition. It also offers many singular contributions:

❖ It is intended primarily to be a one-semester book.
❖ It focuses on a particular set of basic economic concepts.
❖ It emphasizes active learning by the student.
❖ It includes different perspectives.
❖ It places a good bit of responsibility for teaching the course on the instructor.
❖ It encourages the development of critical thinking.

Many of the textbooks that were popular in the 1950s and 1960s were relatively easy to teach from; the material was all there, it was generally straightforward, and it was all familiar to anyone with a graduate degree in economics. Certainly, there was room for classroom innovation and experimentation to make learning economics exciting and lively. But the form and content of the two-semester textbook made it only too easy to lecture on the development of the theory in the text.

However, in the context of the continuing turmoil and confusion of the 1960s and 1970s, many economics teachers became dissatisfied with this approach to introductory economics. They wanted more relevance and applicability of economic concepts. Many were concerned with the lack of balance in the texts—one particular "brand" of economics would be emphasized to the exclusion of others. These teachers wanted their courses to provide more controversy and exposure to different points of view. They wanted less scope and less depth in the development of theory. They wanted to take a more active role in teaching their courses. These kinds of concerns originally inspired us to begin the effort of writing this textbook.

Most textbooks today continue as they have in the past. This text differs from those by introducing a variety of perspectives and providing real-world applications. This revised edition of *Economics: A Tool for Critically Understanding Society* maintains its commitment to focus on some of the most important, essential, and useful economic concepts. It provides up-to-date coverage, but not at the expense of overkill, and it includes additional "Big Picture" segments designed to help students understand the logic behind the economic models without technical details.

This text obviously does not cover every possible topic or economic concept that one might want to teach in the ideal introductory course. Nor are the articles and examples we have chosen the ones that everyone would select. The questions for the students as they read through the text might not be the ones that you would choose to emphasize the essence of a particular concept. However, our experience with this book indicates that it will help students to learn and practice economics and the economic way of thinking as they progress through your course. We believe this book leaves room for and, indeed, requires a substantial amount of imagination, work, and dedication on the part of the instructor. You will have to teach economics, and we hope this text will help you in your task.

One of the most important innovations we have made in teaching our courses is to require the students to read a daily newspaper. Because of our location and the college service it offers, we have used the *New York Times* in this way. The *Wall Street Journal*, the *Christian Science Monitor*, the *Economist*, the *Financial Times*, and the *Washington Post Weekly* are also good supplementary resources and are mailed all over the country. Reading the paper helps students use and reinforce economics—to inform themselves, formulate questions in class, discuss controversial events or proposals, and gain insight into real, current examples of economic problems and the light that economics can throw on them. And, while online publication can provide students with updates on economic events, scanning though newspapers allows students to find articles applicable to economic analysis not only in the front pages and business section but also in the sports and entertainment sections. Combining current events and economics can enable students to develop a critical understanding of the world. Using a newspaper allows the instructor to keep the course relevant and up-to-date. It also confronts the results of a 1990 survey that revealed very low rates of newspaper readership by seventeen- to twenty-nine-year-olds in the United States. (And, while online newspapers are readily available, we find students often miss the larger economic picture.) A more recent study by Princeton economists Alan S. Blinder and Alan B. Krueger found that most Americans rely on television as their most common source of economic information. Unfortunately, they also found those relying on television as their primary source were among the least informed.

We hope this text will encourage you and help you continue to be creative and imaginative in the way you teach introductory economics. It has been a lot of work for us—including many headaches and failed experiments. But then it has also been fun, exciting, and rewarding. Teaching's like that, isn't it?

Suggested One-Semester Course Outline (Fourteen Weeks)

Part 1	Chapters 1–2	Week 1	
	Chapters 3–4	Week 2	
	Chapter 5	Week 3	
Part 2	Chapters 6–7	Week 4	
	Chapter 8	Week 5	Exam 1
	Chapters 9–10	Week 6	
	Chapters 11–12	Week 7	
Part 3	Chapters 13–14	Week 8	
	Chapter 15	Week 9	
	Chapter 16	Week 10	Exam 2
	Chapters 17–18	Week 11	
Part 4	Chapter 19	Week 12	
	Chapter 20	Week 13	
	Chapters 21–22	Week 14	Final Exam

Suggested One-Semester Micro Course Outline (Fourteen Weeks)

Part 1	Chapters 1–2	Week 1	
	Chapters 3–4	Week 2	
	Chapter 5	Week 3	
Part 2	Chapter 6	Week 4	
	Chapter 7	Week 5	Exam 1
	Chapter 8	Week 6	
	Chapter 9	Week 7	
	Chapter 10	Week 8	
	Chapter 11	Week 9	
	Chapter 12	Week 10	Exam 2
Part 4	Chapter 19	Week 11	
	Chapter 20	Week 12	
	Chapter 21	Week 13	
	Chapter 22	Week 14	Final Exam

Suggested One-Semester Macro Course Outline (Fourteen Weeks)

Part 1	Chapter 1–2	Week 1	
	Chapter 3–5	Week 2	
Part 2	Chapter 6	Week 3	
	Chapter 7	Week 4	
Part 3	Chapter 13	Week 5	Exam 1
	Chapter 14	Week 6	
	Chapter 15	Week 7	
	Chapter 16	Week 8	
	Chapter 17	Week 9	
	Chapter 18	Week 10	Exam 2
Part 4	Chapter 19	Week 11	
	Chapter 20	Week 12	
	Chapter 21	Week 13	
	Chapter 22	Week 14	Final Exam

SUPPLEMENTS

For each chapter in the text, the *Online Instructor's Manual* written by Robin Koenigsberg of Regis University, provides teaching suggestions for class and answers to end-of-chapter questions, as well as additional true-false and explain questions. The *Online Test Item File* provides sample exams for each part in the text for use in the classroom. Both the *Online Instructor's Manual* and the *Online Test Item File*, as well as online *PowerPoint* slides for each chapter, are available, via a secure, password-protected Instructor Resource Center Web site (www.pearsonhighered.com/irc).

On the *Companion Web Site* (www.pearsonhighered.com/riddell), you will find chapter-by-chapter web links to additional readings and economic data, an online glossary, and tips on how to use the Internet in your economics course. Also available on the site are multiple-choice question quizzes for each chapter, written by Jim Craven of Clark College and accuracy reviewed by Dennis Debrecht of

Carroll University. If you wish to supplement your course with newspaper subscriptions or economic news sources, ask your local sales representative for details about Pearson's special offers.

The CourseSmart eTextbook for the text is also available through www .coursesmart.com. CourseSmart goes beyond traditional expectations, providing instant, online access to the textbooks and course materials you need at a lower cost to students. And, even as students save money, you can save time and hassle with a digital textbook that allows you to search the most relevant content at the very moment you need it. Whether it's evaluating textbooks or creating lecture notes to help students with difficult concepts, CourseSmart can make life a little easier. See how when you visit www.coursesmart.com/instructors.

Preface

To the Student

ECONOMICS: WHAT'S IN IT FOR YOU?

More than 230 years after the United States became an independent nation, it is one of the most technologically and economically advanced countries in the world. Its complex economic system produces and distributes goods and services daily and provides one of the world's highest standards of living. Yet we are not satisfied, because we, personally and collectively, have many economic problems. Can people find and keep jobs that provide them with the income to support themselves and their families? What are the prospects for improvements in people's economic well-being? Can you find a job that you like? What's more, the United States is not isolated from the rest of the world. Other peoples face similar, as well as different, problems. Unemployment, inflation, energy problems, downsizing, discrimination, deficits, debt, poverty, pollution, resource shortages, underdevelopment, and corruption in business and politics are problems that dominated global headlines in the last third of the twentieth century, and continue into the twenty-first century.

Economics, as one of the social sciences, helps us understand, think, and form opinions about and develop responses to these economic aspects of our social reality. Economics can be a tool that aids us in defining our successes and our failures, as well as in preserving success and correcting failure. It can contribute to our awareness. In an increasingly complex and confusing world, this tool can serve us personally and collectively as we strive to be responsible citizens of our communities, our nation, and our world. This book is dedicated to helping you to acquire that tool.

> We want to make economics as important as baseball and football scores. The minds are out there. It's a question of getting the attention.
>
> —Robert P. Keim, president of the Advertising Council,
> commenting on a public service campaign to "improve public
> understanding and awareness of the system," 1975

> Acting is a business—no more than that—a craft, like plumbing, or being an economist; it's been a good living.
>
> —Marlon Brando, actor, in a television interview with Dick Cavett, 1973

> An inhabitant of cloud-cuckoo land; one knowledgeable in an obsolete art; a harmless academic drudge whose theories and laws are but mere puffs of air in face of the anarchy of banditry, greed, and corruption which holds sway in the pecuniary affairs of the real world.
>
> —A definition of *economist* that won an award
> from the *New Statesman* in England, 1976

The questions in this book are not rhetorical. Each is intended to make you pause and think. Try to answer each question as you go along. Or use them to review each chapter after you have finished reading it.

1. Would you like to be an economist? Why or why not?

2. Why are you taking economics?

3. "Economics has [usually] been a countercyclical discipline; it flourishes when the economy flounders, and vice versa." Why do you suppose that is so?

OBJECTIVES, OR WHAT WE HAVE DESIGNED THIS BOOK TO ACCOMPLISH

Before you begin your formal study, we would like to share the following list of what we consider the most important objectives of an introduction to modern economics:

❖ To produce some "cognitive dissonance." By this, we mean that we hope to present you with some ideas, facts, and ways of thinking that are new or different to you. Our hope is that these will challenge you to think, to work, and to learn. Is capitalism better than socialism? It might be, but then again, it might not be! We hope to open your mind to thinking about alternatives. What is "investment"? It is *not* simply buying a share of stock in a corporation or the stock market! Introductory economics may shake up some of your preconceived ideas and beliefs. And it may reorganize them into a *system* of thought.

❖ To give you perspective on the historical changes in the material conditions, economic institutions, and social relations of human society. The United States has not always been affluent, and capitalism has not always existed.

❖ To introduce you to a system of economic theories and ideas about the economic institutions of societies—and how those ideas and theories have changed over time. Even the conservative Republican Richard Nixon became a Keynesian in the 1970s. (We will learn more about Keynesian economics in Part 3, but basically it is an economic theory that suggests an important role for the government in guiding the overall economy.) But in the 1980s, Ronald Reagan's economic policies were based on a harsh critique of Keynesian economics; he emphasized the primary importance of business activity as opposed to the government. Bill Clinton's economic policies in the mid-1990s relied on an eclectic mixture of market-based, Keynesian theories and monetary policy that emphasized a positive role for government in influencing economic growth. The challenge of Newt Gingrich and the Republican Congress in the mid-1990s over the role of government and taxes and spending was based primarily on conservative thinking. George W. Bush in part continued this conservative tradition. The recent deep recession and financial crisis changed this debate as shortcomings of market freedoms were once again supplemented with additional government involvement in the economy.

- To convey to you *some* of the economic theories that economists, or groups of economists, regard as accurate descriptions and predictors of economic activity. For example, how do the two sides of a market, the buyers and sellers, interact to determine prices? We do not intend to give you a survey of all of economics, but to expose you to some of the most basic and useful economic concepts. There is too much of economics to try to do all of it in one semester or even a year; time is *scarce* (that's an economic concept).

- To focus on some contemporary economic issues—unemployment, inflation, growth, resource shortages, international trade, climate change, poverty and income distribution, multinational corporations, economic growth and development, and others.

- To expose you to the various, and contending, schools of economic thought. Not all economists agree on which theories or even on which problems are the most important. We hope that you will at least appreciate the variety of economic analysis—no matter which, if any, particular set of economic ideas appeals to you.

- To give you practice using economic concepts. We don't want you just to "input" the concepts in your head and "print them out" on tests. We hope that this text gives you opportunities to use economic concepts in solving real-world problems. Our intention is to provide you with real-world situations that allow you to apply economic concepts, ideas, and theories so that you may come to better understand the world you live in (and perhaps to change it!). We enthusiastically recommend that you read a daily newspaper. Regularly reading the newspaper will provide numerous real-world examples of economic problems (to integrate theory and reality). And applying economic concepts will help you understand them and figure out their implications. We may even be able to suggest solutions to some of these problems. How would you eliminate poverty?

- To give you a foundation in economic "literacy." You should be able to interpret some of the jargon of professional economists. You should also be able to identify the variables, ramifications, and possible explanations of and solutions to a variety of economic problems. We hope you develop a facility to evaluate economic ideas critically.

- To demystify economics so that you do not feel that the economy and its problems are too complex to understand and solve. Economics and economic policy ought not to be left only to the economists.

(CALVIN AND HOBBES © 1992 Watterson.Dist. by UNIVERSAL PRESS SYNDICATE. Reprinted with permission. All rights reserved.)

❖ To provide a foundation for future and continued learning. The world is complex. But economics will assist you in thinking critically and independently about our world. It can be one more tool that allows (and encourages) you to assume active citizenship in your community, your society, and your world.

Our hope is that we can excite you about economics, and that the insights you develop will make useful and creative contributions to your pursuit of a rich and meaningful life.

 4. Are there any objectives we have missed? What are they? Do these objectives make sense to you? Why? Why not? In what ways are these objectives consistent with (different from) what you expected from introductory economics?

PART ONE

Economic Methodology, History, and the Development of Modern Economic Thought

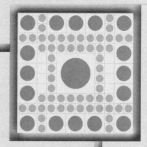

Will capitalism continue for another century? How did the United States come to have a capitalist economic system? In the near future, how will the U.S. economy change? Will it retain world economic leadership? Or, will it begin to lag behind Western Europe and China? Can something be done about the estimated billion people who live on less than $2 per day?

Why does the United States have such an advanced economy? Yet, in the midst of relative affluence, why do child hunger and poverty continue? Is there a reason that a black person is more likely than a white person to be poor and unemployed? Why do women continue to earn, on the average, about 80 percent of what men earn? When there is a boom in the U.S. stock market, who benefits? When the economy slows, who is hurt? How does the United States produce so much food when less than 5 percent of the population is involved in food production?

How will *you* be employed in the future? Will you be rich? Poor? Will you have health insurance? Will the average U.S. workweek continue to rise while those in Europe fall?

These are all predominantly economic questions that affect each and every one of us in our day-to-day lives—either directly or indirectly. We read about these problems in the newspapers, we hear about them on the radio and the television, we listen to politicians talk about them, and we discuss them with our friends and neighbors. They are important and interesting. We have opinions about them—and answers to some or all of them.

Economics is essentially an organized body of knowledge about all of these issues, some of which are current and some of which are perpetual. It seeks to understand and explain these problems and to assist us in solving them. It helps us to think about these problems by indicating important variables and relationships. In Part 1 we begin to examine economic methodology and what the study of economics includes. We then examine economic history and the development of modern economic thought.

Modern economic thinking has been influenced by many economists, among them Adam Smith, Thomas Malthus, David Ricardo, J. B. Say, John Stuart Mill, Alfred Marshall, John Maynard Keynes, Joan Robinson, Thorstein Veblen, and Karl Marx. Many of the economists who contributed to the growing body of economic knowledge were British. Britain's emergence as one of the first capitalist powers, through the spread of its colonial empire and the coming of the Industrial Revolution, accounts for this influence. We can trace many of our theories and ideas about the economy back to these early economists.

This book cannot examine all of the ideas of all of the economists who have made significant contributions to the history of modern economic thought; in this part, we will focus on the development of a few selected and persistent ways of thinking about an economy. Your own understanding of the economy may become clearer as you agree or disagree with some of the most important ideas formulated by past economists.

By examining some of the ideas of these economists as they developed and the historical context in which they emerged, we can gain insights into economic concepts and changing economic institutions, ideas, and theories. Some of this will help us directly in understanding our current economic situation, and it will give us perspective on how the thoughts of past economists have influenced the development of economic systems as well as our understanding of the economy today. We hope that in this course you will learn to use economics to consider the problems that interest and affect you.

CHAPTER ONE

Economics as a Social Science

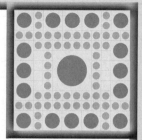

Introduction

What is economics? And what can it do for us?

Economics is the study of how the productive and distributive aspects of human life are organized. The productive aspects include the activities that result in the goods and services that satisfy our day-to-day demands as human beings—for automobiles, cereal, clothes, movies, and so on. The distributive aspects are the ways a society makes these goods and services available to people in the society. Economics studies the history of production, distribution, and consumption of goods and services in different societies and countries, including the ways these aspects have changed over time. It seeks to help us understand the complexities of economic systems in the modern world.

Economics, as a social science, is thus an accumulation of human knowledge about one particular segment of social life: production, distribution, and consumption. Like the other social sciences, including geography, political science, psychology, and sociology, economics focuses on only one part of a rich and complex social life.

In this chapter, we examine economics as a social science. We will be concerned with its goals and methods, as well as its relevance to our lives. In addition, we will introduce briefly different fields in economics and the kinds of things that economists do. Finally, we will see that economists have some disagreements about what economics is and ought to be.

Definitions in This Book

Key economic concepts are indicated in this text by **bold type.** In addition, a glossary at the end of the text defines these important terms.

WHAT IS ECONOMICS?

Teachers of economics are concerned about how best to teach economics. Their concern stems from the importance of economic knowledge in the modern world and the difficulties of teaching that knowledge to students in a way that will prove useful to them. Out of this concern, many economists have attempted to define precisely what the key elements of economic understanding are and to concentrate on teaching these. A reasonable list of key elements of economic understanding would include the following:

* Practicing a reasoned approach to economic issues
* Mastering basic economic concepts
* Possessing an overview of the economy
* Identifying important economic issues
* Applying the concepts to particular issues
* Reaching reasoned decisions on economic issues

These elements provide some insights into the nature of economics as the study of the productive and distributive aspects of human life. Economic understanding encompasses both a body of knowledge and a way of thinking about the economic aspects of social life. It is concerned with practicing a reasoned approach; that is, economics presents an organized and logical way of thinking about economic life. It uses many basic concepts that focus our attention on key variables in economic activity. It provides us with an overall appreciation of the structure and complexity of the economic system in this country as well as those in other countries and in the global economy. It should help us identify the issues that will be important to us in our individual and social lives. In addition, economics helps us to reason and to draw conclusions about specific economic problems, their ramifications, and possible solutions.

In attempting to accomplish all of these tasks, one of the central concerns of economics is the development of **economic theory.** This task relates to the *method* of economics. While economics is concerned with social life and the vagaries of human beings, the development of theory requires that economics be as scientific as possible. An economic theory, for example, would try to explain why the prices of agricultural goods change from year to year as well as to predict how prices might change in the future.

Economists attempt to measure and collect facts about economic activity. In doing so, they try to discover certain patterns in the relationships between different components of economic life. When the facts suggest that these patterns express a constant relationship (in normal circumstances), economists may use them as the basis for economic theories. The theories of supply and demand are examples of such theories. These theories emerged out of observations of the behavior of prices of goods in markets and the ways prices changed over time. The theory developed from efforts to explain these changes. We can use these economic theories to gain insight into how goods and services are valued by society's members, how costly they are to produce, and what price they will sell for in the society, given different circumstances.

The function of economic theory, therefore, is to allow us to examine certain aspects of economic life, discover more or less constant relationships among different economic variables, and predict possible economic events. For example, the theories of supply and demand tells us that, most of the time, a desired article in short supply will command a relatively high price. From this we can conclude (theorize) that if the supply of that article is reduced, then its price is likely to go up even further.

Note that such statements are based on an **assumption**—an *if* statement—followed by a conditional conclusion. Economists love to make assumptions. Much of their theory is based on similar assumptions. In the final analysis, however, their theories must be judged by whether their conclusions and predictions conform with what actually happens in economic reality. In the case of supply-and-demand theory, frequent examples enable us to check the validity of the conclusions and predictions of this economic theory.

For example, in 1973, when the Middle Eastern oil-producing countries embargoed shipments of oil to the United States, Western Europe, and Japan, the supply of oil decreased, and the price *did* increase. Likewise, when there are good crops of wheat in the United States, the price of wheat is likely to go down; when crops are bad because of the weather, the price of wheat goes up. Whenever a freeze occurs in Florida, it sharply reduces the supply of Florida oranges, and this is followed by an increase in the price of oranges. In 2000, oil prices rose again as oil companies raised prices and the Middle Eastern oil-producing countries, now fearing lower returns, reduced supplies to Europe and the United States.

European motorists responding to fuel price increases in 2000.
(© Virginia Mayo/AP/Wide World Photos)

Higher gas prices prompted protests in Europe and complaints in the United States about the cost of filling cars, trucks, and fuel-guzzling sport utility vehicles. From 2004 through 2007, demand by Chinese and Indian industry, growing concerns about Middle East oil supplies, and increased speculation sent prices skyrocketing. In each of these cases, economic reality conforms with economic theory.

These examples highlight the *relevance* of economics. Economics and economic theories are concerned with problems and activities that are important to all of us as individuals and to our societies. The scope of economics can be international, national, regional, local, or personal. The problems and activities that are the subject matter of economics include such pressing concerns as recession, productivity, supplies of natural resources, efficiency, debt, unemployment, inflation, technological development, product distribution, advertising, poverty, alienation, the allocation of scarce resources, income redistribution, taxation, war, and a host of others. Economics identifies such economic problems, describes their ramifications, hypothesizes about their causes, predicts their future development, and prescribes solutions to them. In so doing, economics can build our understanding of the fundamental economic aspects of our social lives.

One Method for Economic Theory

Milton Friedman, a Nobel Prize winner in economics, argued for a particular method in the construction of economic theory. This methodology, which he called "positive economics," has four basic components:

1. The process begins with a set of reasonable *assumptions* about some aspect of economic behavior. For example, in Part 2, one of the most important assumptions that we will make is that the primary objective of firms is the maximization of profits.

2. Next, we try to identify some important economic *concepts* and construct some variables to measure them. For the firm, we will measure profit, cost, revenue, marginal cost, marginal revenue, and other variables. These are all functions of the economic activity of the firm.

3. Based on the assumptions we have made and the concepts we have identified, we develop some *hypotheses* and logical deductions about economic behavior. In the case of the firm, we theorize that the firm maximizes profit at a rate of output where its marginal cost equals its marginal revenue. In Part 2, we will demonstrate this in more detail.

4. The final step is to *test the theory*. Does the hypothesis conform with observable events? When marginal costs do not equal marginal revenues, does the firm alter its decisions so that it can increase its profits?

Friedman emphasized that this method produces abstract economic theory; it simplifies and generalizes. The purpose, however, is to create a model of the economy that will help us evaluate and analyze the real-world economy. A model is an abstraction, or simplification, of the economy, not an exact replica of it.

Source: "Four Basic Components of Positive Economics" from Friedman, CAPITALISM AND FREEDOM. (1962) Copyright © University of Chicago Press. Used with permission.

Economics and Economists

There are many fields within economics, some of which will be introduced in this book. Economic history, reviewed briefly in Chapter 2, focuses on how and why economic activity has changed over time. Urban economics focuses on analyzing the economic operation and problems of cities. Microeconomics is concerned primarily with the activities of smaller economic units, such as the household or the firm, and markets for goods and services. Macroeconomics has the much broader subject of the operation and health of an entire national economy. International economics deals with economic relationships and activities on a global scale. Economic thought treats the development of ideas by economists through the years. Economic development concentrates on theories and problems associated with the economic growth and maturation of national economies. Public policy economics is concerned with the analysis of proposals for dealing with public problems. Political economy highlights the relationships between economic and political institutions and how they affect each other. This by no means exhausts the list of the different fields in economics.

Given this wide variety of fields in economics, economists do many different things. Many people trained in economics as a discipline become teachers of economics in high schools, colleges, or universities. Many work in businesses, informing decision makers on current economic events and future economic forecasts. Since World War II, an increasing number of economists have found employment in government at the local, state, and federal levels. Economists also work for consulting firms, labor unions, public interest or lobbying groups, and international organizations.

With this diversity of employment experiences (and hence allegiances and perspectives), it should not be very surprising to find a healthy amount of "controversy" within the social science of economics. Economists, despite their efforts to build economic theory, often disagree with one another. They may differ about which problems are most important (or even, sometimes, that there are problems!), what the causes of a problem are, and which solutions to a problem are the best. Controversy in economics reflects controversy in life.

Nevertheless, most economists accept a large core of economic ideas. We will study many of these ideas in this book. In addition, economists are unified by the goal of economics: building knowledge about the economic aspects of life.

Much of the debate among economists about what economics is and should be concerns its scope. The famous English economist Alfred Marshall (1842–1924) thought economics could be one of the most precise and scientific of the social sciences because it deals with observable and measurable data in the form of prices, quantities produced and sold, and incomes. In his *Principles of Economics*, he wrote:

> The advantage which economics has over other branches of social science appears then to arise from the fact that its special field of work gives rather larger opportunities for exact methods than any other branch. It concerns itself chiefly with those desires, aspirations and other affections of human nature, the outward manifestations of which appear as incentives to action in such a form that the force or

quantity of the incentives can be estimated and measured with some approach to accuracy; and which therefore are in some degree amenable to treatment by scientific machinery. An opening is made for the methods and the tests of science as soon as the force of a person's motives—not the motives themselves—can be approximately measured by the sum of money, which he will just give up in order to secure a desired satisfaction; or again by the sum which is just required to induce him to undergo a certain fatigue.

Other economists, however, have been less convinced by this argument. They point out that economics, as one of the social sciences, cannot divorce itself from the society in which it exists. The efforts of human beings to understand the world must necessarily be influenced by morality, ideology, and value judgments. In other words, economics cannot be totally scientific because the economist's understanding of the subject matter is affected by his or her evaluation of, opinions about, and conclusions concerning social issues. Economics as a body of thought functions to preserve, protect, and/or challenge existing social life—as well as help us to understand it. For some economists, then, economics should be a part of the effort to understand and *to improve* social existence. Joan Robinson (1903–1983), another English economist, wrote in *Freedom and Necessity*:

> The methods to which the natural sciences owe their success—controlled experiment and exact observation of continually recurring phenomena—cannot be applied to the study of human beings by human beings. So far, no equally successful method of establishing reliable natural laws has been suggested. Certainly, the social sciences should not be unscientific. Their practitioners should not jump to conclusions on inadequate evidence or propound circular statements that are true by definition as though they had some factual content; when they disagree they should not resort to abuse like theologians or literary critics, but should calmly set about to investigate the nature of the difference and to propose a plan of research to resolve it.... The function of social science is quite different from that of the natural sciences—it is to provide society with an organ of self-consciousness. Every interconnected group of human beings has to have an ideology—that is, a conception of what is the proper way to behave and the permissible pattern of relationships in family, economic, and political life.

For Robinson, then, economics must attempt to be scientific and rigorous, but since it is also concerned with the effort to create a better society, it must also devote itself to exploring areas that are more philosophical. It must recognize its ideological elements, and that, as one of the social sciences, it is also involved as a tool of analysis in the formation of public policy.

Along these lines, economists often divide their discipline between "economics" and what is called **political economy.** Economics in this sense is more concerned with explaining what can be measured and with developing theories about "purely" economic relationships. Political economy, on the other hand, is more concerned with the relationships of the economic system and its institutions to the rest of society and social development. It is sensitive to the influence of noneconomic factors such as political and social institutions, morality, and ideology in determining economic events. It thus has a broader focus than economics.

1. "The function of social science...is to provide society with an organ of self-consciousness." What does this mean? How does economics do this?

2. What, according to Robinson, is an ideology? What role do ideologies play in social development?

3. What does Robinson think is the task of economics as a social science? Do you agree with her or not? Would Alfred Marshall?

PARADIGMS AND IDEOLOGIES

Not only do economists disagree about what economics is and should be, they often disagree about which economic problems are important, which theories are correct, and which economic policies are best. This is especially true over time, as the economic problems a society is likely to face change with changing conditions. Along with changes in economic problems and economic institutions, economic theories have also changed. The changes in economic theory and the differences among economists have two results that are useful to keep in mind while studying economics: First, there are different and sometimes contesting kinds of economic theory. Second, different economists begin their study with different assumptions.

The Realm of Theory

Different periods of economic history (and different economic systems) have given rise to new economic theories. New or changed economic conditions and economic institutions have required different explanations and ways of thinking. Stated slightly differently, as crises have developed in economic matters when the old gave way to the new, economic institutions changed. The previous theories and notions became inadequate to explain the new conditions and problems, so economic thought also changed.

Thomas Kuhn, in *The Structure of Scientific Revolutions*, refers to such changes in scientific theory as changes in **paradigms.** A paradigm structures thought about a certain aspect of nature, life, or society. It delineates the scope of a discipline (the questions to be asked about a certain subject and the phenomena to be explained), as well as the method of the discipline (the criteria for accepting explanations).

Paradigms are usually widely accepted as providing a coherent and correct understanding of some aspect of life. However, as time passes, natural and social conditions may change, and new interpretations and new facts may become known. If so, the existing paradigm may be challenged or may be inadequate to explain these changes and a new and more widely accepted paradigm will eventually be developed. An example of this in the field of astronomy was the replacement of the Ptolemaic by the Copernican paradigm. The Copernican paradigm is now widely accepted, because it conforms with what we now know and observe—that the planets revolve around the sun.

Likewise, as economic crises occur and economic conditions change, one economic paradigm replaces another. Before the Great Depression of the 1930s, the dominant economic theory was classical economics, which argued that a laissez-faire, self-regulating market economic system would eliminate economic instability through the flexibility of markets. If overproduction of goods led to a decrease in production and an increase in unemployment, then the markets would respond to correct the situation. Prices would fall and stimulate consumption of those goods, thus eliminating the surplus. Wages would fall and stimulate the hiring of unemployed workers. To explain why overproduction or underconsumption would be unlikely in a laissez-faire market economic system, classical economics relied on Say's law, developed by the French economist J. B. Say (1767–1832), which held that supply creates its own demand. Say theorized that incomes paid out in the process of production of needed goods would always be sufficient to buy what was produced. The flexibility of prices and wages in self-regulating markets would ensure this result. However, when economists observed the severity and persistence of the Great Depression, they questioned Say's law. Consequently, they turned to a new paradigm, Keynesian economics (about which we will learn more in Part 3), which offered an explanation for why depressions occur and what can be done about them.

Not only do paradigms change over time, two contending paradigms sometimes seek to explain the same aspect of economic life. Examining the same events and facts but differing in the use of key concepts and relationships, these contending paradigms offer conflicting (or at least differing) interpretations. At one time or another, or in different places, one or the other might be dominant.

An example of conflicting paradigms is the contrast between orthodox economics and Marxian economics. **Orthodox economics** accepts the assumptions of a competitive market economy and builds a theory around those assumptions. **Marxian economics** assumes a critical stance toward the existing market economic system and attempts to discover how it will and can be changed. Orthodox economics accepts capitalism, and Marxian economics criticizes capitalism and argues for socialism. A third paradigm, **institutional economics**, bridges Marxian and orthodox economics by focusing on the role of changing institutions and power in influencing economic affairs. Throughout this book, we will encounter these different paradigms as they attempt to explain economic life.

The Realm of the Economist

Economists are human beings with differing ideas, theories, assumptions, and ideologies. As economic conditions and institutions have changed, so have economists' ideas, theories, assumptions, and ideologies. In different times and spaces, economists have differed. And in the *same* time and space, economists disagree. One way of clarifying this is to examine **ideology**. E. K. Hunt, in *Property and Prophets*, defines an ideology this way:

> [A set of] ideas and beliefs that tend to justify morally a society's social and economic relationships. Most members of a society internalize the ideology and thus believe that their functional roles, as well as those of others, are morally correct,

and that the method by which society divides its produce is fair. This common belief gives society its cohesiveness and vitality. Lack of it creates turmoil and strife—and ultimately revolution if the differences are deep enough.

At different times, different ideologies may dominate. At one time, Confucianism was the ideology of China. Later, the dominant ideology in China was that of Maoism and socialism. Catholicism and a concern with the next world was at the core of an ideology that dominated Western Europe; later, individualism and materialism held sway.

Ideologies influence the development of theory. For example, the ideology of individualism promoted the development of the economic theory of classical liberalism, and both accompanied the emergence of capitalism as an economic system. More recently, the combination of the ideologies of liberal democracy, the benevolent state, and individualism promoted the acceptance of Keynesian economics along with the emergence of the welfare state. From 1982 to 2007, with an increasing government presence in the economy, many economists (and politicians) with a conservative ideology argued for greater reliance on market forces.

Different ideologies concerning the goals of a society and an economic system may conflict. For example, differences in ideology underlie the division of Western economists today into three broad groups: liberal, conservative, and radical. Each group has its own ideas, theories, and ideologies. These are described in the next section.

4. What is your ideology?

5. Compare and contrast Hunt's definition of ideology with that of Joan Robinson.

CONSERVATIVE, LIBERAL, AND RADICAL ECONOMICS

Milton Friedman (1912–2006) was a prominent conservative economist. John Maynard Keynes offered a liberal solution to the 1930s crisis of capitalism. Adam Smith, while recognized as a conservative today, was a radical in his day. Karl Marx offered a radical critique of capitalism.

What are some of the essential elements of conservative, liberal, and radical ideologies and theories? What are the differences among them? How do they interpret different economic issues, and what different solutions do they offer for economic problems?

Conservative economists focus on the operation of markets in a capitalist, free market economic system. They argue that private ownership of resources under capitalism assures economic and political freedom for individuals in that society. Individuals make their own decisions for their own private gains. Markets, where goods and services are exchanged, will then operate to produce economic well-being and growth for the society and the individuals within it. Markets, through the action of competition, enforce a result that is the best for everyone and uses resources efficiently. Consequently, conservatives see the profit motive as being one of the most important and positive aspects of capital-ism. Firms, to meet their own interests in competitive markets, must produce exactly what consumers want at the lowest price. One further implication of conservative economics is that, since markets operate efficiently and produce economic growth, the government need not take an active role in the operation of the economy (beyond some important, fundamental obligations—see Chapter 12). In fact, most conservatives argue that excessive government inter-vention in the economy is the source of many of our economic problems.

The roots of conservative economics can be found in eighteenth-century clas-sical liberalism. Beginning in Chapter 2, we will encounter the emergence of this body of thought and explore this theory in more detail. Modern examples of conservative economics include "free market" economics, supply-side econom-ics, and monetarism. Conservative economists include Milton Friedman, author of *Capitalism and Freedom* and a Nobel Prize winner; Alan Greenspan, former chairman of the Federal Reserve System; and Robert Barro, *Business Week* columnist and Harvard economics professor. Ronald Reagan and John McCain are examples of politicians who believe in the ideas and the theories of conserva-tive economics. Much of the advertising and educational efforts of corporate America utilize the logic and conclusions of conservative economics. *The Wall Street Journal* and *The Economist* newspapers take a consistently conservative position in their editorials.

Liberal economists accept the structure of the capitalist economic system and its basic institutions of private property and markets. They also agree with conservatives that, for the most part, this free-market system tends to produce efficiency and economic growth and that it protects individual freedom. However, they admit that the operation of the market system may produce problems. For example, it can't guarantee economic stability, it fosters an unequal distribution of income and economic power, often neglects some of the by-products of economic production and exchange such as pollution, and sometimes fails to provide necessary goods and services that can't be produced profitably. Liberals then usually point out that there is a solution to these prob-lems that does not interfere with the basic structure of the economic system; they give the responsibility for addressing these problems to the government. The federal government can take responsibility for trying to achieve economic prosperity and price stability and to avoid economic depressions. It can attempt to redistribute income, and it can attempt to regulate the production of pollution in the economy. And, all levels of government can provide "pub-lic" goods such as parks, roads, schools, and police and fire protection. For lib-erals, the market works economic wonders, but they are qualified wonders; the active involvement of governments in some aspects of the market economy can improve its performance.

The theoretical underpinnings of most liberal economists can be found in Keynesian economics. Some liberals also find the ideas of Thorstein Veblen and other institutionalist economists to be helpful in framing their understand-ing of the economy. We will encounter these theories again in Parts 2 and 4. John Kenneth Galbraith of Harvard University wrote a number of important books about economics and the economy from Keynesian and institutionalist perspectives. Nobel laureate Paul Krugman, who teaches at Princeton University, is another liberal economist and an op-ed columnist for the *New York Times* and author of *The Conscience of a Liberal*. Jimmy Carter, Bill Clinton, and Barack Obama use the ideas and theories of liberal economics. *Business Week* magazine usually presents a relatively liberal editorial policy.

Radical economists tend to be very critical of the structures, institutions, operation, and results of capitalist economic systems. They do not deny that capitalism has been quite successful over the past several centuries in increasing the productive capacity of Western nations and the average standard of living for their inhabitants. However, radical economists suggest that the very operation of a market system based on private ownership creates different classes of people in capitalist societies. On the one hand are those who own productive resources, organize and control productive activity, and have the goal of earning profits for themselves. On the other hand are people who do not own any productive property and who rely on the sale of their mental and/or physical labor to earn a living. Radicals are quick to point out that there are inherent conflicts between these two groups over wages, working conditions, product safety, and economic power. It is this basic class structure of the society, radicals argue, that produces economic inequality, exploitation, and alienation. In addition, they conclude that capitalist production and growth are inherently unable to provide for public goods, ignore the social costs of productive activity, and lead to economic instability. Consequently, the efforts of the state (all levels of government) to deal with these problems

Lower East Side of Manhattan; New York
(© SuperStock.)

are merely Band-Aid solutions because they do not address the root causes—private ownership, production for profit, and a class society.

In the view of radical economists, solving modern economic problems such as poverty, income inequality, discrimination, and pollution requires alterations in the basic economic institutions of the society. Many radicals believe in nationalization, and many want to limit the existing power of corporations. Many would advocate much more significant redistribution of income in the United States (and the world). Some even call for social ownership and control of productive resources in pursuit of social goals of production.

Radical economics finds its roots in both institutional and Marxian economics. Although many radicals find the ideas of both Keynesian and conservative economics useful in understanding how capitalism and markets work, radicals depart in their evaluation of the operation and results of capitalism. For them, the negative aspects outweigh the positive. Samuel Bowles, David Gordon, and Thomas Weisskopf are radical economists who wrote *Beyond the Wasteland: A Democratic Alternative to Economic Decline*. This book contains their analysis of U.S. economic experience and presents a radical economic program for restructuring the economy and addressing many of its long-run problems. In his book *Contours of Descent: U.S. Economic Fractures and the Landscape of Global Austerity*, University of Massachusetts economist Robert Pollin argues that free-market policies have produced extensive poverty and increasing inequality. Along with Robert Pollin, writers for periodicals such as *Mother Jones*, *Z*, and *Dollars and Sense* express a radical point of view. Many of the ideas about economic priorities and policy articulated by Ralph Nader in his 2000, 2004, and 2008 presidential campaigns—for instance, increased income redistribution, significantly reduced military spending, and the promotion of environmentally responsible economic policies—are compatible with radical economics. The Green Party has a radical platform.

Conservatives, Liberals, and Radicals on Poverty

From these brief descriptions of conservative, liberal, and radical economics, it should be possible to identify the basic approach that each would take to understanding a particular economic problem and suggesting solutions for it. But let's develop a single example: poverty. Conservatives tend to argue that poverty exists because of the particular attributes of individuals and their inability to earn high incomes in labor markets. Either they have the wrong skills or few skills, or they don't try or work hard enough. The solution, then, is either "It's appropriate that their economic rewards are low," or "They need to develop their marketable skills." If the society decides that it wants to facilitate the reduction of poverty, the most appropriate way might be through education. Individuals have to develop skills and work harder. Conservatives would not support anti-poverty programs because they represent government involvement with markets. Conservatives think that poverty can be reduced effectively only by the participation of responsible individuals in free markets.

Liberals maintain that, very often, the poverty of individuals is a result of circumstances beyond their control. Consequently, not only would liberals support a public role for education (and job training) to increase people's marketable skills, but, in addition, they would favor direct income redistribution to increase the purchasing power of poor people. This would reduce the burdens of poverty, but it also might create the chance for people to move out of poverty. Liberals would support food stamps and welfare for the poor.

Radicals generally would support governmental redistribution programs and certainly would oppose efforts to take economic benefits away from poor people. However, they would argue that redistribution programs have a very limited effect in eliminating poverty. Governmental programs have reduced poverty, but given the source of unequal incomes in private ownership of productive resources and the fundamental individualism of capitalism, the system cannot tolerate the amount of redistribution that would be necessary to eliminate poverty. Only massive redistribution of income to poor people or a radical restructuring of the institutions and goals of the economic system could significantly reduce the incidence of poverty in the United States.

The analyses of current economic problems are distinctive based on different ideologies and theories. And these differences are reflected in the variety of proposed solutions. Conservatives, liberals, and democratic socialists in the United States each proposed solutions to the financial crisis that began in mid-2007. Many conservatives argued that banks should simply be allowed to fail. These institutions took risks, and the cost is failure. Some liberals argued that these banks (Citi, BankAmerica, Wells Fargo) were "too big to fail," and support government bailout measures for these and other banks in order to protect the financial system and the economy. Democratic socialists proposed another option: Nationalize the banks that are too big to fail. Nationalization would shift the cost from the taxpayer to bank stock and bondholders—those who took risks by purchasing shares and lending to these now failing banks. We will discuss this current financial and economic crisis in the Part 3.

One of the fascinating aspects of modern economics is the controversy that surrounds our understanding of and efforts to deal with these problems. Conservative, liberal, and radical economics have all contributed to that analysis.

6. Which set of economic ideas do you think is dominant in the United States today?

7. Paul Sweezy, a U.S. Marxian economist, has written, "It seems to me that from a scientific point of view the question of choosing between approaches can be answered quite simply. Which more accurately reflects the fundamental characteristics of social reality which is under analysis?" Critically evaluate each of the different perspectives with respect to that statement. How are your answers affected by your own beliefs?

8. What is the difference between theory and ideology?

◆Conclusion

There are many different fields within economics, the social science that focuses on building an understanding of how the economy—production, distribution, and consumption of goods and services—works. Economists do many different things, not the least of which is disagree with each other while at the same time working together to build economic theory. The remaining chapters in Part 1 examine the history and development of economic thought as new developments and institutions require analysis and perhaps different assumptions about economic life.

Review Questions

1. What is economics? Is that what you thought economics is (or should be)?

2. What is the goal of economic theory? What is the test of an economic theory?

3. Why do economists disagree?

4. What is a paradigm? In your life have you ever replaced one paradigm with another?

5. What are the main differences among conservative, liberal, and radical economists?

6. Paradigms can offer contending explanations of the same reality. Sometimes the contention can reflect intense political, social, and economic struggles. Develop some examples of new paradigms for which the people suggesting them have been subjected to neglect, harassment, ridicule, or even punishment.

7. How might conservative, liberal, and radical economists respond to an issue like global climate change?

CHAPTER TWO

The Evolution
of Economic Systems

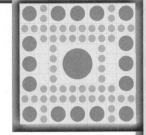

Introduction

The first premise of all human history is, of course, the existence of living human individuals. Thus, the first fact to be established is the physical organization of these individuals and their consequent relation to the rest of nature....

...The writing of history must always set out from these natural bases and their modification in the course of history through the action of men.

Men can be distinguished from animals by consciousness, by religion or anything else you like. They themselves begin to distinguish themselves from animals as soon as they begin to produce their means of subsistence, a step which is conditioned by their physical organization. By producing their means of subsistence men are indirectly producing their actual material life.

The way in which men produce their means of subsistence depends first of all on the nature of the actual means of subsistence they find in existence and have to reproduce. This mode of production must not be considered simply as being the reproduction of the physical existence of the individuals. Rather it is a definite form of activity of these individuals, a definite form of expressing their life, a definite mode of life on their part. As individuals express their life, so they are. What they are, therefore, coincides with their production, both with what they produce and with how they produce. The nature of individuals thus depends on the material conditions determining their production.

—Karl Marx, *The German Ideology* (1845–1846)`

1. What does Marx mean by "the nature of the actual means of subsistence"? What is its relationship to the productive activity of human beings?

Every society is faced with the problem of providing for the day-to-day survival of its people. Production of goods and services on a systematic basis is necessary for the continuance and development of any society or nation. Institutions, traditions, rules, methods, and laws are developed to determine what goods and services will be produced, how they will be produced, and how they will be distributed among the people. According to Marx, the ways in which people organize themselves for the production and distribution of goods and services—the **economic system**—constitutes "the mode of life" of any society.

Individuals and organizations engage in economic activity for particular reasons and according to accepted procedures. This activity is a central and necessary aspect of all human life and societies. It provides us with food, shelter, clothing, and the other necessities of life. The production and distribution of goods and services transforms nature into human uses for survival and sustenance. People's actions in this process determine, to a large extent, their daily contacts and relationships with other people. The results of economic activity—what gets produced and how it gets produced—organized through an economic system, condition the nature, history, and development of a society and its people. Understanding the economic system, then, is fundamental to understanding that society.

To understand the United States economic system, it is necessary to acknowledge the importance of private production and consumption in providing for our day-to-day survival. Consequently, we would want to examine the roles of specialization, division of labor, and markets in the operation of our economic system. It is also important to recognize changes in institutions, productive methods, and material conditions over time. Corporations and labor unions emerged and developed. Technology and the standard of living advanced steadily. Mass production led to the assembly line and automation. Government accepted more direct responsibility for the health of the economy. In other words, the economic system evolved.

ECONOMIC DEVELOPMENT

Over time, all economic systems change. **Economic development** represents progressive changes in a society's ability to meet its economic tasks of production and distribution.

Economic development contains two key elements. One concerns the total amount of goods and services that are produced and available for consumption, and the other concerns institutions. Economic development occurs when a society is able to increase its total output; it experiences economic growth through the generation and usage of its economic **surplus** (more output than necessary for subsistence consumption). Very often a society's ability to produce such growth is a function of the second element of economic development. This concerns the changes in the economic institutions, relationships, and production methods of the society. If the society experiences changes in its economic institutions, relationships, and methods that make it better prepared to produce a growing volume of goods and services for its people, then development will occur. The discovery of new resources will encourage economic development, as will technological improvements in the methods of production. The spread of education and attitudes toward work may facilitate a society's ability to produce goods and services. Economic development is obviously of crucial importance to any society and its continued survival.

The present U.S. economic system, its institutions, and its conditions developed out of previous methods of production and distribution. The historical background lies largely, but not exclusively, in U.S. and European experience. For example, the U.S. market system has its roots in the emergence of trade in the Middle Ages in Europe; the modern corporation has its roots in the development of earlier European and U.S. business enterprises. Yet the foundations of the U.S. labor force have been and are worldwide. An understanding of this background will provide some useful perspective on the current economic system in the United States and the global economy.

2. Marx stated that the "mode of production" of a society constitutes "a definite mode of life on [its] part." What is the "mode of production" in the United States? How does the "mode of production" affect life in the United States? What is the "mode of production" at your college or university?

3. Marx continues, "The nature of individuals thus depends on the material conditions determining their production." What are these material conditions to which Marx refers? In what ways are people in the United States affected by "the material conditions" of production?

FROM FEUDALISM TO CAPITALISM

From time to time, economic change is so wrenching that major transformations occur and completely new economic systems emerge, with new institutions, rules, methods, and laws. Such was the transition from feudalism to capitalism in Western Europe from the twelfth to eighteenth centuries. The change occurred over several centuries but accelerated in the later periods. In the following discussion, we will concentrate on the highlights of this transition to illustrate economic change and to show the historical roots of modern capitalism.

As we have said, all societies must organize themselves for production, distribution, and consumption. If we are clear on what these economic activities are, we will be able to focus on the major differences among economic systems. **Production** refers to the activity that takes the **factors of production** (resources) and transforms them into goods and services. The factors of production are land, labor, and capital. **Land** includes raw materials and the land where productive activity takes place (i.e., farmland or the land on which a factory or office is located). **Labor** is the physical and mental effort of people that is necessary for all production. **Capital** includes the technology, buildings, machinery, and equipment that are used in production, as well as the financial resources necessary to organizing production. **Consumption** is the using up of goods and services. **Distribution** refers to the manner in which goods and services are apportioned among the people of a society. As we will see, feudalism accomplished all of these with institutions and methods much different from those of capitalism.

4. All societies must be able to organize themselves for production, distribution, and consumption. What other economic goals should a society have? List at least five.

Precursors of Feudalism

The ancient empires of Egypt, Greece, and Rome were the precursors of modern Western societies. They were largely agricultural societies that struggled to produce enough food for continued subsistence. *Tradition* and *custom* were primarily responsible for organizing production and distribution. Things were done the way they always had been done. Children tended to follow in the footsteps of their parents. Slaves remained slaves. Peasants were agricultural producers tied to the land for generation after generation. The priests, kings, emperors, pharaohs, and lords continued in the role of the elite upper class removed from production. As economist Robert Heilbroner describes them in *The Making of Economic Society*, these societies had "a mode of social organization in which both production and distribution were based on procedures devised in the distant past, rigidified by a long process of historic trial and error, and maintained by heavy sanctions of law, custom, and belief."

Before we examine feudalism, it is worthwhile to pause and consider economic surplus. Throughout history, the ability to produce an agricultural and economic surplus has been a source of growth and power. If a society can produce more than it needs for consumption, it can use this excess to support an urban population that can pursue nonagricultural production, and it can devote resources to increasing further production. The surplus can be used to further a division of tasks within an economic system and thus to spur economic growth.

By forgoing current consumption, a society can use resources to increase its ability to produce goods and services in the future. A simple example would be using excess grain to feed oxen (instead of eating it) so that more grain could be produced in the future. Another example would be transporting food to an urban area where (fed) artisans would fashion simple tools for agricultural production.

Although the surplus can thus be a source of growth, how a society uses its surplus and who controls its use tell us a lot about that society. Egypt, Greece, and Rome did succeed in producing surplus, but very little was used in a direct attempt to further economic production. Religious and military elites controlled the surplus of these societies and used them to build temples, pyramids, sphinxes, magnificent roads, aqueducts, and buildings that are still with us today. Little of the surplus, however, went to the slaves, peasants, or artisans who were the producers of consumable goods and services, nor was the surplus directed toward improving the productive potential of these sectors of the economic systems. As a result, these societies did not generate significant economic growth.

5. What does the United States do with its economic surplus? Who determines how it is used?

Feudalism

The economic system that dominated Western Europe throughout the Middle Ages was **feudalism**. What exactly was feudalism? What were its major institutions, methods, and customs? The following selection by economic historian E. K. Hunt, from his book *Property and Prophets*, provides us with a concise description of feudalism.

Feudalism
E. K. Hunt

The decline of the western part of the old Roman Empire left Europe without the laws and protection the empire had provided. The vacuum was filled by the creation of a feudal hierarchy. In this hierarchy, the serf, or peasant, was protected by the lord of the manor, who, in turn, owed allegiance to and was protected by a higher overlord. And so the system went, ending eventually with the king. The strong protected the weak, but they did so at a high price. In return for payments of money, food, labor, or military allegiance, overlords granted the fief, or feudum—a hereditary right to use land—to their vassals. At the bottom was the serf, a peasant who tilled the land. The vast majority of the population raised crops for food or clothing or tended sheep for wool and clothing.

Custom and tradition are the key to understanding medieval relationships. In place of laws as we know them today, the *custom of the manor* governed. There was no strong central authority in the Middle Ages that could have enforced a system of laws. The entire medieval organization was based on a system of mutual obligations and services up and down the hierarchy. Possession or use of the land obligated one to certain customary services or payments in return for protection. The lord was as obligated to protect the serf as the serf was to turn over a portion of his crop or to perform extensive labor for the lord....

The basic economic institution of medieval rural life was the manor, which contained within it two separate and distinct classes: noblemen, or lords of the manors, and serfs (from the Latin word *servus,* "slave"). Serfs were not really slaves. Unlike a slave, who was simply property to be bought and sold at will, the serf could not be parted from either his family or his land. If his lord transferred possession of the manor to another nobleman, the serf simply had another lord. In varying degrees, however, obligations were placed upon the serfs that were sometimes very onerous and from which there was often no escape. Usually, they were far from being "free."

The lord lived off the labor of the serfs who farmed his fields and paid taxes in kind and money according to the custom of the manor. Similarly, the lord gave protection, supervision, and administration of justice according to the custom of the manor. It must be added that although the system did rest on reciprocal obligations, the concentration of economic and political power in the hands of the lord led to a system in which, by any standard, the serf was exploited in the extreme.

The Catholic Church was by far the largest owner of land during the Middle Ages....This was also an age during which the religious teaching of the church had a very strong and pervasive influence throughout Western Europe. These factors combined to make the church the closest thing to a strong central government throughout this period.

Thus the manor might be secular or religious...but the essential relationships between lord and serfs were not significantly affected by this distinction. There is little evidence that serfs were treated any less harshly by religious lords than by secular ones. The religious lords and the secular nobility were the joint ruling classes; they controlled the land and the power that went with it. In return for very onerous appropriations of the serf's labor, produce, and money, the nobility provided military protection and the church provided spiritual aid.

In addition to manors, medieval Europe had many towns, which were important centers of manufacturing. Manufactured goods were sold to manors and, sometimes, traded in long-distance commerce. The dominant economic institutions in the towns were the guilds—craft, professional, and trade associations that had existed as far back as the Roman Empire. If anyone wanted to produce or sell any good or service, he had to join a guild.

The guilds were as involved with social and religious questions as with economic ones. They regulated their members' conduct in all their activities: personal, social, religious, and economic. Although the guilds did regulate very carefully the production and sale of commodities, they were less concerned with making profits than with saving their members souls. Salvation demanded that the individual lead an orderly life based on church teachings and custom. Thus the guilds exerted a powerful influence as conservators of the status quo in the medieval towns.

Source: E. K. Hunt. *Property and Prophets*, 3rd edition. Abridged from pp. 5–7, © 1972, 1975, 2003, M.E. Sharpe, Inc., E. K. Hunt. Reprinted by permission of E. K. Hunt.

6. What were the dominant institutions of feudalism? What classes existed in feudal society?

7. How does the feudal "custom of the manor" differ from our modern system of contracts?

8. What did the "religious lords and secular nobility" do with the economic surplus that they controlled?

The Breakdown of Feudalism

As feudalism developed, several new economic activities and trends emerged that eventually created the preconditions for a new economic order. Most notable were changes in technology, urbanization, medieval merchants, the Crusades and exploration, creation of the nation-state, breakdown of the guilds, the rise of Protestantism and individualism, and the decline of the manor and the rise of private property. These factors and others, as sources of change over centuries in Western Europe, eventually led to the destruction of feudal institutions and relationships. These were replaced by a new set of institutions and relationships that we have come to label capitalism.

Changes in Technology.   In about the eleventh century the three-field crop rotation system replaced the two-field system. The widespread introduction of this revolutionary new system allowed for a much more productive use of agricultural land. In this system, all parcels of land would lie fallow every third year, preventing the land from becoming depleted by constant planting. This simple change increased the agricultural surplus and encouraged the use of more grain in supporting field animals. Agricultural production increased even further with greater use of oxen and horses, and later, with consolidation of agricultural lands. In addition, transportation of agricultural goods was facilitated by more horses and improvements in wagon technology.

Urbanization. The increasing agricultural surplus supported an expanding and more urbanized population. Larger urban centers fostered specialization in economic production; the early medieval towns and cities began to concentrate on trade and manufacturing. This specialization led to further increases in production and stimulated trading among the cities and between the cities and the countryside.

Medieval Merchants. Given different specializations of agricultural and manufacturing production in different areas throughout Western Europe, individual merchants during the tenth to fourteenth centuries began traveling from place to place, buying, selling, and trading goods. These transient merchants exposed self-sufficient manors to the variety of products from the rest of Europe and Asia and created interdependencies that whittled away at the traditional patterns of feudal life. This very trade further encouraged the development of regional and urban-rural specialization—a source of increasing economic surplus. It also laid the roots for the later sophistication of European commerce. Traveling merchants were replaced by permanent markets in commercial cities by the fifteenth century.

The Crusades and Exploration. Between the eleventh and thirteenth centuries, the Crusades brought Europeans into contact with a civilization much more concerned with trading and moneymaking. It also exposed them to the wealth of Asia and its goods. This exposure encouraged an effort to expand the trading periphery of Europe. The nations of Europe began to explore Africa and Asia. These explorations ultimately led to the discovery of the New World. The example of moneymaking was not lost either. Merchants financed and profited from the Crusades, while European nations used their newfound exploring capability to establish colonies and reap from them raw materials and precious metals. These new forms of economic surplus financed further development and

CALVIN AND HOBBES © 1990 Watterson. Reprinted with permission of UNIVERSITY PRESS SYNDICATE.

created fledgling capitalist institutions. In fact, the inflow of gold and silver produced such rapid growth that a great price inflation occurred during the sixteenth century in Europe.

Creation of the Nation-State.   An additional factor that contributed to the decline of feudalism and, in fact, supported exploration was the creation of the nation-state. The self-sufficient and decentralized nature of feudalism began to hamper trade as manors attempted to levy tariffs and tolls on merchants. However, as centralization of political power became the goal of certain nobles and lords, these forces were joined by the commercial merchants in the cities. This coalition of economic and political power ensured the emergence of nation-states. By the sixteenth century these newly unified nations within Europe were encouraging trade within and among their countries and exploration across the Atlantic and the Mediterranean. The new nation-states possessed the economic, political, and military power that formed the basis for a new economic order and increased economic growth.

Breakdown of the Guilds.   The replacement of the guilds by the *putting-out system* contributed to the creation of a laboring class of people and to the extension of the market for labor service. Under the feudal guild system of production, independent craftspeople had used their own tools and shops to produce their products and then sold the products to merchants. Production and sales were overseen by the guilds. As trade expanded and the production of manufactured goods increased, the putting-out system began in the sixteenth century to replace the guilds. In this arrangement, a merchant-capitalist gained control of the tools, raw materials, and workplace, and would hire, for wages, skilled individuals to produce the final product. Eventually this system led to the establishment of centralized industrial factories.

Two major elements of this new system differentiated it from the feudal guild system. First, production was controlled by the capitalist—the owner of tools, buildings, and other resources involved in production (i.e., the capital). This person would also arrange for the sale of products. The goal was monetary profit. The guild no longer influenced the production and sale of the goods. Second, this new system created a labor force that depended on the capitalist for work. The craftspeople no longer owned capital; they had only their skills and labor power to sell to the capitalist.

As the putting-out system developed further, markets for goods and resources determined profits for capitalists. These market relationships, rather than the custom and tradition of feudal relations, governed decisions about who would work and for what wages, and how the work would be performed. Industrial production was organized on a capitalist, rather than feudal, basis.

The Rise of Protestantism and Individualism.   Another factor contributing to the decline of feudalism concerned a change in the philosophy of much of the European population as well as a decline in the power of one of feudalism's most powerful institutions, the Catholic Church. The Catholic Church emphasized in its teachings a concern with afterlife and deemphasized material life. In fact, the Church argued against lending money for interest (usury) and profit making; if people were poor, that was their station in this life (it was God's will). This philosophy elevated the role of the Church in the society and economic system and downplayed the importance of the individual. The rise of the Protestant challenge to Catholicism and King Henry VIII's confiscation of Catholic Church lands and installation of the Anglican Church in England weakened the controlling role of the Catholic Church in feudal society.

In addition, Protestantism offered a philosophy more directed toward individual salvation. Calvinism, in fact, provided a justification of profit making as demonstrating service to God in one's "calling." Working hard, earning profits, and plowing those profits back into the business constituted circumstantial evidence that one was among God's chosen. This new religious idea and the Protestant churches as institutions, along with an increased emphasis on political freedom and liberty, supported the creation of a new *individualism*. This spirit, in turn, prompted much of the behavior necessary to the establishment of capitalist institutions.

Decline of the Manor.   One of the most significant trends in the transition from feudalism to capitalism occurred on the manor. Increasingly, the feudal obligations between lords and serfs became monetized. As trade expanded, the need for money caused feudal lords to sell their crops for cash and to put their serfs on money payments for work. In turn, some serfs began to pay rents to the lords for the use of land.

The *enclosure movement* from the thirteenth through the eighteenth centuries sealed the fate of the manorial system. As monetization and trade progressed, lords began to use their manors for cash generation. Common pastureland on the manors, as well as the king's common land, both traditionally accessible to all, were "enclosed" for grazing sheep. The sheep, in turn, were the source of wool to supply the increasing demand throughout Europe for woolen cloth. The effects and methods of this process were widespread. David McNally describes the change in *Political Economy and the Rise of Capitalism:*

> From the late sixteenth century onwards, sections of the gentry took advantage of the weakened status of the village community to launch a sustained offensive against the rights of the small tenants.... And, most important, they undertook to enclose and reorganize lands—a path which tended to raise the productivity of the land by 50 percent on average....[M]odern research suggests that by 1700 three-quarters of all enclosure had already taken place. As a result of this multi-faceted offensive, rents doubled during the half-century from 1590 to 1640.
>
> The landlords' offensive often involved a shift to large-scale capitalist farming in the form of pasturage as well as new crops and rotation patterns which brought more land into productive use year in and year out.

While the enclosures contributed to growing output, trade, and incomes for some, the process also made it increasingly impossible for serfs/tenants to support themselves. In essence, they were forced off the land in search of work for wages. Most gravitated toward the cities.

The combination of the enclosure movement and the putting-out system created a new class of individuals who controlled the productive land

and resources of Western Europe and whose goal was profit. In both the countryside and the city, this centralization of control and ownership resulted in greater economic production. In addition, the changes created a new class of landless, propertyless individuals—people no longer tied to their hereditary lands or their crafts. This was a new kind of labor force: a "free" labor force in which work was not a guarantee and the individual was free to seek work for wages determined by emerging market forces. The members of this labor force responded to the forces of change by attempting to sell their only resource, their labor power, at the best possible wage. They formed the emerging urban working class.

9. From the preceding material, list the feudal relations and institutions that were destroyed by the centuries of change in Western Europe between 1100 and 1800.

10. List the new relationships and institutions that were emerging to form capitalism.

11. What similarities and/or differences do you see between the enclosure movement in Europe and the modern replacement of family farms in the United States by agribusiness corporations?

THE DEVELOPMENT OF PROPERTY IN ENGLAND

Britain is an island (comprising England, Wales, and Scotland) with a total area less than that of Pennsylvania and New York. The Beaker people occupied early Britain; they were followed by the Celts in 800 B.C. The Romans, led by Julius Caesar, arrived in 55 B.C. and departed about A.D. 410. Angles, Saxons, and Jutes arrived in the fifth century, followed by the Vikings in 865.

In 1066, William the Conqueror, with the approval of the pope, invaded England. With his Norman followers, he slew the recently crowned King Harold at the Battle of Hastings, burned houses, and destroyed crops and cattle. William and the Normans confiscated all the land, and William became the chief lord. He redistributed land titles to his favorite Norman subjects, including the Church. About 1085–1086, William ordered a detailed survey of every piece of land in England; it was to include information about the rights by which the land was held. This survey is the *Domesday Book*. William planned to use this information for tax purposes.

Almost two centuries later, in 1215, the barons (landholders), who felt threatened by the Crown, compelled King John to sign the Magna Carta, which would ensure the barons' rights from the encroaching authority of the king. This was a rebellion of feudal lords. The peasants and artisans were not rebelling, and the Magna Carta neither improved nor protected their rights.

A few centuries later, Henry VIII (1491–1547) established the Church of England. He closed the Catholic monasteries and abbeys, confiscated all of the Church land, and appointed his own church officers. As British historian Maurice Keen notes in *The Outlaws of Medieval Legend*, "After that the way was

Property rights were established following the Norman Conquest of Britain by the building of a castle such as this one in York. Its vantage point, overlooking two rivers, assured the property holders that no invaders were sneaking up on them.
(Photograph by Tom Riddell)

clear for the biggest event in our agrarian history—the distribution of all monastery lands to the Tudor millionaires. These landowners—merchants now rather than barons or earls—built themselves...superb mansions."

12. In what ways might these events have helped shape the kind of economic system that developed in Britain?

13. What is a property right? What determines a property right?

Thus, private property emerged in England over the course of several centuries. Its roots lie in conquest by foreign armies under the leadership of individuals who became the medieval nobility. Later on, land was appropriated by kings and distributed to vassals, barons, and the Church. This process was enforced by a combination of military power and monarchical or religious legal authority and was often sanctioned by the Church. As we saw above, the enclosure movement in the later Middle Ages accelerated this formal transfer of land to private owners.

Those Without Property—The Peasants

During the early Middle Ages, the serfs on feudal manors seem to have accepted their lot in life. Their lives had security and certainty, in addition to hard work and perhaps poverty. What complaining there was seems to have been confined to individual peasants or manors. In the later centuries of the Middle Ages, however, as feudal institutions began to change and be replaced by emergent capitalist institutions, the peasants began actively and widely to oppose their rulers.

Beginning in the late fourteenth century and continuing through the sixteenth century, peasant revolts sprang up all over Western Europe. In most cases, the peasants were resisting change and attempting to secure their legal places in the feudal order. They opposed increasing mechanization of agricultural work, the consolidation of plots, the enclosure movement, the seizure of lands, and many of the other changes that signaled the rise of the landed gentry—and the demise of the peasants' rights to land and protection. All of these rebellions were brutally put down by the well-armed nobility. The peasants were leaderless, unorganized, and poorly armed. Their actions did, however, reflect a deep sense of outrage at the costs they bore as a result of fundamental changes in the economic, political, and social order of their day. Out of this history came the legends of Robin Hood and other outlaws of the Middle Ages.

During this period, British people in rural England were totally dependent on the productivity of the land. Those who lived in villages used common land to raise their crops, keep their bees, graze their livestock, and gather their firewood. Without access to land, they would have been without any means to sustain their lives. Over an extended period of time, a series of parliamentary acts converted many of the commons into private property. Whole villages were deserted;

The Significance of Property

Through conquest, appropriation, and legislative act, land in England came to be privately owned. This was one of the bases for the private ownership of productive resources—one of the foundations of capitalism as an economic system. Under private ownership of property, an individual (or a group of individuals, as in a modern corporation) owns and controls a piece of land (or a factory, machine, or product). That ownership allows the owner to use the property, rent it to someone else, or even sell it. The decision about what to do with it rests with its owner.

If we assume that individuals are out to maximize their own self-interest, the property will be used in its most productive or profitable way. The property owner determines a use for the property based on his or her motivations, but also based on the operation of markets—for the property itself, either sold or rented, or for the outputs that it can produce. In other words, the property can be used to maximize the economic return to the owner. The owner has a right to the use and control of that property. And the existence of markets allows owners to seek out the most productive and profitable use for their property.

One necessary implication of property and property rights is that both must be defined within a particular society. Property implies possession and control. It has been, and can still be, determined by force and conquest. Property can be appropriated, willingly or unwillingly. In modern capitalist societies, we have legal documents that convey ownership—deeds, registrations, wills, and stock certificates. In addition, there are legislative, administrative, and judicial dimensions to the definition of property and property rights. Land is surveyed, counties record deeds of land and home ownership, communities pass zoning laws that regulate the use of property, and courts adjudicate disputes among property owners and enforce contracts. Property is an institution that is central to the functioning of markets in a capitalist economy, but it is also an institution that gets its status from the social and political processes of the society.

people who were independent when they could use the common lands became either vagrant or dependent on employment by those who owned the land.

Private Property and the Rise of Capitalism

The formation of truly private property, one of the fundamental prerequisites of capitalism, can be traced to the early history of England. As feudalism faded at the end of the Middle Ages, the notion of property in England was defined in legal terms. Laws conferred or acknowledged the right of ownership and protected the owner's control over the use of property. From the owner's perspective, such property rights and legal protection allowed for maximum earnings from the land and ensured their dominant position in society. From the perspective of the peasants, control of land was torn from them out of their own adversity and weakness through conquest and legal manipulation. This ensured their position at the bottom of society, forcing them into vagrancy or a dependence on wage labor for income. Out of frustration, peasants revolted against the emergence of private property throughout the late Middle Ages.

14. What were the economic roots of the peasant rebellions?
15. What would you predict happened to the distribution of income in England as a result of these changes in property ownership?

Critics of the Institution of Private Property

Socialists and other reform-minded economists blamed the poverty and poor conditions experienced by landless peasants and the working class on the system of private property upon which capitalism was based. Capitalists, these economists wrote, use the productive resources they own for their own benefit, exploiting workers in the process. Workers have no choice but to accept low wages and poor working conditions because they do not own property and therefore must work for someone else in order to survive. Pierre Joseph Proudhon (1809–1865), a French economist, forcefully argued against private property in his essay "What Is Property?" (1840):

> If I were asked to answer the following question: *What is slavery?* and I should answer in one word, *It is murder*, my meaning would be understood at once. No extended argument would be required to show that the power to take from a man his thought, his will, his personality, is a power of life and death; and that to enslave a man is to kill him. Why, then, to this other question: *What is property?* may I not likewise answer, *It is robbery*, without the certainty of being misunderstood; the second proposition being no other than a transformation of the first?
>
> Reader, calm yourself: I am no agent of discord, no firebrand of sedition. I anticipate history by a few days; I disclose a truth whose development we may try in vain to arrest; I write the preamble of our future constitution. This proposition which seems to you blasphemous—*property is robbery*—would, if our prejudices allowed us to consider it, be recognized as the lightning-rod to shield us from the coming thunderbolt; but too many interests stand in the way!...Alas! philosophy

will not change the course of events; destiny will fulfill itself regardless of prophecy. Besides, must not justice be done and our education be finished?

The proprietor, the robber, the hero, the sovereign—for all these titles are synonymous—imposes his will as law, and suffers neither contradiction nor control; that is, he pretends to be the legislative and executive power at once. Accordingly, the substitution of the scientific and true law for the royal will be accomplished only by a terrible struggle; and this constant substitution is, after property, the most potent element in history, the most prolific source of political disturbances. Examples are too numerous and too striking to require enumeration.

Here, Proudhon identifies the holders of private property (business owners, or capitalists) as dictators who have unchecked power over the laborers who work for them. To Proudhon, this power made the relationship between capitalist and worker akin to slavery and gave the capitalist the power to rob workers of a fair price for their labor.

16. *"What is property?...It is robbery."* True or false? What does Proudhon mean by this? What historical developments in the emergence of private property would support this claim?

Proudhon is careful to differentiate **property** from **possessions**. He has no quarrel with people owning *personal* possessions—homes, farms, tools, livestock, furniture, or any of the things we might own and use. He protests the ownership of *impersonal* property that is not used by the owner except to collect rents on land and interest and profits on capital that are produced by others. The difference between property and possessions is an important distinction for many socialist authors. Here is Proudhon's statement about the difference:

> Individual possession is the condition of social life; five thousand years of property demonstrate it. Property is the suicide of society. Possession is a right; property is against right. Suppress property while maintaining possession, and, by this simple modification of the principle you will revolutionize law, government, economy, and institutions; you will drive evil from the face of the earth.

17. To demonstrate your understanding of Proudhon's definition, list five currently familiar examples of "possessions" and five of "property."

Despite the protest by Proudhon and others, the march towards capitalism continued.

EMERGENT CAPITALISM

By the late fifteenth and early sixteenth centuries in England, France, Spain, Belgium, and Holland, modern nation-states involving a coalition of monarchs and merchant capitalists had effectively eliminated the decentralized power of the feudal system. In its place emerged a new type of economic system, the key elements of which formed the historical roots of **capitalism**. Profits became the primary motivation for productive activity. The resources necessary for production and distribution—the raw materials, tools, shops, factories, machinery—were owned by a new class of capitalists. Capitalists used their ownership of capital to organize production, sell goods, and earn profits. The profits, in turn, could be used to enrich the capitalists and to develop more capital. More capital led to more output, more profits, and so on in an accumulation of economic growth.

The sources of this early **capital accumulation process** and the emergence of capitalism were rooted in the increase in trade, exploration (along with colonialism and slavery), the enclosure movement, and the putting-out system. The new class of capitalists developed as the leading force in the economic system, and a new labor force, dependent on wages for income, changed the character of society, as well as the distribution of income. Like feudalism, capitalism would also change and develop, although even today it retains its basic elements of private ownership, profit making, and markets. The earliest form that capitalism took was called mercantilism.

Mercantilism

To build and consolidate their political, economic, and military power, the new nation-states adopted a policy of **mercantilism**. Underlying that policy was the assumption that the foundation of a nation's power and prestige was trading. The object of trading was to accumulate and retain gold and silver bullion, which could be used to finance further trade or to enhance the nation's political and military power. This concern led to exploration to discover and hoard more precious metals. It also led to policies designed to maximize the flow of money into the nation and minimize the flow of money out.

Consequently, under mercantilism, the king designated monopolies in the trade of specific products to minimize the prices of imports and maximize the prices of exports. The state also controlled importing and exporting, levied tariffs on imports, subsidized exports, and controlled shipping extensively. The state thus took a large degree of responsibility in geographic expansion and in controlling economic activity. At first, this sponsorship aided some nascent capitalists, but the state's overriding control over the economy eventually began to burden increasing numbers of individualistic and profit-motivated businesspeople.

Like feudalism before it, mercantilism created a series of internal contradictions that gradually undermined the system. The controlled nature of the economy proved to be a constraint for new capitalist businesses, which wanted more trade and greater access to markets. They began to pressure for change and for a new economic philosophy in which free markets reigned and the king and the monopolists no longer held sway. As we will see in the next chapter, this philosophy, called classical liberalism, was championed by the great economist and philosopher Adam Smith.

❖Conclusion

In this chapter, we began with a description of what an economic system is and showed how economic systems change over time. In particular, we have explored the historical development of economic systems from antiquity to emergent capitalism. In the remaining chapters of Part 1, we will examine how economic thought has changed as well over the years.

Review Questions

1. Discuss the distinguishing characteristics of ancient economic systems.

2. What must an economic system accomplish? Why?

3. Why is surplus a source of economic growth?

4. Explain the transition from feudalism to capitalism, and identify the main differences between the two systems.

5. Of the factors that caused feudalism to decline, which do you think was most important? Why?

6. Under mercantilism, how was the economy organized?

7. Why was the institution of private property important to the economic development of capitalism? Why were some economists critical of private ownership of land and productive resources (the means of production)?

8. What is the importance of markets to a capitalist economic system?

9. Reread the passage by Karl Marx at the beginning of the chapter. Paraphrase his point in the last paragraph. Do you agree with his argument? Why or why not?

10. "The results of economic activity—what gets produced and how it gets produced— organized through an economic system, condition the nature, history and development of a society and its people." Give examples from human history. Give examples from your own experience.

11. "Economic development is obviously of crucial importance to any society and its continued survival." Why is this obvious? What would happen to a society if it didn't experience economic development? What are the advantages of economic develop- ment? Do you think that economic development has advantages for you? What are they?

CHAPTER THREE

Adam Smith, Classical Liberalism, and the Division of Labor

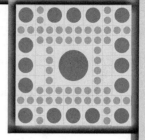

◆ Introduction

I n the eighteenth and nineteenth centuries mercantilist restrictions on economic behavior gave rise to an opposition that ultimately prevailed and drastically reduced the amount of direct state interference in economic affairs. The movement to end mercantilism was spearheaded by a new philosophical and economic body of thought—**classical liberalism.**

Adam Smith was one of the first thinkers to develop a comprehensive description and analysis of this emerging economic system. Property and property rights contributed to the formation of new methods of production, including the division of labor, with specialization of tasks, which promoted an explosive expansion of output. The rise of capitalism also resulted in new ways of distributing income.

Those articulating classical liberal ideas were primarily academics who wanted to transfer control of their national economies from the mercantilism of aristocratic ruling classes that regulated all aspects of production and trade, to an unregulated market system that was thought to be self-regulating. They called this system (from the physiocrats in France) **laissez-faire,** meaning "let it happen," or "let it be." J. B. Say, a French economist, popularized Smith's work, particularly the idea of self-regulating markets.

THE RISE OF CLASSICAL LIBERALISM AND THE INDUSTRIAL REVOLUTION

Adam Smith was born to a prosperous Scottish family in 1723. Smith's father, who died before his son was born, had served as comptroller of customs. His mother was the daughter of a wealthy landowning family. Smith studied at Glasgow and Oxford and at the age of 29 became a professor of moral philosophy at the University of Glasgow.

Adam Smith was influenced by professor Francis Hutcheson, under whom Smith studied at Glasgow University, and by his friend and mentor David Hume. Some of Smith's ideas came from his association with the Physiocrats. He was also influenced significantly by John Locke (1632–1704), whose contributions to the methods of scientific inquiry and political theory were becoming acceptable to most eighteenth-century philosophers. Locke argued for empirical forms of inquiry: "All our ideas come from experience." Smith's first book, *The Theory of Moral Sentiments*, first published in 1759, outlines the ethical and moral aspects of human actions including the social aspects of these actions. In *The Theory of Moral Sentiments*, Smith followed in the footsteps of his Scottish mentors, furthering arguments for what might be called a "moral compass" to guide one's actions and decisions, and establishing a foundation for his later and more famous work, *The Wealth of Nations*, published in 1776. In *The Wealth of Nations* Smith argued forcefully that mercantilist policies interfered with the ability of private individuals and markets to produce maximum social welfare. Smith maintained that, although everyone was basically out to maximize his or her own welfare, private competition in production and consumption would ensure the best possible outcome for all. Self-interest, tempered by competition, would result in increases in the standard of living for everyone. Therefore Smith argued that the state should not be overly involved in economic activity, and that beyond providing for law and order, national defense, and some public goods like roads, the state should take a laissez-faire attitude toward the economic system. Individuals would guide production and consumption. The emerging capitalist class in Western Europe seized on this philosophy and used it eventually to legislate an end to most mercantilist restrictions on trade and other economic activity.

Left to their own devices and the profit motive, English capitalists took early advantage of the technological advances of the Industrial Revolution. The development and introduction of more sophisticated machinery in textiles, transportation, iron production, and other industries led to a phenomenal increase in the productive capacity of the English economic system. The Industrial Revolution, as well as the entrepreneurs who financed and led it, spread throughout Western Europe and to North America.

However, the increase in production was not the only outcome of the Industrial Revolution and emergent capitalism. The factory became the symbol of a new manufacturing society, alongside continuing agricultural and community life. In the factory, working conditions were often unsafe and oppressive. Child labor was a fact of early industrial life. Men, women, and children depended almost totally on factory work for their livelihood. Families flocked to the cities in search of work. Outside the factories, people were crammed into the adjacent slums. Friedrich Engels, in *The Condition of the Working Class in England in 1844*, quotes a government commissioner's description of a Glasgow slum, the "wynds":

> The wynds…house a fluctuating population between 15,000 and 30,000 persons. This district is composed of many narrow streets and square courts and in the middle of each court there is a dunghill. Although the outward appearance of these places was revolting, I was nevertheless quite unprepared for the filth and misery

that were to be found inside. In some bedrooms we visited at night we found a whole mass of humanity stretched on the floor. There were often 15 to 20 men and women huddled together, some being clothed and others naked. There was hardly any furniture there and the only thing which gave these holes the appearance of a dwelling was fire burning on the hearth. Thieving and prostitution are the main sources of income of these people.

1. List three reasons that explain why capitalists and those advocating classical liberalism opposed mercantilism.

2. Early capitalism was unmindful of the social effects of industrialization brought on by the Industrial Revolution. List two ways that the philosophy of laissez-faire might contribute to these social effects.

The emergence of capitalism and a free market for labor encouraged, as well as fed on, the Industrial Revolution. These forces produced rapid economic growth and the factory system, as well as urban slums and adverse working conditions. Central to these changes was the spread of markets for goods and services throughout Western Europe and the world. With the diminution of the roles of tradition, custom, and the state in the economic affairs of Western Europeans, capitalism relied increasingly on *markets* to organize production and distribution. As factors of production, land, labor, and capital all became commodities that were bought and sold on markets for prices. This required the emergence of a market system in which producers made calculations based on prices of resources and products and directed attention toward the accumulation of profits.

Economic activity was thus directed through the operation of these markets and the determination of prices in them. The treatment of land, labor, and capital as commodities contrasted with the feudal system, wherein land and labor were part of the social organization of communities (feudal manors and guilds) and were regulated by social custom, tradition, and institutions. With the emergence of capitalism, land and labor became subject to the market for their occupation and use. In this way, as economic historian Karl Polanyi argues in *The Great Transformation*, capitalism required the subordination of social considerations to the economic dictates of the private market system. Production and distribution were organized, for the society, through markets.

3. Explain the significance of markets in capitalism.

ADAM SMITH AND THE DIVISION OF LABOR

Much of our current thinking about specialization and the **division of labor** has been influenced by the writings of Adam Smith (1723–1790). The **division of labor** involves separating different parts of the production process of any good or service. Instead of one person making each computer, teams of workers make the casings, the chips, the boards, the connections, and the final assembly. **Specialization** results from workers' focusing on and developing expertise in one aspect of the entire process of producing computers. Smith was a Scottish scholar, primarily a moral philosopher, but also the father of modern economics. His writing reflected changes he saw taking place, such as the introduction of modern productive methods, including the assembly line, which were derived from the early development of capitalism during the Industrial Revolution.

The year 1776 is significant because Adam Smith's great book *An Inquiry into the Nature and Causes of the Wealth of Nations* was published. It was the first comprehensive treatise about economics. However, there had been many books and essays about economic matters before Adam Smith, and he used some of these ideas in his book. In his text, Smith created a fairly complete picture of the way an economy behaves and why it behaved as it did in 1776. His observations coincided with the acceleration of the Industrial Revolution and the increasing importance of both domestic and international markets to British capitalists. In *The Wealth of Nations*, Smith also argued for the replacement of mercantilism with competitive markets.

Smith begins *The Wealth of Nations* with this classic description "Of the Division of Labour" in the context of emerging capitalist production:

> The greatest improvement in the productive powers of labour, and the greater part of the skill, dexterity, and judgment with which it is any where directed, or applied, seem to have been the effects of the division of labour.
>
> To take an example from a very trifling manufacturer: but one in which the division of labour has been very often taken notice of, the trade of the pinmaker; a workman not educated to this business (which the division of labour has rendered a distinct trade), not acquainted with the use of the machinery employed in it (to the invention of which the same division of labour has probably given occasion), could scarce, perhaps, with his utmost industry, make one pin in a day, and certainly could not make twenty. But in the way in which this business is now carried on, not only the whole work is a peculiar trade, but it is divided into a number of branches, of which the greater part are likewise peculiar trades. One man draws out the wire, another straights it, a third cuts it, a fourth points it, a fifth grinds it at the top for receiving the head; to make the head requires two or three distinct operations; to put it on, is a peculiar business, to whiten the pins is another; it is even a trade by itself to put them into the paper; and the important business of making a pin is, in this manner, divided into about eighteen distinct operations, which, in some manufactories, are all performed by distinct hands, though in others the same man will sometimes perform two or three of them. I have seen a small manufactory of this kind where ten men only were employed, and where some of them consequently performed two or three distinct operations. But though they were very poor, and therefore but indifferently accommodated with the necessary machinery, they could, when they exerted themselves, make among them about twelve pounds of pins in a day. There are in a pound upwards of four thousand pins of a middling size. Those ten persons, therefore, could make among them upwards of forty-eight thousand pins in a day. Each person, therefore, making a tenth part of forty-eight thousand pins, might be considered as making four thousand eight hundred pins in a day.

Adam Smith (1723–1790)
(Bettmann/Corbis)

4. In what ways might Adam Smith's perceptions have been influenced by the historical time when he wrote this part of the book?

5. Explain the importance of such specialization in Smith's pin factory. Who gains from such specialization?

With this description of the division of labor, Adam Smith highlighted the role of specialization in significantly increasing productive potential. He attributed this great increase in productivity to three factors:

1. "The improvement of the dexterity of the workman necessarily increases the quantity of work he can perform; and the division of labor, by reducing every man's business to some one simple operation, and by making this operation the sole employment of his life, necessarily increases very much the dexterity of the workman."

2. The worker would gain time that used to be lost in moving from one type of work to another.

3. Labor would be made more productive by the application of specialized machinery that would facilitate the division of labor.

Thus, specialization and the application of new technologies during the Industrial Revolution of the late eighteenth and early nineteenth centuries contributed to rapidly expanding output.

An important result of this increase in output accompanying the division of labor was that each worker "has a great quantity of his own work to dispose of beyond what he himself has occasion for." Since every worker is in the same position, **exchange** will take place. Smith puts it this way: "He supplies them abundantly with what they have occasion for, and they accommodate him as amply with what he has occasion for, and a general plenty diffuses itself through all the different ranks of the society." Through the division of labor, economic output will increase, and the existence of exchange will facilitate and further encourage this growth in output. The extension of **markets** (where goods and services are exchanged) throughout the world, the technological revolution, and the division of labor mutually reinforced one another.

6. "And the division of labor, by reducing every man's business to some one simple operation, and by making this operation the sole employment of his life, necessarily increases very much the dexterity of the workman."

   a. Imagine having a job where one simple operation made the sole employment of your life. Do you think that your dexterity might improve?

   b. Do you think that people working on an assembly line would agree with your answer?

Smith traced the emergence of the division of labor in production to the fact that people do exchange goods and services: "It is the necessary, though very slow and gradual, consequence of a propensity in human nature which has in view no such extensive utility: *the propensity to truck, barter, and exchange* one thing for another" [italics added]. Because people have a tendency to exchange, they will begin to specialize in producing what they do best and to trade with others for the other things that they need. Through this process, the division of labor proceeds and economic output increases. Historically, the rapidly spreading and more sophisticated markets in Western Europe tremendously accelerated the development of the division of labor.

Adam Smith further argued that all of this great economic progress derived from the seeking of self-interest by individuals. Individuals enter markets for exchange to benefit themselves. But out of this quest for self-gain, a general good develops in the form of increasing prosperity for all:

But man has almost constant occasion for the help of his brethren, and it is in vain for him to expect it from their benevolence only. He will be more likely to prevail if he can interest their self-love in his favour, and shew them that it is for their own advantage to do for him what he requires of them. Whoever offers to another a bargain of any kind, proposes to do this. Give me that which I want, and you shall have this which you want, is the meaning of every such offer; and it is in this manner that we obtain from one another the far greater part of those good offices which we stand in need of. It is not from the benevolence of the butcher, the brewer, or the baker, that we expect our dinner, but from their regard to their own interest. We address ourselves, not to their humanity but to their self-love, and never talk to them of our own necessities but of their advantages.

General prosperity and economic growth—the wealth of the nation—result from the pursuit of self-interest organized through the division of labor and markets. This is the essence of what Smith calls the **invisible hand**, the force whereby the operation of markets—unfettered by mercantilist regulations—produces general welfare for all, where resources are allocated efficiently.

7. Adam Smith thought the division of labor derived from people's "propensity to truck, barter, and exchange one thing for another." Can you think of examples where this holds true today? Are there other factors that might enter into the division of labor today?

8. "But man has almost constant occasion for the help of his brethren, and it is in vain for him to expect it from their benevolence only. He will be more likely to prevail if he can interest their self-love in his favour, and shew them that it is for their own advantage to do for him what he requires of them."

   a. What does Smith assume about the nature of people's behavior? How did Smith arrive at this conclusion?

   b. If it is an accurate assumption about present behavior, do people have any choice about behaving in any other way?

Side Effects of the Division of Labor

Adam Smith focused on the relation of the division of labor, specialization, exchange, and markets to the wealth of nations. He also showed sensitivity to some side effects of the division of labor. The first of these is a problem that we still experience today: the alienation and boredom of manual labor, the assembly line, and office work. These result from the division of labor and specialization within the workplace, motivated by the capitalist's search for profits and the need to manage labor. Smith wrote about this problem bluntly and graphically in this passage from *The Wealth of Nations*:

> In the progress of the division of labour, the employment of the far greater part of those who live by labour, that is, of the great body of the people, comes to be confined to a few very simple operations, frequently to one or two. But the understandings of the greater part of men are necessarily formed by their ordinary employments. The man whose whole life is spent in performing a few simple operations, of which the effects too are, perhaps, always the same, or very nearly the same, has no occasion to exert his understanding, or to exercise his invention in finding out expedients for removing difficulties which never occur. He naturally loses, therefore, the habit of such exertion, and generally becomes as stupid and ignorant as it is possible for a human creature to become. The torpor of his mind renders him not only incapable of relishing or bearing a part in any rational conversation, but of conceiving any generous, noble, or tender sentiment, and consequently of forming any just judgment concerning many even of the ordinary duties of private life.
>
> His dexterity at his own particular trade seems, in this manner, to be acquired at the expense of his intellectual, social, and martial virtues. But in every improved and civilized society this is the state into which the labouring poor, that is, the great body of the people, must necessarily fall, unless government takes some pains to prevent it.

An additional consequence of this tendency is that the guidance of society must fall to the few, the elite, who are not stupefied by the repetitiveness of their labors. In fact, the division of labor under capitalism not only increased efficiency, it also promoted the control of the capitalist over the work process and the workers. This can also be seen in the emergence of the putting-out system and later the factory system (see Chapter 2). This process effectively splits society into classes—the educated elite and the "great body of the people"—which also have different claims on the income generated by production.

9. Does specialization normally result in workers who are "as stupid and ignorant as it is possible for a human creature to become"? How was this statement of Smith's conditioned by historical time? Do you agree with Smith's conclusion? Why or why not?

THE DISTRIBUTION OF INCOME

Economic production creates value—goods and services that are exchanged in markets. Once this value has been produced, income determines how it will be divided among the people. Early economists, such as Adam Smith, who were beginning to think of economics as a social science, defined and classified income receivers as they appeared at that time. They classified the receivers of the shares of output into the following categories: (1) **laborers**, (2) **landowners**, and (3) **owners of capital**. Smith also named the shares of income that each receives: labor receives **wages**, landowners receive **rent**, and owners of capital receive **profits**.

Each of these shares is received in money income, but this income is only a claim for the real goods and services. Money only has value because it can be used to purchase goods and services. Thus, income distribution determines the distribution of products.

10. Another way of thinking about income in relation to claims on the shares of production is to imagine each dollar in the hands of the income receivers (labor, landowners, and capital owners) as a draft on people's labor. Are there (or will there be) dollar drafts on your labor? Can you refuse to be drafted? Who might be exempt from the dollar draft? If drafted, when do you have to perform your service?

Adam Smith recognized that this division of the national product into shares must bring about some harsh conflicts among the three groups of share receivers:

Envy, malice, or resentment, are the only passions which can prompt one man to injure another in his person or reputation.... Men may live together in society with some tolerable degree of security, though there is no civil magistrate to protect them from the injustice of those passions. But avarice and ambition in the rich, in the poor the hatred of labour and the love of present ease and enjoyment, are the passions which prompt to invade property, passions much more steady in their operation, and much more universal in their influence. Wherever there is great property, there is great inequality. For one very rich man, there must be at least five hundred poor, and the affluence of the few supposes the indigence of the many. The affluence of the rich excites the indignation of the poor, who are often both driven by want, and prompted by envy, to invade his possessions. It is only under the shelter of the civil magistrate that the owner of that valuable property, which is acquired by the labour of many years, or perhaps of many successive generations, can sleep a single night in security. The acquisition of valuable and extensive property, therefore, necessarily requires the establishment of civil government.

The shares of the national product, then, are distributed unequally, primarily because of the unequal distribution of private property (land and capital). While this may lead to conflicts among the different groups of share receivers because each wants to maximize its own share, the government protects private property and, hence, its share of the output.

11. "The acquisition of valuable and extensive property, therefore, necessarily requires the establishment of civil government." Is Smith noting that the purpose of government is to protect the rich from the poor? What is the purpose of government?

In addition to the role played by the state, the operation of markets also resolves the conflict over the division of national output. Each group is out to maximize its position, its own share of production. However, all economic transactions take place in markets for goods and services and, as a result, are regulated by the operation of competition. A worker will not work for a lower wage if he or she can get a higher wage from another employer. A person will not buy a product at a price greater than that of another seller. Smith explains this in the following passage on the "invisible hand":

> Every individual is continually exerting himself to find out the most advantageous employment for whatever capital he can command. It is his own advantage, indeed, and not that of the society, which he has in view. But the study of his own advantage naturally, or rather necessarily leads him to prefer that employment which is most advantageous to the society.
> But the annual revenue of every society is always precisely equal to the exchangeable value of the whole annual produce of its industry, or rather is precisely the same thing with that exchangeable value. As every individual, therefore, endeavours as much as he can both to employ his capital in the support of domestic industry, and so to direct that industry that its produce may be of the greatest value; every individual necessarily labours to render the annual revenue of the society as great as he can. He generally, indeed, neither intends to promote the public interest, nor knows how much he is promoting it. By preferring the support of domestic to that of foreign industry, he intends only his own security; and by directing that industry in such a manner as its produce may be of the greatest value, he intends only his own gain, and he is in this, as in many other cases, led by *an invisible hand* to promote an

end which was no part of his intention. Nor is it always the worse for the society that it was no part of it. By pursuing his own interest he frequently promotes that of the society more effectually than when he really intends to promote it.

Despite the apparent conflict and the motivation of self-gain, the operation of the economic system produces the greatest good for the greatest number. According to Smith, social good results, even though "society...was no part" of directing the activity. Rather, it results from everyone's seeking his or her own advantage.

12. What does Smith mean when he says, "He is in this, as in many other cases, led by *an invisible hand*"? What is an "invisible hand"?

13. Smith says, "But the study of his own advantage naturally, or rather necessarily leads him to prefer that employment which is most advantageous to the society." Can you think of any counterexamples?

THE FLOW OF ECONOMIC ACTIVITY

As we have seen from Smith's analysis above, three factors of production (land, labor, and capital) are combined to create the national product. Each controller of the three productive factors—landlords, laborers, and capitalists—receives a share of the total product transformed conveniently into money and uses it to claim or purchase output. Thus, the controllers of the factors of production receive claims on shares for everything they supply in the production process, and these claims become the demand for part of the total product. Demand for the product is therefore created in the process of supplying the product. Figure 3.1 illustrates this flow of economic activity.

FIGURE 3.1   The Flow of Economic Activity

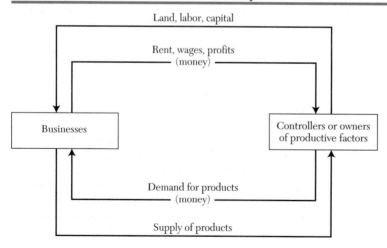

J. B. SAY AND SAY'S LAW

Smith's ideas were widely discussed and popularized by the French economist Jean Baptiste Say (1767–1832). Say argued that removing mercantile control of markets would produce rapid economic progress. As laissez-faire ideas were adopted, growth did take place, but it was accompanied by poverty and recurring swings in economic activity (business cycles). During these cycles, a period of rapid economic growth would be followed by a decline in spending, a glut of goods and services, and a recession. Say's 1803 *Treatise on Political Economy* stated the idea, which became known as **Say's law**, that society should not be concerned with gluts because supply always creates sufficent demand for products:

> It is worthwhile to remark that a product is no sooner created, than it, from that instant, affords a market for other products to the full extent of its own value. When the producer has put the finishing hand to his product, he is most anxious to sell it immediately, lest its value should vanish in his hands. Nor is he less anxious to dispose of the money he may get for it; for the value of money is also perishable. But the only way of getting rid of money is in the purchase of some product or other. Thus, the mere circumstance of the creation of one product immediately opens a vent for other products.

Say assured economists that if markets were left free, there could only be temporary and minor problems of unemployment. He believed this was true because he thought that production (supply) would always create its own demand: The income generated from producing goods and services would always be sufficient to buy the goods and services produced. For example, suppose that in order to supply a product, a local business owner pays out $50,000 in wages to workers in exchange for their labor, $20,000 in rent to the landlord, and keeps $30,000 for herself as profits. The community now has a total of $100,000 in income. What will people do with this money? According to the flow of economic activity (see Figure 3.1), they will spend it on various products. When consumers spend money on products, the money is returned to businesses. Thus, the act of supplying products creates the income that is used to purchase products. Supply (of products) creates demand (for other products). This doctrine was widely accepted by most economists throughout the nineteenth century.

GLUTS

A few economists were concerned about unemployment resulting from more production than people might demand. What if some wrong products are produced, and they are not all purchased? Won't there be unemployment because of insufficient demand in those industries? What if there is more production generally than the people are able to purchase? Economists called this situation a **glut** in the market. Throughout the early history of capitalism, there were recurring gluts that led to economic crises, or recessions. During recessions, businesses could not sell all of the goods they produced, factories lay idle, and unemployment, accompanied by poverty and misery, soared.

Thomas Robert Malthus (1766–1834), a British economist, was one of the few economists concerned about these gluts. In his *Principles of Political Economy* (1820), Malthus observed that while laborers usually spent all of their wages on necessities to maintain their families, capitalists spent only some of their profits and saved the rest. Although Say believed that all money saved would be returned to the economy as purchases of capital goods such as machinery and equipment (investment), Malthus disagreed. Malthus thought that as capitalism progressed, capitalists would earn greater and greater profits while wages would fall. With falling wages, laborers would be less able to purchase the products they produced. But if capitalists' profits were invested in ever greater amounts, then—given the decline in labor incomes—production would increase unsustainably, leading to a glut. As firms decreased output in response to a glut, a recession and higher levels of unemployment would follow.

14. If a recession is caused by too little demand, how might a government go about ending a recession?

Say and others countered the underconsumption argument set forth by Malthus by claiming that whenever a glut of any particular product emerged, markets would immediately adjust through price changes and the reallocation of resources. If one product was overproduced, its price would fall, profits would plummet, and resources would go elsewhere. Activity would shift to those products "most in request." In addition, if capitalists earned greater profits and saved more money (as Malthus feared), this would simply mean greater pools of money for them to use for purchases of additional capital goods (investment). Say believed that any additional savings would be followed in short order by additional capital goods purchases, which would sustain demand in the market. Consequently, gluts would soon be eliminated through the operation of the market system. This reasoning supported the idea of laissez-faire, because no government intervention was needed to solve the problem of gluts.

LAISSEZ-FAIRE

Most classical economists sided with J. B. Say and his conclusion that gluts would be short-lived and minor, and therefore inconsequential. There were significant reasons for this belief in spite of the prevalence of repeated gluts, unemployment, poverty, and economic depressions in capitalist nations.

Economists and business owners (capitalists) were convinced that a self-adjusting economy, free from government controls, was the best system for generating profits and growth. This was Smith's concept of an "invisible hand" directing a free economy to prosperity. The idea of laissez-faire was similar to this "invisible hand." Capitalists wanted to run their own affairs without—well, almost without—government interference.

The idea of laissez-faire is to permit market forces *under competitive conditions* to operate unhindered. Economists said that if the market were permitted to work on its own, it would be most efficient and most advantageous to society. People would demand the products they wanted as they spent their income. This would determine which products would be produced. Competition would ensure that products were produced for the lowest price possible. Doesn't that seem better than having a powerful individual or group of people decide which products will be produced?

Laissez-faire, said the economists, has additional benefits: All of the owners of the factors of production will be directed into the most efficient use of the factors of production by the market. It will be to their greatest advantage to produce the products for which there is a demand in the marketplace. If the owners of the productive factors use them to produce only what they themselves want, no one will purchase the products. There will be smaller shares of national income given to those productive-factor owners who don't follow market demand.

Therefore, the theory went, let the market be; *laissez-faire*; don't interfere with it. It is controlled by an "invisible hand." It will regulate itself. Furthermore, markets will eliminate any gluts and unemployment. Let it be.

All of this is based on the assumption that people will work for their own self-interest. Adam Smith had already asserted the validity of this assumption.

In fact, one of the great ironies of the concept of laissez-faire is that it requires the government to define and enforce its primary institution—private property. Karl Polanyi, in his history of the emergence of capitalism and laissez-faire, *The Great Transformation*, emphasizes the willful creation of a new economic order:

> There was nothing natural about laissez-faire; free markets could never come into being merely by allowing things to take their course. Just as cotton manufacturers— the leading free trade industry—were created by the help of protective tariffs, export bounties, and indirect wage subsidies, laissez-faire itself was enforced by the state.

15. Evaluate the strengths and limits of laissez-faire.

16. What are your assumptions about people's behavior? Are they consistently selfish? Are they consistently altruistic (meaning their actions are based on regard for others)? Which are you? Were we born selfish or altruistic? Are we educated to be selfish or altruistic? If so, by whom or what?

17. Would Adam Smith think it is more patriotic to be selfish or altruistic? Why?

As mercantilist policies were abandoned and laissez-faire policies were adopted in England, the Industrial Revolution and the emergence of capitalist institutions proceeded. During this period, business sought freedom from intrusive state control, and prospered.

Adam Smith argued that it would be better to transfer control of the economy from the self-interest of the ruling class to individual self-interest as expressed in the marketplace. His preference for nontraditional direction led him to perceive the market as an impartial control of resource allocation and income distribution. He hoped the market was impartial, but was it? Smith was aware of the difficulties in his solution. He knew about the ability of combinations of employers to overwhelm the bargaining power of workers, but he continued to support markets free from mercantilist government controls—laissez-faire.

What he may not have fully perceived was that the transfer of market controls from the self-interest of the ruling class to the self-interest of those who had the control of the largest quantities of productive resources was not necessarily the ideal solution for a sick economy. But it may have been an improvement in 1776, when compared with the abuses of mercantilism. Smith thought it would be when he wrote in *The Wealth of Nations* about the allocation of capital by an individual:

> What is the species of domestic industry which his capital can employ, and of which the produce is likely to be of the greatest value, every individual, it is evident, can, in his local situation, judge much better than any statesman or lawgiver can do for him. The statesman, who should attempt to direct private people in what manner they ought to employ their capitals, would not only load himself with a most unnecessary attention, but assume an authority which could safely be trusted, not only to no single person, but to no council or senate whatever, and which would nowhere be so dangerous as in the hands of a man who had folly and presumption enough to fancy himself fit to exercise it.

Conclusion

Property, markets, exchange, division of labor, and specialization emerged in the development of capitalism. Along with these institutions and aspects of changing economic activity, economic theory began to develop to describe, explain, and promote capitalism. In addition to economists contributing to the development of capitalism there were others critical of the lowered standard of living of workers and of contradictions within the capitalist system. These economists were either ignored or viewed as dangerous radicals by the dominant school of economists in the universities and the ruling classes. In this chapter, we have examined the argument for laissez-faire capitalism. In the next chapter, we will explore in more detail Karl Marx's critiques of the development and operation of laissez-faire capitalism.

Review Questions

1. Much of the argument for laissez-faire was based on assumptions about the economy, including Say's law, the assumption that the economy would always be sufficiently competitive, and the notion that consumers were always selfish, rational, and calculating. Under what circumstances might these assumptions fail? What are the implications for the economy if these assumptions do not hold?

2. Proudhon and other economists argued that laissez-faire meant freedom for the capitalist but bondage for workers. Smith, Say, and other advocates of laissez-faire argued that unregulated capitalism meant freedom for all. Are there circumstances under which Proudhon's view is likely to be more accurate? Are there circumstances when Smith's view is likely to be more apt? Explain.

3. Under mercantilism, in addition to assigning trade monopolies to selected merchants and companies, kings extracted taxes from imports and exports to enrich the royal

coffers, funding military and other expenditures. Adam Smith opposed such government intervention in the mercantilist era. What were his objections to mercantilism? What roles did Adam Smith envision for government in the economy?

4. Smith argued that unregulated (laissez-faire) capitalism would lead to substantial increases in income for all. Explain exactly how this was supposed to come about.

5. Smith believed that laissez-faire capitalism would be self-regulating via the invisible hand. Develop an example that illustrates these principles. Using your example, evaluate Smith's argument.

6. Reading Smith in the early twenty-first century, do you find that there are topics that are still applicable to today's economy? If so, which still apply? Do there seem to be areas in which his insight seems faulty? If so, what are those?

7. Have there been times recently when there has been a general glut of goods or services? Has there been a glut of one kind of good? What has been the result? Explain.

8. What reasons can you think of that would cast doubt on Say's law that supply always creates its own demand?

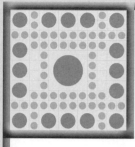

CHAPTER FOUR

Karl Marx and the Socialist Critique of Capitalism

Introduction

As capitalism developed in Western Europe and the United States, a critique of some of its results began to emerge. The conditions of some members of the economy were improving with laissez-faire, but the fate of others was extreme poverty. Why weren't conditions for the poor improving as well? As markets and private property emerged in Western Europe, most people became dependent on wage labor for income. Work was not always available, and many peasants ended up in urban areas, where they inhabited emerging slums and, if possible, worked in the developing factories. Living and working conditions were extremely poor. And with so many competing for jobs, wages were very low. The growing working class during the Industrial Revolution paid the social cost of industrialization in the cities and the factories of Western Europe.

Extreme poverty and poor working conditions led to general strikes (with all workers striking at the same time), revolutions, and political education activities working toward revolutionary change. John Stuart Mill (1806–1873), in his Principles of Political Economy, envisioned a different kind of economy from the one of which he was writing in England in 1848:

> The form of association, however, which if mankind continue to improve, must be expected in the end to predominate, is not that which can exist between a capitalist as chief, and workpeople without a voice in the management, but the association of the labourers themselves on terms of equality, collectively owning the capital with which they carry on their operations, and working under managers elected and removable by themselves.

The socialist critique of nineteenth-century capitalism was developed further in a piece also published in 1848. In this year, Karl Marx (1818–1883) and Friedrich Engels (1820–1895) wrote The Communist Manifesto for the Communist League, *an association of working people in Germany. In the* Manifesto, *Marx and Engels argued forcefully that the capitalist system itself was the source of the poverty and instability experienced by the growing working class. They urged workers to organize themselves for their own protection and to fight for socialism.*

In the Manifesto, Capital, *and subsequent works, Marx produced one of the first systematic analyses and critiques of capitalism. Marx's analysis provides a comprehensive and consistent framework for understanding, evaluating, and criticizing the structure and development of capitalism. For that reason alone, it is important to summarize Marx's system of thought concerning capitalism. In addition, Marxian economics has contributed to the development of economic thought, and Marxism as a political movement promoting socialism and communism has been widespread in the modern era.*

With the fall of the Soviet Union and other communist states in the late 1980s and early 1990s, it might be tempting to think that Marxism is no longer relevant to the modern world. However, the ideas of Marx are alive and well in the social democracies of Europe and in labor movements and intellectual circles around the world. In fact, in a 1999 BBC poll, Marx was voted the "greatest thinker of the millennium." It is important to understand that Marx's primary contributions to the field of economics were his analysis and critique of the evolution of capitalist economies and his description of the problems that invariably result from laissez-faire capitalism. As John Cassidy, economics writer for the New Yorker, *has stated:*

> Marx was a student of capitalism, and that is how he should be judged. Many of the contradictions that he saw in Victorian capitalism and that were subsequently addressed by reformist governments have begun reappearing in new guises, like mutant viruses....[H]e wrote riveting passages about globalization, inequality, political corruption, monopolization, technical progress, the decline of high culture, and the enervating nature of modern existence—issues that economists are now confronting anew, sometimes without realizing that they are walking in Marx's footsteps.
>
> —John Cassidy, "The Return of Karl Marx" (*New Yorker*, October 20–27, 1997)

And, as John Plender observed in the Financial Times, *Marx's ideas are directly relevant in helping us understand the recent financial crisis:*

> in 1893 [Karl Marx] provided as good an account of today's financial implosion as any living commentator. "To the possessor of money capital, the process of production appears merely as an unavoidable intermediate link, as a necessary evil for the sake of money-making. All nations with a capitalist mode of production are therefore seized periodically by a feverish attempt to make money without the intervention of the process of production."
>
> That passage from Das Kapital is a fine description of the financialisation of the economies of the English-speaking countries in recent years and of the resulting credit bubble. As always in financial history, the feverish attempt to make money has now given way to a fevered urge to find someone to blame.
>
> —John Plender, "Shut Out," *Financial Times*, October 17, 2008

This chapter provides a brief introduction to Marxian analysis, along with a discussion of the relevance of Marx's ideas to our understanding of contemporary society.

KARL MARX: POLITICAL ECONOMIST AND REVOLUTIONARY

Marx was born in 1818 in Trier, Germany. His father was a successful lawyer, and Marx began his college career in legal studies. However, he soon switched to philosophy, in which he earned a Ph.D. at the age of twenty-three. Having already become a radical in his student days, he was unable to secure a teaching position. Instead he became the editor of the *Rheinische Zeitung* in Cologne. However, this journal was suppressed by the Prussian government in 1843, and Marx, with his new wife, Jenny von Westphalen, moved to Paris, where Marx was active in left-wing journalism and in the workers' movement. It was there that he met Friedrich Engels and began to study political economy and capitalism.

Over the latter half of the 1840s, Marx's radicalism continually got him in trouble with governments. In 1845, he was expelled from France and moved to Brussels. There he wrote *The German Ideology* and *The Communist Manifesto* with Engels. In 1848 and 1849, several workers' revolutions occurred in Europe, and Belgium sent Marx packing. He first went to Paris and then to Germany. He was soon kicked out of Germany and then out of France again. Finally, in 1849, his family settled in London, where he remained for the rest of his life.

In London, Marx devoted himself to studying political economy and writing. His years there were spent in constant poverty, but he received substantial support from his friend Engels, who had a family interest in a manufacturing firm in Manchester. Marx developed into one of the most profound and widely known critics of capitalism in mid-nineteenth-century Europe. His work had two basic elements: one was his study and writing, and the other was his political activism. He was a correspondent for the *New York Daily Tribune* and published numerous books, the most famous of which is *Capital*. His political activism was as a socialist and communist in the workers' movement. He helped organize the International Working Men's Association—the First International—and was active in workers' struggles throughout the rest of his life.

Marx wrote during the early stages of industrial capitalism. This was a time when it was not uncommon to find child laborers chained to machines and workers regularly losing limbs or even their lives in factories. Most workers lived in desperate poverty. It was in this environment that he developed his critique of laissez-faire capitalism.

MARX'S GENERAL SYSTEM OF THOUGHT

Marx's political activism and his analysis of capitalism were both based on his general theory of social development. This system amounted to a theory of history and of social change. As he put it in *The Communist Manifesto*, "The history of all hitherto existing society is the history of class struggles." This expressed his "materialist conception of history," which emphasized the role of the economic aspects of life in social development. This conception is central to Marx's system of thought and his analysis of capitalism, and we will explore it briefly here.

Dialectics

Marx's general system was based on two philosophical notions: dialectics and materialism. Marx borrowed dialectics from the German philosopher Hegel (1770–1831). **Dialectics** is the study of the contradictions within the essence of things. It emphasizes the idea that all things change and that all things contain not only themselves but their opposites. A rock is a rock, but it is also, at the same time, "not a rock" because it can become a million grains of sand. Consequently, development becomes the struggle of opposites—things becoming other things. Capitalists cannot be capitalists without their opposites, the workers (and vice versa), and capitalists and workers will develop as they interact with and influence each other. Out of this struggle of opposites comes change in which both elements, capitalists and workers, and the thing itself, capitalism, are transformed into something else. The source of change is internal to the social system. Ultimately, Marx thought that the contradictions and conflicts inherent in capitalism would tear it apart, eventually causing it to develop into **socialism** (social ownership and social goals of production influenced by a strong state), and then into **communism** (communal control of the economy and a weak state).

By emphasizing change, contradiction, and the struggle of opposites, dialectics constitutes a challenge to formal logic that concentrates on things as they are and their interrelationships. Marx wrote the following in his preface to *Capital* (1867):

> Dialectic…in its rational form is a scandal and abomination to bourgeoisdom and its doctrinaire professors, because it includes in its comprehension affirmative recognition of the existing state of things, at the same time, also, the recognition of the negation of that state, of its inevitable breaking up; because it regards every historically developed social form as in fluid movement, and therefore, takes into account its transient nature not less than its momentary existence; because it lets nothing impose upon it, and is in its essence critical and revolutionary.

To Marx, one of the main flaws in the theories of orthodox economists was the notion that the economy tended toward stable equilibrium, whereas Marx saw constant change and recurring crises. Marx believed that the key to economics was studying how the economy evolves over time, and Marx sought to discover the "Laws of Motion" that governed the evolution of capitalism via his use of dialectics.

1. Develop your own example that emphasizes the dialectical nature of some thing or process.
2. Why is the dialectic "critical and revolutionary"?

Materialism

The other philosophical notion underlying Marxian economics, **materialism**, concerns the principle that what is basic to the real life of human beings is their activity in the world. Survival is the primary human imperative, and in order to survive, people must work within the existing economic system. We must use our intelligence and energy, along with the materials and resources available to us, to produce (or earn) enough to ensure our survival. To Marx, materialism concerned understanding the world by focusing on real people and their day-to-day activities—especially those concerned with production for continued survival. And, since for most people work determines the structure of their lives, the work process impinges upon all other aspects of life.

According to the materialist approach, to know the world we must study things and their development. In addition, we must study the interrelationships of things: "Things come into being, change and pass out of being, not as separate individual units, but in essential relation and interconnection, so that they cannot be understood each separately and by itself but only in their relation and interconnection." To know the United States, we must study its productive process and how that relates to its laws, beliefs, social classes, patterns of consumption, and so on. Additionally, we must study the history of how all these elements have changed over time and developed.

Materialism contrasts with the notion that change takes place through the development of ideas. For Marx, the source of change rests, ultimately, in actual productive activity.

3. How else could we "know" our world other than through its material aspects?

The Materialist Conception of History: Historical Materialism

From these two philosophical bases, Marx developed his theory of history—the materialist conception of history, or **historical materialism**. All theory requires abstraction and simplification, and Marx's system of generalizations about social development is no exception. Historical materialism states that productive activity is fundamental to human beings and to their societies. Consequently, the organization of production, the economic structure, forms the basis of all societies. All other social institutions and ideas are derived from the economic structure of the society. If the economic structure changes, all other aspects of the society will also change.

Marx formalized his analysis in the following way. The economic structure, or base, is the **mode of production** and consists of the forces of production and the relations of production. The **forces of production** include all the things necessary to produce goods and services: tools, machines, factories, means of transportation, raw materials, human labor, science, technology, skills, and knowledge. Over time, obviously, the forces of production change. The **relations of production** are determined by the relationships among people in the productive process. When the forces of production are organized in a certain way, different classes of people will be defined by their relationship to each other in production. The relations of production, therefore, will be determined by patterns of ownership of productive resources, the nature of property relations, and the division of labor. These will determine a class structure of society. A certain mode of

ECONOMICS
BREAK-UP OF MONOPOLIES
RE-DISTRIBUTION OF WEALTH
BOURGEOISIE
WORKING CLASS
COMMUNITY OWNERSHIP
CAPITALISM
PROLETARIAT
ERIC LOHNAAS

© 1974 by Noah's Ark, Ink. (for *Ramparts* magazine). Reprinted by permission of Bruce W. Stilson.

production, then, consists of specific forces of production and specific relations of production (that is, a specific **class structure**).

In addition, the mode of production is accompanied by the **superstructure** of society, which consists of the society's ideas, institutions, and ideologies, including laws, politics, culture, ethics, religion, morals, aesthetics, art, philosophy, and so on. The purpose of the superstructure is to support the economic base of society. For example, feudalism organized production with certain methods and institutions, and it had its own class structure and superstructure.

Within this framework is Marx's theory of historical change. Oversimplifying somewhat, when the forces of production change, the relations of production—social classes—also will change. This brings about a new mode of production that will, in turn, develop its own specific superstructure. It is in this context that class struggle takes place. Different classes have different interests and visions and thus will do battle over the organization of production and, hence, society. The "old" classes will fight to preserve the old mode of production, and the new will fight for change. One of the most fundamental aspects of this materialist conception of history is that people, by acting on the forces of production, create their own history and social change. Marx sums up his historical materialism in this passage from the *Critique of Political Economy* (1859):

> In the social production which men carry on they enter into definite relations that are indispensable and independent of their will; these relations of production correspond to a definite stage of development of their material powers of production. The sum total of these relations of production constitutes the economic structure of society—the real foundation on which rise legal and political superstructures and to which correspond definite forms of social consciousness. The mode of production in material life determines the general character of the social, political, and spiritual processes of life. It is not the consciousness of men

that determines their existence, but, on the contrary, their social existence determines their consciousness. At a certain stage of their development, the material forces of production in society come into conflict with the existing relations of production, or—what is but a legal expression for the same thing—with the property relations within which they had been at work before. From forms of development of the forces of production these relations turn into their fetters. Then comes the period of social revolution. With the change of economic foundation the entire immense superstructure is more or less rapidly transformed. In considering such transformations the distinction should always be made between the material transformation of the economic conditions or production which can be determined with the precision of natural science, and the legal, political, religious, aesthetic, or philosophic—in short, ideological forms in which men become conscious of this conflict and fight it out.

4. Apply the "materialist conception of history" (historical materialism) to the transition from feudalism to capitalism (see Chapter 2).

5. "It is not the consciousness of men that determines their existence, but, on the contrary, their social existence determines their consciousness." What does this mean? And how does it mean that human beings create their own history?

6. Can Marx's theory of historical materialism be used to explain the recent changes in the Soviet Union and Eastern Europe? How so?

Marx's model of social change thus focuses on the relationships and contradictions among the forces of production, social classes, and the general institutions and ideologies of society. This complex process, according to Marx, determines the development of societies. In that process, the forces of production are of initial importance, but class struggle and ideology in turn become extremely influential.

THE MARXIAN ANALYSIS OF CAPITALISM

From this view of social change and history, Marx proceeded to develop his analysis and critique of capitalism. His conclusion was a condemnation of capitalism and its results, as well as a scientific appraisal of its likely future development and eventual replacement by socialism. Here we will summarize Marx's theory of capitalist development.

Capitalism advances the methods of production, including factories, transportation, and technology, and as it expands, has access to greater supplies of raw materials. Accompanying this mode of production are its own relations of production. Basically, according to Marx, with the advance of the division of labor and private property, there were two main social classes in capitalism. They were defined by their relationship to each other in the productive process. First of all, there were the capitalists, or the bourgeoisie, who owned the means of production, controlled productive activity, and earned profits from the sale of produced goods in markets. Second, there were the workers, the proletariat, who had nothing to sell in markets but their own labor power and, as a result, had to work for wages to survive. The history of capitalism, then, can be seen as the history of the struggle between these two classes.

Marx condemned capitalism because it reduced social relations to impersonal market relations, or the "cash nexus." As he and Engels argued in *The Communist Manifesto* (1848):

> It has pitilessly torn asunder the motley feudal ties that bound man to his "natural superiors," and has left remaining no other nexus between man and man than naked self-interest, than callous "cash payment." It has drowned the most heavenly ecstasies of religious fervor, of chivalrous enthusiasm, of philistine sentimentalism, in the icy water of egotistical calculation. It has resolved personal worth into exchange value, and in place of the numberless indefeasible chartered freedoms, has set up that single, unconscionable freedom—Free Trade. In one word, for exploitation, veiled by religious and political illusions, it has substituted naked, shameless, direct, brutal exploitation.

Within the "cash nexus" that Marx described, workers and capitalists would struggle over wages, the length of the working day, the intensity of work, and working conditions. Additionally, since workers were forced to work for capitalists for wages, and since the capitalists controlled production, capitalism produced **alienation**. Most workers were engaged in mind-numbing, repetitive tasks involving no creativity, which served to sever any connection they might have had to the product that they were producing. In one of Marx's early critical works, *The Economic and Philosophic Manuscripts of 1844*, he described alienation as a consequence of this type of capitalist production. The production of goods was external to the workers; they had no control over their labor or what they produced. Consequently, workers were alienated in their work. They felt dispossessed, and their work was, in essence, forced labor. Alienation, thus, was one more contributor to labor's dissatisfaction with capitalism.

 7. Did Marx deplore the "cash nexus" because it destroyed feudal relationships?

From his early condemnation of capitalism, Marx went on to develop a detailed and lengthy analysis of capitalism in such works as *Wage Labour and Capital* (1849), *The Grundrisse* (1859), *Theories of Surplus Value* (1863), and *Capital* (1867).

Marx accepted the **labor theory of value** as it was developed by Adam Smith and others but turned it to his own purposes. For Marx it became a way of demonstrating the opposition of capitalists and workers and the exploitation of labor in capitalism. Marx contended that the value of all goods and services is a function of the labor that went into them (including both direct labor and the indirect labor embodied in raw materials and capital goods). Workers, in turn, are paid by capitalists to produce goods and services. However, since the capitalists control the productive process and the final output, they will earn **surplus value**. To make a profit, capitalists must pay laborers less than the value of the products the laborers produce. When you graduate from college, you will be hired for a job because the firm that hires you believes you will generate more in revenue for the firm than you will cost in wages (including benefits). The difference between the revenue you generate for the company and the wage you receive is called surplus value. Marx viewed the extraction of surplus value as exploitative. Labor accounts for the value of goods and services, but it receives in return only a portion of that value, since it does not own productive assets or control the production process.

Because of the existence of a mass of unemployed workers (the *industrial reserve army* of the unemployed), the wages of laborers will always hover around "subsistence"—the value of goods and services necessary for continued survival and the reproduction of the working class. Workers can produce enough value in only part of the working day to cover their subsistence needs. The rest of the day they labor to produce surplus value for the capitalist. The more labor that capitalists can get out of the labor power they purchase from workers, the greater the surplus value for the capitalist. Thus, there is an inherent **class conflict** between capitalists and workers. Workers prefer to work fewer hours, with more freedom and flexibility, and for more money. Capitalists prefer workers to work longer, harder, and for less money. To improve the level of profits, capitalists may try to increase the pace and intensity of work, increase supervision over work, or introduce new technology. Workers often resist these trends, sometimes violently. The wage rate hovers around subsistence, but it also varies with the struggle between capital and labor over the level of wages.

Since capitalists derive surplus value and profits from production, and since they operate in a competitive environment in which other capitalists also attempt to earn profits from the same type of activity, they are forced to accumulate capital. **Capital accumulation** is the driving force of capitalism. Profit is used to purchase additional capital goods and thereby increase production. This capital accumulation results in additional profits, which, in turn, will be reinvested in more capital. Capitalists, if they want to stay in business, have no choice about this. If they do not reinvest their profits in new and better forms of capital, they will be driven out of business by their competitors. Marx also emphasized the role of technological development in stimulating capital accumulation.

With a greater stock of capital, which technological improvements make increasingly productive, capitalists must constantly seek out new markets for their ever-increasing supply of products. As Marx observed in The *Communist Manifesto*, "The need of a constantly expanding market for its products chases the bourgeoisie over the whole surface of the globe. It must nestle everywhere, settle everywhere, establish connections everywhere." Similarly, capitalists pursue new markets by attempting to turn anything they can into a way to sell commodities. To choose an obvious example, under capitalism religious holidays such as Christmas and Hanukkah have become major vehicles for businesses to increase sales. Advertisers try to connect caring and loving others with the purchase of commodities. If we care for someone, we are urged to buy a more expensive gift!

8. Has the institution of marriage been commodified? If so, how? What are some other holidays or human institutions that have become commodified?

The process of capital accumulation forms the basis of Marx's understanding of **capitalist instability**. Capital accumulation produces economic growth, but it does so in cycles, with periods of prosperity followed by depression. When production is expanding, capitalists buy more machines, raw materials, and other forms of capital. This also requires them to hire more workers. Doing so depletes the reserve army of the unemployed and begins to drive up wages, which tends to reduce profits. Consequently, capitalists introduce new methods of production that save on the use of labor; more capital-intensive production allows them to produce more with less labor (substitution of capital for labor). In addition, workers lose jobs and the wage goes down as the reserve army is replenished.

This course of action is not without its own contradictions. With more workers out of jobs and with lower wages, capitalists have more difficulty selling what is produced. This tends to reduce capitalists' profits. In addition, with more capital-intensive methods of production, the capitalists reduce relatively the source of profits in production, surplus value generated by labor. This also tends to produce a declining rate of profits. With profits reduced, capital accumulation slows down. All of these effects would combine to produce depressions in economic activity as goods went unsold, profits decreased, workers lost jobs, and capital accumulation slowed. In true dialectical fashion, the expansion, out of its own internal workings, turns into its opposite, a depression. With wage rates depressed, though, capitalists eventually rehire workers because the workers can once again produce surplus value and profits for the capitalists. And out of the depression comes an expansion of economic activity. Capitalism, Marx argued, grew in starts and spurts. The great mass of the people under capitalism, the working class, depends on this unstable process for its livelihood and subsistence.

In addition to this cyclical instability, Marx thought that there were long-run tendencies that would exacerbate the opposition between the capitalist class and the working class. Because of competition, **industrial concentration** tended to occur as capitalists bought out each other or went bankrupt during depressions. The strong survived and came to dominate certain industries. As this occurred, the capitalist class became relatively smaller, as well as relatively more wealthy. Meanwhile, the working class became relatively larger and relatively poorer, as it remained near "subsistence." Marx called this the **immiserization** of the proletariat. And all the while, the capitalist class retained control and the workers were powerless. As a result of continuing instability and these secular tendencies, which reinforce the class structure of capitalist society, the workers would organize for their own class interests. Ultimately, Marx argued, the working-class organizations would overthrow the capitalist system.

The political requirement for workers in the socialist and communist movement was described by Marx and Engels as follows at the end of *The Communist Manifesto:*

> In short, the Communists everywhere support every revolutionary movement against the existing social and political order of things.
>
> In all these movements they bring to the front, as the leading question in each, the property question, no matter what its degree of development at the time.
>
> Finally, they labour everywhere for the union and agreement of the democratic parties of all countries.
>
> The Communists disdain to conceal their views and aims. They openly declare that their ends can be attained only by the forcible overthrow of all existing social conditions. Let the ruling class tremble at a Communistic revolution. The proletarians have nothing to lose but their chains. They have a world to win.

However, this social revolution would not be easy. As Marx emphasized from his general system of social development, capitalism supports itself with its superstructure. The institutions, ideologies, and beliefs of the society defend capitalist economic institutions and social relations. Perhaps most important in this connection is the state. The state, according to Marxian analysis, serves as the "executive committee of the ruling class." The state protects private property and property rights and thereby the class structure of the system. It is in the camp of the capitalists and will actively oppose the workers' movement with all the resources at its command.

9. Evaluate Marx's analysis of capitalism. Does it describe economic reality and the historical development of capitalism? Does it help you understand how capitalism works?

10. Why do you suppose Marx kept getting kicked out of European countries?

SOCIAL REVOLUTION

Marx argued that workers would be exploited, alienated, and condemned to subsistence standards of living under capitalism. He further argued that in their association at work and in their communities, they would be able to analyze objectively their reality and the reasons for this oppression. Consequently, they would organize themselves and transform the whole capitalist system. (Indeed, Marx spent much of his time in political activity with workers.) In *Capital*, he describes the process of **social revolution** as follows:

> Along with the constantly diminishing number of magnates of capital, who usurp and monopolize all advantages of this process of transformation, grows the mass of misery, oppression, slavery, degradation, exploitation; but with this too grows the revolt of the working class, a class always increasing in numbers, and disciplined, united, organized by the very mechanism of the process of capitalist production itself. The monopoly of capital becomes a fetter upon the mode of production, which has sprung up and flourished along with, and under it. Centralization of the means

of production and socialization of labour at last reach a point where they become incompatible with their capitalist integument. This integument is burst asunder. The knell of capitalist private property sounds. The expropriators are expropriated.

Once the death knell of capitalism sounded, what would the socialists, communists, and workers create? What would they do? Although Marx never wrote extensively on this question, a hint at the answer is contained in *The Communist Manifesto:*

The distinguishing feature of Communism is not the abolition of property generally, but the abolition of bourgeois property. But modern bourgeois private property is the final and most complete expression of the system of producing and appropriating products, that is based on class antagonisms, on the exploitation of the many by the few.

In this sense, the theory of the Communists may be summed up in the single sentence: Abolition of private property.

We Communists have been reproached with the desire of abolishing the right of personally acquiring property as the fruit of a man's own labour, which property is alleged to be the groundwork of all personal freedom, activity and independence.

Hard-won, self-acquired, self-earned property! Do you mean the property of the petty artisan and of the small peasant, a form of property that preceded the bourgeois form? There is no need to abolish that: the development of industry has to a great extent already destroyed it, and is still destroying it daily.

Or do you mean modern bourgeois private property?

The proletariat will use its political supremacy to wrest, by degrees, all capital from the bourgeoisie, to centralise all instruments of production in the hands of the State, *i.e.*, of the proletariat organized as the ruling class; and to increase the total of productive forces as rapidly as possible....

These measures will of course be different in different countries.

Nevertheless in the most advanced countries, the following will be...generally applicable.

1. Abolition of property in land and application of all rents of land to public purposes.
2. A heavy progressive or graduated income tax.
3. Abolition of all rights of inheritance.
4. Confiscation of the property of all emigrants and rebels.
5. Centralisation of credit in the hands of the State, by means of a national bank with State capital and an exclusive monopoly.
6. Centralisation of the means of communication and transport in the hands of the State.
7. Extension of factories and instruments of production owned by the State; the bringing into cultivation of wastelands, and the improvement of the soil generally in accordance with a common plan.
8. Equal liability of all to labour. Establishment of industrial armies, especially for agriculture.
9. Combination of agriculture and manufacturing industries; gradual abolition of the distinction between town and country, by a more equable distribution of the population over the country.
10. Free education for all children in public schools. Abolition of children's factory labour in its present form. Combination of education with industrial production, &c., &c.

11. Since the communists would not take your personal possessions away, what kinds of property *would* they "wrest" away?

12. In Marx and Engels's ten-point program, which measures are accepted in the United States? Which are partially accepted? Which are rejected?

Hayek and the Road to Serfdom

Writing in the mid-1800s, Marx saw laissez-faire capitalism as a grave threat to human society. Instead, Marx advocated control of the economy by workers and the communist party. By the 1930s, with Hitler running the German economy under a fascist system and Stalin running the Soviet economy via command-style communism, the idea of centralized state control was getting a bad reputation. It was in this context that Austrian economist Friedrich Hayek wrote his important book, *The Road to Serfdom*. Hayek saw state power as dangerous and coercive. In contrast, he argued that "the system of private property is the most important guarantee of freedom. It is only because the control of the means of production is divided among many people acting independently that we as individuals can decide what to do with ourselves." Hayek insisted that central planners could never duplicate the efficient allocation of resources and generation of information that takes place under the market system. To Hayek, the greatest threat to the economy was state intervention, and any expansion of the role of the state beyond the functions of defense and the provision of welfare and basic social services was a threat to liberty.

As we will see in the next chapter, most economists adopted a position in between those of Marx and Hayek. They accepted the need for government intervention to regulate the worst excesses of capitalism, but they also accepted the market system as an efficient method of allocating resources. Such economists believed in a **mixed economy,** in which some economic decisions were made by government officials and others were made by market mechanisms. The economist who persuaded the world that this was the best approach to managing the economy was John Maynard Keynes.

AN ASSESSMENT OF MARXISM

Marx died more than a century ago, in 1883. What can we say today about the relevance of his analysis of social change and capitalism? Most Americans either reject Marxism or never really study it. The rejection is often based on the fact that several of Marx's predictions have not transpired: the overthrow of advanced capitalism by socialism; the separation of society into only two classes, capitalists and workers; and the creation of a unified and political working class. In addition, Marxism is often associated with the repressive Soviet Union, and socialism as Marx described it has never really been put in place. Socialism and Marxism also offer a direct challenge to two of the basic economic foundations of U.S. society: private ownership of productive property and economic freedom for capital.

On the other hand, Marxian analysis is used by many economists in the United States and the rest of the world to understand economic events. Some aspects of Marxism offer continuing assistance in explaining the structure and development of capitalism. There remain conflicts between workers and capitalists over workplace health and safety, other working conditions, wages and fringe benefits, and the length of the workweek, not to mention downsizing and relocation. This conflict is built into the different interests that they have in the very structure of the economic system. Capitalists seek profits, and workers' demands often limit profits. Although the historical expansion of the middle class has mediated this structure, there are opposing class interests in the operation of the economy, and the classes do struggle over real economic issues in workplaces, bargaining, and public policy. Furthermore, while these struggles have not led to the collapse of capitalism, they have brought about significant changes in its institutions and operation. Marx's analysis of exploitation, surplus value, and class relations can help us to understand this dynamic of U.S. capitalism.

One of the most long-lived aspects of Marxian economic analysis is its theory of the process of capital accumulation. In this treatment, Marx explained capitalism's tendencies toward business cycles, economic concentration, and market expansion. By focusing on the importance of profits and the centrality of capital accumulation, Marx developed a framework that is still useful in understanding recessions and expansions, merger waves, and multinational corporations' penetration of world markets.

Another strength of Marxian analysis is its integration of the micro and macro aspects of economic activity. At the microeconomic level, profits flow from the organization and control of the capitalist mode of production. The process of capital accumulation and the production of surplus value, in turn, provide the framework within which macroeconomic crises are engendered under capitalism.

The fact that Marx was able to anticipate much of how capitalism would evolve in the century after his death demonstrates the strength of Marx's analytical framework. As Marx predicted in *The Communist Manifesto*, globalization, commodification, and the economic concentration of capital have proceeded apace. Where unregulated, capitalists tend to pursue the cheapest labor and least environmental regulations in order to increase profits. The conflicts between capitalists and laborers have waxed and waned. This evidence in support of Marx's insights ensures that his ideas will be studied for many years to come.

Nevertheless, Marx's system retains some limitations and weaknesses. The labor theory of value used by Smith and Marx was supplanted by the development of economic theory that finds value reflected in the supply and demand for products and their resulting prices. Marx did not anticipate the tremendous increase in the average standard of living in the United States (and Western Europe) as governments, sometimes under pressure from labor unions, reformed capitalism. As the economy grew, a good portion of the increasing surplus was in fact apportioned to the middle class and some segments of the working class (although this varies depending on economic conditions and the strength of the working class). The social revolution in advanced capitalist countries anticipated by Marx required more than his prediction: It also necessitated political organization by the working class in the real world. (To his credit, although it is often not included in discussions of Marx, he did recognize this political fact; much of his life was spent in active political organizing among the working class.) Even though there have been communist and socialist parties in the West and in the United States, they have never been strong enough to organize a transition to socialism. Of course, they have not been unopposed. And throughout Western Europe, the social democracy movement reformed capitalism to take into account social issues, rather than eliminating capitalism. Socialism, instead, has emerged where capitalism has been weaker and where societies have not succeeded in dealing with inequality, often in the developing world.

Marx himself would probably be disappointed with the divergence of his ideal of socialism and its reality in much of the present world (particularly wherever it has taken antidemocratic forms). Even so, his ideas have influenced the development and progress of socialism and the pursuit of social goals in China, Cuba, and North Korea, and in countries that once espoused socialism, including the former Soviet Union, Vietnam, Mozambique, and former Yugoslavia (see Chapter 22). And Marxism as a method of analysis still continues to influence the transitions in the post–Cold War world.

❖ Conclusion

In this chapter, we focused on the ideas of Karl Marx and his critique of capitalism. Marx acknowledged that capitalism was a dynamic system that generated rapid economic growth, but he also noted the inequality, poverty, and horrible working conditions that accompanied it in the mid-1800s. In the next chapter, we turn to the ideas of John Maynard Keynes and the rise of the mixed economy as the primary method by which human societies organize their economies today. We also trace the development of the U.S. economy and its evolution into a mixed economy.

Review Questions

1. The dialectic method consists of identifying the forces within the economy that are in conflict and studying those conflicts to understand the evolution of the economy. What are some of the major sources of conflict in the modern global economy? How do you see the global economy changing as a result of these conflicts?

2. The microcomputer revolution and the rise of telecommunications has dramatically altered the modern world. It has changed how we work, what our lives are like, and the class structures of countries around the world. Using the insights from Marx's method of historical materialism, analyze these changes. What were the major changes in the mode of production? How have the relations of production and the superstructure changed as a result?

3. Why do people in the United States tend to reject Marxism?

4. Why is it that some newly independent countries in the world have Marxian governments (i.e., politicians and leaders who rely on Marxian analysis)?

5. What do you think is the weakest part of the Marxian argument?

6. What do you think is the strongest part of the Marxian argument?

7. What is the purpose of Marxian economics?

8. Marx's theories originated more than 100 years ago. Was labor exploited then? Is it now? Why or why not?

9. Using Marx's concept of surplus value, explain why white-collar workers in the United States today are working longer and longer hours.

10. Are most jobs today alienating in nature? What circumstances seem to create alienating work? Is it possible to create workplaces in which alienation is minimized?

11. Marx predicted that capitalist society would become increasingly commercialized and that more and more areas of human society and culture would become vehicles to sell products and increase profits. Is this an accurate prediction? Explain and give examples to support your answer.

12. Marx was very critical of capitalism during its dark age of the mid-1800s. How do you think he would feel about capitalism today?

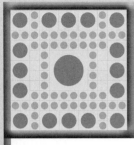

CHAPTER FIVE

The Rise and Fall of Laissez-Faire in the U.S. Economy

◆ Introduction

Despite the conditions of the poor and the socialist and Marxian critiques, laissez-faire capitalism flourished in nineteenth-century England and throughout Western Europe. From 1837 to 1901, Queen Victoria reigned, giving her name to the Victorian Age. This age witnessed increasing commercial dominance over formal and informal institutions that affected social values and behavior. Railway expansion and the telegraph revolutionized transportation and communication, thereby quickening the pace of life. People began to illuminate their homes with electricity. The first cars were on the roads in the United States. The Carnegies, Vanderbilts, and Rockefellers were accumulating their enormous wealth. Coal and oil displaced animals and water power as sources of energy. As a result of these developments, production in the British and the U.S. economies boomed.

However, some economists attempted to call attention to continuing unemployment problems and suggested various ideas for responding to the problems. These economists were either ignored or viewed as dangerous radicals by the dominant school of economists in the universities and the ruling classes. By 1926, John Maynard Keynes was convinced that laissez-faire was no longer an appropriate way of thinking about unemployment. Others had noticed this much earlier, but it was Keynes's contribution in the context of the Great Depression that ultimately signaled the fall of laissez-faire. While calls for laissez-faire grew over the past 30 years, the recession of 2007–2009 has stifled those calls.

THE FLOWERING OF LAISSEZ-FAIRE

As the pace quickened, production increased and more people attempted to succeed in business. A few individuals began to wonder where all of this movement might lead. Among them was the English essayist John Ruskin (1819–1900), one of the great thinkers and writers in the Victorian Age, whose

Brantwood, the elegant home of John Ruskin.
(Photograph by Tom Riddell)

works about art, architecture, and political economy have continuing relevance today. In an 1864 essay named "Traffic," he questions the "ideal of human life" and describes the worshippers of the "Goddess of Getting-on":

> Your ideal of human life then is, I think, that it should be passed in a pleasant undulating world, with iron and coal everywhere underneath it. On each pleasant bank of this world is to be a beautiful mansion, with two wings; and stables, and coach-houses; a moderately-sized park; a large garden and hothouses; and pleasant carriage drives through the shrubberies. In this mansion are to live the favoured votaries of the Goddess; the English gentleman, with his gracious wife, and his beautiful family; he is always able to have the boudoir and the jewels for the wife, and the beautiful ball dresses for the daughters, and hunters for the sons, and a shooting in the Highlands for himself. At the bottom of the bank is to be the mill; not less than a quarter of a mile long, with one steam engine at each end, and two in the middle and a chimney three hundred feet high. In this mill are to be in constant employment from eight hundred to a thousand workers, who never drink, never strike, always go to church on Sunday, and always express themselves in respectful language.

1. Draft a paragraph about your own thoughts on the ideal of human life. Discuss the same kinds of subjects mentioned by Ruskin: houses, environment, transportation, recreation, family, and industry.

2. Ruskin wrote, "There is no wealth but life." What does this mean? Do you agree? Explain.

At the time Ruskin was writing, the majority of people in England lived in poor housing, were paid low wages, and experienced regular periods of unemployment, and their surroundings could best be described as urban squalor. So the Victorian Age was not only a time of general economic growth but also a time of continuing economic disparity. The implications of that disparity offered a potential threat to the existing social, political, and economic order. In *The Victorian Frame of Mind*, historian Walter E. Houghton explains this characteristic of the period:

> To think it strange that the great age of optimism was also an age of anxiety is to overlook the ambivalent reaction which the main social and intellectual tendencies of the period provoked. Expanding business, scientific development, the growth of democracy, and the decline of Christianity were sources of distress as well as of satisfaction....
>
> For all its solid and imposing strength, Victorian society, particularly in the period before 1850, was shot through, from top to bottom, with the dread of some wild outbreak of the masses that would overthrow the established order and confiscate private property.

3. Are wealthy people in the United States today worried about revolution? Why or why not? Are revolutions taking place elsewhere?

THE DEVELOPMENT OF CAPITALISM IN THE UNITED STATES

As capitalism was forming in Europe, many of its institutions and relationships were transplanted to the American colonies. When the colonists eventually removed the yoke of English political and economic control during the American Revolution, they cleared the way for the formation and development of the United States' own form of capitalism. However, they retained their debt to Western civilization, thought, and institutions. This lineage was important to the establishment of emerging capitalist attitudes and institutions in the colonies and their continuance after the Revolution.

Most of the colonists were Protestants who emphasized individualism and hard work. Private ownership of rural and urban production was the dominant form of economic organization. International and domestic trade flourished with the goal of private gain and profit. Markets developed and guided production. In the early years of the new nation, the government utilized mercantilist policies of controlling international trade to foster economic development and to protect the emergence of the United States as a Western nation-state.

Sources of U.S. Development

Throughout its first hundred years as a nation, the United States was primarily an agricultural economy. Through the mid-1870s, agricultural output accounted for more than half of total U.S. production, but by the mid-1880s the value of manufactured goods surpassed the value of agricultural goods. At the same time, the nonagricultural portion of the labor force began to outnumber those who worked on farms. (Later, about 1920, the nation's urban population surpassed the rural population.) Despite the country's being primarily rural and agricultural, the development of industry began early in the nineteenth century. Industrial production accelerated during the middle years of the nineteenth century, stimulated in part by the demands of the Civil War. By the turn of the century, the United States was the world's leading producer of both manufactured and agricultural goods.

What accounted for this tremendous economic achievement? One important source of U.S. economic development, which is often neglected, was the role of the government. In the formative years of the nation, the government played a crucial role in the construction of a federal system in which economic trade flowed freely from one state to another. Indeed, this concern with encouraging trade within the United States was one of the primary reasons behind the construction and ratification of the Constitution. In addition, the government passed tariffs to protect infant industries, established a national currency, and created a legal framework that governed economic transactions. In the nineteenth century, federal, state, and local governments financed and encouraged the development of different forms of transportation that facilitated trade within the expanding nation.

Another source of growth was the vast supply of land and resources available to the United States. The country expanded westward throughout the eighteenth century. This expansion was made possible by conquering one after another of the Native American tribes, by the purchase of land from France and Russia, and by military conquest over Mexico and several European countries that still controlled land in North America. Through what was called Manifest Destiny, the United States eventually controlled the middle part of the North American continent from coast to coast. This expanding geographical territory supplied space for expansion and raw materials for increasing agricultural and industrial production. It also supplied an expanding volume of cotton and wheat exports for sale to Europe. This international market encouraged further agricultural production and made possible imports that facilitated industrial production. At the end of the nineteenth and the beginning of the twentieth centuries, the United States joined Western European countries in the process of expansion beyond their borders. As the United States pursued Manifest Destiny beyond the North American continent into the Pacific, Asia, and Latin America, U.S. imperialism provided raw materials, markets, and investments that fueled further economic expansion.

Technology played a crucial role in the growth and development of the U.S. economy. The adoption of European methods of manufacturing textiles spurred the use of factory production, and the Industrial Revolution in the United States eventually led to the American manufacturing system—relying on interchangeable parts and later the mass assembly line. In agriculture, tractors and combines spurred a tremendous increase in agricultural production.

The American people themselves, both the original colonists and the later immigrants, proved to be an important source of growth and development. Strongly individualistic and dedicated to hard work, they took risks, organized productive activities, educated themselves, invented, worked, and conquered. The United States became a thriving and growing economy through a primarily private economic system based on the efforts of individuals and groups of individuals tied together through an expanding system of national markets for goods and services.

Coincident with all of these sources of growth, many institutions emerged to stimulate development. The banking system, retail and wholesale organizations, and the transportation system facilitated the expansion of economic activity with improved organization and lower costs. Related to the development of these sectors of the economy was the emergence of one of the foremost institutions of U.S. capitalism and economic production, the corporation. A legal combination of individuals, the corporation was a successful device for amassing resources for production. And in several leading industries—oil, the railroads, banking, steel, automobiles, and so on—large corporations led the advance of U.S. growth. In a sense, the history of the corporation and its development is the history of modern U.S. capitalism.

By the middle of the twentieth century, the United States was the dominant economic, political, and military country in the world. It was the most advanced nation in terms of manufacturing and agricultural techniques and production. It had the highest standard of living, on the average, for its almost 200 million citizens. And its people still valued individual economic and political freedom. For the most part, its development had been a success story.

The Situation in the United States and Veblen's Critique

Throughout its history, however, there have also been some negative aspects of U.S. economic development. The conquest and exploitation of the Native American Indians must be counted as—and remain as—a scar in U.S. history. The annexation of much of Mexico is another. Slavery throughout the colonial period and until the Civil War relied on the inhuman subjugation and exploitation of human beings as sources of increased production. As both economic and political power became more concentrated, scandals of political and economic corruption have been rife throughout U.S. history. Private economic power has led to political corruption such as the Crédit Mobilier affair of the 1870s, the Teapot Dome scandal of the 1920s, the savings and loan crisis of the 1980s (see Chapter 16), the technology bubble of the late 1990s, and the financial crisis, that began in 2007.

The latter part of the nineteenth century was marked by the industrialization of the U.S. economy, but it also witnessed the abuses of the "robber barons," entrepreneurs who were generally successful as well as ruthless in their business practices. In the process of consolidating the leading industries of the economy, promoting technological developments, building giant corporations, and amassing great personal fortunes, such men as Jay Gould, Andrew Carnegie, J. P. Morgan, and John D. Rockefeller bilked their partners, eliminated their competitors, underpaid their workers, and/or overcharged many of their customers.

By the beginning of the twentieth century, the United States was the world's leading producer of both agricultural and manufactured goods. U.S. capitalism and markets spread across the North American continent and began to reach out to the rest of the world. Economic output increased dramatically—but this success was not unchallenged. Poverty persisted, a militant labor movement emerged along with a growing working class, periodic financial crises and depressions disrupted the path of growth, and there were continuing problems associated with Native American tribes and the end of slavery. The development of the U.S. economic system was full of successes *and* difficulties.

Thorstein Veblen (1857–1929) was one of the first economists to develop a comprehensive critique of American capitalism. He wrote during a period marked by continuing industrialization and growth, but also by increasing business concentration and recurrent economic depressions. One of his first books, *The Theory of the Leisure Class* (1899), noted the rise of a new class of people in U.S. society, accompanying the economic progress of the Industrial Revolution. These propertied people were privileged to engage in "conspicuous consumption" as testimony to their success. Veblen, in a sarcastic but penetrating style, offered numerous examples of the new leisure class seeking status through the purchase of houses, clothing, and other goods. His tone and insight about "pecuniary emulation" also called attention to the fact that, as in Europe, the industrialization process did not enrich everyone, although it did subject the entire society to the influences of heightened materialism.

In later works, most notably *The Theory of Business Enterprise* (1904) and *Absentee Ownership* (1923), Veblen identified some trends that characterized U.S. economic experience with laissez-faire capitalism. These trends were part and parcel of the American economic success, but they also suggested some future difficulties. Veblen saw a distinction between business and industry. In *Absentee Ownership*, he wrote, "The industrial arts are a matter of tangible performance directed to work that is designed to be of material use to man....[The] arts of business are arts of bargaining, effrontery, salesmanship, make-believe, and are directed to the gain of the business man at the cost of the community, at large and in detail."

This distinction was important to his interpretation of the primary trends in U.S. economic development: a tendency toward business concentration, rapid technological advance, and a constant difficulty with depression. Monopoly resulted from the business instinct to eliminate competition as one of the most effective ways to secure profits. But technological progress also was caused by the business drive for profits. The problem arose because technology constantly pushed the ability of the industrial arts to produce more, but monopoly held back production to get higher prices and profits. The consequence, according to Veblen, was a constant tendency toward depression. The depressions of the 1870s and 1890s in the United States provided real evidence that Say's law should be suspect, and that Veblen's concern with explaining the frequency of high levels of unemployment, if not exactly correct, was at least worth pursuing.

Veblen was an **institutionalist**. The institutionalists were critical of the orthodox school of economics. They argued that the focus of such economists was too narrow and that their method was too abstract. The orthodox economists paid too little attention to the influence of other factors affecting economic behavior. Specifically, the institutionalists, and Veblen as one of their leading figures, argued that analysis of economic events must take account of history, institutions, the pursuit of power, and the complexity of human motivation. Veblen was particularly critical of the prevailing theory of markets, which used supply and demand (see Chapter 7) to predict prices and quantities. These models were based on restrictive assumptions about human behavior. Consumers in general were assumed to be independent, rational, calculating, and self-interested in their pursuit of personal pleasure (hedonistic). These models were also based on the assumption that markets were stable and tended toward equilibrium unless external factors caused a change, in which case the market would simply move to a new equilibrium. The following passage from Veblen's *The Place of Science in Modern Civilization* (1919) demonstrates the institutionalist critique of the orthodox theory of markets and its assumptions about consumer behavior:

> The psychological and anthropological preconceptions of economists have been those which were accepted by the psychological and social sciences some generations ago. The hedonistic conception of man is that of a lightning calculator of pleasures and pains, who oscillates like a homogeneous globule of desire of happiness under the impulse of stimuli that shift him about the area, but leave him intact. He has neither antecedent nor consequent. He is an isolated, definitive human datum, in stable equilibrium except for the buffets of the impinging forces that displace him in one direction or another. Self-imposed in elemental space, he spins symmetrically about his own spiritual axis until the parallelogram of forces bears down upon him, whereupon he follows the line of the resultant. When the force of the impact is spent, he comes to rest, a self-contained globule of desire as before.

4. Do you consider yourself a "self-contained globule of desire"? Are you subject to "buffets of impinging forces"?

Instead of viewing human beings as isolated individuals making rational, informed decisions about what to buy, Veblen preferred a different view of how people make decisions. He believed that peer pressure (or in his words, pecuniary emulation) and advertising influence people's desires, and that cultural institutions, rather than individuals' independent choices, shape their preferences. Veblen identified the wasteful and unproductive side of capitalism, where businesses could make money by forming monopolies and manipulating consumers with advertising instead of producing good products at low prices. These observations led him to oppose laissez-faire and advocate a greater role for government in the economy. Veblen's call was echoed by John Maynard Keynes.

THE GREAT DEPRESSION AND THE KEYNESIAN CRITIQUE OF LAISSEZ-FAIRE

British economist John Maynard Keynes (1883–1946) followed the classical tradition, but in the early 1920s he began to depart from the classical ideas held by most economists. Throughout the late nineteenth and early twentieth centuries, the United States suffered repeated depressions in economic activity.

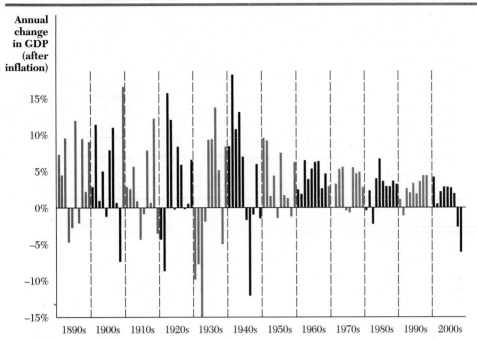

Source: David Wyss, DRI/McGraw-Hill, for the *New York Times*, March 17, 1996; *Economic Report of the President*, 2009, p.284. Bureau of Economic Analysis, http://www.bea.gov/brieprm/gdp.htm.

Periods of prosperity and boom were regularly followed by periods of depression and bust. Figure 5.1 graphically depicts this pattern. In the midst of these depressions, unemployment and economic hardship for many people increased dramatically and tragically. The worst depression occurred in the 1930s, when the decrease in economic activity spread around the world. In 1933, almost one-third of the workforce in the United States was without employment. The Great Depression in the United States was deep and lasted throughout the 1930s. It was also a worldwide depression and its effects were experienced earlier by Britain. In 1929, Keynes was advising the British government to spend freely on public works programs to promote employment. A bit later, President Franklin Roosevelt, confronted by millions of families without any income because laissez-faire capitalism was unable to provide employment in the 1930s, increased the influence of government in the U.S. economy.

In the 1920s, Keynes wrote an essay, "The End of Laissez-Faire," in which he challenged the notion that the search for private interests always led to the greater good for the society as a whole. In particular, he was convinced that capitalism did not automatically produce full employment. He rejected Say's law because his research indicated that there were times when supply did not create enough demand. For example, toward the end of periods of economic expansion, it was often the case that profitable investment opportunities dried up and capital flowed into increasingly risky areas. Inevitably, some investments failed, and these failures undermined consumer and business confidence in the economy, causing declines in consumer spending and in businesses' purchases of capital goods. Because of this lowered confidence, the pool of savings increased and spending declined. More money was now available in the financial sector, but no one wanted to spend or invest while the economy was in decline. Thus, Keynes noted, there could be regular gluts in the economy: An increase in savings might not be matched by an increase in investment if confidence in the economy was low. In response, Keynes believed the state needed to assume responsibility for the overall health of capitalist economies with increases in spending to offset the declines in consumer and investor spending that occurs in recessions. Capitalism might be stronger, he argued, if some decisions were left in private hands; but some others, which were social in nature, ought to be the responsibility of the state.

Keynes thus began to explore the idea that laissez-faire did not always result in the greatest social good. He argued, in fact, that the state should take an active part in certain economic matters, such as maintaining full employment. This emerging argument and the Great Depression of the 1930s signaled the end of laissez-faire. Keynes, while accepting capitalism as an economic system, rejected the classical notion of laissez-faire. His primary argument in reaching this conclusion was that the laissez-faire capitalist economic system could easily permit chronic unemployment and instability. Beginning in the 1930s, and continuing through the rest of the twentieth century, developed countries used Keynes's ideas to establish a mixed economy, which meant smoothing out the rough edges of markets with increasing amounts of government intervention. Governments added welfare and unemployment programs to assist the poor, social security programs to support the elderly, stabilization policies to reduce hardships in recessions, and regulations to improve market outcomes in the areas of health, safety, and the environment. In capitalist economies, the mixed economy became the norm, and economic debates no longer focused on whether or not the government should intervene in the economy, but how much the government should intervene, and in what areas. In Part 3 we will examine in more detail the Keynesian body of thought on instability and the role of the state in the economy.

5. What would Adam Smith think about Keynes's argument? Why?

6. Based on your conception of the U.S. economic system, list its five most important attributes. Are these positive or negative attributes? Are they results of the system? Or are they fundamental characteristics of it?

The Great Depression and the "escape" from it with the increased production and employment brought about by World War II engendered one of the more recent alterations of capitalism in the United States. Given the historical instability of capitalism's growth process, the federal government since the

1930s has taken a more direct responsibility for the overall health of the economy. It has attempted to prevent extremes in the cycles of boom and bust. Some would call this mixed capitalism; others might call it state capitalism. Still others, noting the role of the state and the role of large corporations in the economy, call it monopoly capitalism. And the addition of the economic role of the state constitutes one more major change in the continuing development of U.S. capitalism.

7. What is your name, or label, for our economic system? Why do you call it that?

Joseph Schumpeter, Laissez-Faire, and Creative Destruction

Another prominent economist of the twentieth century, Joseph A. Schumpeter (1883–1950), had great faith in laissez-faire capitalism and opposed government intervention to end recessions, unlike Keynes. Despite the human suffering recessions produced, Schumpeter thought that they were a healthy phase of the business cycle that set the stage for the next expansion. Most economists disagreed, and economists and government officials from the 1930s to the present have widely supported Keynesian stabilization policy.

In addition to disagreeing with Keynes, Schumpeter criticized the static nature of orthodox economics. Schumpeter remarked in *Capitalism, Socialism, and Democracy* (1942), "capitalism...[is] an evolutionary process." Schumpeter believed that economists should focus on evolutionary change, and in particular on the process of **creative destruction** in their analysis:

The opening up of new markets, foreign or domestic, and the organizational development from the craft shop and factory to such concerns as U.S. Steel illustrate the same process of industrial mutation...that incessantly revolutionizes the economic structure from within, incessantly destroying the old one, incessantly creating a new one. This process of Creative Destruction is the essential fact about capitalism.

Schumpeter chided orthodox economists for limiting their studies to "how capitalism administers existing structures, whereas the relevant problem is how it creates and destroys them." For example, Schumpeter thought that when orthodox economists focused on price competition and the entry and exit of similar businesses, they missed key elements of capitalist competition:

In the case of retail trade the competition that matters arises not from additional shops of the same type, but from the department store, the chain store, the mail-order house and the supermarket which are bound to destroy those pyramids sooner or later. Now a theoretical construction which neglects this essential element of the case neglects all that is most typically capitalist about it; even if correct in logic as well as in fact, it is like *Hamlet* without the Danish prince.

Even the process of creative destruction could evolve, according to Schumpeter. In studying the evolution of big corporations in the United States, Schumpeter became convinced that we should not assume that capitalism would always be dynamic and creative. As managers and bureaucrats took over big corporations from the inventors and entrepreneurs that founded them, businesses frequently ceased to be innovative and in fact sometimes hindered innovation. For this reason, Schumpeter thought we might see the end of capitalism—not because of revolution, but because it would eventually cease to function effectively and would have to be replaced with socialism.

In his evolutionary analysis, Schumpeter praised Karl Marx for the scope and depth of his analysis. In particular, as he stated in his *History of Economic Analysis* (1954), he was impressed with how Marx "welded into a single homogeneous whole all branches of sociology *and* economics—a venture that might well dazzle the modern discipline...." However, to Schumpeter, Marx's true claim to greatness as an economist stemmed from the fact that he developed "the only genuinely evolutionary economic theory" of his time.

8. How is the Internet revolution involved in the process of creative destruction (i.e., creating new products and opportunities while destroying existing ones)?

9. Can you think of recent examples where "managers and bureaucrats [who] took over big corporations from the entrepreneurs that founded them..." ceased to be innovative and in fact hindered innovation?

The Post–World War II Experience

Following the demobilization of the economy after World War II, the United States experienced a quarter century of almost unprecedented economic growth and prosperity. During this time, there were periodic recessions, but the average standard of living increased at a rate of about 3 percent per year.

There were several bases for this era of prosperity. One was that the country emerged from the war as the world's leading military, economic, and political power, with its production base fully intact. From this position, it became the leader in establishing a new international economic trading and financial system that stimulated U.S. and Western economies. Following the Great Depression and the war, the federal government, partly based on Keynesian economics (see Part 3), assumed increased responsibility for the general health of the economy and for maintaining prosperity. Building on the labor legislation of the New Deal, which granted labor unions the right to organize and collectively bargain, and the labor peace of that period, big business and organized labor adopted a system of labor relations that minimized conflict and disruptions in production. Corporations themselves became larger and aggressively pursued profit-making possibilities at home and abroad. The result of these and other conditions was vigorous economic growth and the world's highest standard of living.

However, beginning in the late 1960s and early 1970s, some of the bases for the postwar prosperity began to break down, and specific events undermined the overall health of the U.S. economy. Consequently, at the beginning of the 1980s, the economy was plagued with stagflation—high unemployment (stagnation) and relatively high inflation—an energy crisis, and a general economic malaise.

The causes of this "crisis" in the economy were many, and they will be explored to some extent in the remainder of this book. But it is useful to mention a few of them briefly here. The United States lost some of its power in the world, partly as a result of its failure in Vietnam, but also because of the increased power of other countries, including Germany, France, Japan, and the Soviet Union. The United States encountered more effective competition in world markets. Third World countries assumed increased independence, nationalizing some U.S. corporations and adopting independent economic policies. Along these lines, the nations of the Organization of Petroleum Exporting Countries (OPEC) forced the United States to come to grips with expensive and scarce energy resources. The commitment to avoid depressions through the use of governmental economic policies had given the economy an inflationary (as opposed to a deflationary) bias. The relationship between big business and big labor also contributed to an inflationary spiral, with prices and wages moving ever upward. Inflationary expectations further fueled inflation. And there were many other problems as well, including declining productivity, a tax revolt, deregulation, racial and sexual discrimination, and continued poverty.

The Last Decades of the Twentieth Century

In evaluating the operation of the U.S. economy over more recent decades, economists can refer to many standard economic measures—such as the unemployment rate, the rate of inflation, gross domestic product, investment spending, and productivity—that are routinely compiled by government and other economists. By measuring economic activity over time, economists can develop a sense of how the economy is performing. Table 5.1 lists some important economic variables for the United States and shows how they changed over the last half of the twentieth century and into the early twenty-first century.

Table 5.1 Selected Measures of Economic Performance, 1950s–2008

	1950s	1960s	1970s	1980s	1990s	2000–2008
Unemployment rate (annual average, percent)	4.5	4.8	6.2	7.3	5.8	5.1
Rate of inflation (annual average increase in consumer prices, percent)	2.0	2.4	7.8	5.6	3.0	2.8
Average weekly earnings (annual increase, in constant dollars, percent)	2.5	1.4	−0.3	−1.0	0.4	0.1
Output per labor hour (annual average increase, percent)	2.6	2.8	1.9	1.0	1.9	2.5
Real output (annual average increase, percent)	4.0	4.4	3.3	3.0	3.1	2.6
Ratio of profit, after taxes (corporate profits as a percent of stockholders' equity, annual average)	11.3	11.1	12.8	12.2	11.9	12.3

Source: Economic Report of the President, various years.

As Table 5.1 indicates, the U.S. economy performed much less successfully in the 1970s than it did in the 1950s and 1960s. The unemployment rate and the rate of inflation were both higher, on average, than in the previous two decades. Average weekly earnings, after taking inflation into account, actually decreased during the 1970s. The rate of increase in total output per labor hour and the rate of increase in real total output both decreased. The economy was growing at a slower rate, although the rate of profit for corporations was higher than it had been in both the 1950s and the 1960s. In addition, net investment, one of the most important sources of economic growth, was declining as a percentage of total output.

As the United States entered the 1980s, its economic system continued to be plagued with high unemployment and inflation and low rates of economic growth. From 1979 to 1981, real output grew by less than 2 percent per year. The unemployment rate was above 7 percent. Consumer prices were increasing at a rate of 12 to 13 percent a year. The real average weekly earnings for nonagricultural workers in 1980 were less than they had been in 1963. Interest rates were at historic highs. In 1981, the rate that banks charged their best corporate customers for loans was close to 20 percent. The federal deficit was beginning to increase and reached the $50 billion range in 1980 and 1981. And the value of the dollar in international exchange was at its lowest levels for the entire post–World War II period.

These various economic difficulties became a primary concern of economists and the centerpiece of Ronald Reagan's 1980 presidential campaign. The "Reagan Revolution" used the analysis of monetarist and supply-side economics to explain the slowdown in the economy and to develop a package of economic policies that came to be known as "Reaganomics." Very simply, Reagan argued that the country's economic difficulties were a result of too little economic growth. The source of the problem, he contended, was the excessive role of the government in the economy. There was too much regulation of business and too much government spending on social programs, taxes on corporations and individuals were too high, and the increase in the money supply was too rapid. All of this resulted in too much demand for output and not enough production to meet that demand—hence, slow growth and inflation. The solution was to increase the incentives and the rewards for the private sector. This would unleash corporations and individuals, and the nation would witness a massive surge in work and investment. The economy would grow more rapidly, providing economic prosperity with price stability once again.

The policies that President Reagan initiated and Congress passed included a three-year package of cuts in individual and corporate income taxes, reductions in federal spending on a variety of social programs, deregulation in a variety of industries and business practices, and large increases in military spending to restore U.S. power in the world. While the Reagan administration implemented these policies, the Federal Reserve tightened the money supply, as described in Chapter 16.

The immediate result of tighter money and cutbacks in federal spending was a severe recession in the early 1980s. Real output actually declined in 1982, and the unemployment rate rose above 10 percent. In 1983, however, the economy began to recover. Real output increased steadily throughout the mid-1980s, and the unemployment rate began to decline very slowly. Along with the recession, the rate of inflation dropped precipitously to just below 4 percent, but workers' average wages also continued to fall. With the recovery, the rate of growth in productivity (output per hour) began to increase, as did investment spending. As a result of the recession, the tax cuts, and the massive increase in military spending, however, the federal deficit mushroomed to annual levels of close to $200 billion. All of these measurements suggest that there was some improvement in the economy but that significant problems remained at the end of the 1980s.

Table 5.1 provides some information on the overall performance of the U.S. economy during the 1980s. Real output continued to grow at a slower rate than in the 1950s and 1960s, at an average of 3.0 percent annually, although the economy grew continuously from 1982 without recession. The rate of productivity growth was less than half of what it was in the two decades immediately following World War II. With slower economic growth, the average unemployment rate actually increased during the 1980s, while the rate of inflation decreased. Average weekly earnings, adjusted for inflation, continued decreasing and by 1989 were no higher than they were in the early 1960s. Corporate profits, on the other hand, were as healthy as in the 1970s. Meanwhile, the rate of net investment decreased, suggesting continued slow growth in the economy. (Investment is a key determinant of economic growth. It represents spending on capital formation by businesses and expands the ability to produce.) Reaganomics and tight monetary policy by the Federal Reserve certainly led to a reduction in inflation, but they did not produce rampant economic growth, investment, and prosperity. The success, however, was enough to form a basis for George H. W. Bush's winning 1988 presidential campaign.

A number of persistent and emerging problems accompanied these general economic trends. The federal budget deficit was reduced moderately by legislation (the Gramm-Rudman-Hollings Deficit Reduction Act of 1985), but remained in excess of $150 billion in the early 1990s, given Bush's reluctance to raise taxes and congressional resistance to reducing spending on federal social programs. The massive cost of bailing out the many savings and loan institutions that failed during this period compounded the difficulty of deficit reduction. The trade deficit showed some improvement as U.S. exports grew faster than U.S. imports during the late 1980s. But the U.S. economy was increasingly challenged in domestic and global markets by Japanese and European firms. The distribution of income in the United States became more unequal during the 1980s as a result of the 1981 tax cuts, restraints on government social spending programs, and the patterns of growth in the economy. Homelessness became a national concern. At the same time, U.S. military spending was 50 percent higher in real terms than it was at the beginning of the decade. Global environmental problems received increasing public attention. The end of the Cold War held out the promise of reordered priorities.

In the early 1990s, there was a mild recession, just enough to cement George Bush's loss to Bill Clinton in the presidential election. As Table 5.1 shows, the economic news during Clinton's presidency indicates improvement.

The unemployment rate declined by 1.5 percentage points. The rate of inflation fell to half of what it was in the 1980s. Average weekly earnings showed small gains, reversing the trend of the previous two decades. The increase in output per labor hour was the largest since the 1950s and 1960s, while the growth rate for real output reversed its long slowdown. Net investment rose in the late 1990s, the stock market soared as a bubble developed in technology stocks, and government deficits changed to surpluses. The 1990s represented stable growth, high employment, and low levels of inflation.

By early 2000, as George W. Bush was inaugurated president of the United States, growth slowed; unemployment began to rise and the technology bubble that had developed in the stock market burst. The terror attacks of September 11, 2001, left the nation's economy troubled and uncertain about the future. U.S. troops entered Afghanistan in October 2001 and the establishment of a Department of Homeland Security reflected the growing concern with terrorist attacks in the United States. At the same time that U.S. attention turned to terrorism, corporate scandals at energy and telecommunications giants Enron and World Com, and the related collapse of the accounting firm Arthur Andersen, only increased public uncertainty about the economy.

In mid-March 2003, U.S. military forces led a coalition into war with Iraq. Funding needed to support these military actions increased government expenditures. Spending in Afghanistan and Iraq exceeded forecasts and funds needed to rebuild both countries continued to escalate. Budgeted surpluses turned into large and continuing deficits and accelerating levels of economic growth brought about by this fiscal stimulus gradually lowered the unemployment rate.

The economy continued growing until early 2007, but by the end of the year the country had entered the worst recession in 30 years, with some comparing it to the Great Depression of the 1930s. This slowdown in economic growth had consequences on unemployment, with rates approaching double digits in late 2009.

The cause of the dramatic downturn was the financial crisis triggered by bad loans (primarily in the housing market) and what came to be known as "toxic assets" derived from these bad loans in the housing sector. (We will discuss the origins of this financial crisis in Chapter 16.) As a result of these loans and assets that were losing value, banks and other financial institutions halted most lending—even to the best borrowers. Solvent borrowers could no longer find loans available for automobiles, homes, or consumer durables such as washing machines and lawn mowers. The downturn in these industries spread to other sectors in the economy as well. For example, when automobile sales decreased, auto producers cut production and furloughed workers. These cutbacks and layoffs were felt in the industries that supplied auto parts as well as in grocery stores and shopping malls. These firms also begin cutting inventory and staff. The downturn in the housing industry was immediate as well. Builders and buyers could no longer borrow at attractive rates for mortgages and supplies. Homeowners reduced borrowing for home improvements that ranged from floor coverings to furnishings. The financial crisis that began in early 2007 had caused an economic downturn that triggered the recession, the effects of which continued into 2010. This recession was global in its reach as nations throughout the world experienced negative growth and high unemployment.

For almost three decades both Republican and Democratic administrations advocated a return to laissez-faire, publicly declaring a need to reduce the role of the government in the economy from the increases that had occurred at the end of the Great Depression and after World War II. While government spending actually increased during most of this period, the rhetoric was one of free markets and laissez-faire. The liberal programs of state involvement were under attack, from Social Security to Medicare and the welfare system. Liberalism and so-called liberal policies were out of favor, yet government deficits grew in all but three of the 30 years as federal spending continued and taxes were reduced. The rhetoric that free markets would solve economic problems that might arise became more muted during the 2008 presidential campaign as large financial institutions failed or came perilously close to failure, unemployment climbed and economic growth stagnated, and oil prices reached record levels. By the end of the year, President Bush's Treasury Department spent half of the $700 billion TARP (Troubled Asset Relief Program) funds to purchase assets and equity in financial institutions. At the same time, the Federal Reserve pumped reserves into the banking system at extraordinary rates to supply liquidity to prevent a collapse in the financial system. And, at the end of 2008 the U.S. automakers found themselves harmed by the resulting recession. Chrysler and General Motors negotiated emergency loans from the Treasury.

While TARP funds were the beginning of greater government involvement in the economy, the inauguration of Barack Obama in January 2009 brought more government policies to stem the recession and financial turmoil in the United States. The Obama administration worked with world leaders to coordinate actions to calm financial markets. By late January Congress passed a whopping $819 billion stimulus package aimed at programs that would put unemployed workers back to work, along with new tax cuts. The recession continued to gain speed, but financial markets became less volatile. By June 2009, both Chrysler and GM had declared bankruptcy and the federal government, with loans and assistance to the auto industry, found itself owning a substantial portion of major financial institutions and General Motors.

The end to calls for laissez-faire and free-market policies had come once again. And, once again, it was due to the failure of free-market policies to produce the economic stability that the electorate desired. The ideas of John Maynard Keynes were recovered in the stimulus package and in the Treasury's Troubled Asset Relief Program. However, there is significant concern over the magnitude of government spending and tax cuts and their effect on future economic growth.

Still, the U.S. economy has come a long way in its history. It has largely been a history of successful development—not, however, without negative aspects and events. The United States has the world's largest and most industrialized economy. Some questions still face the U.S. economy: Will the recession, once abated, turn into a prolonged period of inflation or, worse, another period of stagflation, as inflation grows and economic growth remains stagnant? Can future budget deficits be controlled? Can productivity growth improve?

Conclusion

In Part 1, we have reviewed economic methodology and the development of economic systems, focusing on capitalism. We have, at the same time, summarized the development of modern economic thought, examining capitalist proponents and its critics. In this chapter we have examined the historical development of capitalism in the United States and how it has changed over time. The ideas of Keynes were influential in assessing solutions for an economy mired in depression. In Parts 2 and 3, we turn to the development of the modern economic theory about how capitalism and markets work—first, in terms of microeconomics, then macroeconomics.

Review Questions

1. List the strengths of laissez-faire capitalism both in theory and in practice.

2. List major shortcomings in the operation of laissez-faire capitalism.

3. How did Keynes reshape the way economists thought about the economy?

4. In what sense can the ideas of John Maynard Keynes be considered a synthesis of the ideas of Smith and Marx?

5. What were the major forces behind the economic success of the United States?

6. What are some current problems facing the U.S. economy?

7. What are the ways in which the ideas of Smith, Marx, and Keynes are incorporated into the structure of the U.S. economy?

THINKING CRITICALLY

TECHNOLOGICAL INNOVATION, THE NEW ECONOMY, AND THE FUTURE

The ideas of Adam Smith and Karl Marx and the intellectual legacy of Joseph Schumpeter continue with us in more ways than we might imagine as we progress into the twenty-first century. Each economist discussed issues of economic growth and conditions necessary for expanding national income. (Also, while we are not focusing on their specific contributions here, Thorstein Veblen and John Maynard Keynes had very important ideas related to technology, technological change, business cycles, and the future of capitalism.) That focus on growth is especially relevant today, with technological change driving the long economic expansion in the United States, lasting from 1991 into 2000. The value of investments traded in the U.S. and global financial markets rose rapidly for those years. The expansion of information and communications technology has also provided the stimulus for capitalism's spread across the globe, as many countries attempt some variation of capitalist development.

The changes amount to more than growth, however. U.S. and global capitalism seem to have entered into a new and different phase made possible by advances in computer and microchip technology and the growth of the semiconductor industry. Satellite technology and the development of fiber optics accelerated a telecommunications revolution. Advances in biotechnology through the human genome project have forever changed the way we approach medical challenges. All the while, the Internet and software developments introduced new ways for consumers and businesses to make purchases. Technology-inspired change transformed all areas of business, from financial operations to marketing, accounting, public relations, advertising, and management practices and strategies.

As every sector of the economy integrated communications and information technology, productivity (output per worker) grew. The services sector of the economy also has expanded. And all of this has taken place on a global scale. During the mid- to late 1990s, stock prices soared as investors poured dollars into high-tech stocks and as industry giants—including AOL and Time Warner, Citibank and Travelers—launched a wave of mergers and buyouts. The wealth generated by this wildly rising stock market, including riches gained (and later lost) in the Internet sector, fueled economic growth through the 1990s and transformed many traditional business methods and markets. Not all of these transformations were used toward productive ends. Complex modeling was used by executives in financial markets to justify taking unwarranted risks, leading to the collapse of financial markets.

While the early economists discussed in these past chapters didn't write about the most recent revolutions in technology, Adam Smith, Karl Marx, and Joseph Schumpeter did introduce important ideas about technological change, innovation, business cycles, economic growth, and the future of capitalism—items that help explain the direction our economy has taken and perhaps help us understand the importance of innovation in economic growth.

Adam Smith and Economic Growth

Adam Smith, whose work we discussed in Chapter 3, didn't foresee the Industrial Revolution that encompassed England as he was teaching about and writing *The Wealth of Nations*. His view of technology nevertheless played a central role in the ongoing development of capitalism. Responding to the free interplay of the forces of supply and demand, Smith confidently noted that the market system would self-adjust through the "invisible hand." The pressure of competition would force capitalists to reinvest profits in new production methods so they would produce better goods more efficiently, helping them retain and capture additional customers and gain a greater share of the market. Capitalists depended on the innovators and the risk takers developing these new processes and the underlying technology to make them more efficient. This constant search for new, more efficient production methods supported Smith's argument that capitalism would advance in periods of growth spurts that would over time improve the progress of society and the well-being of the members of society. (We do, after all, have more pins!) The role for invention was clearly implied in Smith's market system.

Karl Marx, Technical Change, and the Quest for Markets

From our earlier discussion in Chapter 4, we have seen how Karl Marx's analysis of historical change and his capitalist critique incorporated ideas about technology, technological change, business cycles, and the future of capitalism. To Marx, changes in technology would transform the relations of production and eventually the superstructure, ultimately altering society itself. These changes were apparent in the transitions from the early communal societies to the slave societies of Greece and Rome, to the feudal societies of Europe, and finally to the emergence of capitalism in Europe. Indeed, Marx anticipated that capitalism itself would be transformed to a higher stage of development which he defined as socialism, or the first communism.

Marx's theory of capitalist crisis suggested that the capitalist's quest for surplus value would eventually lead to the substitution of capital for labor in the production process to reduce the cost of production. As capitalists invented more and more productive technologies while driving wages down, the result would be a crisis of overproduction. Laborers would no longer be able to purchase all that capitalists produced.

Joseph Schumpeter and Creative Destruction of Technology

In Chapter 5 we noted that Joseph Schumpeter focused on the importance of technical change for the growth process. During the late 1990s and early 2000, Schumpeter's ideas were retrieved from economic history texts and recognized as increasingly relevant in explaining the changes brought about by revolutionary transformations in information and communication technologies. His theories of creative destruction, innovation, and entrepreneurship are today intrinsically associated with the underlying dynamics of capitalism.

The following readings focus on the importance of innovation for economic growth. The article " Catch the Wave" is from a special report, "Innovation in Industry Survey," published in *The Economist* on February 20, 1999. It examines innovation cycles, or "Schumpeter's Waves," over the past two centuries. In May 2009, the Conference Board produced the report "Innovation and U.S. Competitiveness: Reevaluating the Contributors to Growth," that focuses on the importance of innovation as the economy recovers from the 2007–2009 recession. An excerpt from the Conference Board press release outlines major themes of the report.

Read both selections and answer the questions that follow.

Catch the Wave

Think of innovation as "x" in the economic-growth equation—a factor that clearly matters but no-one is quite sure how much. Annual forecasts of gross domestic product (GDP) are no help. They are just statistical measures, laden with guesswork and opinion. They represent the forecaster's view about the difference between an economy's output and its total productive capacity on the one hand, and the state of the country's consumer confidence, stock building and export prospects in the months ahead on the other hand. If that seems tricky, try forecasting economic growth for a number of years into the future. Nobody has done this successfully, because it requires insight into how productivity can be expected to change in the years ahead—among many other things.

From Adam Smith to Karl Marx, economists have struggled to understand productivity growth. But it was not until after the second world war that the beginnings of an explanation emerged. The theory now generally accepted stems from work done on the so-called "production function" by Robert Solow at the Massachusetts Institute of Technology in 1956. This says, reasonably enough, that the output of an economy depends on its inputs—in short, capital and labour. Double the inputs and you get twice the output. To the basic theory, economists have added a rider to account for embarrassing quirks such as the law of diminishing returns. In the revised version, if you add more and more capital to a given labour force, or an increasing number of workers to a fixed amount of capital, the result will be successively smaller increases in output.

So far, so good. But although the production function, like Newtonian mechanics, may be broadly right, it is nowhere near right enough to make meaningful long term predictions. The problem is that, as in Isaac Newton's view of the physical universe, the theory assumes an idealised world—in this case, a heavenly paradise in which perfect competition reigns.

Unfortunately, the real world works rather differently. For instance, if the law of diminishing returns operates as it is supposed to, why have returns on investment in America, Europe and Japan been higher in the second half of the 20th century than in the first half? Why, for that matter, has the gap between the world's rich and poor countries widened rather than narrowed? The theory says that where the stock of capital is rising faster than the work force—as has clearly been true in the industrial countries since the second world war—the return on each additional unit of capital should fall over time. Instead, it has risen over the decades rather than fallen, so something is amiss.

For want of a better explanation, that "something" is now reckoned to be technological progress plus other forms of new knowledge—in short, innovation. In this scheme of things, innovation accounts for any growth that cannot be explained by increases in capital and labour. And although the return on investment may decline as more capital is added to the economy, any deceleration in growth is more than offset by the leveraging effects of innovation. This explains why rates of return have stayed high in rich countries, and why poorer countries have not caught up.

There the economists tend to leave the argument, as if technological progress—along with other new knowledge—were simply to be taken for granted, free as air. However, experience shows that technological know-how, manufacturing experience and market research are not free; they have to be acquired at considerable cost. And once acquired, such proprietary knowledge tends to be hoarded as trade secrets or hedged in by patents and other intellectual-property rights. To ignore such quibbles must be justified if innovation contributed only marginally to economic growth. Yet, maddeningly, this residual, intangible and largely ignored factor seems to account for more than half of all growth. Thus, if this reading is correct, it is innovation—more than the application of capital or labour—that makes the world go round.

Godfather of Innovation

All attempts to understand the effects of technological progress on economic growth pay homage to Joseph Schumpeter, an Austrian economist best remembered for his views on the "creative destruction" associated with industrial cycles 50–60 years long. Arguably the most radical economist of the 20th century, Schumpeter was the first to challenge classical economics as it sought (and still seeks) to optimise existing resources within a stable environment—treating any disruption as an external force on a par with plagues, politics and the weather. Into this intellectual drawing room, Schumpeter introduced the raucous entrepreneur and his rumbustious behaviour. As Schumpeter saw it, a normal, healthy

FIGURE 5.1A Schumpeter's Waves

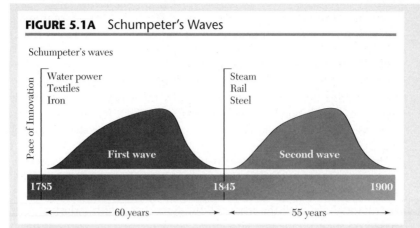

economy was not one in equilibrium, but one that was constantly being "disrupted" by technological innovation.

Others had noticed "long waves" of economic activity before him, notably a Russian economist, Nikolai Kondratieff, who drew attention to them in 1925, using data on prices, wages and interest rates as well as industrial production and consumption drawn from France, Britain and the United States. But it was Schumpeter, the economic radical, who studied them in depth.

In his view, each of these long business cycles was unique, driven by entirely different clusters of industries (see Figure 5.1A & B).Typically, a long upswing in a cycle started when a new set of innovations came into general use—as happened with water power, textiles and iron in the late 18th century; steam, rail and steel in the mid-19th century; and electricity, chemicals and the internal combustion engine at the turn of the 20th century. In turn,

FIGURE 5.1B Schumpeter's Waves

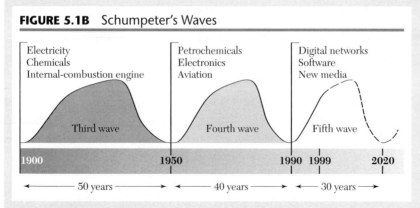

Source: (Figures 5.1A, B) "Schumpeter's Waves" from *Innovation in Industry Survey*, published on February 20,1999 by The Economist. Copyright 1999 by Economist Newspaper Group. Reproduced with permission of Economist Newspaper Group via Copyright Clearance Center.

each upswing stimulated investment and an expansion of the economy. These long booms eventually petered out as the technologies matured and returns to investors declined with the dwindling number of opportunities. After a period of much slower expansion came the inevitable decline—only to be followed by a wave of fresh innovations which destroyed the old way of doing things and created the conditions for a new upswing. The entrepreneur's role, as Schumpeter saw it, was to act as a ferment in this process of creative destruction, allowing the economy to renew itself and bound onwards and upwards again.

By the time Schumpeter died in 1950, the third cycle of his "successive industrial revolutions" had already run its course. The fourth, powered by oil, electronics, aviation and mass production, is now rapidly winding down, if it has not gone already. All the evidence suggests that a fifth industrial revolution—based on semiconductors, fibre optics, genetics and software—is not only well under way but even approaching maturity. This may explain why America shrugged off its lethargy in the early 1990s and started bounding ahead again, leaving behind countries too preoccupied with preserving their fourth-wave industries. If so, then Schumpeter's long economic waves are shortening, from 50–60 years to around 30–40 years.

There is good reason why they should. It was only during the third wave, in the early part of the 20th century, that governments and companies began to search for new technologies in a systematic manner. One of the oldest, Bell Laboratories at Murray Hill in New Jersey, was founded in 1925. Rather than leave the emergence of "new-wave"technologies to chance, all the major industrial countries nowadays have armies of skilled R&D workers sifting the data in pursuit of blockbuster technologies capable of carving out wholly new markets. The tools they use—computer analysers, gene sequencers, text parsers, patent searchers, citation mappers—are getting better all the time, speeding up the process. The productivity of industrial laboratories today is twice what it was a couple of decades ago.

So the fifth industrial revolution that started in America in the late 1980s may last no more than 25–30 years. If, as seems likely, we are already a decade into this new industrial cycle, it may now be almost too late for the dilatory to catch up. The rapid-upswing part of the cycle—in which successful participants enjoy fat margins, set standards, kill off weaker rivals and establish themselves as main players—looks as though it has already run two-thirds of its course, with only another five or six years left to go. Catching the wave at this late stage will depend on governments' willingness to free up their technical and financial resources, invest in the infrastructure required and let their fourth-wave relics go. Failing that, latecomers can expect only crumbs from the table before the party comes to an end—and a new wave of technologies begins, once again, to wash everything aside.

Source: "Catch the Wave" from *Innovation in Industry Survey*, published on February 20,1999 by The Economist. Copyright 1999 by Economist Newspaper Group. Reproduced with permission of Economist Newspaper Group via Copyright Clearance Center.

Innovation Crucial to Recovery and U.S. Competitiveness

May 7, 2009

Innovation is critical to economic recovery and future U.S. competitiveness, and the focus on short-term cost-cutting risks deflecting attention from this crucial economic priority...

The leveling-off of the traditional drivers behind the U.S. economy's competitive edge means that attention and resources must be devoted to better understanding, measuring and fostering innovation...

"Going forward, an economy's competitive edge will depend on its ability to maintain a superior talent pool and knowledge base, along with an environment that encourages and rewards new ideas, products and processes," said Bart van Ark, Chief Economist of The Conference Board and one of the report's authors. "Our report lays this out for the United States—but it's a universal truth."

Today, the scarce and intangible inputs that create a competitive advantage—ideas, knowledge, labor quality (talent)—are much more mobile than the tangible and previously plentiful inputs that gave the United States much of its historical edge. Traditional contributors to growth like land, natural resources and labor quality are maxing out due to the aging of the U.S. population, uncertain immigration trends, continued rising trends in outsourcing and off-shoring, and the technological advances of the 20th century.

These shifts produce a slowing effect on economic growth, while the "knowledge economy's" share of output growth continues to grow in importance. Even the information technology so critical to U.S. economic growth over the past two decades will not translate into further gains without investment in intangible inputs.

Changing this mindset and practice to enhance competitive advantage will require developing new metrics to measure intangibles. The report puts forth a relatively simple framework, presented at the economy level but adaptable for use by companies, that treats innovation as a key source of economic growth along with conventional bricks and machinery, capital, labor force size and skill, and productivity.

"We hear it daily across the global business community: The only way out of this crisis is to innovate our way out," said Gail Fosler, President of The Conference Board and an author of the report. "Innovation is a major element of many of our research projects and executive forums. It should be front and center in strategic planning at all levels of companies and economies."

"This report highlights the critical need to invest in innovation in order to restart economic growth. History suggests that the countries and companies that invest in innovation during the downturn will be the strongest beneficiaries from the recovery—and in fact they'll help to drive that recovery," said Brad Smith, Microsoft Corp. Senior Vice President and General Counsel. "When we look back, successful companies during the Great Depression focused on reducing their debts and cutting their overall costs while sustaining their overall R&D and using innovation to bring new products to market."

Source: Innovation and U.S. Competitiveness: Reevaluating the Contributors to Growth Report #1441-09-RR / The Conference Board http://www.conference-board.org/innovateandcompete

Exercises

Answer the questions that follow.

1. What is the relationship between the process of "creative destruction" and human progress according to Schumpeter?

2. Compare and contrast Schumpeter's core ideas with those of Smith and Marx. Outline key arguments in a debate that the three economic legends might have with one another.

3. What are three ways in which Schumpeter's ideas are relevant for the economy given advances in information and communication technologies? Find support for these three applications in a newspaper article, news or business magazine, or online article. Outline the main factors supporting Schumpeter's theories.

4. If Schumpeter's theory of successive industrial revolutions is correct, where are we now on a historical chart of cycles? Given the recession of 2007–2009, would the authors of "Innovation and U.S. Competitiveness" agree with the Schumpeterian wave analysis outlined in *The Economist?* Do you think Marx would agree or disagree with this interpretation?

5. Are we letting our "fourth wave" relics go? Are there recent government policies that would help us evaluate our commitment to the advance or destruction of the fourth wave? Identify and explain those policies.

6. Explore the items for proposed spending in the stimulus package passed by Congress in January 2009. Are there items that might serve as catalysts for innovation—and potentially drive another Schumpeterian wave?

PART TWO

Microeconomics

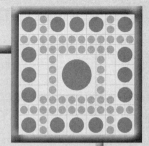

Now that we are about to begin studying modern economic theory, we might pause to ask ourselves what economic theory should do. Ideally, it should have explanatory value to help us understand how economic forces work, predictive power to help us understand what might happen in the future, and relevance to help us solve the economic problems we face. Keep these criteria in mind as you study economic theory in Parts 2, 3, and 4.

Markets have emerged in the Western world as a method of organizing society's production. Markets exist for all of the factors of production and for final consumption goods. Through the information transmitted by markets, producers decide what factors of production to use, and consumers decide what to consume. The information appears in the form of prices. On the basis of these decisions by various economic agents in the society, resources will be used in certain ways to produce certain goods and services. From their participation in production, people will earn certain incomes and will spend them, which will determine how goods are distributed in the society.

Early economists developed theories and concepts to explain these economic activities. The early development of economic thought provided a foundation for modern microeconomics. **Microeconomics** is concerned with describing how the economic system operates to allocate resources, determine incomes, and organize production. Consequently, it focuses on the decision makers—firms, consumers, the government—that determine how resources will be used.

Microeconomics is fundamentally concerned with a major problem facing all contemporary economies: that not enough resources are available to satisfy all the desires of all the economic agents. **Scarcity** is a crucial economic fact of life. Given scarcity, microeconomics also concentrates on how the market system allocates resources by valuing them. Therefore it examines the operation of markets and price determination. Finally, microeconomics is concerned with evaluating how well society allocates and rations its scarce resources. Ideally, society should use resources efficiently. **Efficiency** means the minimal use of scarce resources to achieve the mix of output most highly valued by society.

This section on microeconomics also includes a number of models of economic behavior. Economists use models to focus their analysis on key economic relationships. In a world of boundless complexity, it is literally impossible for economists to consider every factor that might affect the economy. Therefore, economists tend to focus on the most important economic factors and relationships. To do this, they make assumptions that limit the number of variables considered in the relationship being studied, or they may hold variables constant for the time period in question. These assumptions used in economic models can help us to explore key economic relationships in depth. However, if there are circumstances in which the assumptions behind a model do not hold true, inaccurate analyses and predictions may result.

In this part of the book, you will learn to use and apply some basic microeconomic models. These models are used to examine particular economic issues, and we will evaluate the underlying assumptions in some cases to assist in our evaluation of the usefulness of the results.

CHAPTER SIX

Scarcity: "You Can't Always Get What You Want"

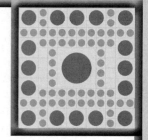

◆ Introduction

Most of us remember the high gas prices of 2008. Few, however, remember an earlier period of equally high gas prices. In the 1970s, the United States experienced an energy crisis. Prices for oil, natural gas, and gasoline increased dramatically. Shortages of petroleum-related products developed and, at times, were serious, driving prices up and forcing long lines at gas stations and even shutdowns of factories and schools. Some observers predicted the shortages would become even more serious.

In 1975, the National Academy of Sciences issued a report warning of future shortages of important resources for advanced industrial societies. The report noted that the United States would continue to depend on oil imports for the next half century and that even the Middle East's oil reserves might be depleted. Other resources in possible short supply included asbestos, tin, copper, helium, and mercury. The academy went on to urge conservation coupled with efforts to increase supplies, substitution, and recycling:

> Because of the limits to natural resources as well as to means for alleviating these limits, it is recommended that the federal government proclaim and deliberately pursue a national policy of conservation of material, energy and environmental resources, informing the public and the private sectors fully about the needs and techniques for reducing energy consumption, the development of substitute materials, increasing the durability and maintainability of products, and reclamation and recycling.

While some reduction in energy use occurred after this crisis in the 1970s, few of the other recommendations were pursued as oil prices fell back to lower levels.

In annual reports on worldwide energy, land, water, and environmental management, the Worldwatch Institute continually warns that the world cannot sustain the rate at which it is using up its resources. Every year, billions of tons of topsoil are depleted, the world population grows, forests are decimated in the Third World, and there is only small progress in the use of renewable energy and recycling.

In the twenty-first century, resource problems continue to plague the global community. Resource shortages pose potential threats to energy-dependent economies, insufficient agricultural production threatens some countries with mass starvation, and soil depletion, overfishing, and deforestation endanger normally replenishable resources. Moreover, the environmental complications of these economic activities pose their own hazards, from oil spills to urban slums to global warming. These are profound challenges to human societies in the new millennium.

Because there are constraints on the availability of resources, individuals, communities, and societies must make choices about the best uses of the resources available to them. Economists have developed concepts to highlight the consequences of these choices, and they have focused on understanding how societies allocate scarce resources.

1. Why are there shortages? What factors play a role in creating shortages?

2. What sorts of actions could be taken to alleviate projected shortages?

SCARCITY: A FUNDAMENTAL ECONOMIC FACT OF MODERN LIFE

Scarcity is one of the fundamental economic facts of modern life. **Scarcity** refers to the limitations on the resources used in production. All societies must develop methods and institutions to produce goods and services and to distribute them to people for consumption. However difficult that task, it is further complicated by the overriding reality of scarce resources and seemingly unlimited human wants and needs. Human societies, and the individual people within them, have certain physical needs for short- and long-run survival. Food, shelter, and clothing must be provided. With the desire to live beyond subsistence and to experience a richer life, the wants of a society are subject to constant expansion.

But the physical and mental resources that can be used to provide for material needs are not subject to constant expansion. This constraint is especially true if we concentrate on the short run—the present and immediate future. The mental capabilities of humans are at a certain stage of development. Physical resources are at a fixed level. There are just so many people who can labor. There is just so much wheat, corn, coal, gas, bauxite, copper, and so forth. With more time, of course, science, technology, and exploration can expand the available resources, but we might also begin to run short of some key resources. In the long run, the problem of scarcity governs the decisions that must be made; society must concern itself with using its resources in the best way possible to meet its needs.

3. Are human wants and needs unlimited? Why or why not? What determines human wants and needs?

4. If wants are not unlimited, does scarcity still exist?

The microeconomic problem for society is to allocate the available resources in the best way possible to meet as many of the needs and wants of its people as it can. This is **efficiency**. A society will be better off if it uses its resources efficiently. This is an incredibly complicated task. How much of our resources should be used to develop nuclear energy? Should we devote more or less to exploring the possibilities of solar energy or growing corn for ethanol production? Should more resources go to housing or to transportation? Should we build automobiles for private transportation or trains for public transportation?

Because of scarcity, we must make choices. In addition to deciding how to organize for production and distribution, a society must develop mechanisms and institutions for making economic decisions—decisions about how best to use the resources that are available. How can we make sure that resources are allocated in the best way possible? Efficiency in the allocation of resources is an important economic objective. Different societies resolve and have resolved this task in different ways—for example, by tradition, by command, and by markets. (Besides efficiency, of course, a society may favor other economic goals, such as economic growth and equitable income distribution.)

In the current U.S. economic system, many of these decisions are made through markets. Clothes are produced because people demand them and are willing to buy them for the prices charged by producers. The prices reflect the costs to the producers for the resources that are used in production. Based on price information, income, and individual tastes and preferences, people decide what to spend money on. We will examine the workings of markets in Chapters 8 to 11 to see how they allocate resources.

Resource allocation also includes public choices about the use of resources. For example, every society desires to protect itself from foreign enemies. Some countries do this by establishing a military force; the threat of physical reaction is intended to forestall aggressive actions by others. In the event of attack or hostile action, the country can use military force to protect the society's interests and possessions. The construction of military force, however, requires the use of resources, which are then unavailable for other uses. This trade-off in the use of resources is what economists call **opportunity cost**—that is, the cost of the resources that is devoted to the production of one category of goods or services and therefore cannot be used in another activity. The opportunity cost of using resources to produce guns, tanks, planes, and other military goods and services is that those resources cannot be used for other purposes. Different societies have made different choices about the size of their military establishments, and thus over the use of their scarce resources.

As in this example, microeconomics is largely concerned with the allocation of resources in society. Are resources being used efficiently? What are the opportunity costs of alternative uses of resources?

THE PRODUCTION POSSIBILITIES CURVE

Economic choices, necessitated by scarcity, have opportunity costs. This fact applies to public choices about how to use tax revenues: Should we build more highways? Should we overhaul the railroad system? Should we expand space exploration? It also applies to analyzing the results of decisions usually made in the private sector: Should we produce big cars? Or little cars? Should we produce cigarettes? Or Power Bars? Or more housing? For these and other uses of resources, choices must be made. Choosing to use resources in a specific way means that they cannot be used for other purposes.

5. What is the opportunity cost of *not* using resources for a particular purpose? For example, what's the opportunity cost of going to work after graduating from high school? By choosing to work, what are you choosing *not* to do?

To illustrate this economic principle—that because the resources needed to produce goods and services are scarce, a society cannot have all of the goods and services it desires—economists have developed a model called the **production possibilities curve**. The basic production possibilities model makes the following assumptions:

❖ The economy is experiencing full employment of all its resources.

❖ The supplies of the factors of production are fixed at one point in time.

❖ Technology is constant (again, at one point in time).

We will apply this model to the public choice between producing military and civilian goods. This requires one further assumption: The economy produces consumer goods and military goods (or "butter" and "guns"), and the resources can be used to produce both types of goods (although some resources are specialized so they will be better than others at producing one type of goods). With our resources (and our assumptions), we can make only limited amounts of both types of goods, so we must choose how much of each type of good to produce. Since our resources are fully employed and limited, we can produce more of one type of good only by producing less of the other. That is, if we decide to produce more military goods, we can do it only by taking resources away from the production of civilian goods and thus produce fewer consumer goods. The opportunity cost of producing more military goods is that we will have fewer civilian goods, and vice versa.

Figure 6.1 shows the resulting production possibilities curve (PPC). If we produce only military goods (point *A* on the PPC, where we are using all our resources for military goods), we can have 50 units of military goods but no civilian goods. At the other extreme (point *D*), if we produce only civilian goods, we can have 100 units of them but no military goods. Or we can produce at point *B* or point *C*, with some military goods and some civilian goods. We have available a whole range of different *combinations* of military goods and civilian goods. The locus of all those possible combinations gives us the production possibilities curve.

At a given moment in time, if a society chooses to have more of one type of good, it must sacrifice some of the other type of good. If a society is currently at point *C* and decides to produce 20 additional units of military goods

FIGURE 6.1   Production Possibilities Curve

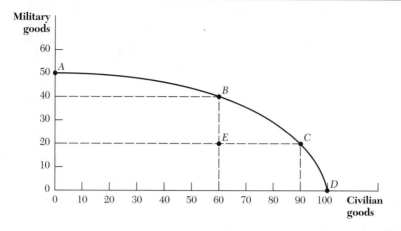

(moving to point *B*), the society will have fewer resources to devote to the production of civilian goods. It will have to reduce the production of civilian goods from 90 units to 60 units. Thus, the opportunity cost of increasing the production of military goods from 20 units to 40 units (the movement from point *C* to point *B*) is the 30 units of civilian goods that the society must give up in the process.

The production possibilities curve is shaped the way it is (concave to the origin) because resources are not completely adaptable to other uses. In other words, some resources are *specialized*. For example, beginning at point *A*, where society is producing only military goods, sacrificing 10 units of military goods will increase the output of civilian goods by 60 units, a substantial increase. This occurs because the resources best suited for producing civilian goods (including pacifists and farmland) are being shifted into production of civilian goods. As the society moves from point *B* to point *C*, it gives up 20 units of military goods for 30 units of civilian goods. Eventually, if society moves from point *C* to point *D*, it gives up 20 units of military goods for only 10 units of civilian goods. This happens because some resources, such as generals and missile factories, are very well suited for the production of military goods but less effective at producing civilian goods. As more and more resources are transferred to producing civilian goods, the *addition* to civilian goods will decline because some resources are specialized and are not easily converted from one use to another. To reflect this phenomenon, the slope of the PPC gets steeper and steeper.

6. What would the PPC look like if resources were not specialized and could be moved easily from one use to another with no loss in efficiency (as in the case of producing more green shirts and fewer blue shirts)?

At any point on the PPC, society is using all of its scarce resources efficiently. If a society were to leave some of its resources unused, or if it were to use its resources inefficiently, then that society would be at a point *inside* the production possibilities curve, such as point *E* in Figure 6.1. A society can attain any point on (or inside) its production possibilities curve with its existing resources and technology. To reach a point beyond the PPC, a society must increase its available resources or increase its efficiency with improvements in its technology.

Economic Growth and the Production Possibilities Curve

Economic growth can occur from technological innovations or decisions to produce greater amounts of **capital goods**. (Economists call the addition of capital goods *investment*.) Capital goods consist of the productive equipment needed to manufacture products. Typical capital goods are machinery, equipment, and infrastructure. Many people consider education to be a capital good (human capital) because it increases productivity, as we will see later in this chapter. Capital goods enhance a society's productive capacity, shifting the PPC out and allowing a society to produce more of all of the goods it desires. Capital goods differ from *consumer goods*, such as food, clothing, and CDs, which are enjoyed by consumers but not used to produce other goods.

Capital goods can be quite important in determining how fast an economy grows. In 1970, the United States was able to produce 2.5 times as many goods per person as Japan was. But in that same year, the Japanese spent more than twice as much per capita on capital goods. In fact, Japan's total capital investment in the 1970s was greater than that made by the much wealthier United States. The result was dramatic economic growth in Japan and mediocre economic growth in the United States. By 1988, Japan was able to produce the same amount of goods per person as the United States because of economic growth generated in large part by Japanese investment in capital goods. The production possibilities curves in Figure 6.2 show that, because Japan devoted a greater amount of resources to capital goods, its economy experienced a greater level of growth in productive capacity, measured on these PPCs as the trade-off between capital and consumer goods. In 1988, Japan's capacity to produce capital goods and consumer goods equaled that of the United States.

One of the reasons that Japan was able to devote a greater share of its resources to capital goods than the United States was that the peace agreement following World War II did not allow the Japanese to maintain a large military. Meanwhile, the United States (and the Soviet Union) was spending vast amounts of money on the Cold War. Military goods, like consumer goods, provide benefits but do not by themselves increase the productive capacity of the economy. As we will see in the next section, devoting so many of a society's scarce resources to military goods generates significant opportunity costs.

FIGURE 6.2   Growth in a PPC from Capital Goods Production

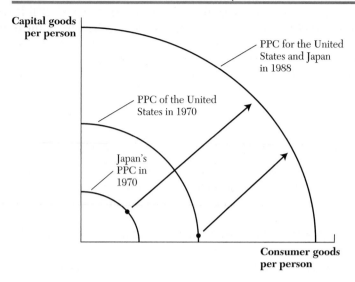

7. Beginning in 1988 and continuing through the early 2000s, the Japanese economy experienced a number of economic setbacks leading to much slower
growth rates for the country, with one result being a reduction in spending on
capital goods (less investment) and another being slower growth rates in
income. During the mid- to late 1990s, the U.S. economy grew at historically
high rates with firms expanding capital goods purchases and incomes also
increasing rapidly.

Using the outermost PPC in Figure 6.2, how can we show the changes in
the spending on capital goods and consumer goods in the United States and
Japan since 1990? What would the new PPCs for the United States and Japan
that result from the changes in capital goods purchases look like? Explain.

MILITARY VERSUS CIVILIAN PRIORITIES

A controversial example of the problem of scarcity in recent years has been
the debate about national priorities. Perhaps the sharpest focus of this debate
has been on military spending versus spending on civilian priorities.
Proponents of military spending want more resources for producing military
goods. They argue that more is needed because of the potential military capabilities of the nation's enemies and because they believe military power is the
best way to assure national security, including protection from terrorist
threats. Critics argue that too many resources are devoted to defense, that
military spending deprives the nation of the use of resources for domestic purposes (e.g., education and health care), and that diplomacy is a better way to
solve international disputes.

The arguments on both sides have become more sophisticated and complex over the years, but at the heart of the matter is an economic choice about how best to use scarce resources. This public issue, though, is not simply an economic question. It is also concerned with philosophy (what is the best way to resolve conflicts? what is social justice? what is security?) and with international and domestic politics.

8. What is national security? What determines whether a nation is secure?

Since World War II, the United States has devoted a substantial portion of its resources every year to military spending. Before the 1940s, with the exception of U.S. involvement in World War I, only about 1 percent of the nation's annual production of goods and services (measured by gross domestic product, or GDP) was devoted to armed forces. In the massive Allied war effort from 1941 to 1945, however, military production dominated the economy. In the period since then, the annual military budget has fluctuated between about 3 and 9 percent of GDP. The 2009 U.S. military budget of $675.1 billion represented 22 percent of federal government spending and 4.5 percent of the nation's GDP. If military-related spending—such as foreign military aid, homeland security, the cost of the wars in Iraq and Afghanistan, and military retirement pay and veterans' benefits—is included, those numbers would more than double. Worldwide military spending in 2008 was $1.464 trillion (41.5 percent of which was U.S. spending, excluding expenditures on the wars in Iraq and Afghanistan). This amounted to about 2.4 percent of global GDP. As Figure 6.3 shows, the United States spends more than 7 times more than China, which has the next largest military budget, and over 27 times more than the states that the U.S. government identifies as security risks. Yet, as the events of September 11, 2001, demonstrated, our massive military budget has not kept us safe from terrorist attacks.

What does all this money buy? About 35 percent of the annual military budget pays for the personnel costs of past and present service people and civilian workers for the Pentagon. About 40 percent of it purchases military supplies, equipment, and weapons: uniforms, food, planes, petroleum, ammunition, nuclear warheads, and so forth. The remainder provides for the general support costs (e.g., construction and maintenance) of the entire military establishment.

The history of this post-1940 shift in the military policy of the United States is rooted in the two world wars, the Cold War, and subsequent "hot" wars and military interventions. For World Wars I and II, the United States mobilized private production and military forces for the war efforts. U.S. peacetime military forces, its standing army and navy, were relatively modest and concerned primarily with defending the borders of the United States. After World War II, however, the United States decided to maintain very large and worldwide military forces. The arguments were that these forces were necessary to *prevent* aggression and that in the post–World War II period the Soviet Union represented a threat to U.S. interests and world peace. The U.S.

FIGURE 6.3 Global Military Spending, 2008 (billions of $)

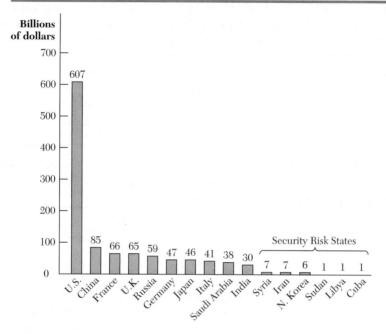

Source: Data from "Recent Trends in Military Expenditure," SIPRI—The Stockholm International Peace Research Institute, www.sipri.org.

arsenal consisted of the personnel in the Army, Navy, Air Force, and Marines and sophisticated conventional and nuclear weapons.

From time to time, a perception of an increased Soviet threat or an active military engagement led to increases in military spending. For example, the Korean (1950–1954) and Vietnam (1964–1975) wars led to increased budgets to finance U.S. participation in the conflicts. In the 1980s and 1990s, U.S. military forces were involved in invasions of Grenada and Panama and in the (Persian) Gulf War. In 2001, U.S.-led forces invaded Afghanistan as part of the war on terror, and in 2003 it invaded Iraq. Both led to an increase in military spending.

As noted above, we can use the concept of opportunity cost to analyze the allocation of resources to military goods and civilian goods. For example, during his first term in office, President Ronald Reagan persuaded Congress to increase spending on national defense by $100 billion to counter a perceived threat from the Soviet Union. This increased military spending was accompanied by decreases in spending on social programs (including food stamps, job training, welfare, and education). Thus the opportunity cost of increased military spending on the Cold War in the early 1980s was the cuts in social programs. Similarly, the 2008 U.S. military budget of $607 billion was more than $303 billion larger than in 2001. Instead of paying for this increase with higher taxes or spending cuts in other areas, President George W. Bush and Congress chose to borrow the money. Yet this too has opportunity costs: The direct costs are the interest payments the government (and taxpayers) must pay on the money borrowed and the stream of payments on these debts in the future, causing U.S. citizens to sacrifice future consumption to pay for current military expenditures and generating an intergenerational transfer of debt.

What are the arguments for and against military use of the scarce material and labor resources of the United States? President Bush and his supporters have argued that the United States must maintain overwhelming military superiority to prevent nuclear war and to be able to attack preemptively states that support terrorism. Moreover, they argue, larger military power will prevent political instability and will enable the United States to protect its vital interests in the Persian Gulf and other regions of the world. Their position is that the rest of the world must perceive that the United States is strong and willing to use its military force; in this way, the United States can contribute to international stability and world peace.

The opponents of this view argue that the United States currently has the capability to blow up the world and deter would-be rogue state attackers. They argue that the United States has more than adequate forces for simple deterrence, and our massive military did not save us from terrorist attacks. In terms of foreign policy, they argue that military power is not the most powerful weapon in promoting peace or U.S. interests in the rest of the world. Rather, diplomacy and economic development would be more useful in creating a more peaceful global environment and reducing anti-U.S. sentiments. Finally, they suggest that a country's national security is determined at least as much by internal health as by military might. Consequently, spending more money on the military and, as a result, denying resources for domestic priorities may actually undermine national security. While the United States is first in military spending, this comes with a substantial opportunity cost, since we are also first among developed countries in poverty and infant mortality.

In his first year in office, President Barack Obama proposed a 2010 defense budget of $663.7 billion, including the costs of the wars in Iraq and Afghanistan. This was a 1.5 percent increase from the 2009 defense budget. While smaller than the increases that President George W. Bush requested during his presidency, this budget indicated a continued emphasis on the maintenance of a large military establishment. However, President Obama also placed a renewed emphasis on diplomacy, indicating a position in between those described above.

9. We can also use the concept of opportunity costs to assess the allocation of resources *within* the military. For example, what is the opportunity cost of continuing to spend billions of dollars on weapons that were originally intended to counter the Soviet threat during the Cold War? Should we instead concentrate our military resources on homeland security and countering the terrorist threat?

10. What are the opportunity costs of increased military spending? What are the possible opportunity costs of not increasing military spending?

11. What is your opinion in this general debate concerning the use of our society's scarce resources? Focus your response on the economic ramifications of the various choices.

12. The Congressional Budget Office has estimated that the federal government could increase its spending on the nation's deteriorating infrastructure—highways, bridges, water and sewer systems, and so forth—by $10 billion a year. Would you support reducing the military budget to do so? Why or why not? Could the federal government spend more on both military and infrastructural programs? Explain.

APPLYING THE CONCEPT OF CHOICE TO PERSONAL DECISIONS

As is implicit in all of the foregoing discussion, decisions about using society's resources require that we compare the costs and the benefits of different uses of resources. Included in the costs are the opportunities forgone by not using resources for alternatives. This balancing of costs versus benefits also occurs in the economic decisions made by individuals, such as choices about work versus leisure, type of work, consumption, and so on.

Consumers weigh the benefits of buying a particular good (say, a home theater system) against its cost (that is, its price). They can also compare the benefits of purchasing a home theater system against the opportunity costs of not buying other goods (things they could have bought for the same price as the home theater system, such as a new flat screen computer and printer). On the basis of such judgments, consumers decide what goods to purchase in markets. (Furthermore, producers take consumers' decisions into account, and resources are allocated through markets to the production of particular goods and services.)

An example of a personal choice about resources is deciding whether to go to college. In making such a decision, an individual must weigh the benefits of going to college against the costs and opportunity costs of doing so. College costs money—for room and board, tuition, travel, books, and so on—and that money cannot be used for anything else. If you are in college, most of you are not working, getting experience, or earning income from a full-time job. On the other hand, a college education will develop your abilities (your human capital), can enrich your later life, and may qualify you for various types of employment. Your years of college also are a privileged period of time and space for growing and maturing in your experiences (curricular and extracurricular) and developing a philosophy of life.

A college education usually prepares people for white-collar, professional, higher-paying jobs. People with college educations, on the average, earn more than nongraduates. The earnings gap between college and high-school graduates is substantial. In 2006, college graduates earned on the average about 83 percent more in annual income. In recent years, college graduates have earned about $1 million more than high-school graduates over their lifetimes. Typically, the unemployment rate of college graduates is less than half that of high-school graduates. Such factors can influence an individual's choice about going to college.

13. What are the benefits of going to college?

14. What are the costs (and opportunity costs) of going to college?

15. Did you make the right decision about going to college? Why or why not?

Conclusion

Scarcity requires choices in both public and private matters. This fundamental economic fact requires societies and individuals to develop institutions and procedures for making hard decisions. Individuals rarely have enough income to buy everything they might want. Governments do not have enough tax money to do everything that their constituents would like them to do. In addition, decisions may result in benefits to someone or some group, while others suffer losses. Decision makers must weigh these costs and benefits in reaching decisions that maximize the use of scarce resources.

One of the most important institutions for facilitating such decisions in a private economy is the market. Markets determine prices for goods and resources. With this information, economic agents can compare alternative courses of action. Producers can decide what to produce and what resources to use. Consumers can decide what goods to purchase. In the next chapter, we will examine the economic theory of markets—how they operate and how prices are determined.

Review Questions

1. From your own experiences, do you think scarcity is really a problem for the United States? Is scarcity a problem in Ethiopia?

2. What is the difference between wants and needs?

3. Are wants and needs really unlimited? If they are, why?

4. How does the concept of opportunity cost help societies and individuals to make choices?

5. Why do economic choices have to be made?

6. Describe examples from your own life when the concepts of scarcity and opportunity cost have influenced your decisions.

7. Why don't the advances of science, technology, and exploration eliminate the problem of scarcity?

8. At the beginning of World War II, why could the United States increase its military output without sacrificing the production of civilian goods and services? Answer using a production possibilities curve.

9. The following table shows production possibilities for Brazil for consumption goods and capital goods:

Consumption Goods	Capital Goods
0	200
50	175
100	145
150	105
200	55
250	0

Graph the production possibilities curve. What are the opportunity costs of increasing the production of consumption goods by successive units of 50? Why might a country want to increase its production of capital goods?

10. Use the graph below, containing a PPC for the small, isolated country of Bucknellica, to answer the following questions.
   a. What is the opportunity cost of moving from point *B* to point *C*?
   b. What is the opportunity cost of moving from point *C* to point *B*?
   c. What factors could cause the Bucknellican economy to be able to achieve point *F*?
   d. What are some factors that might cause the Bucknellican economy to operate at point *E*?
   e. Compute the opportunity cost of one unit of computers for each region of the PPC (*A–B, B–C* and *C–D*). (Hint: In the region from *A–B*, 4 units of computers are equal in terms of resource use to 10 units of beer, so 1 unit of computers is equal to 10/4 or 2.5 units of beer.) Why does the opportunity cost of a unit of computers change as we move from *A* to *D*? Explain.
   f. In terms of economic growth, is there a reason to prefer point *D* over point *A*? Explain.

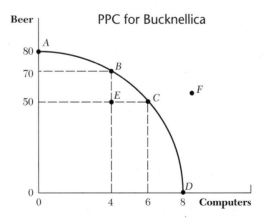

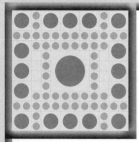

CHAPTER SEVEN

The Theory of Markets

◈ Introduction

Markets guide decisions about resource allocation—that is, how society decides to use its scarce resources. How exactly do markets accomplish this? This chapter will develop the economic analysis of markets to provide some insight into the relationship between markets and resource allocation.

As we saw in Part 1, markets emerged as one of the most fundamental institutions of capitalism. **Markets** are the institutions through which buyers and sellers exchange goods and services. They replaced tradition and feudal authority as the principal organizers of economic activity. Markets exist in capitalism for all consumer goods and productive resources.

Usually, goods and services are exchanged for money. All goods and services, then, must have prices that reflect their values and that govern their exchange. These prices end up guiding production and resource allocation. Producers and consumers use prices as basic information in deciding which resources to use and which products to purchase. Consequently, to see how markets allocate scarce resources, it is essential to understand how markets determine prices.

THE BIG PICTURE

Supply and Demand

The next few chapters introduce more complex economic models that focus on markets and how they work. The Big Picture segments provide an intuitive overview of the models that follow. In this chapter, we develop a model of supply and demand which illustrates how markets work based on the two major groups that participate in any market exchange of a good or service: those who supply the item and those who demand (or purchase) it. Although the graphs depicting supply and demand relationships may seem complex, examining the logic behind the graphs and the models can help in understanding how markets work, and specifically, how prices and quantities in markets respond to the forces of supply and demand.

As an example, consider the market for corn between 2005 and 2006. In September of 2005, corn sold in the U.S. market for $1.72 per bushel (P = $1.72). But higher oil prices and continued instability in the Middle East in the early 2000s had led to to the use of more corn-based ethanol as a fuel substitute for gasoline. In late 2005 new ethanol plants began to come on line. Since these plants used corn to produce ethanol, they purchased more corn. Because of these increased purchases, the demand for corn increased dramatically. This caused the new demand (D) for corn (Figure 7.BP.1) to outstrip supply (S), creating a shortage of corn in the corn market.

FIGURE 7.BP.1 The Corn Market Responds to an Increase in Demand

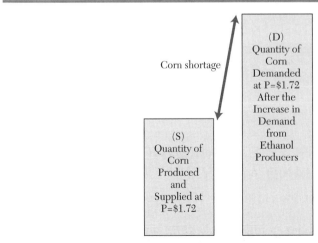

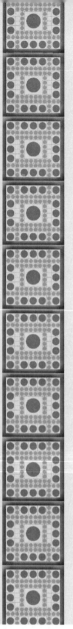

Corn farmers responded predictably to this situation. They reasoned that in the corn market, when more people want your corn (at the current price) than you can possibly supply, then you can increase revenues if you (a) charge a higher price and (b) produce as much of this "hot" commodity as you can in the given time frame. As a result of this reasoning, (a) corn prices rose and (b) corn production (the quantity supplied) increased. As corn prices rose, some people who wished to purchase corn at the old price of $1.72, scaled back on that desire. The market for corn finally stabilized in November 2006 at a price of $2.76 per bushel. At this price, a larger quantity of corn was produced and sold and the demand for corn (D1) equaled the supply of corn (S1) at this price (see Figure 7.BP.2).

In markets where supply exceeds demand (a surplus), the opposite series of events occurs: The excess supply causes producers to (a) reduce prices and (b) lower the quantity produced in that time frame. The market stabilizes at a lower price with smaller quantities produced and sold. Thus, prices and quantities in markets respond to changes in demand as well as to changes in supply. Below, we develop a model of supply and demand to help us understand the intricacies of these changes in markets.

FIGURE 7.BP.2   The Corn Market Responds to an Increase in Demand

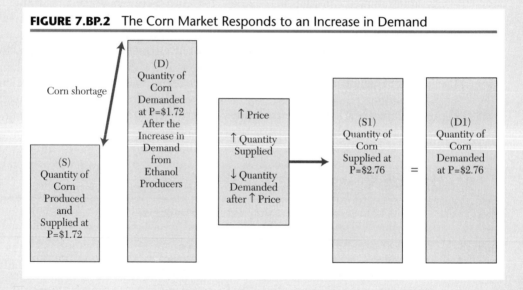

MARKETS AND PRICE DETERMINATION: SUPPLY-AND-DEMAND ANALYSIS

To highlight the economic analysis of markets, we will use as an example the market for college education in the United States. In Chapter 6, we referred to the decision about going to college as an example of a personal choice about the use of scarce resources. How much does it cost? What else could one do with the money? Why should (or shouldn't) one go to college? What

Examining snowboards in a sporting equipment store—a market in action. Markets exist whenever and wherever commodities are exchanged by buyers and sellers.

(© David Young-Wolff/PhotoEdit)

does one sacrifice by going to college for four years? Does it make more sense to enter the labor force right after high school? What are the benefits of a college education?

Obviously, one crucial element in making such an important decision is the dollar cost of going to college. In the following analysis, we will isolate the factors that determine the price of a college education. The analysis will help us to gain some insights into and understanding of how this market operates—how its price is determined and what implications there are for resource allocation. We will develop a method of analysis, the *theory of supply and demand*, that should assist us in understanding the general functioning of markets in a capitalist economy.

1. During the 1970s, the cost of a year at college for tuition, room and board, and fees almost doubled. However, the rise in costs was slightly less than the overall rate of inflation for the same period. In the 1980s, the costs for a year of college more than doubled, increasing much faster than the rate of inflation. During the 1990s, the costs for college nearly doubled again, while prices in general only increased by about 34 percent. And, from 2000–2008, costs for college increased about 26 percent more than prices in general. Why do you think the price of a college education has been continually increasing? What do you think accounts for the fact that since 1980 college costs have increased much more than the prices of most other goods and services? What can be done about this problem? Why is it a "problem"?

To conduct our supply-and-demand analysis, as in all economic theory, we will have to make some assumptions to simplify our model of the market. Despite these simplifying assumptions, our theory will provide us with some tools for understanding the functioning of real markets in the economy. It should also help us understand why market prices change over time. And it might help us develop some possible solutions to economic problems.

We will begin with a fundamental assumption of microeconomics: that economic agents are rational, calculating, fully informed, and motivated by self-interest. We assume that consumers are rational with respect to their purchases and that they try to maximize their own welfare through consumption, given their available spending power (that, through calculations and trial and error, consumers seek to maximize their satisfaction). Generally, we assume that producers calculate costs and revenues and try to maximize their profits from production.

To analyze the market for a college education, we need some additional assumptions and qualifications. First, we will assume that there is, in some sense, a homogeneous product. In other words, we will concentrate on *a* college education as a good that is exchanged in a market of buyers and sellers, assuming away any differences among particular colleges or between private and public universities. Obviously, these differences do exist and account for price differences, but we want to simplify and concentrate on *one* price for a college education. Once we have developed a model of supply and demand, we should be able to use it to account for cost differences at different institutions. We will also assume away the admissions problem (the product is not necessarily available to any buyer who might wish to purchase it), the financial aid dimension (not everyone pays the same price), and the graduation problem (actually getting the product—the diploma—in hand is not merely a matter of paying the costs to the cashier). Finally, although the producer of this product is generally not a profit-making institution, colleges and universities must take their costs and revenues into account, utilize scarce resources efficiently, and charge prices that reflect their costs (minus contributions from alumni, corporations, governments, and other benefactors).

Higher education is a large market in the United States. By the year 2007, this "industry" spent more than $373 billion annually. More than 15 million students are enrolled as undergraduates in more than 2,500 four-year institutions and about 1,700 two-year schools. About 57 percent of the students are women, and about 34 percent are minorities.

U.S. higher education also has a very large comparative advantage in the global economy. The U.S. higher education system is the best in the world, and it attracts students from all areas of the globe. More than 600,000 international students are enrolled in U.S. institutions (about 240,000 as undergraduates), while 242,000 U.S. students study abroad. Of the international students in the United States, 63 percent come from Asia, 14 percent from Europe, 11 percent from Latin America, and 6 percent from Africa.

To see how the market price for a college education is determined, we will begin by examining each side of this market in isolation from the other. For the buyer's side of the market, we will focus on *demand*; for the seller's side of the market, we will focus on *supply*. Then we will put supply and demand together.

Demand

The buyer's side of the market involves the demand for the product. **Demand** is the amount of a particular good or service buyers want, given its price. More specifically, it represents the amounts of a particular good or service buyers are willing and able to purchase at various possible prices.

What determines the demand for any product? Many factors influence the demand for a college education. The essential factor behind the demand for any product obviously is that it is useful to the buyer; it satisfies some want or desire or need. Beyond this, we can list some other influences on the demand for a product: tastes and preferences, income, prices of related goods, number of demanders, and expectations of future prices, among other factors.

Tastes and Preferences.   Consumers' tastes and preferences guide their demand for different goods. Tastes and preferences are influenced by social, political, and cultural forces, as well as by the physical, psychological, and mental requirements of daily survival in the world. Over time, in any given society, tastes and preferences will change and will, in turn, influence changing patterns of consumer demand for different goods and services. Tastes and preferences also differ among different countries.

Throughout the modern history of the United States, a college education has been a valued product. Presumably, it helps prepare people for coping with the world, broadens people's horizons and perspectives, prepares people for professional positions in society, and paves the way for further education. It also helps people gain entry to certain sectors of the labor force.

In recent years, the demand for a college education has been continually increasing (in 1960, there were 6 million students in higher education, less than half as many as today). The primary reason for the increase is that people perceive a college degree to be necessary for obtaining specific types of employment. Indeed, the realities of the labor market suggest that a college education is extremely valuable in this regard. Economists have estimated that the annual rate of return on a college education is about 12 percent (significantly in excess of the return on most financial investments). Consumers' tastes and preferences thus influence the demand for a college education. Throughout the 1960s, the percentage of high school graduates who went on to college steadily increased. In the 1970s, the percentage leveled off, but since 1980 it has increased steadily. In 2006, 66 percent of high school graduates enrolled in college (compared with only 49 percent in 1980 and 45 percent in 1960).

2. Why do you suppose that tastes and preferences changed to cause a leveling off in the percentage of high school graduates who went to college? *Did* tastes and preferences change? Did they change again in the 1980s, 1990s, and 2000s? Why?

Income.   Demand depends not only on the desire to buy, but also on how much consumers have to spend. Spending power, in turn, depends largely on income. And who consumes what products depends on the distribution of income in the society.

Since we have assumed that consumers try to maximize their satisfaction and that they derive it from goods because the goods are useful, we conclude that with more money, consumers will purchase larger quantities of goods and services. During the 1960s, the United States experienced one of its longest periods of prosperity. The real income of the average family increased throughout this period. This increasing income certainly provided the resources for an increasing percentage of U.S. youth to attend college. In the 1970s, however, the increase in average real incomes began to slow down. This probably accounts in part for some of the leveling off in college attendance in the 1970s. When incomes increased in the late 1990s, the demand for college educations also went up. In the recessions of 2001 and 2008-2009, demand declined somewhat.

Prices of Related Goods. The demand for a college education may be sensitive to (and influenced by) the prices of related products. Consumers are very sensitive to the prices of goods they consider to be *substitutes*—goods that satisfy the same need. For example, some substitutes for Coke are Pepsi, other soft drinks, fruit juices, and water; substitutes for plane transportation include train and automobile transportation to the same destination. In the case of the demand for a college education, if some nonprofessional training schools lowered their prices, the demand for college educations might fall, as some people substituted that educational experience for college.

Other goods may be *complementary*. Such goods go together or are consumed together. Examples of complements include computers and computer software, stereo components and CDs, and movies and popcorn. For would-be lawyers, college and law school are complements. An increase in the price of law school might dissuade some of these people from going to college.

Number of Demanders. The total demand for a product is affected by the number of people who desire to consume it. During the 1960s and 1970s, the number of college-age people in the United States was steadily expanding. In the 1960s, with an increasing percentage of youths attending college, the total number of "demanders" in the market increased dramatically. Recently, the increase in the numbers has been less dramatic, although nontraditional students are now increasing their attendance in college.

The number of eighteen-year-olds in the population actually declined by about 25 percent between 1979 and 1994. This had serious implications for the market for a college education in the United States. A number of colleges and universities developed vigorous efforts to recruit nontraditional populations and international students to make up for this reduction in the number of traditional demanders. Some private colleges began to accept part-time students. Many of these factors have had an effect: Students older than twenty-five now make up more than one-third of the 17 million undergraduates enrolled in higher education, and about 40 percent of all students are part-time students. The number of eighteen-year-olds has been increasing slowly since 1995, which is having an impact on the composition of current higher-education enrollments.

Expectations of Future Prices.   If consumers expect the price of a product to change, this tends to affect their demand for that product. For example, if high school graduates expect that the price of attending college will continue to increase in the future, this may cause many of them to enroll right away rather than wait, or they may decide not to go at all.

Notice that, as in the first sentence of this section, economists frequently use the words *tend to*. Their conclusions are often tentative because they are usually based on assumptions and expectations of normal behavior on the part of most economic agents and variables the economists are examining. But not everyone acts the same way! In your own thinking, try to replicate this word usage; the conclusions of economists are not carved in stone and should not be accepted as gospel. Economic theory deals with assumptions and tendencies; if "this" happens, probably "that" will happen.

Miscellaneous Factors.   Other factors also may influence consumers' demands for products. One of these is government policies. In the 1960s the federal government and several state governments significantly increased their support of higher education in the United States. Increased interest in higher education's benefits to the country probably by itself influenced the demand for a college education. In addition, the government support made it easier for more high school graduates to attend college. By significantly expanding public universities and community colleges throughout the country, it also opened up the college experience to people who historically had not had access to higher education in the United States. On the other hand, federal and state budget restraints since 1980 reduced levels of assistance and increased students' reliance on loans and work to finance higher education. These factors make the pursuit of higher education more difficult for many people in the society.

3. What other factor(s) would influence the number of students enrolling in college? (Consider only the demand side of the market.)

Ceteris Paribus and the Demand Curve

If you answered the previous question, "the *price* of a college education," you are on your way to becoming an economist. Economists attempt to isolate the effect of price on the quantity demanded for a product. In analyzing the demand for a product, they acknowledge that all of the factors just described do influence demand. But sometimes simplification helps analysis. Therefore, economists concentrate on the relationship between price and the quantity demanded of a good. To do this, they assume that at one moment of time, all of the other factors are given; then only price will affect the quantity demanded. The other factors (the determinants of demand) are considered to be in a *ceteris paribus* category—a Latin phrase meaning "all other things being equal." *Demand is concerned with the relationship between price and quantity demanded, holding all other things constant.*

So let's make that rather large assumption and see what happens. What is the effect of price on the quantity demanded of a college education? At one moment in time, assuming (again) that there is some average type of college education, there is only one annual price for this product. For 2008–2009, the College Board estimated that the average cost for tuition, room and board, books, and required fees at four-year private universities was $34,132. For public schools, the average cost was $14,333. Since there were more students in public institutions, we will assume that $16,000 was about the average cost for the nation as a whole for a year of college.

We can hypothesize about what would happen to the quantity demanded if the price were higher or lower. In fact, we would expect that *if* the price were lower, people would consume more—the quantity demanded would increase—and that *if* the price were higher, people would consume less—the quantity demanded would decrease. This is true for almost all goods and services: If the price is lowered, the quantity demanded will increase, and if the price is increased, the quantity demanded will decrease. In other words, price and quantity demanded are inversely related. When the price changes, there is a *change in the quantity demanded*—in the opposite direction.

We can state this relationship mathematically as well. A demand equation, generally, would show that the quantity of college education demanded, Q_d, is a function of the price of a college education, P_c, given all of the *ceteris paribus* conditions:

$$Q_d = f(P_c), \textit{ceteris paribus}.$$

To work with numbers, we can construct a hypothetical **demand schedule** (Table 7.1) showing different possible prices and the quantities demanded at those prices at one moment in time. Let's hypothesize about the national market for college educations for a year (again assuming that there is some average education). If the price were $16,000 (about the national average cost in 2008), then about 15 million people would be enrolled in the nation's colleges and universities as students. If, however, the price went up to $18,000 per year, then the quantity demanded would fall to 13 million. Table 7.1 shows several other possibilities as well.

We can also graph the relationship between price and quantity demanded. We call this a **demand curve**. The vertical scale measures price, and the horizontal scale measures quantity demanded. Any point on the graph represents a certain price–quantity demanded combination. Let's take the information from the demand schedule in Table 7.1 and transfer it to the graph. At a price of

Table 7.1   Demand Schedule for College Education

P_c (Cost per Year, Tuition, Room and Board, and Fees)	Q_d (Number of Students, in Millions)
$22,000	9
20,000	11
18,000	13
16,000	15
14,000	17

FIGURE 7.1   Demand Curve

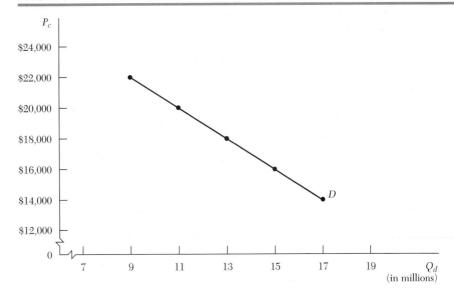

$14,000, the quantity demanded is 17 million; at $16,000, it is 15 million; and so on. Each combination corresponds to a point in Figure 7.1.

If we connect all the price–quantity demanded points, we get a demand curve for a college education during one year in the United States. It shows, hypothetically, all of the possible prices for a college education and the respective quantities demanded. It has a negative slope, reflecting the inverse relationship between price and quantity demanded. At lower prices, the quantity demanded is greater; at higher prices, the quantity demanded is lower. (For convenience, we normally draw demand curves as straight lines.)

The graphs of demand curves and supply curves are very important tools in economics. Make sure you understand how Figure 7.1 was constructed and what it shows.

The demand curve illustrates the buyers' side of the market. Let's turn our attention to the sellers' side of the market and consider it in isolation. After that, we will put the two sides of the market together in our model and get a market price for a college education.

Supply

Now we will focus on the sellers' side of the market. This side involves **supply**—the amounts of a good that will be offered for sale at different possible prices. What influences the supply of a product? What factors determine the number of students that colleges and universities can allow to enroll? Obviously, the price that these institutions can charge students has a lot to do with it. But for the moment, let's discuss other influences. These include resource prices, technology, prices of related goods, sellers' expectations, and the number of sellers in the market.

Resource Prices.   The costs of producing goods and services weigh heavily on the ability of sellers to supply the market. Thus, resource prices help determine the supply of any product offered for sale. In the supply of college educations, if the salaries of professors and other staff increase, the supply tends to shrink or college educations become more expensive. With the rapid inflation of the late 1960s, 1970s, and early 1980s and the moderate price increases from 1985 to 2008, the labor resource costs of running universities skyrocketed as employees demanded commensurate increases in their incomes. Even though dollar labor costs have increased at colleges, in real terms faculty incomes dropped 20 percent during the 1970s due to inflation. This prompted many faculties to form labor unions; there are more than 200 at four-year colleges and almost 400 at two-year colleges. Physical plant workers, cafeteria personnel, and office workers are often in unions on campuses around the country. Increasing costs for food, equipment, maintenance, paper, computers, construction, and energy also have increased total expenses significantly. As a result, the cost of supplying a college education has risen.

Technology.   The techniques of production influence supply. If computers and television sets were used to teach students, to grade their work, and to write letters of recommendation for them, colleges and universities would probably be able to greatly increase the numbers of students to whom they could supply a college education. Other ways of changing the techniques of production involve the use of large lecture classes, sometimes even with video lectures, or computer-assisted learning. (Of course, these might make the process of getting an education a bit less attractive. But that is a *demand* factor.) For the time being, however, the technology of education still relies heavily on human beings and, in some places, on relatively small classes.

Prices of Related Goods.   The ability of suppliers to supply any product to the market will also be affected by the prices of other products. If a college or a university could earn a better return on operating as a summer camp or research institute than offering summer sessions, then maybe it would decide to supply that product instead. Similarly, a college could display paintings and other artwork on its hallway walls, or it could sell wall space to corporate advertisers. Science faculty could use their labs to do research for companies instead of for teaching students.

Sellers' Expectations.   Sellers' expectations about the future will condition their supply of a product to the market. If colleges and universities expect lower enrollments in the future, they might be inclined to try to offer fewer students the chance to go to college now (that is, begin to decrease the supply of the product now). They might do this to prepare themselves for the foreseen lean days ahead. Given the likelihood of continuing high energy prices, some older dormitories might need to be retired, thus reducing the number of spaces available at some schools.

Numbers of Sellers in the Market.   If the number of sellers in the market decreased, it would tend to decrease the supply of the product. And if the

Today's college students expect computer labs, wired dorm rooms, and network facilities, all of which increase the cost of providing a college education.

(The Terry Wild Studio)

number of sellers increased, it would tend to increase the supply. In the late 1970s and early 1980s, a number of colleges and universities in the United States closed their doors. In 1981 there were 3,253 institutions of higher learning in the United States; in 1983 there were 3,111. Since then, the numbers have begun to increase, reaching nearly 4,300 in 2005.

4. Of the five factors described as influencing supply, which, in your opinion, is the most influential in determining the supply of a product? Why?

5. What sorts of factors influence sellers' expectations about their markets?

Ceteris Paribus and the Supply Curve

As we did for the demand curve, we will hold the nonprice influences on supply constant when we create a supply curve. They constitute the *ceteris paribus* conditions for supply. As a result, we will concentrate on the effect of price on the quantity supplied of a product. At one moment in time, we assume that all of the *ceteris paribus* factors (the determinants of supply) are given and consider in isolation the effect of price. *Supply is concerned with the relationship between price and quantity supplied, all other things constant.*

At one moment, there is only one price in existence. But we can hypothesize different possible prices and examine the effects on quantity supplied. If the price were higher, we would expect sellers to increase the quantity supplied. If sellers were offered a lower price, we would expect them to reduce the quantity supplied. For supply, price and quantity supplied are directly related. When the price changes, there is a *change in quantity supplied* in the same direction.

Table 7.2 Supply Schedule for College Education

P_c (Cost per Year)	Q_s (Number of Students, in Millions)
$22,000	21
20,000	19
18,000	17
16,000	15
14,000	13

We can state this as an equation as well. With all other determinants of supply held constant, the quantity supplied of a college education, Q_s, is a function of the price offered for a college education, P_c

$$Q_s = f(P_c), \text{ } \textit{ceteris paribus.}$$

As for demand, we can construct a hypothetical **supply schedule** (Table 7.2), showing different possible prices and the quantities that would be supplied at those prices. Table 7.2 hypothesizes about the total national supply of a college education. *If* the price were only $14,000, then colleges and universities would offer places for only 13 million students. *If* the price were $22,000, then colleges and universities would be willing to offer places to 21 million students. The table includes other possibilities as well.

Again, we can show the supply relationship graphically. We measure price on the vertical scale and quantity supplied on the horizontal scale. Each point in Figure 7.2 represents a certain price–quantity supplied combination. If we connect the five combinations from the schedule in Table 7.2, we get a supply curve for a college education. It shows, hypothetically, all the possible prices

FIGURE 7.2 Supply Curve

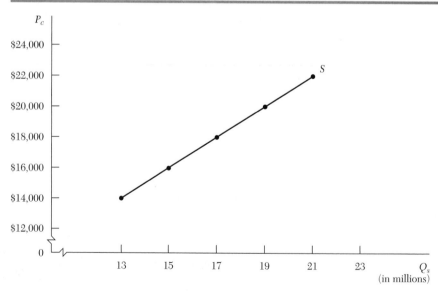

Table 7.3 The Supply Schedule Combined with the Demand Schedule

P_c ($)	Q_d (in Millions)	Q_s (in Millions)
22,000	9	21
20,000	11	19
18,000	13	17
16,000	15	15
14,000	17	13

for a college education and the respective quantities supplied. It has a positive slope, showing the direct relationship between price and quantity supplied; at higher prices, greater quantities will be supplied, and at lower prices, lower quantities will be supplied. (For convenience, we usually draw supply curves as straight lines.)

The supply curve illustrates the sellers' side of the market. The demand curve shows the buyers' side. Let's see what happens when we put them together to look at both sides of the market.

The Market and the Equilibrium Price

Putting the supply and demand schedules together, as listed in Table 7.3 and graphed in Figure 7.3, gives us a hypothetical picture of the market. When we put supply and demand together, the supply and the demand for the product determine a market price. It is an **equilibrium price**. Equilibrium connotes a situation in which the tendency is toward a certain state; once that state is achieved, it will be maintained, in the absence of outside disturbances.

FIGURE 7.3 Market and Equilibrium Price

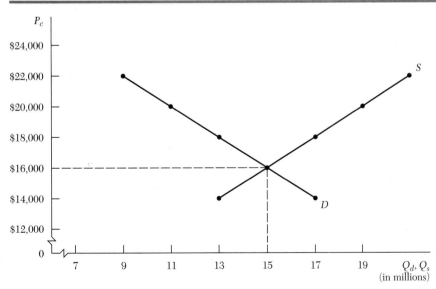

In our example, a price of $16,000 is the equilibrium price. At this price, the desires of buyers and sellers are consistent. Buyers want to buy 15 million places at colleges and universities, and sellers are willing to offer 15 million places. The quantity demanded equals the quantity supplied. Stated mathematically, at $P_c = \$16,000$, $Q_s = Q_d$. On the graph in Figure 7.3, the equilibrium price and quantity exchanged are the point at which the supply and demand curves intersect.

At any other price, Q_s does not equal Q_d, and the price will tend to change because buyers' and sellers' desires are not consistent. For example, at $P_c = \$20,000$, $Q_s = 19$ million and $Q_d = 11$ million. If the price were $20,000, there would be an oversupply, or a **surplus**. That is, 19 million places would be available, but only 11 million students would want to go to college at that price. Sellers would lower their prices to eliminate the excess supply. This has a twofold effect. It reduces the quantity supplied and increases the quantity demanded. We can see this by examining what happens at a price of $18,000. At this price, the quantities supplied and demanded have moved closer together, but Q_s still exceeds Q_d (17 million > 13 million). Suppliers will then lower prices again. This process will continue until $Q_s = Q_d$. This occurs at a price of $16,000. Thus, as shown in Figure 7.4, price changes will eliminate a surplus in the market until the equilibrium price is reached.

In the same way, if the price were below $16,000, there would be a tendency to move toward the $16,000 price. At a price of $14,000, $Q_d = 17$ million and $Q_s = 13$ million. In this case, the quantity demanded exceeds the quantity supplied (17 million > 13 million), and a **shortage** of places at college exists. Purchasers, facing a shortage, begin to bid up the price. Again, this has a twofold effect. It increases the quantity supplied but decreases the quantity demanded. This will

FIGURE 7.4 Surplus Eliminated by Price Decreases

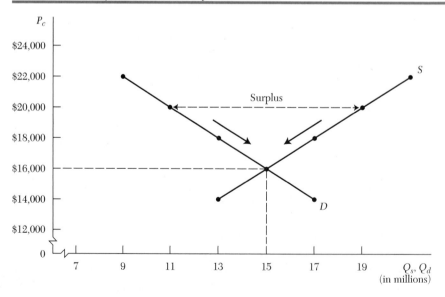

FIGURE 7.5 Shortage Eliminated by Price Increases

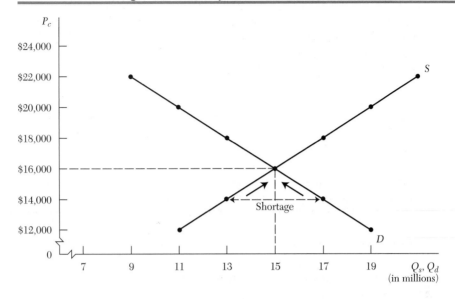

continue until the desires of buyers and sellers are consistent at one price where $Q_s = Q_d$ (see Figure 7.5).

Supply-and-demand analysis has shown us how markets determine equilibrium prices. There is a tendency to establish, or to move toward, the equilibrium price. And once buyers' and sellers' desires are consistent (when the quantity supplied equals the quantity demanded) and there are no outside disturbances, that price will tend to be maintained.

6. Why do sellers lower price when there is a surplus?

7. Why do buyers bid up the price when there is a shortage?

A Tinge of Reality: It's Not a *Ceteris Paribus* World

Our supply-and-demand model so far has included the rather strict and static assumptions involved in our *ceteris paribus* conditions on both sides of the market. However, one of the most useful aspects of this model is that we can use it to accommodate changes in the *ceteris paribus* conditions. In a changing world over time, these other determinants of supply and demand do change. A couple of examples will suffice to illustrate the richness of this approach and the ability of the supply-and-demand model to explain changes in market conditions and prices.

Changes in Demand. First, let's take a change in the demand conditions. We will call this a **change in demand**, and it will cause the whole demand curve to shift. Recall the various determinants of demand (or *ceteris paribus* conditions)—such as tastes and preferences, income, prices of related goods,

FIGURE 7.6 Change in Demand

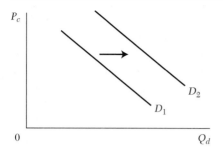

number of demanders, and expectations about prices—and consider the complexity of factors that are behind a demand curve. Any of the determinants could change, or all of them could change. They could move in the same direction (causing an increase or a decrease in demand), or they could influence demand in opposite directions.

Let's examine just one possibility. Assume that in today's economy, for whatever reasons, a college degree is perceived as being more attractive to students. This represents a change in tastes and preferences. What will it do to demand? What effect will it have on the market for a college education?

First of all, it will cause a shift in the demand curve. It causes an increase in demand; the demand curve will shift to the right. At every possible price, the quantity demanded will have increased, and we thus get a new demand curve. This is shown in Figure 7.6 as a shift in the demand curve from D_1 to D_2.

8. What other changes in the determinants of demand might cause an increase in demand, a shift of the curve to the right?

9. What would cause a shift back to the left, a decrease in demand? Give some examples.

What happens in the market? Here we must look at supply and demand together, as shown in Figure 7.7. With the new demand curve, D_2, we get a

FIGURE 7.7 Effect on Market of Change in Demand

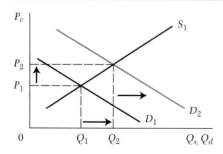

new equilibrium price, P_2, and a new equilibrium quantity exchanged, Q_2, where $Q_s = Q_d$ With an increase in demand, we get a new higher price in the market. Also, the amount exchanged by buyers and sellers has increased in our example (from Q_1 to Q_2). This analysis suggests that one place to look for an explanation of increasing prices in a market is in the dynamic changes in the determinants of demand. The market price of a college education tended to increase from the late 1980s to 2008. Because enrollment (the quantity) also increased, we can conclude that the demand for the product increased. A possible cause was a change in the public's tastes and preferences. A word of caution, however, is in order. Tastes and preferences were not the only determinants of demand that changed during this period of time. For example, the increased number of international students also contributed to the shift in demand. Furthermore, the determinants of supply also were changing. We can conclude, though, that the change in preferences was partly responsible for the increase in demand and the increase in price.

Changes in Supply. The supply-and-demand model can also reflect a **change in supply**. Here we allow the determinants of supply to change. Remember the determinants of supply (the *ceteris paribus* conditions)—resource prices, technology, prices of related goods, sellers' expectations, and the number of sellers. Any or all could change, in the same direction or in opposite directions.

Suppose that in 2010 the prices of the resources used in providing college educations increased. As a result, there would be a change in supply. Suppliers would tend to require higher prices for every different quantity supplied (or they would be willing to offer lower quantities supplied at every possible price). There would be a decrease in supply; the supply curve would shift to the left. The supply curve for a college education shifts from S_1 to S_2, as shown in Figure 7.8.

10. What other factors might cause the supply curve to shift to the left?

11. What factors might cause the supply curve to shift to the right?

FIGURE 7.8 Change in Supply

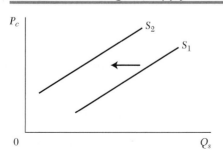

FIGURE 7.9 Effect on Market of Change of Supply

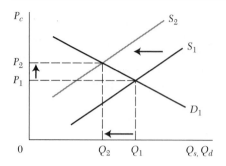

What will this do in the market? Assume that demand conditions are unaltered. Figure 7.9 puts supply and demand together. (We assume that D_1 remains unchanged.) With the new supply curve, S_2, we get a new equilibrium price, P_2, and a new equilibrium quantity exchanged, Q_2, where $Q_s = Q_d$. With this decrease in supply, we get a new higher market price and a lower quantity exchanged.

Again, this analysis may help us to explain price increases by examining what happens to the determinants of supply. If forces are creating decreases in supply for a particular product, that will help to explain the emergence of higher prices for it.

12. What happens if we combine our examples, an increase in demand and a decrease in supply? Show this result in your own graphical illustration.

A Word of Caution

One aspect of learning economics is identifying and defining economic concepts—and doing so precisely. This involves using words carefully. In some sense, it is like learning a foreign language. Some words that economists use have very specific meanings for particular concepts.

What happens on a demand curve if the price of the product changes? We get a *change in the quantity demanded*. If the price increases, the quantity demanded decreases. And if the price decreases, the quantity demanded increases. This represents a movement along a particular demand curve. What happens if one of the determinants of demand changes? We get a *change in demand*. If income increases, the whole demand curve shifts out to the right for most goods. Whenever there is a change in demand, the whole demand curve shifts.

For supply, a change in price causes a *change in the quantity supplied*, which is a movement along a supply curve. A change in one of the determinants of supply causes a *change in supply*, which causes the whole supply curve to shift.

A higher price causes a decrease in quantity demanded and an increase in quantity supplied. If the income of households decreases, the demand for most goods would decrease (there would be a change in demand). What would happen to the equilibrium price, then, if the supply curve stays the

FIGURE 7.10 Effects of a Decrease in Demand

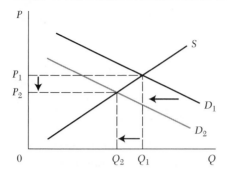

same? Right—price would decrease. And then what happens to quantity demanded and quantity supplied? Right—smaller quantities are demanded and supplied at the new equilibrium. Figure 7.10 shows this result graphically.

APPLYING SUPPLY AND DEMAND

Let's put these principles about supply and demand into practice by examining an application that has drawn coverage from the news media. We'll look at the interaction between supply and demand when gasoline prices rose in 2004.

Gasoline Prices

In April 2004, the Organization of Petroleum Exporting Countries (OPEC) moved to reduce their production of oil by 4 percent. In addition, OPEC sold more oil than usual to China (rapid economic growth in China increased its need for oil) and shipped less oil to the United States. Meanwhile, terrorist attacks in Iraq and Saudi Arabia interrupted oil supplies further. The result was a decrease in the supply of gasoline to the United States. Figure 7.11 shows

FIGURE 7.11 The U.S. Market for Gasoline

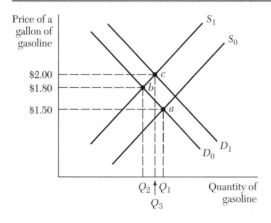

this change as the shift in the supply of oil from S_0 to S_1. As a result, the equilibrium price of gas rose from $1.50 per gallon to $1.80 per gallon, and the equilibrium quantity of gas fell from Q_1 to Q_2, moving the equilibrium from point *a* to point *b*.

While OPEC was reducing the supply of oil, the U.S. recovery strengthened and U.S. consumers continued to purchase larger cars, pickup trucks, and sport utility vehicles with low fuel efficiency and that used much greater quantities of gasoline. Thus, consumer demand for gasoline was increasing during this period. This is shown in Figure 7.11 as the shift in demand from D_0 to D_1. The increase in demand resulted in an additional increase in the equilibrium price from $1.80 to $2.00 per gallon and an increase in the equilibrium quantity of gas from Q_2 to Q_3. The equilibrium moves from point *b* to point *c*. The outcome was a dramatic increase in the average price of a gallon of gasoline from about $1.50 per gallon in 2003 to about $2.00 per gallon in 2004.

13. What has happened to the price of gasoline recently? How can you use supply and demand analysis to explain any price changes?

Price Controls. As gas prices rise, it is sometimes tempting for governments to impose **price controls** to keep prices low for consumers. Specifically, the government could have imposed a **price ceiling**, a legally set maximum price, on gasoline below the new equilibrium price of $2.00. However, as Figure 7.12 shows, lowering the price to $1.80 per gallon would reduce the quantity of gas supplied from Q_3 to Q_s, while also causing an increase in the quantity of gas demanded from Q_3 to Q_d, resulting in a shortage. This would mean that not everyone who wanted to buy gas at a price of $1.80 per gallon would be able to do so, and it would probably lead to long lines at gas stations (and even black markets) as people try to get scarce supplies of gasoline. This is, in fact, exactly what happened when price ceilings were imposed on gasoline and other goods

FIGURE 7.12 The Market for Gasoline with a Price Ceiling

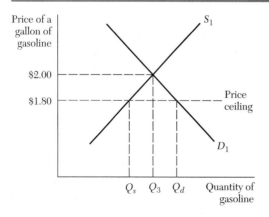

in the 1970s. Many consumers would benefit from lower-priced gasoline (those who could find it), but many others would not be able to purchase as much gasoline as they wanted.

14. Using supply-and-demand analysis, can you think of some other ways that the government could lower the price of gas for consumers without creating a shortage?

15. Burning gasoline contributes to smog and global warming. If our goal were to reduce the quantity of gasoline purchased (instead of keeping its price as low as possible) to reduce pollution, what policies might work?

ELASTICITY

Thus far, we have concentrated on the relationship between prices and quantities supplied and demanded. But if a price changes, *how much* does the quantity demanded change? If the price goes up, *how much* does the quantity supplied increase?

The sensitivity of the demand for (or supply of) a product to changes in its price is called **price elasticity**. This concept is concerned with the relationship between the quantity demanded or supplied and the price of a particular good or service.

Price Elasticity of Demand

All other things held constant, if the price of a college education goes up, the quantity demanded will go down. But how much will the quantity demanded be reduced in comparison with the price increase? The **price elasticity of demand** is a measurement of the sensitivity of changes in quantity demanded to changes in price. It measures the responsiveness of the amount demanded to price changes. (Note that we are using terminology associated with movements along a single demand curve. With all the determinants of demand fixed at one point in time, we focus on the impact of a price change on the quantity demanded.)

The following equation measures the price elasticity of demand:

$$E_d = \frac{\text{percentage change in quantity demanded}}{\text{percentage change in price}} = \frac{\Delta Q_d / Q_d}{\Delta P / P}$$

The percentage change in price is associated with a certain percentage change in the quantity demanded. In calculating elasticity, we ignore the direction of change of each variable and concentrate on the relative relationship between the percentage changes (that is, we take the absolute value of E_d).

If the percentage change in quantity demanded is larger than the percentage change in price, then $E_d > 1$, and we say that the demand for the good is *elastic* with respect to price. Demand is elastic when the quantity demanded is very responsive to changes in price. If the price of digital cameras is reduced by 20 percent and the quantity demanded increases by 30 percent, then $E_d = 1.5$.

In this case, the demand for the cameras is elastic, or relatively sensitive to price changes.

On the other hand, if the price of milk (or beer) increases by 10 percent but the quantity demanded decreases by only 5 percent, then elasticity is 0.5. In this case, we say that the demand for milk (or beer) is *inelastic*, since the percentage change in quantity demanded is less than the percentage change in price ($E_d < 1$). Demand is inelastic when quantity demanded is not very responsive to changes in price.

For example, let's assume a computer store reduced the price of a personal computer model and printer from $2,500 to $2,000. The number of units it sold in a six-month period increased from 100 to 160. We can record these amounts in a table

Price	Quantity Sold
$2,500	100
2,000	160

What is the elasticity of demand? The price decreased by $500, or 20 percent:

$$\frac{\Delta P}{P} = \frac{2,500 - 2,000}{2,500} = \frac{500}{2,500} = 20\%.$$

The quantity demanded increased by 60 units, or 60 percent:

$$\frac{\Delta Q_d}{Q_d} = \frac{160 - 100}{100} = \frac{60}{100} = 60\%.$$

We can use those percentages to find the price elasticity of demand:*

$$E_d = \frac{\text{percentage change in quantity demanded}}{\text{percentage change in price}}$$

$$= \frac{60}{20} = 3.$$

---

*Notice that there is another way we could have calculated the elasticity. We used the original price and quantity as the denominator in our calculations of the percentage changes in quantity and price. If we used the new price and quantity, we'd get the following results:

percentage change in price $= 500/2,000 = 25\%$
percentage change in quantity demanded $= 60/160 = 37.5\%$

$$\text{elasticity of demand} = \frac{37.5}{25} = 1.5$$

There is a way to resolve this difference in the calculated elasticity of demand by taking the average of the old and the new prices and quantities. This is called the midpoints formula:

$$E_d = \frac{\Delta Q/[(Q_1 + Q_2)/2]}{\Delta P/[P_1 + P_2/2]} = \frac{60/130}{500/2,250} = \frac{46.2\%}{22.2\%} = 2.08.$$

The important point, though, is that the elasticity of demand measures the *relative* change in quantity demanded due to the *relative* change in price, to see how sensitive quantity demanded is to price changes.

FIGURE 7.13 Elasticity Along a Demand Curve

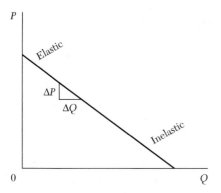

Consequently, the demand for computers is fairly sensitive to price changes; the relative change in quantity demanded is much larger than the relative change in the price.

Elasticity Graphically. On the upper portion of the typical linear demand curve shown in Figure 7.13, the price elasticity of demand is elastic. On the lower portion, it is inelastic. Elasticity changes along the demand curve.

The elasticity of a demand curve does not equal its slope. The slope of the demand curve is the change in the price over the change in the quantity demanded between any two points (the height over the base, the rise over the run, etc.). The slope equals $\Delta P/\Delta Q$. To highlight the difference, we can rearrange the formula for elasticity as follows:

$$\frac{\text{Percentage } \Delta \text{ in quantity demanded}}{\text{Percentage } \Delta \text{ in price}} = \frac{\Delta Q/Q}{\Delta P/P} = \frac{\Delta Q}{\Delta P} \times \frac{P}{Q}.$$

This obviously makes elasticity unequal to the slope of the demand curve.

On the left portion of the demand curve, any percentage change in quantity demanded will be relatively large (since quantity is at low levels), and the percentage change in price will be relatively small. Consequently, elasticity will be greater than 1. On the right portion, percentage changes in quantity will be relatively small, and percentage changes in price will be relatively large. Therefore, elasticity will be less than 1. Moving along the demand curve to the right will reduce elasticity or increase inelasticity.

The Determinants of Elasticity. What determines elasticity, or how sensitive to changes in its price is the demand for a product? Can you think of goods you demand regardless of price? Are there other goods to whose prices you are very sensitive?

Generally, whenever there are substitutes for a good, your demand tends to be elastic. The more substitutes, the more elastic the demand. For example, if the price of green beans increases, most people will substitute other green vegetables. When the price goes up, people will reduce their consumption of green beans by relatively more—that is, we expect the price elasticity of demand for green beans to be greater than 1. On the other hand, if you heat your house with only oil and oil prices increase, you may decrease your use of oil, but not by much. The relative increase in price will outweigh the relative decline in the amount demanded; demand is relatively inelastic because there are no convenient substitutes for oil to run your furnace.

Another example that indicates the importance of substitutes in determining elasticity is the difference between the price elasticity of the demand for a product such as gasoline versus the price elasticity of the demand for one service station's brand of gas (e.g., Exxon). Gas stations with many competitors face price elasticities as high as 6. If one station raises its prices even a few pennies per gallon, consumers will take their business down the street to a gas station where prices are cheaper. (With a price elasticity of 6, a 10 percent increase in price would result in a 60 percent decrease in the quantity demanded!) But consumers as a group use almost the same amount of gas every week, no matter what the price is; we need gasoline for our cars, and there are no close substitutes. In fact, the price elasticity of demand for all brands of gasoline is about 0.2, which is very inelastic.

Goods that are necessities tend to have inelastic demands. For example, in a household with young children, the demand for milk is likely to be relatively inelastic. In fact, the price elasticity of the demand for food is between 0.1 and 0.5. As a student, you have a relatively inelastic demand for books. For these items, the demand is not very sensitive to price changes. The demand for luxuries, however, tends to be elastic. You, and others, are likely to be very sensitive to price changes for CDs, stereos, cameras, expensive clothes, automobiles, and so forth.

For the most part, the relative importance of an item in a household's budget also influences elasticity. High-priced items tend to have elastic demands, and the demand for low-priced items is often inelastic because consumers are less concerned about the price.

Finally, time influences elasticity. The more time consumers have to adjust to price changes for goods and services, the more elastic their demand for certain products is likely to be. For example, people in the United States adjusted their usage of energy as a result of higher oil and gas prices in the 1970s. Cars became smaller and more fuel efficient, people burned more wood as a source of heat, bicycles were used more for transportation, and solar energy was developed. However, with the decline in energy prices in the 1980s and 1990s, these trends reversed, and Americans began driving bigger and bigger cars and using more gas and oil. The steady increase in gas prices from 2002 to 2008 did not cause a significant, immediate decrease in demand. Since the short-run price elasticity of the demand for gasoline is only 0.2, a 20 percent increase in price will decrease the quantity demanded by only 4 percent. But the long-run price elasticity of the demand for gasoline is about 0.8, so we can expect a much larger decrease in the demand for gasoline in the future if gas prices continue to stay high. (With a price elasticity of 0.8, a 20 percent increase in price would result in a 16 percent decrease in the quantity demanded.) If U.S. gas prices rise above a certain point and remain high, the next time consumers need to replace a car, they will be much more likely to choose a fuel-efficient one or to consider other modes of transportation such as bicycles, buses, or trains. (We should note that despite the recent increases, U.S. energy prices are among the lowest in the world. In Europe, a gallon of gas costs about $6.00.)

16. Can you list three ways Europeans have adapted to higher gas prices?

Elasticity and Revenue. Elasticity also holds implications for a firm's revenues or a household's expenditures when the price of a product changes. If the demand for a firm's product is elastic and its price decreases, then the percentage change in quantity demanded in the market will be relatively larger than the price change. The firm's revenues would then increase. (The firm's revenues equal the quantity sold times the price of the product. If the relative increase in quantity exceeds the relative decline in price, then revenues go up.) If a household's demand for a product is inelastic and its price increases, it will decrease its purchases by a relatively lower amount. Consequently, its total expenditures—quantity times price—will increase. Table 7.4 summarizes the possibilities (TR stands for total revenue and equals $P \times Q$). When demand is elastic, the quantity change is relatively larger. When the demand is inelastic, the price change is relatively larger.

It is extremely important for firms to consider price elasticity when deciding what price to charge for their product and how much of that product they should produce. In 2001, the U.S. government released a study stating that the use of growth-promoting drugs on hogs actually resulted in lower hog farm revenues. The increased production caused the price of hogs to fall from $34.80 to $34.02. This resulted in a decrease in total revenue for hog farmers, since the percentage decrease in the price of hogs exceeded the percentage increase in the quantity of hogs purchased. Hog producers face an inelastic demand curve; in fact, the price elasticity of the demand for hogs is estimated to be about 0.4.

Table 7.4   Elasticity (E_d) and Total Revenue (TR)

Inelastic Demand ($E_d < 1$)	Elastic Demand ($E_d > 1$)
% Δ in Q_d < % Δ in P	% Δ in Q_d > % Δ in P
↑ P results in a smaller ↓ Q_d, TR ↑	↑ P results in a larger ↓ Q_d, TR ↓
↓ P results in a smaller ↑ Q_d, TR ↓	↓ P results in a larger ↑ Q_d, TR ↑

Note: Elasticity = E_d = (% Δ in Q_d)/(% Δ in P); Total Revenue = TR = $P \times Q$.

Price Elasticity of Supply

We can also identify the **price elasticity of supply**, or the sensitivity of amounts supplied to price changes:

$$E_s = \frac{\text{Percentage change in quantity supplied}}{\text{Percentage change in price}}.$$

If the elasticity of supply, E_s, is less than 1, the supply of the product is inelastic—that is, the amount supplied is not very sensitive to price changes. If the elasticity of supply, E_s, is greater than 1, then the amount of the good supplied is sensitive to price changes.

Several factors can influence the elasticity of supply. If storage is not possible, then supply will be insensitive to price changes. If you have ten bunches of bananas in your store and the price goes up by 50 percent tomorrow, there is not much you can do to increase the amount of bananas that you have for sale. If you can put an item in inventory, the amount that you have available for sale will be sensitive to price. If the price of pencils goes down, for example, you can store them and reduce the amount you have out for sale. If the price goes up, you can increase the amount you have for sale by taking the pencils out of your inventory. The length of the production process matters as well. The longer the production period, the lower the elasticity of supply. Occasionally a new toy or game is popular (e.g., at holiday season) in the United States. In the short run, the supply is inelastic; consequently, there is a shortage. What happens to price? It rises. With higher prices, in the longer run, the supply becomes more elastic. If it is possible to substitute resources in production, then supply is likely to be more elastic. For example, in the fast-food industry, there are numerous sources of unskilled labor and many sources of hamburger meat, buns, and so forth. Consequently, the supply of fast food is likely to be relatively sensitive to price changes.

Income Elasticity

We can also identify the **income elasticity of demand**. This measures how much the demand for a product changes when income changes. It is expressed by the following equation:

$$E_y = \frac{\text{Percentage change in quantity demanded}}{\text{Percentage change in income}}.$$

When income changes, we know that one of the determinants of demand has changed. Consequently, the entire demand curve will shift. For most goods, if income increases, the demand curve shifts out to the right. The income elasticity of demand, in essence, measures the relative change in the demand curve.

For most goods, the income elasticity is positive, meaning that increases in income result in greater demand for the good. Only *inferior goods* have a negative income elasticity of demand. For example, you might decrease your consumption of cheap meats if your income increased. For some goods, we increase our consumption by only a little bit when our incomes go up. Food products in general fit into this category. The relative increase in the quantity demanded of food will be less than the relative increase in income. For goods like these, the income elasticity of demand is relatively low. For other goods, we increase our consumption a great deal when our incomes go up. The relative change in quantity demanded is larger than the percentage change in income, and the income elasticity of demand is greater than 1. The demand for "luxuries" is elastic with respect to income.

17. Do you think that the price elasticity of demand for a college education is greater or less than 1? Why?

18. For what kinds of goods and services will quantity demanded be relatively insensitive to price changes (i.e., inelastic)? Give some examples.

19. For what kinds of goods and services is the quantity demanded relatively sensitive to price changes (i.e., elastic)? Give some examples.

20. List some goods for which your income elasticity of demand is greater than 1.

Conclusion

In this chapter we have developed a theoretical model of markets to explain how markets determine prices. We have focused on demand and supply, how they are determined, and how they interact in markets. In the next chapter, we will explore the theoretical implications that this has for resource allocation in competitive markets.

Review Questions

1. Use supply-and-demand analysis to explain why your school's tuition and overall charges have been continually increasing the past few years. Address demand factors first and supply factors second, and then put them together.

2. Some colleges have started to announce efforts to cut prices or to limit their price increases. Why would they do this?

3. How are tastes and preferences for goods and services determined in the United States?

4. Markets and prices for different products are interrelated. Why? Can you give some examples?

5. Examine recent issues of newspapers to see how prices of certain products are changing. Use supply-and-demand analysis to explain these changes.

6. How do prices influence resource allocation? Use examples.

7. Assume that the price elasticity of demand for gasoline in the United States is 0.3. If the president wanted to reduce gasoline consumption in the United States by 30 percent, by how much would prices have to be increased?

8. Draw a graph that shows how each of the following events will affect the demand, supply, equilibrium price, and equilibrium quantity of compact discs. Note: Be sure to identify whether or not the demand and supply curves *shift*, or whether you are moving along the demand and supply curves. Assume that the average price of a CD is $20 and that 100,000 CDs are sold each week.

a. The price of DVD audio discs decreases (DVD audio discs can be played in DVD players so the music can be heard in five-speaker surround sound).

b. The Supreme Court declares sharing music files over the Internet legal and the government is no longer able to prevent music file sharing.

c. The technology used to manufacture CDs improves, decreasing the cost of producing a CD.

d. An economic boom causes wages for workers to increase in all sectors of the economy, so CD consumers have more money but CD producers have to pay more to workers.

e. The use of iTunes becomes widespread.

CHAPTER EIGHT

Perfect Competition and Efficiency

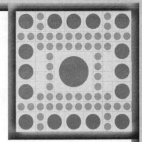

◆ Introduction

To build a model of a perfectly competitive firm, it is necessary to make some assumptions. Microeconomics assumes that in demanding goods, consumers attempt to maximize their satisfaction. Furthermore, we assume that in supplying goods, firms are concerned with profit maximization. In Chapter 7 we saw how supply and demand for a good determine a market price, given certain conditions (i.e., a supply curve and a demand curve). If either the demand curve or the supply curve shifts, or if both shift, we tend to get a new equilibrium price and quantity in that market.

This chapter uses supply-and-demand analysis and develops some new tools to examine the decisions that individual firms make about what rate of output to produce—taking into account information from the market for their product and from the markets for the resources they use. We will develop a model of the firm in a competitive market. This model will demonstrate how profit maximization and competition theoretically produce Adam Smith's "invisible hand." That is, we will discover how competitive markets operate to allocate resources efficiently (to meet the most important demands of the society with the minimum amount of resources).

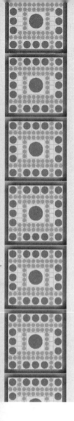

THE BIG PICTURE

Perfectly Competitive Markets

The goal of this chapter is to present the theory of perfectly competitive markets, and to develop a microeconomic model of a perfectly competitive firm. Before we delve into that theory, however, to understand the "big picture" we need to briefly explore how these markets tend to work in practice and why economists tend to prefer outcomes from competitive markets.

Perfectly competitive markets feature many firms producing identical products. This means that no one firm can charge a higher price than competing firms, so prices tend to stay lower than they would with less or no competition. In this environment, firms can make only a modest profit (what economists call a *normal* profit). Because it is difficult to raise prices in the face of so much competition, firms strive to minimize the costs of production. Thus, competitive markets tend to lead to lower prices, smaller levels of profits, and efficient resource allocation (resources allocated to their most productive, least-cost use).

Consumers therefore get the products they want at the lowest possible price. As we will see in Chapter 10, noncompetitive markets do not achieve these results.

PROFIT MAXIMIZATION AND THE COMPETITIVE FIRM

In this section we will examine a particular market, concentrating our attention on the firm (developing a theory of the firm). This is a theoretical market, so we will state some definitions and make some assumptions about the behavior of the buyers and sellers in the market. As an example we will use a local market for pizza.

The **consumer** is the economic unit that demands goods and/or services because they serve some purpose and give the consumer some satisfaction. Consumers in this example include all of the people in the local area who are interested in purchasing and consuming a pizza.

The **firm** is the economic unit that brings goods to the market. It takes raw materials and other resources and transforms them into final consumer goods. Its motivation, or goal, is to maximize its profits. In our example, the firm would be any company that produces and sells pizzas to the general public. This would include small and large restaurants, convenience stores, health food stores, grocery stores, cafeterias, and all other sellers of pizzas.

If we put the firms and the consumers (the sellers and buyers) together, we have a market for pizza. We will assume that this is a competitive market, that is, one characterized by **perfect competition**. We define a perfectly competitive market as one having the following characteristics:

❖ The product is homogeneous.
❖ There are a large number of buyers and sellers in the market.

❖ No *one* buyer or seller can influence the price of the product. (A seller can't raise his or her price, because buyers can go to a competitor and buy.)

❖ There is free entry into the market. (Anyone can be a buyer or seller. There are no constraints on entry.)

❖ There is no need for advertising (since every seller has the same product and charges the same price).

❖ Firms have all the information they need on resource prices, markets, and technology to make rational, profit-generating decisions.

In a perfectly competitive market, there is a market equilibrium price. Can you illustrate this market graphically?

1. Are any of these theoretical characteristics absent from the actual market for pizza in your community? Why?

Let's return to the firm. The firm's objective is to maximize its profits. Profits equal the revenues the firm earns by selling its products minus the costs it incurs to produce those products:

$$\text{profit} = \text{TR} - \text{TC},$$

where TR equals total revenue and TC equals total cost. **Total revenue** is equal to the quantity sold (Q) times the price of the product (P):

$$\text{TR} = P \times Q.$$

The firm obtains revenues by selling its product. The greater the number of pizzas the firm sells, the more money it receives. In producing pizza and bringing it to market, the firm also has certain costs—labor, raw materials, depreciation, rent, interest payments on loans, and the firm's *opportunity cost*. **Total cost** is the sum of all the costs of purchasing the necessary resources for production.

As in Chapter 6, we define the firm's *opportunity cost* as the amount of money the firm could earn by using its facilities and its resources to produce and sell something else profitably (such as hamburgers, subs, ice cream, etc.). The opportunity cost would be the "next best use" of its resources. The firm has some expectation of a "normal profit" from doing business, and therefore must earn at least its opportunity cost (a normal profit) to stay in the business of making pizza. Anything above that is **economic profit**.

If the firm's revenues are just sufficient to cover all of its costs for raw materials, labor, and so on, *and* its opportunity cost, then the firm will earn no economic profits. For example, if the firm's revenues were $100,000, its opportunity cost $20,000, and the costs of all other resources $80,000, it would earn zero economic profits. Its opportunity costs would be covered by the $20,000 of "normal" profits. If revenues exceed costs, then there will be economic profits;

that is, the firm will earn a return over and above its opportunity cost. This gives us the following possibilities for the firm:

TR > TC	Economic profit	The firm's revenues exceed all costs, including opportunity costs.
TR = TC	Normal profit	The firm's revenues equal its costs, including opportunity costs.
TR < TC	Economic loss	The firm's revenues do not cover all of its costs, including opportunity costs.

Profit, revenue, and costs for the firm will vary with the amount of pizza produced and sold. For a firm in a competitive market, the price is determined by the market and will not vary with the number of units that the firm sells (see the third characteristic of a competitive market in the list given earlier). Costs, on the other hand, do vary with output, as we will see in the next section.

2. A small firm's "normal profit" is $75,000 for one year. All of its other costs are $200,000. The firm's revenue in one year is $300,000. What are its economic profits?

SPECIALIZATION, DIMINISHING RETURNS, AND SHORT-RUN COSTS

To study a typical firm's short-run costs, we will construct a hypothetical example for the costs of a small pizzeria. We will then apply these same concepts to an entire competitive market.

Economists define the **short run** as the period in which some resources are fixed and others are variable, whereas in the **long run** all resources are variable. Firms can adjust some (variable) inputs such as labor and materials easily and quickly in the short run, but other (fixed) inputs can be adjusted only with difficulty and time—that is, in the long run. Fixed inputs cannot be changed in the short run in order to increase output. For example, to expand the size of its operations significantly, a pizzeria would need more land, a larger building, more pizza ovens, and more delivery vehicles. These inputs take time to purchase, build, and install, a process that cannot be done at a moment's notice. But on a monthly basis, the firm can change some other inputs quite easily. If our firm wants to increase its output of pizzas, it can hire another laborer or pay existing workers to work more hours, and it can purchase more cheese, sauce, and flour to make pizzas. Thus, labor and materials are considered to be variable inputs, since they can be adjusted easily in the short run. Land and capital (including buildings, machinery, and equipment) are considered fixed inputs because they cannot be adjusted in the short run.

With fixed and variable inputs, our firm also has some costs that are fixed and some costs that are variable. Therefore, in the short run, a firm's total cost (TC) is found by adding together total fixed costs (TFC) and total variable costs (TVC):

$$TC = TFC + TVC.$$

Fixed Costs

The **total fixed costs** are the total costs of the fixed inputs—things like rent, capital costs (payments on machinery purchased on credit or the opportunity cost of that machinery), and property taxes that the firm must pay regardless of how much it produces. Our pizzeria's fixed inputs are land and capital (the building, machinery, and equipment needed to produce pizzas, including pizza ovens, a cash register, tables and chairs, and a truck to deliver pizzas). Since fixed costs are, just that, fixed, they do not go up or down as the firm produces more. Thus, total fixed costs do not change.

In contrast, **average fixed cost**, which is equal to total fixed costs divided by quantity, declines as more is produced:

$$\text{AFC} = \text{TFC}/Q.$$

For example, assume our pizzeria has fixed costs each day of $50. If it produces only one pizza ($Q = 1$), the average fixed costs would be $50/1 = $50. It would have to sell that pizza for more than $50 to make a profit. (Don't forget, in addition to fixed costs, it would have to pay for variable costs such as labor, cheese, sauce, and flour.) However, if the firm produces ten pizzas, then its average fixed costs fall to $50/10 = $5 per pizza. If the firm produces fifty pizzas, then the average fixed cost is $50/50 = $1. This gives us an average fixed cost curve that looks like the one in Figure 8.1. The more the firm produces, the lower its average fixed cost.

Variable Costs

But our firm has more than just fixed costs to contend with. As we noted above, in addition to its fixed inputs such as land and capital, our firm must purchase variable inputs to produce its pizzas. Variable inputs would include labor and the materials necessary to produce pizzas. We will focus our analysis on labor, because it is the most important variable input. Without labor, no pizzas would get made.

Variable (labor) costs are subject to two basic economic laws: the **law of specialization** and the **law of diminishing returns**. The law of specialization refers to the fact that when laborers specialize in one particular task, they gain in skill and dexterity, and they spend less time switching jobs, which improves their efficiency. However, in the short run, when land and capital are fixed, the process of

FIGURE 8.1 Average Fixed Cost

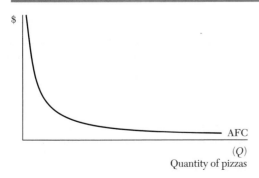

$

AFC

(Q)
Quantity of pizzas

specialization is limited by the size of the firm. Only a certain number of specialized tasks can be done in a small pizzeria. Once the specialized jobs are filled, increasing the output of pizzas becomes increasingly difficult. This is when the law of diminishing returns sets in. According to the law of diminishing returns, in the production of any commodity, as more units of a variable factor of production are added to a fixed quantity of other factors of production, the amount that each additional unit of the variable factor adds to the total product will eventually begin to diminish. In other words, after the specialized jobs are filled, adding more and more labor while keeping other inputs fixed will result in smaller and smaller increases in output. Each laborer gets less efficient after specialization is exhausted.*

To illustrate these fundamental processes of specialization and diminishing returns, suppose our pizzeria has the following fixed inputs: a small dining room with six tables and twenty-four chairs, one cash register, a small kitchen with two pizza ovens, and one truck to deliver pizzas. Suppose also that our firm has enough cheese, sauce, and flour to make as many pizzas as it wants (consider these to be fixed inputs as well for the time being). What will happen as the firm hires laborers at the going wage rate of $8 per hour?

Table 8.1 illustrates how the law of specialization and the law of diminishing returns affects the firm's short-run costs. If our firm hires no laborers, then no pizzas will be produced. It will lose a lot of money, since it must still pay its fixed costs. If our firm hires one laborer for one hour, then that one laborer will have to make the pizzas, cook the pizzas, and deliver them to customers. If our one employee works hard, she can make and deliver six pizzas in an hour. Our

Table 8.1 Marginal Cost and Average Variable Cost of a Pizza

Number of Laborers (L)	Quantity of Pizzas (Q)	Marginal Product of Labor $\left(MPL = \dfrac{\Delta Q}{\Delta L}\right)$	Total Variable (Labor) Cost (TVC = W × L)	Marginal Cost of a Pizza $\left(MC = \dfrac{\Delta TVC}{\Delta Q}\right)$	Average Variable Cost of a Pizza $\left(AVC = \dfrac{TVC}{Q}\right)$
0	0	—	$ 0.00	—	—
1	6	6	8.00	$1.33	$1.33
2	14	8	16.00	1.00	1.14
3	24	10	24.00	0.80	1.00
4	32	8	32.00	1.00	1.00
5	38	6	40.00	1.33	1.05
6	42	4	48.00	2.00	1.14
7	44	2	56.00	4.00	1.27
8	45	1	64.00	8.00	1.42
9	45	0	72.00	—	1.60
10	44	−1	80.00	—	1.82

*It is important to note that the law of diminishing returns can apply to any variable input (not just labor), when all other inputs are held fixed. For example, if our pizzeria added more and more delivery trucks while keeping all other inputs the same, what would happen to output? Would adding a second delivery truck increase output per hour? What about a tenth delivery truck? (With the number of laborers constant, would there be anyone to drive it?)

one laborer ($L = 1$) has produced six pizzas ($Q = 6$) in an hour at a cost of $8 (the wage rate for one hour of work). This worker's **marginal product of labor** (MPL), the increase in output from hiring an additional laborer for an hour, is six pizzas. The **marginal cost** (MC) of a pizza is the increase in cost from producing another pizza, which is equal to the change in **total variable cost** (TVC) divided by the change in quantity:

$$MC = \Delta TVC/\Delta Q.$$

Firms are very concerned with marginal cost because once they know what each unit of output (each pizza) costs, they know what price they need to charge to make a profit on it. In this case, the change in total variable costs was $8 (the cost of hiring one employee for an hour), and the increase in the output of pizzas was six (the number of pizzas increased from zero to six). Thus, the marginal cost of each pizza when one laborer is working for an hour is equal to $8/6 = \$1.33$. Total variable cost is the cost of all variable inputs. Since we are employing one worker for one hour, our current total variable costs are $8.

Now suppose our pizzeria hires a second laborer to work alongside the first one for one hour. The laborers can now specialize in certain tasks. One laborer can concentrate on making the pizzas, and the other can take telephone orders and deliver the pizzas. The two employees together can produce fourteen pizzas in an hour, more than double what one employee could produce on her own, because of specialization. The marginal product of the second laborer is 8, because the output of pizzas increased by eight when the second laborer was hired. The marginal cost of a pizza has fallen, due to specialization:

$$MC = \Delta TVC/\Delta Q = \$8/8 = \$1.$$

Each pizza is now cheaper to produce because of the efficiency gains from specialization.

Hiring a third laborer will increase specialization (and efficiency) even further. Now one employee can make the pizzas, one person can take the orders and run the cash register, and one employee can deliver pizzas (in the process getting to know the town very well, which will improve delivery time). The output of pizzas increases to twenty-four per hour, and the marginal product of the third laborer is 10, because the output of pizzas increased from fourteen to twenty-four. The marginal cost of a pizza has fallen even further, to $8/10 = \$0.80$ (the $8 increase in variable cost divided by 10, the increase in quantity).

However, now that the most important specialized tasks are taken, the law of diminishing returns sets in. Hiring additional laborers will increase the output of pizzas, *but not by as much*. Adding a fourth laborer will increase the output of pizzas to thirty-two, so the marginal product of labor declines back to 8, and the marginal cost of a pizza increases to $1.00. If the firm continues to hire laborers beyond this point, the marginal product of labor declines even further. Eventually, workers start getting in each other's way, and they spend more time standing around and talking than working. The marginal product of the ninth laborer is 0; with a fixed size of operations (land and capital), there is nothing productive for a ninth laborer to do. Adding laborers beyond this would actually *decrease* output. Having too many workers in the small kitchen would prevent work from getting done.

Specialization and diminishing returns determine the shape of the firm's marginal cost and average variable cost curves. As you can see from Table 8.1, as workers get more productive and the marginal product of labor increases, the marginal cost of a pizza declines. When diminishing returns set in and the marginal product of labor declines, the marginal cost of a pizza increases.

The shape of the marginal cost curve determines the shape of the average variable cost curve. Average variable cost (AVC) is equal to total variable cost (TVC) divided by quantity (Q):

$$AVC = TVC/Q.$$

At first, average variable cost is equal to marginal cost; the cost of the first pizza is also equal to the average cost of that pizza. Then, as the marginal cost of each pizza falls below the average variable cost, it pulls the average variable cost of each pizza down as the quantity of pizzas increases. This happens in Table 8.1 as the quantity of pizzas increases from zero to twenty-four; MC < AVC, and AVC falls as quantity rises. When the marginal cost of each pizza exceeds the average variable cost of a pizza, each additional pizza costs more than the average, and this pulls the average cost up. In Table 8.1, this occurs after a quantity of thirty-two pizzas. At a quantity of thirty-two pizzas, MC = AVC. After that point, MC > AVC, and AVC increases as more pizzas are produced.

Together, the law of specialization and the law of diminishing returns give us the marginal cost and average variable cost curves depicted in Figure 8.2. The curves decline at first because specialization improves efficiency and lowers costs. Subsequently, the law of diminishing returns kicks in and the curves increase because efficiency declines, resulting in higher costs.

Average Cost

Now we're ready to construct the firm's **average cost** curve. Recall that total costs are equal to total fixed costs plus total variable costs (TC = TFC + TVC).

FIGURE 8.2 Marginal Cost and Average Variable Cost

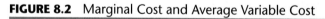

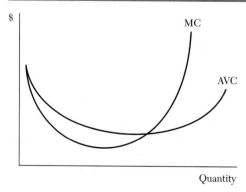

FIGURE 8.3   Average Cost Curve

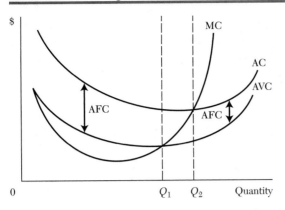

Similarly, average cost (AC) is equal to average fixed cost (AFC) plus average variable cost (AVC):

$$AC = AFC + AVC.$$

If we take the average fixed cost curve from Figure 8.1 and add it to the average variable cost curve in Figure 8.2, we get our firm's average cost curve, which is shown in Figure 8.3. Note that on the graph we do not need to show the average fixed cost curve. It can always be found by taking the difference between AC and AVC (AC − AVC = AFC). As you can see, the AC curve gets closer and closer to the AVC curve as quantity increases. This is because the difference between the AC curve and the AVC curve is average fixed cost (AFC), and as shown in Figure 8.1, AFC gets smaller and smaller as quantity increases.

The short-run average cost curve has a U shape because the average fixed cost curve declines, the average variable cost curve declines at first due to specialization, and the average variable cost curve increases eventually due to the law of diminishing returns. In Figure 8.3, AC falls quickly from a quantity of zero to a quantity of Q_1 because as quantity increases, both of its components (AFC and AVC) are falling. From Q_1 to Q_2, AC decreases slightly as quantity increases. This is because average fixed cost is falling faster than average variable cost is rising (the average variable cost curve increases after Q_1?). After Q_2? AC rises because average variable cost is increasing faster than average fixed cost is falling.

Notice also that the minimum average cost occurs where the average cost curve intersects the marginal cost curve at quantity Q_2. The same process applies here as the one that applies to the average variable cost curve: When MC < AC, each unit costs less than the average, and the average falls as quantity increases. When MC > AC, each unit costs more than the average, so AC increases as quantity increases.

The point where average cost is at a minimum has significance for society as a whole. The level of output that minimizes the average cost of output is the *most efficient rate of output*. It means that society is minimizing the cost of using its resources with respect to the production of a good. In Figure 8.3, Q_2 represents an *optimum level of output*, because it minimizes the per-unit cost of producing that good. Raising or lowering output would increase average cost.

Now that we've analyzed the cost side of the firm, we need to study the revenue side in order to determine how much the firm should produce in any situation.

THE FIRM'S REVENUES

Total revenue (TR), you'll recall, equals the price of the product (P) multiplied by the quantity of the product sold (Q): $TR = P \times Q$. We can also define average revenue and marginal revenue for the firm. **Average revenue** (AR) is revenue per unit, which is equal to price:

$$AR = TR/Q = (P \times Q)/Q = P.$$

Marginal revenue is the change in total revenue from producing and selling an additional unit of output:

$$MR = (change\ in\ TR)/(change\ in\ Q) = \Delta TR/\Delta Q.$$

For a firm in a perfectly competitive market, the price is determined in the market by the forces of supply and demand. The firm is so small a part of the market that it has no influence on the price. Thus, as far as the firm is concerned, the price is fixed, and the firm will earn the same amount of money for each unit sold. For the firm in a perfectly competitive market, $MR = P$. If we were to draw this line on a graph, it would simply be a horizontal line that does not change as quantity changes, as displayed in Figure 8.4.

PROFIT MAXIMIZATION

We are now ready to put the cost information and the revenue information together to describe how a typical firm decides to maximize profits in a perfectly competitive market. The firm's objective is maximum profits (or minimum losses if the business climate is poor). What level of output should the firm produce to get the maximum level of profits? The answer is that the firm should produce as long as marginal revenue is greater than or equal to marginal cost.

FIGURE 8.4 Marginal Revenue Curve

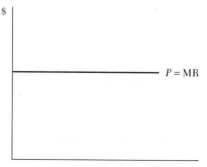

FIGURE 8.5 Marginal Revenue, Marginal Cost, and Profit Maximization

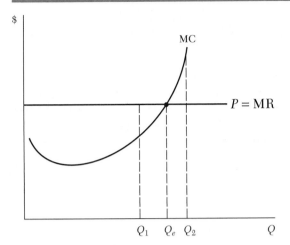

Therefore, *the profit-maximizing quantity will occur where marginal revenue is equal to marginal cost* (MR = MC).

The logic behind the profit maximization rule is quite simple. Every unit that generates more in revenue than it costs will improve the standing of the firm. For example, in Figure 8.5, the firm should produce all units up to Q_e because each unit adds more to the firm's revenue than it costs the firm to produce. If the firm were to stop at Q_1, then it would lose the revenue from the sale of the units between Q_1 and Q_e. However, the firm should not increase production beyond Q_e. At Q_2, the firm is producing units that cost more than they generate in revenue, which would hurt the firm's bottom line. The profit-maximizing quantity always occurs where marginal revenue is equal to marginal cost.

Although the quantity Q_e in Figure 8.5 represents the profit-maximizing or loss-minimizing level of output—the best the firm can possibly do—we don't know how much the firm is making or losing until we add in the other cost information for the firm. Specifically, we need to know the firm's average cost at quantity Q_e. Recall that the firm earns a normal profit when total revenue (TR) equals total cost (TC). Since TR = $P \times Q$ and TC = AC $\times Q$, we can solve for P when TR = TC:

$$P \times Q = AC \times Q$$

$$P = AC.$$

The firm earns a normal profit when the price of its product equals its average cost (including the cost of all inputs plus opportunity costs). Similarly, the firm earns an economic profit when $P > AC$, and it experiences an economic loss when $P < AC$.

3. Why do total costs and total variable costs increase at a *decreasing* rate at relatively low levels of output?

An Example of Profit Maximization in the Short Run

Let's use another simple example of a small firm engaged in the production of pizzas to explore how firms maximize profits. The pizzeria is run by a group of individuals, leases a building outside of Chicago, and owns all of the furniture and equipment in its restaurant. It has borrowed money from BankChicago to finance its business. In this sense, then, it has a certain size of operation for its short-run production expectations. Within this fixed size of operations, it can expand its output of pizzas by using more variable resources—that is, more raw materials and more labor. These variable resources can use the fixed size of operations more or less intensively to produce more or less output. (In the long run, as we will see shortly, all of the resources that the firm uses in production can be expanded or contracted. That is, the firm can change the size of its operation.)

Fixed and Variable Costs. As we saw above, in the short run, the firm incurs both fixed and variable costs. Total fixed costs are the costs that the firm must pay for the fixed resources of production involved in the firm's particular short-run size of operations. These costs do not vary with the rate of output that the firm produces. The firm has a monthly mortgage payment that it gives to the bank to repay the loan it used to purchase its equipment for producing pizzas. The owners of the firm also have an opportunity cost for their participation in the firm's activities. In other words, the owners will get salaries based on what they could earn in some other activity. If these salaries weren't paid, the owners would seek some other jobs in which they could earn their opportunity cost (e.g., as managers of a different restaurant). All of these costs are fixed costs; they are incurred by the firm regardless of the level of output in any particular month. Even if output is zero in the short run, fixed costs are still positive.

Let's assume that the monthly fixed costs of this pizzeria are $1,000. Figure 8.6 illustrates total fixed costs (TFC), with costs measured on the vertical axis and output measured on the horizontal axis. It shows that as output (measured on the horizontal axis) increases, total fixed costs remain constant.

This firm's total variable costs are the expenses for using varying amounts of raw materials and labor to expand output within a fixed-size plant (in the short run). To get greater amounts of output, the firm uses more and more variable resources; consequently, total variable costs increase as output increases. However, given the law of specialization, we know that at first, relatively few added resources will achieve expanded output, and that later, given the law of diminishing returns, the firm will have to add greater amounts of resources to get equivalent additions to output. Therefore, total variable costs will normally increase first at a decreasing rate, then at an increasing rate. Figure 8.6 illustrates what happens to total variable costs (TVC), measured on the vertical axis, as output increases. At rates of output below a quantity of 300, total variable costs increase at a decreasing rate, and at rates of output greater than 300, diminishing returns to the use of variable resources set in, and total variable costs increase at an increasing rate. At a rate of output of zero, total variable costs are zero.

FIGURE 8.6 Total Costs, Total Fixed Costs, and Total Variable Costs

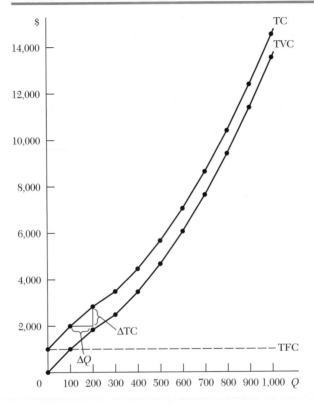

If we add total fixed costs and total variable costs together, we again get the total costs (TC) of production:

$$TC = TFC + TVC.$$

Table 8.2 presents different possible levels of output during a one-month period for our pizzeria and the total fixed costs, total variable costs, and total

Table 8.2 Pizzeria's Costs at Possible Levels of Output

Level of Output	Total Fixed Costs	Total Variable Costs	Total Costs
0	$1,000	$ 0	$ 1,000
100	1,000	1,000	2,000
200	1,000	1,800	2,800
300	1,000	2,400	3,400
400	1,000	3,400	4,400
500	1,000	4,600	5,600
600	1,000	6,000	7,000
700	1,000	7,600	8,600
800	1,000	9,400	10,400
900	1,000	11,400	12,400
1,000	1,000	13,600	14,600

costs of each level of output. Figure 8.6 illustrates total costs. Notice that when output is zero, total costs equal total fixed costs.

Average and Marginal Costs. We can also use this cost information to derive average and marginal costs. As we saw earlier, these cost measures will prove useful in analyzing the firm's profit maximization decisions. Average cost takes the various total costs of production and averages them over each unit of output. For example, at 100 units of output, total fixed costs are $1,000. The average fixed cost for each unit of output is $10. Recall that for each different level of output, average fixed cost is defined as follows:

$$AFC = \frac{TFC}{Q}.$$

In the same way, average variable cost is

$$AVC = \frac{TVC}{Q},$$

and average cost is

$$AC = \frac{TC}{Q}.$$

Since TC = TFC + TVC, then AC = AFC + AVC.

Marginal cost, again, is the additional cost of producing one additional unit of output. It indicates the amount of change in total costs as a result of additional output:

$$MC = \frac{\text{change in TC}}{\text{change in } Q} \text{ or } \frac{\Delta TC}{\Delta Q}.$$

Since fixed costs do not change with the level of output, marginal costs can also be defined as the change in total variable costs as output changes. For example, when the firm moves from producing 100 units of output to 200 units of output, total costs increase from $2,000 to $2,800 (and total variable costs increase from $1,000 to $1,800). Consequently,

$$MC = \frac{2,800 - 2,000}{200 - 100} = \frac{800}{100} = 8.$$

The marginal cost of producing 100 more pizzas (expanding to 200 from 100) is $800, or $8 for each unit. In essence, marginal cost equals the slope of the total costs (or total variable costs) curve in Figure 8.6. Since total costs first increase at a decreasing rate and then begin increasing at an increasing rate, MC will first decrease and then begin increasing.

As shown in Table 8.3, we can use the information in Table 8.2 to derive data on average fixed costs, average variable costs, average costs, and marginal costs. Figure 8.7 graphs the resulting data. AFC, AVC, AC, and MC all vary with the rate of output. In each case, costs are measured in per-unit or marginal terms. The horizontal axis always measures output, and the vertical axis

Table 8.3 Pizzeria's Average and Marginal Costs

Output	$AFC = \dfrac{TFC}{Q}$	$AVC = \dfrac{TVC}{Q}$	$AC = \dfrac{TC}{Q}$	$MC = \dfrac{\Delta TC}{\Delta Q}$
0	–	–	–	–
100	$10.0	$10.0	$20.0	$10
200	5.0	9.0	14.0	8
300	3.3	8.0	11.3	6
400	2.5	8.5	11.0	10
500	2.0	9.2	11.2	12
600	1.7	10.0	11.7	14
700	1.4	10.9	12.3	16
800	1.2	11.7	12.9	18
900	1.1	12.7	13.8	20
1,000	1.0	14.6	15.6	22

measures average or marginal costs. Average fixed cost in Figure 8.7(a) constantly decreases, since it is total fixed cost divided by increasing rates of output. Average variable cost, shown in Figure 8.7(b), is generally U-shaped, reflecting the laws of specialization and diminishing returns. Over a range of output, AVC decreases at first, reaches a minimum at Q_1, and then begins to increase for greater levels of output. At first, when there are increasing returns to the use of variable resources, the per-unit cost of production decreases as output increases. The per-unit amount of resources needed to produce increasing amounts of output decreases. However, beyond Q_1, AVC begins to increase as each unit of output requires the use of increasing amounts of variable resources. This, again, is the result of diminishing returns to the use of variable resources.

FIGURE 8.7 Average Fixed Costs (a), Average Variable Costs (b), Average Costs (b), and Marginal Costs (b)

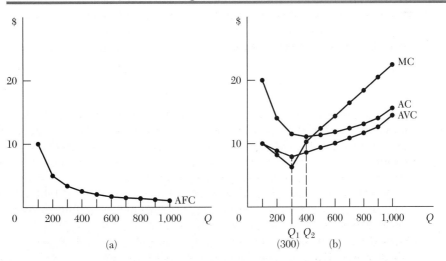

(a)

(b)

Average cost, shown in Figure 8.7(b), is also U-shaped because of the laws of specialization and diminishing returns. Since AC is the sum of AFC and AVC, and AFC is positive and constantly decreasing, AC is above AVC, but the difference between them is constantly decreasing. AC reaches a minimum at the rate of output of Q_2. This is a slightly higher rate of output than Q_1. AVC is increasing, but because AFC is constantly decreasing, it takes a higher level of output for AC to begin increasing (where the effects of increasing AVC begin to outweigh the effects of decreasing AFC).

In Figure 8.7(b), marginal cost is also U-shaped due to the laws of specialization and diminishing returns. Since marginal costs register the *additional* costs of producing greater rates of output, rather than the per-unit costs, marginal costs will more dramatically illustrate the effects first of increasing returns and then of decreasing returns to the use of variable resources.

4. Explain how the law of diminishing returns causes the MC curve to be increasing beyond some rate of output.

5. Why is marginal cost equal to the slope of the total cost curve? What *is* the slope of the total cost curve?

6. If the Los Angeles Dodgers have a team batting average of .275 (that is, on the average they get 275 hits every 1,000 times they come to bat) and they acquire a new outfielder whose batting average is .298, what happens to the team batting average? What if they trade away two players with averages of .260 and .274 for one player with an average of .278? Relate these examples to MC and AC.

7. Explain why the minimum point on the AC curve represents an optimum rate of output.

Price and Profit. Recall that, for a firm in a perfectly competitive market, the price is determined in the market by the forces of supply and demand. The firm gets the price of the product for every unit that it sells, so $P = MR = AR$. If the price of a pizza is \$12, then the firm's revenues per unit are \$12, and its marginal revenues also are \$12. Figure 8.8(a) illustrates total revenues, and Figure 8.8(b) shows price and marginal revenue. These graphs show what happens to revenues, measured on the vertical axis, as output expands.

We are now ready to put the cost information and the revenue information together to describe the profit maximization decision of the pizzeria. Table 8.4 and Figure 8.9 provide information and an illustration of the firm's profit maximization decision. Recall that we have assumed that the firm's objective is to maximize its profits, that in the short run it has a fixed-size of operations (restaurant), that it has access to certain production techniques and technical knowledge, and that it can buy resources in markets for certain prices. What level of output could the firm produce to get the maximum level of profits? The answer is that the pizzeria will produce that rate of output at which the difference between TR and TC is greatest. This also happens to be the rate of output at which MC and MR are equal. *When the marginal cost of producing one*

FIGURE 8.8 Total Revenue (a) and Marginal Revenue (b)

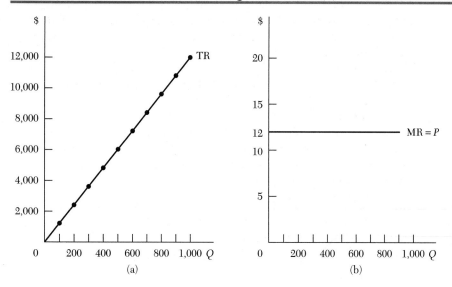

(a)   (b)

Table 8.4 Data for a Firm's Profit Maximization Decision

Output	TC	AC	MC	MR / TR	(and *P*)	Profit (or Loss)
0	$1,000	–	–	0	–	$–1,000
100	2,000	$20.0	$10	$ 1,200	$12	–800
200	2,800	14.0	8	2,400	12	–400
300	3,400	11.3	6	3,600	12	200
400	4,400	11.0	10	4,800	12	400
500	5,600	11.2	12	6,000	12	400
600	7,000	11.7	14	7,200	12	200
700	8,600	12.3	16	8,400	12	–200
800	10,400	12.9	18	9,600	12	–800
900	12,400	13.8	20	10,800	12	–1,600
1,000	14,600	15.6	22	12,000	12	–2,600

more unit of output is equal to the marginal revenue from selling one more unit, the firm maximizes its profits. This occurs at a quantity of 500 in Figure 8.9.

Table 8.4 and Figure 8.9 demonstrate why profits (or TR − TC) are maximized when MC = MR at 500 units of output. (In this numerical example, because we are increasing output in increments of 100, the marginal cost figure is actually an *average* of the marginal cost of producing each added 100 pizzas. As a result, profits are maximized at both 400 and 500 units of output. The firm could pick either rate of output and maximize its profits—at $400. But since MR > MC at 400 units of output, the firm will expand to 500.) At higher rates of output, marginal costs are larger than marginal revenues, and profits decrease. At lower rates of output, marginal revenues exceed marginal costs, and the firm can increase its profits by producing and selling larger levels of output.

FIGURE 8.9 Profit Maximization

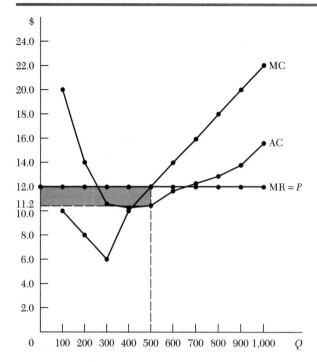

Notice that at a quantity of 500 in Figure 8.9, the price of a pizza is greater than the average cost of producing each unit. That is, for each unit, the revenue that the firm earns exceeds its cost. This is, in fact, profit per unit, since profit = TR − TC:

$$\frac{\text{profit}}{Q} = \frac{\text{TR}}{Q} - \frac{\text{TC}}{Q}$$

$$\text{profit per unit} = P - \text{AC}.$$

As long as price exceeds average cost, the firm earns economic profits of $Q(P - \text{AC})$. Total profits are equal to the area of the shaded rectangle in Figure 8.9. If the price is below the average cost, however, the firm experiences losses. Does this conclusion fit the information in Table 8.4?

What we have just shown summarizes one of the most important results of the economic theory of the firm. A firm will maximize its profits when it produces a rate of output at which its marginal revenues equal its marginal costs. This is its equilibrium rate of output. If a firm expands its output to a point at which MC > MR, its profits decrease. What will it do in response? It will probably reduce its rate of output. The theoretical conclusion would seem to be borne out by what we would expect firms in the real world to do. They will tend to produce that rate of output at which MC = MR.

Figure 8.10 shows examples of a firm earning an economic profit, earning a normal profit, and incurring an economic loss. In each case, the equilibrium

FIGURE 8.10 A Perfectly Competitive Firm Earning an Economic Profit (a), Earning a Normal Profit (b) and Incurring an Economic Loss (c)

Economic Profit

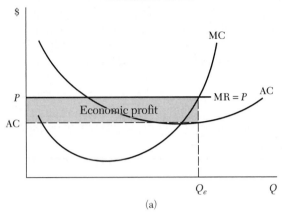

(a)

Normal Profit
(no economic profit or loss)

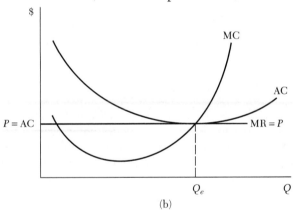

(b)

Economic Loss

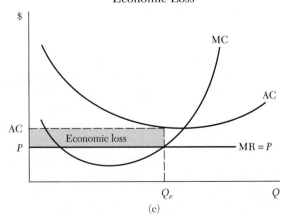

(c)

(profit-maximizing or loss-minimizing) level of output is found at the quantity where MR = MC. The profit or loss per unit is measured by the area between the price (or marginal revenue) curve and the average cost curve for the quantity produced. In Figure 8.10(a), $P > AC$, and the shaded area represents an economic profit. In Figure 8.10(b), $P = AC$, and the firm earns a normal profit. The graph has no shaded area for profit or loss, because a normal profit is already included in the costs of production. In Figure 8.10(c), $P < AC$, and the firm earns an economic loss equal to the shaded area.

8. For our pizzeria, what happens to its profits if it reduces output from 500 to 300? What is the relationship between P and AC at this rate of output? What is the relationship between MC and MR?

9. For Figure 8.9, explain why profits increase if the firm moves from a quantity of 700 to lower levels of output.

10. Construct an AC curve with its own MC curve. What would the firm do if the price of its product passed through the point at which MC = AC? What level of output would it produce? What would its profits be? Would this firm be earning its opportunity costs?

11. From Table 8.4, if the firm produces 800 units of output, what are its profits? What is the relationship between P and AC? Between MR and MC?

The Firm in the Long Run

In the long run, the firm always has more options than in the short run. It can alter the size of its plant. It can change the technology it uses to produce its good or service. For pizza firms, if the market for the product expands or the firm thinks that it will, it can seek a larger facility to buy or rent, borrow more money so that it can purchase more machinery and equipment, hire more workers, take on partners to expand the size of its operation, or relocate its operations. In the long run, the firm can vary all of its production resources; there are no fixed resources.

The long run is no specific period of time; rather, it is that time frame in which people make decisions based on the future. If a pizza firm expects its market to expand in the future, it will adjust for the long run. Or if it expects the market to begin to contract, it can make a different long-run adjustment. In addition, in the long run, firms can enter or leave the industry. The decision to enter or leave is a long-run investment decision for individuals and firms.

In essence, the firm can pick an infinite number of different possible short-run plant sizes in the long run. At any moment in time, the firm is in the short run; it has a fixed-size plant with fixed resources, and it has a corresponding short-run average cost curve. Given the long-run option of different possible plant sizes, the firm will obviously pick the plant size that minimizes the average cost of producing every different possible level of output. For example, in Figure 8.11, there are three different short-run average cost curves representing

Workers make pizzas in a small pizza restaurant.
(© Michael Newman/Photo Edit)

different possible plant sizes for different ranges of output. AC_1 represents the first size plant, AC_2 the second size plant, and AC_3 the third size plant. For Q_1, AC_1 minimizes the average cost of production. So if the firm wanted to produce Q_1, it would pick plant size 1. But if the firm wanted to produce Q_2, it would pick plant size 2, since this minimizes the average cost of that rate of output. Similarly, if it wanted to produce an even larger rate of output, say Q_3 it would pick plant size 3. Notice that this represents a long-run decision. The firm makes a choice of a plant size (or scale of operations) based on its expectations of or experiences with the market. The decision requires time to make arrangements for physical facilities, new and larger equipment, borrowing, and

FIGURE 8.11   Deriving Long-Run Average Costs

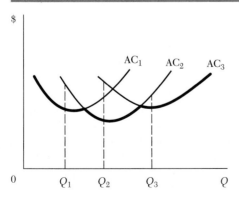

FIGURE 8.12 Typical Long-Run Average Cost Curve

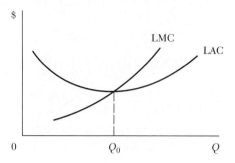

so forth. The firm generates its long-run average cost curve by picking the plant size that minimizes the cost of producing every possible rate of output. It is the heavy line in Figure 8.11.

When we assume that there is an infinite number of possible plant sizes for the firm to choose from, the firm's typical long-run AC curve looks like the one in Figure 8.12. It is U-shaped just like the short-run AC curve (and has its own long-run marginal cost curve, LMC), but for different reasons. The short-run curve was U-shaped because of the laws of specialization and diminishing returns, which assumed that a firm increased output by applying variable resources to fixed resources. In the long run, however, there are no fixed resources; a firm expands output by using more of all resources. If that is the case, then why would long-run average costs (LAC) decrease over a range of output, reach a minimum at Q_0, and then begin to increase?

Economists attribute the shape of the LAC curve to economies and diseconomies of scale. As the firm adjusts its plant size, it alters the scale of its operations. At first, as the firm expands at relatively low levels of output, by building a larger plant, it can take greater advantage of specialization, division of labor, and more advanced technology. (If the pizzeria we analyzed earlier had a much larger kitchen, there would be many more specialized jobs.) The result is lower average costs. The firm experiences **economies of scale:** long-run average costs decrease as output increases. However, beyond some rate of output (Q_0 in Figure 8.12), the firm encounters difficulties in organizing the now larger operation. Coordination and communication make efficient production more difficult. Average costs begin to increase; it costs more to produce each unit of output. **Diseconomies of scale** have set in. As in the short run, the long-run marginal cost curve (LMC) in Figure 8.12 is below LAC while LAC is decreasing and above it while it is increasing.

The shape of the long-run average cost curve defines an optimum plant size. At the rate of output at which LAC is at a minimum, the firm picks the plant size that produces the rate of output at lowest average cost. The firm expands output and plant size throughout the range of economies of scale. At higher rates of output, LAC begins to increase because of diseconomies of scale. At Q_0, the firm produces a rate of output that minimizes the per-unit cost of production.

In fact, in the long run, in competitive industries, firms tend to produce a rate of output that minimizes long-run average costs. Competition forces them to do so.

12. If a firm experienced economies of scale over some range of output and then LAC was constant, what would its LAC curve look like? Does it seem reasonable to you that a firm could keep expanding and not encounter diseconomies of scale? If this happened, what would the optimum size plant be?

13. In Figure 8.12, Q_0 represents the optimum rate of output and the optimum plant size. Does the firm earn its opportunity costs if it gets a price equal to this level of average costs?

COMPETITIVE MARKETS IN THE LONG RUN

In this section, using the model that we developed for the individual firm, we will formulate a general model of the behavior of a competitive market. The analysis focuses on the long-run equilibrium for the firms in the industry and for the entire industry. Although we have concentrated on a single example, the model of a competitive market is intended to be generalizable to all competitive markets or to an entire economy that is competitive. We will also interpret the results of the long-run equilibrium for competitive markets.

In Figure 8.13, with a price of P_1, the firm will produce Q_1, since it is at this rate of output that $MR = MC$. The price is determined in the competitive market for the firm's product. This price is constant, and the firm has no effect on it. Hence, $P = MR$, and the firm can produce as much as it wants at that price. The firm, of course, will produce Q_1, since that is where its profits are maximized. At Q_1 price exceeds AC, so we know that the firm is earning economic profits.

But in the long run, if resources can earn above their opportunity costs, new firms will enter the industry in pursuit of economic profits. In other words, the existence of economic profits provides an incentive for other firms to enter the industry. If economic profits can be made, given the price in the market for pizza and the average costs of production, new firms will enter that market and begin to produce and market their own products.

FIGURE 8.13 The Firm in the Long Run

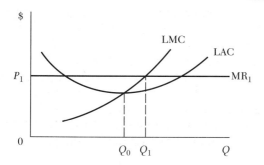

FIGURE 8.14 The Effect of Entry in the Long Run

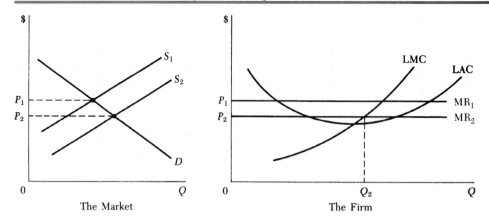

The Market   The Firm

As new firms enter the market, however, the market supply curve shifts out to the right. There is an increase in supply because one of the determinants of supply has changed. This increase in supply, assuming the demand does not change, produces a lower price for pizza, say P_2 (see Figure 8.14). At P_2, the firm will pick a new rate of output, Q_2, at which MR = MC. But P still exceeds AC, firms will continue to make economic profits (albeit smaller than before), and other new firms will enter the market. This further increases market supply and drives down the price of the product.

This process will continue until economic profits no longer exist to provide an incentive for new firms to enter the industry. This occurs at a price of P_3 in Figure 8.15. At this price, the firm picks Q_3, since that is where MR = MC. At this rate of output P = AC, so there are no economic profits. The firm is in equilibrium because it is producing the rate of output that maximizes its profits—even though this means zero economic profits. But the firm does earn

FIGURE 8.15 Long-Run Equilibrium in Competition

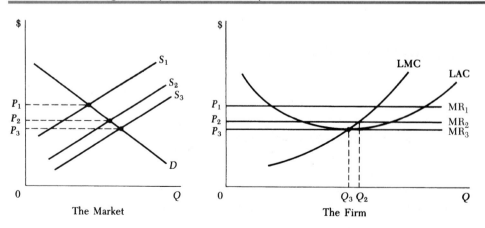

The Market   The Firm

what we called at the beginning of this chapter, normal profits—that is, it covers all of its opportunity costs. The firm collects enough revenues to pay opportunity costs to all of its variable and fixed resources, including a return to the owners of the business equivalent to their opportunity costs. The firm earns as much from its involvement in this activity as it could earn doing anything else. If a firm cannot earn normal profits in the long run, it will exit the market.

Competition and Efficiency

The existence of economic profits encourages new firms to enter the industry until economic profits are eliminated. Firms choose a rate of output that maximizes their profits, which in long-run equilibrium equals zero economic profits, or normal profits. The industry is in equilibrium because there is no incentive for firms to enter or exit the industry. What are the consequences of this result in terms of a society's use of its scarce resources?

Efficiency in production occurs when the per-unit cost of production is minimized. The firm produces at the rate of output that minimizes AC. This means that the amount of resources used to produce each unit of output is minimized. Given resource scarcity, this is an attractive result of the operation of competitive markets. But note how this has happened. Because of competition and free entry, the firm has been forced to produce at the level of output that minimizes average cost! Competition, through the forces that we have analyzed, tends over time to result in efficient production. Firms tend to produce at the optimum level of output, minimizing the per-unit cost of production. So competition tends to produce efficiency.

What assumptions have we made? We assumed that demand was constant and that the cost curves did not change. With these simplifying assumptions, our analysis showed the tendency toward efficiency. Obviously, changes in the real world would make our analysis a bit more complicated, but the essential conclusion remains: Competitive markets tend to result in efficiency in the use of scarce resources.

14. Explain and show in an illustration what happens in our competitive market when the market price goes below P_3 in Figure 8.15. What happens to profits? What do the firms in the industry do? What happens to market supply? To market price? What is the new equilibrium?

15. Do you think that the model of long-run equilibrium—wherein profits attract entry, prices fluctuate, exit of firms is possible, and there is a tendency toward efficiency in production—applies to the example we have been using, the market for pizza? Why or why not? Can you think of some other markets that have demonstrated some of these same characteristics in recent years?

16. In the personal computer market, IBM (now Lenovo) and Apple, the two firms that dominated the market in the 1980s, have faced increasing competition from other PC producers. What has happened to the price of a PC over the past twenty years? What factors explain the price trend?

Another type of efficiency results from long-run equilibrium in competitive markets: **efficiency in resource allocation**. At the long-run equilibrium in Figure 8.15, P_3 equals minimum AC. But P_3 also equals MC at the equilibrium rate of output, Q_3. This is an important result. The price of a product measures the amount of money that people are just willing to spend to purchase one more unit of that good. In other words, the price provides a measure of the marginal benefit that people derive from purchasing a unit of the good or service. The MC of the good (shown by the LMC curve) measures the cost to society of getting additional units of the good. To get one more unit, resources must be paid their opportunity costs. A rate of output that equalizes the marginal cost to society of getting one more unit of a good with the marginal benefit that people get from consuming one more unit maximizes social welfare (with respect to the production of that good). It also implies that resources have been allocated efficiently, given the opportunity costs of resources and given consumers' valuations of goods as shown by their prices.

To demonstrate this, let's consider different rates of output in Figure 8.15. First, take any rate of output lower than Q_3. At all rates of output lower than Q_3, the price of the product exceeds LMC. As output expands, the marginal benefit from getting one more unit of the good is larger than the marginal cost to society of producing it. Expanding output, then, makes a positive contribution to the society's welfare. The additional benefit exceeds the additional cost, so social welfare increases. More resources should be allocated to producing the good.

On the other hand, any rate of output greater than Q_3 results in MC exceeding P. The additional cost of producing one more unit is larger than the extra benefit from getting one more unit for consumers. Consequently, at rates of output above Q_3, social welfare decreases. To increase social welfare requires reducing the rate of output and allocating fewer resources to its production. Therefore, social welfare is maximized at a rate of output of Q_3 at which $P = MC$. This represents efficiency in resource allocation.

The long-run equilibrium tendency of competitive markets is to produce exactly this result! Competitive markets tend to produce efficiency in resource allocation.

Zero economic profits, production at lowest AC, and efficiency in resource allocation are all theoretical results of competitive markets. These results are brought about by the pursuit of profit by firms within the market and by the force of competition itself—the free entry and exit of firms to and from the market and in competition with one another for consumers.

Notice that we have again been using the phrase *tends to* in our analysis of the long-run equilibrium for a competitive market. We have been constructing a model of competition, a theory about how competitive markets work. Given the assumptions that we have made and the concepts that we have defined, we have determined the equilibrium result for competition. This does not mean that such equilibrium exists all the time for every competitive market, or that there won't ever be any economic profits in competitive markets. What it does suggest, though, is that without disturbances (given our assumptions), there are some general tendencies in the operation of competition. The system tends toward equilibrium. And even if it is disturbed—for example, by a change in consumers' incomes or tastes and preferences, by a change in resource prices, or by technological advances—the model that we have developed will allow us to follow through the effects to determine what the new equilibrium will be. In fact, competition encourages adaptability and responsiveness to changes in consumers' behavior.

The "Invisible Hand" and Consumer Sovereignty

What does all this have to do with the "invisible hand" and consumer sovereignty? Remember, Adam Smith's notion of the invisible hand was that the market tends to promote social welfare. **Consumer sovereignty** means that the market follows the "dictates" of consumers, in terms of their tastes and preferences.

Markets and prices indicate to potential producers where profits can be made in the economy. If producers can produce a product at a lower average cost than the price at which they can sell it, then they can earn an economic profit. In addition, producers will attempt to maximize their profits. We can see immediately, then, that producers will probably try to lower their costs, because that increases their profits. Consumers also benefit from this because the price of the product will eventually be lowered due to the cost reduction.

The price reduction following a cost reduction may not be intuitively obvious, so let's examine this theoretical conclusion in more detail. Suppose we have a pizza producer with an MC and MR graph that looks like Figure 8.16. MC_1 represents the firm's costs, and MR is determined by the market price for pizza. This firm then discovers a new and cheaper method of making pizza. As a result, MC falls from MC_1 to MC_2 (each successive unit can now be brought to market for a lower marginal cost).

With the change in costs, the firm makes a new decision about the level of output to produce. Originally, profits were maximized at Q_1; with the new marginal cost curve, the profit-maximizing level of production increases to Q_2. (Since average costs also decrease, the firm also will make larger economic profits, since price is still the same and the firm is now producing more.) At first, the price stays the same; the firm is so small in relation to the market that the additional amount brought to market is not noticeable and has no effect on market price. However, the firm does have larger economic profits (the AC curve would also shift down).

FIGURE 8.16 Change in Costs

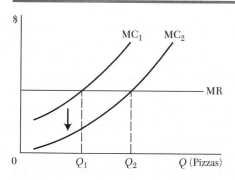

FIGURE 8.17 Change in Market Supply

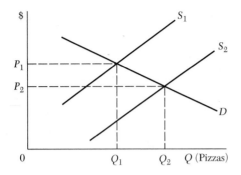

Eventually, other participants in the market notice the improvement this firm made and the extra profits it is earning as a result. These other suppliers begin to use the same or similar cost-reducing methods of production. In addition, the lure of economic profits (a return to the firm over and above opportunity costs) may induce some new firms to enter the market as sellers. (Again, a characteristic of a competitive market is free entry.) What does this do to market supply? It increases it; more pizza will be brought to market. Graphically, in Figure 8.17, we get a new supply curve, S_2; more pizzas are brought to market at each possible price.

Consequently (note we have assumed that D stays the same), the market price will decrease from P_1 to P_2 The cost reduction ended up also reducing the market price! This was brought about through the market and by competition. The market showed that profits could be made, and competition allowed new firms to enter the market. (Note that each producer's profits are lowered to a normal profit because of the price decrease, although each producer will still bring to market the amount that maximizes its profits. Show this using MR, MC, and AC curves.)

Although each producer (firm) is out to maximize its own profits, the market and competition have brought about a situation in which there is an incentive to lower costs and whereby prices are reduced when costs are. Consumers benefit as a result; they get their product for a lower price. The "invisible hand" lives (at least theoretically)! (Go back to Chapter 3 and review what Adam Smith had to say about the "invisible hand.")

In addition, the market responds to consumers' demands. This response is referred to as consumer sovereignty. For example, let's assume that consumers decide to eat out more and, as a result, more and more consumers want pizzas. This change in tastes and preferences (and the increase in the number of consumers in the market) tends to increase the demand for pizza. What effect do these changes have on the market price for pizza? Figure 8.18 shows that the price of pizza tends to increase. What assumption have we made in this illustration? (And is this a realistic assumption? What has happened in recent years in the pizza market on both sides of the market?)

With this increased price, the profits of pizza producers should increase, and they will produce increasing amounts of pizza. Consequently, the desires of

FIGURE 8.18 Change in Demand

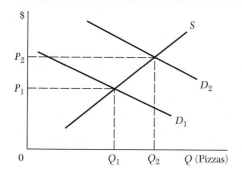

consumers show up in the market and indicate to producers what to do with respect to production. If consumers want more pizza, the market price will indicate that, and the producers will respond by producing more. This is consumer sovereignty. By extension, this process also has implications for resource use in the economy. When production of any good or service is expanded or contracted, the use of resources for that purpose will also increase or decrease.

17. Using Figure 8.18, if a reduction in resource costs allowed a pizzeria to lower its long-run average costs, show what the new long-run equilibrium would be for the firm and for the industry.

◆Conclusion

The competitive market model has some attractive results. Firms earn normal profits. There is a tendency toward an equilibrium at which entry and exit cease. The firms in the market produce a rate of output that minimizes average costs; there is efficiency in production. Output takes place at a rate that maximizes social welfare; when P = MC, *there is efficiency in resource allocation. If products are homogeneous, then there is no need to allocate resources to advertising. Competitive markets are adaptable. Whenever costs change, or supply and demand conditions change, firms register these changes and take them into account in making decisions in pursuit of maximizing their own profits. Since technological change can lower the firm's costs, the firm always has an incentive to try to lower costs, because profits will increase (at least for a while). Competitive markets register the desires of consumers, and those desires guide production and the allocation of resources. The "invisible hand" will bring about cost and price reductions for consumers.*

The competitive market system also links the interdependence of all economic agents in the whole economy. Markets for resources and products provide prices that people use as information in all of the decisions they make about what work they will do, what goods and services they will consume, what business activities they will pursue, and what resources firms will use. As a result of all of these decisions linked by the operation of markets, the scarce resources of society are allocated to meet the needs of people in that society. The competitive market system thus operates to solve the questions of what to produce, how to produce it, and how to distribute it. All of this occurs because of the existence of markets and of competition. Competition and markets guide resource allocation.

If every market were competitive (remember our definition of what that means), then the whole economy would be characterized by efficiency, the operation of the invisible hand, and consumer sovereignty in the long run. Stated differently, the competitive market model in theory produces efficiency and consumer sovereignty. As a result, there is little need for the government to be involved in the economy. If the competitive markets are allowed to operate freely and individuals are allowed to follow their maximizing opportunities, the best economic results are achieved. The competitive model, then, justifies a policy of laissez-faire.

Unfortunately, however, the model of competitive markets is not the same thing as the real economy. The theoretical results of the model of competition we have developed are certainly attractive. In fact, this theory is the basis of the argument that the capitalist system is the best economic system possible. It can be seen in innumerable advertisements from corporate America as well as the ideas of chambers of commerce and the National Association of Manufacturers. Many politicians use the argument to support these pro-business policies in their request for voter support and contributions. But the real world doesn't always duplicate theory, and the results of the model cannot uncritically or without qualification be ascribed to the real world.

It is important to recognize the various ways in which the operation of the real economy departs from the model of competitive markets. Most markets are not, in fact, competitive. For example, large chains such as Domino's and Pizza Hut frequently dominate local pizza markets. Corporations and labor unions, for example, have market power, can influence prices, and have been able to limit the effects of competition. Sometimes markets do not work at all; no one can make profits putting up street signs, for example. The calculation of profits by the firm does not take into account the external costs of production (such as pollution), an omission that can interfere with efficient resource allocation. The operation of resource markets can result in an unequal distribution of income. All of these results of the operation of the real economy limit the extent to which it produces the attractive results of the theoretical model of competition.

In the next four chapters, we will develop some economic theory that analyzes these problems in the operation of the real market system. We will also explore the response of public policy to the existence of these problems connected with the operation of the economy.

Review Questions

1. How accurate is this competitive model with respect to the current U.S. economy? Are its conclusions generally applicable to our economy? Why or why not?

2. Why are profits maximized when MR = MC? Can you explain this logically?

3. Do you think firms really do try to maximize their profits? Do they have other goals? Which are most important?

4. Give some examples of the law of diminishing returns in production. Specify which resources are variable and which ones are fixed.

5. Explain why economic profits cease to exist in competition in the long run (as a tendency). What is the implication of this? Why do firms stay in a market in which there are no economic profits?

6. In Table 8.4, show what happens if the price of pizza increases to $18. Fill in new TR, MR, and Profit columns. What rate of output will the firm choose? Why?

7. Illustrate (with cost and revenue curves) a firm making economic profits in the long run. Show the corresponding market-determined price.

   a. Assume (show) an increase in demand for the product (e.g., rugs imported from India). What happens to market price? What adjustments do the firms in the industry make?

   b. How will long-run equilibrium develop? Illustrate long-run equilibrium for the firm and the industry.

8. a. Complete the table below.

   b. How does the information in the table show the basic economic processes of specialization and diminishing returns?

   c. From the information in the table, plot a graph including AC, AVC, MC, and the firm's demand curve (the Price column). Show the equilibrium (profit maximizing) level of output and the firm's profit or loss on the graph.

      Note: You find a firm's profit maximizing (or loss minimizing) level of output by comparing marginal revenue (price) and marginal cost. A firm should produce a unit as long as marginal revenue is greater than or equal to marginal cost (i.e., a firm should produce every unit that makes the firm more money than it costs the firm). Also, assume that the firm must sell in whole units (e.g., the firm cannot produce at a quantity of 6.5; it must choose either 6 or 7).

   e. Suppose the market price falls to $130. Using the table below, with new Price and TR columns, find the firm's new profit maximizing (or loss minimizing) output (compare Price and Marginal Cost to find the profit maximizing quantity) and compute the firm's new level of profit or loss (compute total revenue and total cost using $130 as the price and using the new profit maximizing quantity). Assume that the firm must produce whole units.

Output (Q)	TVC	TFC	TC	AVC	AC	MC	MR = P	TR	TR – TC (Profit or Loss)
0	0	330					160		
1	100	300					160		
2	150	330					160		
3	180	330					160		
4	260	330					160		
5	380	330					160		
6	540	330					160		
7	764	330					160		
8	1,060	330					160		
9	1,464	330					160		

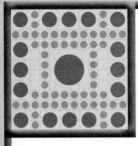

CHAPTER NINE

Noncompetitive Markets and Inefficiency

Introduction

According to neoclassical theory, competitive markets tend to produce consumer sovereignty, provide for the operation of the "invisible hand," and lead to economic efficiency. However, if markets are not competitive—that is, if they do not have all of the characteristics of competition—these results are less likely. In fact, in noncompetitive markets there is likely to be some amount of producer sovereignty, "monopoly" profits (i.e., economic profits not eliminated by competition), and inefficiency. In this chapter, we will define some other models of market structure and examine their results.

MODELS OF NONCOMPETITIVE MARKET STRUCTURES

The competitive market model gives us a standard by which to judge *real* economic markets and other models of market structures. Chapter 8 defined a competitive market and examined its workings and results. In what follows, we will examine some other market structures. With these additional models, we will have a more complete theoretical system for understanding the behavior of firms in the economy and for evaluating their performance.

Before we examine monopoly, oligopoly, and monopolistic competition, we must emphasize that the competitive model is a *model* and that it roughly describes about 10 percent or so of the total private economic activity in the United States. The best examples of competitive markets are those for raw agricultural products—which are homogeneous, are not advertised, have large numbers of buyers and sellers, and can be entered by almost anyone. In the rest of the economy, there are firms and markets from which some or all of these characteristics are missing. The industry may include very few firms, and they may have the market power to control their prices. Products may be differentiated rather than homogeneous. Advertising occurs beyond the simple level of informing consumers about products. And entry into markets isn't always "free" or easy.

THE BIG PICTURE

Imperfect Competition

Economists focus on four different market structures that characterize most firms and industries. In the last chapter, we studied perfect competition. In this chapter, we study the other three market structures: Monopoly, Oligopoly, and Monopolistic Competition. These market structures are all characterized as imperfectly competitive. Figure 9.BP.1 compares all four market structures according to the major characteristics that define them and highlights the key differences among them.

Monopolistically competitive markets are very competitive and easy to enter (and exit). Firms tend to be small, and because of the high degree of competition,

FIGURE 9.BP.1 Market Structures and Their Characteristics

Type of Market	Perfect Competition	Monopolistic Competition	Oligopoly	Monopoly
Ability to influence price	None	Some	Often	Always
Number of sellers	Many	Many	Few	One
Product differentiation	None	Some	None or Some	Unique product
Barriers to entry	None	Few	Substantial	Prohibitive
Can a firm earn long-run economic profit?	No	No	Yes	Yes
Do firms produce at minimum AC?	Yes	No	No	No
Examples	Agriculture, baby-sitting, wooden pallets, concrete	Retail trade such as gasoline stations, restaurants, haircutting establishments	Steel, automobiles, soft drinks, cereal, potato chips, gum	Campus bookstore, local utiliy company, Microsoft Windows (almost)

firms have limited control over their prices. Monopolistically Competitive markets also differ from Perfectly Competitive markets because each monopolistically competitive firm produces products that are slightly different from those produced by their competitors. For example, restaurants compete with each other for diners, but each restaurant has a unique cuisine and location. Product differentiation gives firms an incentive to advertise to attract consumers based on quality differences and to differentiate their product further by brand identification.

Oligopolistic markets differ from markets that are Perfectly Competitive or Monopolistically Competitive because of substantial barriers to entry. For example, in order to enter the automobile manufacturing industry, a firm must have a huge amount of financial capital to invest, access to a vast array of cutting edge technology, a large sales network, and access to a large market of consumers. In such an industry, it is more efficient for a firm to be large, and it is extremely difficult for a new firm to enter the market. Oligopolistic industries tend to be dominated by a few large firms, and oligopolistic firms often advertise heavily to differentiate themselves from competitors.

Monopolies are markets controlled by only one firm. Barriers to entry prevent competitors from entering. Monopolists thus control an entire market, and they are usually able to raise prices and may resist pressures to innovate due to their market domination. For these reasons, governments usually choose to regulate monopolies to prevent abuses. We will begin our more detailed examination of noncompetitive markets by examining monopolies.

The existence and emergence of noncompetitive market structures should not be too surprising. As we demonstrated in Chapter 8, the long-run tendency of competition is to eliminate economic profits. One effective way for a firm to ensure long-run economic profits is to limit the effects of competition, which may involve the elimination of competition.

MONOPOLY

A **monopoly** market structure is one in which there is only one seller of a good or service. The firm is the entire industry. Some monopolies have developed because of the large initial investment required, and only one firm occupies the market. Some monopolies have been established and protected by governments. Many monopolies are legalized because of the confusion that competition would create. At the same time, their prices are usually regulated by public authority. The characteristics of monopoly markets include the following:

❖ There is one seller of a good or service in a particular market.
❖ The product is unique, and there are no close substitutes; buyers must buy the good or service from the monopolist.

- The monopoly has **market power,** meaning it can exercise control over the price of the good or service, since it supplies the total quantity. (In contrast, for the competitive firm, price is determined by the market; the competitor has no influence on the price of its product.)
- Monopolies usually exist because there are absolute **barriers to entry** into the market; no other firm can supply the product because of legal, technological, or geographical factors limiting provision of the good or service.
- The monopoly may or may not advertise.

Examples of legal monopolies are local gas, electric, telephone, cable, and water companies. Professional sports teams in the United States have regional monopolies. As a result of a contract with the National Science Foundation, Network Solutions, Inc., once had a virtual monopoly on the business of assigning Internet addresses. F. M. Scherer, an industrial economist, has estimated that about 6 to 7 percent of private economic output originates in monopolies.

The theoretical results of monopoly markets are that producers tend to restrict output and charge higher prices than they could if there were competition in the market for that monopoly's product. As a result, monopoly markets are less beneficial to consumers, who would prefer to have more of the product at a lower price. Monopolies also interfere with efficient resource allocation. Monopoly power allows a firm to remain immune from competition and to retain monopoly profits. (For these reasons, most monopolies in the United States are regulated.) Monopoly, thus, is less desirable than competition.

Short-Run Equilibrium for the Monopolist

We can demonstrate that monopolies generate an outcome less efficient than competitive markets using a theoretical model of a monopolist operating in the short run. The monopolist faces the entire demand curve for a product, since there are no competitors. Thus, to sell more, the monopolist must lower price. Or if the monopolist raises prices, less will be demanded. As a result, the monopolist's marginal revenue curve will be below the demand curve. Since price must be lowered to sell more, the marginal addition to revenue will always be below the price. This is demonstrated in Table 9.1 and illustrated in Figure 9.1.* This information shows the revenue situation for a typical monopoly firm, with a downward-sloping demand curve and a marginal revenue curve below it. If we assume that the monopoly buys its resources in competitive markets, its MC and AC curves will look like the ones we derived in Chapter 8.

With the cost and revenue data in Table 9.1, we can determine the monopoly firm's profit-maximizing level of output. The same profit maximization rule

---

*Note: In order to simplify the presentation of this material, we are assuming in this chapter that firms sell their product in whole units and that quantity sold is not divisible (i.e., firms cannot produce and sell one-half a unit; they must sell a whole unit). Technically, if the demand curve is a continuous function and output is divisible, then the demand curve and marginal revenue curve would intersect at a quantity of 0 (at the Y axis) instead of at a quantity of 1.

Table 9.1 Monopoly Revenue and Cost

Output (Q)	Price (P)	Total Revenue (TR = P × Q)	Marginal Revenue $\left(MR = \dfrac{\Delta TR}{\Delta Q} \right)$	Total Cost (TC)	Marginal Cost $\left(MC = \dfrac{\Delta TC}{\Delta Q} \right)$	Average Cost $\left(AC = \dfrac{TC}{Q} \right)$
0	–	$ 0	–	$ 5	–	–
1	$10	10	$10	9	$4	$9.00
2	8	16	6	10	1	5.00
3	6	18	2	12	2	4.00
4	4	16	–2	16	4	4.00
5	2	10	–6	25	9	5.00
6	0	0	–10	39	14	6.50

still holds true: The monopolist should produce as long as marginal revenue is greater than or equal to marginal cost, and the equilibrium level of output will always occur where marginal revenue equals marginal cost (MR = MC). In Table 9.1, the profit-maximizing (equilibrium) level of output occurs at a quantity of 3 where MR = MC = $2 and where MR is less than P. At a quantity of 3, P = $6 and AC = $4. This means the firm is earning an average economic profit of $2 per unit over 3 units of output, for a total economic profit of $6.

The same information can be plotted on a graph. Figure 9.2 shows the demand, marginal revenue, average cost, and marginal cost curves for the monopolist from Table 9.1. Notice that the equilibrium level of output occurs at a quantity of 3, where MR = MC. At a quantity of 3, on the demand curve, we get the price of $6. On the AC curve at a quantity of 3, we get an average cost of $4. The difference between price and average cost is the average economic profit of $2. When we multiply this by the quantity of 3, we get total economic profits of $6, which is the area labeled "Economic profit" on the graph.

FIGURE 9.1 Monopoly Demand and Marginal Revenue

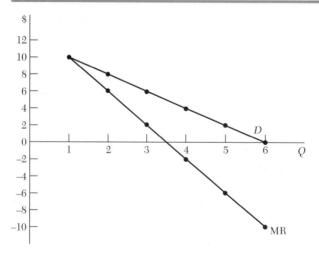

FIGURE 9.2 Monopoly Demand, Marginal Revenue, Average Cost, and Marginal Cost

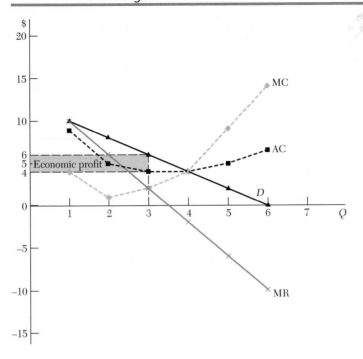

Figure 9.3 illustrates a typical equilibrium result for a monopoly firm. What level of output will the monopoly choose to produce? It will produce Q_m, where MC = MR, because that level of output maximizes its profits. It will charge a price of P_m for that amount of output, because that is the price consumers are willing to pay for that quantity. The monopoly is earning economic profits equal to the shaded area in Figure 9.3, since P is well above AC. And the

FIGURE 9.3 Equilibrium for the Monopoly Firm

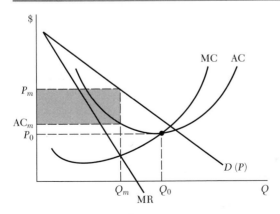

monopoly is producing at a rate of output that does not minimize average costs. (Q_0 is where AC is at a minimum, and P_0 is the minimum AC.)

This illustrates the short-run equilibrium for a monopoly. In this case, the monopolist earns economic profits. However, there is no assurance that even monopolies will always earn profits. If costs are too high or there is no demand for the monopolist's product, a monopoly could suffer economic losses. For example, for many years there was no major-league baseball team in Washington, D.C., because several teams had failed there.

Figure 9.4 shows the alternatives to earning economic profit. In Figure 9.4(a), the monopolist incurs an economic loss. The loss-minimizing level of output still occurs where $MR = MC$. But the price is less than average cost, so the firm is experiencing economic losses. If its profitability does not improve, this firm will eventually go out of business. Figure 9.4(b) shows a monopolist earning a normal profit. The profit-maximizing quantity is where $MR = MC$, and at this quantity, price is equal to average cost ($P = AC$). The price of the product is

FIGURE 9.4   A Monopolist Incurring an Economic Loss (a) and Earning a Normal Profit (b)

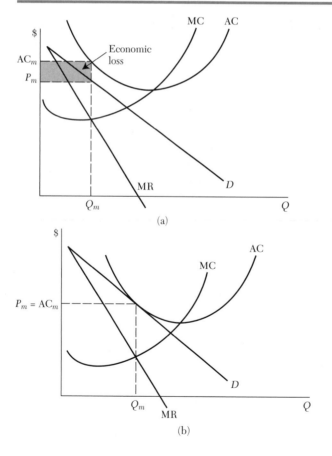

just covering all of the costs of production, including the opportunity costs, earning the firm a normal profit.

Long-Run Equilibrium for the Monopolist

What happens in a monopoly in the long run? Figure 9.5 shows the long-run cost and revenue curves for a monopolist (assuming economies and diseconomies of scale). In the long run, the monopolist has the option of building different-sized plants, and over time the demand curve for the product could change. Given the cost and revenue curves in Figure 9.5, the monopolist produces at Q_{mlr}, the rate of output at which Long Run Marginal Cost (LMC) = MR, and charges a price of P_{mlr} (from the demand curve). P is above AC, so the monopolist earns economic profits. The monopolist is in long-run equilibrium. But in a pure monopoly, even with economic profits, there is no entry into the market; this firm has a monopoly. Therefore, Figure 9.5 shows the long-run equilibrium result for a typical monopoly market. As long as cost and demand conditions remain the same, the monopoly firm produces Q_{mlr}, charges a price of P_{mlr}, and earns economic profits.

Monopoly and Inefficiency

What conclusions can we draw about the theoretical results of monopoly? Economic profits may exist, but because of the monopoly, no entry occurs to seek those extra returns above opportunity costs. The monopolist will not produce at a rate of output that minimizes average cost (Q_0); nothing forces the monopolist to produce at the most efficient rate of output. In monopoly, then, there tends to be **inefficiency in production** (at least from the perspective of the society, since output is not at minimum average cost). The monopoly firm produces the rate of output that maximizes its profits—that is its goal. Moreover, at that rate of output, price exceeds marginal cost. Society values an additional unit of the good or service more than the cost to produce an additional unit.

FIGURE 9.5 Long-Run Equilibrium for the Monopolist

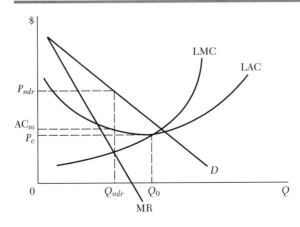

From a social perspective, then, it would be preferable if more resources were allocated to increased production of the commodity. Monopoly thus tends to result in **inefficiency in resource allocation** (since price does not equal marginal cost). Because monopolies usually get economic profits, some resources earn more than their opportunity cost. Finally, some monopolists may engage in advertising, which, although some may be informative or entertaining, requires the use of scarce resources. Consequently, we can see that the long-run equilibrium result of monopoly is significantly inferior to the long-run result of competition. The pursuit of profit, in this case, does not maximize social welfare.

We can also examine the theoretical results of monopoly by focusing on the market, shown in Figure 9.6. If there were competition in the market, new firms would enter, market supply would increase to S_c, and market price would decrease to P_c. (P_c in Figure 9.6 corresponds to P_c in Figure 9.5, the minimum long-run average cost.) Thus, monopoly restricts output, since $Q_m < Q_c$. And monopoly charges higher prices, since $P_m > P_c$. Finally, monopolies earn monopoly profits.

An important conclusion that can be drawn from the monopoly model is that the existence of market power (ability to control supply and price) tends to prevent consumer sovereignty, the attainment of economic efficiency, and the operation of the "invisible hand." The monopoly benefits at the expense of society. This says nothing at all about the further problem of the relationship of economic power to political power. Monopolies, through their economic power and resources, may come to wield undue political power. As a result, monopolies may also tend to disrupt democracy. In the words of Henry Simons, an economist who taught at the University of Chicago, "Political liberty can survive only within the effectively competitive economic system. Thus, the great enemy of democracy is monopoly." Any economic unit tending toward monopoly power, consequently, tends toward these same results.

As a result of these adverse effects of monopoly, the public sector has frequently been involved in regulating the operations and/or prices of monopolies. Many times, the public regulation is in return for governmental granting of a legal monopoly, as is the case with local water service. The usual goal of the public oversight is to increase monopoly output, lower monopoly prices, or

FIGURE 9.6 Monopoly—Output Restriction and High Price

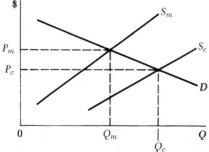

reduce monopoly profits. In these cases, due to economies of scale, it is more efficient to have only one firm supply the product (the firm is called a *natural monopoly*). But the firm must be regulated to prevent it from charging too high a price and producing too low a quantity. (In Chapter 12, we will explore the regulation of monopoly in more detail.)

Occasionally the profit motive itself can limit the existence of a continuing monopoly. For example, a monopoly might produce a good or service for which a close substitute could be developed. Or the monopolist might have some technical advantage that can be duplicated. The very existence of monopoly profits gives other firms an incentive to try to "break" the monopoly. For example, Xerox developed the technique and the machinery for instant photocopying. Given the lucrative results from the monopoly on the technique, other firms developed substitutes and entered the market. Similarly, Apple once had a virtual monopoly on personal computers, but that was "broken" by IBM and numerous IBM-clone producers. The extent to which other firms challenge a monopoly may reduce the adverse theoretical consequences of monopoly.

1. What is so bad about monopolies? What can we do if they exist? What are some possible benefits of monopolies?

2. Analyze Henry Simons's comment above. Do you agree or disagree? Why?

3. Local phone companies sometimes have a monopoly but advertise. Why?

4. In Figure 9.3, explain what would happen to the firm's profits if it produced at Q_0.

5. "Some resources [in monopoly] earn more than their opportunity costs." Can you think of any examples?

Disrupting Regulated Monopolies

An agreement with the National Science Foundation (NSF) originally granted Network Solutions, Inc., of Herndon, Virginia, a monopoly in assigning "domains," or addresses, for electronic mail and Web pages on the World Wide Web. The firm maintained a registry of addresses on the Internet, including those ending in .com for commercial enterprises, .edu for educational institutions, .gov for governmental entities, and .org for nonprofit organizations. Beginning in 1995, Network Solutions (later absorbed by VeriSign) was allowed to charge fees for registering and renewing addresses. The fees were regulated at first by the NSF, but Network Solutions earned substantial economic profits from 1996 to 1999. In 1999, the Department of Commerce and the Internet Corporation for Assigned Names and Numbers (ICANN) opened the market to other firms. Competition in the market for registering domain names caused the price of registering an address to drop from $9 to $6 within a year, and to $5 by 2004. Since 2004, prices have remained low, and in 2009 it cost as little as $6.99. In the process, Network Solutions' profits declined as well.

This example is part of a trend toward introducing competition to markets that were previously regulated monopolies. Long-distance phone service originating in the United States, for example, used to be a monopoly of AT&T, which owned all of the long-distance transmission lines for phone calls. Changes in technology—first fiber optics and satellite transmission and now cell phones—have made it possible to open this market to more competition. Hence, consumers have many options for long-distance telephone service—witness the TV ads and the telephone soliciting campaigns. Do you think that the end of AT&T's monopoly has been good for consumers?

By 2009, twelve states, including New York, Massachusetts, California, and Pennsylvania, were permitting similar experiments in the provision of electricity and natural gas. Traditionally, electric and gas utilities have been monopolies, usually regulated by state utility commissions. The state grants firms exclusive rights to sell electricity and gas, delivered by electric and gas distribution systems, and regulates their prices. The experiments involve letting consumers choose who their supplier will be from among several firms authorized by the state to supply electricity and gas. These firms all use the same distribution system, so there is no duplication of gas transmission pipes or electric lines all over the countryside, but they can offer different prices and services. In 2000–2001, an energy crisis in California caused rolling blackouts and soaring electric bills. Deregulation in California was accompanied by the manipulation of prices by a few large firms (including Enron) and an unstable supply of electricity, rather than low prices, substantial competition, and efficiency.

Nor has the experience been much better in other states. A study by Michigan State University economist Ken Rose found that between 2002 and 2006 average electricity prices rose by 26 percent in regulated states and by 36 percent in deregulated states where rate caps expired. Rose and other industry experts note that the wholesale electricity market is dominated by a few large firms. In markets with too little competition, deregulation gives large firms greater control of the market, which enables them to raise prices. Although electricity prices have fallen slightly in a few of the deregulated states, deregulation has yet to have the positive effects of greater competition, lower prices, and more innovation that government officials hoped for.

MONOPOLISTIC COMPETITION AND OLIGOPOLY

The other two major models of market structure that economists have developed to approximate economic reality are monopolistic competition and oligopoly. Around 80 percent of private economic production comes from firms with monopolistic competition or oligopoly elements. In *Economics and the Public Purpose*, Harvard economist John Kenneth Galbraith estimated that about 50 percent of private production originates in industries that are competitive or monopolistically competitive, and the remainder comes from firms that are monopolies or oligopolies.

Monopolistic Competition

The model of **monopolistic competition,** developed in the 1930s by E. H. Chamberlin and Joan Robinson, is used to describe industries that are close to competitive but have some elements of monopoly. Monopolistic competition has the following major characteristics:

* There are large numbers of buyers and sellers in the market. The firms are all relatively small with respect to the total size of the industry.
* The products are *differentiated*, or distinguished from competitors' offerings by quality and design differences, advertising, and psychological appeal. The products are close substitutes for one another, but each firm tries to create a "monopoly" for its product. A strong stimulus for this behavior is the tendency toward the elimination of profits in competitive industries with homogeneous products.
* Firms have limited control over the prices of their products. Although the firms are small in relation to the market, they sell a differentiated product. Some consumers are loyal to the unique brands of individual firms, even though there are close substitutes. This "monopoly" element gives firms some control over prices.
* Entry into the market is relatively easy, although the costs of differentiation (e.g., for advertising) can be large. Since firms are small, relatively small initial investments make entry feasible.
* Unlike perfect competition, monopolistic competition has an abundance of advertising. The products are not homogeneous, and advertising exists to persuade consumers about the differences. (In 2007, U.S. businesses spent about $280 billion on advertising.)

Some examples of monopolistically competitive industries are retail sales in urban communities, fast-food establishments in any particular area, personal computer and printer stores, processed chicken for retail sales, and clothing.

6. Review the characteristics of monopolistic competition. Does the market for a college education in the United States demonstrate any of these characteristics? How closely does it match the market described above?

Short-Run Equilibrium.   To develop the model of what happens in this type of market structure, let's begin by examining the firm's output and pricing decision in the short run. The objective of a firm in monopolistic competition is the same as that of any other firm, so this decision will be a function of the firm's cost and revenue conditions.

Because the firm has some control over the price it charges for its differentiated product, it will face a downward-sloping demand curve. It can raise its price and not lose all of its sales, which is what would happen in perfect competition because consumers would just go to the firm's competitors if it raises its prices. In monopolistic competition, some consumers will remain loyal to the firm's product and continue to purchase it even though the price has gone up and there are close substitutes. Even so, when the firm raises its price, it will

FIGURE 9.7 Demand and Marginal Revenue for a Firm in Monopolistic Competition

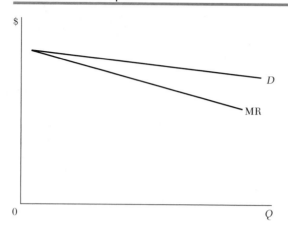

experience a decrease in its sales because there are substitutes. The firm can also lower its price and expect to get a significant increase in its sales because its loyal customers will consume more and because it may also attract business from its competitors (and because the demand for its product is elastic). In other words, the demand curve for a monopolistic competitor is downward sloping and relatively elastic. Because the demand curve is downward sloping, the firm's marginal revenue curve is also downward sloping and below the demand curve. Figure 9.7 shows typical demand and marginal revenue curves for a firm in monopolistic competition.

Since monopolistically competitive firms buy their resources in the same markets as do all other firms, their cost curves will be the same. The typical short-run average cost and marginal cost curves, reflecting the law of diminishing returns, are shown in Figure 9.8. Figure 9.8 gives us the information we need to describe the output and price decision of the monopolistic competitor

FIGURE 9.8 Short-Run Equilibrium for a Firm in Monopolistic Competition

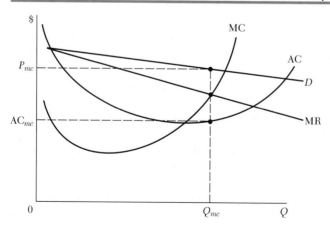

in the short run. Given these cost and demand conditions, the firm produces at Q_{mc}, since that is the rate of output at which MC = MR. The firm will charge a price of P_{mc}, since the market will be willing to pay that price for the amount produced and offered for sale. The firm is earning economic profits because P_{mc} is greater than AC_{mc}. This is the firm's short-run equilibrium position.

Long-Run Equilibrium. What happens in the long run in a monopolistically competitive industry if a firm is earning economic profits? In Figure 9.9(a), with demand curve D_1, the firm is earning economic profits. It can charge a price greater than its average costs ($P > AC$). In Figure 9.9(b), with demand curve D_1, the firm will produce quantity Q_1 where MR_1 is equal to long-run marginal cost (LMC). Since entry is relatively easy, other firms will enter the market in search of returns above opportunity costs. The entry of new firms means new competitors, and this will tend to reduce the sales of every firm already in the industry. This will have the effect of shifting every firm's individual demand curve to the left. After entry occurs, the demand curve in Figure 9.9(a) shifts from D_1 to D_2. In Figure 9.9(b), when the demand curve shifts from D_1 to D_2, the MR curve also shifts from MR_1 to MR_2 (when the price falls for each quantity, the marginal revenue for each quantity also falls). With a new MR curve, we have a new profit-maximizing equilibrium. The new equilibrium quantity is Q_2, which is directly below where MR_2 is equal to LMC. The firm now charges a lower price, P_2, because of the additional competition it faces.

Even after the demand curve has shifted from D_1 to D_2 however, the firm is still earning some economic profits (P_2 is still above the Long-Run Average Cost (LAC) curve). Since economic profits still exist, even more firms will enter, causing the demand curve in Figure 9.9(a) to shift from D_2 to D_3. Notice that D_3 is tangent to LAC. In Figure 9.9(c), with the new demand curve D_3, the firm produces Q_3, charges a price of P_3, and earns a normal profit ($P_3 =$ LAC_3) Since the firm no longer earns economic profits, new firms will stop entering the market, and the market will be in equilibrium. *The firm* also is in equilibrium, earning zero economic profits.

Monopolistic Competition and Efficiency. What are the implications of this long-run equilibrium result for monopolistic competition? $P = AC$, so there are no economic profits. However, P does not equal minimum average cost (at Q_0). The long-run equilibrium in monopolistic competition therefore does not result in efficiency of production. In addition, P exceeds MC, which means that there is inefficiency in resource allocation. From the perspective of social welfare, monopolistic competition results in an underallocation of resources to the production of its goods and services. Since one of the primary characteristics of this market structure is product differentiation, resources also are used in the advertising and promotion of one product over another. From the perspective of the society's use of resources, this represents a waste. Compared with the model of competition, then, monopolistic competition falls short of maximizing social welfare.

On the other hand, the functioning of monopolistically competitive markets has some positive attributes. Relatively free entry by firms when

FIGURE 9.9 Long-Run Equilibrium in Monopolistic Competition

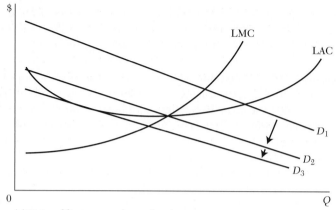

(a) Entry of firms causes demand to decrease.

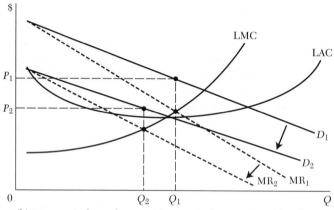

(b) Decrease in demand causes a decrease in the quantity produced and a decrease in price.

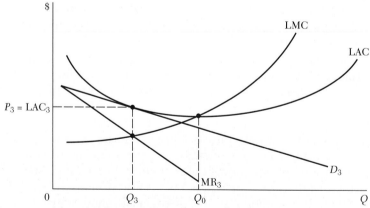

(c) Another decrease in demand causes another decrease in quantity and price until the firm reaches long-run equilibrium.

economic profits exist promotes adaptability; resources are reallocated in response to market conditions. Entry also puts downward pressure on prices, as it does in competitive markets. Product differentiation contributes to one of the wonders of the U.S. economy—variety and choice. When efforts to differentiate products lead to quality improvements, consumers benefit, and firms must be sensitive to consumers' desires. There is also a possibility, however, that product differentiation may not lead to real improvements or that too much choice will only confuse consumers' informed decisions. Finally, in monopolistic competition, entry and limited competition do force firms to produce as efficiently as possible. If firms do not match the costs of other firms, they are in danger of being eliminated from the market by economic losses.

Given the tendency of monopolistic competition to eliminate economic profits in the long run, occasionally the firms in such an industry will engage in efforts to prevent the disappearance of long-run economic profits. A favorite tactic is to stay ahead of the effects of entry by continued differentiation and advertising. By improving the quality, design, or even advertising of a product, a firm may be able to continue earning economic profits in the long run. In addition, monopolistically competitive firms might be able to get legislative protection that controls the entry of firms into the industry. For example, beauty parlors and barber shops must have licenses from the state in order to operate. The licensing requirement restricts entry into the market, and it preserves some economic profits for existing firms.

7. In Figure 9.9(c), show and explain what would happen if the demand for the firm's product (and its close substitutes) decreased (e.g., from a change in consumers' tastes and preferences).

8. In Figure 9.9(c), show and explain what would happen if the costs of production decreased as a result of a technological breakthrough.

9. For the long-run equilibrium result of monopolistic competition, show the effect of an improvement in quality, design, or advertising on the part of one firm attempting to maintain long-run economic profits.

10. Why is the market for processed chicken sold in grocery stores an example of monopolistic competition?

Monopolistic Competition in Fast Foods

It used to offer hamburgers, french fries, milk shakes, and soft drinks—and that was it. Now you can get all of that plus breakfasts, chicken nuggets, salad bars, stuffed potatoes, and more—including occasional "new" products. The fast-food industry in the United States is a good example of a monopolistically competitive industry.

Although McDonald's, Burger King, and Wendy's account for about two-thirds of

Lunch in a familiar setting.

(© Mary Kate Denny/PhotoEdit)

the national hamburger fast-food market, the market is broader than that. The fast-food market consists of hamburger, pizza, chicken, taco, sandwich, and other establishments. And, while McDonald's and other big players dominate the national markets for fast foods, area markets experience stiffer competition, with local and regional firms competing for customers' stomachs and dollars. Also, the fast-food firms must compete in the broader category of commercial dining, a $491 billion industry in 2007.

The market itself has expanded tremendously in the post–World War II period, with mobility and changing lifestyles. The late Ray Kroc took over two hamburger stands run by the McDonald brothers in 1955, and McDonald's hasn't stopped expanding since then. There are now more than 31,000 McDonald's establishments—less than half in the United States and the rest all over the world. Burger King has more than 11,500 outlets.

What characteristics of monopolistic competition are demonstrated by the fast-food industry? Regional markets have a large number of competitors, and entry is relatively easy. You don't have to rival the size or sophistication of McDonald's in order to start a hamburger or pizza joint. The rate of failure also is high, with thousands of restaurants going bankrupt every year. There is obvious and substantial product differentiation. Pizza is not chicken, and hamburgers are not salad. Some hamburgers are frozen, and some aren't. Some are fried, while others are grilled. French fries are notoriously nonstandardized. You can't get a hot dog everywhere. Pizza comes in many styles and qualities. The decors of different places distinguish them from one another. Quality is an issue among the various choices. And, recently, the fast-food industry has become concerned about its junk-food image. Some firms have begun to offer more nutritional and low-fat food items. Finally, since McDonald's first started advertising in 1966, television advertising has become a necessary aspect of the competition for the national fast-food industry. The name of the game is diversification, differentiation, aggressive advertising and marketing, and broad appeal.

Oligopoly

An **oligopoly** is an industry dominated by a few large firms. They are not like small competitive firms, but they are also not monopolists. There is great variety in oligopolistic industries, so economists have developed a number of different models of oligopoly to describe their behavior and results. Oligopoly has the following major characteristics:

❖ A few firms produce most of the output in an industry. These firms are thus usually large with respect to the market, and dominate its activities. Examples include automobiles, computers, steel, aluminum, cigarettes, and chewing gum. In some cases, there may be fewer than ten firms in the entire industry. In others, there may be hundreds of companies, but four or five firms dominate.

❖ The product of an oligopoly may be homogeneous or differentiated. If it is a consumer good, it is usually differentiated to gain consumers' attention and loyalty (e.g., automobiles). And, if it is a raw material sold to other firms, it is usually homogeneous (e.g., steel, copper, or aluminum).

❖ There may be technological reasons for domination of an industry by a few firms. Large-scale operations may enjoy lower costs. Economies of scale may allow only a few firms to constitute the entire industry, given the size of the market. Firms may also have grown large due to mergers. As a result, entry into such markets is difficult. Because of the substantial initial investment, a firm must be large to enter.

❖ The firms in an oligopolistic industry are *interdependent;* their pricing and output decisions affect the other firms in the industry. Each firm must pay close attention to the actions of its rivals. This creates a constant possibility for **price wars** (aggressive price cutting to increase sales) among oligopolists or collusion to avoid those price wars. It can also lead to price leadership or a reluctance to alter price. Despite this interdependence, oligopoly firms do have some control over their prices.

❖ Oligopolies usually have a significant amount of nonprice competition, such as product differentiation and advertising.

Because oligopoly firms are independent, it is difficult to develop one model of what happens in an oligopolistic industry. Depending on how rivals react to price and output decisions, a variety of models are possible, including price wars, collusion, stable prices, and price leadership. We will briefly develop some of these models.

Figure 9.10 illustrates a general possibility for an oligopolist. Because the firm has some control over the price of its product, it has a downward-sloping demand curve and a marginal revenue curve that lies below it. Many oligopolies experience economies of scale. The long-run average cost curve in Figure 9.10 reflects economies of scale; the LAC curve declines over the entire market for this firm's product. The firm does not encounter diseconomies of scale, so there is no limit to the firm's expansion. Given these demand and cost conditions, the firm will pick Q_0 as the rate of output that maximizes its profits (since that is where LMC = MR). The price will come from the firm's demand curve, at P_{oc}. At this price-output combination, the

FIGURE 9.10 Oligopoly Pricing and Output with Economies of Scale

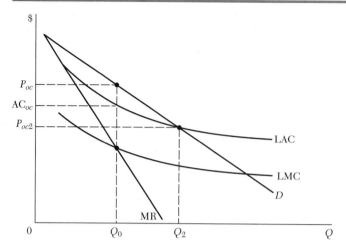

firm earns economic profits, because P is above AC. Since entry is very difficult in oligopoly, these long-run profits are relatively secure.

Price Wars. In oligopoly, however, there is always a possibility of price cutting by rivals. Other firms might try to steal away customers by lowering their prices; this action could spark retaliation. Theoretically, firms could lower prices all the way down to P_{oc2} before encountering losses. As prices decreased, the oligopolists' profits would shrink.

Collusion. In response to a threat of price wars and the possibility of losing all of their economic profits, oligopolists might collude to avoid price competition among themselves. **Collusion,** or agreements to avoid competition and/or to set prices, is illegal in the United States. However, light bulb manufacturers, paperboard companies, and others have been found guilty of price fixing. And oligopolists might avoid price wars through indirect ways of setting prices, such as trade associations, industry meetings, governmental standardization of technical materials, or informal tacit agreements. Given the illustration in Figure 9.10, the firms could simply attempt to set prices as close to P_{oc} as possible. This would maximize their economic profits.

In some international markets, **cartels** are legal and may set prices for their products. A cartel is an organization of producers designed to limit or eliminate competition among its members. One example of a cartel is the Organization of Petroleum Exporting Countries. OPEC consists of eleven oil-producing countries that operate government-owned petroleum industries and sell oil in international markets. OPEC functions as a cartel that sets production quotas and prices for its members. The intention of the cartel is to control the world's supply of oil, avoid price wars among the members, and, consequently, maximize members' joint profits. The members of OPEC in the 1970s and early 1980s dominated the international oil market, and they used this position and their cooperation to control the international price of oil. Later, with the development of more non-OPEC oil sources (e.g., Mexico and Great Britain), OPEC's ability to maintain high prices diminished for a time. But as we have seen, oil prices increased again from 2000–2004 and from 2007–2008, primarily because OPEC countries agreed to reduce production.

In essence, a cartel can accomplish a result similar to that of monopoly. For example, Figure 9.11 shows the combined cost and revenue conditions for a cartel as a whole. The cartel decides to produce a combined output of Q_{oc} and to charge a price of P_{oc}. As is the case in monopoly, output is restricted, and the price is higher than it would be if there were competition. Economic profits exist for the cartel as a whole. The members of the cartel then agree among themselves how to split up the production goal and profits based on their different cost functions, reserves, and negotiating skills. In a market without collusion, the price could fall as low as P_2 if firms were actively competing with each other.

Whether collusion is formal, as in a cartel, or informal, its members often have difficulty maintaining it, even though the reward for doing so is the avoidance of price wars and the accumulation of continued long-run economic profits. If the cartel consists of a large number of countries or firms, it has more difficulty reaching and maintaining agreement on production quotas and price levels. If the products of the cartel are differentiated (e.g., by quality of oil), the cartel has more difficulty establishing consistent price schedules for the varieties of the commodity. If the members of a cartel have different cost conditions in their productive operations, they will have more difficulty agreeing on price levels. Those with relatively high costs will want higher prices, or they will experience lower profits. In the same way, the size of the firm or country in the market will influence its bargaining power in the cartel—that is, different members will have different negotiating power when it comes to

FIGURE 9.11 A Cartel to Ensure Oligopoly Profits

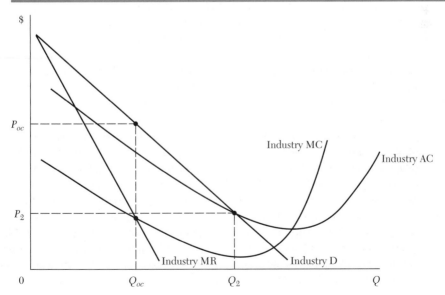

setting production quotas and prices. Additionally, an external force, e.g., the United States, might attempt to disrupt the unity among cartel members through its pursuit of foreign policy objectives.

The characteristic of cartels that most demonstrates their fragility is their tendency toward price breaks. Given the controlled price of the cartel, which will always be higher than the price that might prevail without the cartel, there is a temptation for an individual member to offer lower prices to attract its rivals' customers. If it can get away with secret price breaks, it can increase its sales and profits. The problem is that once one member does so, others are likely to do the same, and then the cartel is faced with a price war and reduced profits for all its members. The other difficulty with cartels in the United States is that they are illegal. For all these reasons, collusive behavior and its ultimate form—the cartel—are difficult to establish and maintain.

11. When OPEC raised its oil prices in 1974, many U.S. analysts argued that OPEC would have difficulty maintaining its cartel. With the passage of time, they suggested, oil prices would fall as OPEC dissolved. What was the basis of this argument? Why did OPEC lose its ability to control world oil prices? To what extent has it regained that ability?

Game Theory

Economists call the study of the strategic behavior of competing, interdependent firms (e.g., oligopolies) game theory. To illustrate, let's construct a model of the behavior of OPEC countries just discussed. First, we will simplify our analysis so that we consider the actions of only two countries, Saudi Arabia and Kuwait, and two strategies, cutting oil production or increasing oil production. Assume for now that Saudi Arabia and Kuwait produce all of the oil output of OPEC. If Saudi Arabia and Kuwait collude and cut production (remember, collusion is the primary purpose of forming a cartel), the world price of oil will increase dramatically, and both countries will make substantial economic profits on their oil, say, $200 billion each.

But suppose Kuwait needs extra oil revenues in order to finance a war with Iraq (exactly what happened in the 1990s). To gain additional oil revenues, Kuwait will have to increase production beyond the amount it agreed to produce. In other words Kuwait will have to renege on its agreement with Saudi Arabia. If Kuwait reneges on the agreement with Saudi Arabia, it can sell more oil at a slightly lower price and reap tremendous benefits. Countries all over the world will want to purchase Kuwaiti oil because it is virtually identical to Saudi oil but costs less. As a result, Kuwait will substantially increase its economic profits from $200 billion to $300 billion. Meanwhile, with Kuwait cutting prices, Saudi Arabia's oil will be more expensive, and few customers will buy Saudi oil. Saudi Arabia's economic profits from oil production therefore decline from $200 billion to $50 billion.

Will Saudi Arabia allow this situation to continue? Of course not. As soon as Saudi Arabia finds out that Kuwait is reneging on the OPEC agreement, it too will increase

FIGURE 9.12 Sample Payoff Matrix

		Kuwait's Strategies	
		Cut Production	**Increase Production**
Saudi Arabia's Strategies	**Cut Production**	Kuwait earns $200 billion. Saudi Arabia earns $200 billion.	Kuwait earns $300 billion. Saudi Arabia earns $50 billion.
	Increase Production	Kuwait earns $50 billion. Saudi Arabia earns $300 billion.	Kuwait earns $100 billion. Saudi Arabia earns $100 billion.

output and lower price. So both countries end up producing a greater quantity of oil at a lower price, which lowers the economic profits for both countries. (With an inelastic demand for oil, the price falls more than the quantity sold increases.) Both countries end up earning economic profits of $100 billion after the increase in production.

The same thing would happen if Saudi Arabia reneged on the agreement and produced more oil instead of Kuwait. In the short term, Saudi Arabia would earn $300 billion after reneging, and Kuwait would earn only $50 billion in economic profits. But in the long term, Kuwait would also increase production and lower prices. Again we end up with both countries earning $100 billion.

We can illustrate this example with the payoff matrix in Figure 9.12. The payoff matrix demonstrates that, if both countries cut production, they both earn $200 billion in profits, which is the largest amount of combined profits possible of any of the four possibilities. If either country reneges on the agreement to cut production, then the country that increases production will earn more economic profits while the other country earns less. But if both countries ultimately end up increasing production, they both end up earning less than they would have if they maintained their collusive agreement and kept production levels low.

How do Saudi Arabia, Kuwait, and other OPEC countries behave in the real world? As we have seen, in the 1970s, they stuck to their production cuts and made vast economic profits. In the 1980s, countries reneged on production agreements, and new competitors entered the oil market, causing oil prices to plummet. But from 1999 to 2008, OPEC again agreed to keep production levels low, and oil prices increased. Maintaining a collusive agreement is difficult, especially where the number of competitors is large. The fewer the competitors, the easier collusion is, but even then, collusion can be unstable.

Price Stability. Another tactic that oligopolistic industries use to avoid price wars involves simply keeping prices stable. If all of the firms in the industry maintain their prices over some period of time, they will avoid the tendency of interdependent firms to engage in self-destructive price competition.

Price Leadership. When oligopolists do change their prices occasionally, they may use one other tactic they have developed to avoid price wars. It is called **price leadership**—the practice of a single firm in an industry announcing a price change, which most if not all of the other firms follow. In some industries, the same firm is consistently the leader. In other industries, the leader may change; it may be one of the giants in the field, or it could be one of the smaller firms. The leader of changes in the *prime rate*, the rate that banks charge their best borrowers, is not always one of the big New York City banks. In addition to this form of price leadership, uniformity in prices that avoids the danger of price wars can also be achieved through the sharing of information in informal contacts (at lunch, golfing, etc.) among the members of firms in an industry or through more formal meetings in conferences and trade associations. The primary goal is the same, though: the protection of oligopoly profits.

Outcomes of Oligopoly.   What are the theoretical results of oligopoly? There is no one model of oligopoly, as we have seen. But, in general, difficulty in entering the market protects oligopolies from the results of competition. Oligopolies have market power over their output and prices, they tend to earn oligopoly profits, and they are somewhat insulated from the dictates of market forces. The force of competition does not require them to produce at the most efficient rate of output. And because they, like other noncompetitive firms, face a downward-sloping demand curve, P will always exceed MC; consequently, oligopolies result in inefficiency in resource allocation. Oligopolies that sell differentiated products also engage in advertising and use scarce resources to convince consumers that their products are better than those of their rivals. Because oligopolies do not face the competition of new entrants into their markets and have market power, some critics suggest that such firms can resist technological change. For example, it might be possible for an automobile company to introduce production and product improvements that would benefit consumers, but because the firm has money tied up in current production techniques and product lines, it puts off introducing changes.

Large oligopolistic firms have enormous resources at their command. They have economic power over plant location, the pace of investment spending in the economy, and the advance of technology. This concentrated economic power can also be translated into concentrated political power, which can pose some difficulties for the operation of democratic institutions.

On the other hand, the defenders of oligopoly and large firms have argued that the pursuit of profit by such firms has spurred technological advancement and economies of scale in many oligopolistic industries. The history of some of the dominant heavy industries in the United States offers proof that economic concentration has accompanied increased output and efficiency. The steel and automobile industries pioneered large factories and the assembly line. The aircraft industry stimulated other industries and transportation in the post–World War II period. More recently, photocopying and computers have revolutionized information processing. With their economic profits, large firms can also afford to establish research and development labs to discover new processes and products. Finally, the persistence of large corporations may lend a certain stability to the operation of the entire economy. Without the rapid entry and exit of competitive markets, oligopolists can plan for the long run and serve the society.

12. Can you think of examples of firms in oligopolistic industries that have not been very sensitive to the wishes of U.S. consumers in recent years? Do you think the increase of global competition, even among very large firms, minimizes the market power of oligopolies (i.e., forces them to be more attentive to change and the preferences of consumers)?

13. Do you think large corporations tend to provide a certain dynamism to the economy, or do you think they obstruct progress?

THE IMPORTANCE OF NONCOMPETITIVE MARKETS IN THE U.S. ECONOMY

The models of noncompetitive market structures are helpful in building a theory of how the U.S. economy operates, because product differentiation and economic concentration are present throughout the real economy. The following data on economic concentration demonstrate the pervasiveness and importance of concentrated markets in the United States.

For the last century, about a third of U.S. manufacturing industries have been dominated by oligopolies, while most of the rest are classified as monopolistic competition. Tables 9.2 and 9.3 show the concentration ratios in

Table 9.2 Share of Value of Shipments Accounted for by the Largest Companies in Selected High-Concentration Manufacturing Industries, 2002

Industry	Four Largest Firms	Eight Largest Firms	Twenty Largest Firms	Total Number of Firms
Cane sugar refining	99%	100%	100%	13
Cigarettes	95	99	100	15
Household laundry equipment	93	100	100	13
Breweries	91	94	96	349
Aircraft	81	94	98	184
Men's and boys' trousers, slacks, and jeans	80	87	94	92
Breakfast cereal	78	91	99	45
Tires	77	93	98	112
Automobiles	76	94	99	164
Computers (electronic)	76	89	95	465
Pens and mechanical pencils	74	81	92	87
Cookies and crackers	67	79	91	296
Women's handbags and purses	67	86	93	99
Dry pasta (spaghetti, etc.)	65	80	88	185
Dog and cat food	64	81	93	176
Creamery butter	58	80	99	33
Semiconductors and related devices	57	64	78	904
Explosives	54	78	93	57
Coffee and tea	51	63	82	258

Source: U.S. Census Bureau, 2002 Economic Census.

Table 9.3 Share of Value of Shipments Accounted for by the Largest Companies in Selected Low-Concentration Manufacturing Industries, 2002

Industry	Four Largest Firms	Eight Largest Firms	Twenty Largest Firms	Total Number of Firms
Ice cream and frozen desserts	48	64	82	364
Audio and video equipment	43	59	78	544
Milk (fluid)	43	54	69	315
Bread and bakery products	39	50	60	9,515
Men's and boys' shirts (except work shirts)	38	53	73	180
Cheese	35	50	73	366
Sporting and athletic goods	23	32	46	2,157
Women's and girls' dresses	22	32	49	525
Jewelry (except costume)	22	31	45	1,923
Women's and girls' blouses and shirts	21	33	57	352
Furniture and related products	11	18	29	21,523
Ready-mix concrete	11	17	28	2,614
Wood containers and pallets	7	10	17	2,792
Signs	5	9	16	6,125

Source: U.S. Census Bureau, 2002 Economic Census.

various U.S. manufacturing industries. The **concentration ratio** is the percentage of total sales in an industry that is accounted for by a specific number of firms. Usually, if the ratio is above 50 percent for the four largest firms in an industry, we say that the industry is an oligopoly. By this standard, all the industries in Table 9.2 are oligopolistic. If one firm had 100 percent of a national market, it would be a monopoly. If the eight largest firms had less than 10 percent of industry sales and there were many other firms in the industry, we would say that the market was close to being competitive. Table 9.3 lists some markets with relatively low concentration ratios; these have some of the characteristics of monopolistic competition. The only manufacturing industries that approach the characteristics of perfect competition in Table 9.3 are signs and wood containers and pallets. In these industries, the product is virtually homogeneous, there are many competitors, and there is easy entry. These two tables demonstrate the importance of concentration in the U.S. economy. Most of the leading sectors of the U.S. economy are heavily concentrated—hence the relevance of models of noncompetitive market structures.

Table 9.4 shows measures of economic concentration in nonmanufacturing industries, including retail trade, information, finance and insurance, health care and social assistance, and accommodation and food services. As you study this table, notice the wide variations in concentration ratios. Some industries are concentrated, while others are not. For example, warehouse clubs and supercenters are heavily concentrated, while the market for florists approaches perfect competition; credit-card issuing is an oligopolistic market, while commercial banking is closer to monopolistic competition; hospitals are oligopolies, while doctors' offices are competitive; and coffee shops are some-what concentrated, while bars and restaurants are not. We have already ex-plored some of the conditions (such as costs of entry) that may influence the degree of concentration. In the next section, we will consider additional factors.

14. Examine Tables 9.2, 9.3, and 9.4. Are you surprised by the high or low concen-tration ratios of any industries in these tables? Do the industries exhibit the characteristics of monopolistic competition and/or oligopoly? Explain.

15. Can you offer explanations for why some of the industries in Table 9.2 (and 9.4) are oligopolies, and why some of the industries in Table 9.3 (and 9.4) are less concentrated?

Table 9.4 Concentration Ratios for Selected Nonmanufacturing Industries

	Four Largest Firms	Eight Largest Firms	Twenty Largest Firms
Retail Trade			
Warehouse clubs and supercenters	92.1%	99.7%	100.0%
Athletic-footwear stores	70.8	79.3	84.6
Department stores	66.4	88.8	99.4
Supermarkets and grocery stores	32.5	45.6	57.3
Clothing stores	28.0	37.8	52.0
Convenience stores	15.5	18.4	21.6
Gasoline stations	8.2	14.7	25.2
Florists	1.7	2.4	3.9
Information			
Cable programming	63.9%	77.7%	91.9%
Cellular and wireless telecommunications	63.4	83.9	91.9
News syndicates	57.7	70.0	83.7
Television broadcasting	50.2	60.9	76.0
Finance and Insurance			
Credit-card issuing	75.8%	87.0%	96.6%
Investment banking and securities dealing	41.3	66.6	83.4
Commercial banking	29.5	41.9	56.3
Insurance agencies and brokerages	9.9	13.4	18.2
Health Care and Social Assistance			
HMO medical centers	90.5%	97.8%	100.0%
General medical and surgical hospitals	71.8	83.7	92.2
Offices of physicians	3.4	4.3	6.2
Child day-care services	2.5	4.4	8.8
Accommodation and Food Services			
Coffee shops	–	66.2%	68.5%
Full-service restaurants	8.6	11.0	15.5
Drinking places (alcoholic beverages)	2.2	2.9	4.2

Source: U.S. Census Bureau, 2002 Economic Census.

The Importance of Noncompetitive Markets in the U.S. Economy **189**

SOURCES OF CONCENTRATION IN THE ECONOMY

Several factors have contributed to increasing concentration and centralization in the economy over the last century. First, legislation and government policy have promoted both competition and monopoly. Governments have granted legal monopolies. In addition, the government has provided support and assistance to several industries with a high degree of concentration—for example, railroads, airlines, defense, and automobiles. On the other hand, antitrust legislation and some regulatory legislation are designed to promote competition. The goal is to control the adverse results of market power by splitting up companies, preventing mergers, prosecuting price setting and other noncompetitive activities, and regulating monopolies. These laws are based on economic arguments; our theory has demonstrated that competitive markets tend to produce efficiency and consumer sovereignty, and that noncompetitive markets, with market power and economic concentration, do not operate as well. One could argue over how well the antitrust laws have been enforced and whether they have prevented the accumulation of economic power by many industries and large firms.

16. Articulate why the government ought to promote competition and prevent extreme economic concentration and market power.

Business policies and practices, including trusts, pools, holding companies, and mergers, also have tended to create monopolies and oligopolies. If competition tends to eliminate economic profits, then one way to ensure long-run profits is to eliminate competition. Many firms have amassed substantial economic power in their markets and in the economy at large. The elimination of cutthroat competition through bankruptcy, mergers, and so on has decreased the number of competitors in many industries. The auto industry comprised more than 100 companies in the late 1920s. Several merger waves in U.S. economic history have produced increased economic concentration. Corporate America experienced a wave of "unfriendly" mergers in the 1980s, in which a company was merged with another against its will. The merger continues to be a strategy of firms to increase market share and economic power.

Technology has developed in some industries to the extent that large-scale operations are necessary for efficiency. This trend promotes large firms and oligopoly. Technology allows some firms to take advantage of economies of scale and outpace their competitors, which then fall by the wayside. An argument in favor of oligopoly, in fact, is that a firm in this market can use some of its oligopoly profits to finance research to further advance technology (and presumably its own oligopoly power!).

Capitalism's economic freedom of enterprise is permissive of the growth of private corporations. With a motive of profit making and a generally laissez-faire attitude by government, the creation of economic power has been tolerated (and even lauded by some) in U.S. economic history.

◆ Conclusion

Whatever the reasons for noncompetitive markets, we can still conclude that they are theoretically inferior to competitive markets in terms of consumers' and society's preferences. Resources are allocated throughout the noncompetitive sectors of the U.S. economy, but noncompetitive markets and prices do not produce the ideals of the "invisible hand," consumer sovereignty, and efficiency, as do competitive markets (theoretically). Adam Smith, where are you, and what would you think?

In the next chapter, we will shift our attention to the operation of resource markets and examine the factors that influence resource prices. One important result of resource markets is that they determine the incomes of resource owners. We will also take a look at the distribution of income in the United States.

Review Questions

1. What are the theoretically adverse results of monopoly markets?

2. What benefits might be derived from oligopoly to offset its inefficiencies and higher prices? Can you give some examples?

3. Why do you think the automobile industry is not competitive, according to our model of competition? What evidence can you cite to show its noncompetitiveness and inefficiency?

4. Why is local water service usually a monopoly? What would happen if it weren't?

5. What would happen to the marijuana "industry" if it were legalized in the United States? What kind of market is it now?

6. If you were the adviser for an OPEC country that had relatively low levels of petroleum reserves, would you advise the setting of high or low prices? Why? What if you were advising a country with extensive reserves?

7. In 2009, the movie *Up* premiered. It was accompanied by a new line of toys. What kind of market is this? Can you think of other examples of this kind of phenomenon?

8. In each of the cases below, match the industry with the market structure (Perfect Competition, Monopoly, Monopolistic Competition, and Oligopoly) that best fits the industry's characteristics. Explain your answer.
   1. Textbooks for your courses that are not available online
   2. Informal baby-sitting services provided by teenagers
   3. Personal computer manufacturing
   4. Legal services (Lawyers)

9. Draw a graph of a Monopolistically Competitive firm earning an economic profit. Include demand, marginal revenue, average total cost, and marginal cost on your graph, and show the profit maximizing price and quantity. Assuming that the cost curves are long-run cost curves, show what will happen to the firm in the long run. Explain carefully.

10. Explain why oligopolists have an incentive to collude or form a cartel. Also, explain why oligopolists in a collusive arrangement might have an incentive to renege on such an agreement.

11. The table below shows cost and revenue data for a Monopoly. Complete the table. Determine the profit maximizing level of output, and compute economic profit or loss at this level of output.

Q	P	TR	MR	TC	MC
0	56			80	
1	54			100	
2	52			112	
3	50			120	
4	48			126	
5	46			134	
6	44			146	
7	42			164	
8	40			190	
9	38			226	
10	36			274	

CHAPTER TEN

Resource Markets and the Distribution of Income

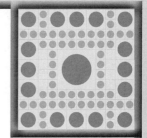

◆ Introduction

In the last two chapters, we developed models of competitive and noncompetitive markets for produced goods and services. As we mentioned previously, there are also markets for the resources used by firms in production. (It's a bit more complicated than that, since some firms produce raw materials used by other firms as factors of production.) The basic resources of the society are mental and/or physical labor, land and its raw materials, and capital.

Resource markets are important for two primary reasons. First of all, resource prices determine costs for firms. Second, since individuals own resources, the operation of resource markets forms the basis of the distribution of income in the society.

In this chapter, we will explore the operation and significance of resource markets—including the determination of resource prices and the allocation of resources throughout the economy. We will also examine the distribution of income in the United States and attempt to explain why it is relatively unequal.

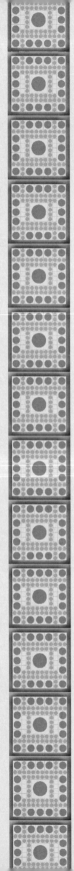

THE **BIG** PICTURE

Resource Markets

Resource markets differ from markets for consumer goods in several key ways.

❖ First, the demand for resources comes from firms producing goods and services, and the supply of resources comes from households. This is different from consumer goods markets where the demand for consumer goods comes from households and the supply of consumer goods comes from firms. In resource markets, consumers supply labor, land or capital, and firms purchase these resources.

❖ Second, the demand for resources is an indirect or *derived* demand: Firms demand resources only because there is a demand for their goods and services. Thus, changes in the demand for a product also cause changes in the demand for the resources used to produce that product.

❖ Third, the demand for a resource is affected by the productivity of that resource. If a resource becomes more productive, then it produces more value for the firm, and the firm will want more of it (assuming the firm can sell more units of output).

Briefly, let's explore some of the implications of the characteristics of resource markets, by focusing on the market for labor, a key resource for all firms.

❖ First, households supply labor and firms demand labor. When laborers decide to work more hours to buy more goods, this increases the supply of labor and puts downward pressure on the price of labor (the wage rate). When firms replace laborers with robots, this reduces the demand for labor and puts downward pressure on wages.

❖ Second, the demand for labor is tied to the demand for the firm's products. For example, when the automobile market is booming, automobile manufacturers hire (demand) more laborers, putting upward pressure on the wages of workers who build automobiles. When the demand for automobiles declines, the opposite occurs: The demand for automobile workers declines and there is downward pressure on wages.

❖ Third, the demand for labor is directly affected by the productivity of labor. If laborers become more productive (due to better technology, or more skills and education), they increase the firm's output and lower the firm's average variable costs of production. Firms usually respond to such events by increasing the demand for labor because of the increased revenue from the additional productivity, which then causes upward pressure on wages.

Thus, in resource markets, the supply of a resource from households, the demand for the firm's products, and the productivity of the resource are major factors in determining the price of the resource and the quantity of the resource purchased in markets. We explore resource markets in more detail below.

THE ECONOMICS OF RESOURCE MARKETS

There are markets for all resources because they are productive; they are used to produce goods and services sold in markets. The demand for resources is thus a **derived demand**, meaning these resources are demanded for the production of the final product.

In the following discussion, for the sake of simplicity, we will concentrate on one resource to illustrate the general operation of resource markets. While we could develop models of the markets for raw materials, land, and capital, we will present a model of the market for unskilled labor as an example. It is one of the broadest of labor markets. The number of people who could work in a McDonald's restaurant or do unskilled work in a factory is about equal to the size of the labor force in the United States—now more than 153 million people. And there are many businesses that hire unskilled workers.

Like all markets, this one has a demand side and a supply side. Figure 10.1 illustrates the market for unskilled labor. On the supply side of the market, there is a positive relationship between wages offered and the amount of unskilled labor supplied by workers. The higher the wage, the greater the amount of labor supplied. On the demand side, there is an inverse relationship between wages and the amount of unskilled labor demanded by employers. The higher the wage, the lower the amount of unskilled labor that employers will want to use.

This market, with large numbers of suppliers and demanders, will determine an equilibrium wage (W_e) and quantity (Q_e) for unskilled workers. That wage influences a firm's potential costs and its decisions about how much of this resource to use (compared with other resources). The wage also determines the decisions that workers make about offering their labor to employers (or not) and influences their incomes.

In a general way, this model applies to other resource markets. To see how resource markets work, let's explore both sides of this market in a little more depth.

FIGURE 10.1 The Market for Unskilled Labor

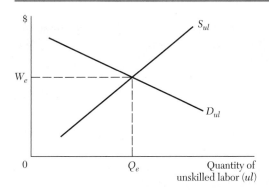

Demand for a Resource

The demand for any resource is derived from consumers' demands for goods and services and from producers' "demands" for profitable enterprise. But we can be much more specific about the nature of the firm's demand for a resource.

Remember, the firm's objective is to maximize profits, the difference between total revenues and total costs. Whenever a firm uses a resource, the firm's costs and revenues are both affected. If a firm uses one unit of a resource, how much will its costs increase? If a McDonald's restaurant hires one more unskilled worker to be a cook, its costs will go up by the worker's wage times the number of hours worked. The firm's costs increase by the price of the resource, and that price is determined in a market. The added cost of the resource, or its **marginal factor cost** (MFC), equals its price:

$$\text{MFC} = \text{price of one additional unit of the resource.}$$

In this case, we find the marginal factor cost of unskilled labor:

$$\text{MFC}_{ul} = P_{ul}$$

where P_{ul} is the price or wage of unskilled labor. Since the market is competitive (i.e., there are many laborers competing for jobs), the firm will be able to use as much unskilled labor as it wants at that price.

The second effect of using more of a resource is that it adds to the firm's revenues if demand is elastic. Why? Because using more resources adds to the firm's output, and that output presumably gets sold in a product market. In fact, the addition to the firm's revenues, which we will call the **marginal revenue product** (MRP) of unskilled labor, equals the **marginal physical product** of unskilled labor (MPP_{ul}) times the marginal revenue of the product (MR_x):

$$\text{MRP}_{ul} = \text{MPP}_{ul} \times \text{MR}_x$$

The marginal physical product is the extra output from adding one more unit of a variable resource. For unskilled labor, MPP_{ul} is the additional output from adding one additional worker to the production process (with other factors held constant). Table 10.1 shows the marginal physical product in terms

Table 10.1 Marginal Physical Product and Marginal Revenue Product of Unskilled Labor

Number Of Workers	Total Output of Big Macs	Marginal Physical Product of Unskilled Labor	Price of Big Macs	Marginal Revenue Product of Unskilled Labor
1	20	–	$4	–
2	27	7	4	$28
3	34	7	4	28
4	40	6	4	24
5	45	5	4	20
6	49	4	4	16
7	51	2	4	8
8	52	1	4	4

of the number of Big Macs produced in one hour as McDonald's hires additional cooks. For example, the MPP of the sixth worker is four Big Macs. Notice that the output from this variable resource follows the law of diminishing returns.

What happens to the extra output in the example? It will be sold for the market price of Big Macs. If we assume, for ease of analysis, that McDonald's is in a competitive market, then the marginal revenue of a Big Mac equals the price of a Big Mac (that is, they are both constant). For this example, we will assume that the price of a Big Mac is $4. The firm's additional revenue from hiring one more unit of unskilled labor—the marginal revenue product of unskilled labor, MRP_{ul}—comes from the extra output produced and then sold. In Table 10.1, MRP_{ul} is found by multiplying the marginal physical product of unskilled labor by the price (marginal revenue) of a Big Mac.

Given that using more of the resource has a marginal effect on the firm's costs and revenues, it should not surprise you that a firm maximizes its profits by choosing the amount of a resource for which the marginal contribution to the firm's revenues equals the marginal contribution to the firm's costs:

$$MFC_{ul} = MRP_{ul}$$

This is illustrated in Figure 10.2. Since MPP_{ul} is decreasing because of the law of diminishing returns and MR_x is constant if the firm sells its product in a competitive market, MRP_{ul} decreases as we add more unskilled labor (along the horizontal axis). MFC_{ul} is equal to the prevailing wage in the market for unskilled labor.

To maximize profits, this firm would use L_e of unskilled labor, since that is where $MFC_{ul} = MRP_{ul}$. If the firm uses less unskilled labor, the firm's revenues from using one more worker exceed the extra cost of using an additional unit (e.g., at L_1). Therefore, expanding the use of the resource would add to the firm's profits. At levels above L_e, the cost of adding the resource exceeds what it adds to the firm's revenues. If the firm uses unskilled labor beyond L_e, the firm's profits will decrease. (Notice that we are assuming the demand for the product

FIGURE 10.2 The Firm's Use of a Resource

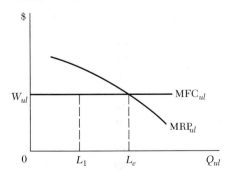

is constant; this is reflected in the marginal revenue the firm receives for selling additional units of output.)

1. Assume that the current wage for unskilled workers is $8 an hour and that the price of a Big Mac is $4. Given the information in Table 10.1, how many workers would McDonald's hire? Why?

Profit maximization leads a firm to choose a specific amount of a resource to use in its productive activities. In addition, the marginal revenue product curve in Figure 10.2 represents the firm's demand curve for this resource. Remember, a demand curve shows the amounts of a good or service that will be demanded at different possible prices. If the price of unskilled labor were lower, with everything else the same, the firm would hire additional workers; if the price were higher, the firm would hire fewer workers. The MRP_{ul} curve, then, gives us the firm's demand for unskilled labor.

The firm's demand for a resource is thus determined by the productivity of the resource, the importance of that resource in producing the good, and the price of the good itself.

2. Using Figure 10.2, explain why a firm would hire fewer workers if the price of the resource were higher.

3. Show what would happen to the demand for unskilled labor if there was an increase in the demand for Big Macs.

Supply of a Resource

As we pointed out earlier in this chapter, in general the amount supplied of a resource increases as its price increases. If the wage for unskilled work increased, for example, we would expect the amount of unskilled labor offered to increase. From the workers' perspective, the wage for labor indicates the opportunity cost of time. An increase in a wage or a salary makes time more valuable and, in most cases, encourages people to work more. From the perspective of an employer, the wage indicates the opportunity cost for the resource; it is what the firm must pay to get that resource to work for it. In a similar manner, buildings and land earn rent, raw materials have prices, capital or money earns interest, and professional workers get salaries.

The sensitivity of a resource to the price offered for its productive services varies over time. That is, the elasticity of supply of a resource can differ in the short run and long run. In the short run, the amount of a resource supplied depends on the mobility of the resource to different possible uses. For example, for unskilled workers, raising the wage at McDonald's could lead to a significant increase in the number of people willing to work there. (Remember, a supply curve is a hypothetical construction; it shows the amounts supplied at different possible prices.) Many individuals are available to work for the relatively low wages in fast foods and would be attracted by a higher wage. This means that the supply of unskilled labor is probably relatively elastic. On the other hand, if wages increased for computer programmers, some time is necessary for the quantity of programmers supplied in the United States to increase, because of the training necessary. For computer programmers, then, the supply is somewhat inelastic in the short run. For buildings and machinery, supply is relatively inelastic in the short run because time is required to construct them or to free existing ones for other uses.

In the short run, the supply of a resource can be elastic or inelastic, depending on the type of resource. Price increases (or decreases) will produce large or small responses in the quantity supplied, depending on the nature and qualities of the resource.

In the long run, the supply of most resources is more elastic. The long-run supply of any resource depends on decisions about the development of resources, which are in turn determined by expected rates of return. People decide to go to college depending on the expected payoff from graduating. That decision consequently influences the supply of professional employees. Decisions about graduate, law, or medical school involve the same calculation, which eventually affects the supply of PhDs, lawyers, and doctors.

These factors determine the supply curves for resources. And, as we suggested at the beginning of this chapter, the supply-and-demand conditions for resources, taken together, produce resource prices. Markets for resources establish resource prices.

What other factors influence resource prices? Legislation may affect the wage paid to certain types of workers, as in the case of the minimum wage. Licensing requirements affect the supply of hair stylists, real estate agents, and many professional workers. Unions can control the supply of certain types of workers through apprenticeship programs, seniority systems, and membership dues. Cartels and trade associations can influence some resource prices. Finally, the general state of the economy and the level of unemployment profoundly affect wages and salaries. The higher the level of unemployment, in general, the lower the wages of unskilled and semiskilled workers.

4. Why would higher rates of unemployment put downward pressure on wages?

5. Wages in Alaska are relatively high. Why would the elasticity of supply for labor partially explain this?

THE ECONOMICS OF THE MINIMUM WAGE

Our assumption that the wage for unskilled labor is determined by the supply and demand for that resource (see Figure 10.1) is a slight oversimplification. In fact, whenever interstate commerce is involved, employers must pay workers at least the minimum wage. This wage is mandated by congressional legislation, and it has progressively increased throughout the post–World War II period. During the 1980s it was constant at $3.35 an hour. In 1990, it increased to $3.80, and in 1991 it increased to $4.20. By early 1996, the minimum wage had increased a nickel, to $4.25, and it increased to $5.15 in mid-1996. In early

Table 10.2   The Real Value of the Minimum Wage, 1950–2009

Year	Minimum Wage in Current Dollars	Price Level (2009 = 1.00)	Minimum Wage in 2009 Dollars
1940	$0.30	0.07	$4.56
1950	$0.75	0.11	$6.62
1960	$1.00	0.14	$7.18
1968	$1.60	0.16	$9.77
1970	$1.60	0.18	$8.77
1980	$3.10	0.39	$8.00
1990	$3.80	0.61	$6.18
2000	$5.15	0.81	$6.36
2005	$5.15	0.92	$5.61
2007	$5.85	0.98	$6.00
2008	$6.55	1.01	$6.47
2009	$7.25	1.00	$7.25

Source: Author's calculations from Bureau of Labor Statistics data.

2007 Congress passed legislation that increased the minimum wage to $7.25 over the following two years. (States may set their own minimum wage higher than this level.)

The fact that the minimum wage has increased seems to indicate that unskilled workers are earning more money today than they did in the past. However, when we consider the value of the minimum wage in real terms, or its actual purchasing power after inflation is taken into account, we see something quite different. The minimum wage in *real* terms is found by dividing the minimum wage rate in any year by the price level in that year. As Table 10.2 and Figure 10.3 show, in 1968 the minimum wage was only $1.60 per hour, but prices were also much lower in 1968 than they are today. In fact,

FIGURE 10.3   The Real Value of the Minimum Wage, 1940–2009

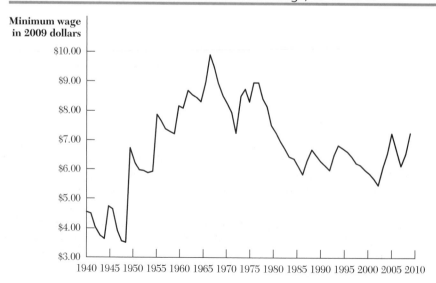

FIGURE 10.4 Effect of Minimum Wage Laws on Unskilled-Labor Market

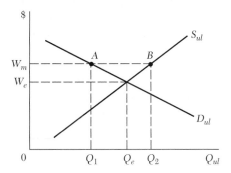

$1.60 an hour in 1968 would buy as many goods as $9.77 an hour in 2009. From the data we can see that the minimum wage in real terms (2009 dollars) has fallen considerably from its peak of $9.77 an hour in 1968 to $7.25 an hour in 2009, a decline of almost 26 percent. At $7.25 an hour, a full-time worker would earn only $14,500 before taxes, which is below the poverty line for a two-person family.

The intent of legislating a minimum wage is to require employers to pay a wage higher than the rate determined by the market for unskilled labor. It is meant to support the incomes of people who work in low-wage jobs, and it was motivated by a concern for fairness. The people who hold low-wage jobs usually have little experience or few skills. In other words, their marginal productivities are relatively low. Also, the products they produce may have low market values. Dishwashers get low wages; doctors, lawyers, and engineers earn much more. In addition, with any amount of unemployment, there is ample supply of unskilled workers.

These factors produce a market that can be illustrated with the supply and demand curves shown in Figure 10.4. The equilibrium wage would be at W_e, but legislation mandates a wage above that, at W_m.

What are the results of the minimum wage? At W_m, employers hire Q_1 of unskilled workers. But Q_2 workers are willing to work at W_m. Hence, there is a surplus of unskilled workers—unemployment of unskilled workers equal to AB. Those who have jobs have higher incomes than they would have at a wage of W_e. But Figure 10.4 shows that the minimum wage has increased unemployment among unskilled workers.

Some economists and politicians have argued that lowering the minimum wage would decrease unemployment. The Reagan administration several times suggested a lower minimum wage for teenage workers. Along with the increase in the minimum wage in 1990, Congress created a "training wage" for teenage workers for six months of initial employment. The basis of the argument lies in Figure 10.4. If the wage were reduced to W_e, there would be an increase in the amount of unskilled labor demanded and a decrease in the amount of unskilled labor supplied. At Q_e, an equilibrium amount would be supplied and demanded—no unemployment in this market! Employers would tend to use more unskilled workers.

But several critical questions can be raised about this analysis. Eight of every ten workers earning a minimum wage are adults age 20 or older. For households with a minimum-wage worker, these wages are a major source of income, representing on average 54 percent of the families' weekly income. Sixty percent of minimum-wage workers are women. Employers might replace older, higher-paid workers with younger, lower-paid workers, which would only shift the incidence of unemployment and would not necessarily reduce the overall amount of unemployment. And what about the difference between Q_2 and Q_e in terms of the amount of unskilled labor supplied? One effect of lowering the minimum wage would be that some teenagers would prefer to spend their summers doing something other than working for a "subminimum wage." Does that mean they are not unemployed?

In reality, raising the minimum wage usually does not create unemployment. To some extent, it may seem to exacerbate unemployment because it could reduce the amount of unskilled labor demanded and increase the amount supplied. But the reasons for unemployment among low-wage, inexperienced, and unskilled workers have more to do with the overall level of economic activity than with the minimum wage.

A number of recent studies indicate that moderate increases in the minimum wage have had *no effect* on the rate of unemployment. The implication is that firms already minimize the number of laborers they need to produce their good or service. Once the minimum wage is increased, firms must continue to hire the same number of unskilled workers in order to supply sufficient quantities to their customers. In other words, the demand curve for unskilled labor is extremely inelastic.

Increases in the minimum wage tend to result in greater worker productivity because workers are more satisfied with their jobs and less likely to change jobs (which reduces training costs and means that more experienced workers stay at their jobs). This offsets somewhat the increase in firms' costs associated with a higher minimum wage, although firms also might increase prices slightly due to higher wage costs.

Because the minimum wage in the late 1990s and early 2000s was very low (in terms of purchasing power) and moderate increases in the minimum wage have had no significant impact on unemployment levels, some economists and activists have called for a "living wage" to be paid to all employees. Paying a living wage would mean setting wages high enough that one full-time worker could support a family. The City of Baltimore passed the nation's first living-wage ordinance, increasing the minimum wage in Baltimore to $7.70 an hour by 1999, enough to support a single parent with one child above the poverty line. Since then, more than 140 cities and towns have enacted living wage laws, many establishing wage rates of more than $10 an hour. However, some economists oppose minimum-wage ordinances because, while small increases in the minimum wage may not affect employment significantly, large increases in the minimum wage could have a much greater effect on employment.

6. What are some arguments for increasing the minimum wage? What are some arguments against raising the minimum wage? Which arguments do you find most compelling?

7. Redraw the graph in Figure 10.4 with a steeper (more inelastic) demand curve and a steeper (more inelastic) supply curve. How do these changes in the graph affect the arguments for and against a minimum wage?

THE DISTRIBUTION OF INCOME

In Chapter 3, we examined the division of income among the different factors of production in a private, market economy: Labor gets wages, landowners get rent, and owners of capital get profits. Adam Smith concluded that any conflict over the distribution of income would be resolved, to the benefit of all, by the operation of the competitive market system. However, there are some other ways of looking at income distribution. A society may decide that the way markets distribute income is undesirable.

In a market system, the distribution of income tends to be fairly unequal. Why? As we have suggested, income is derived from the participation of resources in productive activity. Income is paid to the factors of production for their involvement in the production process. The incomes that individuals earn therefore depend on the resources they own and the prices they command in resource markets. Some individuals have only their unskilled labor power to sell; consequently, they tend to have low incomes. People who possess professional skills, work experience, or capital resources will have higher incomes.

The Size Distribution of Income

What is the actual distribution of income in the United States? A convenient and instructive method of examining the distribution of income is to group people in families and then rank them by income. The result is called the size distribution of income. Table 10.3 shows the size distribution of income for the United States in 2007. It covers all before-tax income—including governmental transfer payments such as Social Security and veterans' benefits, unemployment compensation, and welfare—for the 77.9 million American families.

Table 10.3 Size Distribution of Family Income in the United States, 2007

Grouping	Percentage of Total Income	Income Range ($)
Poorest 20%	4.1	0–27,864
Second poorest 20%	9.7	27,865–49,510
Middle 20%	15.6	49,511–75,000
Second richest 20%	23.3	75,001–112,638
Richest 20%	47.3	Above 112,639
Top 5%	20.1	Above 197,216

Source: U.S. Census Bureau, Table F-1, F-2 (www.census.gov).

When all of the families are ranked by income from the highest to the lowest, we take each successive 20 percent (15.6 million) of the families, add up all of their incomes, and take that income as a percentage of total income. For example, the poorest 20 percent of the families received 4.1 percent of total family income in 2007, the middle 20 percent got 15.6 percent of total income, and the top 20 percent got 47.3 percent. If income were distributed equally, each 20 percent would get 20 percent of total income.

Table 10.3 also shows the ranges of income for each successive 20 percent. For example, families with incomes of $27,864 or less found themselves in the poorest 20 percent. If a family's income was $80,000 in 2007, the family was in the fourth quintile. To get into the top 5 percent of annual family income required at least $197,216.

These statistics indicate a relatively unequal distribution of income. The 15.6 million families at the bottom of the income ladder got only 4.1 percent of total family income, while the same number of families at the top got 47.3 percent. The top 5 percent (the 3.9 million families with incomes over $197,216) receives twenty-four times as much income on average as the poorest 20 percent.

Increasing Inequality in the United States. One of the most discussed trends in the United States recently has been increasing income inequality. As shown in Table 10.4, the share of national income going to the bottom 80 percent of U.S. families has decreased since 1980. Figure 10.5 illustrates that, since 1973, the incomes of the richest 20 percent of U.S. families have grown at a far faster rate than those of any other quintile. The incomes of the poorest 20 percent of U.S. families have barely increased.

Economists believe that a number of factors may be behind these trends. Globalization and the ability of U.S. firms to move their operations overseas has undermined the position of workers in the United States, who must now compete with workers around the world for jobs. Meanwhile, globalization has opened up unprecedented opportunities for those with skills and capital. Improvements in technology, especially computers, increase the demand for skilled workers who can use that technology, but new technologies often replace unskilled workers. The decline of unions in the United States (which we will study in Chapter 11) also may have played a role, since historically unions

Table 10.4 Changes in the U.S. Distribution of Income Since 1950

Year	Poorest 20%	2nd Poorest 20%	Middle 20%	2nd Richest 20%	Richest 20%	Richest 5%
1950	4.5	12.0	17.4	23.4	42.7	17.3
1960	4.8	12.2	17.8	24.0	41.3	15.9
1970	5.4	12.2	17.6	23.8	40.9	15.6
1980	5.3	11.6	17.6	24.4	41.1	14.6
1990	4.6	10.8	16.6	23.8	44.3	17.4
2000	4.3	9.8	15.4	22.7	47.7	21.1
2005	4.0	9.6	15.3	22.9	48.1	21.1
2007	4.1	9.7	15.6	23.3	47.3	20.1

Source: U.S. Census Bureau, Table F-2 (www.census.gov).

FIGURE 10.5 Real Family Income Growth by Quintile, 1947–2006

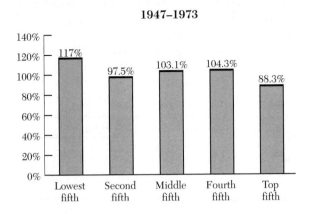

1947–1973

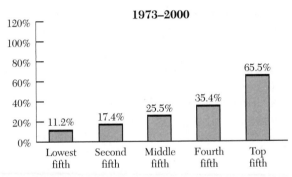

1973–2000

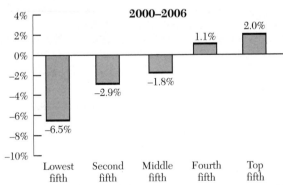

2000–2006

Source: Material taken from Lawrence Mishel, Jared Bernstein, Heidi Shierholz, *The State of Working America, 2008/2009.* Copyright 2009 by Cornell University. Used by permission of the publisher, Cornell University Press.

have represented the interests of less-skilled workers. Furthermore, as we will study in Chapter 12, from 1980 through the early 2000s the government scaled back programs that benefit poorer U.S. citizens while at the same time reducing taxes on the wealthiest citizens.

Many conservative economists are not troubled by increasing economic inequality. They generally believe that people are paid according to their productivity, and higher wages for those at the top are deserved because these people contribute more to the economy than those at the bottom. Also, they argue that increases in income for the wealthy do not harm people at the bottom, who are not worse off than they used to be. (For the bottom 80 percent, incomes have increased since 1973, albeit by much smaller amounts.) Most liberal economists disagree, arguing instead that inequality leads to a host of problems, including crime and the erosion of civil society. As one European official quipped during the economic summit of the G8 (The Group of Eight nations, including Canada, France, Germany, Italy, Japan, Russia, the United Kingdom, and the United States) in Denver in 1997, "Americans keep telling us how successful their system is—then they remind us not to stray too far from our hotel at night." Radical economists dispute the notion that wages are paid according to productivity. They believe that wages for the working class are determined by the degree of working-class power in the economy, and that globalization, technology, and the decline of unions have undermined workers' power while enhancing the power of capitalists. Both liberal and radical economists see economic inequality as a major problem facing the United States early in the twenty-first century.

International Size Distribution of Income. No society has a totally equal distribution of income. However, the degree of inequality varies among the nations. Table 10.5 shows that many of the Western and Northern European countries have distributions of income that are significantly less unequal than that in the United States. At the other extreme, many poor countries in Latin America, Africa, and Asia have very unequal income distributions.

Table 10.5 Income Distribution of Selected Developed and Developing Nations

Country	Year	Gini Coefficient	Poorest 20%	2nd Poorest 20%	Middle 20%	2nd Richest 20%	Richest 20%	Richest 10%
Namibia	1993	0.743	1.4	3.0	5.4	11.5	78.7	64.5
South Africa	2000	0.578	3.5	6.3	10.0	18.0	62.2	44.7
Brazil	2005	0.566	2.9	6.5	11.1	18.7	60.8	44.9
China	2004	0.469	4.3	8.5	13.7	21.7	51.9	34.9
Mexico	2004	0.461	4.3	8.3	12.6	19.7	55.1	39.4
United States	**2000**	**0.408**	**5.4**	**10.7**	**15.7**	**22.4**	**45.8**	**29.9**
India	2005	0.368	8.1	11.3	14.9	20.4	45.3	31.1
United Kingdom	1999	0.360	6.1	11.4	16.0	22.5	44.0	28.5
France	1995	0.327	7.2	12.6	17.2	22.8	40.2	25.1
Canada	2000	0.326	7.2	12.7	17.2	23.0	39.9	24.8
South Korea	1998	0.316	7.9	13.6	18.0	23.1	37.5	22.5
Netherlands	1999	0.309	7.6	13.2	17.2	23.3	38.7	22.9
Germany	2000	0.283	8.5	13.7	17.8	23.1	36.9	22.1
Czech Republic	1996	0.254	10.3	14.5	17.7	21.7	35.9	22.4
Sweden	2000	0.250	9.1	14.0	17.6	22.7	36.6	22.2
Japan	1993	0.249	10.6	14.2	17.6	22.0	35.7	21.7
Denmark	1997	0.247	8.3	14.7	18.2	22.9	35.8	21.3

Source: Data from World Development Indicators, 2008 by World Bank.

FIGURE 10.6 Lorenz Curve and Gini Coefficient Computation

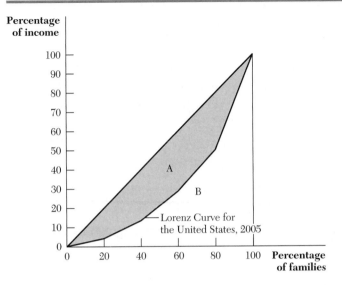

Measuring the Degree of Inequality.

A **Lorenz curve** illustrates the degree of inequality in the distribution of income. Figure 10.6 shows a Lorenz curve based on the distribution of income in the United States in 2005. The horizontal axis measures each 20 percent of the families, and the vertical axis measures their cumulative shares of total income. In 2005, the bottom 20 percent got 4.0 percent of total income, the lowest 40 percent got 13.6 percent, and so on. If income were distributed equally, we would get a straight Lorenz curve at a 45° angle. Instead we get the curved line in Figure 10.6.

To measure the degree of inequality, we can compare the area between the straight line and the Lorenz curve (area *A*) to the area below the 45° line (area *A* plus area *B*). The technical name for this ratio is the **Gini coefficient**. The lower this ratio, the lower the degree of inequality; the higher the ratio, the greater the degree of inequality. In 1970, the Gini coefficient for the distribution of family income in the United States was 0.353 and in 2005, it was 0.440. Figure 10.7 shows that as income inequality in the United States increased from 1970 to 2005, the Lorenz curve shifted out away from the line of perfect equality.

8. List five beneficial effects that might occur from a more equal income distribution. List five negative effects.

9. The Gini coefficient for the United States declined from 0.364 in 1960 to 0.353 in 1970, indicating that the distribution of income became more equal during the 1960s. However, as noted above, the Gini coefficient increased substantially to 0.440 in 2005, indicating greater inequality. What factors might explain those trends? What do you suppose has happened to the degree of inequality in income distribution since 2005? Explain.

FIGURE 10.7 U.S. Lorenz Curve, 1970 and 2005

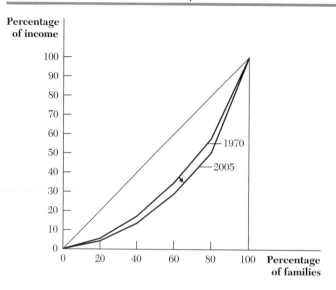

Why is income distributed so unequally in the United States? Fundamentally, it is a function of the ownership of resources and the prices of those resources. Individuals possess different labor and nonlabor resources, and different resources get different prices. Furthermore, the private market system relies on those very differences to allocate and motivate resources.

The Influence of Property

The U.S. economy is basically a capitalist system with private property as one of its most fundamental characteristics. The ownership of land, money, and capital resources is even more unequally distributed than income. Wealth statistics for the United States show that the poorest families have very little in financial and personal assets.

Table 10.6 indicates that the distribution of net worth (assets minus liabilities) in the United States is more unequal than the distribution of income. The median net worth of families in 2007 totaled $120,300, with the median for white families

Table 10.6 Distribution of Financial Wealth in the United States, 2007

Family Income	Median Net Worth
Poorest 20%	$ 8,100
Second poorest 20%	37,900
Middle 20%	88,100
Second richest 20%	204,900
Richest 20%	737,600
Richest 10%	1,119,000

Source: Federal Reserve, *Survey of Consumer Finances.*

Table 10.7 Distribution of Personal Wealth

Asset	Percent of Total Assets Held by Families		
	Bottom 80%	Wealthiest 20%	Wealthiest 5%
Total net worth	15.3	84.7	59.0
Stocks	9.4	90.6	65.3
Other financial assets	9.1	90.9	72.2
Housing equity	34.6	65.4	32.4

Source: Reprinted from Lawrence Mishel, Jared Bernstein and Sylvia Allegretto, *The State of Working America, 2006/2007.* Copyright 2007 by Cornell University. Used by permission of the publisher, Cornell University Press.

at $170,400 and the median for "nonwhite" and Hispanic families at $27,800. Table 10.7 shows the shares of different forms of personal wealth—corporate stocks and other financial assets—owned by the bottom 80 percent, the wealthiest 20 percent, and the wealthiest 5 percent of all families. For example, the wealthiest 5 percent of families held 59 percent of all net worth, 65 percent of all stocks, 32 percent of housing equity, and 72 percent of other (non-stock) financial assets, such as business equity. Other financial assets, including individual checking account deposits, automobiles, and owner-occupied primary residences, are more evenly distributed among the population. Also, as Figure 10.8 shows, the share of household wealth going to the top 1 percent of U.S. families increased steadily from 1976 through 1998, before declining with the recession of 2001.

FIGURE 10.8 Top 1% Share of Household Wealth, 1922–2004

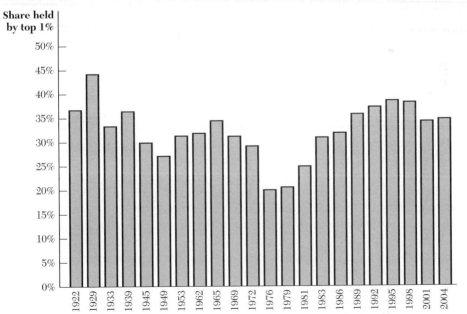

Source: Data from Edward Wolff, reported in Lawrence Mishel, Jared Bernstein, and Sylvia Allegretto, *The State of Working America,* various years. Copyright ©2007 by Cornell University. Used by permission of the publisher.

The unequal distribution of wealth contributes to the unequal distribution of income in the United States. Households with the highest 20 percent of income earn close to 70 percent of the income from owning and renting property. Households in the lowest quintile of the income distribution earn only about 1 percent of the property income generated.

 10. Do you or your family members own any income-producing wealth?

The Influence of Labor Incomes

Approximately 60 percent of personal income in the United States comes from wages and salaries. This percentage is higher for families in the middle of the income distribution. Like property income, income from mental and physical labor is unequally distributed. There are a variety of reasons for the differences in wages and salaries that individuals receive for their contributions to economic activity. The labor that people perform is not homogeneous, and there are differences in the jobs that people hold.

The capabilities, training, and intelligence of individuals have a great deal to do with their respective incomes. Consequently, the distribution of these attributes contributes to an unequal distribution of income. Some people are more productive in certain tasks than others are. For example, someone with physical strength probably can lift and stack more bales of hay in an hour than someone with less strength; someone with mathematical aptitude can balance a firm's books more quickly and accurately than someone without such aptitude. Some people, because of their concentration and motivation, produce more than other people in specific activities over a given period of time. In general, the greater an individual's productivity or contribution to economic output, the higher her or his wages will be.

Different people also have different skills. A large number of people are available for jobs that require minimal skills (e.g., clerks, sales personnel, custodians). As a result, they usually command low wages in labor markets. Others, who make up a smaller segment of the population, have professional skills (doctors, lawyers, economists) or possess unique qualities (athletes, entertainers) that earn them higher incomes. The more specialized the skill or the longer the period of training or education necessary to develop a skill, the higher the wages of people with those skills tend to be. For example, people with college educations, on the average, earn about 50 percent more per year than people with high school diplomas.

Age and experience also contribute to the unequal distribution of income. People who are older and have accumulated work experience tend to be paid more than younger, less experienced workers. An English professor who has taught for twenty years in a university earns more than a colleague who has taught for only two years.

Individuals also have different attitudes and preferences about work and income. Some people have a strong preference for work over leisure. Some people have very strong desires to earn high incomes. In fact, capitalism relies on monetary incentives for productive activity, so it has developed a hierarchy of jobs with different levels of pay. People are motivated to work hard in order to move up the job ladder and to get higher incomes.

Racial and gender differences also have an impact on the unequal distribution of income. As we shall see in some detail in the next section, white males in the United States tend to earn higher incomes than nonwhite males, and males tend to earn more than females.

In addition, differences in the kinds of jobs that people perform contribute to inequality in income distribution. The type of work performed and the conditions surrounding it influence compensation. Dangerous or unpleasant work (e.g., coal mining or garbage collection) is often rewarded with premium wages. Some people, on the other hand, may be willing to give up higher wages in return for significant control over the work that they do. Teachers or people who work for small businesses tend to be paid less than people whose work is more directly controlled by supervisors or institutional demands. The organizational structure of employment also influences wages and salaries. People who work for large corporations tend to earn more. Workers who are members of labor unions usually have higher wages than nonunion workers (see Chapter 11). Finally, the location of a job may influence an individual's remuneration. Someone who works in Idaho tends to be paid less than a person who works in Los Angeles with exactly the same job, skills, and experience.

Many factors account for the differences in the wages and salaries people earn for the work that they do, and these factors help to explain the inequality of income distribution in the United States. Most of the explanations just given imply that market forces play an important role in determining the different wages and salaries individuals receive in our society. The necessity of a medical education, for example, limits the supply of doctors and hence tends to increase their incomes. The widespread demand of moviegoers and video purchasers for films starring Will Smith, Denzel Washington, Brad Pitt, or Cameron Diaz accounts for their astronomical incomes.

On the other hand, many nonmarket conditions also influence people's wages and salaries. In the United States, women do most of the work related to household management and child care, and their work is often unpaid. People's class backgrounds have an impact on the development of their skills and attitudes toward work. Luck—being in the right place at the right time—can influence the jobs and incomes people have.

Income from wages and salaries is somewhat more equally distributed among households than overall income. However, labor incomes tend to be positively related to property income; that is, those with high labor incomes are also likely to have property income. This further contributes to the unequal distribution of income.

11. Why does class background play an important role in determining one's career and salary?

Transfer Income

As we noted earlier, in measuring income distribution, we calculate household income before taxes and include governmental transfer payments such as Social Security and veterans' benefits, unemployment compensation, and welfare payments. While property income is positively related to wage and salary income, transfer income largely goes to those at the lower end of the income distribution spectrum.

Some transfer payments are non-means-tested government programs, including such programs as Social Security, unemployment compensation, and some veterans' benefits. Other programs, including Temporary Assistance for Needy Families (TANF), Supplemental Security Income (SSI), and some veterans' benefits are means-tested, so recipients must meet minimum income and/or other requirements before the transfer is awarded. While the means-tested transfer payments are allocated to low-income individuals and families, Social Security—by far the largest transfer program—is not.

How much do transfer payments influence income distribution in the United States? Table 10.8 shows the impact on income distribution in 2005. The first column shows the distribution of income before any government taxes, transfers, or social insurance programs are included. Column 2 shows what the distribution looks like after including transfer payments such as Social Security. Column 3 shows the effect of including all taxes as well as noncash transfers such as food stamps and subsidized housing.

Without means- and non-means-tested transfer income, income is distributed even more unequally. Without taxes and transfers, the highest 20 percent of income earners would receive about 53.8 percent of the income, and the lowest 20 percent would receive 1.5 percent of the income. If we add back the non-means-tested transfers, the largest of which is Social Security, income distribution approaches the actual 2005 levels. This shows that non-means-tested transfers are a significant contribution to households in lower income brackets. Ultimately, tax and transfer programs do indeed change the distribution of income; in 2005, they accounted for a 6.5 percent decrease in the percentage of income received by those in the highest quintile and a 5.5 percent increase in the percentage received by the lowest two quintiles.

In the mid-1990s, many of the means-tested transfer programs came under attack in an attempt to significantly alter the U.S. welfare system. While we see

Table 10.8 Percentage of Aggregate Income Received by Income Quintiles, 2005

Quintile	Market Income	Post-Social Insurance Income	Total Disposable Income
Lowest 20%	1.5	3.2	4.4
Second 20%	7.3	8.6	9.9
Third 20%	14.0	14.3	15.3
Fourth 20%	23.4	22.8	23.1
Highest 20%	53.8	51.8	47.3

Source: U.S. Census Bureau, *The Effects of Government Taxes and Transfers on Income and Poverty: 2005,* Table 3.

that means-tested transfer programs do contribute income to families in the lower quintiles, they tend to be less significant contributions than non-means-tested programs. Means-tested transfers are often received by women who head low-income households where children are present.

The Influence of Race and Gender

Another characteristic of income inequality in the United States is that blacks earn lower incomes than whites and that women often earn lower incomes than men. The existence of racism and sexism in our society contributes to income inequality in a number of ways. Racism and sexism are systems of social, political, cultural, ideological, and economic domination, whereby one group has less power and control over decisions and resources than another group. Instances of both racism and sexism are manifested in numerous noneconomic ways in the day-to-day life of our society. In addition, racial minorities and women in the United States are systematically less well off in economic terms than white males.

The racial and ethnic composition of the U.S. population is quite diverse and will change dramatically in the near future. Approximately 81 percent of all Americans are white, while 13.5 percent are black, 7 percent are Asian or Native American, and 15 percent are of Hispanic origin (and may be of any race). Blacks, Native Americans, and those of Hispanic origin are more likely to be unemployed than whites. In 2007, the unemployment rate for all white persons over sixteen was 4.1 percent; for blacks, it was 8.3 percent; and for Hispanics, it was 5.6 percent. Members of racial minority populations in the United States are less likely to work in professional and white-collar occupations than whites and are more likely to work in the lower-paying blue-collar and service sector jobs. More than 63 percent of whites work in professional white-collar jobs, compared with only 53 percent of blacks and 39 percent of Hispanics. Correspondingly, blacks and Hispanics are much more likely to be in lower-paying blue-collar or service sector jobs. Table 10.9 illustrates that, in 2007, blacks represented 11.0

Table 10.9 Occupations by Gender and Race in the United States, 1983 and 2007

Occupation	% Female 1983	% Female 2007	% Black 1983	% Black 2007
Engineers	5.8	14.4	2.7	5.3
Lawyers	15.3	32.6	2.6	4.9
Physicians	15.8	30.0	3.2	5.6
College Teachers	36.3	46.2	4.4	5.6
All Occupations	**43.7**	**46.4**	**9.3**	**11.0**
High School Teachers	51.8	56.9	7.2	7.1
Textile Workers	82.1	81.6	18.7	12.8
Elementary School Teachers	83.3	80.9	11.1	10.3
Cashiers	84.4	75.6	10.1	17.4
Health Service Aides	89.2	88.3	23.5	33.6
Nurses	95.8	91.7	6.7	9.9
Secretaries	99.0	96.7	5.8	9.0

Source: Statistical Abstract of the United States, 2009.

Table 10.10 Median Black Family Income as a Percent of White Family Income

Year	Percentage
1955	55.0
1960	55.0
1965	55.0
1970	61.0
1975	61.5
1980	58.0
1985	58.0
1990	58.0
1995	60.9
2000	64.2
2005	60.0
2007	62.4

Source: U.S. Census Bureau, Historical Income Tables, Table F-5.

percent of the workforce in the United States but accounted for only 4.9 percent of lawyers and 5.6 percent of physicians. Hispanics, who represented 14.0 percent of all workers, made up only 4.3 percent of lawyers and 5.2 percent of physicians. Table 10.9 shows that blacks are more heavily concentrated in occupations such as health service aide or textile worker, which tend to be low-paying jobs. The data in Table 10.9 also show that some progress has occurred since 1983. For example, black representation in some professional white-collar jobs increased. But despite these increases, there is still substantial segregation along racial lines (and along gender lines, as we discuss below), with black workers overrepresented in low-wage service and blue-collar jobs.

As a consequence of these factors as well as outright racial discrimination, nonwhites in the United States, on the average, earn less than whites do. The data in Table 10.10 compare the median income of black families with that of white families for various years from 1955 to 2007. The median income of black families has consistently been significantly below that of white families. Some of the decline from 1975 to 1995 reflected an increase in black families headed by women, and some of it reflected the impact of the recessions of the early 1980s and 1990s. The boom from 1995 to 2000 helped to raise black incomes significantly, to 64 percent of white family incomes. However, the recession and sluggish growth of the early 2000s caused median black family incomes to fall relative to those of white families. In 2007, the median income of Hispanic families was 62 percent of the median income of white families, virtually the same as for black families.

The incidence of poverty also differs among racial groups. In 2006, the federal government classified 10.3 percent of whites in the United States as being in poverty. The figure for blacks was 24.3 percent; for Asians, 10.3 percent; and for Hispanics, 20.6 percent.

These data suggest that racial factors have an important impact on the unequal distribution of income in the United States. In a 1982 report to President Reagan, the U.S. Commission on Civil Rights concluded that, despite a generation of civil

Table 10.11 Median Female Worker Income as a
Percent of Median Male Worker Income

Year	Percentage
1960	60.7
1970	59.4
1980	60.2
1990	71.6
2000	73.3
2007	77.8

Source: U.S. Census Bureau, Historical Income Tables, Table P-38.

rights and affirmative-action legislation, discrimination persists "virtually everywhere, at every age level, at every educational level, at every skill level." This statement continues to reflect the reality of poverty data today.

Similarly, women are concentrated in low-paying jobs, tend to work for low-paying concerns, and are "systematically underpaid." A study in 1981, prepared for the Equal Employment Opportunity Commission by the National Research Council (a branch of the National Academy of Sciences) and focusing on the economic position of women, found that "despite the tremendous changes that have occurred in the labor market over the past 20 years, there has been no change in the relative earnings of men and women." When that study was published two decades ago (as the cartoon illustrates), women workers earned sixty cents for every dollar earned by a male worker. Today women earn more—moving the ratio of women's earnings to 78 cents for each dollar earned by male workers. Table 10.11 presents information on the incomes of year-round, full-time female workers compared with the incomes of year-round, full-time male workers from 1960 to 2007. According to Aaron Bernstein ("Women's Pay: Why the Gap Remains a Chasm," *Business Week*, June 14, 2004, p. 58), numerous studies indicate that outright discrimination against women probably accounts for about 10 percentage points of the pay gap. The rest has to do with other factors such as occupational segregation, described below.

The gap between what full-time, year-round male and female workers earn becomes more dramatic when we consider lifetime earnings. According to a

(© 2004 by Nicole Hollander.)

2004 study by economists Stephen J. Rose and Heidi I. Hartmann, "When you look at how much the typical woman actually earns over much of her career, the true figure is more like 44% of what the average man makes" (*ibid.*). The lower long-term income for women stems from the fact that many women take time off from work or work part-time because of family responsibilities. Taking a single year off from work reduces a woman's earnings by an average of 32 percent. Similarly, the hourly wages of part-time jobs average 47 percent less than the hourly wages of full-time jobs, and women more often fill these part-time jobs. As Bernstein (*ibid.*) observes, "speedier progress probably won't happen without more employers making work sites family-friendly and revamping jobs to accommodate women and men as they seek to balance work and family demands."

Over the past four decades, the participation of women in the paid labor force increased substantially. In 1960, about 40 percent of women over sixteen were in the labor force (working for wages or looking for paid work). By 1980, women's labor force participation rate was up to 52 percent. In 2000, it had increased further, to about 60 percent where it remained through 2008.

Men and women remain segregated into different occupations, and usually women are concentrated in the lower-paying occupations. To eliminate occupational segregation in the workplace, 55 percent of the nation's working men and women would have to switch jobs. Almost half of the nation's working women are in occupations that are at least 70 percent female, and one-fifth of working women are in occupations that are at least 90 percent female. As Table 10.9 indicates, women make up 46 percent of the workforce, but in 2007, women constituted 88 percent of health service aides, 92 percent of nurses, 97 percent of secretaries, 81 percent of elementary teachers, and 76 percent of cashiers. Men constituted 86 percent of engineers, 70 percent of doctors, 67 percent of lawyers, 54 percent of college teachers—and 83 percent of tenured and tenure-track economists at Ph.D.–granting institutions. In 2008, women constituted more than half of all management and professional personnel in *Fortune* 500 companies but only 3 percent of CEOs. For many jobs that require equal educational levels and comparable skills, women are systematically paid less than men. The influence of occupation-linked gender differences and sex discrimination thus also contributes to inequality in the distribution of income in the United States.

The high degree of occupational segregation in the United States was highlighted dramatically in the recession of 2007–2009. The industries with the largest job losses from 2007–2009 (including construction and manufacturing) were ones dominated by men, with the result being that 75 percent of the jobs lost were men's jobs. The unemployment rate for men surged to 10.5 percent in May of 2009 while the unemployment rate for women increased to 8 percent. The 2.5 percent-point gap between male and female unemployment was the highest on record. The decline in male employment made millions of women the primary and sometimes the sole breadwinner in the household, which was especially problematic because women tend to earn lower wages than men.

12. Why do economic differences based on race and gender persist in the United States?

13. In recent years, the civil rights and women's movements have challenged racism and sexism. These struggles have led to legislation regarding equal opportunity and affirmative-action programs, as well as to some court cases. In a case in Colorado in the late 1970s, a group of nurses sued the city and county of Denver for sex discrimination. Tree trimmers, sign painters, and repairmen were all paid more than nurses. U.S. District Judge Fred Winner decided against the nurses' claim and concluded, "This is a case pregnant with the possibility of disrupting the entire economic system of the United States of America....I'm not going to restructure the entire economy of the U.S." What was Winner worried about? In a 2004 class action lawsuit, Wal-Mart was accused of sex discrimination. Does the operation of the U.S. economy still require that women be paid less than men (even for comparable work)? Why or why not?

Income Distribution and Child Poverty

Despite the high levels of income on average, substantial numbers of children in the United States still live in poverty. In 2007, some 12.8 million children under the age of eighteen were poor. This represents 17.6 percent of all children. Table 10.12 shows the distribution of child poverty among white and black children under age 18. The risk of black child living in poverty is more than two times that of a white child.

Child poverty is dramatically higher in the United States than in other industrial nations. Figure 10.9 shows the results of a UNICEF study showing that the percentage of poor young people in the United States was the highest of all industrialized nations. The researchers could not fully determine the causes but attributed the possible causes to several factors, including the widest gap between the rich and poor among all of the other countries studied.

The past few decades have seen rapid growth in the number of children in poverty who live in homes where a single female is the head of the household. In 1960, 20 percent of all families below the poverty line were headed by women with no husband present. By 2006, this figure had increased to 53 percent. In 2006, 28.3 percent of all female-headed families with related children were living in poverty (36.6 percent for black families with female heads). The

Table 10.12 Percentage of Children Under Age 18 Below the Poverty Line

Year	All Races	White	African-American
1970	14.9	10.5	41.5
1980	17.9	13.4	42.1
1990	19.9	15.1	44.2
2000	15.6	12.4	30.9
2007	17.6	14.4	34.3

Source: U.S. Census Bureau, Historical Poverty Tables, Table 3.

FIGURE 10.9 Child Poverty in Selected Industrialized Countries, 2007

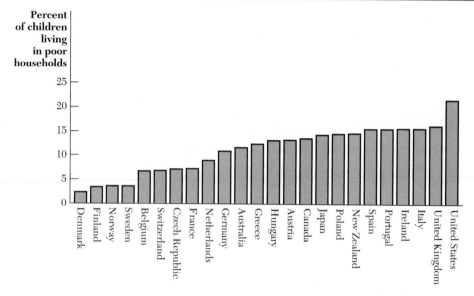

Source: UNICEF, Child Poverty in Rich Countries 2007.

lower incomes received by women have a detrimental effect on these families. Just over half of all poor children live in female-headed households. Single female heads of households in poverty are almost five times as likely as other women to experience unemployment and involuntary part-time work (working less than full time because full-time work is unavailable), and they are almost nine times as likely to have low earnings.

14. What impact does the federal government have on the distribution of income? How does it affect the distribution of income?

Conclusion

In this chapter we have briefly considered the operation of resource markets and the distribution of income in the United States. Resource markets, through the forces of supply and demand, determine the costs of production for firms and the incomes of households. Many factors account for the relatively unequal distribution of income in the United States. People own different resources, the jobs they do are different, and race and gender both influence wages and salaries. Unequal income distribution in turn affects the well-being of families and of the children who live in them.

Review Questions

1. Why is the market for unskilled labor relatively competitive?

2. What influences a firm's demand for a particular resource?

3. A firm tends to use the amount of a resource at which its MRP equals its MFC. Explain why.

4. In the September 17, 1984, issue of *Business Week*, there was an article titled, "The U.S. May Finally Have Too Many Lawyers." Using the economic analysis of resource markets, explain how a surplus of lawyers could happen.

5. Money is a resource; it can be used to finance capital projects. What influences the demand for credit? What influences the supply of credit? What is the price of credit?

6. Polls have reported that a significant majority of people in the United States believe that star athletes, entertainers, and corporate executives are overpaid. In 2008, Tiger Woods earned $128 million ($105 million coming from appearance fees and endorsements) for playing golf and Maria Sharapova earned $26 million for playing tennis. Will Smith had a total income of $80 million in 2005, Cameron Diaz made $50 million, and Oprah Winfrey earned $275 million. Lawrence Ellison, CEO of Oracle, made $193 million in the same year in salary, bonuses, and stock options; and the average CEO of a large company earned almost $13 million. What drives these high salaries? What are the economic effects?

7. Do you think the federal government should develop explicit policies to redistribute income to reduce the inequality of income distribution? Why or why not?

8. What are the sources of inequality in the distribution of income? Which ones might be reformed to reduce income inequality? What political and/or systemic limits are there on the redistribution of income?

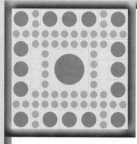

CHAPTER ELEVEN

Corporations and Labor Unions

Introduction

Now that we have examined the economic theory of competitive and noncompetitive market structures and explored the results of different types of firms, it is worthwhile to examine firms as they are encountered in the United States today. The corporation, as a productive unit in the U.S. economic system, has become a dominant institution. In Chapter 9 we saw statistics that showed the impact of the largest U.S. industrial corporations on several economic categories—manufacturing employment, manufacturing assets, and so on. U.S. corporations stand out for consideration in any discussion of production and resource allocation in the United States. Therefore, this chapter concentrates on U.S. corporations, describing what they are and the economic power they have and analyzing what that power implies.

In Chapter 10, we surveyed the operation of resource markets. We suggested that in addition to the forces of supply and demand, labor unions have an impact on labor markets. Labor unions serve as important institutions in the structure of the U.S. economy. The chapter concludes with a brief examination of the history and the effects of labor unions in the economy and how each of these relate to the behavior of corporations.

KINDS OF FIRMS

There are about 30 million businesses in the United States, and more than two-thirds are small businesses. Each year about 1 million new firms are started—many of which fail. Profit-driven businesses fit into one of three major classifications: (1) sole proprietorships, (2) partnerships, or (3) corporations.

A sole proprietorship has a single owner, who has the right to all profits and who bears the unlimited liability for the firm's debts. This kind of business is simple and easy to organize. The owner is in complete control but must be responsible for investing the capital necessary to establish the business. In

FIGURE 11.1 Number and Sales of Each Type of Firm, 2005

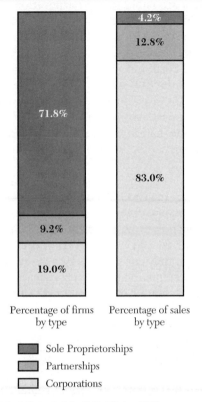

Percentage of firms by type

Percentage of sales by type

- ▇ Sole Proprietorships
- ▨ Partnerships
- ☐ Corporations

Source: U.S. Census Burea. *Statiatical Abstract of the United States,* 2009

2005, sole proprietorships represented 72 percent of all firms in the U.S. economy, yet because they are generally small, they represent only 4.2 percent of all business sales.

A partnership has two or more owners, who share the firm's profits and who bear unlimited liability for the firm's debts. It is often easier to raise the financial resources required to go into business. Partnerships are common in the fields of law, medicine, and accounting. This is the least common form of business organization, making up only 9.2 percent of all firms and accounting for around 13 percent of all business sales.

Figure 11.1 shows the types of business organization in terms of their number and sales.

THE CORPORATION

A corporation is a legal entity that engages in the provision of goods and services for the public. Corporations have legal authority to enter into contracts with other parties. The characteristic of corporations that distinguishes them from other productive units—such as partnerships or proprietorships—is that the individuals who own the corporations, the stockholders, have limited liability. Stockholders are liable to the corporation's creditors only to the extent of the value of their stock. They cannot be sued by creditors. This differs from other forms of business, in which the individuals who operate the business are personally liable to creditors.

This gives the corporation a great advantage in amassing financial resources to underwrite production. Issues of corporate stock can raise capital, and this capital base can be used to raise further capital through bank loans and so forth. Corporations have used this ability to form large productive operations—large plants, nationwide production and distribution facilities, and even worldwide networks. The technological advances of the Industrial Revolution spurred the development of larger and larger corporations, and modern technology continues to do the same. Through these legal advantages and historical developments, many U.S. corporations have grown to be quite large in terms of assets, profits, employees, and economic (and political) power.

How many corporations are there in the United States? And just how large have they grown? In 2005, there were more than 5.5 million corporations in the United States; they constituted 19 percent of businesses but had 83 percent of all business receipts. So corporations handle the vast majority of business transactions in the United States and most of the profits in the economy.

Which corporations are the biggest, in terms of receipts? The largest firms, less than 1 percent of the corporations in the United States, earned more than two-thirds of corporate receipts. Some U.S. corporations have grown very large indeed and dominate certain sectors of the economy. So what? The question is a good one, and the answers to it will differ among those of us in the United States who are affected by corporations. Some will argue that the large size and dominance of corporations are necessary to organize production, provide employment, and produce goods and services efficiently. Others might use economic arguments, pointing out that almost all large corporations are in concentrated industries and are thus theoretically likely to be deficient because of their economic power. (If the economy were perfectly competitive, there would be many more companies, and none would be so dominant.) Others might be less theoretical and say that corporations are only out to make a buck, have too much economic power, and sometimes do things to the detriment of society.

1. Do you think corporations are too big? Too powerful? Why or why not?

2. Why do you think corporations can become so big?

THE ROLE OF PROFITS IN THE CORPORATE SYSTEM

In 1974, the chairman of General Motors, Richard C. Gerstenberg, argued in the *New York Times*, "There is no conflict between corporate profits and social progress. Not one of our grand national goals can be accomplished unless business prospers. Profits fuel the growth of our nation, and our future depends on the profitability of free enterprise." Many would argue that he is correct. We depend on corporate success and profitability for jobs, products, economic growth, technological change, innovation, research and development, and so on. Corporations are in business to earn profits, and in the process of doing so, they provide jobs, investment, goods and services, and economic growth. If they are profitable, they pay taxes that help to finance social programs, and they often contribute to civic and educational endeavors.

However, over the years, a set of counterarguments has informed public sentiments about corporations and led to public opinion polls that at times have concluded that corporate profits are too high. The following list of complaints of corporate wrongdoing and questionable behavior is long and not exhaustive: pollution for decades without cost to the corporation; exploitation of workers (minorities, women, children, illegal immigrants, etc.); taking risks that threaten economic stability; corporate bribery of foreign and domestic officials; political contributions and lobbying to manipulate government policy; high oil company profits in the midst of gas shortages and rolling blackouts in California homes and industries; food additives that destroy our health; disproportionate economic and political power; misleading advertising; and so on—all to make a buck.

Corporations have tended to respond to these criticisms defensively. Gerstenberg charged, "Most [Americans] are ill-equipped to recognize the economics in these issues, much less to recommend the economic remedies. This lack of public understanding," he suggested, "seriously threatens the continuation of our competitive private enterprise system." With the bankruptcy of General Motors and Chrysler and the failure of Lehman Brothers and Bear Stearns in 2009, some have wondered if corporations fully understand the "competitive private enterprise system."

Businesspeople have had plenty of ideas about how to improve the image of business in the country. Small-business leaders suggested the importance of product quality and ethical standards. Many of the executives of the large companies emphasized communication and education, based on the conclusion that the low regard for business comes from a lack of knowledge. Suggested remedies ranged from getting the "media and press on the side of business," increasing corporate involvement in community issues, teaching more courses about free enterprise in high schools and colleges, and making advertising better. "We need to start in the elementary schools, with teachers and students both," said one respondent. An energy executive said, "We need to make people realize that it is business and not the government that provides over 100 million jobs in this country." And a transportation company official added, "We need to make it clear that business profits are not just arbitrarily squirreled away, but reinvested for the benefit of the company, its workers and the public. If we can get this across, we may be able to change the adverse to at least normal." The result has been a pro-business public relations campaign that has infused the media and our schools.

3. Do you have a positive, negative, neutral, indifferent, or balanced view of the corporation's role in the U.S. economy? Have recent events affected your views? Explain.

U.S. CORPORATIONS GO GLOBAL

No treatment of the modern U.S. corporation would be complete without reference to one of the dominant corporate trends in the post–World War II period—the increasing multinationalization of U.S. corporations. We explore this issue in more detail in Part 4 on international economics.

Multinational corporations have productive facilities, offices, and operations in more than one country. Some U.S. multinational companies date back to the end of the nineteenth century. At that time, international activities of most companies involved trade. In the post–World War II period, U.S. corporations began increasingly to invest in productive facilities in other parts of the world. At first, foreign direct investment was directed toward getting around tariff barriers and other impediments to U.S. exports. Much of this investment took place in Western Europe and Canada. In addition, multinationalization could also cut transportation costs for international markets, take advantage of various tax incentives offered by many countries, and cut production costs with cheaper foreign labor. In the 1950s and 1960s, much of this investment by U.S. corporations took place in the underdeveloped countries of Latin America, Asia, and Africa.

In the 1970s the pace of U.S. multinational investment in the rest of the world slowed down somewhat for a variety of reasons. The dollar lost value during the 1970s, making foreign investment more expensive for U.S. corporations. Many developing nations had become more critical about unconditional multinational investment in their countries. Political instability and the expropriation of corporate assets in some developing countries also led to a deterioration of the investment climate, as perceived by U.S. multinationals.

The primary motivation for multinationalization, as with virtually all corporate activity, has always been profitability—from cutting transportation and labor costs to access to raw materials and foreign markets. As the potential profitability of foreign investment was reduced or threatened, U.S. corporations slowed down their overseas expansion. In the 1980s this trend was reversed, and U.S. multinational investments began to increase again. In 2007, the book value of U.S. direct investment in foreign countries was $5,148 billion. The income from these and other foreign investments amounted to more than $348 billion in 2007.

The existence and operation of U.S. multinationals raise a multitude of issues. In some sense, multinational facilities are of crucial importance to the corporations in their search for profits. In 2007, 18.5 percent of the profits of U.S. corporations came from their overseas operations. As far back as 1976, about one-third of U.S. imports came from majority-owned U.S. corporations in foreign countries. Without these international activities, many U.S. corporations would be less profitable than they are.

On the other hand, multinational corporate activities place constraints on the development of U.S. foreign policy. For example, multinationals tend to operate in countries that limit organized labor unions, and often these countries are dictatorial and oppressive in other ways as well. Consequently, U.S. foreign policy may support these regimes and oppose national independence movements as it "protects" U.S. investments. Similarly, policies of the United States toward the Middle East have always been at least partly formed by its importance to U.S. oil companies. In both recent wars with Iraq (1990 and 2003–2009), the U.S. military went to great lengths to safeguard oil stocks in the region.

The relationship between multinationals and Third World countries has created a debate about the effects of these corporations on economic development. Some argue that the multinationals bring jobs and technology and stimulate growth. Others suggest that they cause economic dependence and unequal growth where some individuals prosper while others are exploited and remain mired in poverty. They further argue that corporations take advantage of cheap labor and raw materials but export their profits.

There is no question that wages are a primary motivation for corporations to become global producers in developing countries. When labor is $.07 an hour in Burma, $.22 in Bangladesh, $.51 in India, and $.86 an hour in China, a company that must pay its U.S. labor anywhere from $7 to $35 an hour will seriously consider moving production abroad.

The incentive to relocate production operations in foreign locations (outsource production) is incredible at these low wage rates. Geography is less important when corporations have the advantage of mobile capital resources; easily transferred technology, communications, transportation, computer information and production system technologies; and access to raw materials and other markets. For many larger corporations, becoming a global entity is an imperative to remain competitive. Smaller companies are also discovering opportunities for growth and expansion abroad.

A particularly controversial domestic consequence of U.S. multinationals is the movement of productive facilities out of the Northeast and the Midwest, as well as other parts of the country. Corporations often choose to close down old factories and to relocate new facilities in other parts of the United States or the world. This is a fundamental aspect of the free enterprise system. Capital is mobile, and corporations make decisions about what to do with their capital based on profitability. "Capital flight" may occur in the search for lower taxes, lower wages, less regulation and unionization, or closer proximity to expanding markets. Unfortunately, along with these "run-away shops" go the jobs and, in some cases, the economic health of local communities. Labor unions and communities often react to threats of corporate capital flight with wage and tax concessions, because when corporations close down operations, people lose their jobs, communities lose income and business, and governments lose tax revenues. Occasionally, workers or communities succeed in taking over the legal ownership and operation of corporate facilities rather than letting them leave.

Table 11.1 Sales, Profits, Assets, and Market Value of the Largest U.S. Corporations, 2008

Company	Industry	Sales (billions)	Profits (billions)	Assets (billions)	Market Value (billions)
Wal-Mart Stores	Retailing	$ 378.8	$ 12.7	$ 163.4	$ 198.6
ExxonMobil	Oil & gas	358.6	40.6	242.1	465.5
Chevron	Oil & gas	204.0	18.7	148.8	180.0
General Motors	Cars	181.1	−38.7	148.9	13.2
General Electric	Conglomerates	172.7	22.2	795.3	330.9
Ford Motor	Cars	172.5	−2.7	279.3	14.4
ConocoPhillips	Oil & gas	171.5	11.9	177.8	129.2
Citigroup	Banking	159.2	3.6	2,187.6	123.4
Bank of America	Banking	119.2	15.0	1,715.8	176.5
AT&T	Telecommunications	118.9	12.0	275.6	210.2

Source: Data from Reprinted by permission of Forbes Magazine. © 2009 Forbes, Inc. Available at www.Forbes.com.

4. What effect does capital flight have on workers and communities? What might Adam Smith say about this?

5. In the late 1980s Congress passed legislation that requires notification of shut-downs. Additional legislation has been proposed to grant assistance to workers who want to restart businesses. Does this seem like a good idea to you? How might U.S. multinationals react to these proposals?

Global trade has helped some U.S. corporations grow to enormous size. Table 11.1 shows the sales, profits, assets, and employees of the ten largest U.S. companies, ranked by sales revenue. The largest two—Wal-Mart and ExxonMobil—are also the two largest companies in the world. General Motors, the largest U.S. manufacturing firm, is the world's second-largest car company (after Toyota) and the ninth-largest company in the world. With sales of $378.8 billion, Wal-Mart has more income than most countries in the world, including Austria, Greece, Denmark, Iran, South Africa, Ireland, and Israel.

FREE ENTERPRISE VERSUS REGULATION

A perennial issue surrounding corporate power is the relationship between corporations and the federal government. Corporate officials and their sup-porters constantly complain of governmental regulation and interference with business, such as occupational health and safety legislation and environmental protection legislation. They argue that restrictions on business hamper their initiative and independence in bringing goods to U.S. consumers. Sometimes they even imply that continued regulation will reduce their profits and hence their corporations. These officials see corporations and government as adver-saries. Others argue that if regulation and other governmental controls over business increase the costs of business, corporations then simply pass on these costs to consumers. Those skeptical that unregulated corporations always perform in the public interest counter that while corporations do create jobs and contribute to economic growth, they must be regulated carefully to prevent abuses. Critics believe that only with sufficient laws preserving competition, protecting laborers and the environment, and preventing corporate meddling in politics do corporations actually serve the public interest. Without such safeguards, these economists believe that corporations would often act to further their own interests for greater profits, often to the detriment of society as a whole.

Beyond these perspectives, a more fundamental criticism often voiced by corporate critics is that government regulations protect corporations from competition—government is seen as an ally of business. The government has provided direct assistance in the form of loans to troubled corporations, such as the bailouts of Lockheed and Chrysler in the 1970s and 1980s. Similarly, the Fed helped to orchestrate the private sector bailout of Long-Term Capital Management in 1998. And, during the recession of 2008–2009, the federal government undertook some of the largest bailouts in history, committing trillions of dollars to stave off the worst economic crisis since the Great Depression. This symbiotic relationship has its roots in common goals shared by business and government, such as economic growth, profits, employment, technological advance, and defense. Furthermore, corporations have substantial political power in the government through lobbying, direct campaign contributions, and corporate representatives in all branches of the government. In this view, government usually sides with business interests, usually at the expense of less powerful groups.

A series of corporate scandals in the early 2000s highlighted the debate over government regulation of corporations. In the Enron–Arthur Andersen scandal, investigators discovered that upper managers at Enron used questionable accounting maneuvers to pad earnings, misleading investors in order to boost the company's stock price. The artificially inflated stock price would then allow executives to cash in their stock options at a higher price. Meanwhile, Enron's auditor, the accounting firm Arthur Andersen, overlooked Enron's accounting schemes so as to maintain its lucrative consulting contract with Enron. Subsequently, accounting manipulations were discovered at General Electric, American International Group (AIG), WorldCom, and a host of other large corporations. Another set of scandals surrounding Wall Street research analysts surfaced around the same time. Analysts at Morgan Stanley and Merrill Lynch were found to have pushed dubious stocks on unsuspecting clients for the benefit of the investment bank that employed them.

These scandals shook confidence in U.S. financial markets and prompted calls for renewed regulation of corporations and markets. The U.S. government responded with a modest new regulation, the Sarbanes-Oxley Act of 2002, which requires CEOs to certify the accuracy of their books and mandates that outside auditors concur with the CEO's assessment. While some corporate officials complained that this was overregulation, many corporate critics saw it as a cosmetic reform that did not address fundamental problems in corporate board rooms. Similarly, the National Association of Securities Dealers (NASD) responded to the corrupt practices of research analysts by fining those found guilty of research malpractice and barring them from working within the financial industry. Yet the NASD did not require that research be divorced from investment banking to prevent future conflicts of interest from arising. Thus, the response of regulators to the corporate scandals of the early 2000s had been a modest tightening of controls. Substantial changes in the structures or incentives that existed prior to the scandals have not materialized, and the potential for future abuses due to conflicts of interest still exists.

The financial crisis of 2007–2009 did even more to erode confidence in financial markets. In this case, investment banks and hedge funds made extremely risky investments based on loans to subprime or high-risk borrowers. When the housing market bubble collapsed so did these high-risk investments. As Fed Chairman Ben Bernanke described it in early 2009:

> The proximate cause of the crisis was the turn of the housing cycle in the United States and the associated rise in delinquencies on subprime mortgages, which imposed substantial losses on many financial institutions and shook investor confidence in credit markets. However, although the subprime debacle triggered the crisis, the developments in the U.S. mortgage market were only one aspect of a much larger and more encompassing credit boom whose impact transcended the mortgage market to affect many other forms of credit. Aspects of this broader credit boom included widespread declines in underwriting standards, breakdowns in lending oversight by investors and rating agencies, increased reliance on complex and opaque credit instruments that proved fragile under stress, and unusually low compensation for risk-taking.

The crisis prompted renewed calls for government regulation, and various solutions are being debated in Congress as this book goes to press.

6. What are the pros and cons of government regulation of corporations? Are any regulatory debates making headlines now? What are the issues? How do you think conservative, liberal, and radical economists would respond to the issues?

The Corporate Climate Today

Today, U.S. multinational firms are leaders in global competitiveness. Faced with the new global competition that began in the 1970s with the economic emergence of Japan and West Germany, and newly emerging industrial countries (NICs) including Mexico, Brazil, Taiwan, Singapore, Malaysia, South Korea, and Hong Kong, U.S. global corporations charted a strategy for increasing their competitiveness. This strategy involved the following actions:

❖ Moving some operations overseas
❖ Reducing the wage level and the amount of labor used

- Increasing the use and quality of technology
- Reorganizing the structure and management of the corporation
- Devoting more resources to the training and education of the labor force
- Becoming more flexible and lean

The past decade has been a time of rapid change for global corporations, including the controversial process of downsizing or restructuring. The management revolution that took place forced global firms to reexamine every aspect of their behavior.

Global firms accepted the challenge of focusing on total quality management and continuous improvement. They placed the goals of customer satisfaction and value-added production at the top of their performance objectives. Global competition gave them little choice. These firms also accepted the challenge of entering into new relationships with other firms, many of which had been their traditional rivals. It is common today for firms to form alliances in activities ranging from research and development to the full production of a good or service.

Of all of the forces driving the competitive character of the global economy, none has been as significant as the information system revolution. The use of computer technology in all activities of the firm—design, production, finance, accounting, services, information, sales, and planning—has changed everything. Rapid advances in computer technology and software have pushed the firm into the virtual world of the Internet.

Many firms successfully adapted to the global changes, but others did not. Each firm had to find ways to become more efficient and productive, and it needed a stable and healthy domestic economic context to support its efforts.

The combination of the management revolution (e.g., downsizing, globalization, better implementation of computer technologies), deregulation (including free trade agreements) on the part of governments, and the Internet created a boom from 1990 to 2000 that was very profitable for most U.S. companies and the U.S. stock market. Another merger wave swept the country from 1998 to 2000. Many of these were "megamergers" with purchase prices exceeding $1 billion. In 2000 alone, there were 208 megamergers. Most of these mergers were accompanied by downsizing as merged firms sought to eliminate redundant positions.

While technology companies fueled much of the boom, the inability of most Internet companies to become profitable led to a crash in the value of technology stocks in 2000–2001. Other stocks followed suit as corporate scandals, high energy prices, and high interest rates slowed the economy, ending the boom in early 2001. Looking back on the boom, we see a dramatic economic expansion that generated healthy economic growth, rapid and large gains in stock prices, swelling corporate profits, and a government budget surplus for the first time in decades. Still, there was a downside. The U.S. trade deficit was larger, and downsizing had become a regular occurrence in corporate America. Although workers' productivity per hour increased by 18 percent from 1989 to 1998, workers' average hourly wages increased by only 3 percent over the same period. Despite unemployment rates below 5 percent from 1997 through 2001, many workers were afraid to ask for higher wages because they feared downsizing and firms moving operations overseas.

The recession of 2000–2001 was followed by a period of economic growth, but the recovery did not create the number of jobs that usually accompanies an economic expansion and workers' wages did not increase. From the official end of the recession in November of 2001 until early 2004, the U.S. economy lost 2.2 million jobs, the first time since the Great Depression that an economic "recovery" saw such sustained job losses. During this period, the U.S. continued to lose manufacturing jobs, but job losses also occurred in other areas. Facilitated by inexpensive bandwidth and the Internet, U.S. corporations outsourced millions of jobs in traditional white-collar employments, including engineering, design, accounting, law, insurance, health, and financial analysis. Numbers of young workers left the labor force in response. From 2004–2007, job creation improved and wages finally began to increase. But it was also clear that job displacement from technological advances and outsourcing would continue to occur. The financial crisis and subsequent recession of 2008-2009 hit financial services and manufacturing particularly hard. General Motors was forced to file for bankruptcy protection and millions of workers lost their jobs, with the unemployment reaching 10.2 percent in October of 2009. Some politicians and labor advocates reacted to these events by renewing demands for greater protections for labor and labor unions in global markets.

LABOR UNIONS IN THE UNITED STATES

The role of labor in corporate decision making and growth is crucial. We have noted the influence of labor unions on wage rates and on the decisions that firms make about plant location. In the remainder of this chapter, we will briefly explore the history of labor unions in the United States and the effects they have on the economy.

In 2008, labor unions and employee associations represented just more than 16 million workers, or 12.4 percent of the approximately 130 million people in the public and private sectors of the labor force. There are more than 200 labor unions across the United States, representing industrial workers, secretaries, teachers, and many other employees. Some of the largest and most powerful unions are well known—for example, the United Auto Workers, the Teamsters, and the United Steel Workers. Others are less well known but are of growing importance, such as the United Food and Commercial Workers; the American Federation of State, County, and Municipal Employees; the Service Employees International Union; the United Farmworkers; and the Union of Needletrades, Industrial, and Textile Employees.

Labor unions were formed and exist to promote the interests of their members and other workers. Early unions attempted to do the following:

❖ Get better pay and benefits for their members.
❖ Provide job security for their members.

- ❖ Improve the health and safety of their members.
- ❖ Provide for legitimate representation of their members in the decision-making process of the firms for which they work.

Today, however, unions are often blamed for higher costs, for fewer domestic jobs, and for disrupting economic and community life with strikes and other acts of conflict. How has the impact of labor unions changed over time?

The History of U.S. Labor Unions

Labor unions emerged as a response to the lack of bargaining power that individual workers in a capitalist economy had with their employers over wages, benefits, the control of work, and working conditions. The employer owned the factory and offered employment paying the lowest wages possible. If there was a large pool of unemployed people, an individual employee would not be very successful in demanding higher wages or better working conditions.

In response to this structural reality of capital–labor relations, employees formed associations. Only through such unity could they have the power to protect their interests. In the early part of the nineteenth century, courts held such worker organizations to be illegal restraints of trade, so labor unions were legally powerless to bargain with employers or to strike—to refuse to work. However, in 1842 the Supreme Court ruled that attempts to organize workers into labor unions were not criminal conspiracies. After this ruling, labor unions began to have a national presence. It was also during this period that the economy became increasingly industrialized—a precondition for effective labor organization.

Following the Civil War, the National Labor Union attempted to build a social and political movement around a loose federation of trade unions. However, the craft unions left the organization because they were more interested in union recognition by employers, bargaining with employers over wages, and increasing their wages. In the 1870s and the 1880s, the Knights of Labor attempted to unite all workers against monopolies and to promote the interests of working people. The Knights of Labor organized some successful nationwide strikes against the railroads, but the organization was eventually disbanded because of a lack of internal cohesiveness and as a result of Jay Gould's use of strikebreakers in the 1886 railroad strike.

The modern labor movement can be traced back to the formation of the American Federation of Labor in 1886. The American Federation of Labor (AFL), under the leadership of Samuel Gompers, organized in the crafts, accepted capitalism as an economic system, and focused on obtaining higher wages, better working conditions, and shorter hours through collective bargaining, trade agreements, and strikes. The AFL was a confederation of craft unions, each powerful in its own area, that united in conventions and cooperated in strikes, picketing, and boycotts. The AFL believed firmly in the union shop, requiring all employees in a factory or shop to belong to the union (and this requirement was included in labor contracts with employers). The AFL also supported the strike as the ultimate weapon of organized labor in disputes with employers.

Child labor in a Carolina cotton mill, 1908.
(©Lewis Hine/Bettmann/Corbis)

The AFL shunned direct political activity and also avoided organizing the emerging industrial sectors of the U.S. economy in the late nineteenth and early twentieth centuries. Many of these industrial workers were unskilled, and many were immigrants. Other labor organizers throughout the 1920s and 1930s actively began industrial organizing and eventually formed the Committee for Industrial Organization (CIO). In the 1930s, these forces were successful in forming labor organizations that won the right to represent and collectively bargain for the automobile and steel workers. Also in the 1930s, the **Wagner Act** was passed. This important piece of labor legislation gave all labor unions the legal right to organize and to collectively bargain for their members with employers. Since 1935, labor relations have been overseen by the National Labor Relations Board, which has the authority to spell out the rules of labor organizing for both employers and labor unions.

Since World War II, industrywide contracts have been negotiated by industry representatives and national labor unions in some cases. In other cases, large corporations and large labor unions have reached settlements that establish a pattern for the rest of an industry. During this period there also was a tremendous increase in public employees' unions for police, firefighters, teachers, and so forth. The Taft-Hartley Act, in 1947, allowed states to pass "right-to-work" laws that forbid union shops. Most of the right-to-work states are in the South. The act also allowed the president to order a ninety-day injunction against any strike deemed to threaten "national security" The 1950s saw the merger of the AFL and CIO as a national labor organization—the AFL-CIO—to support workers' interests.

Figure 11.2 shows the size of the organized labor force in the United States. There has been a clear decline in union membership since 1958. Some analysts suggest that the 1980–1992 drop was a result of the Reagan administration's critical stance toward unions. In 1981, President Ronald Reagan fired federal air traffic controllers who went on strike over working conditions. The hostility toward labor unions was also apparent in a National Labor Relations Board that was less hospitable to labor union organizers' disputes with employers. Higher unemployment rates than in the 1960s and 1970s made it more difficult for labor unions to organize, because people were worried simply about getting and holding jobs. Also, much of the job loss since 1980 was in industries with heavy union membership. With reduced output and employment in auto and steel, for example, labor unions lost members. While the service sector has been expanding, it has traditionally had fewer workers organized into labor unions. As globalization has proceeded, employers increasingly threaten workers with moving overseas if they demand higher wages or threaten to strike. This, too, has weakened unions recently.

Labor organization in this country has often been characterized by conflict and occasionally by violence. Capital owners and corporations have always had the power of ownership, and labor has had the power of numbers, unity, and

FIGURE 11.2 The Decline in Nonfarm Unionization, 1948–2008

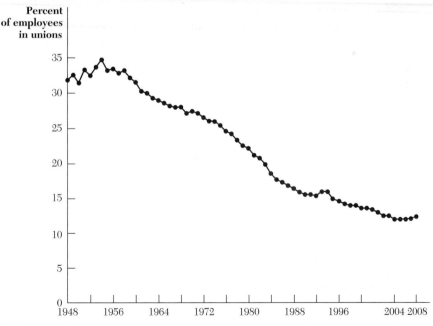

Source: U.S. Bureau of Labor Statistics.

strikes. There have been clear and opposing interests over such issues as the rights of employees to form labor unions, the level of wages, the length of the working day, and working conditions. The interests have clashed, and tempers have flared. Labor organizers were often branded as revolutionaries and Communists. Police have often been used to break strikes, and working people have often responded violently. To some extent the conflict is inherent in the structure of the economy, with private ownership and workers both dependent on labor for their incomes. However, one of the great achievements of modern labor legislation has been to mute this conflict and reduce it to legal and institutional forms that are much less likely to break out into violence.

7. Do any members of your family belong to labor unions? What are their opinions of their unions? What do you think of labor unions? Would you want to be in one? Why or why not?

THE ECONOMIC EFFECTS OF LABOR UNIONS

Labor unions are an important force in the economy and in U.S. society. They affect wages, working conditions, and the lives of union members. They also affect business decisions about location, numbers of employees, and so on. Unions affect communities through civic work, political action, and sometimes strikes. In the following discussion, we concentrate on two of the most significant effects of labor unions on economic conditions: wages and workplace environment.

First of all, what is the general effect of labor unions on wages and employment? Here it will be useful to refer to the supply-and-demand model for a labor market, as shown in Figure 11.3. Assume that there is an organized workforce negotiating with an employer over a new contract. The workers are willing to supply their labor power for wages. The higher the wage, the greater the quantity of labor power they will tend to supply, as shown in the supply curve, S_L. The employer has a demand for labor; the higher the wage, the

FIGURE 11.3 The Effect of Unions on Wages and Unemployment

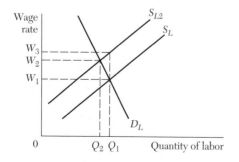

lower the quantity of labor the employer will demand, which is shown in the demand curve, D_L. At the point where the two curves S_L and D_L intersect are the equilibrium wage rate and the equilibrium quantity of labor that will be supplied and demanded.

The labor union is presumably interested in obtaining higher wages for its workers and achieves this goal with the threat of its ultimate weapon, the strike. The workers can shift their supply curve for labor upward to get higher wages. What this means is that it will take a higher wage rate to get union workers to supply the same amount of labor. For example, union workers will only be willing to supply a quantity of labor power Q_1 of if they are offered a wage of W_3. If the employer is unwilling to meet this request for higher wages, the workers may go on strike. Shifting the supply curve upward, to S_{L2}, increases the equilibrium wage rate. It also tends to reduce the equilibrium quantity if the demand curve for labor does not change. Consequently, we can conclude that labor unions tend to increase wages for their members. It has been historically true that labor union members do get higher wages and higher wage increases than nonunion workers (see Figure 11.5 later in this chapter).

8. Data indicate that union workers generally are more productive than nonunion workers. What would this difference do to the demand for labor in Figure 11.3?

On the other hand, the rapid transformation of the global economy has brought increased competitive pressures on U.S.-based companies and concurrent pressures on labor unions to retain their members and successfully represent their interests. Since the early 1970s, U.S. workers have received a smaller share of national income, and their real wages have declined by an average of 10 percent since 1972. Figure 11.4 shows the average real hourly earnings for production and nonsupervisory workers in the private sector. Real wages fell from 1972 to 1996, in contrast with the period from 1947 to 1972, when workers' real wages increased by an average of 79 percent. Real wages have increased since 1996, but not by enough to recover from previous losses. The modern trends of globalization, downsizing, outsourcing, and declining union representation have been associated with a significant worsening of workers' position in the economy.

When we compare real hourly compensation (wages plus benefits) for manufacturing workers in the United States with the compensation of their counterparts overseas, we see that the United States falls in the middle in terms of compensation when compared with other developed countries, as shown in Table 11.2. U.S. manufacturing compensation tends to fall below those countries with strong unions and powerful labor-oriented political parties such as Norway, Denmark, and Germany. But U.S. workers fare better than those in some developed countries, including Japan and Spain. Workers in newly industrialized countries such as Korea and developing countries such as Mexico earn significantly less hourly compensation, which contributes to the trend of U.S.

FIGURE 11.4   Average Real Hourly Earnings, 1964-2008 (in 2008 dollars)

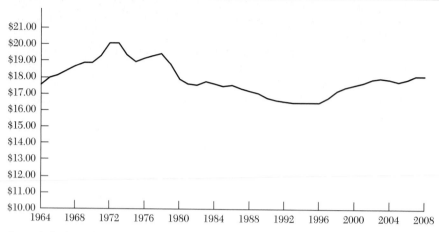

Source: Author's calculations using U.S. Bureau of Labor Statistics data.

Table 11.2   Average Hourly Compensation of Manufacturing Employees, 2007

Country	Hourly Compensation
Norway	$48.56
Denmark	$42.29
Germany	$37.66
Sweden	$36.03
Netherlands	$34.07
Switzerland	$32.88
Australia	$30.17
United Kingdom	$29.73
Canada	$28.91
France	$28.57
Italy	$28.23
United States	**$24.59**
Spain	$20.98
Japan	$19.75
South Korea	$16.02
Czech Republic	$8.20
Mexico	$2.92

Source: U.S. Bureau of Labor Statistics.

corporations moving manufacturing operations to places like South Korea and Mexico.

U.S. workers, however, fare less well than their international counterparts in developed countries with respect to working hours and vacation days. While full-time U.S. workers are guaranteed two weeks of paid vacation per year, many European governments mandate five or six weeks of paid vacation. Workweeks in the United States tend to be much longer as well. The result, as shown in Table 11.3, is that U.S. laborers average more hours of work per year

Table 11.3 Average Annual Hours Worked per Employed Person, 2007

Country	Average Hours Worked
South Korea	2,305*
Czech Republic	1,985
Mexico	1,871
Italy	1,824
United States	**1,794**
Japan	1,785
Canada	1,736
Australia	1,722
United Kingdom	1,670
Switzerland	1,657*
Denmark	1,574*
Sweden	1,562
France	1,561
Germany	1,433
Norway	1,411
Netherlands	1,392

*2006
Source: Data from *OECD Employment Outlook,* 2009

than almost all other developed OECD countries. Table 11.3 also shows that South Korean and Mexican workers face longer work hours, as is often true in newly industrialized and developing countries.

Many of these international differences in wages and work hours can be attributed to the relative strength of labor unions in the various countries. Workers in countries where unions are powerful tend to be paid better and to receive better benefits (including more vacation days) than their counterparts in countries with less powerful unions.

9. What has happened to real wages and to labor compensation as a share of national income in the past few years? What explains these trends? What are some of the consequences of these trends for U.S. labor? The U.S. economy? The global economy?

The second significant effect that labor unions have had on the economy is reforming the institutions and the conditions that surround work in the United States. In negotiations with employers, labor unions have focused on their own members' wages and conditions of employment, but the labor movement has been at the forefront of political efforts to improve the wages and the working conditions for all workers in the country. Legislation at the state and federal level includes workers' compensation, minimum-wage laws, the eight-hour day and overtime, the right of workers to form labor organizations and collectively bargain with employers, improved working conditions, and occupational health and safety regulations. Unions have also supported broad social legislation to improve the lot of working and poor people, including public education, maternity and paternity leave, Social Security, Medicare and Medicaid, environmental protection, civil rights laws, and the government's income-support programs. Over their long history, labor unions have succeeded in gaining legitimacy in our society, winning improved wages and working conditions for members, and promoting general labor and social legislation.

10. Using Internet and library resources, find information about the University of California-American Federation of State, County and Municipal Employees strike that took place in 2008. Why did the strike take place? What were the respective positions of the University of California and the union? What was the settlement? What were the economic consequences of the strike?

The Future of Labor Unions

Over the past three decades, organized labor's position in the U.S. economy weakened somewhat. Now, however, many unions are developing new strategies and approaches for this new economic and global context, becoming more aggressive and assertive in terms of seeking new members and performing their historic functions with more diligence. The president of the AFL-CIO, John Sweeney, has made expanding labor union membership one of his top priorities. Some economists believe that unions no longer have a place in a modern economy, but Michael Yates argues that unions still matter.

Labor-Centered Principles

In his book *Why Unions Matter*, Michael Yates, a professor of economics and labor educator at the University of Pittsburgh at Johnstown, argues that unions bring significant benefit for workers and are the best hope for combating some of the negative trends that have been affecting U.S. workers recently (longer hours, lower wages, downsizing, outsourcing). Yates believes that unions are essential because most workers are powerless on their own:

Let's be honest. Almost every person who works for a living works for someone else. We work in all sorts of jobs, in all types of industries, and under all kinds of conditions. But no matter what the exact circumstances, we do not work for ourselves or for each other, which means that the most fundamental aspects of our work are not controlled by us. Furthermore, our employers try to organize their workplaces so that we cannot exert much control by our own actions. For example, each of us needs to work; we do not labor for the fun of it but to pay our bills and support our families. Yet none of us can guarantee that we will have work on any given day, let alone for an entire working life. If our employer decides to shut down the business, move it, or introduce labor-saving machinery, none of us acting alone can do anything about it....

If we are honest, we must admit that our employers have real power over us. Some of them may be nice and some of them may be nasty, but none of them will spend money just because it would be good for one of us. They know that as individuals we are less powerful than they are. We have only our ability to work to sell, but they have the jobs. In our economic system, these jobs belong to them and not to us, and they can do with them whatever they want. It is a simple but powerful truth that working people and their employers do not face each other as equals. Their employers have the jobs they need, and workers are replaceable....

A worker standing alone is a worker in trouble. For every Michael Jordan, whose amazing talent gives him tremendous power, there are millions of the rest of us, eminently replaceable. Our only hope is to stand together, and,... when we do, we can greatly improve our lots in life. There is no doubt that unions force employers to pay their workers higher wages and to provide them with more and better fringe benefits. And furthermore, unions compel employers to listen to their employees and to respect them as human beings. Employers know these things, and this is why they fight our collective efforts.

Are unions as effective as some economists believe? As Figure 11.5 shows, on average union workers receive $3.70 more per hour in wages and $6.50 more per hour in benefits than nonunion workers. The "union advantage" in total compensation is $10.20 per hour, or 28 percent more than nonunion workers. In addition, union workers are more than twice as likely as nonunion workers to have been employed with their current employer more than ten years, indicating greater job stability. Unions tend to be particularly beneficial for blue-collar workers who have little power in the workplace unless they band together.

In a February 2009 article in the *Monthly Review* titled "Why Unions Still Matter," Yates argued that unions are, in fact, more important than ever: "Because of the electronic revolution, the radical reorganization of the labor process, and the political deregulation of important product and financial markets, employers are more likely to move operations to lower-wage parts of the United States and to poorer countries." To combat these forces, Yates calls for a set of labor-centered principles to advance the interests of working Americans.

1. **Employment as a right**. Unemployment not only wastes the output that the unemployed could have produced, it also wastes human beings and leads to a large number of social problems from arrest and imprisonment to murder and suicide.

2. **Meaningful work**. Human beings have the unique ability to conceptualize work tasks and then perform them. Yet most jobs utilize only a fraction of human ability. This leads to profound alienation and a hatred of work. Instead of seeing labor as the fulfillment of our humanity, we see it as a necessary evil to be avoided if at all possible.

3. **Socialization of consumption**. We waste enormous efforts to purchase goods and services that ought to be provided by society. Examples include education at all levels, health care (including care of the aged), child care, transportation, and recreation (parks, libraries, playgrounds, and gyms). It would be far more efficient to share responsibility for such public needs.

4. **Democratic control of production**. We pride ourselves on having a free society, yet nearly all workplaces are run as dictatorships. Shouldn't we have control over the production of the outputs which we depend upon for our survival? Why should the glass factory that dominated my hometown for nearly a century be able to pack up and leave without the will of the people being considered, much less being decisive?

5. **Shorter hours of work**. At the same time that hundreds of millions of people worldwide cannot find enough work, millions of others are working hours comparable to those who worked during the industrial

FIGURE 11.5 Union Compensation Advantage 2009

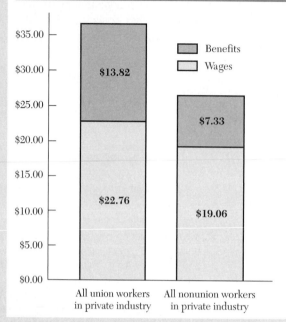

Benefits
Wages

$13.82

$22.76

$7.33

$19.06

All union workers
in private industry

All nonunion workers
in private industry

Source: U.S. Bureau of Labor Statistics.

revolution. People are working too much to enjoy life. Why should this be so?

6. An end to discrimination. What possible justification can there be for the gross inequalities in jobs, incomes, housing, and wealth that exist between those who are white and male and just about everyone else? No just society can be built on a foundation of racial, ethnic, and gender discrimination.

7. Wage and income equality. I can think of no good reason why I should earn four times as much as the men and women who clean the buildings in which I labor and teach. Would I refuse to work if they earned the same as I do? How can

it be justified that a CEO makes tens of millions of dollars per year? For what? Does anyone believe that no one would do these jobs for a lot less?

...In grassroots organizing, based as it must be on rank-and-file control, in struggles for the hearts and souls of our national unions, in alliances with organizations and individuals committed to building the kind of society that is within our grasp, in battles with the employers, whose usefulness becomes less apparent each day, a new labor movement and a new social movement might be born.

Source: Michael Yates, *Why Unions Matter* (New York: *Monthly Review* Press, 1998), various pages; "Why Unions Still Matter," *Monthly Review*, February 2009.

11. Which (if any) of Yates's labor-centered principles do you support? Why? What impact do you think his suggestions would have on the U.S. economy if they were actually implemented?

CORPORATIONS AND LABOR: THE TWENTY-FIRST CENTURY

Today, in the early part of the twenty-first century, U.S. corporations have firmly reestablished their economic and financial dominance in the global economy. This transition, which began in the mid-1970s, has left the U.S. economic landscape radically altered. New relationships exist between corporations and government, corporations and labor, and corporations and communities.

One piece of evidence regarding the reestablishment of corporate dominance over labor is the vast disparity that currently exists between rank-and-file worker incomes and chief executive officer (CEO) salaries. In the past three decades, compensation for top management soared relative to average real wages for workers. In 2007, the average salary and bonus for a CEO of an S&P 500 company was $7.9 million. Including gains from long-term compensation, such as stock options, the average CEO's pay was actually $15.2 million. The highest-paid CEO in 2007 was Steven Jobs of Apple, who was paid only $1 in salary but who earned a total compensation package of $646.6 million. Lawrence Ellison, CEO of Oracle Corporation, set the record for annual CEO compensation in 2001 when he earned $706.1 million for exercising a large quantity of stock options.

The extent to which CEO pay has skyrocketed is clear when it is compared with the wages that average workers earn. According to *Business Week*, the average CEO made 42 times the average worker's pay in 1980, 84 times in 1990, and an astounding 531 times in 2000. The recession and the corporate scandals of 2000–2001 helped reduce this ratio. Still, CEO pay in the United States was 344 times the average worker's pay in 2007. Japanese CEOs earn about 10 times more than what Japanese workers earn, and German CEOs earn an average of 11 times more than German workers.

Some analysts even pointed to U.S. CEO pay as a contributing factor in the financial crisis of 2007-2009. Berkshire Hathaway Chairman and Chief Executive Warren Buffett argued that the main cause of the financial crisis was excessive compensation, which encouraged executives at financial institutions to borrow too much and to take on too much risk without considering the ramifications. Even after the market crashed, many executives continued to get paid very well despite disastrous corporate performances requiring massive government bailouts. High pay despite poor performance led to renewed calls to rein in executive pay.

12. Do you think that the compensation of the nation's top executives is excessive? Explain your answer.

While the issues and arguments put forward by critics of corporations are just as legitimate today as they were decades ago, for most U.S. citizens and the larger global economic community, the corporation is the dynamic organizational engine that drives the growth and prosperity of the global economy. The sustained economic growth and performance of the U.S. economy from 1992 to 2000, highlighted by the phenomenal growth of the stock market and corporate profits (see Figure 11.6), is largely attributed to the success of multinational corporations in the U.S. economy. With the government's policy of deregulation, corporations can do most of what they believe necessary to grow and compete in world markets. Yet, the speculative Internet stock bubble and the corporate scandals that contributed to the recession and slow growth of the early 2000s are also attributed to large corporations. Many of the job losses that occurred from 2002 to 2004 can be linked directly to corporate outsourcing and downsizing, which helped to reestablish corporate profits at the expense of workers (profits increased by more than 20 percent during this period). And, most of the blame for the financial crisis of 2007–2009 can be attributed to large financial corporations. Organized labor and community members will continue to criticize such practices and demand social responsibility from corporations. They insist that corporations be held publicly accountable for their decisions and actions that impact domestic politics, the health and safety of individual workers, the economic viability of individual communities, and the natural environment. It is unlikely that these conflicts will ever disappear.

FIGURE 11.6   Total U.S. Corporate Profits, 1980-2008

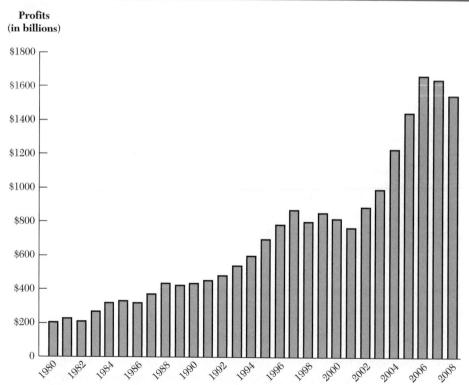

Note: Profit figures include adjustments for inventory valuation and capital consumption.
Source: *Economic Report of the President,* 2009

Conclusion

This chapter focuses on two of the most important economic institutions in the United States: corporations and labor unions. Having stepped outside the realm of pure micro-economic theory, we examined the development, behavior, and importance of corporations and labor unions.

Review Questions

1. Why is the corporation a dominant institution in the U.S. economic system?

2. Why do corporations go global? What are some of the implications of this trend?

3. Why are labor unions an important institution in the U.S. economy?

4. Is the relationship between big corporations and big labor unions adversarial or symbiotic?

5. Do you think U.S. CEOs are worth the large compensation they receive?

6. Corporations have gone global. Will labor unions? Why or why not?

7. In your next job, how much control do you think you will have over your wages, hours, and working conditions? Would Yates's proposals for labor-centered principles improve your position in the workplace? Why or why not?

8. What do you think will be the relationship among corporations, labor, and the government in the next century? What do you think it should be?

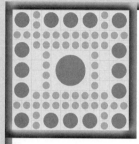

CHAPTER TWELVE

The Economic Role
of Government

Introduction

I n the previous chapters of Part 2, we concentrated on the operation of markets and
their role in allocating resources. We also introduced the importance of corporations
and labor unions as economic factors in the private sector. But the United States has a
mixed economy—one in which business firms and markets in the private sector exist
alongside economic institutions in the public sector. In fact, all the world's economies are
"mixed," with varying levels of public sector involvement.

The **public sector,** in the form of local, state, and federal governmental offices, organizations, and institutions, performs many important economic functions. Think about your
local community. What goods and services are provided by governmental units? The list is
actually quite long, and the activities are fundamentally important to the day-to-day
economic (as well as noneconomic) operation of a community. Public services also provide
capabilities for the long-run survival of a society. Postal service, police and fire protection,
road construction and maintenance, street signs, sewers, parks and recreation services, a
court system, schools, traffic signals, welfare services, and so on are all provided by local,
state, and federal governmental units.

In general, the economic role of government in capitalism results from the failure of
markets to allocate resources to certain tasks or from a public conclusion that the results of
markets are unacceptable. Consequently, governments have taken responsibility for limiting the practice and the results of economic concentration, correcting the inequality of the
distribution of market-determined incomes, providing public goods when markets fail to
supply them, and regulating activities of the private sector that produce external costs to
the rest of society. In this chapter, we will explore each of these aspects of governmental
economic activity in more detail.

THE ROLE OF GOVERNMENT IN THE ECONOMY

Most government intervention in the economy can be grouped under two categories: policies to support the functioning of markets and policies to correct situations when the market fails. Before we consider the government's role in the economy in more detail, it is useful to reflect on the conditions that are required for markets to function efficiently. Markets require an economic framework within which private economic activity takes place, and governments provide that framework. Thus, certain government actions in the economy complement, support, and even make possible private sector activity. For example, a market economy requires clearly defined property rights, including intellectual property, to function efficiently. Property rights encourage owners to invest and innovate, sure in the knowledge that they will be the beneficiaries of successful projects. In countries without clear property rights, such as some dictatorships, business owners are reluctant to invest because the proceeds from their investments can be seized without compensation. Governments provide judicial and legal systems to protect property rights so that productive economic activity can proceed under clear rules and laws.

As we will explore in Part 3, markets also need monetary and banking systems to function efficiently. Money reduces transactions costs (the cost of exchanging goods and services) and facilitates exchange by enabling buyers and sellers to express all products and services in terms of a common unit of currency. A stable, safe banking system also facilitates markets by channeling funds from savers to borrowers, thereby increasing investment and economic growth. Federal regulations that safeguard the health and stability of the banking sector are crucial in this process. Similarly, a stable macroeconomic environment also encourages investment and growth. The federal government utilizes its policy tools to further growth and reduce economic instability.

Another important action of government that supports market activity is the provision of infrastructure, which lowers transactions costs and improves the functioning of markets. Transportation and public utilities are critical parts of the U.S. infrastructure. Where it is prohibitively expensive to distribute products, little market activity will occur. Where the public infrastructure is more elaborate, the cost of exchanging products is lower and more exchange is likely to occur. For example, a new major road attracts investment and commerce to communities near the road.

For markets to function efficiently, both buyers and sellers must have accurate information. People need to know with some degree of certainty how much something is worth to make an informed decision, and they need to be protected from deceptive information, including misleading advertising. Government disclosure and production standards, including labeling requirements, make it easier for consumers to compare products and get the information they need to make an informed decision. Similarly, in financial markets government regulations ensure that stock purchasers get accurate information regarding the value of stocks and that insiders are not able to manipulate markets at the expense of others. Thus, in a capitalist economic system, one major function of government is to create a framework conducive to productive market activity.

However, even after an appropriate framework for markets has been established, when there are market failures the government has to intervene further to ensure that the market system functions efficiently. In response to the various failures of the market system, government has developed many different programs. Public regulation of monopolies and antitrust legislation are intended to control economic concentration. The progressive income tax system and income support, job training, equal opportunity, and affirmative-action programs exist for the purpose of reducing economic inequality. The public use of resources to provide such socially desirable goods and services as education, parks, police and fire protection, and roads results from the failure of the private sector to supply them adequately. Zoning laws, pollution controls, environmental protection legislation, restrictions on child labor, occupational health and safety regulations, and food and drug inspections are meant to correct some of the abuses resulting from the operation of private markets. These public activities have all been developed throughout the history of U.S. capitalism, as well as in other economic systems.

Local, state, and federal governments have created taxation and revenue systems to finance their activities. Through raising money, governments can make a claim on the resources of the society by purchasing them in markets.

All these governmental activities are intensely political and controversial. The decisions about which programs to pursue, how much money to spend on them, and how to raise the revenues to finance them involve public discussion and debate, legislative resolution, administrative direction, and judicial oversight. People, organizations, politicians, political parties, and even ideas are joined in the political process to decide what governments will do and how they will do it.

1. Are there current government programs you consider to be more important than others? Less important? Are there programs you would like to see added? Cut?

Throughout the history of U.S. capitalism, there has been debate about the economic role of the government. At times the debate has been lively and heated. More than two hundred years ago, Alexander Hamilton and Thomas Jefferson argued about whether the country should be an agrarian or industrial society and about what role the federal government ought to play in promoting one or the other. Before the Civil War, the South and the North disagreed about the imposition of tariffs by the federal government as well as slavery. Later in the nineteenth century, a controversial issue was the role of the government in giving land to the railroads and then in regulating their rates. During the Great Depression, there was vociferous debate about the growing role of the government in regulation, relief, public employment, social spending, labor legislation, and even public ownership.

Since that time, along with the growth of government, the debate has continued. During Ronald Reagan's presidency, the discussion was revitalized with a renewed attack on the general role of the government in the economy. One of Reagan's primary campaign themes was that the government was interfering too much in the private sector and that its size and its rules were preventing economic growth. President Bill Clinton echoed these sentiments when he declared, "The era of big government is over." President George W. Bush expressed similar sentiments during his presidency. However, the attacks of September 11, 2001, sparked calls for the expansion of government to fight terrorism. And, the financial crisis and recession of 2007–2009 led to new demands for government regulation and intervention. Only time will tell whether the role of government in the economy will shrink after its role increased to meet new challenges.

Going back to the writings of Adam Smith, we can see that there has always been a case for some necessary tasks on the part of the state in support of the operation of the economy. Smith suggested that the government needed to protect private property, enforce contracts, provide for a monetary system, supply a defense capability, and provide some public goods, such as education and transportation. Beyond that, he believed the role of the government should be circumscribed. Note, however, that what Smith delineated is of fundamental importance to the economy and requires a large and powerful government. Smith said that its powers should be limited—never that it should be weak or small.

Since Smith's time, the general discussion about the role of the government has been partly about the scope of its activities and partly about its limitations within the kind of economic system that we have. To review the debate, it is useful to use the conservative, liberal, and radical perspectives.

Conservatives argue that the state's involvement in the economy limits personal freedoms and that markets, if left alone, will produce economic growth and social welfare. Individuals, pursuing their own interests in business, will provide jobs, technological development, and growth in the economy. Conservatives, consequently, tend to oppose efforts to regulate big corporations, redistribute income, and regulate directly the externalities of the private sector. Such governmental activities interfere with the operation of the "invisible hand." It is largely the conservatives who mount the attacks on the government's role in the economy. (Part of their critique also deals with Keynesian fiscal and monetary policy, which we will discuss in Part 3.)

The liberal position suggests that the operation of the market economy in capitalism tends to produce economic growth and efficiency, along with an emphasis on individual economic freedom. However, liberals acknowledge some of the problems that the development of the economy produces, such as economic concentration, income inequality, externalities, and economic bubbles. Consequently, they think it is entirely appropriate for the government to attempt to correct and address some of those problems. They also argue that such government intervention can, in fact, improve the allocation of resources in society. This position has largely won out in public debate concerning the role of government since the Great Depression.

The radical position begins with the assertion that the government plays a particularly important role in the operation and maintenance of capitalism as an economic system. For example, the state protects private property and the rights of owners to pursue their economic freedom. However, it does not offer the same kind of freedom or protection to poor people. Another way of saying this is that the state's role is constrained by its relationship to capitalism as a particular type of economic system. This point is the basis of the radical critique of liberal policies of government involvement in the economy. There is a limit on the extent of government involvement in the private sector as to redistributing income, regulating externalities, or enforcing antitrust laws. The limit is the requirement of capital accumulation for the growth of capitalism. Without capital accumulation, the economy will stagnate. If state policies interfere with corporate profits or profit expectations, capital accumulation can become endangered. In other words, if state intervention proceeds too far, it may interfere with capital accumulation, and government policies will have to retreat somewhat. Radicals recognize that the political response to the abuses and inequities of capitalism has required and led to governmental programs that address these problems, but ultimately radicals see the government as serving the interests of the wealthy elite.

2. What programs are included in "welfare spending"? Does welfare spending hinder the operation of capitalism? How would you find out if you are right (or if you don't know)? Why does welfare spending take place? What would a conservative say? A liberal? A radical?

3. Are your attitudes toward government spending reflected in these perspectives? Does your attitude vary with particular policies?

THE GROWTH OF GOVERNMENT'S ROLE

The public sector significantly expanded its role in the economy during the twentieth century. Through the political process, governmental institutions make decisions about pursuing particular programs. Table 12.1 presents information on the range of spending programs and the relative priorities of state, local, and federal governments in the United States today. Education is by far the most important category for state and local governments; it accounted for 34 percent of state and local government spending in 2005–2006. In the federal government's budget for fiscal year 2008 (October 1, 2007, to September 30, 2008), national defense, Social Security, income security, and Medicare were the four largest spending categories; they accounted for more than two-thirds of $2.98 trillion in total federal spending.

Table 12.2 presents information on public sector taxes and receipts for various years from 1929 to 2008. The table includes data on the total amount of governmental revenues as well as their percentage share of gross domestic product (GDP), the total value of output for each year. For example, in 1929, total governmental revenues were $11.3 billion, which amounted to 10.9 percent of total output. From even a quick look at this table, we can see that the relative importance of government in the economy has increased significantly over the past 80 years,

Table 12.1 State, Local, and Federal Government Spending

State and Local Government Spending, 2005–2006	
Program	**Spending Level (billions)**
Education	$728.0
Public welfare	$374.9
Highways	$135.4
All other*	$890.1
Total	$2,128.4

Federal Budget Outlays, Fiscal Year 2008	
National defense	$624.1
Social Security	$617.0
Income security	$432.7
Medicare	$390.8
Health	$280.6
Net interest	$248.9
Education, training, employment, and social services	$89.1
Veterans' benefits and services	$84.7
Transportation	$77.7
Administration of justice	$47.4
Natural resources and environment	$30.2
International affairs	$28.8
Commerce and housing credit	$27.8
General science, space and technology	$24.0
Community and regional development	$22.5
Agriculture	$22.0
General government	$16.0
Energy	$0.5
Offsetting receipts	−$86.2
Total	$2,978.7

*Includes health and hospitals, police and fire protection, corrections, interest on debt, parks and recreation, sanitation, administration, housing and urban renewal, protective inspection and regulation, and so on.

Source: Economic Report of the President, 2009.

although government revenues shrank as a percentage of GDP from 2000 to 2008. Revenues in 2008 amounted to more than $4.1 trillion and have increased by almost three-hundredfold since 1929! However, the most useful way to gauge the relative position of any economic variable is to compare it to GDP. Revenues in 2008 were 28.8 percent of GDP. This more than twofold increase in government's share since 1929 represents a shift in the role of government in the economy.

From 1929 to 1940, total revenues increased from 10.9 percent to 17.7 percent of output. Most of this increase occurred in the federal sector in response to the Great Depression. The increase in the share of total revenues from 1940 to 1950 from 17.7 to 24.1 percent resulted from the expansion of the federal government and the retrenchment of state and local governments during World War II. From 1950 to 1970, the public sector continued expanding, and revenues increased to almost 28 percent of GDP. During this period, federal revenues increased their share by less than 3 percent while the share of state–local revenues expanded by almost 50 percent. More recently, the relative

Table 12.2   Public Sector Taxes and Receipts, from Own Sources

Year	Total Government $ Billions	Total Government Percentage of GDP	State and Local Governments $ Billions	State and Local Governments Percentage of GDP	Federal Government $ Billions	Federal Government Percentage of GDP
1929	11.3	10.9	7.5	7.3	3.8	3.6
1940	17.8	17.7	9.1	9.1	8.7	8.6
1950	69.4	24.1	19.0	6.6	50.4	17.5
1960	134.4	25.5	40.5	7.7	93.9	17.8
1970	286.7	27.6	100.8	9.7	186.0	17.9
1980	798.0	28.6	265.9	9.5	532.1	19.1
1990	1,707.8	29.4	626.4	10.8	1,081.5	18.6
1995	2,212.6	29.9	806.1	10.9	1,406.5	19.0
2000	3,125.9	31.8	1,072.2	10.9	2,053.8	20.9
2005	3,620.4	29.8	1,353.5	11.1	2,266.9	18.6
2008	4,157.5	28.8	1,560.4	10.8	2,597.0	18.0

Source: *Economic Report of the President*, 1990, 1997, 2009.

share of governmental revenues in GDP has stabilized and even begun to decline. Total revenues have fallen below 30 percent of GDP, federal revenues are about 18 percent, and state–local revenues have been about 10–11 percent of GDP since 1970.

4. Look at the figures for 1970 and 1980 federal revenues in Table 12.2. When Ronald Reagan ran for the presidency in 1980, he argued that the growth of government was a primary reason for the economic difficulties of the 1970s. Was this an exaggerated claim? What happened to the growth of government from 1980 to 1990? From 1990 to 2000? From 2000 to 2008?

For comparative purposes, Table 12.3 shows the relative importance of government in several economically advanced countries. Government taxes and receipts as a percentage of gross domestic product are higher in all these countries, except Switzerland, than they are in the United States.

We can also measure the size of the government in terms of what it spends. Table 12.4 contains data on governmental expenditures in the United States from 1929 to 2008. In 1929, all levels of government spent $10.3 billion, which was 9.9 percent of output. By 2008, total governmental spending surpassed $4.8 trillion, or 33.3 percent of GDP. In this period, there has been a more than threefold increase in the relative importance of the governmental sector in the economy. The relative share of state and local government spending has increased by 85 percent, while the share of the federal government has increased more than seven times. From 1929 to 1940, most of the growth was in the federal sector as a result of New Deal programs to cope with the effects of the Great Depression. From 1940 to 1970,

Table 12.3 Total Tax and Non-Tax Receipts as a Percentage of Nominal GDP, 2009*

Country	Taxes as a % of GDP
Norway	56.8
Denmark	53.9
Sweden	53.4
France	48.9
Belgium	48.7
Netherlands	47.7
Austria	47.4
Italy	45.5
New Zealand	44.2
Germany	43.0
United Kingdom	41.4
Greece	40.5
Spain	39.5
Canada	39.1
Czech Republic	38.5
Poland	38.2
Ireland	35.4
South Korea	35.3
Australia	34.6
Japan	33.9
United States	**33.4**
Switzerland	33.3

Source: Data from *OECD Economic Outlook*, June 2008.

*Includes fees for services and other collections

the federal share grew as a result of defense spending and expanding social spending. There was also an expansion of federal grants to state and local governments, which contributed to their increasing share. From 1970 to 1980, the share of state and local spending and the share of the federal government increased slightly, reflecting continued growth of social spending in the 1970s. From 1980 to 2008, the share of state and local governments again increased, reaching 14.2 percent of GDP in 2008. Despite the efforts of the Reagan team to reduce the federal government's role in the economy, the federal share increased from 18.4 percent in 1980 to 19.7 percent in 1990. This resulted from increased spending on the military, Social Security, and interest payments on the federal debt. From 1990 to 2000, federal spending decreased to 16.5 percent of GDP, mostly as a result of efforts to reduce the federal budget deficit and the growth of GDP in the late 1990s. Between 2000 to 2008, federal spending in the United States increased relative to GDP. Additional spending on homeland security, the military, an array of pork projects, and stabilization programs in the 2007–2009 recession were primarily responsible.

The government spending in Table 12.4 includes transfer payments. **Transfer payments** are governmental programs that transfer spending power to qualified individuals. Examples include veterans' benefits, unemployment compensation, Medicaid, food stamps, Social Security and Medicare benefits, and Temporary Assistance for Needy Families. Consequently, total government spending

Table 12.4 U.S. Governmental Expenditures

Year	Total Government $ Billions	Total Government Percentage of GDP	State and Local Governments $ Billions	State and Local Governments Percentage of GDP	Federal Government $ Billions	Federal Government Percentage of GDP
1929	10.3	9.9	7.8	7.5	2.5	2.4
1940	18.5	18.4	9.3	9.3	9.2	9.1
1950	61.4	21.3	22.5	7.8	38.9	13.5
1960	122.9	23.3	40.2	7.6	82.7	15.7
1970	294.8	28.4	113.0	10.9	181.8	17.5
1980	842.8	30.2	329.4	11.8	513.4	18.4
1990	1,872.6	32.3	730.5	12.6	1,142.1	19.7
1995	2,397.6	32.4	978.2	13.2	1,419.4	19.2
2000	2,886.5	29.4	1,269.5	12.9	1,617.1	16.5
2005	3,882.6	31.9	1,684.9	13.9	2,197.7	18.1
2008	4,802.5	33.3	2,048.8	14.2	2,753.6	19.1

Note: Intergovernmental grants are counted by the spending source.

Source: Economic Report of the President, 1990, 1997, 2009.

overestimates the claim of government programs on the society's resources. Currently when the government collects Social Security and Medicare taxes from people's wages and salaries (and from their employers), it pays benefits to people who are retired and eligible for Social Security and Medicare. Today resources are transferred through these programs from one set of people (those working now) to another (those retired). People who pay taxes have their spending power reduced, and people who receive benefits have their spending power increased. The money flows through the Social Security Administration, but the federal government makes no direct claim on resources in this transfer program (except for the costs of administering the program). Much of the growth in federal government expenditures as a percentage of output since 1929 has come as a result of the expansion of federal transfer programs.

This conclusion is reinforced by the fact that governmental purchases of goods and services have declined as a percentage of GDP since 1970. In contrast to transfer payments, governmental purchases of goods and services represent **exhaustive spending**. With this type of spending, governments are making claims on society's resources in the pursuit of their priorities. Exhaustive spending includes the purchase of weapons, pencils, government employees' labor, road construction materials, computers, police and fire vehicles, and so forth. By spending on public programs, governments demand the use of resources. This is different from a governmental program that transfers spending power from one group to another.

From 1929 to 1940, total governmental purchases almost doubled their share of output, with almost all of the growth in spending coming from the federal government. From 1940 to 1960, total purchases increased their share of output from 14.2 percent to 21.2 percent. Most of this growth occurred in the federal government sector, with the lion's share being accounted for by purchases of goods and services for national defense. However, from 1950 to

FIGURE 12.1 Public Sector Employment

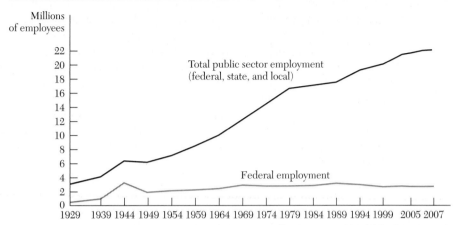

Sources: Advisory Commission on Intergovernmental Relations, *Significant Features of fiscal Federalism*, 1984 ed., (Washington, D.C., 1985) and the U.S. Census Bureau.

1960, there was also a significant postwar expansion in state and local spending, especially for roads and schools. Since 1960, the overall level of government purchases has stabilized at about 20 percent of GDP. Government consequently makes a direct claim on about one-fifth of U.S. output every year.

Public sector employment also demonstrates the growth of government in the twentieth century in the United States. Figure 12.1 illustrates the increase in public sector employment since 1929. In 1929, public sector employees were about 6 percent of the total U.S. labor force; by 2007 this figure had increased to 15 percent. In 2007, more than 22 million people were employed by the federal, state, and local governments, with more than 19 million working for local and state governments and 2.7 million civilians employed by the federal government. The vast majority of the growth in public sector employment since 1950 has come in state and local governments. These workers are employed in education, hospitals, law enforcement, highway work, and general governmental administration.

5. Why has the relative importance of government increased over the past 50 years? Why has it decreased since 1990?

MARKET FAILURE, PUBLIC GOODS, AND EXTERNALITIES

In Chapter 8, we demonstrated that competitive markets operate in a manner that produces efficiency in resource allocation and a maximization of social welfare. The theoretical model of perfect competition proves Adam Smith's contention about the operation of the "invisible hand" in a private market economy—it promotes growth, efficiency, and consumer sovereignty. However, some aspects of economic reality interfere with the attractive theoretical results of competitive markets.

We have already examined one instance when markets fail to produce an efficient allocation of resources. In Chapter 9, we showed that whenever there is imperfect competition in a market, there is also inefficiency in resource allocation. In perfect competition, allocative efficiency occurs because firms in the long run produce at the rate of output where $P = MC$. In Oligopoly, Monopoly, and Monopolistic Competition, firms tend to produce a rate of output in the long run at which P is greater than MC. Because P indicates the extra benefit that consumers derive from one more unit of a good and MC indicates the extra cost of one more unit of the good, society would prefer to have more of that good produced. That is, there is a restriction of output, or an underallocation of resources to the production of that good. Whenever markets are imperfectly competitive, the operation of markets fails to maximize social welfare.

In Chapter 10, we also learned that the distribution of market-determined incomes might fail to satisfy society's concerns with fairness. Consequently, the public sector might decide to redistribute income through taxing and spending programs.

But there are other instances in which markets fail. Private markets organize the exchanges of goods and services between suppliers and purchasers. These exchanges between willing participants are based on the costs to producers and the benefits to consumers of the relevant commodities. The price indicates how much money someone is willing to give up in order to possess something, and it also registers the amount of money a seller must get to turn that something over to someone else. However, this exchange can miss a proper evaluation of the true social benefits and costs of the production and consumption of some goods and services.

Social benefits or costs that occur outside the sale of a good or service are called **externalities**. For example, when someone buys a pack of cigarettes based on that person's demand for them and the producer's costs, there are external effects outside of this exchange. These externalities include the effects of cigarette smoke on other people and smoking-related medical problems the buyers may develop (which may not have been part of the original demand, regardless of required warnings!). These are *external costs* connected with this one good. In a similar fashion, if someone who lives next to you purchases a CD and plays it so loud that you can hear it, and you like it, then you derive an *external benefit* from that exchange. In both cases, the external results are not taken into account in the transaction between the buyer and the seller of the commodity. Whenever externalities are present the operation of markets does not assure an efficient allocation of resources. Markets also fail to allocate resources efficiently when goods generate benefits for large groups of consumers, including those who do not pay for it. For example, public (commercial-free) radio is listened to by thousands of people, but most people choose not to pay for the service. These **public goods** cannot be allocated in sufficient quantities by the market because too many people choose not to pay for a service that they consume (i.e., they choose to be *free riders*).

In all of these instances of **market failure** (where the market fails to register all of the costs or benefits of a transaction, or to produce an efficient result), the public sector may attempt to improve the allocation of resources. That is, governmental programs to limit the effects of economic concentration and to account for external benefits and costs may improve the allocation of resources and increase social welfare.

6. Identify at least one other example of an external cost of a specific exchange. Also, identify one other example of an external benefit.

7. What external costs might be associated with a cigarette smoker's eventual medical bills? What parties might be affected by these bills besides the smoker?

Public Goods

A commodity is considered a public good when it is difficult or impossible to exclude people from using it, even when they do not pay for it, and when its benefits are not depleted when one additional person uses it. For example, freeways are a public good: Anyone with a car can drive on the freeway; one person driving on the freeway does not prevent another person from using it; and people are allowed to drive on the freeway even if they did not help pay for its construction and maintenance. In contrast, a private good is reserved for use by its owner and it is usually used up after it is consumed. If society relied only on markets to allocate resources to public goods, there would be inefficiency in resource allocation. For example, in some cases, the operation of markets either fails to provide any of a good or underallocates resources to it. Consider street signs. Without street signs, businesses would be unable to deliver products, people could not find each other's homes, and general confusion would reign. But street signs are not provided by markets.

The reason is that private markets require suppliers to be able to charge people for the right to possess or consume a commodity. There is property ownership in a private exchange. Someone who owns a bicycle can prevent other people from using it. With street signs, however, there is no ownership, and people cannot be excluded from using them. Everyone on the street can use the street signs, whether or not they helped to pay for them. The firm that put up the street sign could not prevent those who did not pay from using it to identify the street, otherwise the sign would no longer serve its purpose. In this case, no private firm would provide street signs in sufficient quantities because there would be no way to force people to pay for using them. Some people might be willing to pay, but others would choose to be free riders. People will not generally pay for something they can get for free. Consequently, communities have used governmental institutions to provide street signs, and citizens are compelled to pay for them through taxation.

The key issue here is that if it is left up to individuals, society is unlikely to get the optimal quantity of public goods, thereby generating a market failure. Consider national defense as another example. National defense is not depleted when one person uses it. When national defense is provided, every person inside the country is protected, even if she or he did not pay for the service. However, a private firm could not profit from providing national defense because it could not exclude nonpayers from benefiting from the service. The annual bill for national defense is almost $5,000 per household. If several households on a block decided not to pay for defense one year, the whole block would still be protected by national defense (you cannot protect one house and leave others open to attack). However, if more and more households chose not to pay, national defense would be provided in insufficient quantities, resulting in an inadequate military.

Since public goods cannot be provided efficiently by the private sector, we rely on government. Elected government officials decide on the level of public goods that they think the voters want, and voters select politicians to reflect their demand for public goods.

External Benefits

As with public goods, if external benefits are not taken into account, then private markets tend to underallocate resources to the commodity that generates the external benefits. In general, the purchaser of a good that generates an external benefit will benefit the most from that product, but other individuals will receive residual benefits. Because those residual benefits are not incorporated into the market price, the market will tend to provide some amount of the good, but less than the optimal amount.

For example, consider vaccinations. The person being vaccinated gets the greatest benefit from a vaccination, since she is protected from a disease. But a whole host of other individuals benefit from her vaccination. Her employer benefits because she is less likely to fall ill and miss work. Her family, friends, and co-workers benefit because they are less likely to get an illness from her. But these external benefits that flow to people not purchasing the commodity are not reflected in the market price of the vaccination. The marginal benefit going to the vaccination purchaser (marginal private benefit) is reflected in the market price. The demand curve for the product reflects how much the individual consumer values the product (how much benefit is received for each unit). However, because other people benefit from the product but do not pay for it, the market price of the good does not capture society's true benefit. A demand curve that reflected both the individual's marginal benefit and society's external benefit would be shifted up and to the right, reflecting the fact that the product generates a greater value to society than just to the individual, and indicating that an efficient equilibrium would involve more of the product being produced.

Education is another apt example of a good that generates external benefits. Figure 12.2 shows the demand for education based on the collected individual preferences of people for their own education (D_e) and the supply of education based on the resources necessary and their costs (S_e). The market equilibrium is at P_e and Q_e.

But there are external benefits to education that accrue to the whole society. Literacy, the advance of science and technology, culture, and economic intercourse require and benefit from having an educated population. The total social benefits from education, then, include the private benefits to individuals

FIGURE 12.2 External Benefits from Education

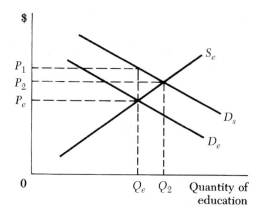

plus the external benefits to society. In Figure 12.2, D_e shows the private demand for education, the marginal private benefit of additional amounts of education. D_s, however, is a "social demand curve" that includes both the private and the external benefits of education. That is, it shows the marginal social benefit of education:

$$MSB = MPB + MEB,$$

where MSB = marginal social benefit, MPB = marginal private benefit, and MEB = marginal external benefit. The marginal external benefit of education is the difference between D_e and D_s.

If the external benefits are not taken into account, there will be an under-allocation of resources to education. At Q_e, the social benefit of education, at P_1, exceeds its marginal cost at P_e (from the supply curve). Society would benefit from increased output of education. In fact, maximal social welfare would occur at Q_2, where the marginal social benefit of additional education equals the marginal cost of education (where the supply and social demand curves intersect). The public sector in the United States, for more than a century, has responded to this situation by providing various forms of assistance to education—the provision of public schools, scholarship assistance, tax exemptions to private educational institutions, funds for teacher training and educational development, and others. In this way, when external benefits are present and markets tend to underallocate resources, public sector provision of the good or service or subsidization can improve social welfare by encouraging increased allocation of resources to the activity. This is called *internalizing* an external benefit. Benefits accruing to those external to the market are brought into the market (internalized) as a result of a pubic sector action. In general, to internalize an external benefit the government tries to increase the quantity of the good that is consumed using revenues taken from those receiving the external benefits. This creates a more efficient allocation of resources.

8. In an interview in the October 1984 *Redbook*, Dr. Benjamin Spock, the famous pediatrician, argued that "the family is the most important thing in life" and that "fathers have just as much responsibility as mothers for caring for their children or deciding who will care for them." Spock went on to suggest that the United States needs more quality day care centers and that there should be subsidies for parents who prefer to stay home with young children. What are the external benefits from good parenting that might justify the use of public resources for child care or home-parenting subsidies? Would you favor such programs? Why or why not?

External Costs

In Chapter 8, we developed the cost curves that the firm faces in making decisions about what level of output to produce (the one that maximizes profits). We also saw how the competitive market encourages firms to produce at the lowest average cost—that is, the rate of output that minimizes the per-unit use of scarce resources. However, this characterization of the competitive firm's behavior poses one large problem.

When firms make decisions about the use of resources and the rate of output, the cost information they take into account concerns their own out-of-pocket, internal costs. But there may be some other costs of production that are external to the firm. These externalities are costs of productive activity that the firm is not forced to bear. For example, in the process of making paper, a paper company may produce air and water pollution. The costs are borne by people who must breathe and smell the befouled air and by the potential downstream users of the dirtied water. These are social costs of production. The firm does not have to pay a price for the use of these resources.

Because these costs do not enter into the firm's calculations, these resources will tend to be overused, and there will be an inefficient use of resources. Therefore, the conclusion that competitive markets tend to produce resource efficiency is true only if there are no externalities in the production process.

9. What other social costs of production, besides pollution, can you identify?

We can illustrate this point graphically. In Figure 12.3a, the graph depicts a perfectly competitive firm where MC represents the marginal private costs that the firm faces at different levels of output, and MSC represents the marginal social costs of production at different levels of output. Marginal social costs include both MC and the marginal social costs that are external to the firm. That is,

$$MSC = MPC + MEC$$

FIGURE 12.3 Marginal Social Costs for a Perfectly Competitive Firm and Market

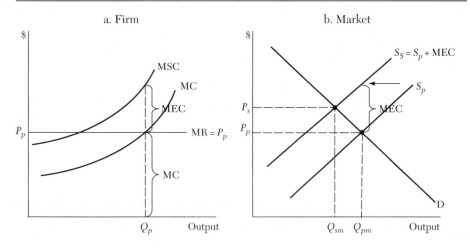

a. Firm

b. Market

at each level of output (Q), where MSC = marginal social costs, MPC = marginal private costs, and MEC = marginal external costs. In attempting to maximize its profits, the firm will produce output Q_p. However, from a social perspective, at Q_p, MSC > P, so resources are overallocated to output of this product—it costs more to society than it is worth. Social welfare is maximized when all external costs of production are incorporated into the price of the product. In Figure 12.3b, we see what happens to the market for this product when all external costs of production are included. With social costs taken into consideration, the market supply curve shifts from S_p to S_s, the market price increases from P_p to P_s and the market quantity decreases from Q_{pm} to Q_{sm}: society produces less of the product and sells it for a higher price.

The government tries to correct the fact that external costs (such as pollution and toxic waste) created by a firm are passed on to society as a whole. The government usually tries to force a firm to reduce the external costs by installing cleaner technologies or by cleaning up the offending emissions or by-products. Instead of regulations that require firms to reduce emissions, the government could impose an emissions tax, which charges a firm for each unit of pollution. The revenues from the emissions tax could then be used to clean up pollution or to compensate those harmed by the pollution. In both of these cases, the government is attempting to reduce the impact of the external costs on society by shifting the external costs generated in the production process back to the polluting firm. Here again, the government is trying to *internalize* an externality.

10. Would an individual firm be willing to take any or all of the social, external costs of production into account? Why or why not?

The existence of externalities in capitalist production has made it necessary for federal, state, and local governments to intervene by requiring firms to consider externalities. Eliminating such externalities as pollution involves costs, so firms will avoid incurring them—because they reduce profits and because the firm faces competition. Consequently, government control forces firms to take the externalities into account. Areas where governmental regulation has emerged include occupational health and safety, noise pollution, hazardous wastes, strip-mined land reclamation, air and water pollution, and the operation of nuclear power plants and disposal of their wastes. In each of these cases, the government has made private firms accountable for the external costs. This has the effect of increasing the product's price and decreasing the output or production of the product, as depicted in Figure 12.3b.

For example, each year industries in the United States generate billions of pounds of hazardous wastes—acids, strong bases, and chlorinated hydrocarbons. In the past, most hazardous wastes found their way to illegal waste dumps, where they pose severe potential health problems for local communities. Douglas Costle, former administrator of the Environmental Protection Agency, noted the dangers in 1980: "These sites with their contents of long-lasting chemicals now represent time capsules releasing their toxic contents into the surface waters, into our groundwaters and seriously degrading our landscapes and our water supply." Some experts have estimated that there are more than 55,000 illegal waste dumps in the United States; the Hooker Chemical Company dump at Love Canal in Niagara Falls, New York, was one of the most widely publicized of these.

Sanitation workers disposing of hazardous paints and chemicals.
(© Bonnie Kamin/PhotoEdit)

Toxic chemicals are linked to higher incidences of cancer among workers and residents of areas where such chemicals were produced. Toxic wastes are considered to be the third largest environmental cause of cancer. The high-tech industry, one of the most rapidly expanding sectors of the U.S. economy, relies heavily on the use of many chemicals (arsenic, strong acids, and solvents) that are poisonous or carcinogenic. Thus, early in the twenty-first century, workers and communities across the United States are faced with a major, continuing environmental hazard in coping with the production, usage, and storage of toxic chemicals and the possible reintroduction of nuclear energy.

As a result of rules established by the Environmental Protection Agency in 1980, companies are responsible for keeping track of their hazardous wastes and ensuring their proper disposal. Firms must take some of the cost into consideration and may not pass all of it along to the public at large. Thus, firms are forced to reduce their external costs, which moves the market closer to a more efficient outcome.

How much of our resources should we devote to dealing with this problem? Environmentalists want increased funding for the cleanup of hazardous waste sites, but the Congress is concerned about spending too much money and overregulating businesses. Who is responsible for the dangerous waste sites already in existence? Who should have to pay for their cleanup? How long will it take? Who will be liable for the health effects of toxic wastes, which may not appear for more than two decades? The externalities associated with one of the most dynamic and important sectors of our economy in the post–World War II period obviously raise some fundamental economic and political questions.

The Tragedy of the Commons: Property Rights and Atlantic Fishing

In the 1990s, fishing in the North Atlantic Ocean had to be suspended for a number of years by several countries, including the United States, Canada, and members of the European Union, because excessive fishing had depleted these traditional fishing areas. The "overfishing" of the North Atlantic is a recent example of what is commonly referred to as the tragedy of the commons. Shared or "common" resources, such as fish in the ocean, or even air and water, can be used freely by anyone. Each individual is able to take resources from and put wastes into the commons. Common resources tend to be abused over time. In the case of North Atlantic fishing, firms kept increasing the size and sophistication of their operations, catching more and more fish each year. Eventually, fish stocks began to dwindle because of this overfishing, but firms in the North Atlantic fishing trade took no action. Firm owners needed to generate income to live on and pay for production costs. Indeed, many small firms began to fish more intensively as fish stocks dwindled in order to preserve their standard of living, make payments on their boats, and cover other production costs. But as fishing became more intense, fish stocks fell so low that most species could no longer replenish themselves. An external cost was created by these firms as a result of catching more fish at the expense of the common resource (and the other people depending on the common resource). But fishing firms do not pay for the cost imposed on the rest of society because no one owns the common resource (ocean fish).

Ultimately, fishing was temporarily banned in the North Atlantic by the National Marine Fisheries Service to allow fish stocks to replenish and North Atlantic fishing is now strictly regulated via a quota system. What we have learned from this and other incidents is that markets tend to overuse and abuse common property resources. In order to safeguard the health of such resources, and to ensure that they are available for future generations, the government is forced to manage the resource to reduce external costs.

11. Explain why no one firm would be likely, *on its own*, to reduce the air pollution or to keep track of and clean up the toxic wastes from its production process.

12. In recent years, there has been intense controversy over acid rain. Many residents of Canada and the northeastern United States, as well as scientific studies, blame pollution from coal-burning, electricity-generating plants and other factories in the Midwest for higher acidity in lakes and rivers. The higher acidity, in turn, has threatened the ecology; in fact, many lakes no longer can support fish life. However, high oil prices in the mid-2000s prompted calls for even greater reliance on coal-burning plants to ensure adequate supplies of electricity.
    a. Explain why acid rain is or is not an externality. What should be done about it? By whom? What difference does it make?
    b. The 1990 Clean Air Act required utilities in the Midwest to use more expensive, low-sulfur coal to reduce acid rain. What might the long-term economic effects of this legislation be?

REGULATION OF ECONOMIC CONCENTRATION

In Chapters 8 and 9, we demonstrated that the theoretical results of competitive markets are superior to those of all forms of imperfect competition. This conclusion suggests that an appropriate response by the public sector would involve attempting to control the effects of imperfect competition and to encourage competition. The regulation of monopoly prices and antitrust policy are both informed by this approach.

Regulating Monopolies

If a monopoly exists, the government has several options. The government can leave the monopoly alone, with the notion that in the long run monopoly profits will provide an incentive for some competition. The government can take over the operation of the activity itself, as in the case of the postal service. It can break up the monopoly so that it has less economic power, as in the reorganization of AT&T in the 1980s. In many cases, governmental units acknowledge the existence of a monopoly, give it legal sanction, and then regulate its prices.

Why would the government allow a monopoly to exist? In the case of a *natural monopoly*, it is actually more efficient to have one firm in the market, but that firm must be regulated in order to achieve a fair price and an efficient out-come rather than the monopoly profit position.

A natural monopoly exists when one firm can supply the entire market output more efficiently than more than one firm can. To see how this works, consider Figure 12.4, which illustrates the demand and cost condi-tions for a natural monopolist. This firm is considered to be a natural monopoly because of economies of scale. The demand curve intersects the average cost curve while the average cost curve is still declining, indicating that the more the firm produces for the market, the lower the cost of the product. The larger the firm is, the more efficiently it is able to produce for the market.

As we learned in Chapter 9, with the goal of profit maximization, the monopolist will produce quantity Q_m, where marginal revenue is equal to marginal cost, and charge price P_m. This will result in a substantial eco-nomic profit for the firm. However, if the government were to use antitrust policies to generate competition in this market, it would not improve the outcome for consumers given the shape of the average cost curve. For ex-ample, suppose the government forced the monopolist to split into three equal-sized firms, each producing one-third of the monopolist's original level of output $(Q_m/3)$. In order to earn a normal profit, these three firms would all have to charge at least AC_3, their average cost of production. But the price that they would need to charge is actually *higher* than the price the monopolist would charge! Clearly, that is not an outcome that benefits consumers or society.

Instead, the government can allow the monopolist to be the only supplier in the market, but it can regulate the price the monopolist is allowed to charge. The government can establish a price ceiling (a legally set maximum price) that pre-vents the monopolist from charging above a certain price. If the goal is to allow the monopolist to earn a fair rate of return, a normal profit, government officials can set the price the monopolist can charge at P_{ac}, where the demand curve inter-sects the AC curve. Since price is just equal to average cost, the monopolist will

FIGURE 12.4 Price Regulation of a Natural Monopoly

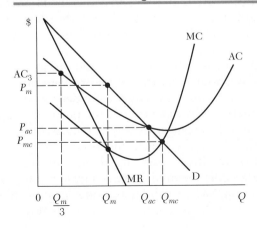

earn a normal profit, the price for consumers will be much lower than the price the monopolist would normally charge ($P_{ac} < P_m$), and the quantity consumers purchase is larger as well ($Q_{ac} > Q_m$). This is called *average cost pricing*—forcing the monopolist to set price equal to average cost so that the firm earns a normal profit, consumers benefit, and the market generates efficiency in production (the good is produced for the lowest cost possible given the size of the market).

Another option the government can choose is *marginal cost pricing*—forcing the monopolist to set price equal to marginal cost, in order to generate maximum social welfare and efficiency in resource allocation. Recall in Chapter 8 it was noted that maximum social welfare is achieved when price is equal to marginal cost, because the opportunity cost of the resources used in production is exactly equal to the benefit to consumers from the product. In Figure 12.4, this occurs where the demand curve intersects the marginal cost curve, at price P_{mc} and quantity Q_{mc}. To achieve this outcome, the government could set a price ceiling on the monopolist at P_{mc}. However, while this outcome would be best for consumers, generating the lowest price and the highest quantity of any of the options we are considering here, we see it is not so good for the monopolist. In this example, at Q_{mc}, $P_{mc} < AC$ and the firm earns an economic loss. The firm would have to shut down if it were required to charge P_{mc}, unless the government subsidized the firm enough to offset losses. Marginal cost pricing is only used in the case of goods that generate significant external benefits, such as public transportation and vaccinations, where society has deemed it worthwhile to subsidize the monopolist and to encourage society's consumption of the good in question.

Governmental price regulation therefore can improve the economic results of monopoly. However, the actual process of price regulation is not quite as easy as Figure 12.4 suggests. Governmental regulators need to have information on the monopoly's costs, its capital assets, and the demand for its products. They cannot regulate the quality of the service provided. Other problems involve the relationships between regulators and the regulated.

The Federal Communications Commission's regulation of AT&T's long-distance phone service prior to 1982 offers some examples. The FCC began with a decision to provide AT&T with a certain rate of return based on the value of its capital assets. Prices were then set so that the excess of revenues over costs produced the determined rate of return. AT&T then had an incentive to exaggerate its capital base as well as its costs so as to increase its profits. Not only did the FCC need to collect a great deal of information, it needed to keep tabs on AT&T's capital and cost estimates. Given the specialized knowledge required to regulate AT&T's business, the regulators were often people familiar with the industry, perhaps through past involvement in it, so there were potential conflicts of interest. (To some extent, the purpose of opening long-distance phone service to other companies was to reduce the regulatory effort, since prices would be influenced by some competition.)

Despite these potential difficulties, price regulation of utility rates throughout the United States does succeed in limiting monopoly pricing power and in requiring monopolies to submit to some degree of public accountability.

Antitrust and Economic Concentration

Based on the economic theory that competition produces a maximization of social welfare and that imperfect competition, in the form of economic concentration, interferes with an efficient allocation of resources, the U.S. government has developed antitrust policies. In general, **antitrust policy** consists of laws intended to limit monopoly and promote competition. Antitrust policy in the United States has always been controversial.

The first national antitrust legislation was the **Sherman Antitrust Act**, passed by Congress in 1890. Political support for the act was based on a reaction to and antipathy toward large and rapacious corporations at the end of the nineteenth century. Farmers, workers, consumers, and small businesses all were, or felt they were, victimized by the railroad, steel, sugar, and other trusts. The act prohibited combinations in "restraint of trade" and price-fixing. Most national corporations and the trusts themselves, however, were not enthusiastic about the new legislation. In fact, the Sherman Antitrust Act was first applied to labor unions as conspiracies in restraint of trade! Since that time, the act has been used to break up some large companies (e.g., the Standard Oil Company), and it has been supplemented by other legislation aimed at preventing mergers that would limit competition or move industries toward "too much" concentration.

In recent years, the antitrust debate has shifted ground to some extent. During the 1980s and 1990s, two merger waves swept the U.S. economy. Mergers occur when one company purchases the stock of another company. In a **horizontal merger**, companies in the same industry are merged—for example, Exxon Oil's purchase of Mobil Oil in 1998. In a **vertical merger**, the merged companies are in different production stages of a particular product, as in the case of the large oil companies that have merged the production, refining, and distribution systems of petroleum products. A **conglomerate merger** takes place when the merging companies do not have similar or related businesses, as was the case with ITT, which once comprised a large number of previously independent companies producing many different goods and services. (ITT grew so large that it became too difficult to manage, and it divested one hundred subsidiary businesses in the 1980s and 1990s.) Antitrust policy has historically been concerned with mergers because they tend to limit competition and to increase economic concentration—with the possible consequences of higher prices, monopolization, and economic inefficiency. In addition, increased economic concentration has always been accompanied by a fear that individual firms will wield increased economic and political power.

Some economists have charged that the merger waves of the 1980s and 1990s increased corporate borrowing and contributed to higher interest rates. Others are concerned about the implications for the concentration of economic and political power if this trend is not checked. Many economists would like to see the antitrust laws enforced more vigorously, and some would even like to see some of the larger corporations broken up.

On the other hand, some liberal economists and most conservative economists would prefer to follow a policy of "benign neglect" toward merger activity and large corporations. They do not see bigness per se as a problem. Even large firms must be sensitive to the market, they argue; if the demand for a product shifts, the firms will respond. Even large firms have an incentive to innovate, because it might increase their profits. Large firms can take advantage of economies of scale, thereby increasing the efficiency of production. Antitrust enforcement, charge these economists, can limit the ability of U.S. firms to compete with overseas companies, or it can prevent a healthy company from swallowing up an unhealthy one, which might improve the overall operation of the merged entity. Furthermore, antitrust litigation costs corporations, and ultimately consumers, billions of dollars in court and legal fees.

During the 1980s, the Ronald Reagan and George H. W. Bush administrations adopted a policy of very lax enforcement of the antitrust laws. The Bill Clinton and George W. Bush administrations did not adopt a very different stance toward preventing corporate mergers. Several mergers of financial institutions may have led to banks that became " too big to be allowed to fail " during the 2007–2009 financial crisis. The Clinton and Bush administrations also participated in the largest antitrust lawsuit of the last decade. The U.S. Department of Justice and nineteen states sued Microsoft for monopolizing the market for personal computer operating systems and engaging in anticompetitive behavior.

The Microsoft Monopoly Case

In November 1999, a U.S. district court ruled that Microsoft was a monopoly and had engaged in anticompetitive practices:

❖ The court stated that there were no viable substitutes for Windows in the market for operating systems for Intel-based personal computers and that it would be prohibitively expensive for a new operating system to gain acceptance in the market. (Everyone was used to Windows, and people were used to applications that ran on Windows.) These circumstances created substantial barriers to entry. Also, Microsoft had a dominant, persistent, and increasing share of the relevant market. The combination of dominant market share and prohibitive barriers to entry indicated to the court that Microsoft Windows did have a monopoly on the relevant market.

❖ The court also held that Microsoft wielded its monopoly power by engaging in anticompetitive practices. Specifically, Microsoft's efforts to take over the Internet browser market from Netscape included predatory pricing (giving away its Internet Explorer browser for free) and

unlawful tying (bundling Internet Explorer with Windows so consumers would have no need to purchase Netscape Navigator).

On June 7, 2000, U.S. District Court Judge Thomas Penfield Jackson ruled that Microsoft should be split into two separate companies, one producing the operating system Windows and the other producing all other Microsoft software applications. The objective of this penalty was to separate the operating system from other software applications so Microsoft could not expand its dominance in operating systems into new areas. Microsoft appealed, and in June 2001, the U.S. Court of Appeals threw out the lower court's ruling that Microsoft should be broken up. However, the Court of Appeals supported the lower court in finding that Microsoft was a monopoly and that it had frequently abused its monopoly power. After Microsoft was (again) found guilty of violating U.S. antitrust laws, the company reached a settlement with the Bush administration and U.S. District Court Judge Colleen Kollar-Kotelly. In the settlement, Microsoft agreed to provisions that were designed to increase competition in the software market. PC makers and users would be allowed to remove the icon for Microsoft applications, but not the underlying software, and Microsoft agreed to license its technology to rivals to build products that seamlessly communicate with computers running Windows software. However, few companies purchased these licenses, and the software market in the United States remained uncompetitive despite the settlement.

In 2004, the European Union also found Microsoft guilty of abusing its monopoly power. After Microsoft and the European Commission, which enforces European Union competition law, failed to agree on a settlement, the commission levied penalties designed to prevent the software company from using its monopoly position as leverage in other software markets. Specifically, Microsoft was fined $613 million, ordered to divulge Windows programming codes to competitors, and forced to offer a version of Windows without its media player. Microsoft paid the fine and complied with much of the ruling, but in December 2005 the EU announced that

Microsoft did not comply fully. In July 2006 the EU fined Microsoft $357.3 million and, in 2008, the EU fined Microsoft an additional $1.44 billion for failure to comply with the 2004 antitrust decision.

As was the case in the United States, the European Commission was responding to Microsoft's use of its monopoly on Windows to dominate most areas of software, including Internet browsers, word processing, servers, and most recently, media players. The commission noted that more than 95 percent of personal computers in the world are powered by Microsoft Windows software, and that Microsoft gradually took over software markets where the dominance of Windows provided an advantage. In contrast, Microsoft was much less successful in markets that have nothing to do with Windows PCs, such as mobile phones. The fact that Microsoft had difficulties competing in non-software markets seemed to indicate to commissioners that its edge in the software market was a product of its monopoly on Windows more than fair competition.

13. Is there a difference between a "bad" merger and a "good" merger? Were the mergers between Exxon and Mobil, Travelers and Citicorp, and Viacom and CBS good or bad? Explain.

14. What are some costs to society of Microsoft's dominance in the market for operating systems? What are some benefits? How might the market for personal computers and software be different in a more competitive environment? Did the antitrust lawsuit against Microsoft produce benefits to consumers? Why or why not?

15. In 1984, a Supreme Court case upheld a law that involved an example of the public (and political) definition of property in Hawaii, where the state took land to reduce economic concentration. In the mid-1960s, eighteen landowners held more than 40 percent of the private land in Hawaii. In writing the majority opinion for the Supreme Court, Justice Sandra Day O'Connor concluded, "Regulating oligopoly and the evils associated with it is a classic example of a state's police powers. We cannot disapprove of Hawaii's exercise of that power.... [It is] a comprehensive and rational approach to identifying and correcting market failure." What is the "market failure"? Is it appropriate for the state to correct it?

POVERTY AND INCOME REDISTRIBUTION

In Chapter 10, we examined the size distribution of income in the United States and explored why it is distributed relatively unequally. One aspect of income inequality is the existence of poverty. Poverty can be both an absolute and a relative concept. In an absolute sense, poverty might refer to a society or individuals within it that cannot easily meet the day-to-day requirements for continued survival. For example, street beggars in an underdeveloped country or homeless people in the United States are poor. But poverty can also have a relative meaning. Even the families in the United States with the lowest incomes are probably better off materially than many families were in the latter half of the nineteenth century. Nevertheless, given the standard of living and the operation of markets in the U.S. economy, it is clear that some people and some families are demonstrably much less well off than most and that survival and development are very difficult for them.

The federal government estimates a level of income called the poverty line. For different family sizes and locations in the country, the poverty line is meant to measure the amount of income required to purchase the basic necessities of life—food, clothing, and shelter. For an urban family of four in 2007, the poverty line was $21,203. All urban families of four with incomes less than this for 2007 are classified as being poor. (Only cash income from work or from assistance is counted.) Given this standard, the federal government estimates the number and percentage of people below the poverty line every year. Table 12.5 shows the number of persons below the poverty line and their percentage of the total population for various years from 1960 to 2007.

In the early 1960s, almost 40 million Americans, more than one-fifth of the nation's citizens, were classified as being poor. In 1973, the number and the percentage reached their lowest levels—23 million people and 11.1 percent of the population. Since then, both the number and the percentage in poverty increased until 1983 and decreased moderately through 1990. In part, the general health of the economy in the 1960s and early 1970s as well as the war on poverty accounted for the reduction in the country's poverty population. From 1973 to 1993, slower economic growth and growing income inequality were

Table 12.5 Persons Below the Poverty Line

Year	Number of Persons (in Millions)	Percentage of Population
1960	39.9	22.2
1970	25.4	12.6
1980	29.3	13.0
1985	33.1	14.0
1990	33.6	13.5
1995	36.4	13.8
2000	31.6	11.3
2005	37.0	12.6
2006	36.5	12.3
2007	37.3	12.5

Source: U.S. Census Bureau, Historical Poverty Tables, Table 2.

associated with higher levels of poverty. The number of people in poverty decreased somewhat from 1993 to 2000 as the economy expanded. Poverty increased, however, with the recession of 2001 and in the jobless recovery of the early 2000s. The poverty rate hovered stubbornly at about 12.5 percent from 2003 through 2007, before increasing sharply in the recession of 2007–2009.

Over the past forty years, the response of the public sector has also had an impact on the incidence of poverty. The case for income redistribution to correct for the inequality of market-determined incomes is at its strongest when directed toward attempts to limit poverty. Poverty is associated with a host of social and economic problems, including homelessness, crime, low-birthweight babies, increased illness, family disintegration, and lower productivity. Thus, poverty imposes significant costs on society. At the height of its postwar prosperity in the early 1960s, the United States recognized the extent of the poverty in its midst and developed public policies to try to eradicate it. A former Catholic lay worker, Michael Harrington, wrote *The Other America*, identifying the extent and incidence of poverty in the country; another Catholic, John F. Kennedy, took up the political challenge of persuading the country to develop federal programs to give relief and promise to its poor.

In 1980, the National Advisory Council on Economic Opportunity in its twelfth annual report on poverty concluded that the progress in reducing the ranks of the poor between the mid-1960s and 1980 almost totally resulted from federal income assistance and antipoverty programs. During the 1970s, the report noted, the number of poor people stayed fairly constant, at about 25 million, and the growth of the economy did not contribute much to the access of poor people as a whole to adequate jobs and earnings. And, while the total number of poor remained stable, the composition of the poverty population became increasingly concentrated among women, the very young, and minorities. The council also predicted that if federal programs for the poor were cut back, the poverty rate would increase.

That prediction was borne out. As part of its overall economic program, the Reagan administration cut back on the growth of many federal programs directed toward the poor, including cash transfer programs such as Aid to Families with Dependent Children and noncash programs such as food stamps, housing assistance, Medicaid, and school lunch subsidies. As a result of these cutbacks and the extremely severe recession of 1981–1983, the poverty rate increased. In 1983, more than 35 million people were classified as poor—15.3 percent of the U.S. population. In the decades since 1983, poverty levels have fallen during boom times and increased during recessions. Since 1995, the government has steadily reduced the amount of money it spends on cash assistance, food assistance, and housing, while increasing spending on education, child care assistance, and other services. This has been part of the major overhaul of federal antipoverty programs that has been termed welfare reform.

The major programs the U.S. government uses to fight poverty include food assistance (food stamps, the women, infants and children special supplemental nutrition program), health care assistance (Medicare, Medicaid), housing assistance, and cash assistance (the earned income tax credit and welfare). Welfare was one of the most potent weapons in reducing poverty in the 1960s and 1970s, but the program has been scaled back and restructured in recent years. Specifically, a major overhaul of the welfare system in 1996 created the Temporary Aid to Needy Families (TANF) program. This new policy imposed strict requirements on welfare recipients, including work requirements and limited lifetime benefits, while shifting money from cash assistance to noncash benefits and services such as child care, education, and job training. Under TANF, the number of people on welfare plunged from 12.2 million in 1996 to 4 million in 2007 and many former welfare recipients were able to find work, causing supporters to view TANF as a major success story. However, poverty levels fell only slightly during the same period, and 40 percent of those who left welfare rolls had no discernible source of income, which helps to explain rising rates of hunger and homelessness. Furthermore, 60 percent of former welfare recipients who did find work were still living in poverty due to the low wages and poor benefits associated with the jobs they were able to find. The recession of 2007–2009 exposed additional problems with the program, in that the number of recipients remained at about the same level while poverty rates increased substantially.

16. Do you think the federal government should contribute income to poor families? Noncash assistance such as food stamps? Training programs for disadvantaged youth? Why or why not? Does society have a public responsibility to reduce poverty? What external costs does poverty have? What is the chance that you will be poor in the future?

17. In 2001, the Census Bureau reported that 32.3 percent of all citizens received at least one form of federal assistance ranging from Social Security to unemployment compensation. In 2006, the government made payments of more than $2.8 trillion to individuals. Further, 20 percent of households received benefits based on need, such as Medicaid, food stamps, public housing, or Temporary Assistance for Needy Families. Why is the impact of the federal government on people's incomes and economic status so widespread? Is it too widespread?

THE LIMITS OF GOVERNMENT'S ROLE

In this chapter, we have focused on the role of government in the economy and the economic arguments that can be and have been made to justify government intervention. During the twentieth century, the liberal view of the state largely won the debate and informed public choices about antitrust policy, the provision of public goods, the regulation of externalities in the private sector, and income redistribution programs. However, some criticisms can be made of government's economic role, and its ability to pursue its objectives efficiently has some inherent limitations. These views served as the rationale for the declining size of government from 1990 to 2008.

As conservatives point out, governmental programs often limit the pursuit of individual freedom in a democratic society. Public provision of goods and services, taxation to finance governmental activities, and regulation all require compulsion. Children must go to school, property owners must pay taxes, factories must clean up their pollution, and so on. Political decisions in a democracy by nature place some limitations on individuals in the interests of the general welfare. The trade-off, which is often only implicit, is a collective good for individual sacrifice. In return for paying taxes, we get schools, parks, national defense, roads, welfare, and so on. As individuals, we might not choose all of the things we get, but as members of local, state, and national communities, we participate in the political decision-making process (to a greater or a lesser extent) and must live with the results. Freedom is not an unqualified right. Nevertheless, there is a fervent debate about the appropriate degree of limitation on individual freedom.

To facilitate the legislative process and to administer public programs, public institutions have been created. Office buildings, legislatures, and other public edifices are physical evidence of the public sector, and the bureaucracies they contain are living and continuing proof of its vitality. To accomplish public objectives, bureaucracies are necessary, but their operation can produce some problems. If there is no measurable output sold in markets (as there is in the private sector), there is no way to calculate success in economic terms. Without profits as an indicator, bureaucracies may have difficulty maintaining efficiency. Roads obviously provide an important public service, but how do we know whether construction companies or road crews are performing at top efficiency? In the private sector, the market theoretically weeds out inefficiency. In the public sector, patronage and/or a civil service system might limit the ability of supervisors to fire employees (justly or unjustly). Finally, bureaucracies develop vested interests in their own programs. Consequently, inertia may affect decisions about the allocation of resources to public programs— rather than having the decision based on the maximization of social benefit compared with the social costs incurred in the use of scarce resources.

The decision-making process in the public sector is imperfect. When we suggest that public involvement in the economy might improve the overall allocation of resources or correct some of the problems of the private sector, we are implicitly assuming that the decision-making process is rational. Through reasoned debate, research on the effects of different programs, cost-benefit analysis, a free press, and democratic procedures and institutions, we may approach rationality. However, the practice of democracy may also veer off from the ideal. Voters and the voting process often emphasize the people, personalities, and parties involved rather than an unemotional, reasoned consideration of the issues. Modern media certainly reinforce the tendency toward superficiality. Special interests have the edge in the political process. Their issues are well defined, their numbers are organizable, and they often have access to significant amounts of money. They lobby, advertise, and persuade, and they are effective in influencing the course of legislating and administering public policies.

As we emphasized at the beginning of this chapter, the government's role in the economy is an issue rich with controversy. In addition, the interpretations of its actual operations and institutions are varied, depending in part on the ideological predispositions of the analysts.

◆Conclusion

Much of the analysis in Part 2 on microeconomics is directly derived from classical and neoclassical economics. In the realm of the market and the firm, the analysis is helpful, although qualified by the historical emergence of noncompetitive market structures and the corporation. We are no longer in the ideal and competitive world of Adam Smith. However, supply-and-demand analysis can still help us understand how markets work to determine prices and allocate resources. And the focus of microeconomics on the firm has caused economists to pay increasing attention to the modern corporation and labor unions. The existence of various market failures, ranging from external costs and benefits to the distribution of income to economic concentration, has also led to the continued development of the role of the public sector in the economy.

In the realm of the operation of the total economy, classical theory has had more severe problems. It contends that the market system will produce growth and full employment. However, this theoretical result conflicts with historical experience. As a result, Keynesian theory emerged to provide an alternative understanding of the macroeconomy. We will explore this theory in Part 3.

Review Questions

1. What is the appropriate role of the government in the economy? What functions should it be responsible for performing?

2. Is it proper for the government to regulate the prices of monopolies? Why or why not?

3. The federal government, in particular, has a number of programs intended to reduce poverty in the United States. Should the government be responsible for this effort? What other possible solutions are there to the problem of poverty? Or is there nothing that can be done about it?

4. Traffic accidents as a result of intoxication are an external cost of the consumption of alcohol. Is this true? Why or why not? If yes, specify what the external costs are. If not, explain. What private and public efforts might contribute to a reduction of this problem?

5. The postal service provides a public good, for example, in the delivery of first-class mail anywhere in the country for the same price. (Before you start thinking of unkind jokes and comments about the post office, consider what has to happen in order for a letter that you put in a box somewhere to get to its recipient, say, all the way across the country.) What is the *external* benefit from postal service? Could the same service be provided by the private sector? Who would object to the private provision of postal service?

6. In March 1990, an Exxon supertanker, the Exxon *Valdez*, crashed into a reef and spewed 11 million gallons of crude oil into Alaska's Prince William Sound.
   a. What were the external costs of this event? Who bore the costs?
   b. Later, fishing firms, tour operators, and the state of Alaska sued Exxon for damages. Why? How could damages be valued?

c. In 1990, a federal grand jury indicted Exxon for violating federal pollution and marine safety laws. What was the purpose of those laws? What steps were taken to make Exxon account for the external costs of this oil spill? What were the effects on Exxon?

7. R. J. Reynolds Tobacco purchased Nabisco foods. Philip Morris Tobacco purchased Kraft Foods and Miller Brewing Company. Why are tobacco firms interested in food companies? What kinds of mergers are these? Do you think antitrust policy should be concerned about such mergers?

8. Many states have laws requiring the use of seat belts in automobiles.
   a. Using concepts from this chapter, what is the logic of these laws?
   b. School buses are not required to have seat belts. Why not? Should they be?

9. In the mid-1990s, welfare reform was summarized by the slogan "workfare, not welfare." From 1996 to 2000, along with a growing economy, millions of welfare recipients moved from welfare to work. Welfare rolls continued to drop between 2000 and 2002, despite the recession and a poor job market. What factors might account for the drop in welfare rolls during an economic slowdown?

10. Suppose that Rex Pharmaceutical devises the first sure-fire cure for the common cold and immediately secures a patent for its discovery, giving it a monopoly on the product. The table below displays cost and revenue for this new product.
   a. Complete the table below.
   b. Based on the data, if Rex Pharmaceutical wishes to maximize profits, how many units of Cold-Be-Gone should it produce? What are Rex Pharmaceutical's maximum economic profits?
   c. If the government decided to regulate the price of Cold-Be-Gone to ensure that more consumers would have access to that drug, what price and quantity would result under Average Cost Pricing and Marginal Cost Pricing?
   d. What is the most appropriate form of regulation in this case? Should the government consider utilizing antitrust laws or revoking or buying out Rex Pharmaceutical's patent? Explain carefully.

Price	Quantity	Total Revenue (TR)	Marginal Revenue (MR)	Total Costs (TC)	Marginal Costs (MC)	Average Total Costs (AC)
$190	0	0		$100		
$170	1	170		$190		190
$150	2	300		$270		135
$130	3	390		$340		113.3
$110	4	440		$400		100
$ 90	5	450		$450		90
$ 70	6	420		$492		82
$ 50	7	350		$542		77.4
$ 30	8	240		$600		75
$ 10	9	90		$666		74

THINKING CRITICALLY

EXPLORATIONS IN MICROECONOMICS—
AFFIRMATIVE ACTION

The debate over reforming or abolishing the nation's affirmative-action policies is a major topic on college campuses and in workplaces around the country. In the past decades, voters, courts, and politicians in seven states have outlawed the use of racial preferences in college admissions, and many other colleges are scaling back their affirmative-action admissions for fear of lawsuits.

Issues present in the current debate over affirmative action reflect not only different assumptions held by conservatives, liberals, and radicals, but also incorporate many microeconomic concepts we have studied, including opportunity costs, resource markets, cost, revenue, income distribution, poverty and discrimination, equality of opportunity versus equality of condition, and access to markets. Below we explore the affirmative action debate in two key arenas: employment and college admissions.

Source: Field Guide to the U.S. Economy: A Compact and Irreverent Guide to Economic Life in America; Jonathan Teller-Elsberg. Nancy Folbre. James Heintz with the Center for Popular Economics

Affirmative Action in Employment

Initially, affirmative-action policies were aimed at increasing employment opportunities for black workers. Executive orders in 1941 and 1961 barred race discrimination in employment, and in 1967 President Lyndon Johnson signed an executive order extending nondiscrimination to include women. At the same time, Johnson emphasized the need for companies to go further to ensure that women and minorities would be actively recruited, hired, and promoted. In 1972, the Equal Employment Act mandated that federal contractors with more than fifty employees take "affirmative action to ensure that applicants are employed and that employees are treated during employment without regard to their race, color, religion, sex, or national origin." These contractors are to have an affirmative-action plan with timetables and goals to correct any shortcomings, which might include an obvious underrepresentation of women or minorities on the company payroll. As a result of suits brought under Title VII of the Civil Rights Act, courts ordered that employers must take steps to ensure nondiscrimination. Complaints are heard by the Equal Employment Opportunity Commission for private employers and the Department of Justice for state and local governments. In 2008, the EEOC received 95,402 charges from employees in private sector workplaces. Most cases are remedied via administrative resolutions or mediation, and in 2008 0.34 percent were litigated. The EEOC obtained $376.6 million in monetary benefits for victims of employment discrimination in 2008.

These affirmative-action programs—executive orders mandating nondiscrimination and the Equal Employment Act—have been under attack for the last two decades.

The Critics

In a 1994 essay titled "Discrimination and Income Differences," economist June O'Neill noted the mounting concerns about affirmative-action policies:

> Generally speaking, I believe that the civil rights movement of the 1960s played a positive role. During the 1970s, however, antidiscrimination policy took a more militant and, in my opinion, a destructive turn as the policy known as affirmative action took center stage. At the federal level, the policy requires that firms holding federal contracts set numerical hiring goals for women and minorities with the threat of loss of their federal contracts if they fail to meet these targets. The setting of hiring goals requires the estimation of available pools of qualified minorities and women that in practice cannot be done with any precision. In consequence, the original standard of the Civil Rights Act, which made discriminatory behavior by employers illegal, has given way to a new standard based almost entirely on numerical results. A firm that does not have the proper composition of women and minorities can be found in violation, even if it has not engaged in any discriminatory act.
>
> There are several things wrong with this new direction. One is that it is a serious departure from the principle of equal treatment under the law, which requires that a person's race, religion, national origin, or gender should not be

the basis for preferential treatment. Affirmative action is intended to help disadvantaged groups overcome the effects of past oppression. But in violating principles of justice and individual freedom to enforce equality, it employs tactics that become reminiscent of a Maoist "cultural revolution."...Moreover, it is not likely to be genuinely helpful. Some who obtain a job through affirmative action may be pleased. But if the job is viewed as undeserved, the process will generate ill will and divisiveness, and perhaps a loss of self-image on the part of the protected minority. Finally, affirmative action has misplaced the emphasis on what is really needed to improve economic status, and in so doing it has given young people the wrong message. In the long run, it is hard work and the acquisition of job skills that ensure success, not jumping ahead in the queue. A better direction for public policy is to provide the resources that are needed to acquire these skills.

—June Elenoff O'Neill, "Discrimination and Income Differences" in *Race and Gender in the American Economy: Views from across the Spectrum*, Susan F. Feiner, ed. (Upper Saddle River, N.J.: Prentice-Hall, 1994). Reprinted by permission of Prentice-Hall.

The Defenders

Defenders of affirmative action argue that despite very limited federal enforcement of affirmative-action policies, they nonetheless have led to small increases in the number of women and minorities in traditionally white male workplaces. One limited, but successful example of this is found in a 1989 class action suit filed against the Shoney's restaurant chain for alleged racial discrimination. After settling the suit out of court for $134.5 million, the company initiated a "turnaround" and began to actively pursue workplace diversity. (For more information on the Shoney's case, see *The Wall Street Journal*, April 16, 1996.) In another example, a 1997 EEOC class-action lawsuit against Publix Super Markets alleged discrimination against women in job assignments and promotions. After an investigation supported the allegations, Publix agreed to a settlement that ensured greater promotional opportunities for women, along with $63.5 million in back pay to current and former female employees.

Class action lawsuits have also improved the workplace environment for women and minorities. For example, in 1998, the EEOC resolved two sexual harassment suits involving large classes of female victims. In one lawsuit, Mitsubishi Motor Manufacturing of America was accused of engaging in a pattern of sexual harassment and then retaliating against female employees who spoke out. In response to the lawsuit, Mitsubishi agreed to pay $34 million in monetary relief to more than 300 female employees. In a second lawsuit, the EEOC charged that Astra USA had engaged in a "continuous pattern of sexual harassment of its female employees." In that settlement, Astra agreed to pay nearly $10 million to more than 80 female victims. In both cases, these settlements are credited with significantly improving the workplace environment. It will be interesting to see if the sex discrimination class action lawsuits against Wal-Mart filed in 2004 and against Citigroup filed in 2009, both still in process when this book went to press, generate a similar result.

In her 1996 book *In Defense of Affirmative Action*, economist Barbara Bergmann notes that affirmative action seldom comes into question when a black or woman candidate is clearly superior to other job applicants. Nor do critics complain about "casting a wide net" to obtain the best applicant pool (thus also casting the net to white males who would otherwise be excluded). The difficult decisions come on the close calls, when there is no clearly superior candidate, when white male, white female, and minority candidates have comparable skill levels and strengths—but they are clearly *not* alike in what they bring to the workplace. Bergmann makes the following observations about such circumstances:

> Some might say that in those hard cases fairness and justice are best served by putting an immediate end to segregation by giving a chance to a highly acceptable black candidate. Others would say that fairness to the "best" candidate overrides all other considerations, and requires that the employer put off ending the segregation for as long as it takes to find that black candidate who will be judged to be the "best." In deciding which side to come down on in these hard cases, we have to balance the value of bringing segregation to a quick end with the value of avoiding violations of a (perhaps imperfect) merit system....
>
> That violations of the merit system occur regularly for purposes other than bringing race segregation to an end—purposes such as helping a nephew or a friend, or taking on someone who will help the sports team—also needs to be taken into account when thinking about the hard cases. When such violations occur, fairness to the displaced "best" candidate is seldom an issue.
>
> It causes no adverse comment when large and important businesses such as the W. R. Grace Company, the Washington Post Corporation, and the New York Times Company place at their head the son or son-in-law of the majority stockholder or the previous head. No protest is made that the company is acting unfairly to a better-qualified non-relative who might otherwise have gotten the position. Nor is there any complaint, even from the stockholders that the company's performance will be degraded by its failure to find the most qualified person. But if the *New York Times* attempts to ensure that it has blacks among its reporters and editors, then resentments arise. That some departures from choosing the "best" are accepted with no complaint at all, while departures made for the purpose of reducing the exclusion of African Americans or women are complained of bitterly, is something that bears thinking about....
>
> The fact is, of course, that in the labor market white males retain largely intact the highly favored position that they had in 1964, the year employment discrimination by race and sex was made illegal. In 1994, among those working full-time, pay for white non-Hispanic males was 49 percent higher than pay for other labor force participants. Differences in skill levels account for some of this pay difference, but nowhere near all of it. Segregation on the job by race and sex remains a common pattern. Opening access for all to the job enclaves that are now the preserves of white males would take a far more rigorous application of

affirmative action techniques than has yet occurred. It would take the introduction of vigorous affirmative action programs into the many workplaces where they have been absent or ignored.

—From *In Defense of Affirmative Action*, by Barbara R. Bergmann. Copyright © 1996 by Basic Books. Reprinted by permission of Basic Books, a member of Perseus Books, LLC.

Many of the concepts discussed in the chapters on microeconomics and earlier chapters apply to the issue of affirmative action. In the following case, Bergmann raises additional questions of affirmative action when viewed through the eyes of an outside observer giving employment advice to the company in question. Read the "Acme and Affirmative Action" case and develop your own recommendations, building on the discussion of affirmative action in employment.

Acme and Affirmative Action

The Acme Company employs 310 machine operators, who operate large machines used in construction, such as bulldozers and cranes. Acme pays them $525 a week, which is good pay for a person without a college education. The personnel manager is concerned that the company has never hired a black in this job. The law says the company has to treat blacks and whites fairly, and he wants to make sure the company is hiring in a fair way.

A machine operator for Acme needs the kind of ability and judgment that an excellent car driver has. The person also needs a sense of responsibility, since careless mistakes could be costly and dangerous. All special training can be given on the job.

Acme had twenty-three vacancies last year, about two a month. Each time there is a vacancy, the employees are asked to spread the word, and an ad is put in the newspapers. Those who apply are given an aptitude test and an interview. The personnel department is then supposed to pick the best applicant.

The company, which is in a city that is half black, got applications last year for the machine operator vacancies from 440 whites and 45 blacks.

Acme's personnel manager reviewed what had happened to the black applicants. He found that they had done about as well as the white applicants on the aptitude test, however, most of the black applicants did not make a good impression on the interviewers. No black had been selected as the best candidate for any of the twenty-three vacancies, although for one of the vacancies a black had been rated third best.

Given this scenario, which of the following actions would you endorse? Briefly explain why.

1. The personnel manager should remind the interviewers to be careful to be fair to blacks. He should tell them that black and white applicants have an equal right to be considered for machine operator jobs.

2. The personnel manager should try to find ways to encourage more black candidates to apply, with a goal of doubling the number of black applicants.
3. The personnel manager should encourage the interviewers to hire at least a few of the blacks who have been judged competent to perform the job.
4. For the next few years, the personnel manager should try to fill at least 10 percent of the vacancies with blacks who have been judged competent to perform the job.
5. To break the pattern of an all-white work force, the personnel manager should ask the interviewers to find competent blacks and hire them for the next five vacancies.

Source: Excerpt from *In Defense of Affirmative Action* by Barbara N. Bergmann. Copyright © 1996 Basic Books.Reprinted by permission of Basic Books, a member of Perseus Books, LLC.

Affirmative Action on Campus

The issue of affirmative action in employment differs somewhat from affirmative action applied to the college admission process. In addition to remedying inequities due to past discrimination, college affirmative-action programs seek to ensure a diverse student body. But affirmative action on college campuses is similar to workplace affirmative action in that it is a controversial topic that arouses passionate opinions on both sides. In the landmark 1978 Bakke decision, the Supreme Court held that because of past discrimination, a "state has a substantial interest that legitimately may be served by a properly devised admission program involving the competitive consideration of race and ethnic origin." Justice Lewis F. Powell Jr. added that universities had a compelling interest in obtaining a diverse student body. Other justices did not support that argument.

In the past two decades, voters, courts, and politicians in several states have outlawed the use of racial preferences in college admissions, and many other colleges are scaling back their affirmative-action admissions for fear of lawsuits. The first of these efforts was Proposition 209, approved by California voters in 1996, which banned affirmative action at all state institutions. Since Proposition 209 was implemented in 1998, enrollment of African American, Hispanic, and Native American students has plummeted at the University of California at Berkeley and other elite state institutions. At Berkeley, between 1997 and 2001, enrollment by African American students fell by 32 percent, enrollment by Hispanic students fell by 23 percent, and enrollment by Native American students fell by 45 percent. Many university officials argue that this decline in diversity interferes with their ability to provide a good education, part of which includes interacting with those from different backgrounds. Nevertheless, foes of affirmative action have celebrated the changes as a much-needed return to a meritocracy.

A major new challenge to affirmative action in admissions came in the form of two lawsuits against the University of Michigan in the late 1990s in which white applicants sued the university for racial discrimination resulting from giving preference to minority candidates. In a landmark decision in 2003, the Supreme Court upheld affirmative-action admissions in principle but threw out an admission policy that was not narrowly tailored. Below we explore the ideas of critics and supporters of college affirmative action programs, and describe the Supreme Court's decision.

The Critics

The critics of affirmative action range from conservatives who decry the government interference in the labor market to those who support government action to end race and gender discrimination but who believe that affirmative action is a flawed policy. Both groups weighed in on the Michigan case.

In early 2003, President George W. Bush issued a statement on the Michigan case, arguing that "the Michigan policies amount to a quota system that unfairly rewards or penalizes prospective students based solely on their race." He called such affirmative-action programs "divisive, unfair and impossible to square with our Constitution." Thus, Bush believed that affirmative-action programs, designed to remedy inequality due to past discrimination, are a form of reverse discrimination.

African American columnist Armstrong Williams opposed affirmative action for different reasons. While acknowledging the problems of racism and discrimination, Williams argued against affirmative action because he saw it as creating a culture of victimhood:

> A shared history of slavery and discrimination has ingrained racial hierarchies into our national identity, divisions that need to be erased. There is, however, a very real danger that we are merely reinforcing the idea that minorities are first and foremost victims.... If the goal of affirmative action is to create a more equitable society, it should be need-based. Instead, affirmative action is designed...to reduce people to fixed categories: at many universities, it seems, admissions officers look less at who you are than what you are. As a result, affirmative-action programs rarely help the least among us. Instead, they often benefit the children of the middle- and upper-class black Americans who have been conditioned to feel they are owed something....It is time to stop. We must reach a point where we expect to rise or fall on our own merits.
>
> —Armstrong Williams,"Admissions Policies Like Michigan's Focus Not on Who, But What You Are," *Newsweek*, January 27, 2003, p. 33.

Criticisms like those of Williams gained additional weight with the 2003 publication of a Century Foundation study indicating that 74 percent of students at America's 146 most selective colleges were from the most privileged 25 percent of the U.S. population, and only 3 percent were from the most disadvantaged 25 percent. Blacks and Hispanics were also underrepresented, making up 12 percent of students at selective colleges compared with 28 percent of the country's college-age population. However, the fact that minority students (28 percent of the population, 12 percent of students) are more likely to go to an elite college than students from the poorest families (25 percent of the population, 3 percent of students) may indicate that middle- and upper-income students from minority groups are the principal beneficiaries of college affirmative-action programs and that they may benefit at the expense of more disadvantaged white students.

The Defenders

Defenders of affirmative action include liberals who advocate using government intervention to correct inequality along racial and gender lines as well as advocates of diversity in universities and the workplace. Microsoft, General Motors, a host of other corporations, and the U.S. military supported the University of Michigan affirmative action programs, filing amicus briefs on behalf of the university. For many institutions, including global multinational corporations, a globalized world demands employees who are comfortable dealing with people from diverse backgrounds. The only way to ensure that college graduates can handle such experiences right out of college is if they encounter them in school. In fact, before deciding to interview students from a particular campus, employers often ask colleges to provide information regarding the diversity and size of the student population to help them determine if the students hail from a sufficiently diverse atmosphere.

In addition to those who see diversity as essential to a well-rounded education, other supporters of affirmative action admissions believe that it is necessary to redress inequality of opportunity. Ronald Dworkin, a professor of law and philosophy at New York University Law School, makes such an argument:

> All of us who are not racists—liberals and conservatives alike—have an instinctive tic against explicit racial classifications, which is understandable given our nation's history of racial injustice. But if we really want a more just society, we must be prepared to re-examine this instinct with an important distinction in mind: we must distinguish between policies whose premises deny equal citizenship and those whose premises affirm it.
>
> Of course, no one should be penalized for his or her race, and no race should be thought to have special rights or privileges. Black applicants have no right to preference now because other blacks suffered from injustice in the past. But affirmative action assumes no such right: it has a forward-looking, not backward-looking, justification. The policy promises a better educational environment and a less racially stratified society for everyone. It recognizes that prejudice has poisoned society for all of us, and that fostering opportunities for different races to study and work together is part of an effective, even if slow-working, antidote.

Is affirmative action unfair? Universities are not honor societies rewarding applicants for past achievements. They have a public responsibility to choose students with an eye to the future—students who will contribute to the institution's educational, academic, and social goals. If a university judges that it can offer a better education to everyone if its student body is racially diverse, then its judgment is no more unfair to anyone than its judgment that it can do better with a geographically diverse class or with athletes as well as scholars. It would, of course, be unfair if a university's judgment were corrupted by bias or favoritism, and universities should be required, if challenged, to offer persuasive evidence rebutting any such claim. But no one's rights are infringed when a university makes an honest and uncorrupted decision about how best to meet its academic responsibilities.

—Ronald Dworkin,"Race and the Uses of Law," *The New York Times*, April 13, 2001, p. A17.

The Supreme Court's Decision

In a 5–4 ruling in June 2003, the Supreme Court upheld the Bakke decision and Justice Powell's view that past discrimination and diversity provided compelling reasons for universities to operate narrowly tailored affirmative-action programs. A university may not use a quota system, but it may consider race or ethnicity as a "plus" factor in a particular applicant's file, while "insuring that each candidate competes with all other qualified applicants." The majority agreed that "student body diversity promotes learning outcomes, and better prepares students for an increasingly diverse workforce and society, and better prepares them as professionals."

However, the Supreme Court struck down one affirmative-action plan that it thought gave too much weight to race, amounting to a quota system that did not consider applicants separately. Furthermore, the Supreme Court anticipated the end of affirmative-action admissions policies, stating, "We expect that 25 years from now, the use of racial preferences will no longer be necessary."

Although the Supreme Court has decided the issue for now, the debate over affirmative action admissions on college campuses is far from over. Several states are considering legislation that would ban affirmative action admissions in their state, following the lead of California and Texas. And conservative groups continue to attack diversity as a legitimate goal for universities to promote. Meanwhile, most universities continue to defend affirmative action admissions and diversity as essential to their educational mission.

Exercises

1. What are the opportunity costs of affirmative-action policies to each of the following groups?
   a. qualified women and minority workers
   b. employers

c. consumers

  d. other employees of the company

  e. society

2. What are the opportunity costs of not using affirmative-action policies to each of the following groups?

  a. qualified women and minority workers

  b. employers

  c. consumers

  d. other employees of the company

  e. society

3. How might Shoney's cost analysis have been affected by its alleged race discrimination? Its revenue stream?

4. Is Bergmann correct in her assessment that few are concerned when sons of corporate leaders (or even coaches) are hired? Why or why not? Does merit have different meanings in different circumstances? Explain.

5. John Bates Clark, one of the early contributors to microeconomic theory, wrote, "The distribution of the income of society is controlled by a natural law, and…this law, if worked without friction, would give to every agent of production the amount of wealth which that agent creates." What does this mean? (Use MRP-MFC to explain your answer.) Does this explain why college-educated women and black men earn lower incomes than college-educated white men?

6. Does affirmative action in college admissions necessarily lower the quality of incoming students? Why or why not?

7. Should children of alumni be given preference in college admissions, as they often are now? Should trumpet players? Football quarterbacks? Explain your answers.

8. Contact the admissions office at your school and find out how they deal with issues of affirmative action and diversity. What methods (if any) do they use to ensure a diverse student body? What "plus factors" are given to students from disadvantaged backgrounds? Do you think your school goes too far or not far enough in this area?

9. If you were in charge of admissions, which of the following applicants would you admit to your school: (1) a minority applicant from a substandard inner city school who finished in the top 10 percent of her high school class and has SAT scores of 1000, just below the national average; or (2) a white applicant from a good suburban school in an affluent neighborhood who finished in the top 50 percent of her high school class and has SAT scores of 1050, just above the national average? Justify your decision. Now construct an argument for admitting the applicant you did not choose.

10. In an article in the January 2004 issue of *The American Prospect*, Lisbeth Schorr, a lecturer in social medicine at Harvard University and director of the Harvard University Project on Effective Interventions, noted that it would take just over $110 billion to create true equality of opportunity for minority students. If the Supreme Court wants to eliminate racial preferences in admissions in 25 years, then she believes certain steps

will have to be taken. These include eliminating racial disparities in birth outcomes, school readiness, public school quality, community programs, and health care. Do you think it is reasonable to expect the elimination of affirmative action admissions without such steps being taken? Would such steps be enough, in your view, to provide true equality of opportunity in college admissions?

11. Watch newspapers and other media for current affirmative-action cases. What are the major issues in these cases? Have any gone to trial? Were any settled out of court? What are the circumstances?

PART THREE

Macroeconomics

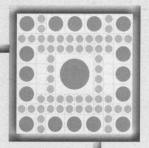

In Part 2, we examined how microeconomics analyzes the behavior of consumers and firms in the U.S. economic system. We focused on the behavior of markets, the different types of market structures, efficiency, scarcity, the nature of the modern corporation and labor unions, and the role of the government.

We will now supplement this microeconomic theory with macroeconomic theory and policy. **Macroeconomics** is the body of economic theory that attempts to analyze the behavior and performance of the whole economy. It describes and explains the dynamics of the institutional and governmental framework of our economic system by focusing on *the total or aggregate performance* of the economy. We begin our discussion of macroeconomics with an exposition of income-expenditures theory, which explains the performance of the economy in terms of employment, income, output, and price levels. A macroeconomic perspective further requires that we explore the relationship between the monetary system and the economy's aggregate performance. We can then use our understanding of monetary theory and policy and the role of governmental fiscal policy (government spending and taxation) to focus on how best to achieve the major macroeconomic goals of full employment, economic growth, and price stability.

While microeconomics focuses on the decisions of individual actors in the economic system, macroeconomics studies the more aggregate behavior of consumers, businesses, and the government, as well as the market for imports and exports. Although we are shifting to the macroeconomic viewpoint of the aggregate, our examination of the markets for goods and services, money, and even labor will use many of the tools of microeconomics. Such microeconomic concepts and methods as markets, supply, demand, equilibrium, and marginal analysis can help us describe and explain aggregate economic behavior. Thus, while the focus of the discussion will clearly be different, macroeconomic theory relies heavily on microeconomic foundations.

Chapter 13 identifies and describes some of the most important goals and problems of macroeconomics. It also introduces the measuring tools of the National Income and Product Accounts (NIPA). In Chapter 14 we begin to explore the theoretical roots of modern macroeconomics and begin to construct an economic model that is used for analyzing economic activity. We continue to build this model and add to it in Chapters 15 through 18. In some of these chapters we include "Big Picture" sections that illustrate an overview of the part of the model that follows. Figure III.1 provides a framework of the structures we will develop in The Big Picture sections that are introduced throughout Part 3. Chapter 15 focuses on the role of government in making fiscal policy. Chapter 16 introduces money, financial intermediaries, and monetary policy. Chapter 17 combines elements of monetary theory and aggregate expenditures theory in examining aggregate supply and aggregate demand. Finally, Chapter 18 explores the major macroeconomic problems of unemployment, inflation, and slower economic growth. It also integrates, summarizes, and critically reflects on the past and present efficacy of contemporary macroeconomic policy in the United States.

FIGURE III.1

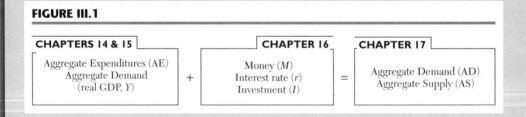

CHAPTER THIRTEEN

Macroeconomics: Issues and Problems

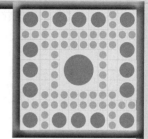

◆ Introduction

This chapter begins our focus on macroeconomics, which examines the economy as a whole. Instead of studying individual parts of the economy, such as firms or labor unions, or concepts such as property and value, we turn our attention to entire sectors that make up our national and international economic system and to aggregate concepts and problems, such as recession, unemployment, inflation, interest rates, taxation, and budget deficits. These topics affect every one of us.

In this chapter, we will examine the goals of macroeconomics, review postwar U.S. macroeconomic trends, develop several tools that will aid our understanding of macroeconomic theory and macroeconomic policy, and define aggregate measures for economic activity in the National Income and Product Accounts. We will begin by considering the importance of macroeconomic theory and some of the ways macroeconomic policy might help to alleviate economic problems.

MACROECONOMIC GOALS

In the early 1950s, the U.S. government accepted as its responsibility three basic macroeconomic goals: (1) economic growth, (2) full employment, and (3) price stability. Government policies should help the economy attain these goals. However, as we will see later, these goals are not necessarily compatible. Despite conflicts among these goals, many would agree that economic growth, full employment, and price stability are reasonable goals. We want people employed. Stable prices are good for most of us. And economic growth has become synonymous with a higher standard of living and economic progress.

Economic Growth

Simply put, **economic growth** is the increased output of goods and services over time. Not only is growth assumed to be necessary and good, but more growth is assumed to be better than less. Economic growth, after all, creates employment and income.

To measure economic growth, economists have developed sophisticated tools that measure the performance of the economy and its annual rate of real growth. By using a method known as national income accounting (explained later in this chapter), they calculate the **gross domestic product (GDP)**—the total dollar value of all goods and services produced in a given year—and monitor its rate of growth. GDP has grown from $2 trillion in 1978 to $14.2 trillion in 2008. The United States continues to have the world's largest GDP. Once we have measured GDP, we can find the percentage change to calculate its growth rate from year to year. Table 13.1 shows recent and historic average growth rates.

During the 1960s and early 1970s, critics challenged the basic assumptions concerning economic growth, arguing that more growth does not necessarily mean an improved standard of living. Others now charge that the GDP merely quantifies the performance of the economy but does not reflect the qualitative dimension addressed by the question, What is the real societal value or cost of increased GDP growth?

Much of this critique stems from a consideration of the environmental aspects of increasing economic growth. Human health and well-being are endangered by toxic wastes and air and water pollution, while acid rain threatens the quality of our food supply. Issues including the demise of the rain forests, climate change, and population growth have reminded us that these are worldwide concerns. Growing ecological awareness in the context of energy and environmental crises has made us examine our values, attitudes, goals, and economic assumptions more intensely.

The economic growth controversy also focuses on issues of income distribution in the United States. Annual increases in economic growth do not lead to more equitable distribution of the increased output. Empirical data support the claim that despite the tremendous increases in GDP since World War II, the distribution of income in the United States did not change significantly until the 1980s, when it became *less* equal. Despite rapid economic growth in the 1990s and mid-2000s, income distribution continues to become even more unequal. Those who advocate economic growth often use the metaphor

Table 13.1 Average Annual Rates of Growth, Unemployment, and Inflation

	1950s	1960s	1970s	1980s	1990s	2000–2008
Real growth rate[a]	4.0%	4.1%	2.8%	2.7%	5.4%	4.1%
Unemployment	4.4	4.8	6.2	7.3	5.8	5.1
Inflation	2.4	2.0	7.1	6.7	2.9	2.8

[a]In current dollars.
Source: *Economic Report of the President*, 1984, 1990, 2001, 2009.

"a rising tide lifts all boats." Indeed, "all boats" did rise during the period from 1993 to 2006, but the "boats" of the most wealthy in the United States rose the most.

Another concern is that economic growth may be too rapid, causing labor and input shortages, which in turn increase prices. In addition, economic growth has not evolved in a stable pattern. The United States has experienced ten major recessions since World War II. The instability characterized by fluctuations of the business cycle has been a primary feature of the postwar era.

Full Employment

The attainment of high levels of employment has been a goal of the U.S. government since the passage of the Employment Act of 1946 following the Great Depression of the 1930s. Congress reaffirmed that goal in passing the Full Employment and Balanced Growth Act of 1978, which set targets of 3 percent inflation and 4 percent unemployment and directed the president to take steps consistent with these goals. These steps might include creating a more favorable business climate and establishing policies for direct federal expenditures, among others. The country has come closest to full employment mostly during times of war, and during the technology boom of the late 1990s.

Unemployment refers to people who would like to have jobs but don't. The Department of Labor defines people as unemployed when they are older than age sixteen, are actively seeking work, do not have a job, and have made some effort to find work during the past four weeks. The unemployment rate is the percent of people without jobs relative to the total number of people in the labor force (those with jobs or looking for jobs). About 63 percent of the U.S. population is in the labor force, and this base is used for the unemployment estimates. By 2008, almost 155 million of the 303 million people in the United States were in the civilian labor force. Table 13.2 shows unemployment rates for selected groups of workers from 1950 to 2008.

1. Does it surprise you that married men typically have lower unemployment rates than other groups of men (see Table 13.2)? Why or why not?

Economists have defined five basic types of unemployment:

1. **Frictional unemployment** is caused by the temporary mismatching of people with jobs because workers change jobs, employers seek new workers, and new people enter the labor market. All labor markets have frictional unemployment; even during the severe labor shortage of World War II, unemployment persisted at about 2 percent.

2. **Seasonal unemployment**, as the name implies, results from changing seasonal demand and supply for labor. Ski instructors seeking jobs in the summer and farmworkers laid off in the winter contribute to seasonal unemployment.

3. **Structural unemployment** presents a more serious problem. It results from permanent displacement of workers due to shifting product demand or technological changes that require new skills. The shift in demand from natural to synthetic fibers created problems of structural unemployment for places such as Fall River, Massachusetts. The mechanical picking of tomatoes caused many migrant farmworkers to become structurally unemployed. Such unemployment is a function of geography, as well as skill level, and mobility.

4. **Cyclical unemployment** is due to the decreased demand for labor during a downturn in the business cycle. The high unemployment of the 1930s was basically a problem of cyclical unemployment. The high unemployment rates of the early 1990s also were predominately cyclical.

5. **Hidden unemployment** is not included in the official unemployment rate and is probably the hardest concept to define and measure. Growing evidence suggests that many people would like a job if they thought one was available, but many have become so discouraged by their past failures to find employment that they have given up trying. Technically, such people are outside the labor force, but as a practical matter, they are unemployed and not offically counted as such. One sign that hidden unemployment exists is the rise in the labor force participation rate (the proportion of the total population seeking jobs) during the early stages of economic recovery. If more people seek jobs as the number of jobs increases, why weren't they part of the labor force when the unemployment rate was higher? In addition, many people work part-time but would prefer to work full-time. These people are counted as being employed.

Table 13.2 Civilian Unemployment Rate by Demographic Characteristics, 1950–2008 (percent)

Year	All Workers	By Sex and Age			Demographic Characteristic			By Selected Group	
		Both Sexes, 16–19	Males, 20 and Over	Females, 20 and Over	White	Black or African American	Hispanic or Latino Ethnicity	Married Men (Spouse Present)	Women Who Maintain Families
1950	5.3	12.2	4.7	5.1	4.9	—	—	4.6	—
1960	5.5	14.7	4.7	5.1	4.9	—	—	3.7	—
1970	4.9	15.3	3.5	4.8	4.5	—	—	2.6	5.4
1975	8.5	19.9	6.7	8.0	7.8	14.8	12.2	5.1	10.0
1980	7.1	17.8	5.9	6.4	6.3	14.3	10.1	4.2	9.2
1985	7.2	18.6	6.2	6.6	6.2	15.1	10.5	4.3	10.4
1990	5.6	15.5	5.0	4.9	4.8	11.4	8.2	3.4	8.2
1995	5.6	17.3	4.8	4.9	4.9	10.4	9.3	3.3	8.0
2000	4.0	13.0	4.1	3.6	3.5	7.6	5.7	2.0	5.9
2005	5.1	16.6	4.4	4.6	4.4	10.0	6.0	2.8	7.8
2006	4.6	15.4	4.0	4.1	4.0	8.9	5.2	2.4	7.1
2007	4.6	15.7	4.1	4.0	4.1	8.3	5.6	2.5	6.5
2008	5.1	17.0	5.4	4.8	4.7	10.0	7.5	3.2	7.9

Source: *Economic Report of the President*, 1990, pp. 338–339; 2003, p. 326; 2008, pp. 334–335.

More than 10 million people (on the average) were unemployed during the recession of 1980 to 1982. (Princeton economist Alan Blinder called them "cannon fodder in the assault on inflation.") Although the number of unemployed fell to 6.5 million in 1989, it quickly rose to 9.4 million in 1992 as the result of the recession that began in 1990. Unemployment rates then trended downward to 4.0 percent in the recovery through 2000. By 2001, the economy was showing signs of recession as economic growth slowed and the unemployment rate increased to 4.7 percent in 2001 and peaked at 6.0 percent in 2003. In late 2003 and 2004, with increases in government spending and tax cuts kicking in to jumpstart the economy, growth had renewed, but joblessness remained stubbornly at 5.6 percent. By 2005, however, unemployment rates had dropped to 4.6 percent. The recession that began at the end of 2007 boosted civilian unemployment rates to 9.4 percent in June 2009. Unemployment has direct social consequences for unemployed individuals, their families, and communities facing closed factories, unemployment lines, and discouraged workers.

Counting the Unemployed. Beyond the real costs to those unemployed and to lost output, there are also problems in simply counting and defining the unemployed in our economy. Critics claim that the national measures of unemployment actually understate the real rate of unemployment. They argue that a different definition and measurement technique would reveal a national "underemployment" rate of 9 to 16 percent.

David Gordon, who taught at the New School of Social Research, called attention to the problem of *underemployment* and suggested that it was a more appropriate measure than the traditional notion of unemployment. As a more meaningful statistic, it would give economists better information and be more instructive to policy makers. Gordon defined underemployment as the number of people who fall into any of the following four categories:

1. *Unemployed people*—those who are actively looking for work but unable to find a job
2. *Discouraged workers*—those who are unemployed and want work but have given up in frustration because they believe no jobs are available
3. *Involuntary part-time workers*—those employed part-time who want full-time work but are unable to find it
4. *Underemployed people*—those who are working full-time but earning less than the poverty level of income as specified by the Bureau of Labor Statistics (for an urban family of four, $21,200 per year in 2008, compared to approximately $13,624 per year paid to a person working full-time at the 2008 minimum wage).

We can use these categories to adjust the traditional measure of unemployment. In May 2009, the Bureau of Labor Statistics reported just over 9.1 million workers who were involuntary part-time employees. This compares to 4.5 million involuntary part-time workers in 2005. Discouraged workers were estimated at 792,000. An additional 1.4 million are marginally attached to the labor market but cite reasons other than being discouraged for not being employed. Such reasons might include transportation problems, family responsibilities, or ill health. When combined with the unemployed, these discouraged and involuntary part-time workers generated an "expanded unemployment rate" of over 12 percent in 2008.

2. Do you anticipate unemployment in your future? Why or why not? What are your "odds"?

3. Does it make any difference how we count the unemployed? Explain.

Costs of Unemployment and Underemployment. Unemployment is an economic (opportunity) cost. Every 1 percent of the labor force that is unemployed represents several billion dollars of potential GDP.

In addition, unemployment has social and psychological costs—crime, family disintegration, and increasing mental health problems, to name a few. An examination of the nature of unemployment in the United States also reveals an identifiable institutionalized process of discrimination according to race, gender, and age. This became increasingly evident as unprecedented numbers of minorities, women, and teenagers entered the labor force after January 1980. In January 2008, when the Bureau of Labor Statistics reported a national unemployment rate that averaged 5.1 percent, the unemployment rate for black or African Americans averaged 10 percent—and more than 30.0 percent for black teens.

A last consideration related to unemployment involves poverty and welfare. In 2007, the poverty rate for those who did not work was more than 8 times the rate for those who worked (21.5 percent versus 2.7 percent), and part-time workers were 6.0 times more likely than full-time workers to fall into poverty. For U.S. citizens who are neither employed nor receiving any form of income from unemployment compensation, Social Security, or disability, welfare is the only way to meet survival needs. In addition, there has been an increase in the percent of part-time jobs. While some workers opt for part-time schedules, some 4.7 million workers who hold part-time jobs prefer to work full-time. Part-time jobs are characterized by lower wages, lower skill levels, more limited promotion opportunities, and fewer benefits than full-time jobs.

Price Stability

One thing that many people have in common is an aversion to **inflation**, which is an upward movement in the general price level. Deflation, in contrast, indicates a downward movement of the general price level. Price stability occurs when there is relatively little movement in the general price level.

The price level is measured by some sort of price index, such as the **Consumer Price Index (CPI)**. A typical price index measures the average level of prices in one year or period as a percentage of the average price level in some base period. The Consumer Price Index is computed by the Bureau of Labor Statistics (BLS). Each month the BLS surveys markets in some fifty urban areas for the prices of 400 "typical" consumer goods and services. The bureau then computes the CPI by measuring the present cost of this "basket" of items as a percentage of the cost in some base period:

$$\text{CPI} = \frac{\text{current cost of basket}}{\text{cost of basket in base year}} \times 100$$

The inflation or deflation rate then measures the percentage change in the price level:

$$\text{current inflation or deflation rate} = \frac{\text{current CPI} - \text{last year's CPI}}{\text{last year's CPI}} \times 100$$

In the 1970s, the U.S. economy experienced frequent periods of inflation. During the 1980s, 1990s, and through 2004, annual rates of price increase remained low overall but began increasing through 2007. Still, price increases have been greater than the overall inflation rate in some selected markets. For example, oil prices reached record levels in 2008 and college students have experienced rapid rises in the cost of tuition each year, as well as higher than average prices for textbooks. Between 2000 and 2006, potential home buyers were confronted by much higher than average housing prices. By 2008, however, the housing bubble had collapsed and home prices were decreasing.

Because rapidly increasing prices often affect our consumption and saving decisions, we tend to have a greater sense of well-being when prices are stable. We don't have to worry (as much) about whether our savings will suffice to send us to college or help maintain our standard of living after we retire. We do know, however, that inflation is not a problem for those who correctly anticipate it and take appropriate precautions. For example, if prices rise by 4 percent and workers are aware of these economic developments, they expect a 4 percent inflation rate. To keep real (inflation-adjusted) wages at the same level, workers will demand at least a 4 percent wage increase. They will also put their savings into assets that will yield at least 4 percent. With these adjustments, workers correctly anticipate inflation and insulate themselves from it. But, if wages rise by only 3 percent with a 5 percent increase in prices, workers' income will lose 2 percent in purchasing power.

Those hurt by inflation include people on fixed incomes, usually the elderly; those working under fixed-cost or fixed-wage contracts; and individuals or institutions who have lent money at an interest rate less than the current rate of inflation. Many contracts now allow for price fluctuations, and many pensions are adjusted for inflation. Financial institutions react to inflationary pressures by charging higher interest rates, or even variable interest rates pegged to bonds that reflect price or inflationary changes. Still, people prefer price stability as a way to avoid the necessity of forecasting correctly and adjusting behavior to that forecast.

During the 1970s, the United States experienced record levels of inflation caused by factors related to demand, supply, and expectations. Owing to the same factors, the 1980s brought an ebbing of inflationary pressures. Several unexpected forces entered into the scenario during the 1970s, all of which heightened the problem of inflation. In 1973, an embargo imposed by the powerful Organization of Petroleum Exporting Countries (OPEC) nations sent energy prices soaring. The reduced supply of oil caused the general price level to rise and output to fall. Shortages and price increases were also felt in the markets for food, metals, and other primary materials.

The 1970s also ushered in a period of increased government regulation. This time, instead of antitrust legislation, the government regulated various aspects of our living and working environments and promoted equal opportunity. While the social benefits of these regulations were widespread, they were also expensive, and these costs initially came on board during the 1970s. Accelerated government expenditures resulting from the Vietnam War added an estimated 3.25 percent to the underlying inflation rate, while the surge in oil prices, first in 1973 and again in 1979, added 4.75 percent. These factors alone explain an inflation rate of 8 percent during the 1970s.

At the beginning of the 1980s, events eased inflationary pressures. Oil prices began to drop as production increased and demand fell. The prices of other raw materials declined as well, due to overproduction in many of the developing nations. Deregulation, or the rollback of government regulations, in a number of industries increased competition and lowered prices. The value of the dollar restrained prices of imported goods, helping to lower inflation in the United States by providing a supply of cheaper imports and by keeping domestic prices in check as U.S. producers struggled to remain price-competitive. Labor made many concessions during the recession of 1980 to 1982, and these "givebacks" kept wages from rising. More importantly, the Federal Reserve cut the growth rate of the money supply to halt the inflationary trends, and lower inflation rates were gained at the cost of high rates of unemployment.

With the Federal Reserve policy continuing to target low inflation rates, the late 1980s through 2004 saw stable prices, averaging growth rates between 2 and 4 percent. This period was accompanied by relatively stable oil and resource prices, slow wage growth, and in the late 1990s, cheap imports. Oil prices began increasing rapidly in 2004 due to concern about Middle East oil supplies and increased oil demand by India and China. The effect of huricane Katrina's disruption of U.S. oil production in late 2005 and the Israel-Lebanon war in 2006 kept oil prices increasing at a robust rate. By the end of 2006, oil markets calmed and prices fell, just before rising to record level in 2008.

The goal of price stability is sometimes achieved due to good economic policy, good luck, or some combination of the two, particularly when factors outside the realm of domestic economic policy tools are operating.

---

4. Which of the three macroeconomic goals—growth, full employment, or price stability—is the most important to you? Why?

5. If you could add another goal to this list, what would it be? Explain.

MACROECONOMIC TOOLS

To achieve the three macroeconomic goals of growth, full employment, and price stability, economists and government policy makers use economic theory to analyze the economy and to formulate macroeconomic policy. The primary macroeconomic tools are monetary and fiscal policy. Let's briefly define each of these and see how they are used.

The Federal Reserve System manages, coordinates, and controls the monetary system of the U.S. economy. Proper management of this system makes available the quantity of money necessary for desired economic growth at interest rates capable of inducing the desired levels of investment and spending. **Monetary policy** consists of tools that can change the amount of money and credit available in the economy. It is administered by the Federal Reserve System to achieve and promote economic growth, maximum employment, and price stability.

Through **fiscal policy**, the government manipulates its expenditures and taxation to attain the basic macroeconomic objectives. Fiscal policy is administered by the executive and legislative branches of the federal government and is coordinated with monetary policy. (See Chapters 15 and 16 for more on fiscal and monetary policy.)

Fiscal and monetary tools have both been part of contemporary macroeconomic policy as it has developed over the past sixty years. Several important issues and problems are associated with this policy. We shall examine a few of these in the context of the economic history of the post–World War II period, when monetary and fiscal policy became mainstays in a U.S. economy aiming to achieve the goals of growth, high employment, and price stability.

The Rise of Pax Americana: 1946 to the 1960s

Just as the Victorian period in the late nineteenth century was dubbed "Pax Britannia," the period after World War II until the middle to late 1960s has been called "Pax Americana." The world seemed ripe for economic quests and successes by the United States. The three decades that followed, however, saw a reduction in U.S. power in the international economic arena. The U.S. position continued to worsen until conditions taking advantage of economic growth, improvements in levels of employment, stable prices, and deficit reductions arose in the mid-1990s.

By the end of World War II, many important institutions characteristic of the U.S. economy were already in place. Monopolies and large corporations had been present since the turn of the century, and the 1930s brought increasing levels of government intervention in the economy. After the prolonged recession and depression of the 1930s and the wartime economy of the 1940s, the setting was ripe for the United States to push ahead and prosper. The 1950s arrived with abundant potential and opportunity; Europe and Japan lay in ruin, and the United States possessed the only productive industrial capacity not debilitated by the war. These industries were immediately called on in the effort to rebuild Europe and Japan, as well as to meet the increased demands for consumer goods and services that had developed in the United States during the war. In the decade following the war, U.S. economic growth skyrocketed. Real weekly earnings increased at an average of 2.3 percent per year. Productivity increases held steady at 3.2 percent, and real GDP growth was about 4 percent. Unemployment averaged 4 percent. When unemployment rose to 5.5 percent in the recessions of 1949, 1954, 1958, and 1960, inflation slowed to 2 percent.

As the prosperity of the 1950s passed into the 1960s, the government began to actively participate in the growth that had earlier been dominated by the private sector. The new federal interstate highway system was the highlight of federal expenditures of the 1950s. These expenditures continued into the 1960s and were joined by a federal Model Cities program that contributed to the U.S. urban infrastructure. In 1964, Congress passed a tax cut specifically designed to increase income—the first planned policy action of its type. Later in the 1960s, the Great Society program was put into place to reduce poverty. Only now are we realizing the successes of these programs—as well as some of their shortcomings. The 1960s also brought the war in Vietnam and a demand for more federal expenditures to finance it.

Also by the 1960s, Japan and the industrial nations of Western Europe had rebuilt their factories, and their economies were strengthened. Increased foreign production challenged U.S. goods in world markets, and U.S. economic growth slowed. In the international sphere, the dollar, which serves as the "key currency" in all international transactions, was coming under economic attack as other nations regained their prewar economic positions. This pressure eventually led to a devaluation of the dollar and a new system for determining international exchange rates.

The Decline of Pax Americana: The 1970s to Mid-1980s

During the 1970s, U.S. economic growth and strength were challenged from several sides. The oil embargo of 1973, coupled with agricultural shortages, showed the vulnerability of the U.S. economy (and others as well) to supply shocks on a world level. A severe recession in the mid-1970s sent unemployment to 9 percent. As the economy began to recover in 1977 and 1978, inflation sky-rocketed to 13.3 percent. In the last half of 1979, the Federal Reserve put in motion a series of credit restraints that sent the economy plummeting into yet another recession. Economic growth slowed, and throughout the decade, growth was due almost entirely to rising employment and not greater productivity. The service sector dominated the employment growth of the seventies, with many dead-end, low-paying jobs providing entry for an expanding labor force.

While the 1970s were marked by record levels of inflation in the United States, the early 1980s witnessed both the highest levels of unemployment since the 1930s and the lowest levels of inflation since the 1960s. In 1981, the economy experienced a recession and modest recovery, then plunged into the deepest recession since the Great Depression. This recession can largely be explained by actions of the Federal Reserve, which was using monetary policy to actively restrict growth in the supply of money between late 1979 and 1982. (Chapter 16 explains these concepts in more detail.)

Monetary ease and historically high government expenditures and tax cuts combined to generate the recovery of 1983 to 1984, which, despite very slow economic growth, persisted until 1989. Unemployment fell as some workers headed back to the factories and many others moved into the service sector. Inflation remained stable at 3 percent, but increases in real weekly earnings averaged only 0.3 percent. The economy, however, had been left with very high real rates of interest, resulting at least partially from large government expenditures and tax cuts creating deficits. Throughout the 1980s, the federal government incurred large and persistent budget deficits. High interest rates hurt the economy by hindering job creation and investment in new plants, equipment, and housing. These high rates of return also attracted foreign money to the United States and kept the value of the dollar high through 1985. This promoted the importation of relatively cheap foreign goods, helping consumers but hurting U.S. producers, who lost out in two ways: Not only were more foreign goods purchased in the United States, but fewer U.S. products were exported to the rest of the world. In the early 1980s, high interest rates also affected debt-plagued developing nations, whose debt payments mounted with each rise in the U.S. interest rate.

6. Why do you think inflation might rise when unemployment is low? Explain.

7. What is debt? How does it arise? Do you worry about going into debt? Why?

The U.S. Economy: The Late 1980s and Early 1990s

During the 1980s, the Federal Reserve continued to increase the money supply, resulting in lower interest rates. During this period of sustained growth and low inflation, a stock market crash in the United States wiped out some $500 billion of wealth, signaling that not all was well with the U.S. economy. By the end of the week of October 19, 1987, nearly $1 trillion of wealth had vanished.*

The repercussions of the crash were felt throughout the world. Quick intervention by the Federal Reserve assured both confidence and sufficient liquidity to underwrite any instability that might spread to the banking and credit industries. Indicators showed the economy to be in reasonable health; the 6 percent unemployment level was the lowest in a decade, prices were stable, and economic growth had been led by a massive consumer spending boom. There were, however, economic as well as structural and institutional problems that prompted the dramatic decline in the New York Stock Exchange on that day, referred to as Black Monday.

After the 1987 crash, the underlying U.S. debt, low saving rate, and institutional problems persisted. The economic recovery of the early 1980s continued, with economic growth averaging just over 3.7 percent between 1987 and 1989. In 1989, unemployment reached its lowest point since 1973, when it fell to 5.3 percent. After this, growth stagnated and an economic slowdown continued through 1992.

A Rebirth of Pax Americana: 1992 and Beyond

A buoyant recovery followed the 1989 to 1992 recession and was characterized by increased investment, strong productivity growth, lower levels of unemployment,

---

*Some people call this wealth "paper wealth." It accumulates from the changing value of stock prices.

and steady economic expansion without any signs of inflation. Indeed, the economic growth experienced in the United States between the trough of the recession in 1991 and peak of the upturn in 2000 was the longest economic expansion on record.

Growth between 1992 and 1997 was accompanied by changes in corporate organization including downsizing. While the rate of growth was initially slow, it increased steadily. The president and Congress paid increasing attention to budget and trade deficits and were successful in reducing budget deficits. The income gap between the haves and have-nots continued to widen, with women and children bearing the brunt of the effects of income redistribution. Although an impressive number of jobs were created between 1982 and 1988 and 1992 and 2000, the number of less-educated workers vying for those jobs reduced the real earnings of high school graduates and dropouts alike. Rank-and-file workers experienced an 18 percent decrease in real (inflation-adjusted) wages between 1973 and 1997, while corporate chief executive officers watched their pay increase by an average of 19 percent (66 percent after taxes). Homelessness became a national problem.

Financial crises in Asia, Latin America, and Russia in 1997 and 1998 failed to stem the economic expansion in the United States. Rather, as countries in these areas experienced a deep economic downturn, their falling currencies and lower wages signaled cheaper exports to the United States. The relatively low prices of imports from these areas kept U.S. prices low.

With inflation well under control, investment continued to increase, and economic growth became even more rapid, reaching an extraordinary level of 6 percent in 1999 before falling to more normal and sustainable rate of 4 percent in 2000. Employment remained strong as growth kept unemployment hovering around 4 percent between 1997 and 2001. With rising income, productivity increases, and moderation in public policy, budget deficits turned into surpluses in 1999 and 2000 for the first time since World War II. Internationally, U.S. growth rates were much stronger than those in Europe and Japan. Despite this remarkable period of economic expansion, the U.S. infrastructure—the stock of highways, bridges, and water and sewer lines that had contributed to growth in the 1950s and 1960s—continued to deteriorate. Fewer U.S. workers were covered by health insurance and the number of uninsured children grew.

By early 2001, a recession was underway. After a decade of uninterrupted and often accelerating growth, postwar unemployment record lows, and vigorous productivity increases, growth did finally slow and a number of economic "shocks" prolonged the slowdown into 2003. In March 2001, the high-flying stock market, largely propelled by technology and .com stocks, began a quick descent, with most stock measures dropping more than 20 percent, wiping out an estimated $4.7 trillion in "paper" wealth from the change in value of stock prices. The Federal Reserve pumped money into the economy and targeted much lower interest rates designed to stimulate investment and consumer spending. Congress passed a series of tax cuts with the hope of increasing the economic stimulus.

In the fall, more economic shocks left the economy reeling. The terror attacks of September 11, 2001, had profound impacts on all aspects of American lives, including the economy. Uncertainty and confusion surrounding the attacks led investors and consumers to be more wary about expenditures. And, while Americans were still trying to deal with the after-effects of September 11 and plan for the future, a series of corporate scandals led to the failure of several large firms, including Enron (the seventh largest firm in the United States in 2000), and Arthur Andersen, one of the (then) "big five" accounting firms. War in Iraq, declared in March 2003, also had economic consequences.

The lowest mortgage rates in four decades, low interest rates, increases in government spending and tax cuts, resilient consumers, and a buoyant housing market stimulated economic activity. By late 2006, economic growth and productivity returned. Initially, lethargic job creation and discouraged workers, accompanied by growing budget deficits and trade deficits (despite a weaker U.S. dollar), continued to cause concern, but by the end of the year and throughout 2007 the unemployment rate remained at a low 4.6 percent. Inflation began to rise in 2007 and 2008 due to high commodity prices, including record oil prices; however, prices stabilized in late 2008. The financial crisis that began in 2007 spread to the rest of the economy in 2008 as consumers cut spending and businesses decreased investment expenditures. Unemployment began to rise, reaching 9.4 percent in mid-2009. Between 2007 and the second quarter of 2009, some $14 trillion in wealth was lost due to decreases in the stock market and the drop in house prices as the housing bubble burst. Because of the global spread of the financial crisis, the U.S. dollar initially rose against most major currencies and the strong dollar dampened an already lethargic export sector. The failure and near failure of several large financial institutions, along with a growing number of U.S. corporations entering bankruptcy, resulted in continuing and increasing job losses. Firms entering bankruptcy included Linens 'n Things, Eddie Bauer, Circuit City, Chrysler, and General Motors. The government injected funds into the economy through the Troubled Asset Relief Program (TARP) and stimulus package, and the Federal Reserve created a number of funding and lending facilities to help supply liquidity to a financial system that had ceased lending and creating credit. Health care and health insurance coverage remained a topic of public discussion as health care costs continued to rise, as did the numbers of uninsured.

As we continue our discussion of macroeconomic goals, we see that while full employment, low inflation, and economic growth are important, other goals also might be beneficial, but little agreement exists as to what these additional goals might be, or which economic problems should have priority.

8. What has happened to the recession since 2009? What has stimulated the rapid or slow or no growth? Has unemployment increased? Inflation? Why or why not?

9. List five macroeconomic goals you think are important for this millennium. Briefly explain your choices.

NATIONAL ACCOUNTING MEASURES

As we chart macroeconomic goals through the next few years, it is important to understand what these concepts mean and how we measure them. The scheme of National Income and Product Accounting was developed to put economic growth measures into perspective. These measures give quantifiable definitions to the activities of the major macroeconomic actors (consumers, businesses, governments, and the international sector) and show how they interact to generate production, consumption, and investment.

To help understand the ways in which the economy continues to change over time, economists collect and analyze data that measure economic variables. Economic measurement is usually designed to aid forecasting and explanation of economic events, or it may be used to compare the size or the value of things. When economists speak of the value of the annual output of a nation, they refer to gross domestic product (GDP), published in quarterly reports issued by the Department of Commerce. The media, politicians, and others who regularly comment on economic affairs await the Commerce Department reports in order to assess whether GDP and its accompanying growth rate are up or down. Economists then assess these results and often qualify them—for example, GDP was up 2.5 percent over last quarter, but prices have been increasing by 3 percent at the same time.

In December 1991, the Bureau of Economic Analysis began to emphasize GDP in place of gross national product (GNP). The distinction between the two accounting measures is that GDP includes the income earned by foreign residents and companies in the United States, but not the income earned by U.S. citizens and corporations abroad. The change from GNP to GDP occurred because GDP more closely follows the short-term economic performance of the economy and because most other countries use GDP as their primary accounting measure.

In fact, for the United States, the difference between GNP and GDP has usually been very small. In a typical year, the income earned by foreign-owned businesses and noncitizens in the United States is very close to the income earned by U.S. citizens and companies abroad. Therefore, the differences between GNP and GDP nearly cancel each other out in the United States. However, in small countries with much business activity by foreign companies, the two measures may be significantly different.

Economists and policy makers use GDP and the rest of the National Income and Product Accounts as the basis for many decisions. We therefore will spend some time looking at the components of these accounts.

There are two basic ways of arriving at final figures for the various accounting measures:

1. The *goods- or expenditures-flow approach* focuses on the prices and quantities of goods and services sold.

FIGURE 13.1 The Income and Spending Flows

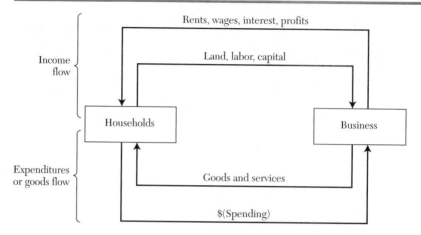

2. The *income-flow approach* focuses on income paid to those producing goods and services.

These approaches appear in the circular flow diagram in Figure 13.1. We can measure either the top part of the circular flow (the income flow) or the bottom part of the circular flow (the goods or expenditures flow) to arrive at equal measures of national income.

The definitions, relations, and data in Tables 13.3 and 13.4 show the derivation of GDP with the goods-flow approach. GDP consists of the total expenditures of the four sectors that purchase goods and services:

$$GDP = C + I + G + (X - M),$$

where C represents the expenditures made by consumers, I is investment expenditures made by the business community, G is expenditures on goods and services by government, and $(X - M)$ represents net exports, or exports (X) minus imports (M). GDP grows or declines due to changes in consumption (C), investment (I), government expenditures (G), and/or net exports $(X - M)$. Figure 13.2 illustrates the percentage change of each of these measures between quarters from 2007 through the second quarter of 2009. Note how the percentage change in consumption spending fell until the first quarter of 2009 as consumers responded to the recession by decreasing their spending. This had the effect of decreasing GDP. Note as well that gross private domestic investment only began to decline in the fourth quarter of 2008. When investment spending falls, it too produces a negative effect on GDP—so GDP will fall, unless decreases are offset by an increase in other measures. The income-flow approach entails summing the various forms of income received from the production process, so when the percentage change in an income stream like wages and salaries falls, GDP will fall unless another income stream, like profits, offsets the decline.

Table 13.3 Relation of Gross Domestic Product, Net National Product, National Income, and Personal Income

The sum of	Billions of Dollars		
	1996	2000	2008
Personal consumption expenditures (C)	5,151.40	6,757.30	10,057.90
Gross private domestic investment (I)	1,117.00	1,832.70	1,993.50
Government consumption expenditures and gross investment (G)	1,406.40	1,743.70	2,882.40
Net exports of goods and services (X – M)	–98.70	–370.70	–669.20
EQUALS: Gross domestic product (GDP)	7,576.10	9,963.10	14,264.60
PLUS: Receipts of factor income from the rest of the world	228.40	370.60	789.30
LESS: Payments of factor income to the rest of the world	237.30	374.90	665.10
EQUALS: Gross national product (GNP)	7,567.20	9,958.70	14,397.80
LESS: Consumption of fixed capital	858.30	1,257.10	1,832.30
EQUALS: Net national product (NNP)	6,708.90	8,701.60	12,565.50
LESS: Indirect business tax and nontax liability	617.90	769.60	–
Business transfer payments	32.20	41.70	–
Statistical discrepancy	–74.60	–87.70	138.10
PLUS: Subsidies less current surplus of government enterprises	17.50	27.90	–
EQUALS: National income (NI)	6,150.90	8,002.00	12,427.40
LESS: Corporate profits with inventory valuation and capital consumption adjustments	654.70	946.20	1,476.50
Net interest	403.30	567.20	682.70
Contributions for social insurance	689.70	705.60	995.70
LESS: Taxes on production (–) M subsides	–	–	983.10
Net Business Transfer Payments	–	–	103.60
PLUS: Personal interest income	1,056.70	1,034.30	–
Personal dividend income	738.20	396.60	–
Personal income receipts on assets	–	–	2,037.70
Government transfer payments to persons	230.60	1,037.10	–
Business transfer payments to persons	23.00	30.70	–
Personal current transfer receipts	–	–	1,869.10
EQUALS: Personal income (PI)	6,451.70	8,281.70	12,100.60
LESS: Personal tax payments	863.80	1,291.90	1,457.30
EQUALS: Disposable personal income (DPI)	5,587.90	6,989.80	10,643.30
LESS: Personal outlays		6,998.30	10,450.70
Personal consumption expenditures (C)	5,151.40	6,757.30	10,057.90
Interest paid by consumers	146.30	212.20	248.90
Personal transfer payments	16.30	28.80	144.50
EQUALS: Personal savings (S)	273.90	–8.50	192.70

Note: Dollars are not constant dollars.

Note: Numbers do not add up to the totals shown because of adjustments or inclusion of minor categories. In 2006, revisions changed the accounting for items shown as dashes (–).

Source: Survey of Current Business, April 1997; April 2001, 2004, 2009.

Table 13.4 Definitions of Primary Account in Table 13.3

___

The sum of

1. *Personal consumption expenditures (C)* consist of the market value of purchases of goods and services by individuals and nonprofit institutions and the value of food, clothing, housing, and financial services received by them as income in kind.

2. *Gross private domestic investment (I)* consists of acquisitions of newly produced capital goods by private business and nonprofit institutions and of the value of the change in the volume of inventories held by business. It covers all private new dwellings.

3. *Government consumption expenditures and gross investment (G)* consist of government expenditures for compensation of employees, purchases from business, net foreign purchases and contributions, and the gross investment of government enterprises. This measure excludes transfer payments, government interest, and subsidies.

4. *Net exports of goods and services (X − M)* measures the excess of (1) domestic output sold abroad over purchases of foreign output, (2) production abroad credited to U.S-owned resources over production at home credited to foreign-owned resources, and (3) cash gifts and contributions received from abroad over cash gifts and contributions to foreigners.

EQUALS

5. *Gross domestic product (GDP)* is the market value of the newly produced goods and services that are not resold in any form during the accounting period (usually one year).

PLUS

6. *Receipts of factor income* from the rest of the world are the moneys received from foreign affiliates of U.S. corporations. The moneys take the form of interest, dividends, and reinvested earnings.

LESS

7. *Payments of factor income* to the rest of the world are the payments to foreign residents of interest, dividends, and reinvested earnings of U.S. affiliates of foreign companies.

EQUALS

8. *Gross national product (GNP)* is the market value of the newly produced goods and services that are not resold in any form during the accounting period (usually one year).

LESS

9. *Capital consumption allowance* is an allowance for capital goods that have been consumed in the process of producing this year's GDP. It consists of depreciation, capital outlays charged to current expense, and accidental damage.

10. *Net national product (NNP)* is the net creation of new wealth resulting from the productive activity of the economy during the accounting period.

___

POTENTIAL PROBLEMS WITH THE NATIONAL INCOME ACCOUNTS

The measures in the National Income Accounts are corrected for inflation with the use of a price index. Also, use of a value-added approach in the measurement process avoids possible double-counting. There are, however, criticisms of the accounts that have not been addressed. Particularly troublesome are issues of what is and what is not included in the National Income and Product Accounts. Let us see how some potential problems have been avoided and discuss some that remain.

Table 13.4 Continued

LESS

11. *Indirect business tax* consists primarily of sales and excise taxes, customs duties on imported goods, and business property taxes. These taxes are collected from businesses and are chargeable to their current costs.

EQUALS

12. *National income (NI)* is the total income of factors from participation in the current productive process.

LESS

13. *After-tax corporate profits* with inventory and capital consumption adjustments subtracts federal and state taxes levied on corporate earnings and depreciation allowances from orporate profits.

14. *Net interest* is interest earnings minus interest liabilities and part of national income.

15. Contributions for ***social insurance*** consist of payments by employees and the self-employed.

PLUS

16. *Personal interest income* includes all interest payments made to persons.

17. *Personal dividend income* includes that part of corporate profits returned to stockholders.

18. *Transfer payments* (government and business) consist of monetary income received by individuals from government and business (other than government interest) for which no services are currently rendered.

EQUALS

19. *Personal income (PI)* is income received by households, as opposed to income earned by households.

LESS

20. *Personal taxes* consist of the taxes levied against individuals, their income, and their property that are not deductible as expenses of business operations.

EQUALS

21. *Disposable personal income (DPI)* is the income remaining to persons after deduction of personal tax and nontax payments to general government.

LESS

22. *Personal consumption expenditures (C)*—this is the same as item 1.

EQUALS

23. *Personal savings (S)* may be in such forms as changes in cash and deposits, security holdings, and private pension, health, welfare, and trust funds.

Real versus Nominal GDP

These definitional relationships ignore many difficult and rather perplexing problems. First, there is the problem of the yardstick, money. This is a very flexible yardstick, since dollars are most often worth more or less as time passes (usually less). To solve the flexibility dilemma, economists use index numbers, meaning they compare a "market basket" of selected goods and services from one accounting period with a similar "basket" from some previous accounting period, or base year.*

---

*In January 1996, the Bureau of Economic Analysis (BEA) released new estimates for the national income and product accounts, moving to a system that uses chain weights instead of fixed weights in the adjustment of real GDP, to remove biases caused by the fixed-weight price system of the past. The formula for this adjustment is no longer as simple as the common market basket example using fixed weights. By adopting the chain-weighting system, the BEA hopes to provide more accurate measures of real GDP. For additional information on these changes, see the 1996 *Economic Report of the President*, pp. 48, 50, and 59.

FIGURE 13.2 Contribution to U.S. GDP Growth, % change on previous quarter (annualized)

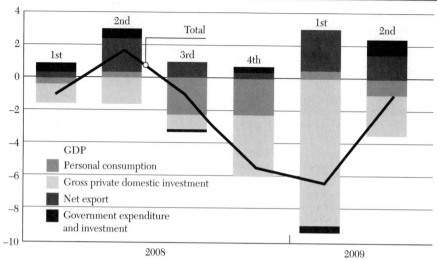

Source: *Thomson Reuters Datastream.*

Thus, they can avoid the perils of price instability by inflating or deflating the dollar value accordingly. For example, if prices increase at a rate of 5 percent during a year, a good that cost $100 at the beginning of the first year would be priced at $105 at the beginning of the next. Using a price index, this item would be valued at $100 in constant dollars. This device allows us to remove the effects of price changes from GDP, so that we can measure the changes in *real* output and better assess the actual physical volume of production in the two periods.

The GDP deflator is a systematized equation that has been shown to be a reasonable indicator of how much the national product has gained or lost due to recession or inflation. For example, in 1979 GDP went up by 12 percent, but prices went up by 11.3 percent, so real GDP increased by only 0.7 percent. Figure 13.3 shows the variation between real and nominal GDP since 1999.

Value-Added Accounting

A second problem encountered in the national income accounting framework is the actual counting process. We can either count the final products produced or sum the amount of value added by each stage of the production process. For example, to enter a loaf of bread into the accounting scheme, we could use the final sale price of the loaf of bread, or we could sum the value added to the loaf of bread by the wheat farmer, miller, baker, grocer, and so on. Both methods should yield the same result, but in the final-product method, there is often a chance of double-counting the components of production. Therefore, the value-added approach is preferred.

What Is Counted in GDP?

The significance of the accounts also has been called into question. These accounts are primarily derived from market transactions with known prices and quantities, but some market transactions are excluded. Excluded transactions include capital gains and losses as well as all illegal transactions. (What would the illegal drug market add to the GDP?) Also excluded is the economic activity of the underground economy—individuals who earn but do not report income on services they render or goods they produce, for example, cash paid for baby-sitting. Barter exchange also is part of the underground economy. The size of the underground economy has been estimated at 5 to 30 percent of GDP. Other industrial nations are estimated to have underground economies comparable to that of the United States.

FIGURE 13.3 GDP in Current and Constant Dollars 1999–2009

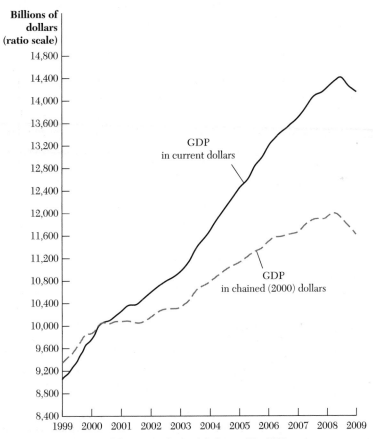

Source: U.S. Department of Commerce, *Economic Indicators*, May 2009.

The accounts also include some imputed values for nonmarket transactions. For example, imputed values are added for owner-occupied homes (room and board services exchanged for). But imagine what would happen to the accounts if we made yet another nonmarket inclusion, the value of unpaid child care provided by parents. If families simply exchanged child care with their neighbors each day and paid one another $50 or more a day (the estimated market worth of child care services), their production would be included in the accounts. These activities are productive; they are services. Currently, however, they are neither measured nor included in the National Income Accounts.

Marilyn Waring, a political economist and former member of the New Zealand Parliament, has suggested in her book *If Women Counted: A New Feminist Economics*, that throughout the world, accounting systems that define productive activity, as well as the economic analysis and teaching that sustain them, automatically exclude the nonmarket activities of women. To this point she quotes retired Harvard economist John Kenneth Galbraith:

> That many women are coming to sense that they are instruments in the economic system is not in doubt. But their feeling finds no support in economic writing and teaching. On the contrary, it is concealed and on the whole with great success, by modern neo-classical economics—the everyday economics of the textbook and classroom. This concealment is neither conspiratorial nor deliberate. It reflects the natural and very strong instincts of economics for what is convenient to influence economic interest—for what I have called the conventional social virtue. It is sufficiently successful that it allows many hundreds of thousands of women to study economics each year without their developing any serious suspicion as to how they will be used.

> —Marilyn J. Waring, *If Women Counted*, HarperCollins Publishers, 1989.

10. How will you be used by the economic system? Does it matter? Why?

11. What are "natural" instincts? Do you trust them?

The National Income Accounts are often misrepresented as an indicator of social well-being. In 1995, Clifford Cobb, Ted Halstead, and Jonathan Rowe published an article in *The Atlantic Monthly* entitled "If the GDP Is Up, Why Is America Down?" The article noted that the U.S. economy was performing in textbook fashion, with productivity and employment increasing and inflation remaining at low levels, but people didn't "feel" better. Indeed, President Clinton later called it a malaise. These authors argued for new measures for economic progress that would "change the social and political landscape":

> The GDP is simply a gross measure of market activity, of money changing hands. It makes no distinction whatsoever between the desirable and the undesirable, or costs and gain. On top of that, it looks only at the portion of reality that economists

choose to acknowledge—the part involved in monetary transactions. The crucial economic functions performed in the household and volunteer sectors go entirely unrecognized. As a result the GDP not only masks the breakdown of the social structure and the natural habitat upon which the economy—and life itself—ultimately depend; worse, it actually portrays such breakdown as economic gain.

Economic "bads," such as pollution and deaths due to lung cancer attributed to smoking cigarettes, actually increase the GDP. These social costs are not subtracted from, but added to the GDP. As we spend more and more to clean up the environment, the spending *adds* to our national product. As cigarette sales increase, GDP increases. As hospital costs for increased numbers of cases of lung cancer and emphysema occur, GDP increases. GDP, in other words, is not a measure of overall welfare.

The environment think tank, Redefining Progress, has constructed what it calls a genuine progress indicator (GPI). The GPI tries to monitor "sustainability"—or the conflict between sustaining human life and the integrity of nature... or living satisfactorily without destroying our environment. Thus the GPI monitors human consumption of resources *and* our contentment with our social, personal, and civic life. In other words, the GPI takes some economic "bads" such as environmental degradation into account. Figure 13.4 compares trends in per capita GPI with trends in per capita GDP in the United States since 1950. Although GDP has risen over that period, the level of GPI has barely changed.

12. Can you give other examples in which individual or societal welfare is diminished but GDP is increased?

Social scientists are attempting to construct a qualitative index that measures social welfare. Thus far, the index is quite crude, but it shows that nations with the highest GDP do not necessarily have the highest social welfare ratings, while a few countries with extremely low GDP have *relatively* high standings on the social welfare index.

The United Nations has constructed a Human Development Index (HDI) that measures a set of average human achievements in a single index. These achievements include life expectancy at birth, adult literacy rate, and per capita income. Table 13.5 lists the top twenty countries according to a recent HDI.

13. Why is it important to collect data on all of these different macroeconomic variables?

FIGURE 13.4 Genuine Progress Indicator and GDP for the United States, 1950–2004

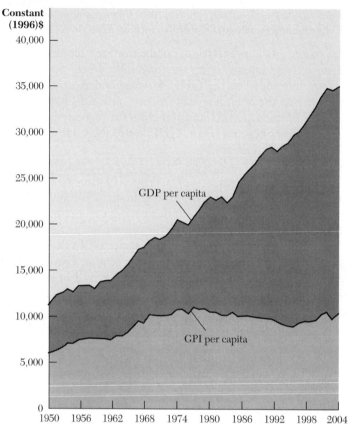

Source: Data from Redefining Progress, *Genuine Progress Report,* 2006. p.4

Table 13.5 Top Countries Rated with the UN's Human Development Index

Rank	Country
1.	Iceland
2.	Norway
3.	Canada
4.	Australia
5.	Ireland
6.	Netherlands
7.	Sweden
8.	Japan
9.	Luxembourg
10.	Switzerland

(continued)

Table 13.5 Top Countries Rated with the UN's Human Development
Index (continued)

Rank	Country
11.	France
12.	Finland
13.	Denmark
14.	Austria
15.	United States
16.	Spain
17.	Belgium
18.	Greece
19.	Italy
20.	New Zeland

Source: Data from United Nations, *Human Development Report.* Copyright © 2008 The United Nations.
Used with permission.

Conclusion

*This brief overview of macroeconomic problems and issues and summary of aggregate
economic measurements provides a conceptual framework for describing relationships
among important economic variables. While it is clear that recent trends in the U.S.
economy have left us with many questions concerning future directions, we need to
ask ourselves, To what extent does contemporary macroeconomic theory adequately
explain our current economic reality? We will attempt to provide satisfactory
answers for this question and develop an understanding of macroeconomic theory and
policy in the following chapters. So let us continue this voyage through macroeconomics by first defining aggregate measures and then interpreting the theory in the
context of its historical roots.*

Review Questions

1. Why do you think full employment, economic growth, and price stability were selected
as the basic macroeconomic goals in the United States? Can you think of other
possible goals? Explain.

2. The three goals are often at odds with one another. Has the relative emphasis
of these different goals changed over time? Why?

3. What do you see as some of the costs associated with unemployment? Inflation?

4. Do events elsewhere in the world affect the U.S. economy? Give some examples.

5. Is it possible to establish an effective body of macroeconomic policy using only fiscal
tools or only monetary tools? Why or why not?

6. Do policy measures aimed at alleviating one set of economic problems sometimes
make others worse? Should a policy action be undertaken to aid one aspect
of the macroeconomy to the detriment of another? Explain.

7. Examine a daily newspaper (e.g., *The New York Times*) for a few days, and see how many articles address macroeconomic issues and problems. Make a list of the macroeconomic terms, concepts, and issues that you find.

8. Why should reports of current levels of GDP be received with care?

9. What do the National Income and Product Accounts measure?

10. Increasing numbers of women have entered the paid labor market during the past three decades. What impact would you expect this to have on GDP? Explain.

CHAPTER FOURTEEN

Macroeconomic Theory: Classical and Keynesian Models

◆ Introduction

The tenets of classical macroeconomic theory formed by Adam Smith, David Ricardo, John Stuart Mill, and others, which focused on growth, were carried pretty much intact through the nineteenth century. Economists in the latter part of that era concentrated more on the microeconomic concepts of utility and production than on the total economy. This chapter will provide a guide to our current understanding of the macroeconomy, discuss four major parts of the classical doctrine, illustrate their use, and then examine the Keynesian critique of classical macroeconomic theory and its inability to deal with high unemployment in the depression-plagued world of the 1930s.

In this chapter, we also will start to construct an economic model that is used for analyzing economic activity and forecasting the outcome of policy measures and/or economic shocks. This aggregate demand–aggregate supply model builds on macroeconomic models of income and output, and adds to that the effect of including money (through monetary policy). We first formulate the Keynesian model, which combines with monetary theory to form the underlying foundation for macroeconomic analysis. We will continue to develop and add to the model over the next four chapters. These building blocks are created from the tools, concepts, and definitions developed in these chapters. Additionally, each stage in the development of the aggregate demand–aggregate supply framework will include a descriptive overview, with a Big Picture feature providing an intuitive guide to a specific theory that is more fully developed in the text.

The completed aggregate demand–aggregate supply graphs resemble the market supply and demand graphs we developed in Chapter 7, but this resemblance is where the similarity ends. Information about financial markets, goods and service markets, and economic policy are reflected in an aggregate demand–aggregate supply analysis, which tells us how those markets respond to economic events, including policy decisions. We will be able to assess aggregate output and price levels for the economy when the model is completed.

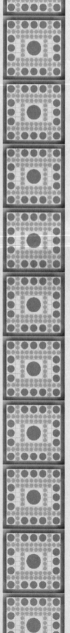

We begin with Keynes's theory which challenged long-standing economic traditions. Some view the Keynesian contribution as a new paradigm, while others view it as simply a major revision of classical theory. The classical model we discuss in this chapter was never formally set up as such by any of the classical economists. Rather, Keynes drew together the foundations from the writings of the classical economists and constructed the model primarily as a foil against which he could contrast his model in The General Theory of Employment, Interest, and Money.

THE **BIG** PICTURE

An Introduction to the Classical Model

If we were to summarize the contributions of various classical and neoclassical economists prior to the Great Depression of the 1930s, they would share the view that a capitalist economy (using an analogy of Cambridge economic historian Mark Blaug) generated its own automatic pilot. If there were disturbances in various markets creating disequilibrium prices, then wages or interest rates would adjust so that equilibrium in markets would once again be attained. For example, if there was not enough saving among the public to generate required levels of investment, the interest rate would be bid up—attracting more saving and lowering investment—and equilibrium would be restored, as we see in Figure 14.BP.1

If there was unemployment, wages would be bid down until employers would be willing to hire those unemployed, thus restoring labor market equilibrium (Figure 14.BP.2).

FIGURE 14.BP.1   Saving and Investment in the Classical Model

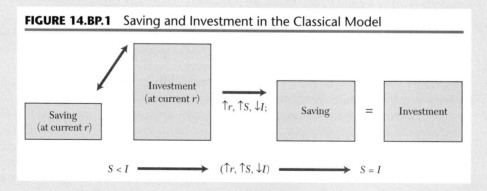

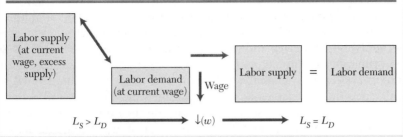

FIGURE 14.BP.2 Labor Market Adjustment in the Classical Model

$L_S > L_D \longrightarrow \quad \downarrow(w) \quad \longrightarrow \quad L_S = L_D$

All one needed to do was wait. The automatic pilot takes over, markets adjust, and equilibrium is restored. But the Great Depression, which was felt throughout the world, found capitalism's markets slow to restore equilibrium. Prices fell and gluts occurred. Wages fell and unemployment increased. The economy crashed before the automatic pilot restored order.

THE CLASSICAL MODEL

We will now discuss four specific elements of the classical model that show how economists analyzed unemployment, inflation, and growth, particularly when the economy suffered during the Great Depression. We will begin by examining the quantity theory of money and the equation of exchange, which was used to show the relationship between money and prices. Next we will briefly examine the goods and labor market, Say's law, and the credit market in the classical model.

The Quantity Theory of Money

A major tenet of classical economic theory is the **quantity theory of money**. Most often this is expressed by the **equation of exchange**:

$$MV = PQ,$$

where M is the money stock in the economy, V is the income velocity of money (the rate of turnover of money), P is the price level, and Q is the level of real national income (real GDP). This equation appears simple enough—perhaps too simple, for when it is examined carefully, it becomes an identity. It is true because it is by definition true. This is because of the definition of velocity—the rate at which money moves through the economy during a given period, or the number of times a piece of money gets spent:

$$V = \frac{PQ}{M}$$

Since national income is a measure of all output (Q) in a country for a year multiplied by the price (P) of each good or service, V is equal, in effect, to

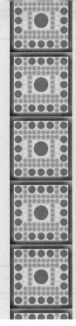

national income in a given year divided by the total amount of money available (on the average) during that year.

The classical economists elaborated further on each of the variables in the equation of exchange. They proposed that each of the variables in the equation is affected by both external and internal forces. Q, or national output, is determined primarily by real factors that change slowly over time, such as capital, technology, resource availability, and labor. The quantity of money (M) would not influence these variables in any significant way. The classical economists argued that the income velocity of money (V), on the other hand, is determined by institutional factors that are also independent of any change in the money stock (M). Some of these institutional factors are population density, custom, transportation factors, the state of the art of banking, and wage payments and practices. With Q and V unaffected by changes in the supply of money, the level of prices (P) is directly related to changes in the quantity of money (M).

Since Q and V were defined as relatively constant, this means changes in the quantity of money produce nearly proportional changes in the price level. Thus, if the quantity of money in the economy doubles, the price level is likely to double as well. In terms of output and employment in the economy, money, therefore, does not matter very much; in terms of wages and prices, however, it matters a great deal. The following equations show this:

$$M\overline{V} = P\overline{Q} \qquad \Delta M = \Delta P$$

Assuming that $\overline{V}$ and $\overline{Q}$ are constant at a point in time, any changes in the quantity of money (ΔM) must lead to changes in prices (ΔP).

The classical economists viewed money as neutral in that it satisfies no direct utility or want. It merely reflects real activity in the economy. It serves as a veil behind which the *real* action of economic forces, such as the growth of the national product and employment, are concealed. Yet money was viewed as a lubricant for the economy, keeping it well oiled and enabling it to run smoothly and effectively. In the classical model, money does not affect the level of output. The labor market plays a role in determining output.

The Goods and Labor Markets in Classical Economics

A second part of the classical model centers on the production of goods, or real output. Equilibrium output is determined by the demand for and supply of labor. Increases in the demand for labor increase output (Q), and decreases in the supply of labor decrease output. In the classical system, the level of output is determined by full employment. The equilibrium real wage defines the level of full employment in the labor force. Anyone willing to work at the prevailing equilibrium wage will be employed—the quantity supplied of labor equals the quantity demanded of labor. Anyone unwilling to work at that wage is regarded as not desiring to work, and therefore not classified as unemployed. As long as wages are flexible (both upward and downward) in the classical world, no conflict will arise. Full employment, as they defined it, is the norm. This fully employed labor force will produce an equilibrium level of goods and services (Q) for the economy.

Say's Law

A third part of classical macroeconomic theory is Say's law, named for the French economist Jean Baptiste Say (1767–1832) which is introduced in Chapter 3. In its oversimplified form, the "law" is often expressed as supply creating its own demand. Businesses in the process of producing or supplying goods and services for the market will pay wages or rents to employees, landlords, and others engaged in producing the product. That income may be used to purchase goods supplied by the firm or goods supplied by other firms. The act of production, which supplies goods to the market, at the same time generates income to workers and others, who in turn demand goods and services in the market and spend the dollars they earn on those products. For every dollar of product produced, a dollar of income is created and spent.

Say's law is the basis of the circular flow diagram shown in Figure 13.1, which is important to both the Keynesian and classical models. The crude circular flow of the classical economists shows the flow of goods and the flow of income. The lower part of the loop shows the movement of goods from the business sector of the economy to the household sector in return for income spent (expenditures). The upper loop shows the transfer of land, labor, and capital from households to business for use in the production of goods and services in exchange for rents, wages, and interest (income).

The supply, or output, that "creates its own demand" consists of the goods and services produced by the firms or businesses. The factors of production (land, labor, and capital) receive returns of rents, wages and salaries, and interest and profits for their part in the production process. Over time, with expanding population, higher income levels in the household sector create more demand for goods and services. The household sector then spends this income on the goods and services that have been produced, thereby creating an income stream for the business sector. As a result, the aggregate expenditures on goods and services by the household sector will equal the aggregate supply of those goods and services produced by the business sector. Equilibrium occurs when aggregate income or output equals aggregate expenditures.

The Classical Credit Market

Thus far we have assumed that Say's law means all income received during the production process will be spent on goods supplied by producers. But what if some of that income is saved? The classical model accounts for both saving and investment in its analysis of the credit or loanable funds market. Any income saved by consumers will flow into the business sector as investment, through the credit or loanable funds market. In this market, a flexible interest rate adjusts to yield an equilibrium between saving and investment.

The classical model assumes that both saving (S) and investment (I) are functions of the rate of interest (r): $S = f(r)$, and $I = f(r)$. The supply of credit comes from people who save. Income not spent is saved in the credit market. The classical economists assumed that higher interest rates cause people to save more because of the higher return on any money they save. Therefore, interest rates are directly related to saving. As Figure 14.1 shows,

FIGURE 14.1 The Classical Credit Market

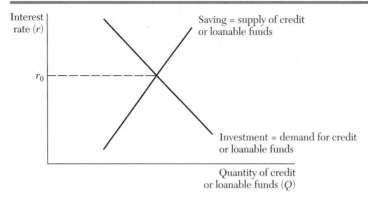

this gives us an upward-sloping curve that represents saving or the supply of credit or loanable funds.

Investment is inversely related to the interest rate. If businesses must borrow funds at high interest rates to finance investments, they will be less willing to borrow and invest. So, at higher interest rates, investment will be low; at lower interest rates, investment will be higher. Investors, like savers, make decisions based on the interest rate. In Figure 14.1 the downward-sloping curve represents investment or the demand for credit or loanable funds. At r_0 the amount saved is motivated by the amount invested; what isn't spent by some is borrowed and spent by others.

FLAWS IN THE CLASSICAL MODEL

Between 1860 and 1929, the U.S. economy generally displayed rapid economic growth. The phases of growth tended to be cyclical, with upswings in economic activity accompanied by downswings, but with an overall upward trend in economic activity averaging about 2 percent per year. We call these recurrent swings in business activity **business cycles**. (See Figure 13.1 for data on U.S. economic performance and cyclical behavior in the economy.) Figure 14.2 shows a hypothetical series of business cycles. Note that periods of growth and peaks are followed by periods of slump and troughs.

FIGURE 14.2 Business Cycles

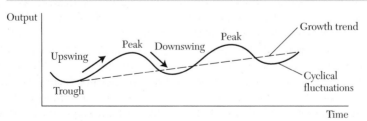

Economists have offered many explanations to account for business cycles. While few classical economists fully explained these fluctuations, economists who followed them offered explanations ranging from increases in sunspot activity to theories suggesting problems in overconsumption and underinvestment, monetary expansion and contraction, and innovation trends. Indeed, compelling arguments have been made for most of these in explaining cycles of growth.

1. If you were to extend Figure 14.2 to include this year, where would the economy be? In an upswing? A downswing? A peak or a trough? Why?

When economic conditions were in the downswing or trough of the cycle, as in the 1930s, classical economic theory explained the resulting levels of unemployment by insisting that those out of work were voluntarily or temporarily unemployed. They believed that businesses could make more employment opportunities by reducing the prevailing wage rate. As wages fell, the amount of labor demanded by businesses would increase. According to classical theory, these unemployed workers would be more than happy to work as long as their wages were above zero. However, during the Great Depression, as wages dropped lower, the number of people out of work actually rose. The classical system failed to explain this.

THE GREAT DEPRESSION

The Great Depression lasted for ten years, from 1929 to 1939, and left enduring imprints on millions of Americans. It resulted from many different phenomena that seemed to culminate all at once. Some people who are interested in business cycles believe that short-, medium-, and long-run cycles all reached bottom at the same time. Certainly, more than just the 1929 stock market crash sustained the Great Depression for such a long period. Despite the robustness of the stock market before its fall, several industries in the economy were essentially weak.

Agriculture and manufacturing were perhaps the most important sectors contributing to the duration of the Great Depression. As the United States grew in the first few decades of that century, the number of agricultural workers fell. Hurt by the exploitation of the rail and storage bosses, and burned by their own speculative activities in land, more and more farmers were leaving or selling out to join the urban migration or to become tenants. The number of independent farms dropped by 40 percent during the 1920s. Output, however, was increasing, and the inelastic demand for farm production did little to help farmers. Unlike the other industries, in which greater supplies meant lower prices and increased demand, demand did not increase for the lower-priced agricultural products. In addition, the European export market declined, as European agricultural production was restored following World War I.

In manufacturing, conditions were mixed. Many people in business foresaw a time of weakness, and although sales, prices, and output were at all-time highs, employers cut back their workforces substantially, especially in the mines and mills. Only in the service and construction industries did employment levels hold their own, for these were areas in which men and women could not yet be displaced by technology. Growth increased throughout the 1920s, but workers were no better off than before. Wages and employment levels simply did not increase. Profits, on the other hand, swelled rapidly, as did the concentration of economic power in the hands of a few wealthy individuals. Profits in 1929 were three times those of 1920. But firms were not reinvesting. This was partially because firms had no incentive to invest; supply was already greater than demand.

The weaknesses in these two industries are directly linked to other causes of the depression: the lopsided distribution of income, with 5 percent of the population receiving about 30 percent of all income, and the lack of new investment by the business sector. In addition, the existing banking system was troubled. A series of unexpected and urgent demands by customers on some poorly managed banks created fear among all bank depositors, so that even economically sound banks were subjected to "runs" (when large numbers of depositors withdrew their money) and potential failure. Some 5,000 of the nation's banks failed during the Great Depression. Other factors added to the instability: Several European governments defaulted on U.S. loans, and in the United States, Congress adopted a balanced-budget philosophy that, by increasing taxes and reducing government expenditures, helped to worsen an already bad situation.

From this description, you can see that the U.S. economy had fundamental problems at the time of the stock market crash. From the widespread prosperity of the early 1920s, the late 1920s saw a lack of capital formation, overproduction of goods and services, and an agricultural glut, in addition to international disequilibrium and deep-seated psychological effects of the crash. All these led to prolonged instability, which caused many businesses, organizations, and institutions to collapse and brought havoc to the lives of unemployed workers, the heads of failed businesses, and their families and friends. The depression of the 1930s was a time of severe unemployment and poverty for the men, women, and children who endured it. More than one-third of the nation was unemployed or living in poverty. Conditions were abysmal for all but a few of the well-to-do.

As conditions worsened worldwide, the U.S. Congress passed the Smoot-Hawley Act imposing a 45 percent tariff on a third of U.S. imports. Other nations retaliated with high tariff barriers to protect their domestic industries from U.S. imports. Retaliation led to even higher tariffs and very high prices on all imported goods. World trade slowed dramatically. During this same period there was a severe contraction in the supply of money, which worsened financial conditions. Between 1929 and 1932, in the United States, 85,000 businesses failed, and stock values decreased from $87 billion to $19 billion. Manufacturing and farm income decreased by 50 percent. By 1933, the GDP had declined from $104 billion in 1929 to $56 billion, and unemployment stood firmly at 25 percent, with 12 million people unemployed. Despite the human misery that swept the nation, Secretary of the Treasury Andrew Mellon advised, "Liquidate labor, liquidate stocks, liquidate the farmers, liquidate real estate."

ENTER JOHN MAYNARD KEYNES

The most important work of John Maynard Keynes (1883–1946) came at a time when the classical model was most under fire because of its inability to account for continued and worldwide depression with the masses of unemployed in the 1930s. Keynes watched the economic importance of his native Britain continue to wane after World War I, as the rapid growth of the United States and continental Western Europe accelerated. He developed his ideas and critique of the classical model slowly over a long period of time. Much of his writing was highly critical of the British authorities. Keynes was one of the first to recognize the implausibility of the British attachment to the gold standard for international payments and to object to the Versailles Peace Treaty after World War I. (He believed correctly that it would be impossible for Germany to meet the reparations called for by the treaty.)

During the 1930s, the major question being asked in each world capital was what to do about the depression. According to the classical doctrine, the simple remedy was to reduce wages to eliminate the excess supply of workers. But wages were falling, and more unemployment resulted, not less, violating Say's law. Supply was not creating its own demand. The circular flow was not working as it should. Markets were not adjusting to an equilibrium position as laissez-faire predicted. Classical theory and economists who were following these classical tenets were in a quandary.

Keynes focused on unemployment and argued, "The postulates of the classical theory are applicable only to a special case and not the general case ... and not ... those [conditions] of the economic society in which we actually live." In so doing, he illustrated the futility of the classical scheme, particularly Say's law and the limited circular flow.

Capitalism's Savior

John Maynard Keynes is endlessly fascinating. A product of Eton, Cambridge, and the British Treasury, he was also a member of the Bloomsbury group, that influential collection of writers, artists, and intellectuals in London that included Virginia Woolf and E. M. Forster. A top academic and public policy polemicist, he also ran an insurance company and made a fortune in the markets. The philosopher Bertrand Russell considered Keynes's mind the "sharpest and clearest" he had ever encountered. "When I argued with him," Russell said, "I felt that I took my life in my hands, and I seldom emerged without feeling something of a fool."

But it is as an economic innovator that Keynes is best remembered. Keynes changed how economists study business cycles, price levels, labor markets, and economic growth. His insights have largely kept downturns in the business cycle over the past half century from turning into depressions. "Keynes's lasting achievement is the invention of macroeconomics," says Deidre McCloskey, an economic historian at the University of Illinois at Chicago.

Indeed, Keynes can lay claim to playing a crucial role in saving capitalism and, perhaps, civilization during the Great Depression. Despite millions of unemployed workers in the industrial nations, economic orthodoxy demanded that government do nothing or, worse yet, tighten the purse strings. Little wonder that the totalitarian solutions of fascism and communism exerted such pull. U.S. Treasury Secretary Andrew W. Mellon expressed a widespread sentiment among elites when he said in 1930 that the depression would "purge the rottenness out of the system. High costs of living and high living will come down. People will work harder, live a more moral life. Values will be adjusted, and enterprising people will pick up the wrecks from less competent people."

Keynes battled against such harsh counsel. With his landmark 1936 book, *The General Theory of Employment, Interest, and Money*, he persuaded a generation of thinkers and leaders to abandon a near-theological belief in balanced budgets. He showed how economies could get trapped in recession or depression—and argued that government could break the spiral by borrowing to finance public spending that stimulated consumer activity and restored business confidence. His ideas helped create

the golden era of postwar growth, and two institutions he championed in the 1940s still operate on a global scale, the International Monetary Fund and the World Bank.

Keynes is the philosopher-king of the modern mixed economy. It's a sign of his influence that there are no true believers in laissez-faire left. We are all Keynesians now. Governments routinely run deficits during downturns to increase the overall level of demand and, hence, employment. And many economists believe Japan's long stagnation in the 1990s largely reflected timid policy makers unwilling to boldly use the levers of fiscal and monetary policy.

Like Adam Smith and Karl Marx before him, Keynes believed economics wasn't merely about studying the efficient allocation of resources. For him, the good life meant beauty, art, love, morality—the passions that define civilization—and the value of economics lay in its pursuit of the stability and wealth that would allow our passions to flower.

Source: "Capitalism's Savior" by Christopher Farrell, *Business Week*, reprinted from the April 12, 2004, p. 20, issue of *Bloomberg Businessweek* by special permission, copyright © 2004 by Bloomberg L.P.

© Hulton-Deutsch Collection/CORBIS

Today in the United States there is a resurgence of support for Keynesian economics. As the recession that began in the fourth quarter of 2007 deepened, many economists looked to lessons learned from the past to find solutions for that crisis. As we explore topics in both fiscal and monetary policy (Chapters 16 and 17), we will see evidence of this reemergence of Keynesian ideas.

THE BIG PICTURE

The Keynesian Model

Part 1: Consumption, Saving, Investment, and Income

During the 1930s, nations mired in the Great Depression suffered massive levels of unemployment; little if any investment; falling prices (deflation); and reduced production. John Maynard Keynes's *The General Theory of Employment, Interest, and Money*, published in 1936, offered a macroeconomic analysis that challenged the time frame for market adjustment and the argument that the economy was best left unregulated. One message of the Keynesian theory is that market forces won't reliably generate full employment in a society. Market forces take too long—and are perhaps too weak—to return an economy to full employment in a timely way. In addition, the economic and social costs are too high to wait for market adjustment in the national and international markets for goods and services.

Several Keynesian assumptions about economic behavior differed from some assumptions of the classical model. For example, Keynes viewed full employment as *one possible equilibrium*; the classical model viewed full employment as *the only equilibrium* possible. Keynes noted that the economy could be in equilibrium when labor was fully employed, when it was underemployed, or even when it was over fully employed.

Equilibrium in Keynes's theory occurred when aggregate expenditures equaled aggregate output or national income—and that could be at full employment or not. Keynes noted that unemployment was part of the normal process of economic expansion and contraction in capitalist economies. Economies based on capitalism to this point displayed a history of expansion when employment increased, followed by economic contraction that left large numbers of people unemployed for substantial periods of time, without any sign of an automatic pilot reversing the trend. But, for Keynes, there was hope that an economy enduring recession and unemployment could be restored to full employment quickly with government borrowing and government spending. Since the economy could be in equilibrium below full employment, there was no reason to think the economy would reach full employment—or adjust on its own. Thus, a *decisive actor* replaced the automatic pilot.

Two building blocks of the Keynesian model are the consumption function; viewing savings and investment adjustment through income, not interest rate changes; and the Keynesian multiplier.

Consumption   Income can either be consumed or saved and Keynes viewed both consumption and saving as functions of income, so that as income increased, consumption would increase—but not by as much as the increase in income—with the remaining income saved (Figure 14.BP.3). By examining the relationship between income and consumption expenditures in a country over time, we find that as income rises, consumption also rises, and that there is a fairly stable relation between consumption and income.

FIGURE 14.BP.3   Saving, Consumption, and Income

Consumption		
	=	Income
Saving		

Savings Equals Investment   In Keynes's explanation of macroeconomic relationships, just as in the classical system, in equilibrium, saving must equal investment. Keynes argued that consumers most often make spending decisions based on changes in their income, not changes in interest rates in the economy. If we think about what drives our decision, say to purchase a new pair of jeans, it is our income that we consider, not the current interest rate. So, since in the Keynesian model consumption and thus saving are functions of income, it is changes in income that equate savings and investment. For example, if investment is greater than saving, increased investment will generate higher levels of income that will raise both consumption and saving, and the economy reaches equilibrium (Figure 14.BP.4).

The Multiplier (k)   In the circular flow we examined in Chapter 3, we observed that business payments to the factors of production (income in the form of wages, rents, and profits) would be used by households to purchase goods and services produced by businesses (Figure 14.BP.5).

FIGURE 14.BP.4 Saving, Investment, and Income in the Keynesian Model

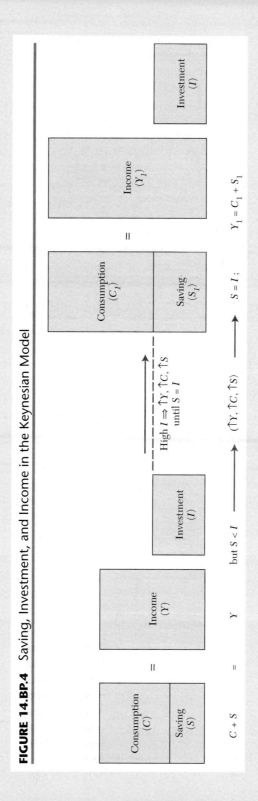

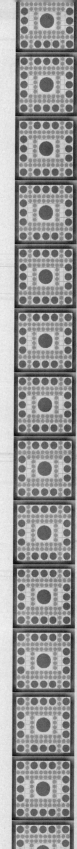

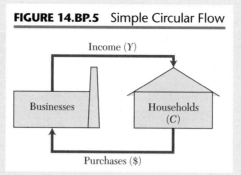

FIGURE 14.BP.5   Simple Circular Flow

Income (Y)

Businesses

Households
(C)

Purchases ($)

But Keynes pointed out that not all of income households earn will be spent on business-produced goods and services. Some will be saved—a leakage from the circular flow (Figure 14.BP.6).

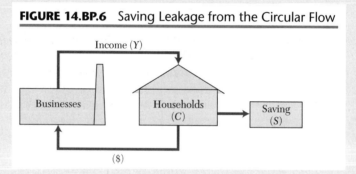

FIGURE 14.BP.6   Saving Leakage from the Circular Flow

Income (Y)

Businesses

Households
(C)

Saving
(S)

($)

To restore equilibrium to the system, business must *inject* investment expenditures that add new facilities, technology, and tools, as we see in Figure 14.BP.7.

But Keynes saw these investment expenditures as a source of higher income since investment has a multiplier effect on income. In other words, an increase in investment will increase income by much more than the initial investment expenditure.

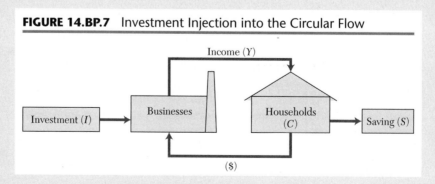

FIGURE 14.BP.7   Investment Injection into the Circular Flow

Income (Y)

Investment (I)

Businesses

Households
(C)

Saving (S)

($)

Let's see how that works. First, the initial investment expenditure becomes income in the economy. The expenditure on that investment is received by the seller as income (Figure 14.BP.8).

FIGURE 14.BP.8 Initial Investment Received as Income

Investment = Income

When income is received, some will be spent or used for consumption—perhaps on groceries and shoes, and the rest on replacement materials (glass, concrete). The amount spent on consumption adds to the income stream. If consumption (C) averages three-fourths of income, 75 cents of each dollar of income (Y) is spent as consumption and 25 cents is saved. So here C_1 is added to I as part of income. Now the grocer and shoe dealer and concrete supplier have additional income—three-fourths of which will be consumed; one-fourth saved. The three-fourths adds income. The multiplier continues through this responding effect to finally increase income by the multiplier times the change in investment. The multiplier depends on the percent of income that is consumed and saved. For our example, when consumers spend three-fourths of their income, the multiplier is 4. An increase in investment spending of $1,000 would result in an increase in income of $4,000. The higher the percentage of expenditure out of each dollar, the higher the multiplier. (If a nation's public spends four-fifths of each dollar of income, the multiplier is 5.) We can see each of these additions to income from the initial $1,000 investment in Figure 14.BP.9.

To see how this works in a possible real-life example, consider a business that invests $100,000 in new computer equipment. This generates $100,000 in income for the computer manufacturer. Using a multiplier of 4 (above), the computer manufacturer will spend three-fourths of the $100,000, or $75,000, on purchases from suppliers, workers, and other goods or services. The suppliers and workers will continue the spending cycle, with three-fourths of $75,000, or $56,250, worth of purchases—perhaps on CDs, groceries, gasoline, amusement parks, and so forth. The spending cycle continues until the total increase in income generated by the $100,000 investment in computer equipment increases income by $400,000, which equals the multiplier (4) times the initial investment ($100,000). We can see the result of the initial investment expenditure leading to the continuing responding effect in Figure 14.BP.10.

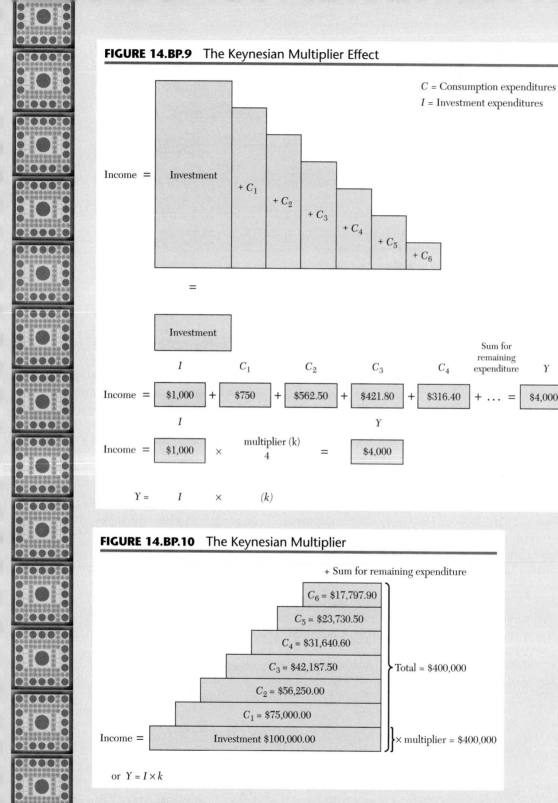

FIGURE 14.BP.9 The Keynesian Multiplier Effect

C = Consumption expenditures
I = Investment expenditures

Income = Investment $+ C_1$ $+ C_2$ $+ C_3$ $+ C_4$ $+ C_5$ $+ C_6$

=

Investment

	I		C_1		C_2		C_3		C_4		Sum for remaining expenditure		Y

Income = \$1,000 + \$750 + \$562.50 + \$421.80 + \$316.40 + … = \$4,000

I Y

Income = \$1,000 $\times$ multiplier (k) 4 = \$4,000

$$Y = I \times (k)$$

FIGURE 14.BP.10 The Keynesian Multiplier

+ Sum for remaining expenditure

C_6 = \$17,797.90
C_5 = \$23,730.50
C_4 = \$31,640.60
C_3 = \$42,187.50   Total = \$400,000
C_2 = \$56,250.00
C_1 = \$75,000.00

Income = Investment \$100,000.00 $\times$ multiplier = \$400,000

or $Y = I \times k$

The Keynesian Model: The Details

Keynes defined aggregate expenditures as the sum of consumption expenditures, investment expenditures, government expenditures, and net exports. He and some contemporary economists recognized that there are leakages (transfers of funds out of the income and spending flows) and injections (additions of funds to these flows). Leakages include saving, taxes, and purchases of goods and services in international markets (imports). With each of these leakages, income flows out of domestic economic activity and thus out of the circle in the circular flow diagram of the classical economists. Saving and hoarding remove money from the spending stream and occur when households, deciding that future consumption is better than present consumption, put their money into savings accounts at banks, into the stock market, or under their mattresses. Taxes leave the spending stream of the household and business sectors and are turned over to the government. Imported goods and services from other nations increase the goods and services received by households but reduce the total domestic spending, since these dollars go abroad to pay for the goods and services received.

In contrast to leakages, funds can enter into or be added to domestic economic activity. These injections into the income and spending stream may take the form of government spending, investment, and the sale of goods in international markets (exports). Government spending, like consumer spending, increases the income received by the business sector, since government and consumer purchases are made of business products. Government spending may also go directly to the household sector in the form of wages, transfer payments, or income supplements, which in turn will increase spending as well. **Investment** occurs when the business sector creates new capital in the form of new plants,

FIGURE 14.3 The Circular Flow with Leakages (L) and Injections (IN)

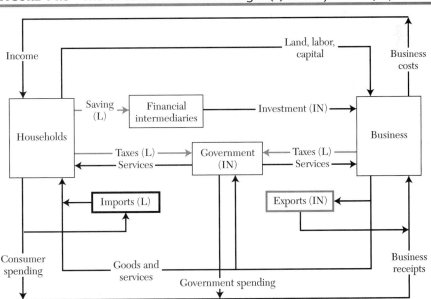

additions to equipment, and the buildup of inventories, or existing stocks of goods and services. Investment is, in effect, business spending. Exports create an injection into the income stream, since businesses have a new market for their products and receive income. Figure 14.3 illustrates the dynamics of these flows, with leakages indicated as (L) and injections as (IN).

For the economy to be in equilibrium, the injections must equal the leakages. As a result, aggregate expenditures for goods and services in the economy will equal the aggregate output or income. This establishes an equilibrium level of income and output that may or may not be at full employment. According to Keynes, an economy can have an infinite number of equilibrium positions, one of which is at full employment. The equilibrium depends on the level of spending in the economy. The classical economists, however, saw one and only one equilibrium—the one that exists at full employment.

Keynes recommended that governments use spending policies to counter cyclical upswings and downswings. These policies could cure a full range of economic maladies. In a depression, increased government spending would increase the levels of income, employment, and output. To ward off inflation, government spending could be cut and/or taxes increased.

The Keynesian model has remained a prevailing economic paradigm for the past half century. It has not always been successful, and economists have continued to add to and revise its core. Despite the challenges of the 1980s, however, it still solidly forms the basis for much of New Keynesian macroeconomic theory and is the basis for current economic policy. The late Nobel Prize recepient and monetarist Milton Friedman perhaps stated it best when he said, "We are all Keynesians now."

THE KEYNESIAN ECONOMIC MODEL

In the discussion that follows, we will describe the assumptions, methods, and implications of the full Keynesian model, exploring the sources of spending and how they affect aggregate output or GDP in any period.

Consumption

To begin our construction of a simple Keynesian model, we will first examine the assumptions and hypotheses for the consumption function. The importance of consumption on economic activity is fairly straightforward. In 2007, the U.S. population spent 83 percent of personal income on goods and services. Consumption is simply purchasing of goods and services, spending of income for necessities and luxuries. The level of consumption depends on many things, including income, interest rates, price levels, and expectations, along with the other financial assets the consumer might possess. But as one might well expect, consumption is primarily a function of income. In our simplified version of the Keynesian model, we will express consumption as

$$C = f(\text{DPI}),$$

FIGURE 14.4 The Consumption Fuction

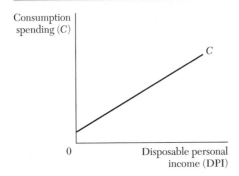

where C is the consumption of individuals over some period of time, DPI is disposable personal income, and f is a functional notation (see Table 13.4).* In what Keynes called a "fundamental psychological law," he states, "As a rule and on the average, [people] are disposed to increase their consumption as their income increases." In other words, as your income increases (perhaps after graduation and upon securing a better job), your consumption spending will rise as well—but, says Keynes, not by as much. This relationship can be expressed graphically with consumption (C) measured on the vertical axis and disposable personal income (DPI) on the horizontal axis. Since consumption is an increasing function of disposable income, as DPI increases, C will also increase (see Figure 14.4).

What happens to the income *not* spent on consumption? People save it. *Saving* is any part of income that is not spent on consumption. There is nothing left to do with it. (Burning it isn't rational, and Keynes assumes that we are all rational.) We can express the relationship between income, consumption, and saving as follows:

$$DPI = C + S,$$

where DPI is disposable personal income, C is personal consumption expenditures, and S is personal saving. Saving is a residual of consumption.

Saving occurs when individuals defer present consumption and keep the funds for future use. People save for many different reasons: precaution or fear of what might lie ahead, financial independence, or pride or avarice. In contrast to the classical model, which assumes that saving is a function of the rate of interest, Keynes assumed that consumption expenditures are a priority, and we save whatever funds are left after we make these consumption expenditures. No matter how much a high interest rate

---

*Studies have shown consumption to be a linear function of income, or $C = a + b$ DPI where C is the consumption of individuals over time, a is the intercept of the consumption function (or C where DPI = 0), b is the slope of the function, and DPI is disposable income (that is, GDP – depreciation – taxes – undistributed corporate profits + transfer payments). DPI, then, is income that a household has available for consumption spending. Since a is positive, individuals must consume some amount of food, clothing, and shelter even if they have no income.

might make us want to increase our saving, we pay for food, housing, and other necessary consumption expenditures first. Whatever is left can be saved. So in the Keynesian model, saving, like consumption, also is a function of income:

$$S = f(\text{DPI})$$

2. Do you or your family behave as though $S = f(\text{DPI})$ or $S = f(r)$? Which comes first, the mortgage or rent payment, grocery and clothing expenditures—or saving?

Before we proceed further in the analysis of consumption and saving, it is important to establish a reference position (or helping line) to make it easier to discuss the relation of the level of consumption spending to the level of income. This helping line is a 45° line from the origin of the consumption-income axis (see Figure 14.5). The 45° line represents the locus of equilibrium points where total spending equals total output or disposable personal income (DPI). If firms produce $3.0 trillion worth of goods and services, and spending in the economy equals $3.0 trillion, we will be at point A on the 45° line. Each of these points is on the 45° line, which bisects the origin and represents a level of spending just equal to a corresponding level of disposable personal income (DPI). Here and throughout the Keynesian analysis, we assume that *prices are constant*.

We can now use the relationship between expenditures and income in examining consumption. Since the 45° line bisects the 90° angle, at any point on the 45° line, income (DPI) will equal consumption. For example, at point A, DPI = C = $3.0 trillion; at point B, DPI = C = $4.0 trillion. If we superimpose the consumption curve on this 45° line, we can compare the relationship of consumption spending to the actual level of disposable personal income in the economy.

FIGURE 14.5 The 45° Line

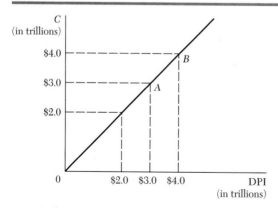

FIGURE 14.6 The Consumption Function and the 45° Line

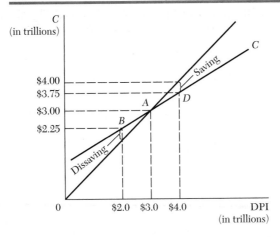

In Figure 14.6, at point *A*, consumption and disposable personal income are equal, since the consumption curve passes through the 45° line at that point. Saving equals 0 (since $S = \text{DPI} - C$, and $3.0 trillion − $3.0 trillion = 0). At point *D*, however, consumption (*C*) is less than disposable personal income, indicating that saving occurs. Since disposable personal income is $4.0 trillion and consumption is only $3.75 trillion, $0.25 trillion must be saved. At point *B*, consumption is greater than disposable personal income; income is $2.0 trillion, but consumption spending is $2.25 trillion. Dissaving is taking place to allow the desired level of consumption. Dissaving consists of borrowing or drawing down other financial assets in order to purchase products for current consumption. Individuals on low fixed incomes frequently dissave, as do young people starting families or households. (Note that even when income is 0, there is some amount of consumption spending.)

3. Do you dissave now? Do you expect to dissave in the next year or two? Draw a curve on the graph in Figure 14.7 indicating what you expect your consumption pattern to look like for the rest of your life. At what periods do you think you might be dissaving?

FIGURE 14.7 Your Consumption Function

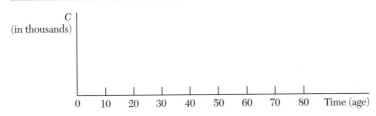

Table 14.1 Data for Hypothetical Consumption Function

DPI (in Trillions)	C (in Trillions)	MPC = ΔC/ΔDPI
$2.0	$2.25	0
		0.75
3.0	3.00	
		0.75
4.0	3.75	

Marginal Propensity to Consume

From the information given thus far, we can determine two ratios: the average propensity to consume (APC) and the **marginal propensity to consume (MPC)**. APC is simply C/DPI. MPC is the ratio between the *change* that occurs in consumption with some given change in disposable personal income:

$$MPC = \Delta C / \Delta DPI,$$

where Δ is a symbol for change, C is consumption, and DPI is disposable personal income. In the previous example, if disposable personal income increases from $3.0 trillion to $4.0 trillion, consumption increases from $3.00 trillion to $3.75 trillion. The change in disposable personal income is $4.0 trillion – $3.0 trillion, or $1.0 trillion; the change in consumption is $3.75 trillion – $3.00 trillion, or .75 trillion. The MPC, then, is $\Delta C/\Delta DPI = \$0.75$ trillion / $1.0 trillion, or 0.75 (see Table 14.1). For every additional dollar of disposable personal income, consumers use $0.75 for consumption and save the remaining $0.25 (see Table 14.1 and Figure 14.8).

The relationship $MPC = \Delta C / \Delta DPI$ is also the slope of the consumption function* (see Figure 14.8). Note that the consumption function is a straight line only when MPC is constant at all levels of disposable personal income.

FIGURE 14.8 Marginal Propensity to Consume

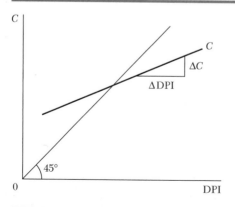

---

*MPC is the slope of the consumption function, or b in $C = a + b$ (DPI).

This will seldom occur in practice, since each individual as well as each income-earning group reacts differently to changes in income. However, to simplify the analysis, in most cases we will assume a constant MPC (and thus a straight-line consumption function).

4. How might your reaction to a change in income be different from that of Warren Buffett, Tiger Woods, J. K. Rowling, or Oprah Winfrey? From that of a poor person?

Saving

Given that saving is a residual of consumption (DPI = $C + S$, so $S = \text{DPI} - C$), we can analyze the saving function as we did the consumption function. Data for a saving function are derived in Table 14.2 and graphed in Figure 14.9.

Marginal Propensity to Save

We can also express the average propensity to save (APS) and the **marginal propensity to save (MPS)**. APS is the ratio of saving to disposable personal income, S/DPI. MPS is the ratio of the change in saving to any change in disposable personal income:

$$\text{MPS} = \Delta S / \Delta \text{DPI}$$

In Table 14.3, we find MPS using the data for S we derived earlier.

Table 14.2 Derivation of Saving Function from Consumption Data

DPI (in Trillions)	C (in Trillions)	S = DPI – C (in Trillions)
$2.0	$2.25	–$0.25
3.0	3.00	0.00
4.0	3.75	0.25

FIGURE 14.9 The Saving Function

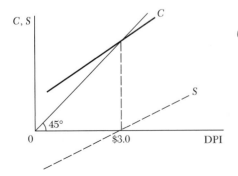
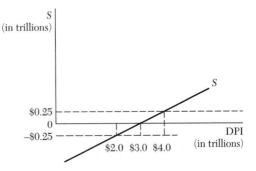

Table 14.3 Data for Hypothetical Saving Example

DPI	S (in Trillions)	MPS = ΔS / ΔDPI
$2.0	–$0.25	
		0.25
3.0	0.00	
		0.25
4.0	0.25	

Note that MPS + MPC = 1. This must be true, since the change in C and the change in S must add to the whole of every new dollar of disposable personal income.*

Consumption and Real GDP

We have just seen how consumption (C) changes when disposable personal income (DPI) changes. What causes changes in disposable personal income? Disposable personal income changes whenever real GDP (Y) changes or when there is a change in tax rates. As long as tax rates are constant (which we will assume they are for this analysis), real GDP (Y) is the only influence on disposable personal income. In equations we can write this as follows:

$$DPI = Y - Tx$$

because we are assuming that

$$Tx = 0, DPI = Y$$

Consumption therefore depends not only on disposable personal income, but also on real GDP. In the sections that follow, we will add other variables that determine real GDP (Y), including investment expenditures, government expenditures, and net exports.

Investment and the Two-Sector Model

The simplest Keynesian model describes the behavior of two sectors in the economy: the household and business sectors. This simple model ignores the government and foreign sectors. We represent total spending by individuals and businesses as follows:

$$AE = C + I,$$

where AE is income or real GDP, C is consumption, and I is investment. In equilibrium, $Y = AE$; all aggregate expenditures (AE) become someone's income (Y). This relationship is derived from expenditures flow in the circular

---

*$DPI = C + S$
$\Delta DPI = \Delta C + \Delta S$
$\Delta DPI / \Delta DPI = \Delta C / \Delta DPI + \Delta S / \Delta DPI$
$1 = MPC + MPS$

flow diagram in the National Income Accounts examined in Chapter 13, Figure 13.1. Consumption represents spending by households, and investment consists of business spending on additions to plants, equipment, inventories, and newly constructed housing. Inventories may be goods of any type, from raw material inputs to intermediate and finished products. Together, consumption and investment make up the aggregate expenditures for goods and services produced. In the preceding sections, we learned about consumption, but we know little about investment.

In this simple two-sector model, we assume that investment is determined outside the model itself.* For example, if Microsoft decides to invest $1,000, it makes the decision without considering the variables included in this model. Expected profits, interest costs, or business confidence might be more important to investment decisions than income and consumption levels. Graphically, then, investment would be constant at all levels of GDP, as shown in Figure 14.10.

In the two-sector model, we know that aggregate expenditures (AE) equal consumption plus investment $(AE = C + I)$ and that the resulting GDP (Y) can be spent or saved $(Y = C + S)$. For equilibrium in the macroeconomy, income (Y) and expenditures (AE) must be equal $(Y = AE)$. A level of spending produces a level of income, which, in turn, generates the same level of spending, and so on (as in the circular flow of activity). Putting these two equations together tells us that in the two-sector Keynesian model, the only leakage, saving, must equal the only injection, investment. This describes the equilibrium condition for the model: when aggregate income $(Y = C + S)$ equals aggregate expenditures $(AE = C + I)$, then $S = I$.

$$Y = AE$$
$$C + S = C + I$$
$$S = I$$

FIGURE 14.10 The Investment Function

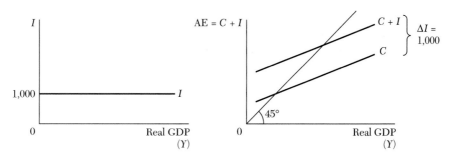

*Investment in a more sophisticated model is a function of changes in income, since as GDP increases, businesses will likely increase their level of investment. Investment decisions also depend on interest rates, expected inflation, expected profits, depreciation, and other factors. Investment fluctuates over time and plays a major role in accounting for business cycles. With a more sophisticated model, our analysis can include investment decisions more typical of businesses. For simplicity, however, we use the less complex model and assume that investment decisions are given and constant.

Table 14.4 Data for Hypothetical Investment Function

Y	C	S	I_p	I_a
$6.0 T	$5.75 T	$0.25 T	$0.25 T	$0.25 T
6.5	5.50	0.50	0.25	0.50

Several factors are important in the $S = I$ relationship. First, saving and investment are done by two different groups of people for totally different reasons. Second, realized (or actual) saving must equal realized (or actual) investment. There is no guarantee that the dollar amount of investment *planned* by the business sector will be the same as the saving planned in the household sector.

Using the data in Table 14.4, which assumes planned investment spending of $0.25 trillion, we can illustrate this with an example. I_p equals planned investment, and I_a equals actual investment. Figure 14.11 shows that the equilibrium income level in this simple model is at point A, where the $C + I$ line intersects the 45° reference line. This graph is sometimes referred to as the *Keynesian cross*. Here, AE = $C + I$ = $6.0 trillion, C = $5.75 trillion, and I = $0.25 trillion. All higher and lower levels of income are not at equilibrium; planned S does not equal planned I, and planned aggregate expenditures do not equal planned aggregate income. At $Y = $ AE = $6.0 trillion, $C + I = C + S$ and aggregate expenditures equal real GDP. Only at the $6.0 trillion equilibrium point does planned investment equal actual investment ($I_p = I_a$).

FIGURE 14.11 Equilibrium Level of Income

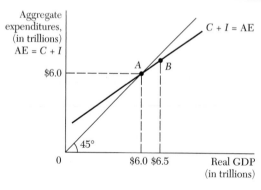

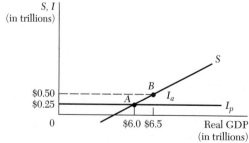

At disequilibrium position B, $C = \$6.0$ trillion, $S = \$0.50$ trillion, and $Y = \$6.5$ trillion. Here, intended saving is greater than intended investment, since saving is $0.50 trillion and investment is only $0.25 trillion. With I_p at $0.25 trillion, there will be an unplanned increase in inventories; some of the goods produced will not be sold, because consumers desire to increase their saving balances. At $Y = \$6.50$ trillion (GDP), $C + I = $ (only) $6.25 trillion (and $C + S = \$6.50$ trillion). Aggregate output is greater than aggregate expenditures. Total output is $6.50 trillion, but total spending is only $6.25 trillion. Therefore, inventories increase by $0.25 trillion. Since the increase in inventories is counted as investment, I_a will increase to $0.50 trillion. Actual saving equals actual investment.

5. In the next time period with an accumulation of inventories, what do you expect the I_p response of business would be? What does this do to the equilibrium level of income where aggregate expenditures equal real GDP and $S = I$?

Since planned S is greater than planned I, however, this is not an equilibrium position. With increased inventories, which were unplanned, producers will cut back production and lay off workers. As output is cut, income will also be reduced. This movement will continue until an equilibrium is reached where aggregate expenditures equal aggregate output or income. This new equilibrium occurs at point A, where $C + S = C + I$, and where planned S of $0.25 trillion equals planned I of $0.25 trillion. This equilibrium may be or may not be at full employment. Unlike the classical model, the Keynesian model may have equilibrium conditions at greater than full, less than full, or full employment.

Changes in Investment and the Keynesian Multiplier

Once the economy is in equilibrium, it tends to remain unchanged until some disturbance occurs, such as a change in the level of investment. Suppose investment increases from $0.25 trillion to $0.45 trillion, a change of $0.20 trillion. This change is graphed in Figure 14.12.

How much does income increase as a result of this $0.20 trillion increase in investment? What is the new equilibrium level of income? Here, the **Keynesian multiplier (k)** has its effect. When additional investment enters the model, the equilibrium level of income (Y) increases by some multiple of the change in investment. This multiple (called the Keynesian multiplier) equals $1/(1 - \text{MPC})$ or the ratio between the change in income and the change in investment ($\Delta Y / \Delta I$).

To demonstrate how the multiplier works, consider a nursery that decides to expand by adding a greenhouse costing $200,000. The first round of spending is $200,000, which is added to the income stream. The contractor and workers who built the greenhouse now have the $200,000 (as income)

FIGURE 14.12 An Increase in Investment Spending

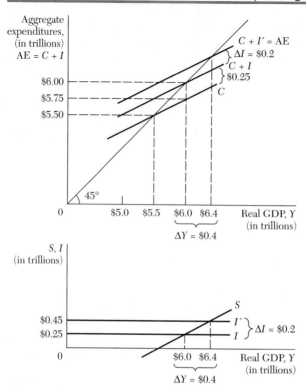

and will respend it according to the MPC. If the MPC is 0.5, the contractor and her workers will spend $100,000 and save the remaining $100,000. The $100,000 then enters the income stream (as other people's income); half of that will be spent and half saved in the third round. Table 14.5 illustrates this process.

Table 14.5 Keynesian Respending Effect

Expenditure for Greenhouse			
$\Delta I = \$200,000$	ΔY	$\Delta C = 0.5 \, \Delta Y$	$\Delta S = 0.5 \, \Delta Y$
Round 1	$200,000	$100,000	$100,000
Round 2	100,000	50,000	50,000
Round 3	50,000	25,000	25,000
Round 4	25,000	12,500	12,500
Round 5	12,500	6,250	6,250
Round 6	6,250	3,125	3,125
Etc.			
Total*	$400,000	$200,000	$200,000

*The rounds continue until they have generated $200,000[1/(1 − 0.5)] = $200,000 × 2 = $400,000 in new income. The initial increase in spending is multiplied through the economy.

In the example of a nursery adding a greenhouse, the MPS of 0.5 yields a multiplier of 2. Thus, the $200,000 increase in investment will generate $400,000 of new income. In Figure 14.12, an increase in I of $0.2 trillion will produce a new equilibrium level of $Y = \$6.4$ trillion? (representing a "multiplied" increase in Y of $0.4 trillion).

6. What is the new level of consumption in Figure 14.12 at $Y = \$6.4$ trillion? What is the level of saving?

A Simple Derivation of the Multiplier

The Keynesian multiplier gives us the amount of income (GDP) generated by an increase in spending. We know that at equilibrium in the Keynesian model, $\Delta I = \Delta S$ If both sides of this identity are divided by ΔY the right side of the equation becomes MPS:

$$\frac{\Delta I}{\Delta Y} = \frac{\Delta S}{\Delta Y} = MPS = \frac{1}{\text{the multiplier}}.$$

To get the multiplier (k), we invert the equation:

$$k = \frac{\Delta S}{\Delta Y} = \frac{\Delta Y}{\Delta S} = \frac{1}{MPS}.$$

Since MPC + MPS = 1, we can restate this in terms of MPC:

$$\frac{\Delta Y}{\Delta I} = \frac{1}{1 - MPC} = k.$$

Example: Given MPC = 0.75

$$k = \frac{\Delta Y}{\Delta I} = \frac{1}{1 - 0.75} = \frac{1}{0.25} = 4.$$

In this example, for each ΔI, real GDP (Y) will increase by 4 times ΔI.

The Three-Sector Model

To add a bit more realism, we can add the government sector to the simple two-sector Keynesian model. *Government expenditures* (G) are purchases of goods and services by the government during a given period. Like investment, we will assume in this extension of our simple model that government spending is determined outside of the Keynesian model. For example, Congress decides to spend $G = G_0$. This means there is a given level of government spending for goods and services at all levels of income, as shown in Figure 14.13.

Once we add government spending to the model, aggregate expenditures become $AE = C + I + G$, as shown in Figure 14.14. Now, in our three-sector model, we have

$$AE = C + I + G,$$

where aggregate expenditures (AE) equal the sum of consumption (C), investment (I), and government expenditures (G). In our three-sector model, real GDP (Y)

FIGURE 14.13 The Government Spending Function

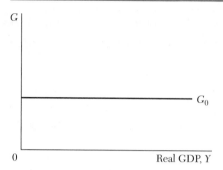

will equal the sum of consumption (C), saving (S), and—now that we have introduced the government—taxes (Tx):

$$Y = C + S + Tx$$

Given our definition of disposable personal income (DPI), we can also state this as:

$$Y = DPI + Tx$$

In equilibrium, $Y = AE$, so the two sides of our three-sector model are equal:

$$C + S + Tx = C + I + G$$

To simplify, we subtract C from both sides of the equation, in equilibrium (when $Y = AE$):

$$S + Tx = I + G$$

The 45° line again represents equilibrium points where aggregate spending equals aggregate output or income. Expenditures for goods and services are now made by consumers, investors, *and* the government, creating the aggregate expenditures graph for the three-sector economy. The equilibrium level of income is Y_a where $AE = Y = C + I + G$. At any other level, $Y \neq C + I + G$.

FIGURE 14.14 The Keynesian Model with C, I, and G Spending

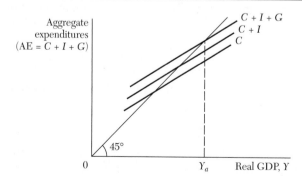

Government expenditures include expenditures by state and local governments as well as by the federal government. Currently, about 17.5 percent of the GDP is made up of purchases by the government. The government buys a wide range of goods and services, from paper to computers to military equipment. The government makes such purchases to support its normal operations or as part of programs designed to stimulate the economy when the business cycle is declining, as Keynes suggested in his *General Theory*. Transfer payments from the government are not included as part of these government purchases. (We will examine the effect of transfers in Chapter 15.)

The size of G may change. Indeed, the government may make decisions that will affect the level of income in the economy. These expenditures are often aimed at *directly* changing the level of income—perhaps from a level not at full employment to a new equilibrium level at full employment. Government expenditures for goods and services are subject to the Keynesian multiplier just as investments are. Government spending becomes income that enters the spending flow as recipients consume and save at increased levels by their MPC and MPS. Any increase in G will increase Y by an amount equal to $\Delta G / (1 - \text{MPC})$.

We can analyze the results of government spending by looking at a purchase of a new defense system at a total cost of $0.5 trillion. Figure 14.15 shows that aggregate expenditures have increased from the equilibrium position at $8 trillion (where AE = C + I + G). If the marginal propensity to consume remains at 0.5, the multiplier is 2. The increase in income that results from the purchase of the defense system is $k \times \Delta G = 2 \times \$0.5$ trillion $= \$1.0$ trillion. The new equilibrium level of income is therefore $9 trillion ($8 trillion + $1 trillion).

FIGURE 14.15 Effects of Increased Government Spending on the Equilibrium Level of Income

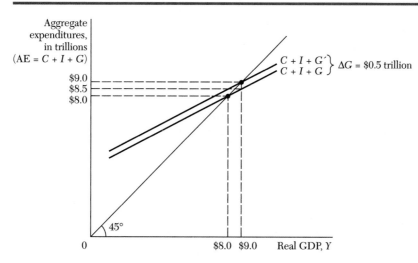

An increase in government allocations for research for the space program and NASA will boost the economies of Huntsville, Alabama; Houston, Texas; and Cape Canaveral, Florida, as well as increasing the enrollments in aerospace engineering courses. Cuts in government expenditures reverse the Keynesian multiplier effect. A decrease in defense spending, such as military base closures, will have the effect of contracting the economies of Alameda, California, and Charleston, South Carolina. Entire communities will be affected by the decreasing income and increasing unemployment levels.

7. What kinds of government spending programs would stimulate growth in your area? What are a few government spending programs that would help us all?

The Four-Sector Model

Thus far, we have extended our economic model by adding *injections* of investment expenditures and government purchases of goods and services into the spending flow and observing how the Keynesian multiplier affects each of them. There is, of course, one more injection into the spending stream, and that comes from the foreign sector through foreign trade. Whenever U.S. goods and services are exported to other nations, dollars flow into the U.S. economy in payment for these exported goods. These dollars then enter the spending stream as injections. On the other hand, imports take money out of the income flow, since goods and services come into the country in return for dollars that flow out of the U.S. income stream and into the income stream of the exporting nation.

In dealing with both of these flows, we will use the quantity *net exports*, which is simply $X - M$, where X represents exports and M accounts for goods and services imported into the nation. If $X - M$ is positive, then money is flowing into the U.S. income stream. If $X - M$ is negative, then money is flowing out of the U.S. income stream as imported goods and services flow in. A positive net export figure ($X - M > 0$) will mean additional income, as Y expands. If net exports are negative ($X - M < 0$), Y will fall.

We can express this four-sector model as an equation:

$$AE = C + I + G + (X - M)$$

Now aggregate expenditures (AE) equals the sum of consumption (C), investment (I), government expenditures (G), and net exports ($X - M$). Real GDP (Y) is still equal to the sum of consumption (C), saving (S), and taxes (Tx):

$$Y = C + S + Tx$$

As noted previously, we can also say that real GDP equals disposable personal income (DPI) plus taxes: $Y = \text{DPI} + Tx$. In equilibrium, $Y = \text{AE}$, so the sum of their components is equal:

$$C + S + Tx = C + I + G + (X - M)$$

We can simplify by subtracting C (consumption) and M (imports) from both sides of the equation. Thus, in equilibrium (when $Y = \text{AE}$),

$$S + Tx + M = I + G + X$$

The equilibrium level of income is at the point where the total for expanded aggregate expenditures intersects the 45° line. When imports to the United States exceed exports, more goods and services are coming into the country and more income (money) is going out of the country. Net exports are negative. The equilibrium level of income will be lower.

Domestic and foreign economic policies may directly affect import or export expenditures or both. We will direct our attention to some of these policy effects in Chapter 15.

THE BIG PICTURE

Chapter 14 Wrap-Up

Thus far The Big Picture has looked only at two sectors in the economy: consumers, through their consumption expenditures (C), and businesses through investment expenditures (I). And we discovered how investment expenditures work through the Keynesian multiplier (k) to increase income (real GDP) by more than the initial investment expenditure.

We must now complete our examination of aggregate expenditures (AE)—which to this point includes only investment (I) and consumption (C) expenditures. To complete the model we must also add government expenditures (G) and the expenditures of the international sector, which we defined in Chapter 13 as net exports ($X - M$).

Thus, if we put the features of the Keynesian model together using the building blocks we've explained above, we see that equilibrium in this model is where aggregate expenditures (AE) is equal to aggregate output or real GDP (Y) (see Figure 14.BP.11).

FIGURE 14.BP.11 The Keynesian Model—Four Sectors

CHAPTER 14

Aggregate Expenditures (AE = $C + I + G + [X - M]$)

=

Aggregate Output (real GDP = $Y = C + S + Tx$)

Consumption (C)	Investment (I)	Government (G)	Net exports ($X - M$)
Consumption (C)	Savings (S)		Taxes (Tx)

Conclusion

We have examined the impact of the Keynesian multiplier on several sectors of the economy and noted that income (output) expands by the value of the multiplier times the value of the injection. Prices do not change in the Keynesian model as a result of changes in aggregate expenditures. In this chapter we have examined only how changes in injections affect income. The next chapter will explore the effect of changes in leakages, including saving and transfers, and Chapter 17 will explore the complications that arise from price changes. We have made many assumptions about investment and spending decisions; the economy is somewhat more complex than our model. Nevertheless, the model helps us begin to understand how the macroeconomy functions.

The Keynesian model gives us a theoretical framework within which to analyze how the aggregate economy operates and to examine the sorts of macroeconomic problems one might expect to encounter and how we might develop stabilization policies to try to correct them. If real GDP exceeds aggregate expenditures, we can expect a lower level of national income. Conversely, if aggregate expenditures exceed real GDP, we would expect an expansion of economic activity and a higher equilibrium level of national income. An equilibrium level is where real GDP (Y) equals aggregate expenditures (AE = C + I + G + [X − M]).

Review Questions

1. What phenomena caused the Great Depression? Why did it continue for so long? Why did it affect so many sectors of the economy?

2. What did your grandparents or your great-grandparents and their families do during the Great Depression? How were they affected by the economic conditions of the time?

3. Why would the classical economists distinguish between real factors and monetary ones as influences of the variables in the equation of exchange? What is the implication of prices increasing as the quantity of money increases?

4. Why might Keynes's theory be called a "depression theory"? Can you make a few arguments as to why it might command a more general use?

5. What were Keynes's major criticisms of the classical theory?

6. What are leakages? Why are they called leakages? How do leakages differ from injections?

7. Why must leakages equal injections in the Keynesian world for an equilibrium level of income to exist?

8. In the Keynesian circular flow diagram (Figure 14.3), do leakages and injections ever leave the economy permanently? How are they fed back into the economy?

9. If depressions become self-fulfilling prophecy, can inflationary periods also be self-fulfilling? What would you expect the Keynesian prescription to be in such a case?

Use the information in Figure 14.16 to answer Questions 10–17.

10. Explain in words why the equilibrium would be $4 trillion if there were no saving, investment, or government spending. What would be the level of output at this income level?

FIGURE 14.16 A Problem on the Keynesian Model

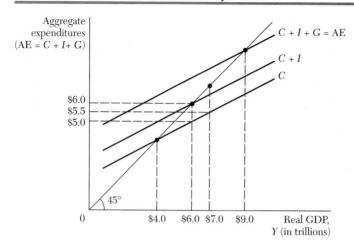

The intersection of income or output (AE) and aggregate expenditures (Y) = $9.0 trillion.

11. Why would the consumption function (if extended) intersect the spending axis at a positive value? What does this mean? Is it realistic?

12. The slope of the consumption function tells us that as real GDP increases, consumption (increases/decreases) but at a (slower/faster) rate. Is this realistic?

13. What assumptions are required to draw an investment function parallel to the consumption function? How realistic are these assumptions? What is the amount of desired investment in Figure 14.16?

14. Assuming no government expenditures, what is the level of saving at $Y = \$6$ trillion? What is the level of desired investment at $Y = \$6$ trillion? Why is $Y = \$6$ trillion an equilibrium level (with $C = I$)?

15. What would be the level of saving if the real GDP (Y) were at $7 trillion? What is the level of desired investment at this level? What forces are at work at a real GDP of $7 trillion? What will be the equilibrium level of real GDP?

16. What is the MPC in Figure 14.16?

17. Assume that real GDP is $6 trillion but real GDP of $9 trillion is needed to generate enough jobs for full employment. What level of government spending will be necessary to achieve full employment?

18. Why is there a multiplier effect for injections into the U.S. economy? What determines the multiplier?

19. How do net exports affect real GDP? Can real GDP be reduced by net exports? How?

CHAPTER FIFTEEN

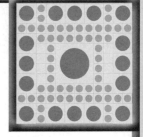

Fiscal Policy: Government Spending and Taxation

◆Introduction

For the past fifty years, the federal government has been officially committed to maintaining employment, price stability, and output. The **Employment Act of 1946** states,

> The Congress hereby declares that it is the continuing policy and responsibility of the Federal Government to use all practicable means consistent with its needs and obligations and other essential considerations of national policy, with assistance and cooperation of industry, agriculture, labor, and state and local governments, to coordinate and utilize all its plans, functions, and resources for the purpose of creating and maintaining, in a manner calculated to foster and promote free competitive enterprise and the general welfare, conditions under which there will be afforded useful employment opportunities, including self-employment, for those able, willing, and seeking to work and to promote maximum employment, production, and purchasing power.

Within the framework of these economic objectives, the government establishes and implements its **fiscal policy**—actions of taxation or government spending that are designed to change the level of income.

According to Keynesian theory, when poverty, unemployment, or inflation rises, the government has tools to try to fix each problem. The existence of unemployment and poverty suggests a need for government spending and/or transfers. These may take the form of unemployment and welfare benefits, food stamps, Medicaid, or a variety of other payments, or they may be purchases of goods and services. Other possible remedies are increases in employment opportunities and decreased tax levels. The government may try to stimulate employment by directly adding programs that put people back to work—for example, through a series of tax credits or advantages for those

*firms increasing employment and investment. Recently we have seen several of these poli-
cies implemented as part of the government stimulus package aimed at alleviating the
recession that began in late 2007. To combat inflation, fiscal policy requires spending reductions and/or tax increases. Cutbacks of all types and tax increases restrict household
and business spending. Fiscal policy can also be used to affect aggregate supply; for example, a tax cut might be designed to lower business costs, increasing supply.*

*While normally we think of the federal government as the major purchasing, borrowing,
and taxing authority, state and local governments are very active in the process as well. In some
cases, however, state and local governments exacerbate economic problems (pursuing* procyclical
rather than countercyclical *measures—for example, spending during times of economic expansion rather than during times of contraction and cutting spending during recessions.).*

*Fiscal policy is also subject to the constraints of the political process. At the federal level,
the president receives advice on fiscal policy from the Council of Economic Advisors (CEA)
and the National Economic Council created in the 1990s to coordinate policy making.
Some of the advice is accepted and successfully makes its way through the bureaucratic
channels, but other advice does not. In addition, the president receives advice from the
Office of Management and Budget. Meanwhile, in addition to its own committees,
Congress has the Joint Economic Committee and Congressional Budget Office to assist in
legislative decisions on government spending and taxation. Policy studies in all these bodies
are constantly ongoing. Often the dynamics of these public offices, plus the host of private
organizations engaged in economic research, lead to a profusion of mixed analysis and
advice. Since each advisory body has its own priorities and operates under its own assumptions about economic growth, policy recommendations vary widely.*

*This chapter will explore how each type of fiscal action works. Some fiscal policies may di-
rectly affect the level of imports and/or exports as well as the domestic economy. We will explore
these implications and deal with the shortcomings and advantages of using fiscal policy to address economic problems. We will also explore the budget process of fiscal policy's major player, the
federal government. The discussion of the federal budget includes the impact of federal debt on
the economy, balanced budgets, and the difference between structural and cyclical budget deficits.*

FISCAL POLICY

The tools of fiscal policy may be selected to resolve a particular problem, or they
may occur automatically with a given change in economic conditions. The former uses constitute **discretionary fiscal policy**. The automatic, nondiscretionary
forms of fiscal policy are called **built-in stabilizers**. Examples of built-in stabilizers include the progressive income tax system, unemployment insurance, and all
other compensatory programs that come into effect when income levels are low
and that are shut off when income levels are high. As economic activity decreases
during a recession, income is lost. This threatens additional decreases in economic activity. However, as unemployment increases, unemployment compensation *automatically* increases income and spending to slow a cumulative decrease in
economic activity. Additionally, during a recession, people find themselves in
lower tax brackets, which reduces the tax bite on individuals as their incomes fall.

1. If income is increasing at a highly inflationary rate, how do progressive income
   taxes help to stabilize the economy automatically?

THE BIG PICTURE

Fiscal Policy

When government officials pass a bill to increase public spending on the interstate highway system or to repair the nation's infrastructure, once undertaken, these projects work like expenditures on investment. As we saw in Chapter 14, an increase in investment spending worked through the multiplier through respending. Fiscal policy also works through the multiplier to increase income in the economy by more than the initial policy expenditure. In our example, if Congress approved a $10 billion expenditure on the highway system, we would find that the initial $10 billion spent would increase national income through the multiplier. This first $10 billion could be spent to employ designers, engineers, and asphalt firms and to purchase concrete and orange safety barrels. (We will follow the same analogy we developed in the Big Picture in Chapter 14, with consumers spending three-fourths of new income and saving the remaining one-fourth.) After this first round of spending, the designers, engineers, firm owners, concrete makers, and so forth would spend three-fourths of the $10 billion (or $7.5 billion) on supplies, labor, and other goods and services. Next, laborers, suppliers, and others will spend three-fourths of this new $7.5 billion (or $5.63 billion) of income on groceries, clothing, entertainment, and other goods and services. And the process continues until the initial $10 billion expenditure on highways results in $40 billion in income in the economy.

Instead of authorizing expenditure increases or cuts (which work in reverse), policy makers might consider a tax policy. This would involve tax cuts (to increase income) or tax increases (to decrease income). Tax policies also have a multiplier

FIGURE 15.BP.1 The Effect of Expenditure and Tax Policies on Income.

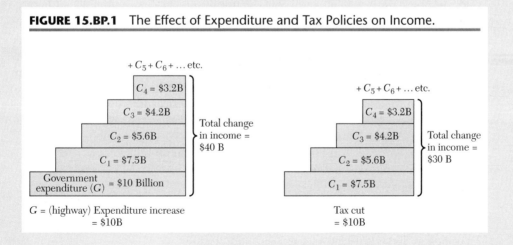

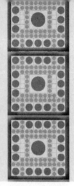

effect, but the tax multiplier is not as large as the investment and government expenditures multiplier since some portion of the income received from a change in tax policy is saved. Because there is no initial one-time expenditure, the effect is to reduce the multiplier by 1. In our earlier example, the expenditure multiplier was 4, and this tax multiplier would be 3 (or 4 – 1). The effect on the economy of reducing taxes by $10 billion to increase income would cause total income to increase by $30 billion, or by $10 billion less than by increasing highway expenditures by $10 billion. Figure 15.BP.1 illustrates the difference in the two outcomes.

Government Spending

The government often adopts a fiscal policy position when politicians and public opinion consider employment levels to be inadequate—for example, if the full-employment level of income is thought to be at $5.7 trillion and income is currently $5.1 trillion. In this situation, a substantial amount of unemployment is likely, and the government can opt for fiscal action that will increase employment and boost the level of income by $0.6 trillion ($5.7 trillion – $5.1 trillion).* In its arsenal of policies are spending, taxing authority, and the ability to issue transfer payments (income supplements such as Social Security and welfare paid to individuals). Since transfer payments are not for current productive services, they are not included in the yearly national product accounts but enter the income-spending flow as part of the personal income tally.

Government spending on goods and services such as military operations, the space program, and public buildings will have the largest expansionary impact on income in the economy, since the full amount of spending enters the economy in the first round. In the case of transfer payments and tax reductions, some of the impact in the first round is "leaked" into savings. Table 15.1 provides an example of the difference.

In the example, the equations show the amount of government spending or tax reductions necessary to increase the level of income by $0.6 trillion (or $600 billion), assuming MPC in the economy is 2/3. The first set of equations addresses government spending. With an MPC of 2/3, we can use the formula $k = 1/(1 - \text{MPC})$ to determine that the multiplier is 3.[†] Knowing the multiplier ($k = 3$) and the desired level of income ($\Delta Y = \$600$ billion), we have enough information to determine the necessary amount of government spending (ΔG):

$$\Delta Y = k \times \Delta G$$

$$\Delta G = \Delta Y/k = \$600 \text{ billion}/3 = \$200 \text{ billion}$$

---

*Conversely, we could establish an example in which inflation was the primary problem, with income being above the full employment level. For example, income could be at $5.7 trillion, with the full employment level at $5.1 trillion. In that case, the policy measures would be the opposite of those we discuss in the following sections.

[†] $k = \dfrac{1}{1 - \text{MPC}} = \dfrac{1}{1 - \frac{2}{3}} = \dfrac{1}{\frac{1}{3}} = 3$

Table 15.1   Multiplier Effect of Government Expenditures and Tax Cuts

Spending Sequence	$\Delta G = \$200$ billion	$\Delta Tx = \$300$ billion
Round 1		
(direct expenditure)		(indirect expenditure $\Delta Tx \times$ MPC $= \Delta Y$)
	$\Delta G = \Delta Y = \$200B$	$\Delta Y = \$300$ B $\times$ 2/3 $= \$200B$
Round 2		
($\Delta Y \times$ MPC)	$\$200$ B $\times$ 2/3 $= \$133$ B	$\$200$ B $\times$ 2/3 $= \$133$ B
Round 3	133 B $\times$ 2/3 $= \$90$ B	$\$133$ B $\times$ 2/3 $= \$90$ B
Round 4	90 B $\times$ 2/3 $= \$60$ B	90 B $\times$ 2/3 $= \$60$ B
Round 5	60 B $\times$ 2/3 $= \$40$ B	60 B $\times$ 2/3 $= \$40$ B
Round 6	40 B $\times$ 2/3 $= \$27$ B	40 B $\times$ 2/3 $= \$27$ B
Round 7	27 B $\times$ 2/3 $= \$18$ B	27 B $\times$ 2/3 $= \$18$ B
Round 8	18 B $\times$ 2/3 $= \$12$ B	18 B $\times$ 2/3 $= \$12$ B
Round 9	12 B $\times$ 2/3 $= \$8$ B	12 B $\times$ 2/3 $= \$8$ B
etc.	Total $\$600$ B	Total $\$600$ B

Our policy recommendation, then, is that the government build a (big) dam at a price of $200 billion to increase income by $600 billion to the full employment income level of $5.7 trillion. This is illustrated in Figure 15.1.

Although the example shows that the needed increase in income is $600 billion, policy decisions certainly are not made by such quick calculations. Partisan politics and economic philosophies play a crucial role in these decisions. We might recommend the construction of a dam, but each of the 435 representatives and 100 senators has his or her own plan, which often involves a particular congressional district or state. This and the following examples describe technical economic "solutions" to extremely complex economic, political, and social problems—what theoretically needs to happen to achieve economic goals. This is one reason "shovel ready" highway projects that are spread across the country have bipartisan support.

2. Clip a recent newspaper article on some federal, state, or local economic issue. What, besides the economics of the problem or policy, does the article address?
3. In the example you found, are the various positions based on ideology, economic theory, or rhetoric?

Tax Policy and Income Effects

If the government decides it wants to accomplish the desired income increase of $600 billion through a cut in taxes, it must decide how much of a tax reduction is needed to generate new increases in income equal to the $600 billion. Since tax cuts are initiated through a different channel for their progression

FIGURE 15.1   Effect of Increased Government Spending

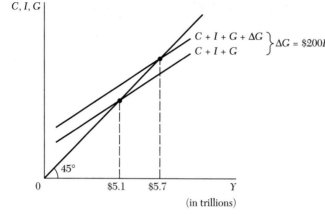

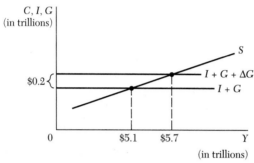

within the economy, we must address the behavior of leakages, rather than the effects of injections on spending flows. The crucial difference between the effect of leakages and that of injections occurs during the first round of spending.

Instead of $200 billion being directly spent on a dam, the $200 billion in tax cuts goes into the pockets and bank accounts of the taxpayers. According to the marginal propensities given, taxpayers will save part of the $200 billion and spend the remainder. With an MPC of 2/3, the first action is to consume 2/3 of $200 billion, or $133 billion, and save $67 billion. Thus, only $133 billion *initially* enters the total income stream, instead of the $200 billion that would enter in the case of government spending.

The *tax multiplier* is therefore less than the spending multiplier—in fact, 1 less*:

$$k - 1 = k_{tx}$$

$$k_{tx} = -MPC/(1 - MPC)$$

---

*This can be derived as follows:
$$-k_{tx} = [1/(1 - MPC)] - 1$$
$$= \frac{1}{(1 - MPC)} - \frac{(1 - MPC)}{(1 - MPC)} = \frac{MPC}{(1 - MPC)}$$
$$k_{tx} = -MPC/(1 - MPC).$$

(Note the negative sign for the tax multiplier, since a tax *cut* will increase income.) Using our previous example, to get a $600 billion increase in income with a tax multiplier of 2 (because $3 - 1 = 2$), the following decrease in taxes must occur:

$$\Delta Y = -k_{tx} \times \Delta Tx$$

$$\$600 \text{ billion} = -2 \times \Delta Tx$$

$$\Delta Tx = -\$300 \text{ billion}$$

In other words, as detailed in Table 15.1, taxes must be reduced by $300 billion to increase income by $600 billion. (The impact of a tax cut on equilibrium income is outlined at the end of the chapter.)

Transfer Payments

The logic behind the macroeconomic effects of changes in transfer payments is essentially the same as those of tax cuts. Transfer payments, however, redistribute income, while tax cuts may not. Looking at the impact of transfer payments on the economy, we find that the income of households will increase. In our example, the change in spending during the first round will be two-thirds of $300 billion, since part of the transfer will be consumed and the remainder will be saved. The **transfer multiplier**, like the tax multiplier, is $k - 1 = k_{tr}$ (note that the transfer multiplier is positive, since an increase in transfers will increase income). Transfer expenditures worth $300 billion would be necessary to raise income by $600 billion.

4. If Social Security transfers were to increase by $4 billion and if MPC were 0.9, how much of an impact would this transfer package have on the economy?

The government, of course, might choose one or any combination of tax, spending, or transfer alternatives. It also might decide to pass legislation to encourage new consumer or investment spending. Tax credits and incentives have been used in recent years to stimulate certain industries that might be suffering more than others. During a housing slump in 1974, Congress gave a 5 percent income tax credit to purchasers of newly constructed homes. In 2009 an $8,000 tax credit was offered to first-time home buyers. These measures were designed to pick up a depressed housing industry, as well as to stimulate economic activity in general. Unemployment benefits were extended during the 1990–1993, 2001, 2007–2009 recessions so that those who were unable to find jobs during the normal benefit period could receive an additional six weeks of benefits.

PROBLEMS WITH FISCAL POLICY

With these "mechanical" fiscal fixes firmly in mind, it is well to remember that problems are likely to arise in the determination of fiscal policy. The political machinery involved in fiscal decisions is often slow, the product of many lags. Additionally, policies of state and local governments offer their own brand of fiscal effects, which more often than not are ill-timed for national objectives because of interest costs, spending capacity, and political considerations.

Lags and Lumps in Fiscal Measures

From the discussion thus far, it seems that full employment in the economy requires only a mighty snap of the government purse strings. Several rather sticky problems emerge in the deployment of these strings, however. One problem encountered early on is the time it takes simply to recognize that a problem exists—in other words, a *recognition lag*. Another is trying to estimate MPC and thus the multiplier effect that each expenditure might have on the economy. Additionally, government spending tends to be lumpy. Projects are normally large and are generally confined to a reasonably small geographical area. Constructing a flood wall in Lewisburg, Pennsylvania, will probably not help alleviate unemployment in Dubuque or Detroit.

Legislation also tends to move slowly through Congress. By the time funds are allocated, new and different problems might emerge. During this time, higher resource prices might increase the inflation rate, and the expenditure of government funds would only add to the problem of rising prices. The enactment of tax policies takes time. For example, the 1964 tax cut was proposed in 1963 and approved after more than a year of hearings. This particular tax cut was an example of Keynesian economics well thought out and proposed, but legislative reluctance delayed the cut for over twelve months. Oftentimes a conflict between the president and the Congress leads to bitter policy debates. We refer to the undue passage of time before a proposed policy measure is signed into law as the *legislative lag*.

Execution presents another delay in transferring the legislation into action. Tax policies tend to be faster and more efficient after passage, but spending packages may be hung up in a bidding and allocation process for months. This has been called the *implementation lag*.

Finally, once the legislation for government spending or tax cuts is enacted and executed, time passes before the policy becomes effective. Results from empirical econometric models show that this *reaction lag* can be as long as a year or more before even part of the policy has affected GDP.

Procyclical Tax and Spending Policy

In the introduction to this chapter, we mentioned that policies of state and local governments have their own fiscal effects. These governments are active in spending and taxing as well as in issuing transfers. Often, however, they use their tools at the "wrong" time in the business cycle. Federal fiscal policy is usually designed to counter inflationary and recessionary trends in economic activity. Yet local government spending often occurs when fiscal "good times" prevail. Voters more readily approve bond issues for schools, libraries, or parks during boom periods, so these construction projects add to the boom. In the same vein, when times are hard, state and local governments often have difficulty financing new spending projects that might stimulate the economy, thus reinforcing a recession. The recession that began in 2007 caused state and local governments to lay off workers, reduce work hours, and cancel projects as growing unemployment rates and lower income and corporate tax revenue diminished state treasuries.

5. What does Keynesian theory tell you about this kind of spending? What would be the economic effects?

6. Is there any salvation to the procyclical spending of state and local governments? (What happens when bond issues to finance libraries and schools are passed?)

FISCAL POLICY IN ACTION: THE AMERICAN RECOVERY AND REINVESTMENT ACT (ARRA) OF 2009

The American Recovery and Reinvestment Act (ARRA) is the name of the $787 billion stimulus package created to counter the recession that began in late 2007. The act was signed into law on February 17, 2009, and is the largest single stimulus package in U.S. history. The act includes funds for tax cuts, infrastructure investment, expansion of unemployment benefits, education and training, health care, and energy. Table 15.2 lists the overarching categories within ARRA and the funds that are allocated to each of these areas. Tax cuts account for 37 percent of the allocation and relief to state and local governments accounts for 18 percent.

According to Recovery.gov, the website developed for ARRA to provide up to date information and transparency for the general public, the act is designed to:

❖ Save and create more than 3.5 million jobs over the next two years.

❖ Take a big step toward computerizing Americans' health records, reducing medical errors, and saving billions in health care costs.

Table 15.2 American Recovery and Reinvestment Act Funding

Category	Amount ($Billions)
Tax Relief*	$288
State and Local Fiscal Relief**	$144
Infrastructure and Science	$111
Protecting the Vulnerable	$81
Health Care	$59
Education and Training	$53
Energy	$43
Other	$8

*Tax Relief includes $15 billion for Infrastructure and Science, $61 billion for Protecting the Vulnerable, $25 billion for Education and Training, and $22 billion for Energy, so total funds are $126 billion for Protecting the Vulnerable, $74 billion for Educational and Training, and $65 billion for Energy.

**State and Local Fiscal Relief prevents state and local costs to health and education programs and state and local tax increases.

Source: http://www.recovery.gov

- ❖ Revive the renewable energy industry and provide the capital over the next three years to eventually double domestic renewable energy capacity.
- ❖ Undertake the largest weatherization program in history by modernizing 75 percent of federal building space and more than one million homes.
- ❖ Increase college affordability for seven million students by funding the shortfall in Pell Grants, increasing the maximum award level by $500, and providing a new higher education tax cut to nearly four million students.
- ❖ As part of the $150 billion investment in new infrastructure, enact the largest increase in funding of our nation's roads, bridges, and mass transit systems since the creation of the national highway system in the 1950s.
- ❖ Provide an $800 Making Work Pay tax credit for 129 million working households, and cut taxes for the families of millions of children through an expansion of the Child Tax Credit.
- ❖ Require unprecedented levels of transparency, oversight, and accountability.

Expenditures for projects fundable through ARRA were to be made between 2009 and 2011. The Congressional Budget Office (CBO) has estimated several scenarios for ARRA outcomes. Figure 15.2 shows CBO estimates

FIGURE 15.2 Difference Between Potential GDP in CBO's Baseline and Actual GDP With and Without the Impact of the American Recovery and Reinvestment Act of 2009.

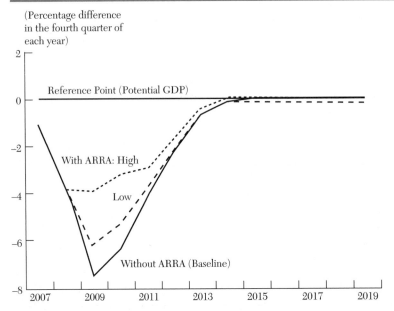

Note: CBO's January 2009 baseline projection of potential gross domestic product (GDP) is set as a reference point. The projection of actual GDP without the effects of the American Recovery and Reinvestment Act of 2009 (ARRA) is CBO's January 2009 estimate, as presented in *The Budget and Economic Outlook: Fiscal Years 2009–2019*. The projections of actual GDP with the effects of ARRA incorporated (the high and low estimates) reflect a range of assumptions.

Source: Congressional Budget Office.

for "high" returns from ARRA projects and tax relief, predicting a lower downturn in GDP and a faster recovery, and a "low" estimate, projecting a much greater decrease in GDP (but not as large as the reduction in GDP without ARRA) and a slower recovery. The baseline illustrates the CBO's estimates of the recession without ARRA. Despite this stimulus package, it will take some time for the expenditures and tax policies to have a full effect on the economy.

At the time ARRA was enacted, a number of prominent economists called for a much larger stimulus package to combat the economic downturn. As the economy worsened during 2009 with growing numbers of unemployed workers and increased business failures, more economists called for a second round of stimulus, noting that while ARRA was working, still more was needed.

7. What are the implications of over one-third of the stimulus package targeted at tax relief? Explain by comparing the effects of the tax multiplier to those of the expenditures multiplier.

8. Has a second round of stimulus been requested by the president or passed by Congress? What are the implications of this action or inaction?

FISCAL POLICY IN AN OPEN ECONOMY

Thus far, we have examined the effects of fiscal policy in our three-sector closed economy of domestic households, businesses, and government. Since international economic activity plays an increasingly important role in U.S. transactions, we need to examine how the foreign sector or net exports (as we are representing the foreign sector) responds to fiscal policy. We can examine two specific effects on net exports: responses to changes in interest rates and responses to changes in currency value. Both affect national income.

Fiscal policy, such as an increase in government expenditures or a tax cut financed by an increase in government borrowing, may cause interest rates to rise in the short run as the government increases its demand for credit. Higher interest rates on government bonds will make U.S. government securities more attractive to both domestic and foreign investors than foreign security offerings with lower interest rates. An increase in the demand for U.S. bonds by foreign investors will create an increased demand for dollars by foreign individuals and institutions and a decrease in the supply of dollars offered by U.S. investors in foreign security markets. This will cause the value of the dollar to increase with respect to other currencies. Each dollar will purchase a larger volume of foreign goods, so imports should increase. On the other hand, U.S. products (exports) will cost more to those desiring U.S. goods, so the demand for U.S. exports should fall because of their relatively higher prices on international markets.

When we account for this effect of fiscal policy actions in an open economy, we see that it acts in opposition to the initial fiscal policy designed to increase levels of income and output. With imports rising and exports falling, net exports $(X - M)$ will fall. In our aggregate expenditure analysis, where $Y = C + I + G + (X - M)$, the increase in G may, through a higher interest rate, cause an appreciation of the U.S. dollar and thus a decrease in net exports. The expenditures multiplier therefore will be less effective in the presence of an international market. In contrast, tax cuts financed by lowered government surpluses rather than by increased government borrowing should stimulate consumption spending. Some of this increased consumption will be spent on imported goods and services, but overall, income (Y) should rise.

A second effect of fiscal policy in an open economy is the effect of output on exchange rates. Here, however, the effects on imports and exports are offsetting, so the total effect is assumed to be zero. As increased government expenditures or tax cuts increase income, those who receive this additional income will be inclined to increase their expenditures on goods and services. Some of this increased demand will be for international products. The demand for imports should increase as incomes rise. This increased demand for imports will yield a greater supply of dollars in the currency markets as U.S. customers exchange dollars for imported goods. The increased supply of U.S. dollars will have the effect of decreasing or depreciating the value of the dollar in the international market. A lower-valued dollar will increase the demand for U.S. exports and decrease the demand for imports in the United States. In this case, fiscal policy in an open economy most likely has a neutral effect. An initial increase in import demand will be followed by a rise in exports and a fall in imports as the dollar depreciates in value, so the original fiscal policy stimulus maintains its effectiveness.

THE FEDERAL BUDGET

The federal government's fiscal policy is directly related to the federal budget. During the 1980s, 1990s, and after 2002, the public and politicians objected to the size of the federal government, the size of the budget deficit, and its effects. As illustrated in Figure 15.3, the level of the federal budget deficit increased dramatically in the 1980s, with annual deficits of more than $150 billion and the total accumulated debt of around $1 trillion in 1980 increasing to more than $5 trillion by 1997. Then, between 1998 and 2000, federal surpluses halted the growing debt. After 2002, federal budget deficits sharply increased until faster economic growth and higher tax receipts reduced the deficit level in 2005 through 2007. With the recession that began in late 2007, large deficits resumed; the largest deficit on record was expected in 2009.

In the United States, a few deficit watchers have always been alarmed at prospects of deficits and their implications, but when large deficits were projected to continue throughout the 1990s, deficit reduction became an important political and economic issue. Some have pointed to the large budget deficits incurred by the ARRA as reason not to fund a second stimulus package. A slower recovery, however, would also generate larger budget deficits over a longer period of time.

FIGURE 15.3 The Fedral Budget Surplus or Deficit, 1935–2009

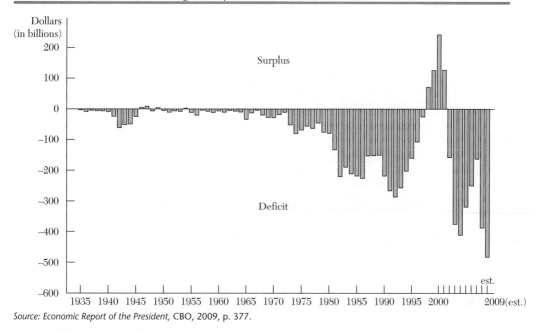

Source: *Economic Report of the President,* CBO, 2009, p. 377.

The Federal Budget and the Economy

Just as the budget of a family or business determines the direction, priorities, and obligations of that unit, the federal budget determines the direction, prior- ities, and obligations assumed by the nation. The federal budget consists of ex- penditures (such as direct purchases of goods and services) and receipts (such as taxes). Elements of fiscal policy are directly reflected in the annual federal bud- get, which not only indicates a president's view about fiscal and social policy, but also reflects electoral policies and the process of government. The budget that the president proposes and Congress passes, in what is now a yearlong process, reflects what the government will do and what priorities it will set. As is the case with household budgets, receipts are balanced against expenditures. If receipts are greater than expenditures, a surplus results; if expenditures ex- ceed receipts, there is a deficit.

The most obvious source of federal government revenue is tax receipts. Individual income taxes provided 45 percent of the roughly $2.6 trillion col- lected in 2007. As shown in Figure 15.4, the importance of individual income taxes has grown since the 1940s. Social Security taxes now provide the next largest single receipt, having increased from only 11 percent in 1950 to 33 per- cent in 2007.

Corporate income taxes provided a substantial portion of federal receipts during the 1950s and 1960s, but as a result of the Reagan tax cut package of 1981, the corporate share of the total tax burden shrank to 6.2 percent in 1983. The Economic Recovery Tax Act, as it was called, cut personal income tax rates by 23 percent over three years. The measure also accelerated the rate at which businesses could take depreciation deductions, and gave other

FIGURE 15.4 Tax Type as a Percentage of Government Revenue, 1940–2007

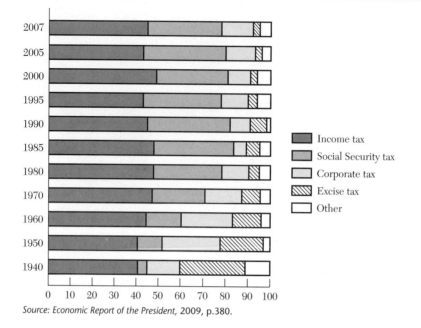

Source: *Economic Report of the President,* 2009, p.380.

deductions and additional loopholes to individuals and businesses alike. The much-heralded Tax Reform Act of 1986 reduced corporate tax rates, elimi- nated the investment tax credit (which had saved corporations billions in taxes), and made depreciation allowances stricter. The corporate share of taxes increased to 11.4 percent in 1988 and in 2007 corporate taxes con- tributed 14 percent to total revenues.

The other side of the federal government's budget is expenditures. Table 15.3 shows federal expenditures both as the proportion of the budget going to se- lected areas and as a percentage of GDP for selected years. Military expendi- tures, while not changing dramatically as a percentage of the federal budget, increased dramatically as a percentage of GDP during the 1980s. In 1988 total defense expenditures were $290 billion, or 6.0 percent of GDP. Thanks to the end of the Cold War and the breakup of the former Soviet Union, U.S. defense expenditures were $294 billion, or roughly 3 percent of GDP by 2000. However, the Iraq war has brought additional military expenditures, and sub- stantial increases have occurred in Social Security and Medicare expenditures. At the same time, interest payments on the federal debt have declined as a per- cent of GDP, thanks to lower interest rates.

Most budgeted programs were, in fact, cut as part of the Reagan and Bush programs to enhance the role of the private sector while reducing the role of government. However, since military, agriculture, Social Security, and interest expenditures increased so significantly in the 1980s, Reagan was unable to keep his campaign promise of reducing government's role. Under his administra- tion, expenditures rose to a peacetime record of 23.7 percent of GDP in 1983.

Table 15.3 Government Expenditures as a Percentage of Budget Outlays and GDP, 1975–2009 (Selected Categories)

Selected Expenditure	1975 % Budget Outlay	1975 % GDP	1980 % Budget Outlay	1980 % GDP	1985 % Budget Outlay	1985 % GDP	1990 % Budget Outlay	1990 % GDP	1995 % Budget Outlay	1995 % GDP	2000 % Budget Outlay	2000 % GDP	2005 % Budget Outlay	2005 % GDP	2007 % Budget Outlay	2007 % GDP
National defense	26.5	5.3	23.2	4.8	26.7	6.0	23.9	5.2	18.0	3.7	16.4	2.8	20.0	4.0	21.5	4.0
Education/health	13.2	2.6	9.2	1.9	6.6	1.5	7.7	1.7	11.2	2.3	11.9	2.1	14.2	2.8	10.3	1.9
Social Security (includes Medicare)			26.1	5.4	26.9	6.1	27.7	6.0	29.8	6.8	33.9	6.0	20.0	3.96	22.8	4.2
Medicare	—		—		—		—		—		—		12.1	2.4	14.6	2.7
Income security	33.3	6.7	15.0	3.1	13.5	3.0	11.8	2.6	14.5	3.0	13.8	2.4	14.0	2.7	14.2	2.6
Net interest	9.5	1.9	9.1	1.9	13.7	3.1	14.7	3.2	15.3	3.2	12.8	2.2	7.4	1.4	9.2	1.7
Agriculture	0.5	0.1	0.8	0.2	2.7	0.6	0.9	0.2	0.6	0.1	2.2	0.4	1.1	0.2	0.7	0.1
Total budget	20.0		20.7		22.6		21.7		20.9		17.5		19.8		18.6	
Surplus/(deficit)	(2.8)		(2.1)		(5.0)		(3.8)		(2.2)		0.8		(4.0)		(1.3)	

Source: Economic Report of the President, 1989, pp. 316, 398, 399; February 1996, p. 369; February 2006, p. 380; February 2009, p. 380.

During the Clinton administration, government expenditures as a percentage of GDP declined to 17.5 percent of GDP. In 2005, the G. W. Bush administration saw government expenditures rise to 19.8 percent of GDP, decreasing to 18.6 percent in 2007.

By grouping these outlays another way, we can see why policy makers had such a difficult time reducing the deficit. Figure 15.5 shows the discretionary, non-defense–discretionary and nondiscretionary spending as a percentage of the total budget using assumptions based on the 2010 fiscal year budget. Discretionary spending is voted on annually. The government automatically spends money on these mandatory programs. The largest of these entitlements are Medicare and Social Security, which grow as increasingly large numbers of the population reach retirement age.

The combination of tax reductions and expenditure increases led to then-record **budget deficits** between 1980 and 1993. Although the federal budget deficit has been larger when measured as a percentage of GDP, deficits comparable to those registered during the 1980s through the mid-1990s have seldom been recorded during a time of peace or economic growth. In July 2009, U.S. federal debt stood at $11.6 trillion. The United States is the largest debtor nation in the world.

In the early 1990s, in an attempt to deal with large actual and projected deficits, Congress passed the Balanced Budget and Emergency Deficit Control Act (better known as Gramm-Rudman-Hollings), which mandated a balanced budget by 1993 and required automatic spending cuts in military and nonmilitary expenditures if Congress and the president failed to meet annual deficit reduction targets in the federal budget. Those targets were never achieved, in part because of the money spent to bail out failing savings and loan institutions in the late 1980s (see Chapter 16). In 1990, Congress enacted spending cuts and tax increases to cut the deficit. The Budget Enforcement Act limited discretionary

FIGURE 15.5   Federal Spending by Budget Category (FY 2010 Budget)

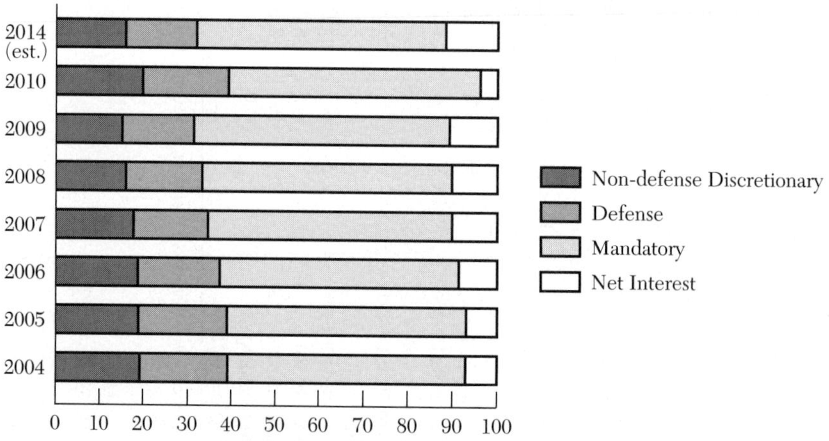

Source: Data from OMB, *Historical Tables, FY 2010 Budget.*

spending and ensured that new entitlement programs would not worsen the deficit. Unfortunately, these were enacted at the same time the 1990 recession began, so tax receipts did not rise as they were expected to and government spending increased to offset the higher unemployment levels generated by the recession. In 1993, Congress passed a five-year deficit reduction plan designed to cut spending and increase revenue. Deficits fell from $290 billion in 1992 to $164 billion in 1995. In 1996, a seven-year plan to balance the budget was passed, and, by 1998, thanks in part to a surging economy resulting in increased tax revenues, the government realized its first surplus since the 1960s. Forecasts were mildly optimistic through 2000 but weakened in 2001 with tax reductions curbing receipts and increases in military and homeland security expenditures. Surpluses turned quickly into deficits as tax cuts continued and military expenditures grew. Economic growth rebounded with these fiscal stimuli until the fourth quarter of 2007, when the economy entered a deep and prolonged recession. The ARRA was implemented to attack the downturn with tax cuts and increased expenditures.

9. Which categories of federal government expenditures have grown most rapidly over the past two decades? Which revenues have seen the greatest growth?

10. What is the forecast for the deficit this year?

Federal Deficits and Surpluses

Deficits in the federal budget give rise to the **national** (or **federal) debt**. The national debt is the debt or obligation of the federal government and is the accumulation of annual budget deficits. When expenditures are greater than revenues, the government must borrow the difference to finance its spending. The government finances its deficits by borrowing from the public through the sale of treasury bills and bonds. Treasury bonds are debt issues of the government that guarantee the repayment of the original investment plus a specified rate or amount of interest. The Treasury Department sells them to the public, to government agencies, and to institutional investors. Surpluses cause some to wonder about the future of treasury bond sales. In the remainder of this chapter, we examine concerns related to federal deficits and federal surpluses.

The national debt has been one of the great conversation topics of Americans concerned with its growth and size. The historical record indicates that all forms of debt increased dramatically after World War II. In the 1960s, the total federal debt was $300 billion, and in 2007 it reached $9 trillion. The debt more than tripled during the 1980s, stabilized in the late 1990s, and has expanded since.

We might ask why the debt is so worrisome to citizens, as well as to economists and policy makers. The government could eliminate it quite simply by assessing every man, woman, and child in the country an additional $37,900 (in 2009), their per capita share of the national debt. But more important facets of the debt need to be examined. The federal debt did not overly concern the majority of U.S. economists until the 1980s. To understand why such an issue is being made of the debt, we need to examine how debt that accumulated before the 1980s differs from debt that accumulated during the 1980s and after.

The Budget Deficit Through Leakages and Injections.   One way to examine the federal deficit in terms of the problems deficits bring to our economy is to analyze aggregate expenditures. In Chapter 14, we noted that in equilibrium, all leakages out of the economy must equal all injections into the economy:

$$\text{Injections} = \text{leakages}$$

$$G + I + X = S + Tx + M$$

We can also restate this by subtracting M from both sides of the equation:

$$G + I + (X - M) = S + Tx,$$

where G represents government expenditures, I is investment expenditures, $(X - M)$ is net exports, S is saving, and Tx is taxes. We can rearrange the terms in this equation to show the federal budget deficit or surplus:

$$G - Tx = S - I - (X - M).$$

We know that the deficit or surplus is represented by government expenditures less receipts, or $G - Tx$. If taxes (receipts) are less than government expenditures, there is a deficit.

Reviewing this budget equation clarifies the government's options. If tax receipts are chronically less than government expenditures, the deficit must be offset by one or a combination of factors represented on the right side of the equation just given. The government can fund its expenditures by borrowing savings balances from the private and public sectors. This leaves fewer funds for private investment. Or it can increase borrowing from abroad, thus increasing its obligations to foreign citizens and institutions.*

What's the Problem with Deficits?   Before the 1980s, most of the national debt accumulated during war years, especially during World War II and the Vietnam War. Until early 1982 and begining again in 2001, the debt as a percentage of national income continued to fall. As long as GDP was rising faster than the debt each year, there were only three major concerns:

1. Does the debt compete with other uses of credit?
2. Who pays the interest?
3. Who owns the debt and receives the interest?

---

*We can also express this in our national accounting framework, since

$$Y = C + I + G + (X - M),$$

where

$$Y = C + S + Tx$$

Now substitute and simplify:

$$C + S + Tx = C + I + G + (X - M)$$
$$S + Tx = I + G + (X - M)$$
$$G - Tx = S - I - (X - M)$$

The question of alternative financing sources is particularly cause for concern when the economy is operating at close to full employment. The government can increase taxes or borrow. Either action reduces the spending potential of another sector. Tax increases reduce the spending power of consumers and businesses. Borrowing, or enlarging the debt, may force interest rates up because government bond issues will have to be offered at a higher yield to attract enough buyers. Most of these bond issues will be sold to financial intermediaries, corporations, and others, so government spending will tend to take place at the expense of investment (instead of consumption); the financial intermediaries would otherwise lend to corporations for investment purposes rather than buying government bonds. This crowding out of private investment may occur when the economy is expanding. If there were severe levels of unemployment and excess capacity, interest rates would probably not have to rise with the new government bond issues, and businesses would be reluctant to invest anyway, no matter how low the interest rate fell.

Large budget deficits cause concern for future levels of economic growth, which in turn affects wealth and future living standards. While there are many uses for funds made available by businesses and household saving, there is a limit to that saving. National saving consists of private saving and government saving. Government saving is the budget surplus, or the part of its revenues the government does not spend. If the government must borrow from private saving to finance its deficit, it may divert funds from domestic investment. This is a particular problem when savings rates fall markedly. Figure 15.6 shows that the national saving rate fell from around 8.0 percent of GDP in the 1950s

FIGURE 15.6 Net National Saving and Personal Saving as a Percent of GDP (1930–2005), Budget Deficit as a Percent of GDP (1950–2005)

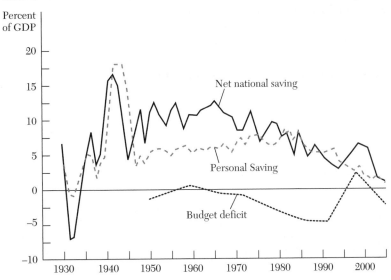

Source: GAO analysis of NIPA data from the Bureau of Economic Analysis (BEA). GAO Report, GAO-06-628T.

through the 1970s to 3 percent in the first half of the 1980s and to 2.4 percent in the last half. The national saving rate rose to 5 percent of GDP in the 1990s, only to fall to 2 percent in 2005. Private saving dropped from 9 percent in the 1950–1980 period to 6 percent in the 1980s. Private saving continued to fall through the 1990s, reaching 1 percent in 2004. Government deficits thus consumed many of the resources that had to be parceled out among a variety of credit demands. If interest costs rise, the higher costs can lower the demand for housing and reduce investment. Many economists believe that deficits must remain low if the nation is to achieve long-term prosperity.

The second, more obvious, concern over who owns the debt arises with regard to repayment. It is one thing to pay the interest to ourselves and quite another to owe it to someone else. In 1985, about 11.5 percent of the debt was owned by foreign individuals and governments. By 2007, this figure approached 25 percent. We will examine the links between borrowing from international sources and the U.S. government debt in Chapter 20.

11. Why did the foreign-held debt increase? Do you think it will continue to do so? Why or why not?

It would be naive to assume that all of us own some of the debt (government bonds) held equally within the U.S. public. Some of us own much more of the debt than others, and the richer we are, the more debt (or bonds) we are likely to own. The poorer among us hold few if any bonds. Institutions and middle- and upper-income individuals use government bonds as a safe and profitable way to hold their savings. Lower-income groups tend not to have substantial savings, since they consume most if not all of their income.

This brings us to the final problem of the interest payments on the debt. In 2008, the debt cost taxpayers more than $253 billion in interest payments. Since the interest payments come from budget receipts, and budget receipts come from taxation, this pattern of interest payments and ownership leads to a redistribution of income in the economy, from bottom to top. Almost everyone pays taxes, some of which are used to pay the interest on the debt. But only individuals who own government bonds receive these interest payments. This is a concern for some economists and politicians.

12. Is ownership of the debt of some concern to you?

13. What groups benefit from the redistributive effects of the debt?

Historically, the debt has financed wars, higher levels of employment and income, and inflation. In the 1980s, it financed additional military and Social Security expenditures and lower taxes. Some argue that the results are a bargain at $37,900 (in 2009) per person! While many economists believe that deficits are an urgent problem, others believe that part of the debt funds much-needed public investments in education, infrastructure, the military, consumer protection, and other public goods.

Cyclical and Structural Deficits and Surpluses

The Keynesian philosophy toward budgets was that deficits should accumulate during recessions, when additional government expenditures are necessary to boost the economy by stimulating aggregate expenditures, and governments should accumulate surpluses during times of prosperity. The results would be a cyclically balanced budget. Granted, the amounts spent during the recessions might not equal the amounts accumulated during prosperity, but on the whole they would more or less even out. In the United States, however, during the 88 quarters between 1960 and 1981, only four surpluses were recorded. After that, 18 more years passed until the next surplus, recorded in 1999.

When deficits accumulate as a result of economic downturns, they are called **cyclical deficits**, measured by the economic cost of the recession in terms of added expenditures due to unemployment and lost tax receipts. During the recession of the early 1990s, higher levels of unemployment and lower incomes meant that cyclical factors were acting with structural factors to create a much larger than projected federal budget deficit. Cyclical surpluses occur in economic upturns when strong employment and growth yield higher tax receipts. The surpluses of 1999 and 2000 were cyclical surpluses and the 2009 deficit was a cyclical deficit.

Deficits that accrue during times of prosperity or high employment are called **structural deficits**. They result from the structure of federal receipts and expenditures, regardless of the level of economic activity. Between 1960 and 1980, structural deficits averaged less than 2 percent of GDP until 1983, when they reached 2.9 percent of GDP. With economic growth between 1993 and 1995, the cyclical component of the deficit shrank. In 1995, there was a negative cyclical component, since unemployment was below 5.7 percent (the unemployment rate used to calculate "full employment"). With unemployment levels at or below this level in 2005 and 2006, large federal deficits were primarily structural.

The structure of federal receipts and expenditures can also produce structural surpluses. Structural surpluses would occur if the economy were at full employment when the government accrued surpluses. Some economists argue that structural surpluses are detrimental to the economy. According to this argument, surpluses act as a drag on future economic activity by shifting savings from private to public sources. In the 1960s, this phenomenon was called "fiscal drag." Higher tax returns lowered private saving, possibly lowering consumption and limiting loanable funds for private investments.

14. Are cuts in federal expenditures possible? Why or why not?

15. Have any tax cuts or tax increases been passed since 2009? Have new or different types of taxes been proposed? What are they?

16. How large was the federal deficit last year? How large is the federal debt?

17. What would be the effect on income of a decrease in government spending of $0.3 trillion and a tax cut of $0.3 trillion? Is this a balanced budget?

18. Economists have called an unemployment rate of 5.7 percent "full employment." Is there recent evidence that this rate should be changed? If so, what evidence?

Conclusion

This chapter has highlighted how fiscal policy works through the tax, transfer, and spending multipliers. For a wide variety of reasons, fiscal policy is not always efficient, but it is most often effective—at least when estimated by Keynesian models. We have also seen the growing concern with structural budget deficits and the desire to balance government receipts against expenditures in periods of economic growth. Chapter 16 will introduce money into the Keynesian model of the economy; this provides yet another set of tools for achieving policy objectives.

Review Questions

1. What fiscal policy recommendations would you make to combat unemployment and recession?
   a. What fiscal measures would you recommend if the economy were in the middle of a prolonged period of inflation?
   b. Would you favor a tax policy over a curb on government spending? Why or why not?
   c. What might be the end result of your policy?
   d. How long do you expect the lags to last before your policy would be enacted?

2. What are the differences between automatic stabilizers and discretionary fiscal policy?

3. Would you ever recommend a balanced budget for the federal government? Why or why not? If so, when?

4. Can federal budget deficits be beneficial to the economy?

5. How might deficits limit the productive potential of the economy?

6. Are structural deficits more cause for concern than cyclical deficits? Explain.

7. If MPC = 0.8, what would be the effect of a $10 million tax cut and a $6 million increase in government purchases?

Note

The body of this chapter dealt only with the effect of injections (government spending, investment, and net exports) on equilibrium income. Now we examine in more detail the effect of leakages or withdrawals in the Keynesian model. We will focus specifically on taxation, although the analysis is similar for other withdrawals, including transfers. In the two-sector model, the only leakage we encountered was saving. When saving increases (S to S') and consumption decreases (C to C'), the saving schedule shifts up and to the left, while the consumption schedule shifts down and to the right, and equilibrium income moves to Y_1 in Figure 15.A.

Just as all injections— C, I, G, and $(X - M)$—are components of aggregate expenditures and are graphically represented as part of the aggregate expenditures function, all leakages or withdrawals are represented on an aggregate leakage curve. To illustrate our aggregate leakage curve, we

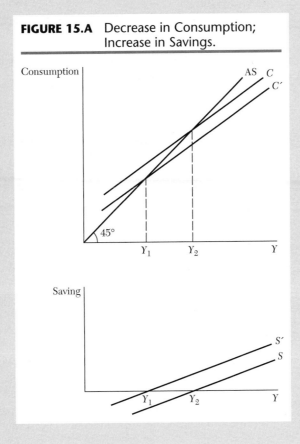

FIGURE 15.A Decrease in Consumption; Increase in Savings.

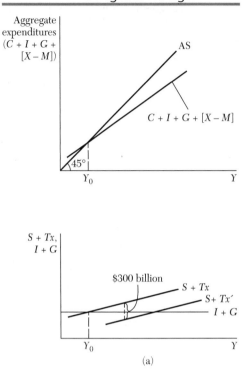

FIGURE 15.B Impact of a Tax Cut
(a) Tax decrease of
$300 billion is shown as
a negative leakage.

Aggregate expenditures $(C + I + G + [X - M])$

AS

$C + I + G + [X - M]$

45°

Y_0

Y

$S + Tx,$
$I + G$

$300 billion

$S + Tx$

$S + Tx'$

$I + G$

Y_0

Y

(a)

again expand the model from two to three sectors by adding the taxation leakage to the saving schedule. We add the exogenous tax leakage to the savings function, which in this analysis gives the leakage function its slope (MPS), just as the consumption function gives the injection function or aggregate expenditures curve its slope (MPC). The leakage curve represents positive and negative tax and saving changes. (A tax increase would represent a positive leakage; a tax decrease would represent a negative leakage.) An increase in saving or taxes will shift the leakage curve up and to the left. A decrease in saving or taxes will shift the curve down and to the right; thus, at every level of income, leakages are lower.

Returning to the previous example of a $300 billion tax cut, we arrive at the new equilibrium income after a series of three steps (see Figure 15.B). These three steps occur simultaneously but are shown as a series to clearly demonstrate each part of the

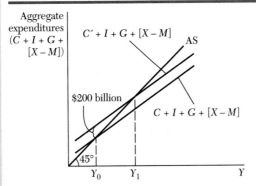

FIGURE 15.B (Continued)
(b) Consumption increase as a result of the addition to income from the tax cut ($\Delta C = 2/3 \times$ $300 billion = $300 billion).

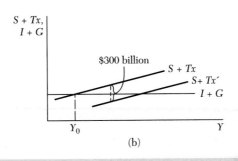

(b)

adjustment process. The steps describe how people respond to a cut in taxes. (Note that this is not a cut in the tax rate.) The cut brings an increase in income, but how is that increase allocated? Our answer conforms to what we learned in Chapter 14. Part of the $300 billion will be consumed, and part will be saved; the MPC and MPS tell us how consumption and saving are allocated. In the first step, Figure 15.B(a), the saving–tax leakage curve shifts down by $300 billion, as taxes are cut by that amount. Second, since income initially rises by the amount of the tax cut, individuals will boost their consumption by MPC times the tax reduction (2/3 × $300 billion = $200 billion). In Figure 15.B(b), we see the effect of this increase in consumption as the aggregate expenditures curve shifts up by $200 billion. At this point, there is an equilibrium level of income in the

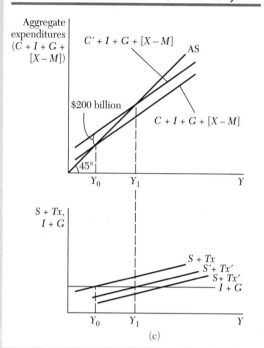

FIGURE 15.B (Continued)
(C) Saving increases as a result of the addition to income from the tax cut ($\Delta S = 1/3 \times$ $300 billion = $100 billion).

(c)

upper, aggregate expenditures graph, but not in the lower, leakage graph. To arrive at equilibrium in both the upper and lower graphs, we must complete the final step. Just as individuals increase consumption by MPC times the tax reduction, they will increase their saving by MPS times the tax reduction ($1/3 \times$ $300 billion = $100 billion). Thus, the saving–tax leakage curve shifts up and to the left—by $300 billion, as shown in Figure 15.B(c). In the final analysis, income increases from Y_0 to Y_1, or by $600 billion. To arrive at this result more directly, we can multiply the tax multiplier by the change in taxes:

$$- k_{tx} \times \Delta Tx = \Delta Y$$

$$- 2 \times - \$300 \text{ billion} = \$300 \text{ billion}$$

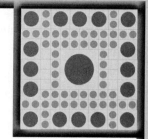

CHAPTER SIXTEEN

Financial Markets, Money, and Monetary Policy

 Introduction

Money *is an asset accepted in exchange for the goods and services we want to purchase. The role of money and the operation of the markets for money and other financial instruments are important in economic decision making and policy making, and economists do not always agree on the way money works through the economy or on its potential impact.*

Key players in the market for money and other financial instruments are institutions called **financial intermediaries,** *which hold the funds of savers and make those funds available to borrowers. Financial intermediaries include commercial banks, savings and loan institutions, mutual savings banks, finance companies, credit unions, life insurance companies, mutual funds, and pension funds. They provide financial services demanded by consumers in a changing society. Depository institutions have been more directly linked to Federal Reserve Board (Fed) actions than other financial intermediaries, although the recent financial crisis has expanded the role of the Fed.*

To begin examining money and a group of financial intermediaries accepting deposits of savers, we will first look at the uses of and demands for money. Next, we will examine the money supply, including the ways the Fed can increase and decrease the money supply and the role of money in the Keynesian model. Finally, we examine monetary policy, and the role of the Federal Reserve and monetary policy in the recent financial crisis.

THE USES OF MONEY

Money is important to economics because of its uses. Some say that money is as money does. Few individuals hold dollars for the sheer joy of counting or stacking them.

Money is valued for the goods and services that it buys—for its use as a **medium of exchange**. It is commonly accepted in payment for goods and services.

Before money was institutionalized, barter economies prevailed; people simply exchanged goods and services. Of course, problems arose when two parties could not agree upon objects to trade or when there was no double coincidence of wants. For example, barter fails if one trader desires shoes and has only nuts to offer in exchange, while the shoemaker wants only leather in exchange for shoes. Larger problems would arise if one had only assets that could not be divided, such as a horse to trade for less valuable objects.

Because it is an accepted medium of exchange, money can also be used as a measuring rod for the value of each good or service—in other words, as a **unit of account**. In our economy, goods are measured by a dollar amount. In shopping we observe that a pound of nuts is priced at $4.69, a pair of shoes at $85.98, and a horse and buggy at $5,753. In Chapter 13, we used money as our unit of account in measuring the National Income Accounts of GDP and NNP. Firms use money to account for the flow of goods and services produced and sold.

Besides its unique role as a medium of exchange and unit of account, money has two functions that it shares with other assets (things of value that are owned). Money may serve as a **store of value**. To be a store of value, an asset must hold its value into the future. Some other assets that serve this function are stocks, bonds, precious metals, gems, and property. Money may also be a **standard of deferred payment**. Standards of deferred payment are assets accepted by others for future payment.

1. What assets would you accept as payment for your work?

DEMAND FOR MONEY

The four uses of money are associated with the three categories of demand for money. The **transactions demand**—the only category recognized by the classical economists—indicates the amount of money balances that individuals desire for transaction (purchasing) purposes. This demand corresponds to money's function as a medium of exchange and is often constant with a given level of income and pattern of consumption expenditures.

People also have a **precautionary demand** for money, or a demand for money to hold to meet unforeseen expenses. John Maynard Keynes wrote about this demand as a separate category in *The General Theory*. We observe this precautionary demand as we try to hedge our risks by saving, perhaps for the proverbial "rainy day" or for some other reason.

2. Divide your demands for money into transactions and precautionary balances. What percentage of your money balances do you hold for each?

FIGURE 16.1 Precautionary and Transactions Demand for Money

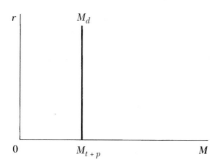

The precautionary demand, like the transactions demand, is generally constant; people at certain income levels will tend to save or keep a relatively fixed proportion of their income for precautionary purposes. Figure 16.1 shows a demand curve for the transactions and precautionary balances plotted on a price-quantity axis. (This adds money to the array of goods and services for which there is a demand—and later, of course, a supply.) The quantity of money (M) is measured along the horizontal axis, and the price of money, represented by the interest rate (r),* is measured along the vertical axis. The vertical line M_d indicates that at all rates of interest, the precautionary and transactions demand will be constant for a given individual at a given income level.

The third demand for money (or, as he called it, liquidity preference[†]) recognized by Keynes is the **speculative demand**. This demand arises from people's desire to maximize their returns on the funds left over after satisfying their transactions and precautionary demands. The speculative demand for funds is inversely related to the interest rate. If the interest rate is high, people will hold relatively few speculative or liquid balances. Instead, they will exchange these speculative money balances for bonds or other assets. If the interest rate is low, individuals may decide to wait and see what happens to interest rates in the future. If interest rates rise, people want to avoid being locked into low-yielding assets, so they prefer to hold (speculative) cash or money balances. One can plot the speculative demand for money with respect to interest and the quantity of money, since $M_{spec} = f(r)$, as shown in Figure 16.2.

At extremely high interest rates, the speculative demand for money balances approaches 0, whereas at very low rates of interest, people will desire to hold only money balances. This low-interest range in which the demand for money is perfectly elastic is called the Keynesian **liquidity trap**. Keynes pointed out that at extremely low rates of interest, people believe interest rates can go no

---

*The price of money is the rate of interest, since a person who buys or borrows money pays for it at the prevailing rate of interest. Although there is a wide array of interest rates in the economy at any one time, depending on such factors as risk and time until the asset matures, we will focus on *an* interest rate, assuming that all of them behave similarly.
[†]Liquidity is the degree of "moneyness." One hundred percent liquid suggests that all of one's assets are in cash and/or demand and checkable deposits. Stocks and bonds and property are assets of somewhat lesser levels of liquidity, since they cannot immediately be converted into cash.

FIGURE 16.2   Speculative Demand for Money

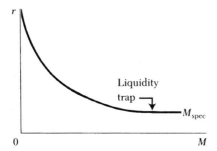

lower and can only rise. To buy bonds would be courting disaster, so people hold on to their cash. This liquidity trap area becomes important when discussing various aspects of monetary policy, a topic we will return to later in the chapter.

If we combine all three demands for money, we obtain the total demand for money, which is plotted in Figure 16.3. This demand curve for money, like all demand curves, indicates that the quantity demanded varies inversely with price. As the interest rate rises, people will hold smaller money balances, down to the amount needed to satisfy transactions and precautionary demands.

Changes in the Demand for Money

Like other demand curves, the demand for money may not remain constant over time. Shifts, or changes in demand, are often caused by a change in the level of income. For example, if an individual's income increases from $40,000 a year to $45,000 a year, that person's demand for money will more than likely increase. The reason is that the demand for precautionary and transactions balances increases as income increases. Figure 16.4 shows how changes in income affect the demand for money.

FIGURE 16.3   Total Demand for Money

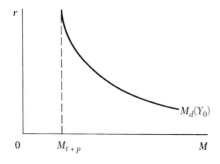

FIGURE 16.4 The Effect of Income Changes on the Demand for Money

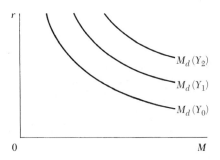

SUPPLY OF MONEY

Unlike the supply of most goods and services, the total supply of money is controlled not by individual firms, but by the Federal Reserve System, more commonly known as the Fed.

The Fed

To mend an ailing national banking system by promoting stability in the banking system, the Federal Reserve Act of 1913 established the **Federal Reserve System** (the **Fed**) as the central bank in the United States. The Fed is an independent agency of the government, established by Congress to centralize control over the banking system and the money supply. Figure 16.5 shows the basic organizational structure of the Federal Reserve System.

Members of the Board of Governors of the Federal Reserve System, appointed to 14 year terms by the president with congressional approval, coordinate and regulate monetary policy in the United States. The chair of the Board of Governors acts as spokesperson for the entire system. The Federal Open Market Committee (FOMC) directs Fed sales and purchases of U.S. Treasury bonds, and the other councils advise. The 12 regional Federal Reserve Banks and their 24 branches throughout the country oversee operations of the member commercial banks in their districts. Figure 16.6 shows the locations of these regional banks.

The Monetary Control Act of 1980 stipulated that the Federal Reserve can require that *all* banks and depository institutions in the country hold reserves (or a percentage of deposits). The passage of this act gave the Fed control over the reserves placed on money held in commercial banks, savings banks, savings and loan institutions, and credit unions.

3. Congress established the Federal Reserve as an independent agency of the federal government (that is, outside the operational control of Congress or the president). List arguments supporting an independent agency.

4. Who is the current chair of the Fed?

FIGURE 16.5 Federal Reserve System

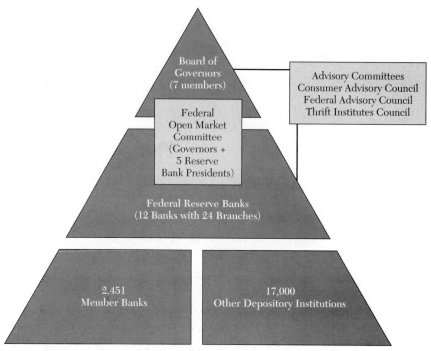

Source: Board of Governors of the Federal Reserve System, *The Federal Reserve Today*, p. 2.

FIGURE 16.6 Boundaries of Federal Reserve Districts and Their Branch Territories

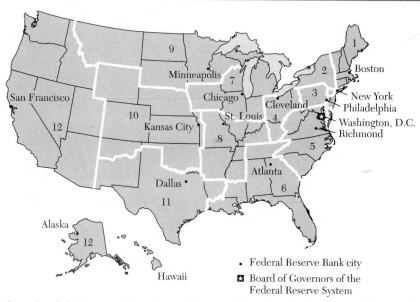

Source: Board of Governors of the Federal Reserve System, http://www.federalreserve.gov/otherfrb.htm

Regulation of Financial Markets

Operating within the U.S. financial markets are many institutional players, all of them subject to some degree of regulation. Commercial banks are the oldest financial intermediaries. Savings banks and insurance companies emerged in the late nineteenth century, while credit unions, real estate trusts, investment banks, bank holding companies, and finance companies developed in the twentieth century. A number of innovations in existing financial institutions occurred in the 1980s, and changes resulting from new regulation and deregulation legislation continued throughout the 1990s.

There is a long history of financial market regulation in the United States. Financial institutions have seen periods of total control and regulation, as well as periods that might be called banking anarchy. The current period of regulation resulted from controls instituted after the Great Depression, as Congress enacted legislation to avoid the recurrence of widespread banking failures. Investors as well as depositors wanted protection from financial market failures. The federal and state governments responded with laws and regulations designed to assure the safety of the financial system. Federal deposit insurance agencies began insuring a variety of deposits, and agencies began to regulate the activities of financial institutions. However, in the 1980s and in 1999, Congress moved to eliminate at least some of the regulations dating from the 1930s.

Regulation limited the kinds of loans and assets each type of financial institution could issue and possess. As a result, the financial industry was segmented into largely different types of institutions with little competition among them. Commercial banks, for example, specialized in commercial loans to businesses, while savings and loan institutions generated home mortgages. Started by builders in the 1870s, savings banks made money available to people wanting to buy the builders' products.

Perhaps the most onerous of the depression-era regulations was **Regulation Q**, which placed ceilings on the interest rate financial institutions could pay for time and savings deposits. The purpose of interest ceilings was to "restrain excessive price competition," which was thought to be one of the causes of the 1933 banking collapse. The interest ceiling was above the market rate of interest through the mid-1960s, so until then it caused no concern. After 1966, market rates rose above the interest ceiling on several occasions. This effectively prevented financial intermediaries from attracting money and then lending it. Instead of depositing their funds in financial intermediaries, people withdrew their dollars and put them into stocks or other assets to get higher returns. Instead of **financial intermediation**, there was **disintermediation**. To avoid interest ceilings, financial intermediaries began creating new financial instruments, since only time and savings deposit accounts were then subject to Regulation Q. But the Federal Reserve was not to be caught short. While Regulation Q covered only two types of accounts in 1965, twenty-four types were covered by 1979.

Because of these rapid financial innovations, Congress came under pressure to deregulate financial markets. The regulation of the 1930s had limited competition and the ability to work within the market system to bid for funds. By the end of the 1970s, the mood toward regulation had substantially changed as described in the 1984 *Economic Report of the President*:

> In the 1930s, financial instability was attributed to the natural operation of competitive markets, and this view supported a very substantial extension of regulatory controls over financial markets. More recently, however, a renewed respect for the efficiency of competitive markets has developed, as well as increased recognition of the costs of regulation. Regulation tends to spread in unproductive directions and often causes industries to evolve less efficiently than they otherwise would. For these reasons, the promotion of efficiency by furthering competition is also an important regulatory goal. The purpose of regulation should not be to protect poorly managed individual firms from failure, but rather to prevent such failures from shaking the stability of the financial system as a whole. Regulation should be designed to achieve stability of the system, while individual firms are afforded the maximum possible freedom to compete and innovate.

In the early 1980s, financial deregulation significantly changed the rules of the game in the financial markets. Between 1980 and 1984, most interest rates on federally insured deposits were deregulated, allowing banks and thrift institutions (savings and loan institutions, savings banks, and credit unions) to freely determine the rate of interest they paid on most types of deposits. This added both competition and uncertainty to a vast financial system. The deregulatory activity was started by the Monetary Control Act of 1980 and extended by the Garn–St. Germain Depository Institutions Act of 1982. The Monetary Control Act set lower reserve requirements for all nonmember banks, established the Fed as the lender of the last resort for depository institutions, and eliminated Regulation Q. The Garn–St. Germain Act authorized all financial institutions to offer interest-bearing checking accounts and extended the power of regulators to promote mergers for depository institutions that were failing. It also expanded the lending and deposit powers of thrifts. This permitted some new lending and investing powers, including commercial and real estate loans by savings and loan institutions.

Following deregulation, the rate of bank failures and instability increased, and the savings and loan industry nearly collapsed. Continental Illinois, a major U.S. national bank, paved the way for bank failures in the late 1980s and early 1990s. Unable to arrange a merger for this ailing giant, the Federal Deposit Insurance Corporation (FDIC), which insures deposits of most banks, took over operations. Other failing banks and thrifts were either merged with institutions believed to be more stable or liquidated. Many have therefore questioned the wisdom of aspects of this particular financial deregulation.

Two major reforms in bank regulation took place in the 1990s. In 1994, Congress set nationwide standards for banks wishing to expand or operate branches beyond their home state boundaries. Late in 1999 the Gramm-Leach-Bliley Act was passed by Congress allowing commercial banks to engage in investment banking activities in order to compete more effectively with other financial intermediaries. This legislation revoked part of the Glass-Steagall Act of 1933 designed to protect the public from financiers who might fund some investment activities while denying funds to equally worthy activities. From the late 1990s there was continuing pressure to avoid increased regulation of financial markets and financial instruments. With repercussions from the financial crisis that begun in 2007, there have been increased calls for greater regulation; however, financial institutions have continually resisted further regulation. In late 2009 several measure to regulate financial markets and instruments were under investigation in Congress.

Banking and Thrift Instability, 1980s and 1990s Style

Deregulation posed enormous problems for the nation's commercial banks and savings institutions. Nearly eight times as many banks closed between 1980 and 1990 as closed during the 1970s. Some 1,570 savings institutions closed their doors or merged with other depository institutions during this period. The government's response to the turmoil in the thrift industry cost U.S. taxpayers an estimated $500 billion or more.

A number of thrifts were in financial difficulty prior to deregulation. Initially chartered to provide mortgage funds to the housing market, savings and loan institutions were legally restricted to holding only mortgages as assets. After World War II, amidst a large upswing in purchases of single-family homes, the demand for mortgages rose, and savings institutions prospered despite the long-term, low-interest nature of these mortgages. Thanks to Regulation Q limiting the interest rate that could be paid to depositors, tax benefits to the industry, and federal insurance guarantees to depositors, savings institutions could thrive as long as interest rates remained low. However, interest rates rose markedly in the 1970s, and savings institutions had to pay higher interest rates to attract deposits. Their profits were squeezed, since the long-run returns on the mortgages already in their portfolios remained fixed at low rates, even though new mortgages reflected the higher rates. Furthermore, the institutions faced geographic restrictions on their customer base, so institutions in agriculture and oil-producing states were especially fragile. Energy and agricultural prices plunged in the 1980s, and increasing numbers of firms in the Midwest and Southwest failed, rendering many loans worthless. Deregulation freed these institutions to engage in potentially more lucrative but riskier areas of investment. Thrifts diversified into office buildings, commercial loans, and some direct purchases of franchises. At the same time, federal depository insurance was increased from $40,000 per account to $100,000 per account, so thrifts sought out larger deposits by offering more attractive rates of return. They hoped the new channels of investment open to them would more than offset the higher interest rates they were paying for funds. The risk for bankers (and depositors) was limited, since most deposits were insured.

During this same period, federal budget cuts, combined with a spirit of deregulation, reduced the number of bank examiners hired to oversee these more risky (and sometimes fraudulent) activities. The reduction in regulation and inspection, along with an overextension of risky loans, left many institutions with deposit liabilities in excess of the value of their assets. These ingredients completed a recipe for widespread thrift failure.

With the mounting failures draining federal deposit insurance funds, Congress in 1989 enacted the Financial Institutions

Reform, Recovery and Enforcement Act (FIR-REA). This law provided funds to merge or liquidate failing thrift institutions and prevent the thrift failures of the eighties from recurring. FIRREA created the Resolution Trust Corporation (RTC) to manage a bailout of the savings and loan industry through the early 1990s. Among its charges, the RTC was to sell houses, apartment buildings, golf resorts, office buildings, and other assets of failed thrifts. Much of the real estate sold at bargain-basement prices, recouping only a small fraction of the moneys lost. These massive sales depressed real estate markets and new construction in communities with the highest levels of RTC sales.

FIRREA also eliminated other thrift regulatory agencies and established several new agencies in their place. The law established more stringent capital standards, requiring thrifts to meet the higher capital requirements of banks. Regulators continued to examine bank and thrift capital requirements through the 1990s.

Economists estimated that in the early 1990s, closing or selling insolvent thrifts cost taxpayers some $10 million for each day the S&Ls stayed open.

5. List some of the opportunity costs of the thrift bailout. (What could have been purchased with these amounts?)

6. Some economists argue that markets function more efficiently without regulation. Explain why deregulation of the S&L industry worked so poorly.

Measures of the Money Supply

Besides controlling the amount of credit in the system of depository institutions (which is often referred to as the banking system), the Fed also regulates the money supply. Because a number of financial assets are "used" as money, economists measure the money supply in broader terms than currency used for exchange. They use measures of the money supply called **monetary aggregates**, which include measures for M_1 and M_2. Figure 16.7 details the components of each measure.

The most narrowly defined monetary aggregate includes most of the "money" that we use for our day-to-day transactions and is called M_1. M_1 includes coins and currency plus demand deposits (checking accounts), traveler's checks, and other checkable deposits (including NOW and ATS accounts*) held by the public. In 2009, currency and coins accounted for about 51 percent of M_1, demand deposits for 26 percent, other checkable deposits for 21 percent, and traveler's checks for 0.3 percent. The total

---

*Negotiable order of withdrawal (NOW) accounts are interest-bearing checking accounts. They became legal throughout the United States on November 1, 1980, with an initial maximum interest rate of $5^1/4$ percent. NOW accounts may be issued by all depository institutions. ATS accounts are automatic transfer service accounts.

FIGURE 16.7 Components of the Monetary Aggregates, July 2009

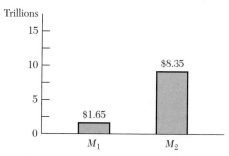

M_1 includes currency, traveler's checks, demand deposits, and other checkable deposits.
M_2 includes M_1, small-denomination time deposits, savings deposits and money market
deposit accounts, money market mutual fund shares (noninstitutional), overnight
repurchase agreements, and overnight eurodollars.

Source: Board of Governors of the Federal Reserve System, *Statistical Release,* May 28, 2009.

money supply measured as M_1 stood at \$1.6 trillion in mid 2009. M_1 has
historically grown at an annual rate of around 5 or 6 percent. In 1990,
the growth rate of M_1 was only 4 percent, but it increased to 14 percent in
1992 as the economy slowed. After 1995, the annual change in M_1 averaged a
2 percent increase.

An expanded monetary aggregate M_2 includes M_1 and adds other short-term
accounts that are easily converted into money. M_2 equals M_1 plus short-term
time and savings accounts and other interest-bearing accounts, including
money market deposit accounts, noninstitutional money market mutual funds,
and some other very liquid assets.* In 2009, M_2 was \$8.3 trillion—over five
times the value of M_1.

Some economists believe that the use of the M_2 definition better explains
consumption and other decisions made in the economy. Other economists,
however, believe that the Federal Reserve—when reflecting on policy actions
that will result in changes in the money supply—really looks at the availability
of credit in the economy rather than any precise M_1 or M_2 definition. For example, if the Fed concludes that credit is too tight, it will take measures to increase credit availability by increasing the money supply.

Although the Fed is responsible for initiating changes in policies to alter the
money supply, individual depository institutions allocate the money to the
public. To a large extent, their allocation reflects the interest rates in the economy. If interest rates are low, depository institutions are reluctant to lend large
quantities of money and risk being locked into low-yielding assets. On the
other hand, if interest rates are high, the depository institutions will be more

---

*Money market mutual funds (MMMFs) and money market deposit accounts (MMDAs) are
funds issued to savers and backed by holdings of high-quality short-term assets. MMDAs are
federally insured bank deposit accounts.

FIGURE 16.8 The Money Supply

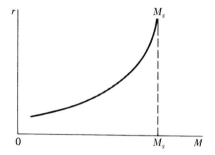

willing to lend money *if it is available to them* (or if the Fed has allocated additional money by implementing policies that increase the money supply). We can illustrate this by constructing a money supply curve. The interest rate is on the vertical axis, and the quantity of money is on the horizontal axis, as in Figure 16.8.

When we combine the supply and demand curves for money, the intersection of the two curves signifies equilibrium in the money market, as shown in Figure 16.9. At point E the quantity of money demanded equals the quantity supplied at an interest rate of r_0. In equilibrium, there is no excess demand or supply. If the Fed allows the money supply to increase, then the M_{s0} curve will shift to the right (M_{s1}) usually resulting in a lower interest rate (r_1) as in Figure 16.10. A decrease in the money supply will shift M_{s0} to the left (M_{s2}) and increase the interest rate (r_2) Later in this chapter, we will look at the tools with which the Fed changes the money supply. First we will examine the process by which commercial banks "create" money and how this money works within the Keynesian model.

Suppliers of Money

All financial intermediaries facilitate the exchange of money, but commercial banks and other depository institutions also have the power to "create"

FIGURE 16.9 Equilibrium in the Money Market

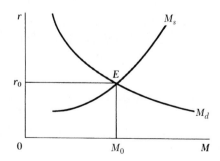

FIGURE 16.10 Changes in the Money Supply

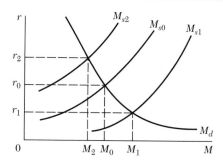

money. They create money on the basis of a **fractional reserve system** of deposit balances. The Fed requires that every depository institution hold reserves, setting aside a certain percentage of its total deposits in its vault or in the nearest Federal Reserve Bank to ensure safety and the ability to meet deposit withdrawals. The **reserve requirement** (the percentage of reserves that must be held) varies according to the asset size of the depository and the type of account. Table 16.1 lists the most recent reserve requirements mandated by the Fed.

 7. Why isn't there a 100 percent reserve requirement?

An example of the money creation process should help clarify what happens to a deposit in a commercial bank or other depository institution. For simplicity's sake, we shall use a 10 percent reserve requirement for demand deposits and begin with a newly created $1,000 deposit. With this deposit, new deposits in the depository or banking system increase by $1,000, and required reserves increase by $100. This leaves the commercial bank with $1,000 minus $100, or $900. The prudent (profit-maximizing) banker would use the $900 to generate loans and investments of an equal amount.

Table 16.1 Reserve Requirements of Depository Institutions

Type of Liability	Requirements	
	Reserve Percentage (%) of Liabilities	Effective Date
(Net Transaction Accounts)		
$0 to $10.7 million	0	12/31/09
More than $10 million to $55.2 million	3	12/31/09
More than $55.2 million	10	12/31/09
Nonpersonal time deposits	0	12/27/90
Eurocurrency liabilities	0	12/27/90

Source: www.federalreserve.gove/monetarypolicy/reservereq.htm

Perhaps you are in the market for a $900 loan. If our friendly neighborhood banker decides you are creditworthy, you may receive the "extra" $900. If you spend the $900 on new stereo components, there is a good chance that the full $900 will enter the banking system when the Stereo Shack deposits its daily balances. The banking system then has another deposit, this time one of $900. It must hold 10 percent of $900, or $90, as the reserve requirement on the *new* $900 deposit. Total new deposits are now $1,900, and total new required reserves are $190 in the banking system. And what will happen to the $900 minus $90, or $810, left in the bank? Of course, it becomes a potential source for increases in loans and investments. Table 16.2 shows the final result of the initial $1,000 demand deposit.

Rather than carrying this process to its final result, we can more easily find the total amount of money "created" by using the following formula:

$$\Delta R \times 1/r_{dd} = \Delta DD,$$

where ΔR is the original change in reserves, r_{dd} is the reserve requirement on demand deposits, and ΔDD is the total change in demand deposits. We can substitute numbers from our example:

$$\$1,000 \times 1/(1/10) = \Delta DD$$

$$\$1,000 \times 10 = \Delta DD$$

$$\$10,000 = \Delta DD$$

Table 16.2 Money Creation: Example

Position of Depository Institution	New Deposits	New Loans and Investments	Required Reserves
Original depository institution	$ 1,000.00	$ 900.00	$ 100.00
2nd depository institution	900.00	810.00	90.00
3rd depository institution	810.00	729.00	81.00
4th depository institution	729.00	656.10	72.90
5th depository institution	656.10	590.49	65.60
6th depository institution	590.49	531.44	59.05
7th depository institution	531.44	478.30	53.14
8th depository institution	478.30	430.47	47.83
9th depository institution	430.47	387.42	43.05
10th depository institution	387.42	348.68	38.74
11th depository institution	348.68	313.81	34.87
12th depository institution	+ 313.81	+282.43	31.38
Sum of 12 depository institutions	$ 7,175.71	$ 6,458.14	$ 717.61
Sum of remaining depository institutions	+ 2,824.29	+ 2,541.86	+ 282.39
Total for system as a whole	$10,000.00	$9,000.00	$1,000.00

Note: Totals may not be accurate due to rounding.

From $1,000, with the stroke of a pen, depository institutions can "make" $10,000—representing $9,000 of *new* money.

Before we accept this fountain pen magic, however, we must take note of several conditions. The first is that an individual bank or depository institution acting alone cannot create money. The process must operate throughout the whole system. To more easily understand this, imagine that a single depository institution tried to expand or create money on its own. Based on the $1,000 increase in its reserves with the $1,000 deposit, the institution loaned $9,000. What happens to that depository institution when someone comes to withdraw or use the funds the depository institution has just lent? As you might imagine, many problems can result, one being that the bank cannot maintain its reserve requirement.

8. What other difficulties might this depository institution run into?

A second point to remember is that the simplified money creation process as described works only if there are no leakages in the system. Leakages can occur in several places. Individuals may decide to place their funds elsewhere, either outside the depository institutions or in hoards. If they do not deposit the funds, then there are no reserves to expand upon. Consumers may place some funds in time accounts. These funds have lower reserve requirements, so the money multiplier is larger. Consequently, such deposits will lead to an even greater expansion of the money supply.

Another leakage may appear within the financial system itself. Bankers and other deposit managers may decide that they can earn greater profits by holding assets other than loans or securities. Perhaps they believe their liquidity is too low and desire to place their remaining funds (or excess reserves) in more short-term assets, such as government bonds. In either case, there is a leakage of funds that do not reenter the demand deposit flow for an indefinite period of time. Indeed, the amount of assets that depository institutions hold in loans or securities is approximately 60 percent of their total portfolio.

Caution should therefore be the byword when examining the money creation process. Nevertheless, the process does suggest that commercial banks and other depository institutions can expand the money supply by "creating" demand deposits. In addition, the simple formula $\Delta R \times r_{dd} = \Delta DD$ approximates the amount of money that the system can create from a new deposit.

9. What happens to the money supply when people take $1,000 out of their depository institution deposits?

The Myth and Mystique of Money

In the following excerpt from "Commercial Banks as Creators of Money," Yale economist James Tobin tries to steal our thunder in explaining the multiple money creation process in a principles text:

Perhaps the greatest moment of triumph for the elementary economics teacher is his [her] exposition of the multiple creation of bank credit and bank deposits. Before the admiring eyes of freshmen [s]he puts to rout the practical banker who is so sure that [s]he "lends only the money depositors entrust to him [her]." The banker is shown to have a worm's-eye view, and his [her] error stands as an introductory object lesson in the fallacy of composition. From the Olympian vantage of the teacher and the textbook it appears that the banker's dictum must be reversed: depositors entrust to bankers whatever amounts the bankers lend. To be sure, this is not true of a single bank; one bank's loan may wind up as another bank's deposit. But it is, as the arithmetic of successive rounds of deposit creation makes clear, true of the banking system as a whole. Whatever their other errors, a long line of financial heretics have been right in speaking of "fountain pen money"—money created by the stroke of the bank president's pen when she approves a loan and credits the proceeds to the borrower's checking account.

In this time-honored exposition two characteristics of commercial banks are intertwined. One is that their liabilities—well, at least their demand deposit liabilities—serve as widely acceptable means of payment. Thus, they count, along with coin and currency in public circulation, as "money." The other is that the preferences of the public normally play no role in determining the total volume of deposits or the total quantity of money. For it is the beginning of wisdom in monetary economics to observe that money is like the "hot potato" of a children's game: one individual may pass it to another, but the group as a whole cannot get rid of it. If the economy and the supply of money are out of adjustment, it is the economy that must do the adjusting. This is as true, evidently, of the money created by bankers' fountain pens as of money created by public printing presses.

The commercial banks possess the widow's cruse [an expression implying unending supply]. And because they possess this key to unlimited expansion, they have to be restrained by reserve requirements.

Excerpt from J. Tobin,"Commercial Banks as Creators of Money," in BANKING
AND MONETARY STUDIES, D. Carson, ed. © 1963 Irwin.

THE BIG PICTURE

Money and the Keynesian System

In Chapters 14 and 15 we saw how increases in spending—whether by businesses (as investment) or the government (as expenditures or taxes) worked through the multiplier to increase income by amounts greater than the original spending increases or tax cuts. Similarly, we saw how decreases in investment or government spending or increases in taxes would reduce income by more than the original spending cut or tax increase through the multiplier. In the sections just above we saw how equilibrium in the money market, where the supply of money M_s equals the demand for money M_d is at an interest rate (r). In Figure 16.BP.1 we see that this interest rate is at r_0.

With just one more piece of information we can see how increases in the money supply will—in our Keynesian analysis—impact investment decisions and thus income. Increases in investment as seen in Chapter 14 work through the multiplier to increase income by more than the original investment. (Decreased investment will have the opposite effect on income.)

The key to linking monetary policy and the money supply to investment decisions is the interest rate. In Figure 16.BP.2 we see a demand for investment graph, with interest rates (r) on the vertical axis and the quantity of investment (Q_I) on the horizontal axis. This demand curve is downward sloping, illustrating that at high interest rates, the cost of investment funds is high and managers will need to earn very high returns from any investment made—thus the demand for investment is low at high rates of interest. As interest rates fall, investment demand increases as money to fund investment activities becomes cheaper.

When the Federal Reserve increases the money available and interest rates fall, businesses will find investment opportunities more attractive at these lower interest rates. As they undertake these additional investments—these new investment expenditures work through the Keynesian multiplier to increase income—by more than the initial investment expenditure. Thus we have another possible policy aid to expand income.

Figure 16.BP.3 illustrates the effect of this additional investment. In Chapter 14 we traced the process of a business investing $100,000 in new computer equipment

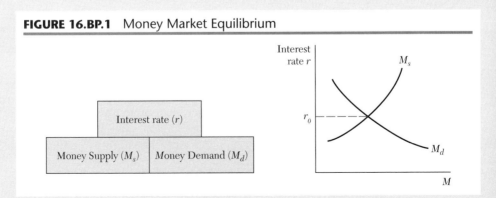

FIGURE 16.BP.1 Money Market Equilibrium

FIGURE 16.BP.2 Investment Demand

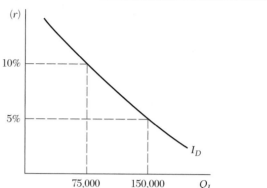

and how this generated income for the computer manufacturer and the responding effect through the multiplier. Now suppose that owners of a golf course decide that lower interest rates make it possible for them to install a watering system that costs $150,000. When interest rates were high, the cost of the system was too high and the returns to making such an investment decision too small. So this additional investment is triggered through lower interest rates. This generates $150,000 in income for the firm manufacturing the automatic watering systems. Using a multiplier of 4 (from Chapter 14), the watering system manufacturer will spend three-fourths of the $150,000, or $112,500 on purchases of components, equipment rental, labor, and other goods or services. Again, the component suppliers and workers will continue the spending cycle, with three-fourths of $112,500 or $84,375 worth of purchases—perhaps on vacations, rent, travel, food, and so on. And the spending cycle continues until the total increase in income generated by the $150,000 investment in watering equipment generates increased income of $600,000, which equals the multiplier (4) times the initial investment ($150,000).

If the Federal Reserve contracts the money supply, interest rates will rise (*cet. par.*) and investment will drop—and thus income will fall.

FIGURE 16.BP.3 Money, Interest Rates, Investment, and the Keynesian Multiplier

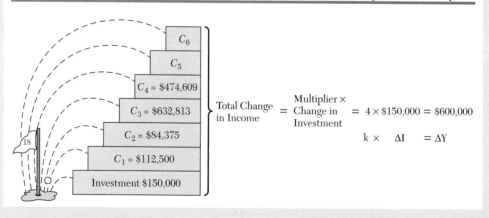

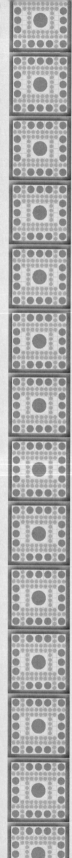

MONEY AND THE KEYNESIAN SYSTEM: THE DETAILS

Money can be an integral part of the Keynesian system. In Chapters 14 and 15, we saw that the gist of the Keynesian system is that changes in consumption, investment, and government spending can effectively be used to expand or lower the level of income in the economy. Money can and most often does work within the Keynesian sphere to allow income changes as well. Changes in the money supply often directly influence both the business and household sectors in their investment and consumption decisions.

An increase in the supply of money will lower the interest rate (see Figure 16.10), just as (*ceteris paribus*) any increase in supply will decrease the price of a product. As Figure 16.10 shows, an increase in M_s from M_{s0} to M_{s1} lowers interest rates from r_0 to r_1. These interest rates and the demand for investment are shown in Figure 16.11. As money becomes "cheaper," investors reconsider their present levels of investment. Low interest rates will encourage businesses to borrow from commercial banks and to spend these funds on new buildings and equipment (i.e., investment); high rates, on the other hand, deter investment decisions. This is expressed graphically in Figure 16.11 as an inverse relationship between the rate of interest (r) and the level of investment (I), or $I = f(r)$. As the interest rate falls from r_0 to r_1, investment (in housing, equipment, or plants) will expand from I_0 to I_1.

Returning to the Keynesian model developed in the last two chapters, we can again examine the effect of an increase in investment. This time, however, the investment increase is stimulated by a reduction in the interest rate, generated by an increase in the money supply (see Figure 16.10). As the money supply increases from M_{s0} to M_{s1} in Figure 16.10, the interest rate decreases from r_0 to r_1. As this occurs, investment increases from I_0 to I_1 (see Figure 16.11). Finally, this increased investment, working through the multiplier, generates a new higher income level, Y_1 as in Figure 16.12. (Remember, $I_1 - I_0 = \Delta I$, $Y_1 - Y_0 = \Delta Y$, and $\Delta Y = k \times \Delta I$.)

10. When the Fed decreases the money supply, what happens to interest rates? The level of investment? The level of income? Employment?

FIGURE 16.11 The Interest-Investment Relationship

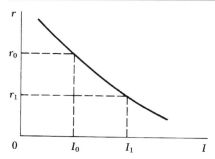

FIGURE 16.12 Income Response to a Change in Investment

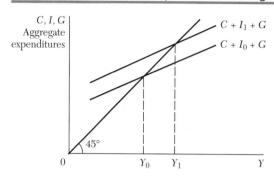

The Liquidity Trap

Keynes relied more on fiscal policy for the stimulation of aggregate expenditures because he expected that during times of depression the economy would operate in the area of the liquidity trap. In this area, no matter how much the money supply increased, the rate of interest would fall no lower. And the business community's grim expectations of the future would discourage any further investment activity, even with low rates of interest. As we can see in Figure 16.13, changes in the money supply within the range of the liquidity trap will have no effect on interest rates. And if interest rates are unchanged, the levels of investment and income also will remain the same, yielding no effect on aggregate expenditures. For example, as interest rates in Japan fell to almost zero in 2001, some characterized Japan as experiencing a liquidity trap at that time.

Keynes also believed that business and consumer expectations could change during depressions, thereby thwarting the effect of monetary policy. For these reasons, economists often say that increasing the money stock to increase investment is much like pushing on a string. In *The General Theory*, Keynes expressed substantial doubt about the ability of monetary policy—a policy that changes the money supply—to rescue the economy from a severe depression. Yet, during the past four decades, we have seen the power of monetary policy to affect the levels of aggregate expenditures in the economy. During this period, the Fed has played an active role in determining aggregate expenditures, a practice that has

FIGURE 16.13 Money Supply Increase in the Liquidity Trap

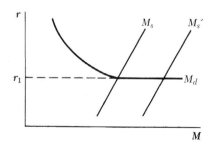

drawn frequent criticism. Still, monetary policy has continued to be an important tool for economic stabilization.

MONETARY POLICY

Some critics have argued that the Fed is too powerful, too independent, and too business-oriented. Others believe that the money supply is much too important to be left to the discretion of mere mortals. In this section, we shall examine the tools that enable the Federal Reserve to control the supply of money and credit in the economy and outline effects of international markets. After a review of the Greenspan years, we shall examine recent Federal Reserve policy and the interaction between monetary and fiscal policy.

Tools of the Trade

To affect the level of income in the economy, the Fed has at hand several tools. The two primary tools are (1) reserve requirement changes and (2) open-market operations. On occasion—for example, during World War II—the Fed has implemented several selective credit controls on home mortgages and consumer credit. The only credit control that it regularly uses is the margin requirement for stocks, which stipulates the percentages of payment that must be in cash on any security purchase. In March 1980, the Fed responded to President Carter's request for tighter credit to help quell the inflationary trends by announcing new controls on consumer and business credit. It quickly withdrew these controls when evidence showed they were dramatically worsening the recession of 1980. In 2008 and 2009 the Fed extented its power considerably, introducing a number of new tools to stem the growing financial crisis and ensure the stability of the financial system. The Fed can also use moral suasion in pursuit of its economic goals; that is, it can attempt to persuade relevant economic actors to engage in or refrain from certain activities. Since 2003, changes in another tool, the discount rate, have been pegged to the fed funds rate (see below).

Reserve Requirements. As we saw earlier in Table 16.1, each depository institution must keep a reserve requirement at the Federal Reserve or as cash in vault. The Board of Governors of the Federal Reserve can change the levels of reserves required at any time. In general, the central bank views its ability to change reserve requirements as its most powerful tool and uses this tool with utmost discretion. Since a change in reserve requirements of only 1 percent alters the monetary situation geometrically, changes in reserve requirements have been infrequent since 1935, when this tool became available. In more recent years the Fed has altered the size of liabilities on which reserves are held.

Critics claim that this tool works like an ax rather than a scalpel. An example shows why. Assume the Fed wants to restrict economic activity by reducing the money supply (e.g., to fight inflation). If banking assets are at $400 billion with 10 percent reserve requirements, some $40 billion is being held as reserves. If reserve requirements are increased by 1 percent, to 11 percent, some $44 billion must be held. This takes $4 billion out of the money supply immediately, as loans and investments are called in to increase reserves to the new level. More would be taken out of the system later through multiple deposit contraction—the reverse of the multiple deposit expansion explained previously.

11. In the example just given, what might happen to interest rates? Why?

12. What would happen if reserve requirements were lowered by 1 percent? How much would member banks be required to hold? What would happen to the "extra" money (or excess reserves)?

An increase in reserve requirements can absorb large changes in *excess reserves*, or additional moneys held by depository institutions, such as those that occurred during the 1930s when substantial amounts of gold flowed into the country. A reduction in the reserve requirement may offset a large loss in reserves. In either case, a change in reserve requirements announces a change in Fed policy to the public as well as to the banks and other depository institutions. Critics of the Fed suggest that other means are more appropriate for the announcement of policy changes.

Open-Market Operations.   The Fed is engaged daily in **open-market operations** through the activities of the Federal Reserve Open Market Committee. Activities in the open market involve purchases and sales of government bonds, bills, and notes at the Federal Reserve Bank of New York. These actions affect the money supply as well as interest rates. To increase the money supply and economic activity (e.g., to combat recession), the Fed actively buys bonds (Treasury issues). Buying bonds takes them out of the hands of the banks and other depository institutions and increases the money supply by exchanging the bonds for money (in the form of a check or cash from the Fed). If, on the other hand, the Fed wants to reduce the money stock, it will step up bond *sales* to commercial banks and other depository institutions, this time increasing the holding of bonds at banks and decreasing their holding of reserves.

As discussed in the box below titled "Interest Rates, Bond Prices, and the Money Supply," the effect on interest rates of these bond sales and purchases is inversely related to the money supply. When bond sales reduce the money stock, interest rates must increase in order to attract businesses as well as households to purchase the bond offerings. Otherwise, investors would place their funds elsewhere. Bond sales, then, encourage interest rates upward as they compete with other assets for the public's cash balances. Once the sales have been made, the interest rate will also rise because of the shortage of money.

Open-market operations are the Fed's most important tool. They take place on a day-to-day basis, and the Fed's Open Market Committee meets regularly to decide how open-market operations should affect the money supply and interest rates.

13. How do bond purchases by the Fed affect interest rates in the economy? Why?

Interest Rates, Bond Prices, and the Money Supply

We can use an example to illustrate how the interest rate is related to the price of bonds and to the purchase of a bond by the Federal Reserve. First, assume you receive a $100 government bond for your birthday. In the fine print on this bond, the U.S. government promises to pay you $100 at the end of ten years. Obviously, the people who gave you the bond did not pay $100 for something that is worth $100 at the end of ten years; they paid less.

To find the price they paid, we can examine a present-value table such as Table 16.3. The *present value* of your $100 bond payable in ten years is the amount it is worth today; more generally, present value is what a dollar at the end of a specified future year is worth today. Examining the abbreviated present-value table in Table 16.3, we find that the present value depends on the interest rate. At an interest rate of 10

percent, the present value is $38.50; if the interest rate were 15 percent, the price of the bond would be $24.70. As the interest rate rises (from 10 to 15 percent), the price of the $100 bond falls (from $38.50 to $24.70). There is an inverse relation between the rate of return (interest rate) and the price of the bond. In essence, the bondholder earns interest on the bond every year it is held.

When the Federal Reserve purchases bonds (not $100 savings bonds, but $100,000 and larger denominations of U.S. Treasury bonds, notes, and bills) in the open market in order to increase the money supply, the demand for bonds increases, so the price of bonds rises (Figure 16.14). The interest rate is inversely related to price, so the interest rate falls. Thus, as the Fed buys bonds, increasing the money supply, interest rates fall.

Table 16.3 Present Value of $100.00

| Year | Interest Rate | | | |
	3%	7%	10%	15%
1	97.10	93.50	90.90	87.00
2	94.30	87.30	82.60	75.60
3	91.50	81.60	75.10	65.80
4	88.90	76.30	68.30	57.20
5	86.30	71.30	62.00	49.70
6	83.80	66.66	56.40	43.20
7	81.30	62.30	51.30	37.60
8	78.90	58.20	46.60	32.60
9	76.60	54.40	42.40	28.40
10	74.40	50.80	38.50	24.70

Note: The formula for finding the present value entries in the table is $P = R/(1 + r)^t$. The present value, P, equals the future return, R (in this case, $100), divided by $(1 + \text{rate of interest})^t$, where t is the number of years to maturity. (In our example, $t = 10$ years.)

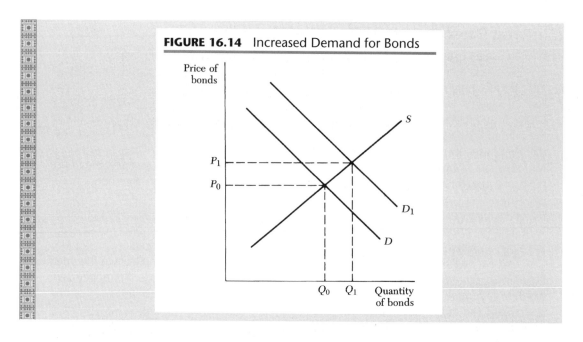

FIGURE 16.14 Increased Demand for Bonds

The Discount Rate. The Federal Reserve also establishes the **discount rate**—the rate at which a bank or depository institution can borrow from the Fed. Often, institutions borrow from the Fed to protect their reserve position. They typically present collateral consisting of bonds, which the Fed discounts for short-term borrowing purposes. In 2003 the Fed adopted a policy that "tied" the discount rate to the fed funds rate (see below). If the Fed increases the fed funds target rate, for most banks and other depository institutions the discount rate will be 1 percent greater than the fed funds target. This will ensure that funds are available when there might be a shortage of liquidity within the banking system. This rate is called the *primary credit rate*.

In "emergency" situations, the Fed may serve as "the lender of last resort," with the discount rate historically providing liquidity. The Fed stood ready in this capacity immediately after the stock market crash of October 1987. Alan Greenspan, then chairman of the Fed's Board of Governors, issued the following statement on the day following the crash: "The Federal Reserve, consistent with its responsibilities as the nation's central bank, affirmed today its readiness to serve as a source of liquidity to support the economic and financial system." This brief statement seemed to reassure financial markets, particularly as the Fed took necessary actions to ensure adequate liquidity to the financial system. To calm the uncertainty accompanying the terror attacks of September 11, 2001, Greenspan issued a similar statement, again ensuring liquidity.

The Fed Funds Rate. For more than two decades, the interest rate on federal funds (fed funds) instruments has played an important role in Federal Reserve monetary policy. The fed funds instruments are overnight or very short-term loans in which one bank lends another some of its deposits at the Fed. (Typically, these deposits are at the Fed to meet reserve requirements.) If a bank has deposited more money at the Fed than is necessary to meet its reserve requirements, the bank may lend those excess deposits to banks needing additional reserves. The **fed funds rate** is the interest rate that banks charge when they lend these reserves for short periods of time. The Fed can "target" the fed funds rate by using its reserve requirement and open-market operations tools. In recent years, the Federal Reserve Open Market Committee has voted to raise or lower targets for the fed funds rate. The Fed usually uses open-market operations to meet the fed funds target rate.

Lags in Monetary Policy

As is true with fiscal policy, lags or delays are inherent in monetary actions. Economists have classified these lags into two major types: the *inside lag* and the *outside lag*. The inside lag comprises a *recognition lag* (the time it takes for the Federal Reserve authorities to recognize there is a problem in the economy) and an *action lag* (the time of recognition until the time some policy is implemented). These lags are usually a function of measurement and forecasting.

After the action takes place, there is an outside lag before the impact of the policy (either partial or total) is felt in the economy. The length of impact lags is a subject of dispute among economists and economic models. Monetarists—economists who favor monetary policies over fiscal policies—argue that the impact lag with monetary actions is much shorter than the one estimated by their Keynesian counterparts.

Monetary Policy in an Open Economy

Monetary policy has two types of effects on international markets in an open economy. One is an interest effect, similar to but not the same as that experienced in fiscal policy in an international environment. The second is an effect on prices due to monetary changes.

If the Fed takes some policy action to increase the money supply (to expand the economy), interest rates will fall. In international financial markets, demand for U.S. assets, which yield a return attached to this lower interest rate, will decline. This will decrease the demand for dollars, shifting the dollar demand curve to the left, such as the shift from D_0 to D_1 in Figure 16.15. At the same time, because of the lower interest rates, U.S. investors will seek higher-yielding securities in the international arena. As U.S. citizens trade their dollars or dollar-denominated securities for higher-yielding foreign securities, the supply of dollars in the international market will increase, shifting the dollar supply curve to the right (the shift from S_0 to S_1 in Figure 16.15). These changes in the demand for and supply of dollars in the international financial markets will depreciate the value of the dollar (bid the value of the dollar down with respect to other currencies currently in demand).

This lower-valued dollar will create a demand for U.S. exports, since they are now cheaper to foreign citizens. At the same time, imports into the United States will decline, since imports now cost more of the lower-valued dollar. Net exports

FIGURE 16.15 Demand and Supply of Dollars in the International Market

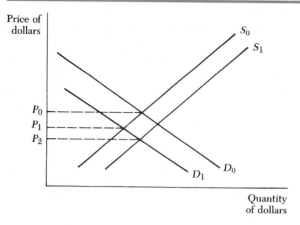

(X – M) will rise. This increases aggregate expenditures and income, thus reinforcing the monetary expansion also designed to increase aggregate expenditures.

Monetary policy will also produce a long-run price effect in the international financial markets. To the extent to which increases in the money supply lead to increases in domestic prices, foreign exchange markets of U.S. trading partners will be affected. If the increase in the money supply brings about a 5 percent increase in prices of domestic products, this price increase will be felt in both domestic and international markets.

Let's look at the effect of this type of policy on trade between the United States and Japan. A 5 percent increase in the price of U.S. products will decrease the demand for or purchase of U.S. products by the Japanese (assuming an elastic demand for U.S. exports). This will cause a decrease in the demand for dollars, since the Japanese are purchasing fewer U.S. goods. This decrease causes the demand curve for dollars to shift to the left (from D_0 to D_1 in Figure 16.15). At the same time, a 5 percent increase in domestic prices makes Japanese products relatively less expensive in the United States. As U.S. consumers increase their demand for Japanese products, they supply more dollars to the international market, thus shifting the supply curve for dollars to the right, as in Figure 16.15.

Both of these actions serve to lower the value of the dollar and appreciate the value of the yen. From here on out, consumer reactions are reversed. The Japanese will resume purchasing U.S. products. Although prices did increase, the yen appreciation offsets this price increase. Likewise, demand for Japanese products will fall back to previous levels. Despite the price effects produced by monetary policy, after currency adjustments, the level of exports and imports should remain about the same.

14. After income has increased due to monetary expansion, what will be the reaction in international markets?

A Brief History of Monetary Policy

The Fed has powerful tools, and its independence gives it the authority to carry out the monetary policy it views as best. During the 1950s and 1960s, the Fed followed its collective instinct in managing money matters. After economists severely criticized this policy in the mid-1960s, the Fed began to target interest rate levels in adjusting the nation's money supply. This type of policy, despite outcries from monetarists, continued until the fall of 1979. Monetarists believe that control of the nation's money supply is far more important than control of interest rates. In contrast, the Keynesians rely heavily on interest rates to transmit the effects of monetary policy to the economy.

In 1982, amidst low inflation and economic recession, the Fed, under chairman Paul Volcker, began increasing the monetary growth rate and paid more attention to interest rate targets. Low inflation continued and, coupled with economic growth, left the recession of the early 1980s behind. By 1987, when Alan Greenspan assumed the chairmanship of the Fed's Board of Governors, the economic recovery was into its fifth year.

Greenspan's Fed: 1987–2005

Looking for a conservative Republican to replace Paul Volcker as chairman of the Federal Reserve Board of Governors, the Reagan administration in 1987 turned to Alan Greenspan. Greenspan had served as chair of the Council of Economic Advisors beginning in 1974 under President Nixon and continuing through the Ford administration. Known as a meticulous observer and student of statistical data of all economic markets, Greenspan played a more activist role in fine-tuning the economy, carefully watching leading indicators that might suggest greater levels of inflation. Indeed, the first Bush administration criticized his tolerance of higher interest rates at the expense of slower economic growth and argued that the Fed did not do enough to lower interest rates to ward off the recession of the early 1990s.

Fed policy actions during the Greenspan years were often credited for bringing economic stability in the late 1980s and setting the stage for economic growth between 1995 and 1999. As illustrated in Figure 16.16, Greenspan's Fed

FIGURE 16.16 Federal Open Market Committee (FOMC) Intended Federal Funds Rate, and Discount Rate, and Primary Credit Rate

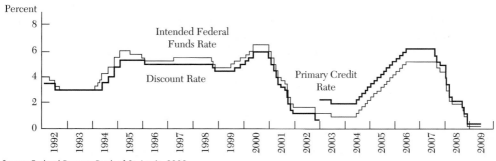

Source: Federal Reserve Bank of St. Louis, 2009.

raised the fed funds and discount rates to reduce inflationary tendencies during the late 1980s. During the recession of 1990–1991, the Fed lowered these rates. The series of prolonged reductions in the fed funds targets and discount rates helped the economy to rebound into a period of prolonged economic growth, which continued into 2001. Fear of inflation began to spread in the mid-1990s, and between 1994 and 2000, the Fed responded by increasing the fed funds targets and discount rates several times. The Fed continued to monitor for potential inflationary activity until early 2001 as the technology bubble collapsed, when it abruptly lowered the discount rate and fed funds targets, hoping to avert a serious economic downturn, and continued lowering the targets until mid-2004, when growth expanded and inflationary pressures returned in the form of higher oil prices. The Fed quickly targeted a higher fed funds rate.

15. Why can't the Fed target both the money supply and interest rates?

16. Plot what has happened to the general level of interest rates and to M_1 and M_2 since this book has been published. (This information is published monthly in the *Federal Reserve Bulletin*.) What does the Fed appear to have been targeting?

In the mid-1990s, the press portrayed Greenspan as the "poster boy for the new economy." Economic growth was exploding at a rate of 6.5 percent. The Fed helped the U.S. economy maintain growth in spite of currency crises in Mexico, Asia, Russia, and Latin America, as well as fears of a "Y2K" meltdown of computer systems at the turn of the millennium in the United States and abroad. During this period, a hedge fund called Long Term Capital Management made massive money-losing speculative transactions in financial instruments of the Russian, Asian, and Latin American markets.* The New York Fed helped to avoid panic by orchestrating a bailout of the fund by private companies.

By early 2001, however, many who had sung Greenspan's praises were wondering whether he had lost his touch and reacted too slowly. Greenspan's Fed tried to engineer a "soft landing" for the economy, which would see continuing growth, albeit at a slower rate. The stock market, as described in the next section, declined dramatically and the economy abruptly slowed, with unemployment rising to 6 percent in 2003. Monetary policy kept interest rates low and while business investment lagged, consumer spending continued. Housing construction and mortgage refinancing led some to conclude that a "bubble" might have developed in the housing sector—as housing "wealth" fueled consumption expenditures and consumer borrowing. Economic growth rebounded and in late 2004 the Fed initiated policies to target higher interest rates as raw material and oil prices increased inflationary expectations. Through all of this, Greenspan, initially appointed to chair the Fed by President Reagan in 1987, ended his career at the Fed on January 31, 2006, and was succeeded by Ben Bernanke.

---

*Hedge funds engage in very speculative trades (or "bets") for wealthy individuals. They remain largely unregulated.

Bernanke's Fed

In the fall of 2005, President George W. Bush announced his choice of Ben S. Bernanke to replace Alan Greenspan as chairman of the Board of Governors of the Fed and President Obama has recommended renewal of his appointment. The former Princeton University professor has held many Federal Reserve roles and his nomination was easily approved by Congress. Before his appointment, Bernanke favored a program of "inflation targeting," which has been adopted by both the European Central Bank and by the Bank of England. Time will tell if inflation targets become part of U.S. Federal Reserve policy making. Bernanke's Fed continued to target higher fed funds rates through the end of 2007.

The financial crisis that emerged at the end of 2007 sent the fed funds rate plummeting. It reached a 0.5 to zero percent target by the end of 2008 and remained at that target through 2009.

17. Are you convinced that there is a relationship between the money supply and prices? Why or why not?

18. Have inflation rates increased? What is the current inflation rate?

19. What Federal Reserve policies helped the United States avoid a recession since 2009? Were there two consecutive quarters of negative growth in the economy?

Stock Markets Bubble Trouble in the Greenspan Era

In early October 1987, the Dow Jones Industrial Average (one measure of U.S. stock market performance) was at 2,700 points. On October 19, 1987, two months after Greenspan was sworn in as chairman of the Federal Reserve Board of Governors, the Dow dropped 508 points, losing $1 trillion in (paper) wealth and 20 percent of its value. By the end of the month, the Dow stood at just 1,700.

The Greenspan Fed moved to ensure liquidity of financial intermediaries and reassured the stumbling financial markets with a simple one-line statement reinforcing the Fed's role as a lender of last resort. This was enough to steady markets and begin an era that often characterized Greenspan as legendary—an almost mythical figure who steps in at exactly the right time to reassure the financial system.

Between 1991 and 1996, U.S. productivity boomed, reflecting growth in the high-technology "New Economy" sectors. The Dow Jones Industrial Average and the then-fledgling NASDAQ Composite Index (an index for the NASDAQ, an exchange for smaller, often high-tech companies' stocks) galloped to all-time highs. With the Dow reaching 10,000 points, Greenspan on December 5, 1996, tried to moderate the growth by referring to it as "irrational exuberance." Nevertheless, money continued to pour into the stock market, which reached a peak on March 10, 1999.

By many accounts, the rapid increases in stock prices during the late 1990s represented a "bubble" in the stock market. Bubbles are nothing new. In the late 1500s and early 1600s, speculation in tulip bulbs drove prices of some bulbs to exorbitant levels. Prices eventually crashed, and many speculators were left penniless. Similarly, as graphed in Figure 16.17, a bubble in the

Dow grew and burst between 1924 and 1932, and Japan's Nikkei stock average experienced a bubble between 1982 and 2001. The NASDAQ's bubble also burst. Between the end of 2000 and beginning of 2001, investors in U.S. stock markets lost more than $5.2 trillion of (paper) wealth. Some critics blamed Greenspan for the accompanying slowdown in the economy. We must be careful, however, not to confuse stock market performance with economic performance. The stock market is just one part of the U.S. economy.

Between 2001 and March 2004, the NASDAQ and Dow recovered from their 2001 lows. But, as the Federal Reserve prepared to pare the growth of the money supply and increase interest rates, stock market volatility resumed. As interest rates began to rise, concern arose that the developing housing bubble might crash and dampen the longer-run future of an economic recovery as consumers faced the repayment of high debt levels and potentially lower home values. By the end of 2006, housing prices began to fall and inventories of unsold housing grew significantly. The housing market did crash with an estimated $7 trillion in lost house wealth due to lower prices. The Dow also suffered a more than 50 percent decline between October 2007 and March 2009.

FIGURE 16.17   Stock Market Bubbles

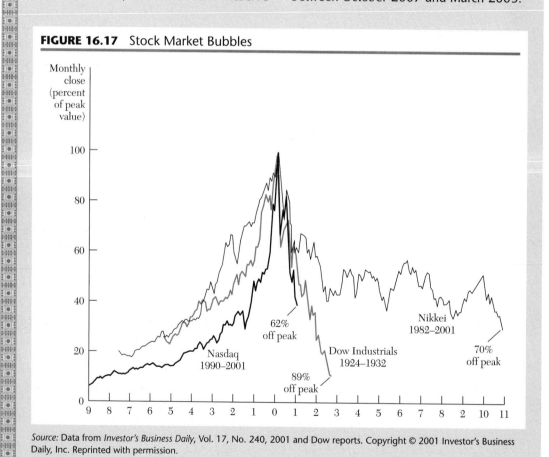

Source: Data from *Investor's Business Daily*, Vol. 17, No. 240, 2001 and Dow reports. Copyright © 2001 Investor's Business Daily, Inc. Reprinted with permission.

ENTERING THE GLOBAL FINANCIAL CRISIS: THE COLLAPSE OF THE HOUSING BUBBLE, 2007–2009

After the technology, or .com bubble burst in 2000, the Federal Reserve began increasing the supply of money to ensure enough liquidity to avoid a recession, as people with stock wealth lost an estimated $7 trillion. The Fed continued to lower the fed funds target rate through 2004, also responding to the economic downturn after the terror attacks of September 11, 2001 (see Figure 16.6). Earlier in this chapter we noted that as the money supply increases interest rates fall, and as interest rates fall there is more borrowing for investment and for consumer spending. Since the Federal Reserve made funds widely available, financial intermediaries (such as banks) lent to customers wanting to purchase consumer goods, as well as build and purchase homes. Shortly thereafter, some economists warned of a housing bubble that was building in the United States and in several European countries. Rising house prices helped homeowners feel wealthier, and those who lost wealth as stock prices crashed after the technology bubble regained wealth as they watched equity in their houses increase. Between 2002 and 2006, home prices rose far faster than the historical average and were rising faster than the cost of rental homes as well—indicating that the price increase was not because of a limited supply of housing. As house prices rose, some homeowners increased their consumption, often borrowing funds based on their increased home value; others opted to purchase larger homes, while others entered a housing market that had heretofore eluded them because of low income or poor credit. This increased borrowing by individuals who might not be able to repay these loans, and financial intermediaries lending to these borrowers, contributed to the global financial crisis that began in late 2007, but other factors were even more important.

Banks try to lend to the best customers first. There is less risk that these borrowers will default on loan payments. These are individuals with a good credit rating, who pay bills on time, and who have an income stream large enough to ensure loan repayment. After the "good borrower" market is saturated and if funds are still available to lend, banks lend to higher-risk borrowers. Between 2000 and 2007, an abundant money supply and low interest rates ensured that financial institutions had ample funds for lending. Banks and mortgage companies began to lend to "subprime" borrowers—those with a poor credit rating or without a wage or income stream that would suggest with certainty that the borrowed funds could be repaid. Most of these subprime loans had variable interest rates; that is, the interest rate on the loan changed as interest rates changed in the economy. While interest rates remained low, subprime borrowers could more than likely make loan payments. When interest rates rose, however, the amount owed on these loans increased, making it harder for people who had taken on larger mortgage obligations to make monthly payments on the loan. As long as housing prices continued to rise and interest rates remained low, loan payments were made. Homeowners were participating in the "American Dream" of owning their own home, or owning an even larger home, and some speculators were hoping for quick profits from rising house prices.

But why would banks and mortgage institutions lend to subprime, high-risk borrowers? First of all, financial institutions had a lot of funds to lend. A low fed funds target rate generated increased liquidity through the money supply, and, at the same time Asian countries and Middle East oil-producing countries transferred surplus funds from international trade into the United States. A second reason was *securitization*: the bundling of various kinds of loans (mortgage loans, credit card loans, auto loans, etc.) and "repackaging" them into instruments with characteristics borrowers might want. The repackaged loans are then resold as bonds or collateralized mortgage obligations (CMOs) to investors, who are often other financial intermediaries. A bank that lent funds to a subprime borrower might quickly sell that loan to another financial intermediary (perhaps an investment bank) for repackaging. Thus, despite having made the loan, the bank would no longer hold any risk from that loan. With securitization there was little reason for mortgage lenders to care whether a loan they made would be repaid or not. After all, the loan is very quickly moved out of the lender's portfolio.

Still, the effects of the housing market collapse on the economy would have been much milder if it was simply high-risk or subprime borrowers not repaying loans on houses. The economy would have experienced a mild downturn rather than a great recession. Indeed, other financial innovations (besides securitization) caused the deepening and widening of the crisis that propelled not only the United States but other economies of the world into the deepest recession since the Great Depression.

Some financial intermediaries (such as investment banks Goldman Sachs, Lehman Brothers and Bear Sterns, and the insurance giant AIG) created a financial instrument called a credit default swap (CDS). Credit default swaps were sold to institutions purchasing bonds or CMOs that were based on mortgages (some subprime) as the underlying asset. These CDSs basically "insured" purchasers if there was a default on the instrument (the bond or the CMO), or if the institution issuing the bond or the CMO went out of business. These CDSs were complex (often running hundreds of pages) and were ultimately "bets." Purchasers of CDSs were betting that if there were defaults on the subprime mortgages that comprised the securitized loans they purchased (as bonds and CMOs), the CDSs would pay off. Issuers of the CDSs were "betting" that the subprime mortgages would be paid. CDS issuers were also firms that bundled and sold securitized loans. To attract buyers to purchase a bundle of loans (as a bond or CMO), financial institutions such as Bear Steams, Lehman Brothers, and Citibank would also offer to sell a CDS to the purchaser. This certainly made purchasing bonds or CMOs containing subprime loans more attractive because of the risk. A default on the estimated $1.3 trillion of subprime loans would have caused a setback for the U.S. economy, but with an estimated $600 trillion of unregulated CDSs sold worldwide, a financial crisis ensued, followed by the Great Recession.

In early 2007 there were some signs (including financial institution failures) that something might be amiss in financial markets, but authorities didn't seem to recognize the potential severity of the problem until late in 2008. In March 2008, investment bank Bear Stearns suffered great losses from the sale of CMOs and CDSs. The Fed agreed to absorb $30 billion in Bear Stearns liabilities before JP Morgan Chase purchased the company at a fire sale price. By September, other Wall Street and Main Street financial institutions were also under pressure. Lehman Brothers went into bankruptcy, while Merrill Lynch sold itself to Bank of America and Wachovia sold itself to Wells Fargo. By the end of the month, all remaining major investment banks in the United States had reorganized as bank holding companies, making them eligible for Federal Reserve loans. The Fed also bailed out the insurance giant American International Group (AIG), as its losses in the CDS market continued to mount.

Between 2008 and mid-2009, some 87 bank failures were reported. This compares to no failures between 2003 and 2004 and three in 2007.

FEDERAL RESERVE RESPONSE TO THE FINANCIAL CRISIS

Financial institutions in the United States (and throughout the world) responded to the growing crisis in late 2008 by refusing to lend—thus freezing credit markets. Loans dried up—even to the best borrowers. This meant that businesses relying on loans for investments or inventory purchases could not make those investments or replace depleted inventories. The Federal Reserve immediately reduced the fed funds rate (see Figure 16.6), hoping to unfreeze credit markets by pouring liquidity into the financial system. By the end of 2008, the Fed had more than doubled the funds on which the money supply is based. It had extended loans to banks and other financial institutions and purchased commercial paper (IOUs issued by one firm and purchased by another). It had expanded the monetary policy tools beyond open market operations, the discount rate, and reserve requirements. The list now includes the tools below.

Each of the tools listed in the box below were created by the Federal Reserve to add additional liquidity into the financial system and to reduce the possibility of a system collapse. Figure 16.17 illustrates the size of Fed actions through these tools in nominal dollars.

Federal Reserve Monetary Tools Created in Response to the 2007–2009 Financial Crisis

❖ *Interest on Required Reserve Balances and Excess Balances*—Interest that eliminates an implied tax on required reserves and excess reserves.

❖ *Term Auction Facility*—Allows the Fed to auction term funds to depository institutions.

❖ *Primary Dealer Credit Facility*—Allows the Fed to give overnight loans to primary bond dealers to facilitate the operation of financial markets.

❖ *Term Securities Lending Facility*—Promotes liquidity and aids the functioning of financial markets by offering to loan Treasury securities held by the Fed against eligible collateral.

❖ *ABCP MMMF Liquidity Facility*—The asset-backed commercial paper money market mutual fund liquidity facility provides additional liquidity by allowing the Fed to lend to depository institutions and bank holding companies for the purchase of high-quality commercial paper from money market mutual funds if certain conditions are met.

❖ *Commercial Paper Funding Facility*—Another measure for the Fed to provide liquidity to the commercial paper market.

❖ *Money Market Investor Funding Facility*—Allows the Fed to provide liquidity to investors in the U.S. money market.

❖ *Term Asset-Backed Securities Loan Facility*—A funding facility supported by the Troubled Asset Relief Program (see below) designed to help depository institutions meet the credit needs of households and small businesses.

Source: http://www.federalreserve.gov/monetarypolicy/abcpmmmf.html. For a more complete description of these new monetary policy tools, go to the web site.

THE **BIG** PICTURE

Financial Crisis 101

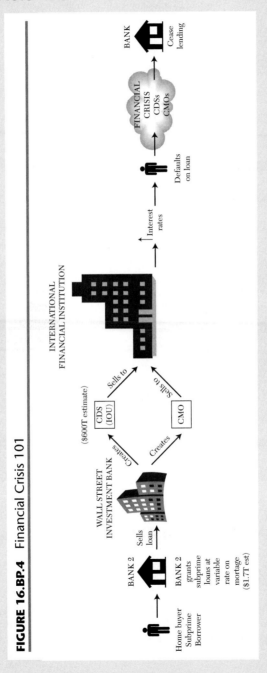

FIGURE 16.BP.4 Financial Crisis 101

FIGURE 16.17 Bailout Costs vs Big Historical Events

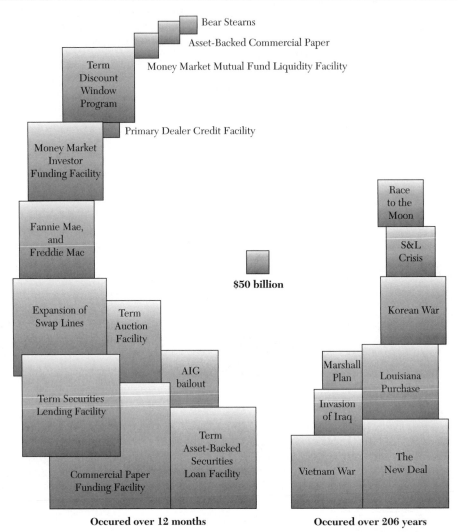

Source: http://www.ritholtz.com/blog/2009/06/bailout-costs-vs-big-historical-events/, Barry Ritholtz–June 18th, 2009.

THE TREASURY BAILOUT PLAN—EESA AND TARP

As uncertainty continued throughout the world, financial markets and officials at the U.S. Treasury also responded to the growing financial crisis. In early October, Congress passed the Emergency Economic Stabilization Act (EESA) of 2008. The EESA authorized the Treasury to spend $700 billion under the Troubled Asset Relief Program (TARP). The first TARP funds were aimed at unfreezing credit markets by injecting funds into the largest banks in the United States chiefly through the purchase of preferred stock in those banks. The Treasury continued to purchase shares in large and smaller banks as well. Despite this infusion of funds, credit was slow to expand. Initially the program was set up to purchase "troubled" or so-called "toxic" assets and sell those assets in private auctions, but as of mid-2009 the details for that program were still being worked out. TARP funds were also used as loans to ailing auto companies General Motors and Chrysler and to AIG. Additional programs have emerged under TARP to help homeowners refinance mortgages, unfreeze credit markets for student and small business loans, and continue investment in institutions the Treasury deems important to U.S. financial stability.

MONETARY AND FISCAL POLICY

Models constructed to measure the effectiveness of monetary and fiscal policy yield different results if underlying assumptions used in the models differ. Monetarists emphasize velocity as the mode of transmission, and the Keynesians stress the rate of interest.

Monetarists assume that there can be no effective expansion of fiscal policy unless it is accompanied by an increase in the money supply. Why? The government *must* finance its expenditures with increases in taxes or by debt issue. Either method transfers money from one sector of the economy to another. As government spending proceeds and GDP increases, if the money supply has not grown, consumers and investors will find themselves short of cash and will begin to try to increase their liquidity by selling their financial holdings. This will increase bond sales even further, driving the price of bonds down and the interest rate up. As the interest rate rises, business investors are crowded out of financial markets by the government, so GDP doesn't change. Spending is just transferred from one sector to another.

For Keynesians, however, the reason for government spending is to stimulate an economy in which neither business *nor* households are spending. The government at least gets the process started. Expansionary fiscal policy increases economic activity. This encourages spending by consumers and businesses in the future.

In practice, monetary policy is very effective at slowing the economy but not very effective when used to stimulate economic activity. The presence of an international sector tends to reinforce the income and output effects of monetary policy.

Coordination of Monetary and Fiscal Policy

We have seen how monetary and fiscal policy may provide a powerful punch when used together to stimulate economic recovery. However, coordinating the two policies at times other than an economic and financial crisis may be problematic. Since the Fed determines monetary policy, and fiscal expenditures are in the hands of Congress and the president, policy decisions sometimes offset one another or are not complementary. For example, the Fed reacted to the high inflation rates of 1980 by attempting to reduce the money supply in order to decrease aggregate expenditures. On the other hand, Congress decreased taxes, which increased aggregate expenditures. High interest rates created by the tight money supply tended to counteract the desired investment effects from lower tax rates. The chairman of the Federal Reserve Board now regularly informs Congress of impending Fed action so that there are no surprises, but policies may still offset one another.

Some people have called for a reduction in the Fed's independence in order to achieve greater coordination of monetary and fiscal policies. Critics of this suggestion argue that to have either the legislative or the executive branch of the government control the Fed would make the money supply a political tool—as surely as many fiscal expenditures and taxing decisions already are. They argue that we could expect regular increases in the money supply in election years and decreases after elections. Whatever the solution, an effective economic policy clearly requires that monetary and fiscal policy at least be aimed in the same direction.

20. What is the Fed doing today to defeat the forces of inflation? Is its policy being coordinated with the executive branch?

21. What kinds of "political mischief" might occur if the monetary authority were controlled by the executive branch?

Conclusion

By examining the institution of money and the institutions that extend and regulate monetary instruments in the economy, we have discovered rather powerful tools by which the economy has been regulated over the past several decades. This regulation has focused on monetary ease during economic downturns and monetary restraint during periods of inflation. While monetary policy may have strong economic effects, changing institutions, financial instruments, lags, velocity changes, and internal financing of corporate investment may at times offset or thwart an intended monetary policy action. In the following chapter, we will see how changes in the money supply and demand, coupled with fiscal changes, affect aggregate expenditures in the economy and the importance of aggregate supply.

Review Questions

1. Explain the differences among the transactions, precautionary, and speculative demands for money. List five factors that influence your demands for money.

2. Why is a barter economy unsuitable for today's world?

3. What is the difference between M_1 and M_2? Is it important to distinguish between them? Does it really matter what the money supply is? Discuss.

4. Suppose you discovered $50,000 of old dollars stuffed in a mattress in your dorm.
   a. What would be the effect of the $50,000 of "new money" on the banking system? Explain.
   b. What would be the effect if you spent the money on a new BMW?
   c. What if you stuffed the money back into the mattress?

5. How do the demands for money relate to Keynesian income and employment theory?

6. Which of the monetary policy tools is used most actively by the Fed? Under what situations would the Fed use another tool?

7. Why do monetarists argue that fiscal policy is ineffective in adjusting the economy?

8. What are some of the factors that inhibit the successful implementation of monetary policy?

9. In what kinds of situations is fiscal policy more effective than monetary policy? In what kinds of situations is monetary policy more effective than fiscal policy?

10. What would be some of the complications of finding the proper mix of monetary and fiscal policy?

11. If the economy were experiencing high unemployment and moderate inflation, what would be the appropriate monetary policy? Why?

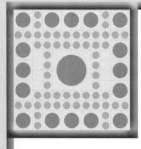

CHAPTER SEVENTEEN

Aggregate Demand and Aggregate Supply

THE **BIG** PICTURE

Introduction   In Chapters 14 through 16, we developed the building blocks of Keynesian macroeconomic theory, including the multiplier, the components of aggregate expenditure, and financial markets. In this chapter we add another building block to our macroeconomic theory: the analysis of prices using a model of aggregate demand (AD) and aggregate supply (AS).

Although Keynes himself pointed out limitations to his theory of aggregate expenditures, the shortcoming of the Keynesian analysis that has most bothered modern economists is the lack of an analysis of prices. In the "real world" economy, since the 1960s, the United States has experienced price changes sometimes larger, sometimes smaller. These changes have occurred not just on certain goods and services, but across the whole economy. In this chapter, we will develop an analysis of aggregate demand and aggregate supply that allows us to illustrate how changes in economic policy or changes in other economic variables affect aggregate prices and output. From this analysis, we will be better able to examine the potential stabilizing effects of policy changes, an issue central to the ongoing debate over stabilization policy.

Aggregate demand is the total quantity of goods and services demanded by households, businesses, government, and the international sector at various prices. The aggregate demand curve illustrates the sum of these sector demands, showing the negative relationship between the aggregate output of goods and services, or real GDP demanded, and the overall price level. **Aggregate supply** is the total quantity of goods and services firms are willing to supply at varying price levels. The aggregate supply curve illustrates the relationship between the aggregate output supplied by all firms and the overall price level. The aggregate demand curve for the economy is downward sloping, while the aggregate supply curve generally illustrates a positive relationship between the price level and GDP, depending mostly on the time frame we choose to examine. Both Figure 17.BP.1 and Figure 17.1 show the relationship between aggregate demand and aggregate supply. Equilibrium is the point where aggregate demand equals aggregate supply.

FIGURE 17.BP.1 Aggregate Demand and Aggregate Supply

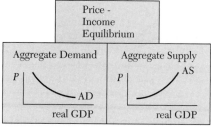

AGGREGATE ANALYSIS

We will save derivation of the aggregate demand curve for a more advanced course in macroeconomic theory, but we will show logically why the curve is downward sloping and examine economic variables that are reflected by shifts in the aggregate demand curve. Recognizing that in macroeconomic theory, an analysis of supply has historically accompanied one of demand, we will then turn our attention to factors important to aggregate supply. We will also attempt to understand why supply policies are often precarious in their outcome. We will discuss the views of supply-side economists in the 1980s and the results of supply-side policies during the Reagan administration.

Aggregate demand has served as the center of economic theory and policy for the past four and a half decades, and Keynesian solutions have remained at the helm of economic thought and have often been preferred by policy makers. Our analysis of aggregate demand and aggregate supply will allow us to understand the role of economic policy variables as well as of supply shocks and productivity changes on real income and prices.

AGGREGATE DEMAND

The aggregate demand curve relates the price level to real output (or real GDP) in the overall economy. It shows how the demand for goods and services varies with the price level. This is possible since all points on the aggregate demand curve are equilibrium points in both the money (financial) market and the market for goods and services. Exogenous changes in both the money and goods markets affect the aggregate demand curve and thus prices and real GDP.

Although this particular aggregate demand curve looks like demand curves we saw in Part 2 on microeconomics, it is very different. A price rise is not analogous to a jump in the price of butter that prompts us to switch to margarine

FIGURE 17.1 Aggregate Demand and Aggregate Supply

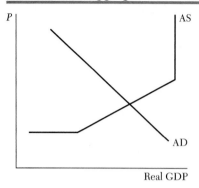

or some other substitute. A price increase signals that *all* domestic prices are rising, including the prices of domestically produced substitutes.

Conditions for Goods and Money Market Equilibrium: A Review

Equilibrium positions in the goods market are found at every point on the aggregate demand curve. Recall from Chapter 13 that the components of the goods and services market are

$$C + I + G + (X - M) = \text{aggregate expenditures},$$

where C is consumption expenditures, I is investment expenditures, G is government expenditures, and $X - M$ is net foreign expenditures (net exports). This market is at equilibrium when aggregate expenditures equal aggregate output of goods and services.

We saw in Chapter 16 that, in the money market, equilibrium is achieved when money supply equals money demand. The aggregate demand curve is derived from equilibrium conditions in both markets. Therefore, at any point on the aggregate demand curve, aggregate expenditures are equal to aggregate output, and money supply equals money demand.

Prices are measured by some weighted price index such as the GDP deflator, and are represented by P on the vertical axis in Figure 17.2. Real income and output changes are represented by real GDP on the horizontal axis. We have assumed that the aggregate demand curve is downward sloping, showing an inverse relation between prices and real GDP. While we do not have all the tools necessary to derive this relationship here, we can intuitively show that this relationship is plausible by asking ourselves what happens to aggregate demand when there is a general rise in prices. If we aren't careful, however, we are likely to arrive at an answer that would yield a downward-sloping aggregate demand curve, but for the wrong reasons. Since our experience has been more as consumers rather than as economists, we are likely to conclude that a general rise in prices will decrease the real income of consumers, thus reducing consumption expenditures. Aggregate

FIGURE 17.2 Aggregate Demand

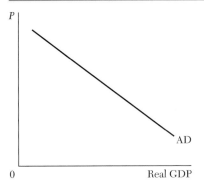

expenditures for goods and services would decline, leading to a decrease in GDP. But price increases yield additional revenues for producers, which they may share with the household sector through wage increases or higher dividends. If production is unchanged, then income would stay the same, so our assumption about the effect of an increase in the general price level on the goods market is a bit premature.

If, however, we look to the money or financial market, we will arrive at a better answer to our question about the slope of the aggregate demand curve. If there is a rise in prices, and if the Federal Reserve does not increase the growth rate in the money supply, the demand for money will increase, since consumers will need more money to keep their levels of consumption if velocity is constant. (With M constant and P rising, the demand for money increases.) As the demand for money rises, interest rates will rise. (Figure 17.3 shows that in response to an increase in the overall price level, money demand increases from M_{D0} to M_{D1} and with M_s constant, interest rates rise from r_0 to r_1.) This means that less money is available at every interest rate for investment by the business sector (see Figure 17.4) and for expenditures by consumers. So, with everything else remaining the same, a rise in prices means that the same amount of (nominal) money balances must be used to purchase goods and services at higher

FIGURE 17.3 Money Demand with a Price Increase

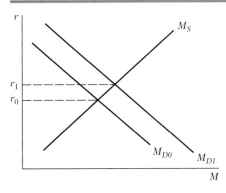

FIGURE 17.4 Demand for Investment Funds

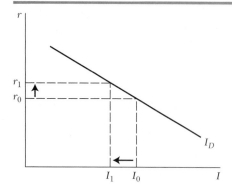

prices. Interest rates will be bid up, demand for funds for investment and consumption purposes will fall, and thus aggregate expenditures will fall. This analysis logically gives us the downward-sloping aggregate demand curve and the inverse relation between prices and real GDP. On the graph in Figure 17.5, we can see that a price increase from P_0 to P_1 decreases real GDP from GDP_A to GDP_B, a movement from point A to point B on the aggregate demand curve.

Two other relationships explain the inverse relationship between prices and real GDP. As prices rise, the real wealth of people holding money balances declines. Those who are holding money balances cannot purchase the same quantity of goods and services as they did at lower prices, so the demand for goods and services falls, as does real GDP. Secondly, when prices increase in the United States, we can expect net exports $(X - M)$ to decline, since the prices of domestic goods have increased relative to foreign goods. U.S. exports are relatively more expensive, so the international market will demand fewer U.S. exports. Again, price increases will lower GDP—hence the movement from point A to point B in Figure 17.5.

Conversely, a decrease in the price level will raise the aggregate quantity of goods and services demanded. Three reasons account for this: The real interest rate falls due to a greater availability of money balances, since the real money

FIGURE 17.5 Movement Along the Aggregate Demand Curve

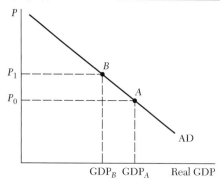

supply increases as prices fall. The real wealth of persons holding money balances increases when prices fall. Net exports increase as prices of domestic goods fall relative to prices of foreign goods.

Shifts in the Aggregate Demand Curve

The analysis of aggregate demand allows us to observe how exogenous changes affect aggregate demand and thus the overall price level *and* the level of real GDP. The aggregate demand curve describes the economy in equilibrium in both the market for goods and services and the money market. Any exogenous or induced change that results in a shift in the aggregate expenditures curve or in the demand or supply curve of money will by definition cause a shift in the aggregate demand curve. As we saw in Chapters 14 and 15, with prices remaining constant, increases in government expenditures (G), investment expenditures (I), exogenous consumption expenditures (C), and net exports ($X - M$), as well as tax cuts and an increase in the money supply, will increase income in the goods market and will cause the aggregate demand curve to shift outward to the right. In Figure 17.6, the aggregate demand curve AD_0 shifts to the right to AD_1. At every price level, real GDP is higher on AD_1. Tax cuts or increases in G, C, I, net exports ($X - M$), and the money supply cause the aggregate demand curve to shift to the right, away from the axis, as shown by AD_1 in Figure 17.6. With this shift, at every price level, GDP is higher.

We can now envision the effects of monetary policy and fiscal policy and changes in autonomous spending on price levels as well as on real income and output. Table 17.1 summarizes the effects of policy changes on aggregate demand.

1. The 2010 federal budget called for income tax reductions, with the less wealthy receiving greater returns from these cuts. The budget proposal also included increased spending. Using the preceding analysis of aggregate demand curves, illustrate and explain what these curves predict would happen to aggregate demand.

FIGURE 17.6 Shifts in the Aggregate Demand Curve

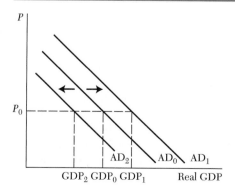

Table 17.1 Effects of Monetary and Fiscal Policy on Aggregate Demand

Policy	Effect of Policy	Effect on Aggregate Demand (AD)
Monetary Policy	Increase in money supply	AD curve shifts to the right.
	Decrease in money supply	AD curve shifts to the left.
Fiscal Policy	Increase in G	AD curve shifts to the right.
	Decrease in Tx	AD curve shifts to the right.
	Decrease in G	AD curve shifts to the left.
	Increase in Tx	AD curve shifts to the left.

While we are primarily interested in policy changes that can shift the aggregate demand curve, several non-policy-related factors can cause a shift in the aggregate demand curve. An increase in real wealth will cause an outward shift. When stock market prices rose dramatically in 1999, holders of corporate stock increased their wealth, and their demand for goods and services increased. The increase in housing prices produced the same result. The increased equity in their homes caused homeowners to increase their borrowing and thus increase their demand for goods and services. Decreases in wealth due to the dramatic downturn in house prices in 2007 caused the aggregate demand curve to shift to the left.

Expectations also influence shifts in the aggregate demand curve. If consumers and investors become increasingly optimistic about the economy, aggregate demand may shift to the right. An expectation that the inflation rate will rise will produce the same result, as consumers and investors purchase durable goods now while prices are lower than those they predict in the future. On the international front, if real income rises abroad so that foreign citizens have more to spend, we can expect an increased demand for domestic goods and services. Again, the aggregate demand curve will shift to the right. All of these shifts indicate that real GDP is higher at every level of prices, as shown in Figure 17.6.

2. List the conditions unrelated to economic policy that would cause the aggregate demand curve to shift to the left, indicating lower real GDP at all price levels.

SHORT-RUN AGGREGATE SUPPLY

The short-run aggregate supply shows the relationship between the output that is hypothetically supplied by the nation's producers of goods and services in response to changes in the price level. In the short run, producer responses will be restrained by the level of plant or factory capacity available for producing additional output and by the speed at which the prices of inputs or factors of production respond to the increase in the overall price level. Many economists believe that there is a delay between a rise in the general price level and resulting increases in prices for raw materials and labor. We will assume that in the short run, input prices do not change. Our examination of long-run aggregate supply will account for increases in resource prices in response to increases in overall prices.

Producers respond to increases in demand by increasing production, since increases in demand tend to bid output prices up and, with factor costs stable, to increase producer profits. Thus, we must examine the level of plant capacity available in the economy to trace the level of real output (GDP) that can be supplied at various price levels, given increases in demand. Tracing these responses will give us a curve that represents short-run aggregate supply.

If the economy is in a severe recession or depression, plenty of plant capacity will be available for producing additional products. Excess labor and capital will be available for the production process, since by definition, high levels of unemployment and low levels of output mean that greater increases in output (GDP) can be made available without producers incurring large costs. Thus, if the economy were operating at a point such as point A in Figure 17.7, a small increase in demand—to point B—would increase real GDP without an overall price increase or with only a very small increase.

At the other extreme, if the economy is operating near or at full capacity, large quantities of output are already being produced. By definition, at full capacity, no new output can be produced. Producers are literally using every available machine, worker, and plant as much as is possible. At point C in Figure 17.7, an increase in demand—to point D—can only bid up the level of prices. Little or no additional output will be forthcoming.

Most often the economy is operating somewhere between these two extreme possibilities of short-run aggregate supply responses. More normally the economy might be at point E. At this point, if demand is increased—to point F —there will be increased GDP in the form of goods and services, and there will be a modest increase in the overall price level.

The upward slope of the aggregate supply curve is partly due to diminishing returns and partly due to resource and factor costs (particularly fixed wages) rising less rapidly than prices when demand for additional output increases. Moving along the aggregate supply curve illustrates the effect of increased aggregate demand at different levels of output and different price levels. Thus, the aggregate supply curve shows us the price level associated with each level of output, where firms will produce a profit-maximizing output at a fixed wage rate and a given level of productivity.

FIGURE 17.7   Short-Run Aggregate Supply

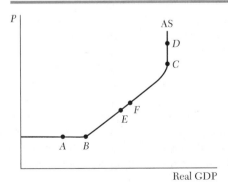

Causes of Shifts in the Short-Run Aggregate Supply Curve

The short-run aggregate supply curve may shift for many reasons, including changes in the labor market, supply shocks, and government policies that affect supply. Positive factors that cut costs, such as technological innovations, will cause the aggregate supply curve to shift to the right. Negative factors, such as rising costs, will cause a shift to the left. Let's examine some conditions that will cause such shifts.

Labor market forces have had and continue to have effects on the aggregate supply curve. Increases and decreases in the labor force are obvious causes of a shift. Over the past four decades, women have entered the U.S. labor force in record numbers. Increases in the labor supply will, of course, increase aggregate supply and shift the curve to the right. Any factor that makes people want to work less—such as attending school, avoiding higher taxes, or pursuing more leisure activities—will cause a shift to the left.

Expectations also cause the short-run aggregate supply curve to shift. If producers expect higher inflation in the future, they will adjust short-run production levels to reflect the expected price hikes. Expected crop failure or surplus will also be reflected in the short-run aggregate supply curve as drought or perhaps freezing weather affects the production level of various crops.

3. If most producers expected prices to rise in the near future, which way would the short-run aggregate supply curve shift? Why? Illustrate with an example.

Most of us are familiar with price changes for domestic and imported resources, another factor affecting the aggregate supply curve. The oil price increases of the 1970s created supply shocks throughout the world, causing a leftward shift in the short-run aggregate supply curve. **Supply shocks** are unexpected events that cause increases in prices. They occur when the cost of producing a wide variety of products increases dramatically, causing the aggregate supply curve to shift to the left and thus push prices upward. During the 1970s, the United States and the world economy experienced a variety of supply shocks, which sent prices soaring. The most noteworthy supply shock occurred in 1973 and 1974, when the powerful OPEC nations placed an embargo (restriction on the import or export of a good) on oil exports. The reduced supply of oil products to many nations of the world severely curtailed production and increased prices, as shown by the shift from AS_0 to AS_1 in Figure 17.8. The price level on AS_1 is raised for each level of real output.

Other, less noteworthy supply shocks have affected the prices and output of many goods and services throughout the world. Price increases of raw materials and/or agricultural products have often been the cause of these shocks. The price increases may be caused by weather—from drought to floods, earthquakes and hurricanes—and by wars, both of which are beyond the control of policy makers. Large, rapid, and perhaps unexpected currency depreciations may also

FIGURE 17.8 A Supply Shock

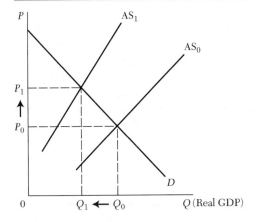

result in dramatic price increases or a supply shock for a nation heavily reliant on imported goods.

During the 1998–2000 U.S. economic expansion, low prices of imported goods affected the aggregate supply curve. In the late 1990s, many Asian economies, weakened by recession and its accompanying high unemployment, produced and exported goods very cheaply. A strong dollar and weakening Asian currencies ensured that exports to U.S. markets would be priced even lower. These cheap imports pressured U.S. producers to keep prices low so that their products could remain competitive in international markets. The low prices in an increasingly global marketplace served, in effect, as a "reverse supply shock." In contrast, from 2004 through mid-2007 as the U.S. economy grew, price pressures on the supply side were felt in some commodities markets, including copper and oil.

4. List other possible shocks to a nation's aggregate supply.

5. List some other factors that would be the reverse of shocks and would increase the nation's supply.

6. List five ways that the government might increase production of the supply of goods and services to the public (i.e., shift the AS curve to the right).

Long-Run Aggregate Supply

Many economists believe that in the long run, the aggregate supply is a vertical line at the full-employment level of output; as new resources and technologies develop, this vertical line shifts to the right. According to this view, in the long run, economic policy will have only price effects unless productivity or technology improves. Before we examine these factors that cause shifts in long-run aggregate supply, we will illustrate how equilibrium is reached using the short- and long-run aggregate supply curves with the aggregate demand curve.

Arriving at Equilibrium

Now that we have introduced the concept of aggregate supply, let's see how changes in aggregate demand will lead first to equilibrium with short-run aggregate supply and then move to an equilibrium on a long-run aggregate supply curve. In our previous analysis in Chapter 13, we assumed that any increase in aggregate expenditures increased real output or real GDP but left prices unchanged. (In Figure 17.9 the entire multiplier effect is seen on the horizontal part of the short-run aggregate supply curve AS.) However, under normal economic conditions, the short-run aggregate supply curve slopes upward. As aggregate demand increases from AD_0 to AD_1, perhaps due to increased government expenditures or decreased taxes, the effect of the expenditure increase is shown as increased real income, GDP, or output; GDP rises from GDP_0 to GDP_1. Moving along the short-run aggregate supply curve AS_0, real GDP increases (from GDP_0 to GDP_1) as do prices (from P_0 to P_1). Equilibrium is found where $AS_0 = AS_1$ at point B. Equilibrium moves from point A to point B. As the economy reaches its capacity to produce additional goods and services, further increases in aggregate demand push up prices.

Is this a stable equilibrium? No. Firms may be happy with this adjustment, but workers will not be. Prices have increased from P_0 to P_1, so workers' real wages have fallen. Workers will not be satisfied with a reduction in their real wages and will insist on a nominal wage increase during the next round of wage negotiations. Since the short-run aggregate supply curve was derived within the context of a model that assumed nominal wages were set and unchanged, any increase in the nominal wage, which increases producers' costs of production, will cause the short-run aggregate supply curve to shift. Responding to the increase in nominal wages, the short-run aggregate supply curve shifts from AS_0 to AS_1 in Figure 17.9. Now we find our short-run equilibrium position at D, where GDP has fallen from GDP_1 to GDP_0 and P has increased from P_1 to P_2.

If there are no additional exogenous changes, there will be no more tendency for movement in the economy. We can see that the long-run aggregate supply

FIGURE 17.9 Equilibrium with Aggregate Demand and Long-Run and Short-Run Aggregate Supply

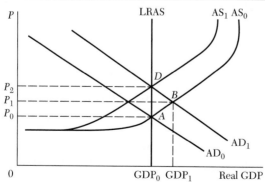

curve (LRAS) is vertical at GDP_0. (If, as we will see later, technology improves in the long run, LRAS would shift to the right, and so would real GDP.)

We examine the short-run aggregate supply curve to see the effect immediately after some fiscal, monetary, or other stimulus to aggregate demand has been introduced, before the economy has time to adjust to these changes in the long run. Firms will adjust their production levels based on the changes in aggregate demand. They will try to increase output to meet the increased demand at a higher price level, since, as we learned in Chapter 7, supply is a function of price. Short-run effects are particularly important to economists who see stabilization policy as important to fine-tuning the economy, and to an understanding of the economy that we face from day to day. Perhaps Keynes expressed the concerns of those economists interested in the short run best when he remarked, "In the long run, we are all dead."

Shifts in the Long-Run Aggregate Supply Curve

Since the long-run aggregate supply curve is not responsive to price changes, it is vertical. Any shift in the long-run aggregate supply curve will reflect a change in the quantity of resources available, a change in the productivity of resources, a change in technology, or perhaps some institutional change that affects resource efficiency or productivity. Each of these will increase or decrease output at all price levels and thus cause the LRAS curve to shift. These factors are mostly insensitive to price changes and are not *immediately* affected by short-term macroeconomic policy.

Productivity

An important source of shifts in the long-run aggregate supply curve comes from increases and decreases in labor **productivity**, or the amount of output produced by a unit of input, in this case, a laborer. Increased productivity shifts the LRAS curve to the right, indicating more output at each price level. The importance of productivity growth is that it allows for noninflationary increases in real GDP, as shown in Figure 17.10.

FIGURE 17.10 Impact of Productivity Increases on Long-Run Aggregate Supply

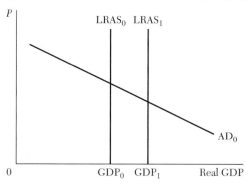

Table 17.2 Growth of U.S. Output per
Person-Hour Worked, 1973–2007

Period	Average Annual Growth
1973–1980	0.6%
1980–1981	0.7%
1981–1990	0.9%
1990–1995	2.2%
1995–2000	3.1%
2000–2007	2.3%

Source: Bureau of Labor Statistics, 2000, 2008.

Productivity is difficult to measure. One problem is the measurement of actual output. As the nation's labor force has shifted from industrial production to service activities, physical output is more difficult to measure. Approximately 18 percent of the nation's nonagricultural workers produce a tangible product. The rest produce services that can be measured in dollars only by examining the number of hours worked. Furthermore, the lack of accounting for quality improvements in manufactured goods has in the past understated U.S. productivity figures. Increases in the numbers of temporary workers paid by temp agencies rather than firms tends to overstate productivity increases.

In the 1970s and 1980s, economists and politicians were concerned with the apparent decline in the growth rate of U.S. productivity. Gains in labor productivity, measured as output per person-hour worked, appear to have been sluggish until the 1990s. While the average annual growth of output per worker was 1.9 percent between 1950 and 1973, Table 17.2 shows it grew 0.6 percent annually between 1973 and 1980, and it averaged less than 1 percent until the 1990s. In contrast, between 1960 and 1973, productivity increased by more than 4 percent annually in Germany and by more than 5 percent in Japan. Since 1979, productivity increases have averaged between 2 and 3 percent in Germany and 3 and 4 percent in Japan (see Figure 17.11).

Recent trends in the United States show productivity gains have slowed after averaging 3.1 percent annually between 1995 and 2000. Productivity normally increases during a recession, so this increase would have been expected in the early 1990s. During the second half of the 1990s, increases in investment spending, particularly in information and communications technology, are believed to have sparked further increases. Historically, productivity increases as labor has more capital to work with, more education, and more training. Despite rapid growth rates in output per worker in Japan and Germany, U.S. workers remain the most productive in the world, with the average worker producing some $28 worth of goods and services per hour and more than $49,000 worth of goods and services annually.

Economists often attribute slowdowns in worker productivity to a slowdown in innovation and technological change. Other culprits that have been cited as contributors to slowdowns in productivity growth include slower growth

FIGURE 17.11 Output per Manufacturing Employee in Selected Countries

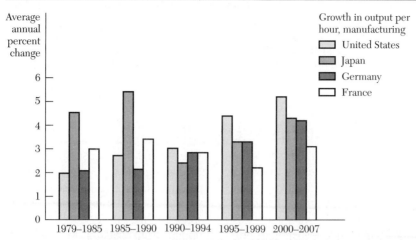

Source: Bureau of Labor Statistics "International Comparisons of Manufacturing Productivity" 1950-2005, BCS 2009.

of private and public investment expenditures, flagging funding for research and development efforts, increased costs of health and safety regulations, and high energy prices during the 1970s. In 2006, slowing productivity rates were partly attributed to cost-cutting options. Aggressive cost-cutting after 2001 sparked productivity increases, but further cost reductions are limited. A reduction in investment in high tech has also been linked to a slowing of productivity growth.

7. Why would slower growth of investment expenditures contribute to decreases in productivity growth rates? How would increased energy costs contribute?

Labor and capitalists, however, sometimes hold different views of policies to increase productivity. Corporations would suggest tax cuts for business to stimulate capital investment and other incentives for research and development and thus shift the aggregate supply curve to the right, providing lower prices at each level of output. Labor, on the other hand, would argue for training programs and higher wages to improve productivity growth. That approach requires that output increase faster than the costs of training and pay increases.

Princeton economist William Baumol and his associates have argued that while productivity is a concern, it should be viewed in a long-run rather than a short-run context, and that increases in U.S. and U.K. productivity growth over the past decade must be sustained to have a long-run impact, since rising productivity and resulting economic growth can help rising debt levels. In discussing recent trends in productivity in their article "Pause Stirs Concern That Growth in Productivity May Be Flattening," Mark Whitehouse and Tim Aeppel write:

Productivity matters for everyone, because it provides the essential ingredient that makes nations rich. When companies produce more for each hour their employees work, they can pay higher wages or reap bigger profits without having to raise prices. Annual productivity growth of 2 percent would more than double inflation-adjusted wages over 40 years, all else being equal. Add another percentage point in productivity growth, and wages would more than triple.

—*The Wall Street Journal*, November 3, 2006, p. 1.

Aggregate Supply and Economic Growth

Thus far in our examination of macroeconomics we have seen how changes in aggregate demand and in aggregate supply affect real GDP, our primary measure of economic performance. Economic growth, remember, is defined as the change in real GDP from one year to the next and is in part determined by the growth in the labor force (or quantity of labor), by physical and human capital accumulation, and by advances in technology. Politicians and policy makers often discuss plans to increase the economy's growth rate, but even a seemingly slow rate of growth has a profound impact over the long term. Compounded over many years, growth at a rate of just 1 or 2 percent contributes greatly to the size of a nation's economy.

Figure 17.12 shows real growth in the U.S. economy over the past century. Over that period, real GDP per person grew on average at about 2 percent annually. Between 1960 and 1973, GDP growth per person averaged 4.2 percent, but between 1975 and 1985, the growth rate fell to 1.1 percent per year. It then rebounded a bit, averaging 2.1 percent between 1990 and 2004.

Factors that cause changes in medium and long-term economic growth are the same factors that cause shifts in the long-run aggregate supply curve: changes in labor productivity and discoveries of new technologies or innovations. What is responsible for these? Often, investment (funded from saving) in new capital or public investment in a nation's infrastructure will increase worker productivity. Investment in human capital has historically improved productivity as well. This investment may take the form of public-sector expenditures on education and training or private expenditures on worker training.

New technological innovation may be fostered by investment expenditures on research and development—for instance, Defense Department research and development expenditures that led to the Internet*—or simply "learning by doing." Once a technical innovation that may improve productivity occurs, investment in capital (perhaps through equipment expenditures) employing this technology or innovation makes it available to the labor force. There is a crucial link between technology, science, and knowledge; advances in one serve as a catalyst for advances in another.

---

*Internet technology is a product of Department of Defense expenditures during the Cold War. The Advanced Research Projects Agency (ARPA), set up by the Eisenhower administration in 1957, began exploring computer communication, and in 1969 ARPAnet linked four research universities. During the 1970s ARPAnet expanded, and other networks were established—again, mostly linking universities. Research reports and articles were read and discussed on e-mail (electronic mail) and electronic discussion groups. In the 1980s, establishment of a communication standard, or protocol, allowed for the development of the Internet.

FIGURE 17.12 Economic Growth in the United States, 1895–2005

Real GDP per person (thousands of 1996 dollars)

World War II

Great Depression

Source: Data from Christina D. Romer, "The Prewar Business Cycle Reconsidered: New Estimates of Gross National Product, 1869-1908," *Journal of Political Economy* Vol. 97(1989); *National Income and Product Accounts of the United States; Historical Statistics of the United States Colonial Times to 1957* (U.S. Department of Commerce, 1960); *Economic Report of the President,* 1999; Michael Parkin, *Economics,* 5th ed., Addison Wesley, 2005. p. 463; and www.gov/fls/flsgdp.pdf, 2006.

Productivity, along with increases in the labor force, increases in capital, and changes in technology, has a powerful effect on aggregate supply and on the nation's standard of living. Therefore, now that we have developed the theory of aggregate supply and understand how various factors influence it, we must examine how our theory of supply relates to economic policy.

SUPPLY-SIDE ECONOMIC POLICY

In 1975, a handful of academic economists, together with politicians and journalists, began to reexamine the problems of the U.S. economy from a different perspective than mainstream Keynesian economics. The focus of the reexamination was on the "supply side." As we have seen previously, the orthodox Keynesian approach to the problems of inflation and unemployment focused on the demand side of the economy. If the economy showed signs of recession or depression, the verdict was that the economy was suffering from insufficient aggregate demand. If there were inflationary trends, then aggregate demand was too robust. Supply-side economists argued that those policies tended to be inflationary; once the government had initiated spending for particular programs, spending was hard to reduce.

Rationale for Supply-Side Economics

Neither Keynes nor the classical economists totally ignored the supply side of the market in their economic analysis, but the policies Keynesians designed were predominantly aimed at either shoring up a weak aggregate demand or calming one that was excessive. To them, income or output was a function of aggregate demand.

Proponents of the supply-side approach argued that federal, state, and local governments had stifled production and incentive in the United States with their emphasis on policies leading to increased spending, taxation, and regulation. They argued that higher tax rates (particularly progressive taxes) and increased government regulation reduced incentives, while spending fueled inflation.

Supply-side advocates argued that increased tax rates inhibited production and reduced output as people substituted leisure activities for productive activity and did more work in which they had less skill. This would reduce the time spent in more productive economic activities, which because of higher taxes were less financially rewarding, and lead to an inefficient allocation of economic resources. Further inefficiencies would occur if tax-deductible goods became less desirable than those that were nondeductible. Finally, advocates of a supply-side approach pointed to the declining productivity in the United States and argued that lower corporate tax rates would generate more business investment and thus increase productivity.

This theory also predicted increased saving and perhaps increases in the rate of saving. Supply-side economists argued that lower tax rates would induce more saving in the private sector; the tax reductions would leave people more income from which to consume and save. If the government also reduced its spending, additional investment funds would become available. Greater investment should lead to lower interest rates and economic growth.

In summary, advocates of the supply-side approach to economic policy saw tax rates as extremely important in determining total output in the economy. They believed that decreases in tax rates caused individuals and businesses to substitute such productive activity as work, investment, and specialization for nonproductive activities. This would result in a more efficient allocation of resources. Total economic output would rise with lower tax rates.

8. How do taxes directly affect supply? Illustrate on a graph of aggregate supply and aggregate demand how a tax cut works.

Supply-Side Critics

Some economists sympathized with the notions put forth by advocates of the supply-side approach but noted that policies to stimulate supply-side increases take long periods of time before having noticeable effects on the economy. Indeed, they added, some of those policies might increase aggregate demand at the same time.

Another supply-side argument that came under fire was the assertion that lower tax rates would provide incentives for people to work more, since they could "keep" more of their income. Critics of this notion argued instead that higher tax rates had forced some people to work more than they would like to simply to maintain their standard of living. These people already had two jobs or worked overtime to keep the same level of income in the face of high tax rates. It was hard to conceive of them working more, yet easy to envision their working less if the tax rate fell.

Tax cuts for businesses had critics as well. Although in theory the cuts should stimulate investment, the critics questioned whether these funds would in fact be spent on new, productive activities. They cited corporate mergers in the 1980s, such as the purchase of Montgomery Ward by Mobil Oil, and Nabisco by R. J. Reynolds, as examples of corporate spending that created no new jobs or productive output for the nation.

Finally, the supply-side aspects of 1980s economic policies tended to shift the distribution of income. Wealthy individuals benefited far more than middle- and lower-middle-income groups. In absolute-dollar amounts, the benefit to those earning less than $10,000 a year was minimal, if not negative.

The Federal Reserve set the recovery of 1983–1984 in motion by pumping up the growth rate of the money supply in 1982, at the same time Congress increased military spending and enacted tax cuts. This stimulated a *demand-led*, rather than a supply-led, recovery, although business tax cuts did kick in somewhat higher levels of investment as the recovery mounted. The effects of supply-side policies of the early 1980s had decreased economic growth rates while increasing unemployment and budget deficits. Tax incentives to individuals and businesses had unexpected outcomes: decreases in the personal saving rate and investment expenditures as a percentage of national income.

THE BIG PICTURE

And the Big Picture Concluded

In this chapter we have completed the construction of the aggregate supply–aggregate demand model that allows us to analyze and show the effects of prices when economic policies are implemented. While the aggregate demand–aggregate supply graphs resemble the market supply graphs we developed in Chapter 7, this resemblance is where the similarity stops. Information about money markets, goods and services markets, and economic policy is reflected in the aggregate demand–aggregate supply analysis, telling us how those markets respond to economic events, including policy decisions. We can now assess aggregate output and price levels for the economy. Figure 17.BP.2 outlines the path we have taken to develop this model to this point in Part 3.

FIGURE 17.BP.2 Construction of the Aggregate Demand–Aggregate Supply Model

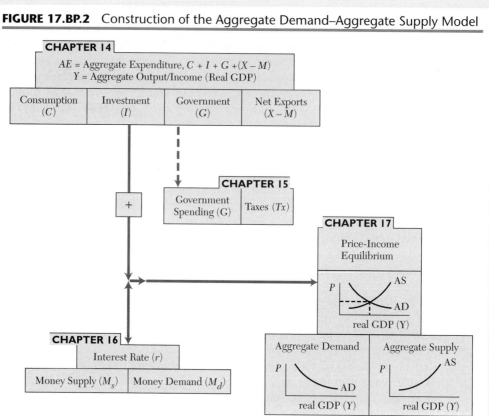

Conclusion

Because price stability is one of the three macroeconomic goals, we need to be aware of price changes that may result from supply shocks—such as oil or energy shortages and productivity changes. With this in mind, we move to Chapter 18, where we examine stabilization policy and the trade-off between inflation and unemployment. This chapter illustrates The Big Picture in action.

Review Questions

1. How is monetary policy related to aggregate demand?

2. What incentives do supply-side policies attempt to improve? Are incentives important in economic analysis?

3. Explain the relationship between supply-side tax policies and "demand-side" policies. Are the two interrelated? Explain.

4. Why is it difficult to increase output and thus expand economic growth through supply-side policies?

5. What was the last supply shock to occur in the United States? Explain its significance.

6. What were some of the reasons for the slowdown in productivity in the late 1970s and early 1980s? Increases in the 1990s?

7. Does it matter whether productivity is viewed in the short or long run? How does one increase productivity?

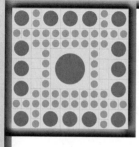

CHAPTER EIGHTEEN

Unemployment, Inflation, and Stabilization Policy in a Global Economy

❖ Introduction

As the United States entered the twenty-first century, it was experiencing the longest period of sustained growth on record. But as the economic slowdown in 2001 was exacerbated by the terror attacks on the World Trade Center and the Pentagon, policy makers began again to reconsider policies concerning unemployment and inflation. During the years of economic growth in the 1960s, some economists declared the business cycle "dead," only to have it roar back in the 1970s and 1980s. From the economic experiences of those decades, economists not only learned about trade-offs, but they also discovered how economic variables might respond to policy.

The previous chapters dealing with macroeconomic theory and policy have touched only slightly on the controversy that surrounds most policy decisions. We have hinted that there is some conflict between the monetarists and the Keynesians about solving these problems and that there might be other contending opinions. Conservatives, liberals, and radicals see different sorts of problems and different sets of solutions. One issue, which we shall focus on in the first part of the chapter, is the trade-off between the macroeconomic goals of unemployment and inflation. An even more troublesome situation happens when inflation and unemployment occur at the same time, resulting in what economists call **stagflation**.

We will begin by examining unemployment and inflation, the trade-off between the two, and the implications for stabilization policy. From there we will outline the views of several competing schools of economic thought to see how (or, in some cases, if) we can effectively use macroeconomic policy to reach societal goals.

THE TRADE-OFF: UNEMPLOYMENT AND INFLATION

Given the economic goals of price stability, full employment, and growth, Keynesian macroeconomic policy prescriptions advise us that increased spending and/or increases in the money supply may be necessary to attain full employment, with price increases as a side effect. On the other hand, if policy makers attempt to curb inflation through monetary and fiscal measures, income will fall—and so will employment. We seem to be between a rock and a hard place. But an even more difficult problem emerges when the economy develops high inflation as well as high unemployment rates.

The Phillips Curve

At one time, economists believed they had a rather simple answer to questions dealing with the trade-off between full employment and price stability. Economist A. W. Phillips studied the British economy for 100-plus years and found a rather stable relationship between increases in the wage rate and the rate of unemployment. High rates of unemployment were associated with low wage increases, and wage increases appeared to be related to the general rate of inflation. In the 1960s, U.S. economists Paul Samuelson and Robert Solow related rates of price increase to rates of unemployment and found that inflation and unemployment were inversely related. High inflation rates were associated with low unemployment rates and vice versa. When plotted, this downward-sloping relationship between the inflation rate and the unemployment rate came to be known as the **Phillips curve**.

If the Phillips curve is valid, then the matter of priorities seems to be rather straightforward. Economists could present a menu of the various trade-offs that were possible—perhaps a 4 percent inflation rate with a 5 percent unemployment rate, or a 2 percent inflation rate with a 6 percent unemployment rate. Through the democratic process, the electorate would establish which combination it desired, and the policy makers would fine-tune the economy to obtain this trade-off. If the economy had 5 percent inflation and 4 percent unemployment but the electorate and policy makers desired 4 and 4.5 percent rates, then economic policy should be ever so slightly more restrictive.

During the 1960s, the United States had one of its longest periods of uninterrupted economic growth, inflation averaged around 2 percent (although it accelerated to over 5 percent by the late 1960s), and the unemployment rate declined from 6.7 percent in 1961 to 3.5 percent in 1969. (Figure 18.1 graphs these rates, which are listed in Table 18.1.) But the 1970s and early 1980s presented a vastly different picture. In 1971, the unemployment rate climbed above 5.9 percent while the inflation rate rose to nearly 5 percent. By 1981, the unemployment rate reached 7.6 percent, and inflation was 10.3 percent. As inflation dropped to between 3 and 4 percent, unemployment peaked at 9.6 percent in 1983 and declined somewhat to 7.5 percent in 1984. The idea of a simple trade-off between inflation and unemployment had broken down. It took increasingly higher levels of unemployment to reduce inflation by increasingly smaller amounts.

Despite the generally inverse relationship between unemployment and price pressures, the trade-off appeared to worsen, leading some economists to suggest that the Phillips curve had shifted. By "connecting the dots" between the annual points plotted between 1960 and 1968 and between 1969 and 1974 on Figure 18.1, we show a shifting Phillips curve. After that time, connecting the

FIGURE 18.1 The Phillips Curve and the U.S. Economy, 1960–2008

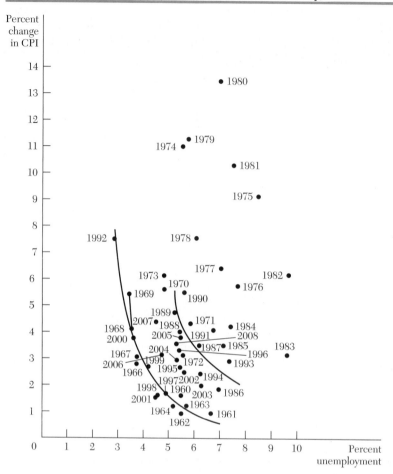

dots creates an upward and then a downward spiral, indicating a longer upward movement in the 1970s and early 1980s, followed by a more recent downward trend in the late 1980s and the 1990s, renewing the idea of a trade-off.

Some economists attributed shifts in the Phillips curve in the 1970s to supply shocks the economy received during those years. These included the very high increases in oil prices caused by the OPEC embargo, increased prices of agricultural products, and the increased prices of foreign goods brought about by the fall in the dollar's value in 1973. This period generated critiques of the Phillips curve, with Edmund Phelps and Milton Friedman arguing that inflationary expectations might be generating the higher levels of inflation and unemployment.

The 1990s brought the U.S. economy low levels of unemployment and inflation, accompanying a record number of months of sustained economic growth. As economic activity slowed in 2001–2003, higher unemployment levels peaked at 6 percent in 2003 while prices remained low. As the recovery gained momentum in 2004, job growth was initially sluggish and inflationary pressures

Table 18.1 Inflation and Unemployment in the U.S. Economy, 1950–2008

Year	Inflation Consumer Price Index*	Inflation Year-to-Year Change	Unemployment Rate	Year	Inflation Consumer Price Index*	Inflation Year-to-Year Change	Unemployment Rate
1950	24.1	1.3%	5.3%	1980	82.4	13.5%	7.1%
1951	26.0	7.9	3.3	1981	90.9	10.3	7.6
1952	26.5	1.9	3.0	1982	96.5	6.2	9.7
1953	26.7	0.8	2.9	1983	99.6	3.2	9.6
1954	26.9	0.7	5.5	1984	103.9	4.3	7.5
1955	26.8	−0.4	4.4	1985	107.6	3.6	7.2
1956	27.2	1.5	4.1	1986	109.6	1.9	7.0
1957	28.1	3.3	4.3	1987	113.6	3.6	6.2
1958	28.9	2.8	6.8	1988	118.3	4.1	5.5
1959	29.1	0.7	5.5	1989	124.0	4.8	5.3
1960	29.6	1.7	5.5	1990	130.7	5.4	5.5
1961	29.9	1.0	6.7	1991	136.2	4.2	6.7
1962	30.2	1.0	5.5	1992	140.3	3.0	7.4
1963	30.6	1.3	5.7	1993	144.5	3.0	6.8
1964	31.0	1.3	5.2	1994	148.2	2.6	6.1
1965	31.5	1.6	4.5	1995	152.4	2.8	5.6
1966	32.4	2.9	3.8	1996	156.9	3.3	5.4
1967	33.4	3.1	3.8	1997	160.5	1.7	4.9
1968	34.7	3.7	3.6	1998	163.0	1.6	4.5
1969	36.7	5.5	3.5	1999	166.6	2.7	4.2
1970	38.8	5.7	4.9	2000	172.2	3.4	4.0
1971	40.5	4.4	5.9	2001	177.1	1.6	4.7
1972	41.8	3.2	5.6	2002	179.9	2.4	5.8
1973	44.4	6.2	4.9	2003	184.0	1.9.	6.0
1974	49.3	11.0	5.6	2004	185.9	3.3	5.5
1975	53.8	9.1	8.5	2005	195.3	3.4	5.1
1976	56.9	5.8	7.7	2006	201.6	2.5	4.6
1977	60.6	6.5	7.1	2007	207.3	4.1	4.6
1978	65.2	7.6	6.1	2008	NA	3.1	5.1
1979	72.6	11.3	5.8				

*The Consumer Price Index (CPI) measures changes in the "cost of living" (1982 – 1984 = 100). The inflation rate is the percent change in CPI.

Source: Economic Report of the President, 2009, pp. 334,353,357.

edged prices upward. The economy continued to grow at an accelerated rate through 2005 and early 2006. Growth slowed to modest levels in late 2006 as prices continued to rise. In addition to concerns about levels of employment and price stability, significant concerns about trade deficits and other structural problems remained. In a nation with one of the world's highest standards of living, homelessness persists, and the infant mortality rate remains among the highest of the industrial nations. Continuing increases in poverty levels, especially among the young, are particularly troublesome, as are the growing numbers of workers without health insurance. Even in periods of low inflation and unemployment, these troubling economic issues remained unsolved.

INFLATION

We have defined inflation as a rise in the general price level. We can expect price increases to accompany a growing, viable economy, but if these price increases are larger than increases in productivity or real output would dictate, they are inflationary. Table 18.1 indicates what has happened to prices in the past half century, measured as changes in the Consumer Price Index (CPI). These numbers reflect revisions that government economists have made to the way they measure inflation, beginning in 1995. The revisions lowered the level of inflation from earlier years by about 0.68 percentage points per year. The purpose of these changes was to provide a more accurate measure of inflation experienced by consumers. Note the lower rates of inflation in recent years.

1. On the average, how much would something that cost $200 in 1967 cost in 2007? How much have prices increased since you were born?

2. Does any information in the table surprise you? If so, what surprised you? (If not, what met your expectations?)

From our analysis of aggregate demand and aggregate supply in Chapter 17, we can see that any action that shifts the aggregate demand curve to the right or the aggregate supply curve to the left causes price increases and possibly inflation. We can classify the prevailing types of inflation according to the possible cause of each: demand-pull inflation, cost-push inflation, and expectations-generated inflation. These types of inflation can occur simultaneously or independently.

Demand-pull inflation is a rise in the price level attributed to excessive aggregate demand. Aggregate demand can increase for a number of reasons, including increases in autonomous consumption, investment, government spending, net exports, and the money supply or decreases in taxes or saving. We can view this graphically in Figure 18.2, where AS represents the aggregate

FIGURE 18.2 Demand-Pull Inflation

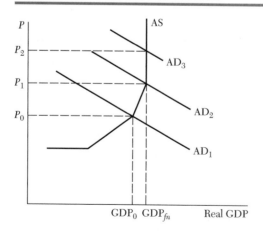

supply curve, and AD represents aggregate demand. All are plotted with respect to real output (real GDP) and the general price level (P). A rightward shift of the aggregate demand curve from AD_1 to AD_2 increases both prices and real output in the short run as real GDP increases from GDP_0 to GDP_{fn} and prices increase from P_0 to P_1. As income levels increase, the demand for goods and services will rise. Initially, as demand increases, prices are bid up, output increases, and more laborers are hired to produce products. If resources are fully employed and aggregate demand continues to rise, as illustrated by a shift from AD_2 to AD_3, there is no increase in GDP, only an increase in prices. From our analysis in Chapter 17, we know that the higher aggregate demand in the face of limited supply will cause shortages of goods and services and the need for additional labor to increase production. The increased demand for goods and services, raw materials, and labor may even exceed the capacity to generate new output.

A simple remedy for inflation generated by increased aggregate demand is to cut back on spending and the money supply. The same technique can thwart inflationary expectations. Reductions in the growth rate of the money supply are particularly effective (and painful).

Cost-push (or supply) **inflation** puts the responsibility for price increases on rising costs of production. From the analysis of demand and supply in Chapter 7, we found that as production costs increased, the supply curve shifted to the left, leading to higher prices. A few of the cost factors that might cause a shift in the supply function are wages, raw material prices, interest rates, and profits. In Figure 18.3 higher costs bring about increases in price as well as a reduction in output. In the long run, producers will be able to reduce wages because of higher levels of unemployment, and output will return to the original level (GDP_{fn}).

Cost increases can come from many places, including increases in raw material prices, labor costs, and higher profits. As market structures have become more concentrated, some large corporations have gained more ability to administer prices for their own benefit—which in most cases means to increase prices and profits. During the 1970s, resource shortages pushed the prices of some goods upward. The lack of supply created a bottleneck in the

FIGURE 18.3 Cost-Push Inflation

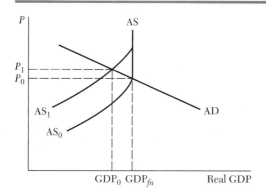

production process, with limited amounts of raw materials forthcoming, even at higher costs.

Unlike aggregate demand inflation, cost-push or supply inflation has no simple remedy. Resource shortages are difficult to prevent. Cartels that withhold raw materials are hard to bargain with. Controls placed on wages and prices, and other types of incomes policies, do not seem to work very well, when viewed in a historical context. Indeed, controls often lead to contrived shortages, as suppliers hesitate to continue production when they cannot recoup rising costs.

If businesses respond to higher output and profits sparked by an increase in aggregate demand by hiring additional workers, more jobs become available, and unemployment falls. If the current rates of inflation are expected to continue, *expectations-generated inflation* may occur. Workers, trying to restore the purchasing power of their wages, press for increases based on inflationary expectations. Once workers attain higher wages, the aggregate supply will decrease to reflect the increased costs to firms. With these higher costs, profits fall, and firms cut back on output. Now real GDP falls back to its original level, but prices are now at a higher level.

While expectations may seem an unlikely candidate for economic analysis, inflationary expectations are at times important in explaining inflation. Each time we expect inflation, we tend to generate inflationary price increases. Yale economist William Nordhaus stated this well:

> Inflation is a highly inertial process. It will go along to whatever rate it has been going at until it is shocked to a different level....From 1973 to 1980 we had 6 to 9 percent inflation built into the wage and price system. It [higher inflation] was built into contracts. It was built into expectations. The recession [1980–1982] beat it down to 5 percent and now we have lower inertial rates.

Inflationary expectations directly affect aggregate supply. As wages increase because workers expect inflation, costs to firms increase. Firms then pass on these increased costs to consumers in the form of higher prices. On the demand side, expectations of higher interest rates generate consumer and business borrowing and expenditures. These activities increase aggregate demand and drive up prices.

When inflationary expectations are low, inflation is easier to moderate with monetary and fiscal policy. In the 1970s, when inflationary expectations were high, the fiscal policies employed were largely ineffective. They resulted in increased unemployment without significantly lower inflation. From the late 1980s through the late 1990s, expectations remained low and thus aided in maintaining stable prices. As the U.S. and industrial economies expanded from 2004 through 2006, inflationary expectations increased as rising oil and commodity prices and consumer demand pushed prices upward.

THE IMPACT OF UNEMPLOYMENT AND INFLATION

Although policy makers and politicians would prefer to have the low inflation *and* low unemployment characteristic of the late 1960s and late 1990s, when unemployment or prices begin to rise, policy makers must respond to those changes. Decisions must be made about which goal, full employment or price stability, is preferable. Economists studying this question have found that higher unemployment and higher inflation affect different groups in different ways.

According to a study by Princeton economist Alan Blinder, former member of the Federal Reserve Board and Council of Economic Advisors, and Northwestern University economist Rebecca Blank, the unemployment rate for teens increases at two times the base rate, and unemployment for the elderly increases at about half the base rate. Blinder and Blank also made the following observations:

> The burden of unemployment is distributed unequally across age, race, and sex groups. In particular, nonwhite and young workers are more severely affected. On the other hand, female and older workers—who are also typically low-wage workers—are not as sensitive to changes in general unemployment levels.

They conclude, "The business cycle is not neutral in spreading the burden of unemployment. Certain workers experience much larger increases in unemployment when the general economy turns down than others." Blank and Blinder also found that whites, males, and the middle-aged receive a larger share of unemployment compensation than do unemployed workers in other categories.*

Inflation particularly hurts creditors and those on fixed incomes, while borrowers in general benefit. The poor seem to be hurt less by inflation than the rich. Prices generally rise for consumers at all income levels, but so do wages and salaries. However, the income from and worth of wealthy people's assets are more readily eroded by inflation.

3. What effect will supply shortages have on the trade-off between inflation and unemployment when unemployment is increasing?

4. How might inflation benefit a person who borrows money? Is this always so?

STABILIZATION POLICY: AN INTERNATIONAL PERSPECTIVE

Unemployment and inflation concern policy makers throughout the world's industrial and developing nations. The 1990s brought generally low rates of unemployment and inflation in the United States, Germany, and Japan, but several other industrial nations experienced substantially higher unemployment. Table 18.2 shows recent unemployment and inflation rates in some of the nations that actively compete with the United States in international markets.

Many of the European nations listed in the table have chosen more aggressive social programs than those in the United States for dealing with the effects of unemployment. These more generous programs have at least partially resulted in higher taxes. As Figure 12.3 illustrates, the United States, along with

*Rebecca M. Blank and Alan S. Blinder, "Macroeconomics, Income Distribution and Poverty," in Sheldon H. Danziger and Daniel Weinberg, eds., *Fighting Poverty: What Works and What Doesn't* (Cambridge, MA: Harvard University Press, 1986), p. 191.

Table 18.2 Unemployment and Inflation Rates in Selected Countries, 2007

Country	Unemployment Rate	Change in Consumer Price Index
United States	4.6%	2.9%
Australia	4.4	2.3
Canada	6.0	2.1
France	8.3	1.5
Germany	8.4	2.1
Italy	6.1	1.8
Japan	3.9	0.1
Sweden	6.1	2.2
United Kingdom	5.3	4.3

Source: Statistical Abstract of the United States, 2009, Tables 1321 and 1311.

Japan and Korea, has a relatively lower tax burden than the other industrialized nations. At the same time, many of these nations have also experienced higher government deficits.

MACROECONOMIC SOLUTIONS: THE ALTERNATIVES

While the Keynesian aggregate expenditures model we have explored commends the use of monetary and fiscal policy in stabilization efforts, other economic models and theories question the effectiveness of intervention. The dilemma is what to do—not so much about inflation and unemployment but about government budgets, trade deficits, economic and productivity growth rates, and the myriad of other economic problems that surround us in the context of a complex and increasingly interdependent world economy. Traditional Keynesian remedies, declared deficient during the stagflation of the 1970s, returned with renewed vitality to the New Keynesians by the end of the 1980s, and attained even greater importance in 2008 and 2009.

Ever an evolutionary theory, Keynesianism is becoming more eclectic, encompassing some of the better ideas presented by other schools of macroeconomic thought in the 1980s. These include a larger framework on which consumers base their expectations of the future and a reaffirmation that, along with fiscal policy, monetary policy is important to stabilization efforts. As Keynesians returned to the limelight, popular movements of the 1970s and 1980s lost favor. To better understand the status of stabilization policy, we will briefly summarize some of the theories and policies of contending schools of thought and review their standing in the early twenty-first century.

Monetarist Solutions

Monetarists believe that growth rates of money control inflation and business cycle activity. Monetary policy, therefore, is the most effective way to stabilize the economy, although most monetarists prefer a nondiscretionary rule rather than small changes in policy that aim to fine-tune the economy. Monetarists contend that only money matters, since increases in money allow fiscal policy to be effective in the long run. (Actually, it is monetary policy that is effective.) The monetarists focus on the long run and avoid short-run solutions.

Boosted by the failures of Keynesian theory and policy to explain and counter the stagflation of the 1970s, the monetarists entered the 1980s with their theories at the top of the hit parade. But even the 1970s and certainly the following two decades dealt monetarists a cruel blow. Predictions fell by the wayside. Velocity was unstable, as was the demand for money. The money supply proved hard to target. Inflation of the 1970s proved not to be a monetary phenomenon, and inflation predicted in the 1980s failed to materialize. The monetarists fell from favor.

Supply-Side Solutions

Although supply-siders fell from favor at the end of the 1980s, the election in 2000 of George W. Bush helped them regain some power in policy-making circles. In the 1980s, wishful thinking proved no match for the economy that resulted from supply-side policies. Marginal tax rate policies designed to stimulate investment and incentives brought about increased unemployment, decreased saving and investment, large budget deficits, and increased income and wealth inequality. We discussed supply-side economics at length in Chapter 17 and will not repeat those arguments here. Economists accept the supply-side idea that marginal tax rates can help to increase incentives and investment, but most economists see them having a rather small effect on overall economic activity. Supply-side stabilization policies should not be disregarded, but their stabilization effect is small.

New Classical Solutions

The New Classical or Rational Expectations school of macroeconomic thought gained support and prestige during the 1970s and early 1980s. Its abstract theoretical and mathematical model, based on classical assumptions of pure and perfect competition, appealed to a number of academic economists. New Classical economists argue that firms and workers acquire, assess, and utilize information very quickly and rationally. For example, in our prior discussion of inflation, economists subscribing to the New Classical view would argue that as soon as laborers realized policy makers were trying to stimulate demand, they would adjust their consumption and wage demands, making the "short-run" Phillips curve trade-off even shorter and making the long-run aggregate supply and vertical Phillips curves the only appropriate ones for examining policy actions. Short-run stabilization policy would be useless, since rational people would react immediately and "outguess" the policy. Only policy "surprises" would be effective. Rational individuals would use all information, not just past data about prices or income. Policy makers could introduce or curb inflationary expectations simply by appointing a new Federal Reserve chair known to be easy or tough on inflation. New Classical economists would rely on perfectly competitive markets—ones without collusion, price fixing, or monopoly—to chart the best course for the economy.

When economists examined the evidence from the late 1970s and 1980s, New Classical theories fell short. According to the theories, inflation could be reduced without an increase in unemployment. With the Federal Reserve decreasing the growth rate of the money supply, economic actors should have adjusted their inflationary expectations downward, avoiding high levels of unemployment. But that period showed the short-run Phillips curve to be alive and well, and Rational Expectations remains a theory without an accompanying reality.

Post-Keynesian (Managed Capitalist) Solutions

Post-Keynesians, distrustful of solutions that rely solely on market activity, and the long-run timing of such solutions, and relying heavily on the role of demand in the economy, recommend adoption of an incomes policy to determine an annual noninflationary rise in all types of income. This would involve controls over the rates of increase in personal and business income. Tax incentives would assure compliance. The post-Keynesians believe that government and business should jointly make decisions for long-run public and private investment, and that employment and growth policies are central to a recovery and economic restructuring.

In the 1980s, post-Keynesian alternatives such as wage and price controls faded from sight as means to combat inflation or reduce unemployment. In the postwar era, however, every president until Ronald Reagan at some point flirted with controls or guidelines. Nevertheless, outside of the political machismo derived from controls, there has been little evidence that the particular types of controls instituted have been effective.

Feminist Economists' Solutions

Feminist economists note the failure of present economic models to predict and address real-world concerns of women, children, and men. They seek to go beyond formal economic models based on what they see as oversimplified assumptions about human behavior. For example, feminist economist Nancy Folbre has pointed out that while Adam Smith noted the role that competitive markets play in our lives (see Chapter 3), the expanding role of the market has sometimes come at the cost of care for others. Smith considered this problem but, according to Folbre, "didn't take it seriously, because he optimistically assumed that people were not all that selfish". He considered love of family, duty to others, and loyalty to country the hallmarks of an advanced civilization. The book that launched his career was entitled *The Theory of the Moral Sentiments*. In it he wrote:

> However selfish soever man may be supposed, there are evidently some principles in his nature, which interest him in the fortune of others, and render their happiness necessary to him, though he derives nothing from it, except the pleasure of seeing it.

Folbre, too, considers a more caring macroeconomics, where societal goods other than wealth are factors:

> Extending family values to society as a whole requires looking beyond the redistribution of income to ways of strengthening cultural values of love, obligation, and reciprocity....
>
> We could encourage greater civic participation, offering tax credits and other incentives for the provision of care services that develop long-term relationships between individuals and communities. We could discourage residential and cultural segregation by class and ethnicity. We could defend and enlarge our

public spaces. Our educational institutions could encourage the development of caring skills and community involvement. Among other strategies, we might invite young people to repay the money invested in them through national service rather than simply through taxes.

Policies designed to promote care for other people appear unproductive only to those who define economic efficiency in cramped terms, such as increases in GDP. The weakening of family and social solidarity can impose enormous costs, reflected in educational failures, poor health, environmental degradation, high crime rates, and a cultural atmosphere of anxiety and resentment. The care and nurturance of human capabilities has always been difficult and expensive. In the past, a sexual division of labor based upon the subordination of women helped minimize both the difficulties and the expense. Today, however, the costs of providing care need to be explicitly confronted and fairly distributed.

> —Nancy Folbre, *The Invisible Heart: Economics and Family Values*,
> New Press, 2001, pp. 229–230.

Feminist perspectives on economics, such as the one seen here, often expand the scope of the traditional meaning of stabilization policy, pushing it beyond indicators such as inflation and unemployment rates.

Radical Solutions

Radical economists argued that the stagflation of the 1970s was symptomatic not only of a failure of Keynesian theory and policy but also of a fundamental breakdown of U.S. capitalism. Radicals viewed U.S. capitalism as experiencing a long-term structural crisis, explained not by factors external to the economy but by the business cycle. A radical critique of Keynesian theory and policy challenges the "theory of the state," with the state as the legitimate arbiter of societal conflicts resulting from interest groups' political behavior and lobbying. Arguing that the state consciously guides the economy and cyclical instability in order to serve the needs of the dominant economic class, Raford Boddy and James Crotty summarize the functional analysis of a recession in the business cycle:

> It is the economic function of the recession to correct the imbalances of the previous expansion and thereby create the preconditions for a new one. By robbing millions of people of their jobs, and threatening the jobs of millions of others, recessions reduce worker demands and end the rise of labor costs. They eventually rebuild profit margins and stabilize prices. During recessions inventories are cut, loans are repaid, corporate liquidity position is reversed. All the statements of Keynesian economists to the contrary notwithstanding, recessions are inevitable in the unplanned economy of the United States because they perform an essential function for which no adequate substitute has thus far been available.
>
> —Raford Boddy and James R. Crotty, "Who Will Plan the
> Planned Economy?" *The Progressive*, February 1975.

Radicals see increases in concentration and specialization of production by domestic and multinational corporations as expanding both their political and their economic power. An increasingly symbiotic relationship between government and business explains the structural transformation of U.S. capitalism since World

War II, prohibits the possibility of genuine democracy in the United States, and clearly depicts an underlying class character of government functions and policies. Radicals view stabilization policies as outside the interests of workers and the democratic process.

5. What are the top five macroeconomic issues today? Select one of those issues and explain how conservatives, liberals, and radicals respond. How might a feminist economist respond to that issue?

Conclusion

We must increasingly adapt our theory and policy within the context of the existing U.S. and world economies, finding solutions that are effective within this context. The U.S. economy is far different from what it was in the post–World War II era. The workforce is changing, and the economic base, which was continually regenerated through economic growth, is no longer industrial. Additionally, policy decisions must reflect the fact that the U.S. economy in this century is greatly dependent on the other nations of the world. As government leaders plan for economic growth in the United States, they must do so within a world context. Today around 10 percent of the products made in the United States are exported to other nations. Exports plus imports made up about 20 percent of the U.S. GDP in 2004, compared with 12.4 percent of GDP in 1970 and less than 10 percent in the 1960s. If the economies of U.S. trading partners are unhealthy, we cannot expect the U.S. economy to remain vigorous.

This chapter completes our discussion of macroeconomics. We have seen that the Keynesian approach to economic policy has carried us a long way from the classical approach. Yet problems still exist, and new approaches may be needed to deal with future problems. Many of these issues are increasing our attention toward macroeconomics and the functioning of specific markets. Before we look further at policy, however, we need to broaden our perspective and see what is happening in international economics. An understanding of the global arena is necessary to appreciate the full complexity of macroeconomic problems.

Review Questions

1. What is the basis for the trade-off or inverse relationship between inflation and unemployment? Why can't there be zero unemployment and zero inflation?

2. Do you think fighting inflation is more important than fighting unemployment? Why or why not?

3. What competing theories explain inflation in the economy?

4. What structural elements in the economy limit the effectiveness of fiscal and monetary policies?

5. How does avoiding a boom avoid a recession? What is the resulting impact on inflation?

6. What are the main schools of thought with respect to macroeconomic stabilization policy? What are the main issues of contention? Does the recent macroeconomic performance of the U.S. economy suport the ideas of one school more than another?

THINKING CRITICALLY

SPEND ME TO THE MOON

In examining macroeconomic theory and policy, we have seen how and why both monetary and fiscal policies are important to economic growth and stabilization. While at times complicated by the increasing globalization of economic activity and fluctuations beyond U.S. borders, stabilization policies, when employed, have had some success in calming national and international markets. As you might expect, opinions about macroeconomic goals and the policies the government or the Fed should pursue to accomplish them are often linked to belief systems (as we learned in Chapter 1). We understand how monetary and fiscal policy works. We understand the limitations and the strengths of monetary, spending, and taxation policies. But one of the most often asked questions is, What should U.S. or Fed policy be? In answering this question, conservative, liberal, and radical perspectives play an important role in establishing the dialogue and the parameters of discussion.

Between 1999 and 2000, economists representing every perspective applauded the Fed's use of monetary policy to sustain a buoyant and growing economy (although some believed even higher growth could have been generated with lower interest rates). However, economists from each paradigm criticized the Fed's failure to recognize hints of recession in early 2000 and its tardy response. While many questioned whether or not the Fed once again was slow to recognize inflation expectations in 2004, neither monetary or fiscal authorities recognized the extent of the housing bubble or the effects of tax regulation of financial institutions since the 1980s. While there is some agreement among economists about the effect that expenditures have on GDP (and on employment and prices) there is little agreement about who should do the spending—businesses, consumers, or the government—or just whose taxes should be cut or increased. There is also disagreement about the priority of economic goals and objectives. Some prefer targeting full employment, while others would rather focus on inflation, with these inflation fights continuing through the economic recession and financial crises that began in 2007. Some economists, including Jamie Galbraith at the University of Texas, focus on links among factors, such as how increased income inequality tends to signal economic downturns in the overall context of unemployment and inflation. (For more information about this linkage, visit the Utip Inequality Watch Web site at utip.gov.utexas.edu.) Some conservatives have resisted surpluses, arguing that politicians would spend any excess revenues on new programs or expansion of existing programs. Over past decades, persistent and ongoing deficits have effectively squelched serious public policy discussions about new spending programs—after all, when can nations "afford" to discuss innovative policies focusing on public goods?

Over the years, one group of economists has as a goal continued reduction of structural deficits and paying down the accumulated federal debt. They focus on the short- and long-run effects of lower interest rate costs on the federal budget and the economy. To them, the opportunity cost of a large deficit is high.

Other economists, such as the late Robert Eisner, a past president of the American Economic Association who taught at Northwestern University, have argued that part of the federal deficit amassed from government spending can be seen as a good thing when viewed in the context of public investment expenditures. Eisner argued, "Much of the debt goes to pay for physical assets—roads, buildings, schools, the defense system—which ought to be separated, as is done by corporations, into a capital budget." He further argued that "budget deficits not only do not inhibit real growth but also that deficit spending is what promotes national growth, prosperity and savings."

So after the dust settles on the Great Recession of 2007–2009, what should a macroeconomic policy aimed at long-term growth look like? As you might expect by now, economists (and politicians) are of at least three different minds on this question. One group, favoring tax cuts, argues that by putting funds into the pockets of taxpayers, greater consumer spending will stimulate business investment, innovation, and long-term growth. Yet even among those favoring tax cuts there are disagreements over who exactly should receive the tax advantages. Should the benefit fall to wealthier taxpayers, in middle or lower income groups? Certainly tax cuts will stimulate economic activity, but is it the best way to stimulate long-term growth?

Certainly not, argues another group, pointing out that tax cuts and spending used separately or together are fine to reverse cyclical downturns in economic activity—but they note that until 2009, structural, not cyclical, deficits have left the United States burdened with a large public debt that may slow down long-term growth. Interest payments must be made on the debt and deficits potentially generate higher interest rates from government borrowing in times when monetary authorities are restraining monetary growth. Critical of the advocates of tax cuts, this group argues that the resulting reduced government revenues simply add to structural deficits. Tax cuts may not have expiration dates and may not be changed after the cycle has reversed. (They also remind us that the political leaders in the United States have shown little fiscal or budgetary restraint in curbing expenditures despite the reduction in revenues.) Their argument, then, is that minimizing or eliminating structural deficits and "paying down" or repaying cyclical deficits during economic upswings (or booms) leads to lower interest rates—thus stimulating long-term economic growth.

A final group argues that neither deep tax cuts nor "buying" lower deficits will ensure long-term growth. They argue that government spending in areas such as education, science, and technology inspires innovation producing long-term investment payoffs. Indeed, in his book *The Internet Galaxy*, Manuel Castells writes about ARPANET, the predecessor of the Internet:

> However, to say that ARPANET was not a military oriented project does not mean that its Defense Department origins were inconsequential for the development of

the Internet. For all the vision and all the competence these scientists displayed in their project, they could never have commanded the level of resources that was necessary to build a computer network and to design all the appropriate technologies. The Cold War provided a context in which there was strong public and government support to invest in cutting-edge science and technology, particularly after the challenge of the Soviet space program became a threat to U.S. national security.

In excerpts from the article, "Forget Bush and Gore; Our Economy Needs Another Khrushchev," Barry Bluestone, professor of political economy at Northeastern University, continues the debate in the tradition of Professor Eisner—but with a twist. Bluestone argues that the great growth in technology generating the productivity surge in the late 1990s was initiated not by Reagan, Clinton, or Greenspan, but by government expenditures that started during the Cold War era. (The Cold War began at the conclusion of World War II and ended in 1989 with the fall of the Berlin Wall and the collapse of the Soviet Union.) These expenditures resulted in defense projects and a space program, which brought miniaturization, computer technology, Teflon, and the Internet, among other innovations. Bluestone argues that the vast expenditures on research and development necessary to fund such projects can be generated only through the deep pockets of the government. Research and development budgets of individual companies—while large when added together—are simply too shallow and unfocused to yield impressive and prolonged results. He also argues that emphasis on education and training in science and mathematics had an enormous impact on today's economic expansion, and that too little interest in these areas bodes ill for the future. So, argues Bluestone, it is not tax cuts or deficit repayments but investment expenditures in science and technology, that stimulate long-term economic growth.

David Leonhardt is also concerned about long-term economic growth as the economy emerges from the 2007–2009 recession. In "The Big Fix," a February 1, 2009, *New York Times Magazine* article Leonhardt raises questions about "where sources of real growth will come from." While Bluestone points to the "deep pockets" of the government, Leonhardt focuses on areas President Barak Obama has outlined that "lay a new foundation for growth," outlining the short-term costs and long-term benefits of public investment in green technology, health care, and education.

Exercises

Read the excerpts from the Bluestone and Leonhardt articles, and answer the following questions.

1. In what ways are Bluestone's arguments similar to Schumpeter's analysis of long waves of economic cycles? How long are the time lags in cycles as predicted by each economist? How would each economist stimulate the economy to yield such technical advances? List the ways macroeconomic policy can stimulate growth. Are any of these policies consistent with Leonhardt's concerns?

2. Look at recent articles or information about the telecom industry, which after explosive growth and huge investments in capital during the late 1990s faced grave economic difficulties when the tech bubble crashed. Contrast this to the development of the first telephone network by AT&T—a government-protected monopoly. Using information in Chapter 7 about competitive and noncompetitive markets, could different government policies in these two eras have yielded different outcomes? Explain.

3. Explain the policies Bluestone and Leonhardt might recommend be used to stabilize the economy. Can the concerns highlighted by Leonhardt be dealt with using Bluestone-type recommendations? Explain.

4. Use the Keynesian-cross diagram and the model of aggregate demand and aggregate supply to show the effects on GDP and prices of spending of the sort Bluestone and Leonhardt recommend. How would the multiplier effects work?

5. Bluestone believes that an emphasis on math and science education during the Cold War advanced today's developments in science and technology. Are you a science or a mathematics major? Are you planning on enrolling in a number of science and mathematics courses during your undergraduate years? Why or why not? What is currently happening to math and science enrollments? Who is receiving Ph.D.s in the sciences and mathematics? What jobs are available for scientists and mathematicians?

6. Eisner and Bluestone seem to think that if the government accumulates deficits to fund expenditures that advance society, we should simply consider the future return to the private sector (and perhaps resulting surpluses) to be a cost of "doing the public's business." Others, particularly groups such as the Concord Coalition, see deficits as bad at all times. Examine Bluestone's arguments, and take a look at information from the Concord Coalition (www.concord.coalition.com), then assess your own position on deficits.

7. In the debate over government tax and expenditure policies, what underlying assumptions of conservatives, liberals, and radicals inform their positions, as detailed in the Bluestone and Leonhardt articles?

8. According to Leonhardt, what are the costs of not "remaking" the U.S. economy and making public investment in areas that generate faster long-term growth?

9. What is an "investment gap"? According to Leonhardt, will simply filling an investment gap restore U.S. growth? Explain. What are some of the potential short-term effects of these public investment efforts?

10. Leonhardt quotes economist Paul Romer as saying "The choices that determine a country's growth rate 'dwarf all other economic policy concerns.'" Why are these choices so important? What can get in the way of growth and growth policies? Why do some kinds of economic activity promote more growth than others? Why is it necessary to have public rather than private investment for these efforts?

Forget Bush and Gore; Our Economy Needs Another Khrushchev

Barry Bluestone

...the conventional wisdom holds that it took three initiatives to restart the American growth machine. The first was Reagan's effort to get government regulation and social spending under control beginning in the 1980s. The second was President Clinton's getting the deficit under control after 1993. And the third was the amazing prowess of Federal Reserve Chairman Alan Greenspan in keeping inflation under control despite strong consumer demand and extraordinarily low unemployment.

In the bad old days, according to this logic, regulations undercut corporate intentions to invest, while public borrowing forced up interest rates to the point that borrowing became too expensive. The threat of inflation dampened enthusiasm for new capital improvements. Consequently, productivity suffered and economic growth slowed.

The annual growth in the nation's real gross domestic product fell from 4.4 percent in the 1960s to 3.2 in the 1970s to 3.0 in the 1980s and finally to only 2.3 percent during the first half of the 1990s. Only *after* Clinton and Congress moved decisively to reduce the federal deficit, and only after Greenspan snuffed out any hint of inflation, could the economy grow again.

That story sounds plausible, and the timing seems exquisite. Yet it's mostly wrong. The best data tracking the U.S. economy reveal that corporations were already investing heavily before the 1990s even though deficits were soaring and we were still worrying about inflation. Moreover, the investments were paying off, the proof being that productivity completely rebounded in the United States' manufacturing sector by the mid-1980s. It was the service sector that was dragging down overall productivity growth, but even in that labor-intensive sector, productivity began to pick up by the early 1990s. So even before we reined in federal deficits and stopped inflation cold, the economy was perched to take off.

Our rapid growth today has its roots in a technological revolution that has been underway for nearly three decades. Since it takes so long for business to move up the "learning curves" of new technologies, and often longer still to diffuse those technologies throughout the economy, there has always been a long lag time between the introduction of innovations and their payoff in the marketplace.

After the introduction of the steam engine in the early nineteenth century, it took nearly two decades for the new technology to yield a growth premium. Only after years of tinkering with that revolutionary technology and teaching a generation of mechanics how to use it did the steam engine provide for a sustained period of economic growth. The same lag pattern occurred between the introduction of the electric motor at the end of the nineteenth century and the realization of long-term growth we witnessed at the beginning of the twentieth century.

The lag phenomenon has recurred with the revolution brought about by the integrated circuit, the computer, and sophisticated software. It took more than two decades for the information-age technology to become sufficiently user-friendly that it could revolutionize production in nearly every goods-producing industry and in the service sector. During the same period, we were educating a work force to operate these marvels. As a result, productivity is now rising at better than 3 percent a year—three times faster than during the early 1990s. Tied to a labor supply growing at 1 percent annually, we have seen better than 4 percent growth for the past five years, every bit as high as we enjoyed during the booming post–World War II era.

Whom do we have to thank for all this? Reagan? Clinton? Greenspan? A more likely candidate is Nikita Khrushchev. Behind the information-age revolution were investments the federal government made beginning decades ago in basic research, education, and training. Khrushchev, the podium-thumping leader of the Soviet empire, challenged the United States to a nuclear arms race and then a space race beginning at the end of the 1950s. We took that challenge.

Massive computing power stuffed into the cramped quarters of missile cones was needed to guide ICBMs and rockets. The government, therefore, paid for the development of the first integrated circuits and microprocessors. Software was needed for the instruction sets for those minicomputers, and the government paid for that as well. The personal computer and all that followed were the direct descendants of those federally sponsored Cold War research projects. Later, it was the Department of Defense's investment in the ARPANET that led to the modern-day Internet.

Without those investments, today's ubiquitous e-commerce would never have come about—or at least it would have been delayed by decades. Moreover, money the federal government poured into science and math education after the launch of Sputnik in 1957 was critical for preparing a generation of scientists and engineers who developed all the new technology.

Alas, Khrushchev is gone, the Cold War is over, and Americans refuse to lavish money on the civilian side to anywhere near the extent we once did on the military. As a result, the federal government has been unwittingly destroying vital elements of the public-private research partnership....

Constrained by the number-one goal of paying down the federal debt as fast as possible, the amount spent on federal research and education has been plummeting, and these new initiatives would do little to reverse that downward trajectory. Back in the mid-1960s, federal spending on research and development was equivalent to 2.15 percent of the gross domestic product. Today, it has fallen to only .8 percent. Over the same period, federal spending on education as a proportion of the GDP has declined by almost half, from 1.07 percent to .56 percent. If *all* of President Clinton's spending plans for education were implemented over the next five years, the share of discretionary spending by the federal government allocated to this vital area would increase from just 5.0 percent to 5.8 percent—and basic research would fare no better. As a percentage of GDP, both education and basic research would continue to decline.

It would be nice to think that the private sector could make up the difference. But increased cost pressures from global competition and the deregulation of such industries as telecommunications have made it more difficult for private firms to set aside funds for basic research. Such investment is highly speculative, the payoffs are distant, and it is often impossible to restrict the benefits to those who paid for the research in the first place. As a result, while private research support is growing, only a small fraction pays for the kind of basic research that powers technological revolutions. And, of course, the private sector finances only a small portion of basic education.

So where is Khrushchev when we need him? We need something like the civilian equivalent of the Cold War to assure us of a continuing stream of technological breakthroughs that can fuel sustained prosperity.

There are many candidates for such government-sponsored research investments. Mounting a fully financed "war on cancer" and other medical scourges is one. Adding to the research on nanotechnology and biotechnology are two more. Certainly we could use more research into alternative fuel supplies and other efforts aimed at the problem of global warming.

On the education front, the federal government could underwrite a program to assure every child in the United States a prekindergarten year of schooling to help them get off on the right foot. Further expansion of federal backing for science and math education could be important as well, especially given the fact that the proportion of college students majoring in science and engineering has not increased since the 1970s....Unfortunately, the tax-cut nostrums of the Republicans and the debt obsession of many Democrats divert our attention from the growing federal-investment deficit that could ultimately condemn the nation to slower growth.

Source: Barry Bluestone, "Forget Bush and Gore; Our Economy Needs Another Khrushchev," *The Chronicle Review*, Jan. 5, 2001, pp. 311–312. Copyright © Barry Bluestone. Used with permission.

The Big Fix

David Leonhardt

I. Whither Growth?

The economy will recover. It won't recover anytime soon. It is likely to get significantly worse over the course of 2009, no matter what President Obama and Congress do. And resolving the financial crisis will require both aggressiveness and creativity. In fact, the main lesson from other crises of the past century is that governments tend to err on the side of too much caution—of taking the punch bowl away before the party has truly started up again. "The mistake the United States made during the Depression and the Japanese made during the '90s was too much start–stop in their policies," said Timothy Geithner, Obama's choice for Treasury secretary, when I went to visit him in his transition office a few weeks ago. Japan announced stimulus measures even as it was cutting other government spending. Franklin Roosevelt flirted with fiscal discipline midway through the New Deal, and the country slipped back into decline....

Once governments finally decide to use the enormous resources at their disposal, they have typically been able to shock an economy back to life. They can put to work the people, money and equipment sitting idle, until the private sector is willing to begin using them again. The prescription developed almost a century ago by John Maynard Keynes does appear to work.

But while Washington has been preoccupied with stimulus and bailouts, another, equally important issue has received far less attention—and the resolution of it is far more uncertain. What will happen once the paddles have been applied and the economy's heart starts beating again? How should the new American economy be remade? Above all, how fast will it grow?

That last question may sound abstract, even technical, compared with the current crisis. Yet the consequences of a country's growth rate are not abstract at all. Slow growth makes almost all problems worse. Fast growth helps solve them. As Paul Romer, an economist at Stanford University, has said, the choices that determine a country's growth rate "dwarf all other economic-policy concerns."

Growth is the only way for a government to pay off its debts in a relatively quick and painless fashion, allowing tax revenues to increase without tax rates having to rise. That is essentially what happened in the years after World War II. When the war ended, the federal government's debt equaled 120 percent of the gross domestic product (more than twice as high as its likely level by the end of next year). The rapid economic growth of the 1950s and '60s—more than 4 percent a year, compared with 2.5 percent in this decade—quickly whittled that debt away. Over the coming 25 years, if growth could be lifted by just one-tenth of a percentage point a year, the extra tax revenue would completely pay for an $800 billion stimulus package.

Yet there are real concerns that the United States' economy won't grow enough to pay off its debts easily and ensure rising living standards, as happened in the postwar decades. The fraternity of growth experts in the economics profession predicts that the economy, on its current path, will grow more slowly in the next couple of decades than over the past couple. They are concerned in part because two of the economy's most powerful recent engines have been exposed as a mirage: the explosion in consumer debt and spending, which lifted short-term growth at the expense of future growth, and the great Wall Street boom, which depended partly on activities that had very little real value.

Richard Freeman, a Harvard economist, argues that our bubble economy had something in common with the old Soviet economy. The Soviet Union's growth was artificially raised by massive industrial output that ended up having little use. Ours was artificially raised by mortgage-backed securities, collateralized debt obligations and even the occasional Ponzi scheme.

Where will new, real sources of growth come from? Wall Street is not likely to cure the nation's economic problems. Neither, obviously, is Detroit. Nor is Silicon Valley, at least not by itself. Well before the housing bubble burst, the big productivity gains brought about by the 1990s technology boom seemed to be petering out, which suggests that the Internet may not be able to fuel decades of economic growth in the way that the industrial inventions of the early 20th century did. Annual economic growth in the current decade, even excluding the dismal contributions that 2008 and 2009 will make to the average, has been the slowest of any decade since the 1930s.

So for the first time in more than 70 years, the epicenter of the American economy can be placed outside of California or New York or the industrial Midwest. It can be placed in Washington. Washington won't merely be given the task of pulling the economy out of the immediate crisis. It will also have to figure out how to put the American economy on a more sustainable path—to help it achieve fast, broadly shared growth and do so without the benefit of a bubble. Obama said as much in his inauguration speech when he pledged to overhaul Washington's approach to education, health care, science and infrastructure, all in an effort to "lay a new foundation for growth."

For centuries, people have worried that economic growth had limits—that the only way for one group to prosper was at the expense of another. The pessimists, from Malthus and the Luddites and on, have been proved wrong again and again. Growth is not finite. But it is also not inevitable. It requires a strategy....

III. The Investment Gap

One good way to understand the current growth slowdown is to think of the debt-fueled consumer-spending spree of the past 20 years as a symbol of an even larger problem. As a country we have been spending too much on the present and not enough on the future. We have been consuming rather than investing. We're suffering from investment-deficit disorder.

You can find examples of this disorder in just about any realm of American life. Walk into a doctor's office and you will be asked to fill out a long form with the most basic kinds of information that you have provided dozens of times before. Walk into a doctor's office in many other rich countries and that information—as well as your medical history—will be stored in computers. These electronic records not only reduce hassle; they also reduce medical errors. Americans cannot avail themselves of this innovation despite the fact that the United States spends far more on health care, per person, than any other country. We are spending our money to consume medical treatments, many of which have only marginal health benefits, rather than to invest it in ways that would eventually have far broader benefits.

Along similar lines, Americans are indefatigable buyers of consumer electronics, yet a smaller share of households in the United States has broadband Internet service than in Canada, Japan, Britain, South Korea and about a dozen other countries. Then there's education: this country once led the world in educational attainment by a wide margin. It no longer does. And transportation: a trip from Boston to Washington, on the fastest train in this country, takes six-and-a-half hours. A trip from Paris to Marseilles, roughly the same distance, takes three hours—a result of the French government's commitment to infrastructure.

These are only a few examples. Tucked away in the many statistical tables at the Commerce Department are numbers on how much the government and the private sector spend on investment and research—on highways, software, medical research and other things likely to yield future benefits. Spending by the private sector hasn't changed much over time. It was equal to 17 percent of G.D.P. 50 years ago, and it is about 17 percent now. But spending by the government—federal, state and local—has changed. It has dropped from about 7 percent of G.D.P. in the 1950s to about 4 percent now.

Governments have a unique role to play in making investments for two main reasons. Some activities, like mass transportation and pollution reduction, have societal benefits but not necessarily financial ones, and the private sector simply won't undertake them. And while many other kinds of investments do bring big financial returns, only a fraction of those returns go to the original investor. This makes the private sector reluctant to jump in. As a result, economists say that the private sector tends to spend less on research and investment than is economically ideal....

Even so, the idea that the government would be playing a much larger role in promoting economic growth would have sounded radical, even among Democrats, until just a few months ago. After all, the European countries that have tried guiding huge swaths of their economies—that have kept their arms around the "commanding heights," in Lenin's enduring phrase—have grown even more slowly than this country in recent years. But the credit crunch and the deepening recession have changed the discussion here. The federal government seems as if it was doing too little to take advantage of the American economy's enormous assets: its size, its openness and its mobile, risk-taking work force. The government is also one of the few large entities today able to borrow at a low interest rate. It alone can raise the capital that could transform the economy in the kind of fundamental ways....

IV. Stimulus vs. Transformation

The Obama administration's first chance to build a new economy—an investment economy—is the stimulus package that has been dominating policy discussions in Washington. Obama has repeatedly said he wants it to be a down payment on solving bigger problems. The twin goals, he said recently, are to "immediately jump-start job creation and long-term growth." But it is not easy to balance those goals....

Sometimes a project can give an economy a lift and also lead to transformation, but sometimes the goals are at odds, at least in the short term. Nothing demonstrates this quandary quite so well as green jobs, which are often cited as the single best hope for driving the post-bubble economy. Obama himself makes this case. Consumer spending has been the economic engine of the past two decades, he has said. Alternative energy will supposedly be the engine of the future—a way to save the planet, reduce the amount of money flowing to hostile oil-producing countries and revive the American economy, all at once. Put in these terms, green jobs sounds like a free lunch.

Green jobs can certainly provide stimulus. Obama's proposal includes subsidies for companies that make wind turbines, solar power and other alternative energy sources, and these subsidies will create some jobs. But the subsidies will not be nearly enough to eliminate the gap between the cost of dirty, carbon-based energy and clean energy. Dirty-energy sources—oil, gas and coal—are cheap. That's why we have become so dependent on them.

The only way to create huge numbers of clean-energy jobs would be to raise the cost of dirty-energy sources, as Obama's proposed cap-and-trade carbon-reduction program would do, to make them more expensive than clean energy. This is where the green-jobs dream gets complicated.

For starters, of the $700 billion we spend each year on energy, more than half stays inside this country. It goes to coal companies or utilities here, not to Iran or Russia. If we begin to use less electricity, those utilities will cut jobs. Just as important, the current, relatively low price of energy allows other companies—manufacturers, retailers, even white-collar enterprises—to sell all sorts of things at a profit. Raising that cost would raise the cost of almost everything that businesses do. Some projects that would have been profitable to Boeing, Kroger or Microsoft in the current economy no longer will be. Jobs that would otherwise have been created won't be. As Rob Stavins, a leading environmental economist, says, "Green jobs will, to some degree, displace other jobs." Just think about what happened when gas prices began soaring last spring: sales of some hybrids increased, but vehicle sales fell overall.

None of this means that Obama's climate policy is a mistake. Raising the price of carbon makes urgent sense, for the well-being of the planet and of the human race. And the economic costs of a serious climate policy are unlikely to be nearly as big as the alarmists—lobbyists and members of Congress trying to protect old-line energy industries—suggest. Various analyses of Obama's cap-and-trade plan, including one by Stavins, suggest that after it is fully implemented, it would cost less than 1 percent of gross domestic product a year, or about $100 billion in today's terms. That cost is entirely manageable. But it's still a cost.

Or perhaps we should think of it as an investment. Like so much in the economy, our energy policy has been geared toward the short term. Inexpensive energy made daily life easier and less expensive for all of us. Building a green economy, on the other hand, will require some sacrifice. In the end, that sacrifice should pay a handsome return in the form of icecaps that don't melt and droughts that don't happen—events with costs of their own. Over time, the direct economic costs of a new energy policy may also fall. A cap-and-trade program will create incentives for the private sector to invest in alternative energy, which will lead to innovations and lower prices. Some of the new clean-energy spending, meanwhile, really will replace money now flowing overseas and create jobs here.

But all those benefits will come later. The costs will come sooner, which is a big reason we do not already have a green economy—or an investment economy.

V. Curing Inefficiencies

Washington's challenge on energy policy is to rewrite the rules so that the private sector can start building one of tomorrow's big industries. On health care, the challenge is keeping one of tomorrow's industries from growing too large.

For almost two decades, spending on health care grew rapidly, no matter what the rest of the economy was doing. Some of this is only natural. As a society gets richer and the basic comforts of life become commonplace, people will choose to spend more of their money on health and longevity instead of a third car or a fourth television.

Much of the increases in health care spending, however, are a result of government rules that have made the sector a fabulously—some say uniquely—inefficient sector. These inefficiencies have left the United States spending far more than other countries on medicine and, by many measures, getting worse results. The costs of health care are now so large that it has become one problem that cannot be solved by growth alone. It's qualitatively different from the other budget problems facing the government, like the Wall Street bailout, the stimulus, the war in Iraq or Social Security.

You can see that by looking at various costs as a share of one year of economic output—that is, gross domestic product. Surprisingly, the debt that the federal government has already accumulated doesn't present much of a problem. It is equal to about $6 trillion, or 40 percent of G.D.P., a level that is slightly lower than the average of the past six decades. The bailout, the stimulus and the rest of the deficits over the next two years will probably add about 15 percent of G.D.P. to the debt. That will take debt to almost 60 percent, which is above its long-term average but well below the levels of the 1950s. But the unfinanced parts of Medicare, the spending that the government has promised over and above the taxes it will collect in the coming decades requires another decimal place. They are equal to more than 200 percent of current G.D.P.

During the campaign, Obama talked about the need to control medical costs and mentioned a few ideas for doing so, but he rarely lingered on the topic. He spent more time talking about expanding health-insurance coverage, which would raise the government's bill. After the election, however, when time came to name a budget director, Obama sent a different message. He appointed Peter Orszag, who over the last two years has become one of the country's leading experts on the looming budget mess that is health care. . . .

"One of the blessings in the current environment is that we have significant capacity to expand and sell Treasury debt," he [Orszag] told me recently. "If we didn't have that, and if the financial markets didn't have confidence that we would repay that debt, we would be in even more dire straits than we are." Absent a health care overhaul, the federal government's lenders around the world may eventually grow nervous about its ability to repay its debts. That, in turn, will cause them to demand higher interest rates to cover their risk when lending to the United States. Facing higher interest rates, the government won't be able to afford the kind of loans needed to respond to a future crisis, be it financial or military. The higher rates will also depress economic growth, aggravating every other problem. . . .

Orszag would begin his talks by explaining that the problem is not one of demographics but one of medicine. "It's not primarily that we're going to have more 85-year-olds," he said during a September speech in California. "It's primarily that each 85-year-old in the future will cost us a lot more than they cost us today." The medical system will keep coming up with expensive new treatments, and Medicare will keep reimbursing them, even if they bring little benefit. . . .

VI. Graduates Equal Growth

A great appeal of green jobs—or, for that matter, of a growing and efficient health care sector—is that they make it possible to imagine what tomorrow's economy might look like. They are concrete. When somebody wonders, What will replace Wall Street? What will replace housing? they can be given an answer.

As answers go, green jobs and health care are fine. But they probably aren't the best answers. The best one is less concrete. It also has a lot more historical evidence on its side.

Last year, two labor economists, Claudia Goldin and Lawrence Katz, published a book called "The Race Between Education and Technology." It is as much a work of history—the history of education—as it is a work of economics. Goldin and Katz set out to answer the question of how much an education really matters. They are themselves products of public schools, she of New York and he of Los Angeles, and they have been a couple for two decades. They are liberals (Katz served as the chief economist under Robert Reich in Bill Clinton's Labor Department), but their book has been praised by both the right and the left. "I read the Katz and Goldin book," Matthew Slaughter, an associate dean of Dartmouth's business school who was an economic adviser to George W. Bush, recently told me, "and there's part of me that can't fathom that half the presidential debates weren't about a couple of facts in that book." Summers wrote a blurb for the book, calling it "the definitive treatment" of income inequality.

The book's central fact is that the United States has lost its once-wide lead in educational attainment. South Korea and Denmark graduate a larger share of their population from college—and Australia, Japan and the United Kingdom are close on our heels.

Goldin and Katz explain that the original purpose of American education was political, to educate the citizens of a democracy. By the start of the 20th century, though, the purpose had become blatantly economic. As parents saw that high-school graduates were getting most of the good jobs, they started a grass-roots movement, known as the high-school movement, to demand free, public high schools in their communities. "Middletown," the classic 1929 sociological study of life in Indiana, reported that education "evokes the fervor of a religion, a means of salvation, among a large section of the population."

At the time, some European intellectuals dismissed the new American high schools as wasteful. Instead of offering narrowly tailored apprentice programs, the United States was accused of overeducating its masses (or at least its white masses). But Goldin and Katz, digging into old population surveys, show that the American system paid huge dividends. High-school graduates filled the ranks of companies like General Electric and John Deere and used their broad base of skills to help their employers become global powers. And these new white-collar workers weren't the only ones to benefit. A high-school education also paid off for blue-collar workers. Those with a diploma were far more likely to enter newer, better-paying, more technologically advanced industries. They became plumbers, jewelers, electricians, auto mechanics and railroad engineers.

Not only did mass education increase the size of the nation's economic pie; it also evened out the distribution. The spread of high schools—by 1940, half of teenagers were getting a diploma—meant that graduates were no longer an elite group. In economic terms, their supply had increased, which meant that the wage premium that came with a diploma was now spread among a larger group of workers. Sure enough, inequality fell rapidly in the middle decades of the 20th century.

But then the great education boom petered out, starting in the late 1960s. The country's worst high schools never got their graduation rates close to 100 percent, while many of the fast-growing community colleges and public colleges, which were educating middle-class and poorer students, had low graduation rates. Between the early 1950s and early '80s, the share of young adults receiving a bachelor's degree jumped to 24 percent, from 7 percent. In the 30 years since, the share has only risen to 32 percent. Nearly all of the recent gains have come among women. For the first time on record, young men in the last couple of decades haven't been much more educated than their fathers were.

Goldin and Katz are careful to say that economic growth is not simply a matter of investing in education. And we can all name exceptions to the general rule. Bill Gates dropped out of college (though, as Malcolm Gladwell explains in his recent book, "Outliers," Gates received a fabulously intense computer-programming education while in high school). Some college graduates struggle to make a good living, and many will lose their jobs in this recession. But these are exceptions. Goldin's and Katz's thesis is that the 20th century was the American century in large part because this country led the world in education. The last 30 years, when educational gains slowed markedly, have been years of slower growth and rising inequality.

Their argument happens to be supported by a rich body of economic literature that didn't even make it into the book. More-educated people are healthier, live longer and, of course, make more money. Countries that educate more of their citizens tend to grow faster than similar countries that do not. The same is true of states and regions within this country. Crucially, the income gains tend to come after the education gains. What distinguishes thriving Boston from the other struggling cities of New England? Part of the answer is the relative share of children who graduate from college. The two most affluent immigrant groups in modern America—Asian-Americans and Jews—are also the most educated. In recent decades, as the educational attainment of men has stagnated, so have their wages. The median male worker is roughly as educated as he was 30 years ago and makes roughly the same in hourly pay. The median female worker is far more educated than she was 30 years ago and makes 30 percent more than she did then.

There really is no mystery about why education would be the lifeblood of economic growth. On the most basic level, education helps people figure out how to make objects and accomplish tasks more efficiently. It allows companies to make complex products that the rest of the world wants to buy and thus creates high-wage jobs. Education may not be as tangible as green jobs. But it helps a society leverage every other investment it makes, be it in medicine, transportation or alternative energy. Education—educating more people and educating them better—appears to be the best single bet that a society can make....

The Obama administration has suggested that education reform is an important goal. The education secretary is Arne Duncan, the former school superintendent in Chicago, who pushed for education changes there based on empirical data. Obama advisers say that the administration plans to use the education money in the stimulus package as leverage. States that reward good teaching and use uniform testing standards—rather than the choose-your-own-yardstick approach of the No Child Left Behind law—may get more money.

But it is still unclear just how much of a push the administration will make. With the financial crisis looming so large, something as sprawling and perennially plagued as education can seem like a sideshow. Given everything else on its agenda, the Obama administration could end up financing a few promising pilot programs without actually changing much. States, for their part, will be cutting education spending to balance their budgets....

Economists don't talk much about cultural norms. They prefer to emphasize prices, taxes and other incentives. And the transformation of the American economy will depend very much on such incentives: financial aid, Medicare reimbursements, energy prices and marginal tax rates. But it will also depend on forces that aren't quite so easy to quantify.

Orszag, on his barnstorming tour to talk about the health care system, argued that his fellow economists were making a mistake by paying so little attention to norms. After all, doctors in Minnesota don't work under a different Medicare system than doctors in New Jersey. But they do act differently.

The norms of the last two decades or so—consume before invest; worry about the short term, not the long term—have been more than just a reflection of the economy. They have also *affected* the economy. Chief executives have fought for paychecks that their predecessors would have considered obscenely large. Technocrats inside Washington's regulatory agencies, after listening to their bosses talk endlessly about the dangers of overregulation, made quite sure that they weren't regulating too much. Financial engineering became a more appealing career track than actual engineering or science. In one of the small gems in their book, Goldin and Katz write that towns and cities with a large elderly population once devoted a higher-than-average share of their taxes to schools. Apparently, age made them see the benefits of education. In recent decades, though, the relationship switched. Older towns spent less than average on schools. You can imagine voters in these places asking themselves, "What's in it for me?"

By any standard, the Obama administration faces an imposing economic to-do list. It will try to end the financial crisis and recession as quickly as possible, even as it starts work on an agenda that will inspire opposition from a murderers' row of interest groups: Wall Street, Big Oil, Big Coal, the American Medical Association and teachers' unions. Some items on the agenda will fail.

But the same was true of the New Deal and the decades after World War II, the period that is obviously the model for the Obama years. Roosevelt and

Truman both failed to pass universal health insurance or even a program like Medicare. Yet the successes of those years—Social Security, the highway system, the G.I. Bill, the National Science Foundation, the National Labor Relations Board—had a huge effect on the culture.

The American economy didn't simply grow rapidly in the late 1940s, 1950s and 1960s. It grew rapidly and gave an increasing share of its bounty to the vast middle class. Middle-class incomes soared during those years, while income growth at the very top of the ladder, which had been so great in the 1920s, slowed down. The effects were too great to be explained by a neat package of policies, just as the last few decades can't be explained only by education, investment and the like.

When Washington sets out to rewrite the rules for the economy, it can pass new laws and shift money from one program to another. But the effects of those changes are not likely to be merely the obvious ones. The changes can also send signals. They can influence millions of individual decisions—about the schools people attend, the jobs they choose, the medical care they request—and, in the process, reshape the economy.

Source: David Leonhardt. "The Big Fix," February 1, 2008. *The New York Times.* From the *New York Times,* © August 13, 2009 the *New York Times.* All rights reserved. Used by permission and protected by the Copyright Laws of the United States. The printing, copying, redistribution, or retransmission of the Material without express written permission is prohibited.

The Washington Post.

PART FOUR

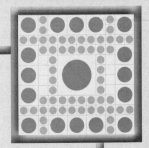

International Economics and Finance

With each passing decade, the nations of the world grow increasingly interdependent. When weighing various macroeconomic policy options, U.S. decision makers must consider international economic conditions. In the past, economists were primarily concerned with domestic monetary and fiscal policy and any perceived impact international activities might have on these policies. As far as international issues were concerned, decision makers examined the value of a nation's currency, or its exchange rate; the balance of payments; and perhaps protectionist tendencies that might exist in the world economy. Today, however, more complex questions arise involving volatile exchange rates; the economic power of an increasingly unified Europe; the integration of Eastern Europe and the former Soviet Union into the Western market system; China and India's rapid economic growth; the changes in various international institutions such as the International Monetary Fund, the World Bank, and the World Trade Organization; the outcome of the UN's Millennium Development Goals focused on reducing global poverty and arresting the global HIV/AIDS pandemic; the world's challenge to reduce its dependence on nonrenewable energy, especially petroleum, and to develop renewable and sustainable energy resources; and the world's need to address the pressing environmental challenges from global warming and climate change to issues dealing with fishing, grazing, soil, water, food, air pollution, and biodiversity. All of this is in the context of global instability and uncertainty related to the U.S. war in Iraq and terrorism. These trends and questions challenge the dynamics of twenty-first-century globalization.

Global economic activity has become more integrated by technological change transforming production, finance, trade, information systems, and communications throughout the world. These changes have caused economic and financial markets to become more integrated, and this increased interdependence has affected national political decisions, social and environmental policy, and culture.

In Part 4 we will explore all of these issues and questions. Chapter 19, "International Trade and Interdependence," examines the recent history of world trade, the role of trade in the U.S. economy, the theory of free trade, the case for protectionism, and the recent experience with trade integration and liberalization. Chapter 20, "International Finance," explores the concepts of the international balance of payments and exchange rates including the recent history of the U.S. dollar. Chapter 21, "The Economics of Developing Nations," focuses on the reality of global poverty, the basic economic problems of developing nations, and competing schools of thought on development and underdevelopment. Finally, Chapter 22, "Modern Economic Systems," will revisit the concepts of capitalism and socialism, explore the liberal and coordinated market economies that make up the developed world, and contrast the economic transitions toward market capitalism that have taken place in Russia and China. The concept of sustainability will be examined in the context of the world's environmental and energy challenges. The final "Thinking Critically" section focuses on the issues related to the future of globalization.

CHAPTER NINETEEN

International Trade and Interdependence

❖Introduction

As we have noted previously, interdependence among nations is a major feature of the modern world economy, and this will be a salient theme throughout the remainder of this book. To understand this concept properly and apply it to the problems we will be examining, we must be more specific. By the term economic interdependence, we mean that all countries are affected by the events of an economic nature that occur in many other countries. For example, many industrialized nations rely on developing nations for raw materials and other resources. In turn, many developing nations import manufactured finished goods from industrialized nations. The degree of interdependence is, of course, different for every nation. For example, the Japanese economy is seriously affected by increased oil prices yet relatively unaffected by Costa Rica's decision to increase banana prices. On the other hand, the Costa Rican economy, also strongly affected by an oil price increase, has the flexibility to shift its imports of steel from the United States to Japan.

Economic interdependence describes the effect of the complex international flow of goods, services, and capital among nations. It helps us understand how individuals, businesses, and nations must first exchange their currencies before exchanging goods and services. To acquire Japanese Toyotas, a U.S. auto importer must first exchange dollars for yen in a currency market. Then, the automobile transaction can be completed.

Financial markets are interdependent as well. For example, if real interest rates fall in Germany and at the same time rise in the United States, investors are likely to sell their German bonds and invest the proceeds in U.S. bonds generating a better return. If Mexico experiences political instability or increasing inflation, domestic and foreign investors will likely transfer funds from Mexico to the United States or Europe. Information and communications technology has increased both the magnitude and speed of these transfers and facilitated international interdependence.

The nature of this contemporary interdependence involves not only the exchange of goods and services but technology transfers, financial capital movements, and factors affecting the *international division of labor. For the past four centuries, raw materials and resources as well as technology provided the impetus for trade. Indeed, much of the motivation for the geographical explorations of the fifteenth century was the search for trade routes and later for colonies from which raw materials could be exported cheaply. Later, with the Industrial Revolution, the ability to manufacture and export products cheaply became a motivation for trade. While capital has always been highly mobile, seeking the highest profits worldwide, today the transfer of technology has made it very easy to set up operations in places where wages and other production costs are low. Increasingly, industrialized nations are losing jobs and exports to developing countries, which offer an abundance of low-wage labor.*

INTERNATIONAL TRADE AND INTERDEPENDENCE

The 1990s brought forward a decade of rapid globalization. This globalization was characterized by the increased volume of international trade in goods and services, financial flows and services, the migration of labor, and technological changes in the areas of communications, information, finance, and production. The global economic and financial system was fundamentally transformed in this decade. Combined with a prevailing economic philosophy that focused on the benefits of free markets, free trade, unrestricted capital flows, and deregulation, there were distinct uneven outcomes between nations and between citizens within nations. By the end of the 1990s, there was a worldwide anti-globalization movement calling into question the efficacy of the liberalization character of the new global system.

The first decade of the twenty-first century has seen the continuation of this debate as the rapid and impressive economic growth of both China and India benefited from markets open to them. In this decade China and Japan have used their large trade surplus to buy U.S. debt, thus financing both public and private U.S. expenditures financed by borrowing. The global financial crisis and great recession that began in late 2007 and continued through 2009 left the global financial and economic system facing many serious challenges and questions. In addition, the issues of global poverty, unemployment, public health, environmental degradation, energy sustainability, food supply and prices, and climate change present serious long-term challenges for the global community.

WORLD TRADE

Figures 19.1 and 19.2 show the rapid process of globalization and trade liberalization that has resulted in a sustained increase in the growth of world real GDP growth. Figure 19.3 shows the slowing of the world trade volume, beginning in 2007. In Fig. 19.1, we can observe that the trend for world real GDP growth rose to around 4 percent by 2005, yet fell dramatically in 2009 to a negative 1.6 percent. It is expected to recover to its historic trend line after 2012. Figure 19.2 shows that between 2000 and 2007, emerging and developing economies grew at rates between 4 and 8 percent while advanced economies grew rates of 3.5 percent or less. The economic downturn in late 2007 slowed emerging and developing economies growth rates to 2 percent, while advanced economies saw growth fall by −4 percent. Nevertheless, the International Monetary Fund in its 2009 *Global Prospects and Policies Report* estimates a return to positive trends when the recession ends.

FIGURE 19.1 The Rapid Growth of Globalization

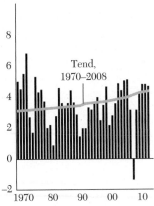

Note: *Annual percent change unless otherwise noted.*

The global economy is undergoing its most severe recession of the postwar period. World real GDP dropped in 2009, with advanced economies experiencing deep contractions and emerging and developing economies slowing abruptly. Trade volumes fell sharply, while inflation subsided quickly.

Source: IMF Global Prospects: Policies, Chapter 1, 2009.

The Impact of International Trade on the United States

Since the early 1980s, international trade has continued to become a larger and larger share of the U.S. economy. By 2000, imports of goods represented 13 percent of the GDP and exports of goods represented 8 percent of the GDP, together representing more than 20 percent of the GDP. Since the early 1980s, the United States has experienced a trade deficit. By 1987, the trade deficit had increased to $40 billion. With a change in policies and a determined depreciation of

FIGURE 19.2 Real GDP Growth—1970–2010

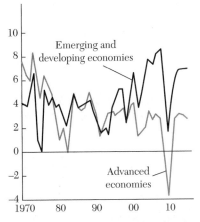

Note: Annual percent change unless otherwise noted.

Source: IMF Global Prospects: Policies, Chapter 1, 2009.

FIGURE 19.3 World Trade Volume (goods and services)

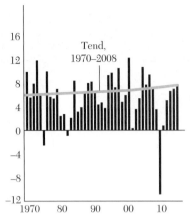

Note: Annual percent change unless otherwise noted.

Source: IMF Global Prospects: Policies, Chapter 1, 2009.

the U.S. dollar (to make exports more competitive and imports more expensive), the U.S. trade deficit narrowed in 1991 to less than $10 billion. Yet, in the 1990s, globalization and the global movement toward the liberalization of trade and markets along with a returning strong U.S. dollar produced a trend toward larger trade deficits. This process accelerated from the period 1997 to the present.

Table 19.1 GDP and Merchandise Trade by Region, 2006–2008 (Annual % change at constant prices)

	GDP			Exports			Imports		
	2006	2007	2008	2006	2007	2008	2006	2007	2008
World	3.7	3.5	1.7	8.5	6.0	2.0	8.0	6.0	2.0
North America	2.9	2.1	1.1	8.5	5.0	1.5	6.0	2.0	−2.5
United States	2.8	2.0	1.1	10.5	7.0	5.5	5.5	1.0	−4.0
South and Central America[a]	6.1	6.6	5.3	4.0	3.0	1.5	15.5	17.5	15.5
Europe	3.1	2.8	1.0	7.5	4.0	0.5	7.5	4.0	−1.0
European Union (27)	3.0	2.8	1.0	7.5	3.5	0.0	7.0	3.5	−1.0
Commonwealth of Independent States (CIS)	7.5	8.4	5.5	6.0	7.5	6.0	20.5	20.0	15.0
Africa	5.7	5.8	5.0	1.5	4.5	3.0	10.0	14.0	13.0
Middle East	5.2	5.5	5.7	3.0	4.0	3.0	5.5	14.0	10.0
Asia	4.6	4.9	2.0	13.5	11.5	4.5	8.5	8.0	4.0
China	11.6	11.9	9.0	22.0	19.5	8.5	16.5	13.5	4.0
Japan	2.0	2.4	−0.7	10.0	9.5	2.5	2.0	1.5	−1.0
India	9.8	9.3	7.9	11.0	13.0	7.0	8.0	16.0	12.5
Newly industrialized economies (4)[b]	5.6	5.6	1.7	13.0	9.0	3.5	8.0	6.0	3.5

[a]Includes the Caribbean.
[b]Hong Kong, China; Republic of Korea; Singapore and Chinese Taipei.

Source: World Trade Secretariat 2009.

Table 19.2 World Merchandise Trade by Region and Selected Country, 2008 ($bn and %)

	Exports		Imports	
	Value 2008	Annual % change 2000–2008	Value 2008	Annual % change 2000–2008
World	15,775	12	16,120	12
North America	2,049	7	2,909	7
United States	1,301	7	2,166	7
Canada	456	6	418	7
Mexico	292	7	323	7
South and Central America[a]	602	15	595	14
Brazil	198	17	183	15
Other South and Central America[a]	404	14	413	14
Europe	6,456	12	6,833	12
European Union (27)	5,913	12	6,268	12
Germany	1,465	13	1,206	12
France	609	8	708	10
Netherlands	634	13	574	13
Italy	540	11	556	11
United Kingdom[b]	458	6	632	8
Commonwealth of Independent States (CIS)	703	22	493	25
Russian Federation[c]	472	21	292	26
Africa	561	18	466	17
South Africa	81	13	99	16
Africa less South Africa	481	19	367	18
Oil exporters[d]	347	21	137	21
Non-oil exporters	133	15	229	16
Middle East	1,047	19	575	17
Asia	4,355	13	4,247	14
China	1,428	24	1,133	22
Japan	782	6	762	9
India	179	20	292	24
Newly Industrialized economies (4)[e]	1,033	10	1,093	10
Memorandum Items				
Developing economies	6,025	15	5,494	15
MERCOSUR[f]	279	16	259	14
ASEAN[g]	990	11	936	12
EU (27) extra-trade	1,928	12	2,283	12
Least Developed Countries (LDCs)	176	22	157	17

[a]Includes the Caribbean. For composition of groups see the Technical Notes of WTO, International Trade Statistics, 2008.
[b]The 2007 annual change was affected by a reduction in trade associated with fraudulent VAT declaration. For further information, refer to the special notes of the monthly *UK Trade First Release.*
[c]Imports are valued f.o.b.
[d]Algeria, Angola, Cameroon, Chad, Congo, Equatorial Guinea, Gabon, Libya, Nigeria, Sudan.
[e]Hong Kong, China; Republic of Korea; Singapore and Chinese Taipei.
[f]Common Market of the Southern Cone: Argentina, Brazil, Paraguay, Uruguay
[g]Association of Southeast Asian Nations: Brunei, Cambodia, Indonesia, Laos, Malaysia, Myanmar, Philippines, Singapore, Thailand, Viet Nam.

Source: World Trade Secretariat 2009.

Table 19.3 World Exports of Commercial Services by Region and Selected Country, 2008 ($bn and %)

	Exports		Imports	
	Value 2008	**Annual % change 2000–2008**	**Value 2008**	**Annual % change 2000–2008**
World	3,730	12	3,470	12
North America	603	8	473	7
United States	522	8	364	7
South and Central America[b]	109	11	117	10
Brazil	29	16	44	14
Europe	1,919	13	1,628	12
European Union (27)	1,738	13	1,516	12
Germany	235	15	285	10
United Kingdom	283	12	199	9
France	153	9	137	11
Italy	123	10	132	12
Spain	143	13	108	16
Commonwealth of Independent States (CIS)	83	22	114	22
Russian Federation	50	23	75	21
Africa	88	14	121	16
Egypt	25	12	16	11
South Africa[a]	13	13	17	15
Middle East	94	14	158	16
Israel	24	6	20	7
Asia	837	13	858	11
Japan	144	10	166	6
China[a]	137	—	152	—
India[a]	106	—	91	—
Four East Asian traders[c]	271	11	247	10

[a]Secretariat estimates.
[b]Includes the Caribbean. For composition of groups see Chapter IV Metadata of WTO International Trade Statistics, 2008.
[c]Chinese Taipei; Hong Kong, China; Republic of Korea and Singapore.

Note: While provisional full year data were available in early March for 50 countries accounting for more than two-thirds of world commercial services trade, estimates for most other countries are based on data for the first three quarters (the first six months in the case of China).

Source: World Trade Secretariat 2009.

Table 19.4 Merchandise Trade: Leading Exporters and Importers, 2008 ($bn and %)

Rank Exporters	Value	Share	Annual % Change	Rank Importers	Value	Share	Annual % Change
1. Germany	1,465	9.1	11	1. United States	2,166	13.2	7
2. China	1,428	8.9	17	2. Germany	1,206	7.3	14
3. United States	1,301	8.1	12	3. China	1,133	6.9	19
4. Japan	782	4.9	10	4. Japan	762	4.6	22
5. Netherlands	634	3.9	15	5. France	708	4.3	14
6. France	609	3.8	10	6. United Kingdom	632	3.8	1

Table 19.4 Continued

Rank Exporters	Value	Share	Annual % Change	Rank Importers	Value	Share	Annual % Change
7. Italy	540	3.3	10	7. Netherlands	574	3.5	16
8. Belgium	477	3.0	10	8. Italy	556	3.4	10
9. Russian Federation	472	2.9	33	9. Belgium	470	2.9	14
10. United Kingdom	458	2.8	4	10. Korea, Republic of	435	2.7	22
11. Canada	456	2.8	8	11. Canada	418	2.5	7
12. Korea, Republic of	422	2.6	14	12. Spain	402	2.5	3
13. Hong Kong, China	370	2.3	6	13. Hong Kong, China	393	2.4	6
- domestic exports	17	0.1	—	- retained imports	98	0.6	—
- re-exports	353	2.2	—				
14. Singapore	338	2.1	13	14. Mexico	323	2.0	9
- domestic exports	176	1.1	13				
- re-exports	162	1.0	13				
15. Saudi Arabia[a]	329	2.0	40	15. Singapore	320	1.9	22
				- retained imports[b]	157	1.0	31
16. Mexico	292	1.8	7	16. Russian Federation[c]	292	1.8	31
17. Spain	268	1.7	6	17. India	292	1.8	35
18. Taipei, Chinese	256	1.6	4	18. Taipei, Chinese	240	1.5	10
19. United Arab Emirates[a]	232	1.4	28	19. Poland	204	1.2	23
20. Switzerland	200	1.2	16	20. Turkey	202	1.2	19
21. Malaysia	200	1.2	13	21. Australia	200	1.2	21
22. Brazil	198	1.2	23	22. Austria	184	1.1	13
23. Australia	187	1.2	33	23. Switzerland	183	1.1	14
24. Sweden	184	1.1	9	24. Brazil	183	1.1	44
25. Austria	182	1.1	11	25. Thailand	179	1.1	28
26. India	179	1.1	22	26. Sweden	167	1.0	10
27. Thailand	178	1.1	17	27. United Arab Emirates[a]	159	1.0	20
28. Poland	168	1.0	20	28. Malaysia	157	1.0	7
29. Norway	168	1.0	23	29. Czech Republic	142	0.9	20
30. Czech Republic	147	0.9	20	30. Indonesia	126	0.8	36
Total of above[d]	13,120	81.4	—	Total of above[d]	13,409	81.7	—
World[d]	16,127	100.0	15	World[d]	16,415	100.0	15

[a]Secretariat estimates.
[b]Singapore's retained imports are defined as imports less re-exports.
[c]Imports are valued f.o.b.
[d]Includes significant re-exports or imports for re-export.

Source: WTO Secretariat 2009.

Table 19.5 Leading Exporters and Importers in World Trade in Commercial Services, 2008 ($bn and %)

Rank	Exporters	Value	Share	Annual % change	Rank	Importers	Value	Share	Annual % change
1	United States	522	14.0	10	1	United States	364	10.5	7
2	United Kingdom	283	7.6	2	2	Germany	285	8.2	11
3	Germany	235	6.3	11	3	United Kingdom	199	5.7	1
4	France	153	4.1	6	4	Japan	166	4.8	11
5	Japan	144	3.9	13	5	China[a]	152	4.4	—
6	Spain	143	3.8	11	6	France	137	3.9	6
7	China[a]	137	3.7	—	7	Italy	132	3.8	12
8	Italy	123	3.3	12	8	Spain	108	3.1	10
9	India[a]	106	2.8	—	9	Ireland[a]	103	3.0	9
10	Netherlands[a]	102	2.7	8	10	Korea, Republic of	93	2.7	12
11	Ireland[a]	96	2.6	8	11	Netherlands[a]	92	2.6	10
12	Hong Kong, China	91	2.4	9	12	India[a]	91	2.6	—
13	Belgium[a]	89	2.4	16	13	Canada	84	2.4	5
14	Switzerland	74	2.0	15	14	Belgium[a]	84	2.4	16
15	Korea, Republic of	74	2.0	20	15	Singapore	76	2.2	6
16	Denmark	72	1.9	17	16	Russian Federation	75	2.2	29
17	Singapore	72	1.9	3	17	Denmark	62	1.8	16
18	Sweden	71	1.9	13	18	Sweden	54	1.6	13
19	Luxembourg[a]	68	1.8	5	19	Thailand	46	1.3	22
20	Canada	62	1.7	2	20	Australia	45	1.3	18

Table 19.5 Continued

Rank	Exporters	Value	Share	Annual % change	Rank	Importers	Value	Share	Annual % change
21	Austria	62	1.7	12	21	Brazil	44	1.3	28
22	Russian Federation	50	1.3	29	22	Hong Kong, China	44	1.3	7
23	Greece	50	1.3	16	23	Norway	44	1.3	12
24	Norway	46	1.2	13	24	Austria	42	1.2	8
25	Australia	46	1.2	15	25	Luxembourg[a]	40	1.2	8
26	Poland	35	0.9	20	26	Switzerland	37	1.1	10
27	Turkey	34	0.9	22	27	United Arab Emirates[a]	35	1.0	—
28	Taipei, Chinese	34	0.9	8	28	Saudi Arabia[a]	34	1.0	—
29	Thailand	33	0.9	11	29	Taipei, Chinese	34	1.0	−2
30	Malaysia	30	0.8	5	30	Poland	30	0.9	25
	Total of above	3,135	84.1	—		Total of above	2,835	81.7	—
	World	3,730	100.0	11		World	3,470	100.0	11

[a]Secretariat estimates.

Note: While provisional full year data were available in early March for 50 countries accounting for more than two-thirds of world commercial services trade, estimates for most other countries are based on data for the first three quarters (the first six months in the case of China).

Source: World Trade Secretariat 2009.

FIGURE 19.4 International Trade–Goods and Services, Percent of GDP

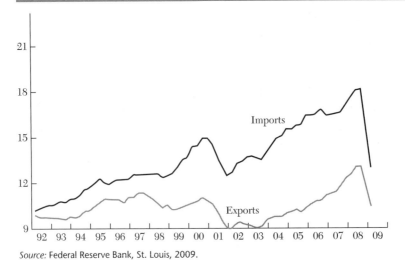

Source: Federal Reserve Bank, St. Louis, 2009.

Figure 19.4 shows the share of exports and share of imports as a percentage of the U.S. GDP. Together, exports and imports were 29 percent by 2008 (18 percent for exports and 13 percent for imports). As a consequence of accelerated demand for imports over exports, Figure 19.5 shows that the U.S. trade deficit reached record levels before plummeting in 2009 as a

FIGURE 19.5 Trade Deficit in Goods and Services, Billions of Dollars, Monthly Rate

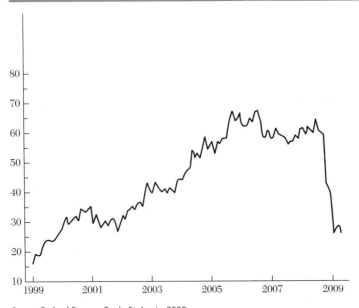

Source: Federal Reserve Bank, St. Louis, 2009.

FIGURE 19.6 U.S. Goods Export & Import Shares, 2008

Goods Export Shares, 2008

(a) Share from United States, 2008

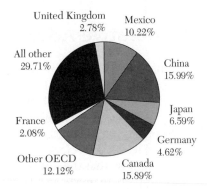

Goods Import Shares, 2008

(b) Share to United States, 2008

Source: Research Division, Federal Reserve Bank of St. Louis, 2009.

result of the global recession. By 2006, the U.S. trade deficit was more than $600 billion and was at a level that represented more than 6 percent of the GDP. (As we will see in Chapter 20, many experts are concerned that in the long run the United States cannot finance or sustain this level of trade deficit.) More than two-thirds ($400 billion) of this trade deficit is with China and Japan.

The United States trades with many countries, and Figure 19.6, shows that Canada is the major trading partner with the United States. In 2008 the United States exported over 20 percent of its goods to Canada and imported nearly 16 percent of its goods from Canada, while 16 percent of the goods entering the United States came from China, China received only 5.5 percent of U.S. exports.

THE MODERN THEORY OF INTERNATIONAL TRADE

Modern economic interdependence and the influence of multinational corporations led to more complex national trade questions in the 1990s. Before examining those questions, however, we need to understand why trade takes place. The simple answer to this question relies on the **theory of comparative advantage,** which suggests that free trade is most beneficial to world economies. We shall examine the theory behind international trade, a few of the more convincing arguments for protection, and current trends toward free trade as well as the critics of such attempts.

THE BIG PICTURE

Comparative Advantage

The theory of comparative advantage explains why nations gain from specialization in production and trade. Two countries will benefit if they both specialize in producing goods in which they have a relative advantage and trade those goods freely. One way to think about this is by comparing the resources or inputs it takes to produce two goods, textiles and computers, in two countries, the United States and Mexico, and examine how each might benefit from specialization and trade.

Suppose that the United States is more efficient in producing both textiles and computers than Mexico. (Using the same amount of inputs, the United States can produce more computers and textiles). Suppose furthermore that the United States is twice as productive in textile production and four times as productive in computer production. We can say that the United States has an *absolute* advantage in both goods, that is, it can produce both textiles and computers more efficiently). However, if we look at the relative advantage of each nation, we find that the United States has a relative (and absolute advantage) in producing computers, while Mexico has a relative (but not an absolute) advantage in producing textiles.

Production with same resource inputs:

United States	Mexico
200 Textiles	100 textiles
400 Computers	100 computers

The United States can produce computers relatively more efficiently than it can produce textiles and Mexico can produce textiles relatively more efficiently than it can produce computers—given the same input or resource requirements. Thus, the United States has a *comparative* advantage in computers and Mexico has a *comparative* advantage in textiles. Given that the United States has limited resources, the United States will benefit from specializing in computer production, and importing textiles from Mexico, which should specialize in textile production, and Mexico will benefit from trading textiles for computers. When each country specializes in the good that it is relatively best at producing and trades that good freely, total production or output of both goods increases. After trade occurs, the standard of living in both countries increases.

This is illustrated in Figure 19.BP.1 below. Before trade occurs, both countries produce both goods. Given that the United States can produce either 200 Textiles or 400 Computers with its resources, suppose it decides to devote 1/4 of its resources to producing 50 Textiles and 3/4 of its resources to producing 300

FIGURE 19.BP.1

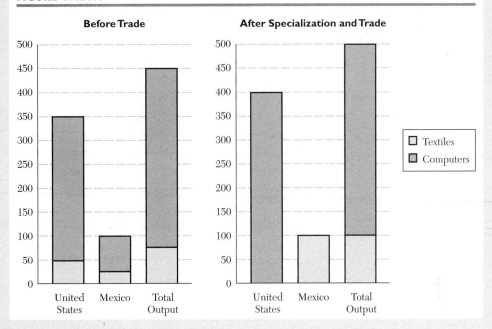

Computers. Similarly, Mexico can produce either 100 Textiles or 100 Computers, and chooses to produce 25 Textiles and 75 Computers. Total output of both countries is then 75 Textiles and 375 Computers before trade. After trade, the United States specializes entirely in computer production, producing 400 Computers, and Mexico specializes entirely in textile production, producing 100 Textiles. Production of both goods has increased, and both countries can now consume more of both goods due to specialization and trade based on comparative advantage.

If this process is extended to more countries, then specialization and trade based on the theory of comparative advantage should increase global efficiency and enhance the standard of living of all trading countries. The section below outlines the theory of comparative advantage in more detail, and then lays out some of the problems with this theory when applied to the modern global economy.

Who Trades What, and Why?

How does an individual nation assume its place in the world economy? Why does one nation specialize in production of groundnuts; a second, textiles; a third, aircraft; and a fourth, financial services? One of the first economists to deal with this question was Adam Smith, and in 1817 David Ricardo refined Smith's ideas to develop the general approach that we still use today. This approach to understanding trade is based on two basic concepts, absolute and comparative advantage.

Some assumptions will greatly facilitate matters by allowing us to deal with the essentials. In our hypothetical world, we have two nations, producing two goods. Perfect competition exists everywhere, there are no transportation costs, and labor and capital cannot move between the two nations. The costs of production in terms of labor hours are assumed to be as follows:

	Cost to Produce 1 Unit (Hours of Labor)	
	Wheat	Cloth
United Kingdom	10	20
France	15	45

Under these assumptions, the United Kingdom can produce both goods with less labor cost than can France. The United Kingdom, therefore, has an absolute advantage in producing both wheat and cloth, and France has an absolute disadvantage in each. Having an **absolute advantage** simply means that a nation can produce goods (in this case, both wheat and cloth) more efficiently than another.

This does not mean, however, that the United Kingdom produces and exports both goods and that France produces neither of them. To find out what production and exchange will take place, we must examine the production trade-off ratios between products within each nation; that is, we must see how much cloth must be given up to produce more wheat. In our example, one unit of wheat is produced in the United Kingdom with half the amount of labor time that it takes to produce a unit of cloth; with other factors constant, one unit of cloth will exchange for two units of wheat. In France—again, because of the relative costs of production—one unit of cloth can be exchanged for three units of wheat. This gives us the following internal rates of exchange of cloth for wheat:

United Kingdom 1 cloth = 2 wheat   comp adv
France 1 cloth = 3 wheat

or

United Kingdom 1/2 cloth = 1 wheat
France 1/3 cloth = 1 wheat   comp adv

By comparing the internal rates of exchange in each of the two countries, a trader might reason, "If I could buy one unit of wheat in Paris, ship it to London, and exchange it there for cloth, I could get one-half of a unit of cloth; if I exchanged it in France, I would get only one-third of a unit of cloth. My gain from this trade is one-sixth of a unit of cloth. On the other hand, taking one unit of cloth from Paris to London and exchanging it for wheat would bring me only two units of wheat, whereas I could have gotten three units of wheat at home in France. I lose one unit of wheat in the process." Note that taking one unit of cloth from London to Paris results in a gain of one unit of wheat (two units of wheat in the United Kingdom but three units in France).

[Handwritten margin notes:]

$\frac{10}{W} = \frac{20}{C}$

$C = 2W$

$20C = 10W$

$\frac{100h}{car} = \frac{300h}{Robot}$

$R = \frac{300}{100} C$

Germany $R = 3C$ comp adv

US $R = 4C$

Germ. $C = \frac{1}{3} R$

US $C = \frac{1}{4} R$ comp adv

$\frac{150}{C} = \frac{600}{R}$

$R = \frac{600}{150} C$

Our trader would quickly conclude that France has a comparative advantage in the production and export of wheat, even though France has an absolute disadvantage in both goods. By similar reasoning, we conclude that the United Kingdom has a comparative advantage in the production of cloth. A **comparative advantage** means that one nation can produce a product relatively, not absolutely, more efficiently than another nation. (A nation with an absolute advantage can produce a variety of products more efficiently than another.) Trade is expanded when nations produce products where they possess a comparative advantage.

Although the assumptions underlying this theory are "unreal" in today's world, economists since David Ricardo's time have shown that his comparative advantage model is valid for a world of many nations producing many different goods. Other economists have demonstrated that dropping the assumptions of perfect competition and zero transportation costs reduces the gain from specialization and trade but does not invalidate the theory. The only assumption crucial to these results is labor immobility. If workers migrated freely from country to country, we could have exchanges of labor rather than exchanges of products.

Comparative Advantage and Output

In the following example, we can see what happens to total output of two goods (here, units of wheat and cloth) when trade occurs. We can also use a production possibilities curve to help us understand the effect of trade on total output. Unlike our previous example, we don't know the amount of labor involved in the production of each of these outputs, nor do we know the size of the labor forces. While we cannot calculate total output precisely, the production levels shown in Table 19.6 are consistent with our hypothetical costs and rates of exchange.

For the production levels given, France has the absolute advantage in the production of both products. If neither country is involved in international trade, each must use part of its resources to produce some of each product to meet domestic demand. If France uses half of its resources to produce wheat and half to produce cloth, cloth production will be 400 units and wheat production 1,200 units. If Brazil divides its labor resources so that six-sevenths produce wheat and one-seventh produces cloth, 600 units of wheat and 100 units of cloth will be produced. Total world output will be that shown in Table 19.7. Figure 19.7 shows the production possibilities curves for this example.

1. In what product does Brazil have the comparative advantage? Why would France want to trade with Brazil at all?

Table 19.6 Total Country Production

	Units per Year		
	Wheat		**Cloth**
Brazil	700	or	700
France	2,400	or	800

Table 19.7 Total World Output Without Trade

	Units per Year	
	Wheat	**Cloth**
Brazil	600	100
France	1,200	400
Total	1,800	500

The two countries can expand total output by specializing. France has a comparative advantage in wheat production, and Brazil has a comparative advantage in cloth. If each country produces only its specialty, world output expands as shown in Table 19.8.

FIGURE 19.7 Production Possibilities without Trade

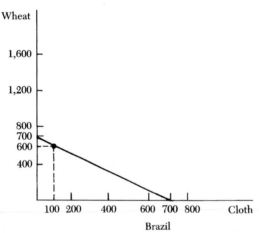

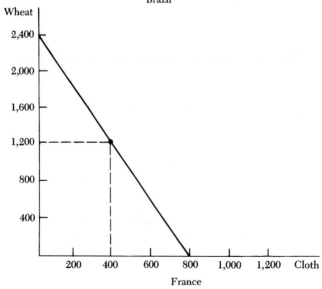

Table 19.8 Total World Output with Specialization

	Units per Year	
	Wheat	**Cloth**
Brazil	0	700
France	2,400	0
Total	2,400	700

With trade, the countries can exchange some of their expanded output so that both countries have both products. Of the wheat France produces, it uses some for domestic consumption and exports the rest. Of the cloth Brazil produces, it uses some for domestic consumption and exports the rest. After trading, many results are possible, but we might get a result similar to that shown in Table 19.9. In this case, the countries exchange 1,000 units of wheat from France for 500 units of cloth from Brazil. Figure 19.8 shows the production possibilities curves of Brazil and France with trade.

2. Who has gained what through specialization and trade?

3. In the example just given, what are some other possible combinations of exchange?

Thus, if each nation specializes in the product in which it has a comparative advantage, world output of both commodities is increased—in this case by 600 units of wheat and 200 units of cloth. If specialization and trade result in some reasonable distribution of this gain, both countries are better off than they would be in the absence of trade. This is the essence, then, of the argument for free trade.

Terms of Trade

In the example from the previous section, not only can we determine whether Brazil and France can benefit from specialization and trade, we can also examine exchange ratios or **terms of trade** in which both will gain. By looking at the internal or domestic production ratios within each nation—the production possibilities in Table 19.6—we can determine how much wheat must be given up in order to produce an additional unit of cloth. Brazil can produce 700 units of

Table 19.9 Total World Output with Specialization and Trade

	Units per Year	
	Wheat	**Cloth**
Brazil	1,000	200
France	1,400	500
Total	2,400	700

FIGURE 19.8 Production Possibilities with Trade

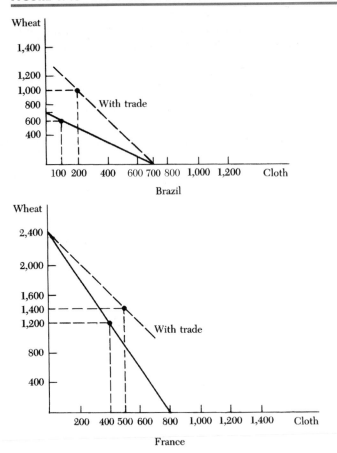

Brazil

France

wheat or 700 units of cloth during a year, so producing an additional unit of wheat necessarily means reducing cloth production by 1 unit. France can produce 2,400 units of wheat or 800 units of cloth, so the internal production trade-off is 3 units of wheat for each additional unit of cloth produced. To produce an additional unit of cloth, French wheat production must be reduced by 3 units.

With the internal production trade-off at 1 unit of wheat for 1 unit of cloth in Brazil (1W:1C) and 3 units of wheat for 1 unit of cloth in France (3W:1C), we can look for a terms of trade somewhere between those two ratios and show that each nation will gain from trade. The simplest trading ratio within that range is 2W:1C. Both nations gain with a 2:1 terms of trade. Brazil is able to exchange 1 unit of cloth for 2 units of wheat (twice as much as domestic production would allow), and France is able to exchange 2 units of its wheat for 1 unit of cloth, rather than sacrificing a full 3 units for an additional unit.

Several other trading ratios are possible in this example. In practice, the final terms of trade will depend on the bargaining strength of each nation as well as other economic and political factors. Each nation will want to negotiate the best possible terms of trade for itself.

To measure the terms of trade, we compare import and export price ratios—that is, we measure the price a country pays for imports and the price it receives for exports. We can express this as an index number:

$$\text{terms of trade} = \frac{\text{index of export prices}}{\text{index of import prices}} \times 100$$

For example, suppose the U.S. export price index was 113 in 1997 and the import price index was 95, both beginning from a base year of 1992 (at 100). In this case, the terms of trade would be $113/95 \times 100 = 119$. The terms of trade over the 1992–1997 period increased from 100 to 119, a 19 percent improvement. This improvement in terms of trade allowed the United States to give up 19 percent less in exports to obtain the same amount of imports.

For developing countries, the terms of trade is a very important influence on their capability to carry out their development plans and strategies. If their terms of trade decline, they have to pay relatively more for imports than they receive for their exports (that is, they must pay greater amounts of exports in return for imports).

Problems with the Theoretical Assumptions of Free Trade

This theoretical model of comparative advantage clearly shows that international trade benefits the trading nations. Since the 1800s, this theory has become the rationale for most economists' belief that free trade is good and anything that interferes with it—such as tariffs, quotas, and other protectionist measures—is, by definition, bad. But the theory itself has serious problems. As is often the case in economic analysis, these problems involve the assumptions of the model.

When Ricardo first developed the theory of comparative advantage, he assumed that costs remain constant no matter what the level of production. Therefore, a nation could increase its production to satisfy the needs of other nations without increasing its own costs. But modern economics has documented, to the satisfaction of most, that since production is subject to diminishing returns, it is also subject to increasing costs—sooner or later, depending on what is being produced. In such a case, the increased costs may cancel out much, if not all, of the benefits of comparative advantage.

Ricardo also did not consider the large transportation costs that may be involved in international trade. These often raise the costs of imported goods considerably over those produced domestically and cancel out some of the benefits of international trade.

Finally, Ricardo assumed that the factors of production that are mobile within a country may be immobile internationally. These days labor still is fairly immobile, but capital funds move freely internationally. It is not so easy, as the modern era has shown, for a country to abandon production of one product and move resources into the production of another without serious reallocation problems. Further, moving resources from one industry to another can cause serious political difficulties beyond the practical economic realities.

Despite these limitations, the theory of comparative advantage does provide a useful perspective for viewing the trading process. However, it cannot alone explain the much more complicated process of the internationalization of world production.

Restrictions to Free Trade: Protectionism

Free trade exists if there are no barriers to the export and import of goods and services. But, historically, when unemployment, job loss, reduced profits, and recession threaten a nation, domestic industry, or region, the predictable response is a call for increased protection of domestic goods and thus domestic jobs.

Nations use several types of trade restrictions, but the most common have been tariffs and quotas. **Tariffs** are simply taxes on goods imported or exported, while **quotas** are limits on the quantities of goods imported or exported. More recently, orderly marketing agreements (OMAs) have been popular. OMAs are nonmonetary barriers that absolutely or quantitatively limit imports and thus limit the choice between imported and domestic goods. Importers reap the profits from the higher prices commanded by the limited supply (assuming that there is a relatively inelastic demand for the product).

In general, tariffs and quotas succeed in their objective—they protect a special interest at the expense of the whole population. In other words, a few people are helped a lot, while all citizens are hurt a little because they pay higher prices for the goods and services on which tariff duties are imposed.

Arguments for Protectionism.   Nations establish trade barriers for many reasons. Most often protectionist measures are designed to protect some interest in the home country. Special interest groups in the United States often appeal to Congress for protection. Industries also seek protection from "unfair trade practices." For example, some governments subsidize particular industries, giving those products a price advantage over other viable producers. Representatives of new industries also use the "infant industries" argument that they need help to gain a foothold in world markets already flush with producers that might "overpower" the infant industry in a competitive marketplace. This argument is common in developing nations hoping to diversify their primarily agricultural base with a new industry. With time, however, particularly in the industrialized countries, the infant industry might grow to be a major competitor in the market, offering a better product at a better price.

Included in the protectionists' argument is another reason for tariff levies—retaliation. Governments have often increased tariffs in response to increases by trading partners. The 1930 Smoot-Hawley tariff, for example, set off a worldwide round of tariff increases. This "do unto others as they have done unto you" philosophy has also been used simply for the sake of self-esteem. As a result, consumers in both nations pay the higher price. At worst, such retaliation can compound recession into worldwide depression. During the 1930s, international trade almost disappeared—one important factor in the length and depth of the Great Depression. In the 1990s, the United States threatened retaliatory action against French wine.

At times Congress has considered proposals that it levy tariffs for the purpose of raising revenue, since the proceeds from the tax are collected by the government. This is well and good, but there are many more effective ways of raising revenue. Besides, if the tariff prices the imported good above that of the domestic product, the government will not collect any revenue, since the consumer will be priced out of the import market and will purchase only the domestic product.

Another protectionist argument centers on the need to reduce the competition of cheap foreign labor to protect domestic labor and domestic wage rates.

Protection is also very sensitive to political cycles. For example, during presidential elections, some candidates propose protectionism to win political support from some areas of the United States hurt by exports.

Other arguments on trade policy have run from the rather dry and abstract to the invective. The "national defense" argument falls into both categories. The merchant marine and the oil industry have argued for protection, since they are essential in times of national emergency.

4. Congress adopted import quotas to protect the oil industry for "defense" reasons from 1954 to 1973. How did these protective quotas, designed to encourage U.S. oil production, work during the OPEC oil embargo of 1973? As a consequence, what happened to domestic reserves of oil?

Costs of Protectionism.   Despite the many arguments in support of protectionist policies, an analysis of the consequences for consumers in each nation and the overall international trading system shows that one group may gain while another loses, and the entire trading system often suffers. The practice of protectionism results in all consumers paying higher prices for goods and services. The higher cost of imported goods may contribute to inflationary pressures. Protected jobs and firms may be sheltered from the competitive dynamics of the market, which would normally force them to allocate their scarce resources more efficiently and more productively.

The costs of protectionism can be high. Australia's Center for International Economics in 1990 concluded that if all regions in the global trading system reduced their tariff and nontariff barriers by 50 percent, the total gains from freer trade, measured in terms of increases in worldwide output, would be around $740 billion (more than $130 per person). A 1988 report issued by the Organization for Economic Cooperation and Development (the OECD, which includes the twenty-two advanced Western countries) concluded that agricultural protectionism cost the OECD countries about $72 billion a year. With free trade in agriculture, the study argues, personal incomes would increase by 1 percent, and less than 1 percent of the workforce would be displaced. The cost per farm job saved was estimated at $20,000 per year. In addition, free trade in agriculture would potentially increase Third World nations' agricultural exports by $30 billion a year.

In the 1997 *Economic Report of the President*, the Clinton administration noted the costs and benefits of free trade:

> Defenders of free trade can do it a disservice by promoting it as a way to create more jobs or to reduce bilateral trade deficits. Jobs, the unemployment rate, and the overall balance of payments [see Chapter 20] are ultimately a consequence of macroeconomic policies, not trade barriers. The real objective of free trade is to raise living standards by ensuring that more Americans are working in areas where the United States is comparatively more productive than its trading partners. In a full-employment economy, trade has more impact on the distribution of jobs than on the quantity of jobs.

> —*Economic Report of the President*, 1997, p. 21.

U.S. Steelmakers Accuse China of Dumping

Since late 2007 and throughout 2008, there has been a discernable rise in U.S. imports of steel from China and Canada. As a consequence, U.S. steelmakers have asserted that China is flooding the United States markets with steel subsidized by the Chinese government, thus enabling exporters to sell steel in the United States at prices below the cost of production. This practice, if true, is called **dumping**, which is illegal in international trade law.

As a consequence, U.S. steelmakers want the U.S. government to impose higher import tariffs (taxes) so that domestic producers can hold on to market share that they are losing and at the same time recover from the recession and the crisis in the U.S. automobile market.

The World Trade Organization allows countries to raise their import tariffs on goods that have suffered from dumping. But, the case most be proved and won for this to be given approval. This is an example of what generally takes place in the context of a global slowdown in trade. China no doubt needs to keep its steel plants operating to maintain employment for thousands of its citizens. The United States has the same motivation.

Source: Wall Street Journal. "U.S. Steelmakers to Seek Higher Tariffs," by John W. Miller. Copyright 2009 by Dow Jones & Company, Inc. Reproduced with permission of Dow Jones & Company, Inc. via Copyright Clearance Center.

FIGURE 19.9 Monthly U.S. Steel-Product Imports from China

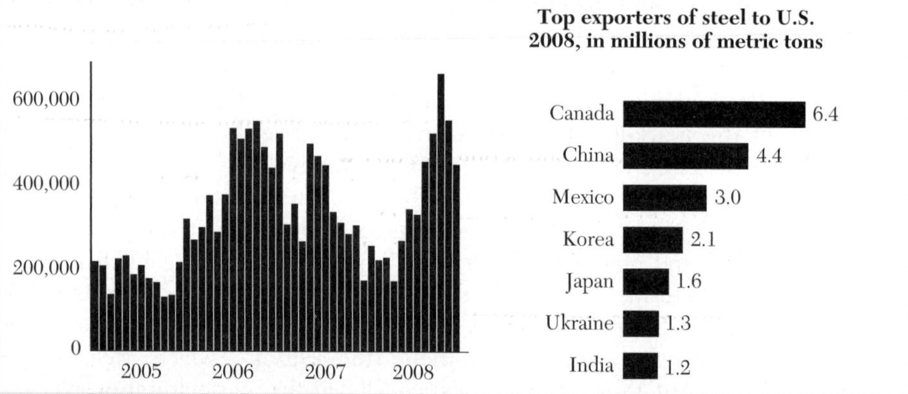

Top exporters of steel to U.S.
2008, in millions of metric tons

Canada	6.4
China	4.4
Mexico	3.0
Korea	2.1
Japan	1.6
Ukraine	1.3
India	1.2

Source: *Wall Street Journal.* "U.S. Steelmakers to Seek Higher Tariffs" by John W. Miller. Copyright 2009 by Dow Jones & Company, Inc. Reproduced with permission of Dow Jones & Company, Inc. via Copyright Clearance Center.

One major issue in recent trade negotiations has been the large agricultural subsidies of developed countries, including the United States, Canada, Japan and the European Union. These subsidies benefit developed-country farmers at the expense of poor farmers in developing countries. And, the subsidies encourage production in locations that have a higher opportunity cost, thereby reducing economies efficiency.

INTERNATIONAL TRADE ISSUES

As the volume of world trade has grown, nations have joined together in agreements to reduce trade barriers between them and to move toward freer trade. These agreements have included establishing trading blocs among a group of specific countries to reduce barriers among themselves (increasing both trade and the size of the market), as well as multinational agreements to reduce barriers throughout the world. Among the trade agreements important to the United States (as well as to the other countries involved) are the North American Free Trade Agreement (NAFTA) signed in 1992, and the Asia-Pacific Economic Cooperation (APEC) agreements joining twelve Asia-Pacific countries. Meanwhile, the integration of Europe continued with the Maastricht Treaty officially establishing the European Union in 1993. The decade of the 1990s brought much progress on the trade front. The WTO advanced the liberalization and globalization dynamics and established an economic and political framework for advancing free markets and along with them the goal of free trade. By the beginning of the twenty-first century, the .com bubble had burst and the results of the 1990s experience with globalization, trade, and financial liberalization policies documented the winners and losers, with results unevenly distributed. A strong antiglobalization movement emerged at the WTO meetings in Seattle in 1999 with protesters in the streets. Following the terror attacks on September 11, 2001, and subsequent wars in Afghanistan and Iraq (2003), the WTO-led push for enhanced trade liberalization began to crumble. Following the Seattle experience, the Doha Round in 2001 again focused on the importance of linking trade liberalization with the development goals and objectives of developing nations, which argued that trade liberalization was not contributing to their development agenda. The Doha Round encountered nothing but difficulty. The followup meetings in Cancun, Mexico, in 2003 collapsed after the fourth day, with the majority of members from the developing countries walking away in anger. The more recent meetings in Hong Kong in 2005 were no more successful. In 2006 there was a faint-hearted effort to breathe life back into the Doha agenda at the meeting of the World Economic Forum in Davos, Switzerland, but there were no expectations that anything would come of it. In the opinion of many experts, by 2006 it appeared that the era of multilateral trade liberalization was over. However, many critics and experts, like Joseph Stiglitz (author of *Making Globalization Work*, 2006), argue that there is a comprehensive set of proposals for reform that would make it possible for trade liberalization to work. This would effectively mean creating a fair trade environment in which all subsidies and trade restraints are eliminated. His point is that this is not the case today, especially for the advanced countries, even though they claimed to advocate free trade.

Much criticism has been leveled at China over the past few years as it has moved to protect several of its domestic markets, including books, songs, and movies. The following article, "W.T.O. Rules against China's Limits on Imports," examines the arguments and the ruling of the World Trade Organization after multiple complaints of protectionism.

W.T.O. Rules Against China's Limits on Imports

HONG KONG — The World Trade Organization gave the United States a victory on Wednesday in its trade battle with China, ruling that Beijing had violated international rules by limiting imports of books, songs and movies.

The W.T.O. panel decision in Geneva buttresses growing complaints from the United States and Europe that China is becoming increasingly nationalistic in its trade policies. It also offers some hope that China will remove its restrictions on media and reduce rampant piracy of intellectual property, though the country can appeal.

But even if China changes its policy in light of the decision, Western companies could struggle to increase their sales anytime soon. The ruling does not affect a quota that caps at 20 the number of foreign films that can be released in Chinese movie theaters each year.

Also, because of piracy, Chinese consumers are so accustomed to paying very little for DVDs, or downloading movies or songs free on the Internet, that American movie companies already sell authorized DVDs of their movies for much less in China than in the United States—and still struggle to find buyers.

Still, Ron Kirk, the United States trade representative, praised the panel's legal finding. "This decision promises to level the playing field for American companies working to distribute high-quality entertainment products in China," Mr. Kirk said, "so that legitimate American products can get to market and beat out the pirates."

For the American media industry, the ruling essentially means that the W.T.O. supports demands by United States movie studios, book and newspaper publishers, and record labels that they be allowed to sell more directly to the Chinese consumer, rather than first going through a middleman, often a state-owned enterprise, as China has required. It does not necessarily mean the Chinese consumer will have access to a broader array of American films, books and music — although those industries hope that may eventually occur.

"American companies now have the right to trade without going through a Chinese intermediary at the border," said James Bacchus, a lawyer at Greenberg Traurig in Washington who represented the China Copyright Alliance, a consortium of media companies, in the case. ...

Either side may appeal the panel's ruling. It is difficult, although not impossible, for a panel decision like this one to clear the way for the petitioning country to impose trade sanctions on the country that broke the rules.

The ruling goes to the heart of one of the biggest trade issues pending between China and the West: whether intellectual property, like copyrighted songs, books and movies, should be granted the same kind of protection from discriminatory trade practices as manufactured goods.

China has enjoyed double-digit economic growth through most of the last three decades in part because of rapid expansion of exports, virtually all of which have been manufactured goods. But Chinese imports have grown much more slowly, particularly if imports of goods for export are excluded, like computer chips from Japan that are assembled in China into consumer electronics for shipment to the United States.

One reason for the slow growth in imports has been China's restrictions on imported books, movies and other content. Demand is met by pirated copies made in China; the latest Hollywood movies are on DVDs on street corners across China within days of their release, at a cost of $1 or less— much less in inland cities and for the buyer who bargains aggressively.

The Chinese government had no immediate reaction to the decision, which was released late at night Beijing time. Chinese state media also initially ignored the decision. Officials sometimes wait a day or two to respond to adverse trade developments. ...

The panel stopped short of endorsing an American request for a ruling on whether Chinese censorship had unfairly restricted imports. The panel said that this question was outside its purview; for the same reason, the panel also declined to rule on whether China's approval processes were too onerous for would-be distributors of imported entertainment.

Like the United Nations, the W.T.O. has limited power to enforce decisions. But criticism from the W.T.O. can shame countries, and panel rulings against other countries have frequently become the basis for bilateral or multilateral negotiations that result in policy changes.

The Bush administration filed the original complaint in 2007, partly to head off possible legislation requiring a more confrontational trade policy toward China. The Obama administration now faces pressure from the Democratic majority in Congress to take more assertive action in response to China's trade surplus during the current recession, and could use the ruling as evidence that the issue is already being addressed. It may also use the victory as a precedent to take more cases against China to the trade organization, said Gary Clyde Hufbauer, a trade expert at the Peterson Institute for International Economics.

But while China has lost two other W.T.O. panel rulings in the last 13 months, regarding high taxes on imported auto parts and lax enforcement of counterfeiting laws, China has not changed its policies in either case.

"They've got a poor record of compliance. They keep filing appeals," said Lyle Vander Schaaf, a partner in Washington at the law firm Bryan Cave who specializes in W.T.O. dispute panels and has not advised either side in any of the three panel decisions against China.

—Tim Arango and Gerry Shih contributed reporting from New York and Helene Cooper from Washington.

1. What exactly are intellectual property rights? What is the issue of piracy with regard to intellectual property rights? Why is it so difficult to resolve this kind of issue?

2. Why would China want to cap the official inflow of foreign films at 20 per year?

3. What are the likely impacts and consequences of the World Trade Organization decision?

Next, we will briefly examine the experience of the North American Free Trade Agreement between the United States, Canada, and Mexico.

North American Free Trade Agreement (NAFTA)

In 1992, the North American Free Trade Agreement joined Canada, the United States, and Mexico into a multilateral trading bloc. NAFTA provides guiding principles for the reduction of tariffs on goods traded among these countries over fifteen years, until trade barriers no longer exist among the three. The NAFTA agreement was signed by President Bush in 1992 and ratified by Congress in late 1993, despite considerable debate in the 1992 presidential campaign (with Ross Perot opposing NAFTA and Bill Clinton supporting a modified NAFTA agreement). Some changes were negotiated in the areas of the environment and job loss.

NAFTA was hotly debated. Opponents argued that job losses would off-set increased profits to manufacturers and lower consumer prices. Supporters argued that more jobs and increased wealth would result for all three nations. Since implementation in 1994, critics point to data validating their predictions. In the first two years of the agreement, Mexico imported fewer U.S. goods than in previous years; at the same time the level of Mexican exports to the United States rose dramatically. Even supporters of the agreement adjusted their earlier prediction of U.S. job growth. A currency crisis in the Mexican peso complicated interpretation of early results of the treaty. While some argue that the jury is still out on NAFTA, others—politicians and economists alike—look ahead to more free trade agreements in South America and the establishment of a Free Trade Area of the Americas (FTAA).

Since NAFTA began, proponents and critics have been studying the experience in order to be able to argue that it has indeed been successful or that it has been a disappointment or, even, a failure. By 2007, there had been several major and highly reputable studies on the performance of NAFTA (the World Bank, Institute for International Economics, AFL-CIO, etc.). Obviously, everyone can make a case for his or her position. Nevertheless, this is a very controversial and important debate as it sheds light not just on the experience of NAFTA but the recent passage of the Central American Free Trade Agreement (CAFTA).

The following article by James Parks, "NAFTA, CAFTA Not Working" (AFL-CIO, September 12, 2006), is an example of the case that critics make of NAFTA and CAFTA.

NAFTA, CAFTA Not Working

James Parks

They are the twin pillars of recent U.S. trade policy—NAFTA and DR-CAFTA. And neither of them is working.

After 12 years, NAFTA (North American Free Trade Agreement) has not brought prosperity to working people in Mexico, Canada and United States, as promised.

And like NAFTA and other bad U.S. trade agreements, DR-CAFTA (Dominican Republic–Central American Free Trade Agreement) does not contain enforceable workers' rights or environmental protections. The agreement, which went into effect in January, is already failing after just eight months, according to a report released Tuesday.

In testimony submitted Sept. 11 to the Senate Finance Subcommittee on International Trade for NAFTA hearings, AFL-CIO Policy Director Thea Lee noted that "rather than encouraging sustainable and equitable growth, NAFTA has contributed to the loss of jobs and incomes of workers, while enriching the very few."

NAFTA's main outcome has been to strengthen the clout and bargaining power of multinational corporations, to limit the scope of governments to regulate in the public interest and to force workers into more direct competition with each other, while assuring them fewer rights and protections. The increased capital mobility afforded by NAFTA has hurt workers, the environment and communities in all three NAFTA countries.

Since 1994, the U.S. combined trade deficit with Mexico and Canada has ballooned from $9 billion to $127 billion, Lee says. The Department of Labor has certified that well over half a million U.S. workers lost their jobs due to NAFTA, and the nonprofit Economic Policy Institute (EPI) estimates the skyrocketing NAFTA trade deficit contributed to the loss of more than 1 million jobs and job opportunities.

Mexican workers haven't fared any better. Real wages in Mexico are actually lower today than before NAFTA went into effect in 1994, and the number of people in poverty grew from 62 million to 69 million through 2003, Lee says.

The NAFTA model was the starting point for CAFTA. In *Monitoring Report: DR-CAFTA in Year One*, prepared by the Stop CAFTA Coalition, Katherine Hoyt of the Nicaragua Network, one of the members of the coalition,

says CAFTA has fueled the deterioration of workers' rights. For example, according to the report:

❖ Few collective bargaining agreements exist with noncompany unions in the free-trade zones of Central America, and corporations continue to fire union leadership in order to quash organizing efforts.

❖ Despite promises from the El Salvadoran government and the Bush administration, the cost of living is increasing, including the price of food. The White House had assured Salvadoran farmers that increased food exports from the United States would lead to lower food prices.

❖ In Nicaragua, funds from a program to support farmers are going to rich, powerful large producers, not to small farmers who desperately need them.

❖ Using a section of CAFTA, El Salvador's government is preparing a new law to privatize the nation's water system, an action that traditionally leads to huge cost increases and the loss of water by poor farmers and workers.

With Congress poised to consider new NAFTA-type trade agreements with Peru and Colombia, lawmakers need to take a look at what has happened in Central America and Mexico, Lee says:

Trade agreements must include enforceable protections for workers' core rights and must preserve our ability to use our domestic trade laws effectively. They must protect our government's ability to regulate in the public interest, to use procurement dollars to promote economic development and other legitimate social goals, and to provide high-quality public services. Finally, it is essential that workers, their unions and other civil society organizations be able to participate meaningfully in our government's trade policy process, on an equal footing with corporate interests.

The success or failure of any future trade and investment agreements will hinge on government's willingness and ability to negotiate agreements that appropriately address all of the social, economic and political dimensions of trade and investment, not just those of concern to corporations. Unfortunately, NAFTA is precisely the wrong starting point.

1. What is the case against NAFTA?
2. Can you find information (data) that would support or contradict this argument? What is it?
3. What are the lessons of NAFTA for CAFTA?
4. What would make for a more "fair" agreement?

The WTO and GATT

Despite debates over protectionism, much of the post–World War II period has seen an overall reduction in the excessive protection of the Great Depression years. Nations have, of course, disagreed as to which goods should be exempt from tariff reductions and where tariff levels should be set. Protectionist tendencies are particularly prevalent during periods of severe recession as countries compete for shrinking markets. Still, primarily through international negotiations in organizations such as the **General Agreement on Tariffs and Trade (GATT),** treaties increase trade through agreed-on reductions in tariffs.

Ninety-nine nations participated in the General Agreement on Tariffs and Trade, Multilateral Trade Negotiations, or the Tokyo Rounds, which concluded in 1979 after five years of negotiation over tariff reductions and the elimination of nontariff impediments and distortions to trade. In 1986, GATT attempted to reduce barriers in Punta del Este, Uruguay, and continued through 1993. Delegates negotiated reductions in both tariff and nontariff barriers, on everything from intellectual property, including patents and copyrights, to services such as telecommunications.

The most controversial part of the Uruguay Round was the agreement to establish the World Trade Organization (WTO) as the institution responsible for governing international trade. The WTO represents more than 120 countries. The WTO has the duty of implementing the agreements in the Uruguay Round by administering the agreements and providing a forum for settling disputes. The WTO replaced GATT as the central institution working to eliminate trade barriers. In its early years of existence, the WTO had its share of critics and supporters. Critics argued that the WTO oversteps its bounds in issues of national sovereignty. As the WTO makes more decisions, the organization has come under increased scrutiny from its supporters, who want increased powers and enforcement of those powers, and critics, who want to reduce WTO's importance.

European Integration

Twelve European nations with a total population of 320 million and a GDP rivaling that of the United States formally merged into the European Union in 1993. There are currently 27 member states with a population nearing 500 million. The latest in a series of European organizational efforts beginning in 1952 with the European Coal and Steel Community, the EU trading bloc was designed to liberalize trade between member nations, encourage cooperation in intergovernmental and security affairs, and facilitate the movement toward a single currency. The economic goal of the EU is to synchronize economic policies promoting European economic growth and stabilization. Gains from integration are predicted at around 6.2 percent of combined GDP, or $230 billion.

Continued integration efforts are not easy. Strikes by French farmers and German miners emphasize the discord within member nations, as the EU places regional economic decisions above national ones. The EU is opening its doors to trade with the rest of the world, and thus opening a growing European market to U.S. products, even though trade among member nations receives greater emphasis. For U.S. trade, the future direction of EU economic policy is an important one. The majority of EU members moved to a common currency (the euro) in January 2000.

12. If a nation encourages free trade, what happens to the laborer whose job is threatened by increased domestic demand for imported substitutes?

Japan as a Neomercantilist Trading Partner

While NAFTA, APEC, FTAA, the WTO, and the European Union aim at reducing the potential for trade wars, fears of such disputes have not vanished.

In particular, some concern persists regarding Japan's remaining neomercantilist trade policies. Some policy makers working on Japan trade issues have concluded that prior to the mid-1990s, Japan's trade policies were mercantilist in nature and that free trade interrupted their organized markets.

Japanese exports to U.S. markets account for more than half of Japan's total trade surplus. Needless to say, there is concern over Japanese trade policies, which are generally exclusionary and sometimes violate international trade law. The strategies with which the Japanese encourage strategic industries often puts U.S. domestic competitors at a disadvantage.

U.S. government and trade officials and businesspeople have long been frustrated with the Japanese. Intensive rounds of bilateral trade negotiations have increased the frustration on both sides. Tariff barriers *have* fallen over the past few years, but other restrictive practices have made entry into some Japanese markets difficult.

Conclusion

With protectionist measures, there is always an undercurrent of possible retaliation and trade wars similar to those of the 1930s, during which time international trade almost disappeared. In the past decade, however, the fear of retaliation seems not to have been an issue. Increasingly more economists are calling for the introduction of trade strategies as an improvement on free trade.

Developing countries are especially concerned about protectionist tendencies. They need to increase their exports in order to earn much-needed dollars and foreign currencies with which to repay the enormous debt that they have accrued in the past. A quota on imported steel would greatly affect a nation such as Brazil, which relies heavily on steel exports to earn foreign exchange. These nations have learned to play the game of protection as well. Several of the developing countries are using import controls as well as export subsidies to improve their trade positions. This trend has been caused by a minimal weakening of inflationary activity and the persistence of high unemployment levels.

Protection or free trade? Retaliation? Negotiated trade agreements? More than 30 years ago, in his 1977 presidential address to the twelfth biannual convention of the AFL-CIO, George Meany declared, "Free trade is a joke and a myth, and a government policy dedicated to 'free trade' is more than a joke—it is a prescription for disaster. The answer is fair trade—do unto others as they do unto you—barrier for barrier, closed door for closed door."

The 2001 U.S. economic recession that followed the collapse of the technology bubble and boom of the late 1990s resulted in a worldwide economic slowdown. The critics of globalization, free trade, and economic liberalization gathered more and more influence. This put enormous pressure on the World Trade Organization and other regional economic integration initiatives. By 2003 and into the early months of 2004, WTO trade discussions broke down in Cancun, Mexico, and Miami, Florida. Rising protectionist sentiment was visible throughout the global economy especially as the global economic downturn caused by the financial crisis threatened jobs and slowed economic growth.

From 2005 to 2009, the Doha Round talks continued to produce little if any progress. The Bush administration continued to be preoccupied with the Iraq War and the ongoing war in Afghanistan. The twin deficits (budget and trade) persisted in the face of sluggish economic growth. Oil prices continued to rise as the increased demand for petroleum from China and India and speculation by oil traders pushed prices to the highest nominal and real levels ever—over $145 per barrel. As growth remained robust in emerging nations and with China's appetite for natural resources to fuel its 10 percent growth rate, a commodity boom emerged, causing prices for raw materials to soar. This generated a strong trade dynamic and allowed many emerging nations to generate a favorable trade surplus. Yet, by late 2007, signs of the emerging global financial crisis were self-evident and the global recession was underway. The global recession continued through early to mid-2009. With the economic downturn, the slowdown in international trade, and soaring unemployment rates, protectionist policies emerged.

There can be no doubt that arguments over free trade will continue in the future, and the effects will be felt on currencies and domestic policies. In the next chapter, we measure international trade and survey the historical development of the institutions that permitted international exchange to develop and flourish in an increasingly interdependent world. We will also see how these institutions sometimes failed to develop appropriate policies for the ever-changing and complex world economy.

Review Questions

1. What factors have brought about the dynamic process of globalization and international economic interdependence?

2. What are some of the more dominant trends with respect to international trade? What can be said of the role and position of the United States with regard to international trade?

3. What is the basic theory of free trade? What are the pros and cons of free trade in theory? In practice?

4. What are the arguments for protectionism?

5. What is the reality of farm subsidies in the United States? Should they be maintained, reduced, or eliminated? Explain.

6. What has been the overall experience of NAFTA given its goals and objectives?

7. What since 2000 has been the trade relationship between the United States and China? What are the apparent benefits and costs of this relationship to each country?

8. What has the global financial crisis and economic recession done to global economic growth and international trade since 2008?

9. How would you categorize President Obama's trade policy and strategy? Do you agree or disagree with it? Explain.

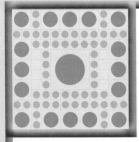

CHAPTER TWENTY

International Finance

Introduction

Having considered the theory and the recent history of international trade, we shall now turn our attention to issues of international finance and to accounting for the international exchange of goods, services, investment, and other capital flows. Monies flow from one nation to another when citizens or institutions of a given nation decide to lend to or borrow from foreigners and to import or export goods and services.

We begin our examination with a discussion of the **balance of payments,** which is the accounting scheme that governments and international organizations use for measuring trade and capital flows between nations. We shall then move to a discussion of exchange rates and review how they respond to trade and financial transactions. Our discussion of exchange rates includes how international trade flows alter these rates, and how systems of exchange have changed over time.

THE BALANCE OF PAYMENTS

All nations must eventually adjust their national economic policies to meet the demands of the international trading and financial system. Nations commonly keep track of these demands with a mechanism called the balance-of-payments accounting system. A balance-of-payments account is a statement of a nation's aggregate international financial transactions over a period of time, usually one year. The balance of payments is a statement that shows the exchange of a country's currency for foreign currencies for all of the international transactions of a country's citizens, businesses, and government during a year. It helps nations keep track of the flow of goods and services into and out of the country. In this accounting statement, all international economic and financial transactions must have either a positive or a negative effect on a nation's balance-of-payments accounts. Table 20.1 shows the effects of possible transactions.

Table 20.1 Credits and Debits in a Nation's Balance of Payments

Credits (+)	Debits (−)
1. Any *receipt* of foreign money	1. Any *payment* to a foreign country
2. Any *earnings* of an investment in a foreign country	2. Any *earnings* on domestic investments by a foreign country
3. Any sale of goods or services abroad (*export*)	3. Any purchase of goods and services from abroad (*import*)
4. Any gift or aid *from* a foreign country	4. Any gift or aid *given* abroad
5. Any *sale* of stocks or bonds abroad	5. Any *purchase* of foreign stocks or bonds
6. Any foreign investment in this country	6. Any investment in a foreign country

The balance-of-payments accounting statement is divided into three major classifications: the current account, the capital account, and the financial account. (In June 1999, the Bureau of Economic Analysis changed the way that it accounts for financial transactions in its international account. The BEA had previously used only a current account and capital account; by adding the financial account, the BEA conforms more closely to the international guidelines of the International Monetary Fund.) For each of these accounts, subtracting payments from receipts results in an account balance.

The Current Account

The **current account** includes the import and export of all goods and services, investment income, and most unilateral transfers during a year. Exports of goods and services create a receipt of income, while imports of goods command payments abroad, resulting in an outflow of income. Table 20.2 shows the magnitude of these components of the current account for 2005, 2007 and 2008.

By far the largest category under the current account is the export and import of goods—cars, steel, raw materials, machines, and so forth. In 2007 U.S. goods exported totaled $1.148 trillion, and goods imported totaled an outflow $1.98 trillion. The balance referred to as the **balance of trade** represents the value of exports of goods and services minus the value of imports. For 2007, the balance of trade was −$700.4 billion. The balance is negative because payments were larger than receipts in 2007.

Besides merchandise trade, the current account records investment income and services of various types. When we total all of the transactions in the current account, we get the current account balance. For 2007, this balance was −$706 billion.

Just as we examined the budget deficit within the framework of our leakages and injections model of National Income Accounting, we can look at trade deficits within the same context. In equilibrium, leakages equal injections:

$$\text{leakages} = \text{injections}$$

$$S + Tx + M = I + G + X$$

Table 20.2 U.S. International Transactions, 2005, 2007, and 2008

Transaction	Amount (in millions)		
	2005	2007	2008
Current Account			
(1) Exports of goods and services and income receipts	$1,749.9	$2,463.5	$2,591.3
(2) Goods, balance-of-payment basis	894.6	1,148.4	1,277.0
(3) Services	380.6	497.2	549.6
(4) Income Receipts	474.6	817.8	764.6
(5) Imports of goods and services and income payments	−2,455.3	−3,082.0	−3,168.9
(6) Goods, balance-of-payment basis	−1,677.4	−1,967.8	−2,117.2
(7) Services	−314.6	−378.1	−405.3
(8) Income Payments	−463.4	−736.0	−646.4
(9) Unilateral current transfers, net	−86.1	−112.7	−128.1
(10) Balance on current account = (1) + (5) + (9)	−791.5	−731.2	−706.0
Capital Account			
(11) Capital Account transactions, net	−4.4	−1.8	1.0
Financial Account			
(12) U.S.-owned assets abroad, net (increase/financial outflow excluding financial derivatives (−))	−426.8	−1,289.9	−0.1
(13) U.S. official reserve assets, net	14.1	−0.1	−4.8
(14) U.S. government assets, other than official reserves assets, net	5.5	−22.2	−529.5
(15) U.S. private assets, net	−446.4	−1,267.5	481.9
(16) Foreign-owned assets in the United States, net excluding financial derivatives (increase/financial inflow (+))	1,212.3	2,057.7	534.1
(17) Foreign official assets in the United States, net	199.4	411.1	477.7
(18) Other foreign assets in the United States, net	1,012.7	1,646.6	177.7
(19) Financial Derivatives, net	N/A	6.5	N/A
(20) Balance of capital financial flows = (16) − (12)	785.4	767.8	537.0
(21) Statistical discrepancy (sum of above items with sign reversed)	10.4	−41.3	−129.3
Balance of payments =	0	0	0
(1) + (5) + (9) + (11) + (12) + (16) + (20) + (21)			
Balance of trade = (2) + (3) + (6) + (7)	−716.7	−700.4	−695.9

Source: Bureau of Economic Analysis, *Survey of Current Business,* June 2006, July 2009.

Next, we can rewrite the equation in terms of the current account balance, which is in deficit in this case:

$$X - M = S - I - G + Tx,$$

where I is domestic investment, G is government expenditures, $X - M$ is net exports (and here serves as a measure of the current account deficit or surplus), S is private domestic saving, and Tx is domestic tax receipts.

$$(X - M) = S - I - (G - Tx),$$

where $X - M$ is the current account balance and $G - Tx$ is the government deficit. This balance is linked to fiscal and/or saving imbalances.

The Capital Account

The amount in the nation's **capital account** is small. The only transactions included are a few unilateral transfers that had been included in the current account until the Bureau of Economic Analysis changed its accounting for financial transactions in 1999. The BEA provides the following definition:

> The newly defined capital account consists of capital transfers and the acquisition or disposal of nonproduced nonfinancial assets. They are major types of capital transfers and are debt forgiveness and migrant's transfers (goods and financial assets accompanying migrants as they leave or enter the country). "Other" capital transfers include the transfer of title to fixed assets and the transfer of funds linked to the sale or acquisition of fixed assets, gift and inheritance taxes, death duties, uninsured damage to fixed assets, and legacies. The acquisition and disposal of nonproduced nonfinancial assets includes the sales and purchases of nonproduced assets, such as the rights to natural resources, and the sales and purchases of intangible assets, such as patents, copyrights, trademarks, franchises, and leases.

Although these capital account transactions are relatively small in the U.S. accounts, they are more important to other countries and may become more important to U.S. accounts. In 2007, these transactions amounted to −$1 billion.

The Financial Account

The financial account includes all financial flows in and out of the United States. U.S. financial outflow represents the purchase of capital assets outside of the United States by the government, citizens, or corporations. The dollars used to purchase these assets flow out of the country. In return, the government, citizen, or business now owns an asset abroad. U.S. citizens or businesses might make bank deposits in other countries, purchase foreign stocks and bonds, or even buy foreign productive facilities (a plant, office, McDonald's franchise, etc.). All of these activities produce an increase in U.S. assets abroad, or an outflow of dollars—a payment in the balance of payments. On the other hand, if U.S. residents were to sell their foreign assets and bring the proceeds back home, this would be recorded as a receipt. In 2007, the net outflow of U.S. private assets amounted to −$1.23 trillion, which represented payments in the financial account. Financial inflow into the United States, which occurs when foreign governments, institutions, corporations, or individuals increase their assets in the United States, amounted to $2.1 trillion in 2007. In Table 20.2, entries in the financial account in 2008 are significantly different from other years because of the global financial crisis. Note the vast change in row 12 for U.S.-owned assets abroad. These dropped by $1 trillion between 2007 and 2008. This was due to dramatic changes in row 15 because of U.S. claims reported by banks. Looking at foreign-owned assets in the United States, U.S. liabilities reported by banks is reflected in changes in row 18. The world credit market crisis is reflected in the financial account of the balance of payments in 2008.

1. What do we lose by foreign direct investment in the United States? What do we gain when it occurs?

Balancing the Accounts

The balance of payments always "balances." Whatever surplus (net inflow) or deficit (net outflow) these transactions generate is offset by the use of official reserve assets of the U.S. government and the statistical discrepancy.

The *statistical discrepancy* category is in one sense an accounting mechanism for balancing the accounts. It is simply the total of the items in the current, capital, and financial account measurements with the sign reversed. One reason this account is necessary is that the measurement of all international transactions is extremely complex. The government cannot accurately measure all of these transactions, particularly illegal ones; some transactions, both legal and illegal, will escape measurement. For 2007, the deficit in the U.S. current, capital, and financial account items indicates an outflow of dollars. This number could represent any one or a combination of possible activities. The deficit would put downward pressure on the dollar, reducing its value and "balancing" the deficit. Alternatively, other nations could hold on to the dollars that they had received because of U.S. imports from their countries or U.S. capital flows to their countries. They might want to hold these dollars for future use. Whatever the specifics, to compensate for the imprecision involved in attempting to measure all international economic activities, the statistical discrepancy category mechanically balances the international accounts.

2. If investment by Canada in the United States results in a "receipt" or positive effect on the U.S. balance of payments in the financial account, is this investment necessarily good for the United States? Why or why not?

3. What would be an example of a merchandise export? A government transfer payment? If you took $1,000 out of your bank account in the United States and put it in a bank in London, what effect would it have on the balance of payments accounts?

Trade Deficits

When reporters, economists, and politicians speak of balance-of-payments deficits (outflows of dollars) and surpluses (inflows of dollars), they may be referring only to the transactions in the current account or the current and financial accounts—and not in the balancing cash, gold, or bond transactions. The *basic balance* includes the balance on the current account added to the long-term capital movements. This basic balance normally shows a payments deficit (payments < receipts) or surplus (receipts > payments).

If we look only at the merchandise balance in the current account (the balance of trade), we find that the U.S. "balance" has historically been a surplus.

In every year from 1893 until 1971, merchandise exports exceeded merchandise imports. Beginning in the 1970s, however, the balance of trade has shown deficits—large ones in the late 1970s and even larger in the 1980s and late 1990s, after simply large deficits in the early 1990s. The trade deficits of the early to mid-1970s resulted primarily from the large increase in the price of imported oil. During the first half of the 1980s, the trade deficits were caused by a very strong dollar, which made U.S. goods much more expensive than imported goods. This price shift decreased U.S. exports and increased foreign imports. In the latter half of the decade, the value of the dollar fell, and the trade deficit began to decrease in 1988, having reached a record $152.9 billion in 1987. Deficits in the trade balance continued to narrow until 1992. Since 1992 trade deficits climbed to record levels. Figure 20.1 shows the pattern for international transactions balances between 1983 and 2008.

Trade deficits in the current account have been offset by larger financial inflows into the United States, which have reduced the deficit in the basic balance. Until recently the financial account has historically run deficits, since it records U.S. corporate investment in foreign nations.

> During the period when imports by Americans do exceed our exports to the rest of the world, foreigners must accept additional dollar securities in exchange for our excess imports. In different words, we finance the excess imports by borrowing from the rest of the world or by selling U.S. assets to foreigners. This accommodating flow of credit or capital to the United States is an inevitable corollary of the trade deficit.
>
> —Martin Feldstein, "Why the Dollar Is Strong," *Challenge*, January/February 1984

FIGURE 20.1 Current Account, Trade, and Investment Income Balances

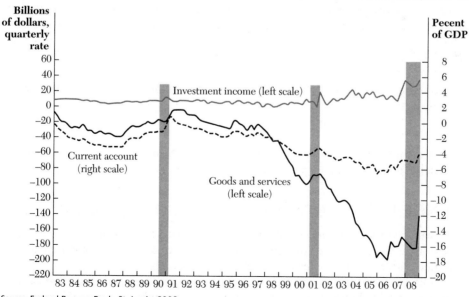

Source: Federal Reserve Bank, St. Louis, 2009.

One of the problems a nation encounters in trade, just as in life, is that it must pay for the goods and services received. An individual can use either cash or an IOU to offset a debt. In the international sphere, several alternatives are available. Payments are accepted in cash (dollars), gold, or special drawing rights (a bookkeeping form of international money).

If a nation's exports exceed its imports, it will have attained a balance-of-trade surplus. The reward for this is increased employment and income at home. The penalty is higher prices. Why? As exports of goods and services rise, income (Y) and hence GDP increase. As income increases, consumption increases. As consumption increases, more dollars are competing for fewer domestic goods, and prices will tend to rise.

A trade deficit (imports greater than exports) earns a nation's economic and political leaders criticism and economic disadvantages. Strains are placed on the value of a nation's currency with respect to other currencies. If these strains become too severe, the country's currency will **depreciate** (be worth less) with respect to other, stronger currencies, so imported goods will cost more. On the other hand, exports should become cheaper and thus more attractive to foreign nations. In following sections of this chapter, we will see how this happens.

A country cannot do away with a trade deficit simply by removing or reducing a "big" item on the balance-of-payments statement. For example, it is not true that, as opponents of foreign aid have argued, this expenditure caused deficits in the basic trade balance for many years. Much foreign aid is "tied"; that is, it must be spent on goods produced in the United States. So if the United States cut foreign aid by $1 billion, U.S. exports might be reduced by as much as $800 million. The gain would be very small indeed. Many of the items in the balance of payments are related to other items in this way.

It is, however, legitimate to note that when a particular item is in surplus, the country has the freedom to run up a deficit in some other item without creating pressure against its currency. This sort of situation can be created in either of two ways: There may be items that in the working out of "basic economic forces" generate a surplus, or other countries in the world economy may "allow" deficits to exist without exerting pressure for policy measures that would reduce them. An example of the former is the flow of investment income into the United States. In the past, the net income on U.S. investments abroad allowed the United States to, among other things, increase its ownership of factories and mines in other countries and finance military expenditures abroad. An example of the second situation would be the willingness of countries to hold onto dollars accumulated from U.S. deficits because dollars are valuable to them.

EXCHANGE RATES AND THE BALANCE OF PAYMENTS

As we mentioned earlier, trade imbalances can create pressures on a nation's currency. Let's examine how the value (exchange rate) of the dollar is determined and how it influences the balance of payments.

The value of a nation's currency, the exchange rate, is determined by the supply of and demand for that currency. The supply of a nation's currency

THE BIG PICTURE

Exchange Rates

The supply and demand model (developed in Chapter 7) is used to determine exchange rates. There are a number of determinants that affect exchange rates, and this can make fluctuations in exchange rates difficult to understand. But the logic behind the supply and demand model for exchange rates, and thus behind fluctuations in exchange rates, is straightforward. When international actors (including consumers, investors, businesses, speculators, and governments) want more of a particular country's goods, services, or assets, they will demand more of that country's currency to pay for those goods, services, or assets. As shown in Figure 20.BP.1, any increase in the demand for a nation's currency will cause that currency to increase (or appreciate) in value relative to the currency of its trading partner (whose currency will in turn decrease, or depreciate, in value). When international actors want less of a particular nation's goods, services, or assets, they will demand less of that nation's currency. Any decrease in the demand for a nation's currency will cause that currency to decrease (or depreciate) in value relative to the currency of its trading partner(s). There are, of course, a number of variations to this story, and we explore the nuances of changes in exchange rates in the rest of the chapter.

FIGURE 20.BP.1 The Market for Dollars Responds to an Increase in Demand

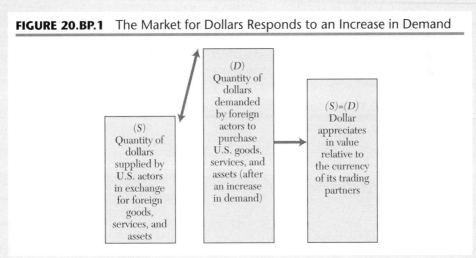

FIGURE 20.2 An Increase in the Supply of Dollars

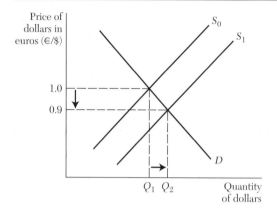

comes from the country's central bank as well as its citizens who desire to purchase foreign goods, services, securities, and other assets. For example, the supply of U.S. dollars would increase if the Fed supplied more dollars in order to purchase foreign currencies, if U.S. citizens wanted to purchase more imported goods, or if U.S. investors wanted to invest in foreign asset markets. Figure 20.2 shows that an increase in the supply of dollars in exchange for euros causes the value of the dollar in terms of foreign currency to depreciate (decrease in price relative to the euro). A depreciation of the dollar means that each U.S. dollar buys less foreign currency than it used to, making foreign goods more expensive to purchase.

The demand for a nation's currency comes from foreign citizens who want to purchase the home country's goods and assets. For example, the demand for dollars would increase if the prices of U.S. goods fell relative to foreign goods (causing foreign citizens to desire more U.S. goods), if foreign citizens wanted to invest more in U.S. bonds, or if foreign citizens wanted to hold more dollars as assets. As Figure 20.3 shows, an increase in

FIGURE 20.3 An Increase in the Demand for Dollars

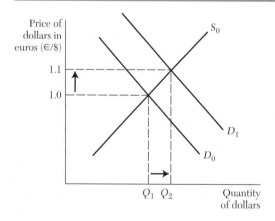

the demand for dollars by European citizens would shift the demand curve for the dollar to the right, causing the dollar to appreciate (increase in price relative to the euro). An appreciation of the dollar means that each dollar can purchase more foreign currency than it used to, making foreign goods cheaper to U.S. citizens.

The Dollar and the Euro In fact, the dollar was strong relative to the euro from 1999 to 2001 and weak from 2001 to 2009. As the U.S. economy slowed in 2001, the stock market plummeted, and the Fed slashed interest rates to try to stave off a recession. Normally, economists would expect declining stock prices and low interest rates on bonds to scare off foreign investors, causing a decrease in the demand for dollars and a depreciation of the dollar.

   While the dollar fell with respect to the euro and other European currencies, including the pound and kroner, Asian currencies held up the sagging dollar—at least for a while. During much of the period from 2003–2008 the United States was very dependent on Asian central banks to finance the current account deficit.

Determinants of Exchange Rates To understand shifts in the supply and demand curves for a currency, we must understand the determinants of exchange rates. Table 20.3 lists some of the factors that cause shifts in the supply of and demand for a currency. The supply of a currency is affected by the central bank's decisions to supply more or less of the currency, as well as domestic consumer and producer decisions regarding foreign goods, services, and assets. The demand for a nation's currency is affected by the demand for a nation's products and the prices of those products. The lower the price of the products, the greater the demand, and thus the greater the demand for the nation's currency, since currency is needed to purchase the products. Other factors that often influence exchange rates include tastes and preferences for the country's products, productivity increases, the inflation rate, and the domestic interest rate relative to other countries' rates. In Figure 20.4, an increased demand in the United States for Japanese-produced Toyotas increases the demand for yen and thus increases the exchange rate of the yen in terms of dollars. Each dollar will purchase fewer yen as the price of yen in dollars rises. From the opposite perspective, the price of dollars in terms of yen has decreased.

   Given the current U.S. trade deficits, we might expect the value of the dollar to be falling with respect to many other currencies, since the demand for U.S. exports is low (contributing to a low demand for dollars) and the demand for imported goods is high (contributing to a large supply of dollars). But other factors affect the demand for a nation's currency. Nontrade pressures, which are not influenced by the demand for a nation's products, might dramatically influence the value, or the exchange rate, of the dollar. Currencies are used not only to purchase goods and services, but also to make money—that is, to earn a rate of return, or interest. The Fed's tightening of monetary policy in the fall of 1979, in late 1989, and from 1997 to 2000 did curb the growth rate of the money supply, but the resulting higher interest rate and a growing confidence that the United States was a "safe haven" for assets created a demand for dollars

Table 20.3 Shifts in the Supply and Demand for a Currency (Dollars)

Determinant Change	Supply of Dollars	Demand for Dollars	Value of the Dollars
U.S. prices increase.	U.S. citizens want cheaper foreign goods; supply of dollars increases.	Foreign citizens want fewer U.S. goods; demand for dollars decreases.	Depreciates
U.S. demand for foreign goods, services, and assets increases.	U.S. citizens want more foreign items; supply of dollars increases.	Foreign citizens do not change the amount of U.S. goods they purchase; demand for dollars does not shift.	Depreciates
Foreign demand for U.S. goods, services, and assets increases.	U.S. citizens do not change the amount of foreign goods they purchase; supply of dollars does not change.	Foreign citizens want more U.S. items; demand for dollars increases.	Appreciates
U.S. productivity increases, lowering the prices of U.S. goods.	U.S. citizens prefer cheaper U.S. goods to many foreign goods; supply of dollars decreases.	Foreign citizens want more U.S. goods now that the price has fallen; demand for dollars increases.	Appreciates
U.S. interest rates increase.	U.S. investors move their money from foreign banks back to U.S. banks to get a higher return; supply of dollars decreases.	Foreign investors put more money in U.S. banks to get a higher return; demand for dollars increases.	Appreciates

FIGURE 20.4 Supply and Demand for Toyotas and Yen

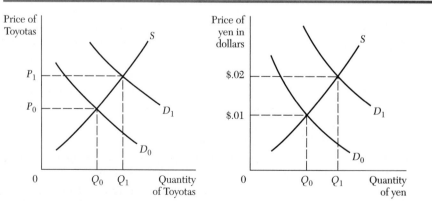

FIGURE 20.5 Supply and Demand for Dollars When U.S. Interest Rates Increase

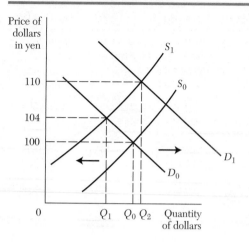

among foreign corporations and investors. In early 2009, foreign investors were again attracted to the U.S. safe haven.

To illustrate this, we will assume that before the Fed initiative, $1 would purchase 100 yen. In Figure 20.5, a Fed reduction in the growth rate of the money supply is shown by the shift in the supply curve of dollars from S_0 to S_1. A higher interest rate created by the reduced money supply will attract foreign investment and thus increase the demand for dollars. This is shown by a shift in the demand curve from D_0 to D_1.

In this example, the dollar has become very strong. Therefore, it commands or purchases a larger quantity of other foreign currencies and thus more foreign goods and services. Before the Fed's contractionary monetary policy, $1 would purchase 100 yen, but with less supply and greater demand, $1 purchases 110 yen. Japanese products have become relatively cheaper for U.S. consumers. That will tend to increase Japanese (foreign) imports, which increases the tendency for the U.S. balance of trade to run a deficit. At the same time, 1 yen commands fewer dollars, its buying power having fallen from $.010 worth of U.S. products to only $.009 worth. Therefore, each U.S. product costs Japanese consumers more. Even though the prices of U.S. products have not changed in absolute terms, for a Japanese consumer they are relatively higher, since the yen's dollar-purchasing power has declined. As a result, fewer U.S. goods are exported to Japan, leading to further deterioration in the balance of trade. In this example, the dollar has appreciated, or gained in value with respect to the yen, while the yen has depreciated, or lost value with respect to the dollar.

The Value of the Dollar Since the 1970s

During the 1970s, the U.S. dollar experienced a spectacular decline in value relative to other major trading currencies. Beginning in the fall of 1979, the dollar began an upward roll, eventually reaching new highs against most

Discount store, Tokyo, Japan.
(Eddie Stanger/SuperStock, Inc.)

major currencies (major currency index) in early 1985 (see Figure 20.6). The decline in the 1970s reflected major weaknesses in the U.S. economy: slow growth, an impressive economic challenge by Germany and Japan, and relatively high and continuing inflation in the United States. Factors responsible for sustaining the high dollar value in the 1980s included the high U.S. budget deficits, high real interest rates, and low levels of inflation with respect to those in other industrial nations. The dollar peaked against the yen in 1985 at $1 = 260 yen.

Between 1985 and 1993, the dollar began to drop, particularly in relation to the German mark and the Japanese yen. In September of 1985, the Group of Five (the United States, United Kingdom, France, West Germany, and Japan—also known as G-5), agreed in the Plaza Accord* to intervene in foreign exchange markets to lower the value of the soaring dollar in order to promote more even-handed economic growth.[†] After 1993, the dollar had fallen to its post–World War II low against the yen at $1 = 100.9 yen. The dollar had depreciated more than 50 percent from its peak in 1985, as interest rates in the

---

*The Plaza Accord was so named after the location of the September 1985 meeting at New York City's Plaza Hotel.
[†]Currency intervention occurs when a nation (or nations) purchase (or sell) the currency of a particular nation to establish a higher (or lower) rate of exchange. In this case, the G-5 nations agreed to sell dollars so as to lower the dollar's value with respect to other trading currencies. This is truly a managed float!

FIGURE 20.6 EXCHANGE RATES

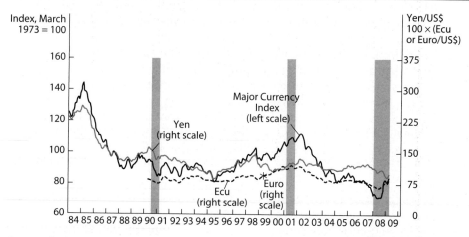

Source: Federal Reserve Bank of St. Louis, 2009.

*ECU–the precursor to the Euro.

United States and oil prices continued to fall. Since 1993, the dollar strengthened against the yen and many other major currencies and by early 1997 had moved to 125 yen per dollar.

The period between 1971 and 1997 shows a complete cycle of exchange rate movements that respond to domestic inflation, interest rates, and intervention in currency markets. Some economists argue that the U.S. merchandise trade balance was not reduced by a greater magnitude during the period of dollar decline because many foreign producers cut their profit margins in order to keep export prices low and thus maintain their share of the market. These economists also point out that the dollar depreciation was much greater with respect to the yen and German mark than to other currencies. Thus, prices of goods imported from those areas remained attractive to U.S. consumers.

4. What kind of sale on U.S.-produced goods were Japanese consumers and businesses treated to with the fall in the value of the dollar between 1985 and 1993? How would U.S. retailers advertise such a deal?

In 1997 the value of the dollar was again turning upward. The threat of increased inflation caused the Fed to institute a somewhat more restrictive monetary policy and thus an increase in interest rates in the United States. Japanese investors, still concerned with domestic banking and stock market crises, moved some of their funds to the United States and Europe to seek higher yields and perhaps greater stability. As the movement continued, the U.S. trade balance felt increased pressure as imports became more attractive to U.S. consumers and exports lost their exchange advantage in international markets.

The U.S. dollar continued to grow stronger from 1997 to the early months of 2001. As Figure 20.6 illustrates, the weak dollar of the late 1970s gave way to the strong dollar of the early 1980s, only to weaken from 1985 to 1990. From 1990 to 1995, the dollar maintained its general strength but was weaker to the yen and stronger to the euro. From 1995, the dollar began its rise for the remainder of the decade, growing stronger against the yen and the euro. Much of the strength of the dollar was related to the increased demand for dollars generated by the strong foreign demand for U.S. financial instruments and for direct investment in the United States. In addition, the demand for U.S. exports began to increase in the late 1990s.

The U.S. dollar, as measured by the major currency index in Figure 20.6, strengthened from 1999 to the beginning of 2002. After 2002, the dollar declined through 2006 into early 2008, with the U.S. economic downturn. Continued concerns about the U.S. economic recovery, contributed to the dollar's fall. By mid-2008 the dollar had strengthened against many major currencies as investors perceived the U.S. dollar as a safe haven. By mid-2009 the dollar again began to lose value, particularly against the euro. The growing U.S. trade and current account deficit and the domestic budget deficit were also major factors contributing to this decline.

THE FUTURE OF THE INTERNATIONAL FINANCIAL SYSTEM

As the twenty-first century began, global capital markets became more integrated. Economic policy makers and central bankers from all countries realized that their ability to control their respective domestic economies, in the context of rapid global change, was increasingly more difficult and less effective. Capital was highly mobile. It could move quickly. Currency values were increasingly volatile.

The countries with the eight largest industrial economies (the United States, Canada, United Kingdom, France, Germany, Italy, Russia, and Japan), together known as the G-8 countries, responded by voluntarily coordinating some of their economic policies. Their ongoing effort to cooperate has been mildly successful. Still, without the discipline of an enforcement mechanism, countries tend to do only what is self-serving and politically expedient. Annual economic summits have served largely to bring together the members of the G-8 for public relations, ritual identification of the problems they face collectively, and only moderate cooperation.

By 2006, the global economy was marked by rapid and dramatic forces of change. Developing countries in Asia, Latin America, and Africa were moving toward market economies and democratic governments. Other nations in transition in Eastern Europe, Central Europe, and the Commonwealth of Independent States were also following the path toward establishing market economies, drawing enormous attention to the potential opportunities afforded by these emerging market economies. In these countries there was a new interest in stock and bond markets, along with investment scandals, such as the one in Albania in 1997, which produced riots and a governmental crisis. Increased capital flows in the form of direct private foreign investment in these countries led many international commercial banks and investment banks to aggressively establish themselves there.

From the 1990s to the early years of the twenty-first century, China and India emerged as powerful new players in the global economy. Western Europe continued to adapt to the changes and challenges of European economic integration and monetary union for most of the EU members. West Germany's integration with East Germany slowed the locomotive for European economic growth a bit. And while all this had been taking place, the competitive pressures of the marketplace were pushing even more rapid change.

The mid-1990s found Japan coming out of three years of recession, only to have its economy collapse again in 1998 as fears of a currency crisis gripped Asia and spread to Latin America. In 2001, Japan continued to try to solve many internal financial and political problems as well as confront new competitive pressures in its own backyard. By 2004, the United States and the global economy were entering a period of synchronized growth and economic recovery. But the U.S. occupation of Iraq, the terrorist train bombing in Madrid, and the continued instability in the Middle East provided a context for an underlying concern about the prospects for continued growth and stability.

Economic growth continued until 2008 when the effects of the financial and economic crisis began to spread. The effects of the housing market bubble bursting lasting through 2009. The low interest rates that provided for easy access to credit and financing generated housing price increases, near zero savings, and rising household debt in the United States. Regulators were late to recognize the potential consequences of this situation while it was brewing. When the crisis hit, both the U.S. and global economy went into a tailspin. Global growth and international trade slowed dramatically, or ceased, as frozen credit markets prevented even the most basic economic activities, such as borrowing and lending, from taking place.

At the end of 2009, the United States was left with twin deficits including a budget deficit due to the growing public debt and a considerable current account deficit. Major issues and challenges for the United States remained, including restoring economic growth, fiscal integrity, and re-regulating the financial sector to prevent another crisis. There was also the need for international coordination and cooperation to address the structural and regulatory aspects of the current crisis. Indeed, European leaders called for a new international conference similar to that held in Bretton Woods after World War II (see box below) to focus on institutions and policies and regulations to provide sound footing for future world trade and finance. Another issue for such a conference would be the future role of the U.S. dollar in the global economy. The United States has depended on borrowing from other countries to finance both public and private spending. In the following article, "China's Leader Says He Is 'Worried' Over U.S. Treasuries," Michael Wines, Keith Bradsher, and Mark Landler report on China's growing concern about U.S. policies and its ability to repay debt in the future.

Exchange Rate Systems: An Historical Perspective

Some type of international financial system is required to deal with the "imbalances" in the balance-of-payments positions among nations. If the United States, for example, has an overall balance-of-trade deficit with the rest of the world, some mechanism must exist for "balancing" that deficit. Throughout the history of modern world capitalism, several different systems have existed for accomplishing this task, including fixed and fluctuating exchange standards.

The Gold Standard

Gold served as the external form of payment in the international system from the Middle Ages until the twentieth century. Under a gold standard, a country's currency is convertible into gold at a fixed price. The price of the currency expressed in terms of gold is known as its *parity value*. The United States and the United Kingdom once defined their currencies in terms of gold. As a result, surpluses and deficits in the balance of payments were equivalent to a certain amount of gold.

This mechanism was relatively simple and had some attractive results. The flow of gold from the United Kingdom would reduce the money supply in the United Kingdom and increase it in the United States. As an automatic reaction, prices would fall in the United Kingdom and rise in the United States, since less (more) money would tend to force prices downward (upward) and since gold was a part of the money supply. Consumers in each country would then respond to the price changes. Exports of U.S. goods would tend to fall, and those of the United Kingdom would tend to increase. Consequently, the balance-of-payments surplus of the United States would tend to decline, all without any government intervention.

The concept of liquidity is vital to trade in that transactions require some standard of "moneyness" that is universally accepted, and the trading parties must have this liquidity. Under the gold standard, if countries do not have enough gold reserves (or gold mines) to facilitate trade or if output of goods and services outstrips the output of gold, a liquidity crisis results. The health of domestic economies is therefore at the mercy of the world's ability to produce gold. In practice, the gold standard limited the amount of international trade that could be financed and tended to restrict some domestic economies. As nations and trade grew, the limited gold resources could not satisfy the needs of world trade.

The International Monetary Fund and the Bretton Woods System

Two world wars separated by the Great Depression dealt fatal blows to the gold standard. The framework for the system that forms the official organizational structure of today's international financial negotiations was formulated in 1944 at a conference in Bretton Woods, New Hampshire, and became known as the **Bretton Woods system.** The institutional arrangements settled on were to be overseen by a new organization, the **International Monetary Fund (IMF).** The IMF was established to provide an institutional framework for monetary cooperation and consultation when problems arose. It was charged with facilitating expansion and balanced growth of trade with high levels of domestic income and employment.

To accomplish this goal, the participants established a system of fixed exchange rates. Under the fixed exchange system, currencies were defined in terms of one another. The IMF was to provide for stable exchange rates between currencies. Consistency was assured, with each nation defining its currency in terms of both gold and the U.S. dollar. The U.S. dollar maintained a passive role in the Bretton Woods system because it was chosen to serve as the key or reserve currency, making it as acceptable as gold in international transactions. The Bretton Woods system functioned with this fixed exchange system until 1973.

International Monetary Crisis

The IMF was created and designed to guarantee the working of the Bretton Woods system, but problems sent the fixed exchange system into periods of confusion and disarray, never quite fulfilling the dreams of its creators. According to the design of the Bretton Woods system, exchange rate adjustments should occur in cases of persistent balance-of-payments difficulties. However, because the dollar was the reserve currency and essential for international liquidity, necessary dollar adjustments were avoided. In addition, more serious trouble lay deeper than this. Currency realignments were rare under the Bretton Woods system. Many believed depreciation was a sign of national weakness, while appreciation was viewed not as a sign of strength but as a compromise to a weaker economic position. Many nations' exchange rates were out of kilter, since they remained at essentially the same parity rates that existed at the end of World War II.

With ever-increasing deficits in the balance of payments, U.S. policy remained much the same during the 1960s. During this period, the IMF virtually conceded its operations to the Group of Ten, consisting of the ten most economically powerful countries in the world. At their meetings they discussed and acted at any indication of weakness in currency operations—but prompt realignment of parity rates did not occur. A system of emergency capital flows developed, with funds being shuttled from one weak currency to the next. This led only to greater instability within the Bretton Woods system.

In August 1971, President Nixon introduced the New Economic Policy (NEP), which, along with domestic wage and price controls, called for a temporary 10 percent surcharge on all imports as well as a "temporary" halt in the convertibility of dollars into gold. (This temporary condition still exists, and it is now understood that August 15, 1971, marked the complete end of the gold exchange standard. Although U.S. citizens have not been able to exchange their dollar holdings for gold from the U.S. Treasury since 1934, foreign dollar holders continued to exchange dollars for gold until this suspension.) Under the burden of inflation and the high costs of the war in Vietnam, the U.S. balance-of-payments deficit was larger and more pressing than it had been at any time in the nation's history.

Floating Exchange Rates

On December 18, 1971, President Nixon committed what a few years earlier would have been political suicide and devalued the dollar. The "historic" Smithsonian agreement called for an 8 percent devaluation of the dollar and a realignment of other currencies to reflect the lower value of the dollar. As pressures continued, nations began to let their currencies float (adjust to daily changes in the supply of and demand for each currency).

Since 1973, *de facto* currency depreciations or appreciations occur without official IMF sanction. The overvalued dollar was allowed to seek its own worth in the somewhat free international currency markets. The IMF was given the power to "oversee the exchange rate regime, adopt principles to guide national policies, and encourage international cooperation."

In the years since the introduction of floating exchange rates, the international monetary system has adjusted surprisingly well, even though the central banks of most major industrial countries have intervened at one time or another to "manage" or intervene in their exchange rates. Floating exchange rates have presented special problems for developing economies, however. Because few of these nations had well-developed currency markets, they tied or pegged their currency to that of their major industrial trading partner. A developing nation whose currency was pegged to the British pound found that its currency, like the pound, depreciated by almost 25 percent between mid-1975 and the end of 1976. These kinds of exchange rate movements can cause severe inflationary pressures in developing countries where inflation is often a persistent problem.

China's Leader Says He Is "Worried" Over U.S. Treasuries

BEIJING — The Chinese prime minister, Wen Jiabao, spoke in unusually blunt terms on Friday about the "safety" of China's $1 trillion investment in American government debt, the world's largest such holding, and urged the Obama administration to offer assurances that the securities would maintain their value.

Speaking ahead of a meeting of finance ministers and bankers this weekend near London to lay the groundwork for next month's Group of 20 summit meeting of the nations with the 20 largest economies, Mr. Wen said that he was "worried" about China's holdings of United States Treasury bonds and other debt, and that China was watching economic developments in the United States closely.

As the financial crisis has unfolded, China has become increasingly vocal about what it perceives as Washington's mismanagement of the global economy and financial system, joining a chorus of foreign critics of unbridled American capitalism. On Thursday, for example, France and Germany rebuffed American calls to coordinate a global stimulus package at the G-20 meeting, saying financial regulation should come first.

In January, Mr. Wen gave a speech criticizing what he called an "unsustainable model of development characterized by prolonged low savings and high consumption." There was little doubt that he was referring to the United States....

With budget deficits mounting rapidly, the United States needs China if it is to finance all that new debt at low interest rates.

"President Obama and his new government have adopted a series of measures to deal with the financial crisis. We have expectations as to the effects of these measures," Mr. Wen said. "We have lent a huge amount of money to the U.S. Of course we are concerned about the safety of our assets. To be honest, I am definitely a little worried."

He called on the United States to "maintain its good credit, to honor its promises and to guarantee the safety of China's assets." What he did not mention was that Chinese investments in the United States helped drive the debt-fueled boom of the last decade, during which China grew increasingly dependent on the American market—a point that was driven home earlier this week when China reported a record 26 percent drop in exports in February.

He stopped short of any threat to reduce purchases of American bonds, much less sell any of them, underscoring the two countries' mutual dependency.

Some specialists say that China's investment in American debt is now so vast that it would be impossible for Beijing to unload its Treasury securities without flooding the market and driving down their price....

While economists dismiss the possibility of the United States defaulting on its obligations, they say China could face steep losses in the event of a sharp rise in United States interest rates or a plunge in the value of the dollar.

Mr. Wen praised China's comparatively healthy economy and said his government would take whatever steps were needed to end the country's slump. He also predicted that the world economy would improve in 2010....

Mr. Wen's confident performance also underscored the growing financial and geopolitical importance of China, one of the few countries to retain enormous spending power despite slowing growth. It has the world's largest reserves of foreign exchange, estimated at $2 trillion, the product of years of double-digit growth.

Economists say at least half of that money has been invested in United States Treasury notes and other government-backed debt, mostly bonds issued by the Treasury and government-sponsored enterprises, Fannie Mae and Freddie Mac.

Much of the Treasury debt China purchased in recent years carries a low interest rate and would plunge in value if interest rates were to rise sharply in the United States. Some financial experts have warned that measures taken to combat the financial crisis — running large budget deficits and expanding the money supply — may eventually lead to higher interest rates.

"The United States government is going to have to sell a huge amount of paper, and the market may react by demanding a higher interest rate," said Nicholas R. Lardy, an expert in the Chinese economy at the Peterson Institute for International Economics. "This will force down the price of outstanding treasuries, imposing large paper losses on the Chinese."

The conflicting financial currents pose a dilemma for Beijing. The smaller the United States stimulus, the less its borrowing, which could help prevent interest rates from rising. But less government spending in the United States could also mean a slower recovery for the American economy and reduced American demand for Chinese goods.

The sharp narrowing of China's trade surplus with the United States may result in reduced Chinese purchases of American bonds in any case. By some accounts, China's trade surplus could fall by as much as half this year, to around $155 billion. That would leave China with fewer dollars to buy foreign bonds, particularly as the pace of investment flows into China has also slowed sharply.

During her visit here last month, Secretary of State Hillary Rodham Clinton publicly assured China that its American holdings remained a reliable investment. But the sheer size of China's holdings of American debt ensure that the countries' partnership will endure, some analysts say. "The only possibility, really, is that China will have to hold these bonds until maturity," said Shen Minggao, the chief economist at Caijing, a Beijing-based business magazine. "If you start to sell those bonds, the market may collapse."

Michael Wines reported from Beijing, Keith Bradsher from Hong Kong, and Mark Landler from Washington.

❖Conclusion

With all of these changes taking place, what will become of the international financial system? A number of factors currently drive this system with interactive effects. The context of these changes is a competitive system characterized by deregulation, free markets, and innovation. Deregulation and innovation have generated exchange rate volatility as financial entities have applied new computer and information system technologies to their operations and the development of new products and services.

Clearly, these issues confound simple Keynesian solutions to macroeconomic problems. As we move further into this millennium, global policy makers will continue to be challenged to find workable solutions that promote worldwide economic stability.

In Chapter 21 we examine the role of emerging nations in the future of the international financial system. As a nation's economy continues to grow, it experiences particular pressures on energy (fossil fuels especially), natural resources, and the environment.

Review Questions

1. What is the international balance of payments? What does it mean to have a balance-of-payments surplus or deficit?

2. What kinds of activities contribute positive credits (+) to a nation's balance of payments?

3. How can you use the National Income Accounting framework to illustrate a trade deficit?

4. What has been the experience of the United States with trade deficits and current account deficits since 1990?

5. What has been the experience of the U.S. dollar since 2000? What is the situation for the U.S. dollar today?

6. What are the primary determinants of the value of a nation's currency (exchange rate)?

7. What can explain the appreciation of the dollar? The depreciation of the dollar?

8. What have been the yen/dollar and euro/dollar relationship since 2006? What is your analysis of these relationships?

CHAPTER TWENTY-ONE

The Economics
of Developing Nations

◆ Introduction

According to the United Nations, by the year 2020 approximately 80 percent of the world's population (an estimated 8 billion) will be living in developing countries. What will this mean in terms of global poverty? The competition for global resources? The economic growth and development needs of these countries? Relations between the more-developed and less-developed countries?

By the early 1960s, it had become common practice to refer to nations as being part of either the First, Second, or Third World. Those in the First World were the Western industrialized market economies, while those in the Second World were members of the socialist planned economies. The remaining nations fell into the category of the Third World. The nations of the Third World were the developing nations of Asia, Africa, the Middle East, and Latin America. Most of these nations had achieved political independence by the early 1960s and found themselves caught between the First and Second Worlds in terms of both the Cold War and their own quest for economic development.

By 1960 the economic gap between the developed and developing world had widened to such an extent that the United Nations declared the 1960s to be the "Development Decade." Since then, the global community and many international institutions such as the World Bank and the International Monetary Fund have devoted considerable resources to bring about economic development in the Third World over the last fifty years. These efforts, as we shall see, have produced mixed results, great controversy, and an emerging consensus on the future direction of development.

COMMON CHARACTERISTICS OF DEVELOPING NATIONS

Despite great diversity among developing nations, they share a set of common characteristics. A developing nation typically has the following attributes:

❖ Low standard of living

❖ Low level of labor productivity

❖ High rate of population growth

❖ High and rising level of unemployment and underemployment

❖ Dependency on agricultural production and primary product exports

❖ Vulnerability in international political, economic, and financial relations

Global Poverty

At the end of the twentieth century, about 1.2 billion people lived in abject poverty (surviving on $1 a day or less). As shown in Table 21.1, the number of people living on less than $2 a day decreased slightly from 2,654 million in 1990 to 2,564 million in 2005. These 2.5 billion people represented 47 percent of the world's population. The strong global economic growth that took place from 2002 to 2005 resulted in these numbers actually declining from the 2002 levels. (The deep global recession of 2008–2009 pushed these numbers back up but it was not clear just how much by the end of 2009.) In South Asia and sub-Saharan Africa, 75 percent of the population is classified as poor. By comparison, Latin America and the Caribbean had a poverty rate of 24.0 percent and Europe and Central Asia only 16.1 percent. Although over the past decade poverty rates have improved significantly East Asia, sub-Saharan Africa and South Asia have not seen improvement. The Great Recession of 2007–2009 may well slow improvement in these poverty rates.

Global poverty on such a scale is even more dramatic when looked at in terms of the *distribution* of global income. A 2005 IMF study revealed that 77 percent of the world's people earn 15 percent of its income.

Table 21.1 Number of People in the World Living on Less than $2.00 per day (millions)

	1990		2002		2005	
	millions	**percent**	**millions**	**percent**	**millions**	**percent**
East Asia & Pacific	1,274	(79.8)	954	(51.9)	729	(38.7)
China	961	(84.6)	655	(51.2)	474	(36.3)
Europe & Central Asia	32	(6.9)	57	(12.0)	42	(8.9)
Latin America & Caribbean	96	(21.9)	114	(21.6)	94	(17.1)
Middle East & North Africa	44	(19.7)	51	(17.6)	51	(16.9)
South Asia	926	(82.7)	1,084	(77.1)	1,092	(73.9)
India	702	(82.6)	813	(77.5)	828	(75.6)
Sub-Saharan Africa	393	(76.1)	536	(75.6)	556	(72.9)
Total	2,765	(63.4)	2,795	(53.3)	2,594	(47.0)

Source: World Bank, *World Development Indicators,* 2008, p. 11.

Underdevelopment: The Reality and Significance

It is difficult—if not impossible—for those of us living in a modern advanced nation such as the United States to understand what it would be like to live in poverty in a developing nation. Denis Goulet, a professor at the University of Notre Dame, has put it eloquently:

> Underdevelopment is shocking: the squalor, disease, unnecessary deaths, and hopelessness of it all! No man understands if underdevelopment remains for him a mere statistic reflecting low income, poor housing, premature mortality, or underemployment. The most empathetic observer can speak objectively about underdevelopment only after undergoing, personally or vicariously, the "shock of underdevelopment." This unique cultural shock comes to one as he is initiated to the emotions which prevail in the "culture of poverty." The reverse shock is felt by those living in destitution when a new self-understanding reveals to them that their life is neither human nor inevitable. The prevalent emotion of underdevelopment is a sense of personal and societal impotence in the face of disease and death, of confusion and ignorance as one gropes to understand change, of servility toward men whose decisions govern the course of events, of hopelessness before hunger and natural catastrophe. Chronic poverty is a cruel kind of hell, and one cannot understand how cruel that hell is merely by gazing upon poverty as an object.

—Denis Goulet, *The Cruel Choice*, Atheneum, 1975

1. Have you ever been to a developing country? Did you see the kind of underdevelopment described in the quotation? If not, can you imagine this kind of reality?

The Hidden Hunger

Nicholas D. Kristof
BISSAU, Guinea-Bissau—

The most heartbreaking thing about starving children is their equanimity.

They don't cry. They don't smile. They don't move. They don't show a flicker of fear, pain or interest. Tiny, wizened zombies, they shut down all nonessential operations to employ every last calorie to stay alive.

We in the West misunderstand starvation—especially the increasing hunger caused by the global economic crisis—and so along with Paul Bowers, the student winner of my "win-a-trip" contest, I've been traveling across five countries in West Africa, meeting the malnourished.

At the extreme, they were like Maximiano Camara, a 15-month-old boy here in Bissau, who was so emaciated that he risked failure of major organs. His ribs protruded, his eyes were glassy, his skin was stretched taut over tiny bones.

(Doctors try to help but are overwhelmed: One was showing me Maximiano when a nurse rushed in from another room carrying a baby who had stopped breathing. The doctor paused, revived that child on the next bed, handed her back to the nurse, and then calmly resumed his discussion of Maximiano.)

Even if Maximiano survives, hunger may leave him physically stunted. Or poor nutrition may have already withered the development of his brain.

It's impossible to know if Maximiano was starving because of the economic crisis or because of chronic malnutrition here, but the hardships in the developing world have been exacerbated by elevated food prices and declining remittances from workers abroad.

The World Bank has estimated that United Nations goals for overcoming global poverty have been set back seven years by the global crisis. It calculates that increased malnutrition last year may have caused an additional 44 million children to suffer permanent physical or mental impairment.

Yet one of the great Western misconceptions is that severe malnutrition is simply about not getting enough to eat. Often it's about not getting the right micronutrients—iron, zinc, vitamin A, iodine—and one of the most cost-effective ways outsiders can combat poverty is to fight this "hidden hunger."

Malnutrition is not a glamorous field, and so it's routinely neglected by everybody—donor governments, poor countries and, yes, journalists. But malnutrition is implicated in one-third to one-half of all child deaths each year; the immediate cause may be diarrhea, but lurking behind it is a deficiency of zinc.

"That image of a starving child in a famine doesn't represent the magnitude of the problem," notes Shawn Baker of Helen Keller International, a New York-based aid group working in this area. "For every child who is like that, you have 10 who are somewhat malnourished and many more who are deficient in micronutrients.

"Lack of iron is the most widespread nutrition deficiency in the world, and yet you can't really see it," he added.

In my column last Sunday, I wrote about women dying in childbirth. One reason so many die of hemorrhages is that 42 percent of pregnant women worldwide have anemia, according to the World Health Organization.

And here in Guinea-Bissau, 83 percent of youngsters under age 5 suffer from iron deficiency.

An American or European typically has a hemoglobin, or Hb, level of 13, while anemic women and children in Africa are sometimes at 5 or below.

"In Europe, we get worried when Hb drops to 9, and then we consider a transfusion," said Dr. Annette Kröber, a German working at a Doctors Without Borders clinic for malnourished children in Sierra Leone. "Here, when we get Hb up to 6, we're very happy."

The general rise in food prices (in part because of American use of corn for ethanol) is leading to more micronutrient deficiencies. One study found that a 50 percent rise in food prices in poor countries leads to a 30 percent drop in iron intake.

One solution is to distribute supplements to vulnerable people, or to fortify foods with micronutrients. A panel of prominent economists produced the "Copenhagen Consensus" on which forms of aid are most cost-effective, and it ranked micronutrient supplements as No. 1 (malaria prevention was No. 12, sanitation No. 20, and microfinance No. 22).

Americans typically get micronutrients from fortified foods, and the same strategy is possible in Africa. Helen Keller International is helping Guinea's leading flour mill fortify its products with iron, folic acid and vitamin B (zinc is coming soon). We visited the mill, and managers said that the fortification costs virtually nothing—a tiny fraction of a penny per loaf of bread—yet it will reduce anemia, maternal mortality and cognitive impairments around the country.

None of this is glamorous, but it's hugely needed—and truly a bargain.

2. What does the author mean by the phrase "hidden hunger"?

3. What is the primary misconception about malnutrition and why is this important for being able to address the problem?

4. How have rising food prices contributed to this problem?

5. What seems to be a much needed solution to this problem?

Underdevelopment is an economic as well as human condition. In economic terms, we tend to think of an underdeveloped country as having a low per capita income and a low per capita gross domestic product. A developing country usually has a large percentage of its labor force in agriculture. It typically has a shortage of domestic savings, so it must rely on external capital and technology to stimulate investment and economic growth. Such a country usually depends on a small number of primary exports (raw materials and food crops) and some manufactured goods. It typically has balance-of-payments problems that stem from current account deficits (deficits in trade and investment income). In addition to the climate disaster, poverty and AIDS and other diseases, developing countries also suffer from large external debts, which require sizable debt servicing (interest and principal payments). Payment of the debt involves outflows of interest and principal to foreign creditors.

While many economists tend to discuss underdevelopment in economic terms, others have expanded the economic aspect to include categories such as productivity, equity, sustainability, and empowerment. The box below emphasizes each of these categories as a part of a more fully developed definition of what constitutes not just economic development but human development. (This paradigm has been developed by the United Nations.)

Components of the Human Development Paradigm

The human development paradigm contains four main components:

❖ *Productivity*—People must be enabled to increase their productivity and to participate fully in the process of income generation and remunerative employment. Economic growth is, therefore, a subset of human development models.

❖ *Equity*—People must have access to equal opportunities. All barriers to economic and political opportunities must be eliminated so that people can participate in, and benefit from, these opportunities.

❖ *Sustainability*—Access to opportunities must be ensured not only for the present generations but for future generations as well. All forms of capital—physical, human, environmental—should be replenished.

❖ *Empowerment*—Development must be by people, not only for them. People must participate fully in the decisions and processes that shape their lives.

Source: *Human Development Report*, 1995.

6. Are there any other goals that you would add to this list? Explain.

7. What kinds of policies and programs would be necessary to reduce global poverty 50 percent by 2015?

8. What would you say is the global public health challenge?

BASIC ECONOMIC PROBLEMS OF DEVELOPING NATIONS

To complete our basic profile of a developing country, we turn to a more detailed discussion of the basic economic problems of developing nations. These problems include economic growth, population, macroeconomic instability, international trade and finance, and environmental problems.

Millennium Development Goals

In 2000, the United Nations presented its Millennium Development Goals. The economic optimism for the global economy going into the twenty-first century provided a positive context for these lofty yet necessary goals for the global community. Each of the goals had selected targets to be met by 2015.

The Millennium Development Goals

1. Halve the proportion of people living on less than a dollar a day.

2. Ensure all children complete primary school.

3. Educate boys and girls equally.

4. Reduce the mortality rate among children under five by two-thirds.

5. Reduce the maternal mortality rate by three-quarters.

6. Halt and begin to reverse the spread of HIV/AIDS, malaria, and other diseases.

7. Halve the proportion of people without access to safe water and sanitation.

8. Increase aid and improve governance.

Economic Growth

The primary consideration for developing countries is increasing the rate of economic growth. The essence of seeking higher levels of economic growth is to produce more goods and services to improve the population's material standard of living. Economic development, in its most basic sense, is the process of improving standards of living and well-being by raising per capita income.

As we have seen, economic growth depends on a number of factors. In a macroeconomic context, it involves increasing consumption, investment, government spending, and trade. In a microeconomic context, it involves physical resources, labor resources, and technology as applied to production. Microeconomic concerns oblige us to think in terms of efficiency and productivity. Macroeconomic issues require us to think in terms of savings flowing to investments in productive activities. Taken separately or together, these two perspectives on economic growth frame a context for understanding the challenges of economic development.

Table 21.2 Emerging and Developing Economies: Real GDP (Annual percent change)

	Average 1991–2000	2001	2002	2003	2004	2005	2006	2007	2008	2009	2010*	2014*
Emerging and developing economies	**3.6**	**3.8**	**4.8**	**6.3**	**7.5**	**7.1**	**8.0**	**8.3**	**6.1**	**1.6**	**4.0**	**6.8**
Regional groups												
Africa	2.4	4.9	6.5	5.5	6.7	5.8	6.1	6.2	5.2	2.0	3.9	5.4
Sub-Sahara	2.4	5.0	7.3	5.2	7.1	6.2	6.6	6.9	5.5	1.7	3.8	5.4
Excluding Nigeria and South Africa	2.8	5.5	4.6	4.5	7.1	7.2	7.6	8.2	6.9	2.3	5.3	5.6
Central and eastern Europe	2.0	0.0	4.4	4.9	7.3	6.0	6.6	5.4	2.9	-3.7	0.8	4.0
Commonwealth of Independent States[a]	—	6.1	5.2	7.8	8.2	6.7	8.4	8.6	5.5	-5.1	1.2	5.3
Russia	—	5.1	4.7	7.3	7.2	6.4	7.7	8.1	5.6	-6.0	0.5	5.0
Excluding Russia	—	8.9	6.6	9.1	10.8	7.4	10.2	9.9	5.3	-2.9	3.1	5.9
Developing Asia	7.4	5.8	6.9	8.2	8.6	9.0	9.8	10.6	7.7	4.8	6.1	8.8
China	10.4	8.3	9.1	10.0	10.1	10.4	11.6	13.0	9.0	6.5	7.5	10.0
India	5.6	3.9	4.6	6.9	7.9	9.2	9.8	9.3	7.3	4.5	5.6	8.0
Excluding China and India	4.7	2.9	4.8	5.8	6.3	6.1	6.1	6.4	5.1	0.9	2.8	6.1
Middle East	4.0	2.6	3.8	7.0	6.0	5.8	5.7	6.3	5.9	2.5	3.5	4.5
Western Hemisphere	3.3	0.7	0.6	2.2	6.0	4.7	5.7	5.7	4.2	-1.5	1.6	4.3
Brazil	2.5	1.3	2.7	1.1	5.7	3.2	4.0	5.7	5.1	-1.3	2.2	4.5
Mexico	3.5	-0.2	0.8	1.7	4.0	3.2	5.1	3.3	1.3	-3.7	1.0	4.9
Memorandum												
Real per capita GDP												
Emerging and developing economies	2.0	2.4	3.4	4.9	6.1	5.8	6.6	7.1	4.8	0.3	2.5	5.3
Africa	-0.2	2.4	4.0	3.0	4.2	3.4	3.7	3.8	2.7	-0.4	1.5	3.0
Central and eastern Europe	1.5	-0.5	3.8	4.4	6.8	5.5	6.6	5.1	2.6	-4.1	0.4	3.6
Commonwealth of Independent States[a]	—	6.5	5.6	7.8	8.4	6.9	8.4	8.6	5.5	-5.1	1.5	5.3
Developing Asia	5.8	4.5	5.6	6.9	7.4	7.9	8.7	9.5	6.6	3.7	4.6	7.4
Middle East	1.7	0.3	1.8	4.8	3.8	3.6	3.1	4.0	3.7	0.3	1.4	2.1
Western Hemisphere	1.6	-0.7	-1.0	0.8	4.5	3.4	4.2	4.3	2.8	-2.8	0.3	3.2

[a]Mongolia, which is not a member of the Commonwealth of Independent States, is included in this group for reasons of geography and similarities in economic structure.

Source: IMF, *World Economic Outlook, 2009*, p. 5.

*2010 and 2014, projected estimates.

As Table 21.2 shows, the economic growth experience of emerging and developing economies was very positive from 1991 forward with real GDP growth rates moving from 3.8 percent in 2001 to a high of 8.3 percent in 2007. Real per capita growth rates mirrored the trajectory of real GDP, improving from 2.4 percent in 2001 to a high of 7.1 percent in 2007. (Regional groups had some degree of variation, with China and India posting the largest gains and Africa continuing to lag behind the rest of the global community.) The global recession of 2008 and 2009 clearly reversed these gains in the near term. The expectation was that by 2014, a stronger period of economic growth would evolve, with higher GDP per capita growth as well.

Population: Undermining Economic Growth

In 2000, the world's population reached the 6.0 billion mark. The United Nations and the World Bank projected that global population would reach 8.8 billion by the year 2030. Of these, 7.4 billion (or 84 percent) of humanity will be living in the low- and middle-income countries.

Figure 21.1 shows world population growth from 1950–2050. Table 21.3 illustrates the growth of world population from 1975 to 2003, with projections for the year 2015. The low- and middle-income countries have made some progress in reducing the average annual population growth rate from 2.5 percent between 1965 and 1975 to 2.1 percent for low-income countries and 1.4 percent for middle-income countries between 1975 and 2003. Yet this reduction has not been enough

FIGURE 21.1 World Population: 1950–2050

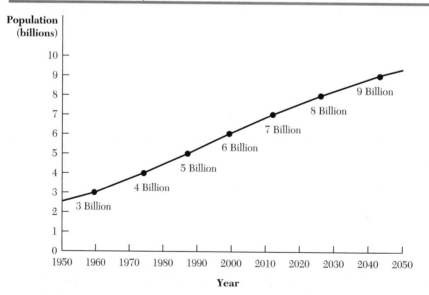

The world population increased from 3 billion in 1959 to 6 billion by 1999, a doubling that occurred over 40 years. The Census Bureau's latest projections imply that population growth will continue in the 21st century, although more slowly. The world population is projected to grow from 6 billion in 1999 to 9 billion by 2043, an increase of 50 percent that is expected to require 44 years.

Source: U.S. Census Bureau, International Data Base, June 2009 Update.

Table 21.3 Population

	Total Population* (millions)		Annual Population Growth Rate (%)	
	2003	2015	1975–2003	2003–2015
Developing Countries	5,022.4	5,885.6	1.9	1.3
Least developed countries	723.2	950.1	2.5	2.3
Arab states	303.9	386.0	2.7	2.0
East Asia and the Pacific	1,928.1	2,108.9	1.4	0.7
Latin America and the Caribbean	540.7	628.3	1.9	1.3
South Asia	1,503.4	1,801.4	2.1	1.5
Sub-Saharan Africa	674.2	877.4	2.7	2.2
Central and Eastern Europe and the CIS	406.3	396.8	0.4	−0.2
High Income	948.3	1,005.6	0.7	0.5
Middle Income	2,748.6	3,028.6	1.4	0.8
Low Income	2,614.5	3,182.5	2.1	1.6
World	6,313.8*	7,219.4*	1.6	1.1

*Reprinted from the UN Human Development Report, 2005. © United Nations Publications. All rights reserved.

Source: United Nations, *Human Development Report*, 2005, http://hdr.undp.org/statistics/data/pdf/hdr05_table_5.pdf.

to halt the rapid increase in population growth from 2.4 billion in 1965 to 4.1 billion in 1990 to 6.3 billion in 2003. The age structure (number of persons in specific age groups) in the least developed countries is such that 35 to 50 percent of the population is under age 15, and the women in this category are in or entering their peak fertility years. So, even if the average annual population growth rate is declining, say from 2.5 percent to 1.7 percent as is projected, the absolute size of the population is still increasing dramatically.

Even more striking is the situation in much of Africa. In sub-Saharan Africa, the average annual population growth rate has been about 3 percent for more than 25 years. This is more than a full percentage point above the world average and more than three times the average for high-income countries, where the population growth rate is less than 1.0 percent.

9. What do these data mean in the context of economic development and the economic growth data examined earlier?

The population growth and pressure in the poorest nations will continue in the context of a projected slowdown in the growth of the global economic system. With more mouths to feed as the number of the world's poor increases, the ability of nations to realistically increase their standard of living by increasing the real per capita GDP will be all the more difficult, if not impossible. Any improvement requires major changes on many different fronts, not the least of which is population control.

The basic issue is that for economic progress to take place, the rate of economic growth has to exceed the rate of population growth. This has not been happening in the Third World.

Macroeconomic Instability

Developing nations share with everyone the same basic overall goal of sustained economic growth with price stability. Yet, unlike the more advanced industrialized countries, their ability to practice traditional Keynesian stabilization policies has proven to be more limited. Many analysts have pointed out that the basic Keynesian theoretical and policy framework evolved out of unique circumstances—the crisis of a well-developed capitalist market economy in the 1930s—and it has been refined in that context ever since. In many developing nations, however, the state of development of free markets and other economic institutions presents unique complexities when it comes to developing policy prescriptions for inflation and unemployment. In other words, traditional Keynesian stimulus policies (increased government spending, lower taxes, lower interest rates, etc.) may not be sufficient to trigger higher growth.

Moreover, in developing nations, inflation rates may be as high as 25 percent to more than 1,000 percent. High rates of inflation have the same negative consequences on the economy as in advanced market economies, but to a greater degree. From a policy perspective, developing countries typically resort to conventional Keynesian stabilization policies: reducing government spending, increasing taxes, and reducing government deficits. These usually result in slower growth and higher unemployment, neither of which poor developing countries can tolerate. Contractionary fiscal policy is usually matched with a tight monetary policy, but reducing the growth rate of the money supply and increasing interest rates only worsens the contraction of the economy.

Unemployment in developing countries is also a critical problem, and official government unemployment statistics tend to understate its severity. This is a result of political considerations, as well as different methods of determining unemployment than in more advanced market economies. When a country announces that its unemployment rate is only 6 percent, the actual rate may be closer to 30 percent or even more in rural areas. The difficulty in measurement comes from the fact that large numbers of people work outside of formal labor markets. In the informal labor market, there is no official record of work, wages, or taxes. People working in the informal labor market may exchange labor for goods and/or services, or they may work occasionally for cash for which there is no official record.

Furthermore, while formal unemployment is a problem, *underemployment* is a much greater problem. Many people working in the formal labor market are working only a few days or hours a week while seeking full-time employment. In many developing countries, underemployment rates are estimated to be in the range of 40 to 50 percent.

Government policies to address unemployment and underemployment are usually the standard Keynesian expansionary prescription: increase government spending, lower taxes, increase the money supply, and lower interest rates. But these policies are difficult to implement because inflation is severe

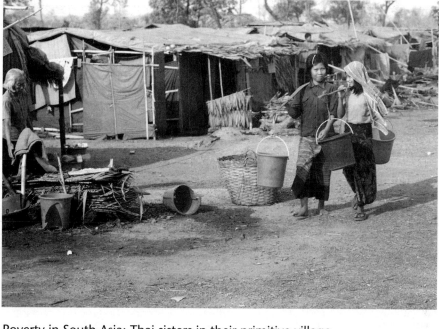

Poverty in South Asia: Thai sisters in their primitive village.
(Mark Richards/PhotoEdit)

and governments confront large internal deficits and demanding external debts. For this reason, many leaders champion the growth of the informal sector.

The global recession that began in 2008 and continued through 2009 and 2010 had a devastating impact on global employment. The International Labor Office estimated that global unemployment soared to 50 million people in 2009. While China has been the fastest-growing nation in the world and tens of millions of people have migrated from the rural areas to the urban areas seeking employment, this economic crisis has had a decisive impact on rising unemployment in China as the following article, "China Fears Tremors as Jobs Vanish from Coast," describes. Because of this situation and the possible political consequences, China initiated its own economic stimulus spending program to generate jobs for those who had lost jobs.

China Fears Tremors as Jobs Vanish from Coast
Andrew Jacobs

TANJIA, China — Tan Tianying might not look like a troublemaker, but she and millions of other workers like her have government leaders fretting about the country's stability.

A shy, delicately built seamstress who makes aprons and coveralls in Guangzhou,

Ms. Tan, 24, is part of an army of migrants, 130 million strong, who have flocked to cities for jobs, but whose prospects for continued employment are increasingly dim.

As the global economic crisis deepens and the demand for Chinese exports slackens, manufacturing jobs in the Pearl River Delta and all along the once-booming coast are disappearing at a stunning pace. Over the last few months, more than 20 million migrant workers have been cast into the ranks of the unemployed, depriving impoverished towns like Tanjia of the much-needed income the workers sent home.

Since December, hundreds of employees at Ms. Tan's uniform factory have been let go and wages have been cut by a third as orders from the United States dry up. Last year, 2,400 factories in and around Guangzhou closed.

"I hope I still have a job," Ms. Tan said this month, a few hours before leaving Tanjia on a train for the 10-hour ride that in recent years has carried away most of the town's working-age residents. "I don't want to go back to being a poor farmer."

In a nation obsessed with social harmony, the well-being of China's mobile work force has become the top priority for a government that has long seen its fortunes tied to those of the country's 800 million rural dwellers. Mao's revolution, after all, was fueled by embittered peasants, and it has not gone unnoticed in Beijing that decades of heady growth has fed a widening gap between urban residents and those who live in the rural interior.

Although the government has not released updated information about rural unrest, officials have been strategizing about how best to keep large protests and riots from spreading, should the dispossessed grow unruly.

This week, more than 3,000 public security directors from across the country are gathering in the capital to learn how to neutralize rallies and strikes before they blossom into so-called mass incidents. At a meeting of the Chinese cabinet last month, Prime Minister Wen Jiabao told government leaders they should prepare for rough times ahead. "The country's employment situation is extremely grim," he said.

To ameliorate the hardship of idled migrants, the central government has announced a series of initiatives that include vocational training, an expansion of rural health care and crop subsidies to ensure that those who return to the land can make a living despite a slump in agricultural prices. A $585 billion stimulus package introduced in November, much of it weighted toward labor-intensive construction projects, is also expected to absorb some of the newly unemployed.

But here in Tanjia and the surrounding countryside of northeast Hunan Province, most people say they have yet to see much in the way of government largess. As the Lunar New Year came to an end two weeks ago, many migrants who had come home for the holidays were anxious to return south, where they hoped to reclaim their old jobs or find new ones.

About 40 percent of the town's 2,000 residents work outside the province, and their remittances have been a lifeline for the children and elderly people who remain behind. Much of that money has been spent on motorcycles, high school educations and new homes, some trimmed with Corinthian columns and ceramic dragons, that are the brick-and-mortar embodiment of this newfound prosperity.

Ms. Tan's family home, like those of her neighbors, is a work in progress. Since 2005, her mother, father and brother, all migrant workers, have poured $15,000 into the two-story house, but they still need another $9,000 for appliances, fixtures and a white tiled facade. "We have no savings," said her father, Tan Liangsheng, 52, a haggard-looking man who recently lost his job as a construction worker. "All our hard work and bitterness is invested in this house."

Just behind him sat the mud-brick structure where the extended Tan clan used to live.

In some ways, Tanjia's residents are luckier than most. Unlike China's drought-stricken north and its chronically arid west, Hunan Province is well watered and blessed with a temperate climate that allows farmers to grow food much of the year.

Still, with 64 million people squeezed into an area the size of Kansas, most people make do with tiny plots of land; in Tanjia the average size is a tenth of an acre. "Maybe we won't starve to death, but life would become very difficult if everyone came back home," said Long Feng, 29, who works at a car repair shop in Shenzhen, not far from the Hong Kong border.

In Zhuzhou, the nearest city of any consequence, government officials are not very concerned about a surge in jobless farmers.

Chen Shuxian, director of Zhuzhou's employment center, said he was more worried about the 3.7 million people who live in and around his booming city, people who have become accustomed to relatively comfortable lives. "They have cellphone bills and rent to pay," he said. "The migrants don't have a lot of expectations and they can always fall back on the land and their family savings."

Such sentiments are common in China, where rural laborers are often viewed as dime-a-dozen workhorses capable of enduring enormous hardship. He Xuefeng, a professor who studies rural life, said many manufacturers believed the most productive workers were spent by 40.

"As workers grow older, they can't work as quickly or accurately, so they are naturally eliminated," said Mr. He, who teaches at Huazhong University of Science and Technology in Hubei Province. "The financial crisis will simply speed up that process by two or three years and force them to return home earlier."

After he lost his job at a glass factory in Guangzhou last year, Wang Liming, 39, returned to his home on the outskirts of Zhuzhou thinking he could find employment nearby. Things turned more dire after his wife lost her job just before the New Year festivities.

He acknowledged that there was work to be had in Zhuzhou, but those jobs generally pay less than $100 a month, about half what a semiskilled assembly line position pays in Guangzhou.

"I couldn't even afford my daughter's high school tuition on that kind of salary," he said, standing in front of his home, a half-built box that lacks windows and a refrigerator.

A gruff, chain-smoking man, Mr. Wang said the decade he spent in the south turned him off to agricultural work. "I hate working the fields," he said as his neighbors nodded in agreement. Even if they wanted to, he and his fellow villagers could not make much money from farming: some of the best patches of land have been swallowed up by Zhuzhou's rapid development, including the electric generating plant that dominates the view from his front door.

Asked about his plans, Mr. Wang shook his head, glanced at his cellphone and said he was waiting for friends in Guangzhou to call him about a job. "I'm just hoping the phone rings," he said.

International Trade

In the international sector, developing nations have been trying to reduce their historic current account and balance-of-payments deficits. In addition, virtually all developing countries are trying to diversify their export sectors by moving away from traditional dependence on one or several primary commodity exports (such as oil, coffee, and cotton).

The nations that have been implementing export diversification strategies with some success are called **newly industrializing countries (NICs)**. This group includes Hong Kong, Taiwan, Singapore, Malaysia, the Philippines, South Korea, Brazil, Mexico, and Argentina. These countries have allowed foreign firms to set up operations that have generated a sizable export capability in manufactured goods and hence contributed to increased employment and income.

Policies to promote export growth and reduce imports are designed to improve the overall trade balance. But many developing countries have argued that the terms of trade—the price of *developed* countries' exports relative to the price of *developing* countries' exports—has turned against them. The deteriorating terms of trade, they contend, contributes to their current account deficit and the balance-of-payments deficit.

Table 21.4 documents the balance of payments on current account from 1999–2007 for developed economies, economies in transition, and developing economies. By 2003 the global economic recovery (from the prolonged 2000–2002 recession) began to reveal itself as developing countries reported a current account surplus of $224.6 billion, the economies in transition a current account surplus of $30 billion, and the developed economies reported a current account deficit of $317 billion (demonstrating a resurgence in their demand for imports). By 2007, as the global economy continued to expand, the developing economies registered a current account surplus of $776 billion (from a strong demand for commodities and rise in the prices of major commodities) and the economies in transition had a current account surplus of $60 billion. In 2007, the developed countries had a current account deficit of $555 billion. (The United States alone, as we saw in the last two chapters, had a current account deficit of over 6 percent of the GDP, or over $700 billion in 2007.)

Figure 21.2 indicates that in 2003 real exports for emerging economies reached a growth rate of 20 percent, for advanced economies a growth rate of 10 percent, and for the world economy a growth rate of 14 percent. With the onset of the global recession in late 2007 and into 2008, the growth rate for exports fell to 10 percent for emerging economies, to 6 percent for advanced economies, and to 8 percent for the world economy.

Figure 21.3 tracks the current account positions (as a percent of GDP) of four regions from 2000 to 2008. In 2004, the Middle East reached a high of 12 percent, Asia a weak 2 percent, Latin America less than 1 percent, and Emerging Europe a negative 6 percent. The Middle East was enjoying the positive and dramatic impact of rising oil prices (which would peak at $145 per barrel) in 2007. By early 2007, the global recession had taken its toll on Asia, Latin America, and Emerging Europe (falling to 6 percent, − 1 percent, and − 7 percent respectively). Yet, because of firm oil prices, the Middle East continued to improve its current account position to a level of 23 percent of its GDP.

International Finance and Development

As we saw in the previous chapter, when a currency is depreciated, exports are cheaper and thus more competitive and imports are more expensive. The theoretical result is an increase in exports, a decrease in imports, and an improvement in the trade balance, the current account, and the overall balance of payments.

Table 21.4 Balance of Payments on Current Account, by Country or Country Group, Summary Table, 1999–2007 (billions of dollars)

	1999	2000	2001	2002	2003	2004	2005	2006	2007
Developed economies	-182.6	-322.8	-265.2	-287.7	-317.8	-330.7	-505.0	-597.7	-555.3
Japan	114.5	119.6	87.8	112.6	136.2	172.1	165.7	170.4	211.0
United States	-299.8	-417.4	-382.4	-461.3	-523.4	-625.0	-729.0	-788.1	-731.2
Europe[a]	25.8	-27.2	21.8	66.2	90.5	144.5	87.0	51.8	19.1
EU-15	11.3	-60.5	-6.8	38.6	48.9	107.6	25.6	-6.0	-28.9
New EU member States	-23.2	-21.8	-18.6	-20.2	-27.4	-41.7	-35.7	-53.5	-79.9
Economies in transition	21.4	47.0	31.0	25.3	30.7	56.7	81.0	89.5	60.3
South-eastern Europe	-2.5	-1.3	-2.2	-5.0	-5.4	-7.0	-7.2	-8.0	-13.9
Commonwealth of Independent States	23.9	48.3	33.2	30.4	36.1	63.8	88.2	97.4	74.2
Developing economies	39.8	102.3	78.1	127.4	224.6	274.5	485.1	685.0	776.0
Net fuel exporters	-7.9	79.5	32.6	29.5	76.7	121.6	279.1	360.4	336.4
Net fuel importers	47.7	22.9	45.5	97.9	147.9	152.9	205.9	324.7	439.6
Latin America and the Caribbean	-55.8	-47.3	-52.5	-15.2	9.1	21.5	37.0	50.2	18.7
Net fuel exporters	-22.8	-14.1	-21.1	-0.6	11.0	12.6	26.6	35.3	21.0
Net fuel importers	-33.0	-33.2	-31.4	-14.6	-1.8	8.9	10.4	14.8	-2.3
Africa	-11.4	18.4	5.2	-7.7	2.6	12.3	35.5	53.7	29.6
Net fuel exporters	-2.3	26.7	12.0	-2.4	11.4	27.7	56.4	81.7	66.5
Net fuel importers	-9.1	-8.3	-6.8	-5.3	-8.8	-15.4	-20.9	-27.9	-36.9
Western Asia	3.0	37.8	32.2	23.9	44.9	63.1	152.5	190.5	181.5
Net fuel exporters	7.7	50.3	32.4	27.1	52.3	77.6	174.9	216.6	221.2
Net fuel importers	-4.7	-12.4	-0.2	-3.2	-7.3	-14.5	-22.4	-26.1	-39.7
East and South Asia	103.9	93.4	93.3	126.4	167.9	177.5	260.0	390.7	546.3
Net fuel exporters	9.4	16.6	9.4	5.4	2.0	3.7	21.2	26.8	27.8
Net fuel importers	94.5	76.8	83.9	121.0	165.9	173.9	238.8	363.8	518.5
World residual[b]	-121.5	-173.5	-156.0	-134.9	-62.5	0.6	61.1	176.8	281.0

[a]Europe consists of EU-15, new EU member states, plus Iceland, Norway, and Switzerland.
[b]Statiscal discrepancy.

Sources: IMF, *World Economic Outlook*, October 2008; and IMF, *Balance of Payments Statistics*.

FIGURE 21.2 Real Exports (percent)

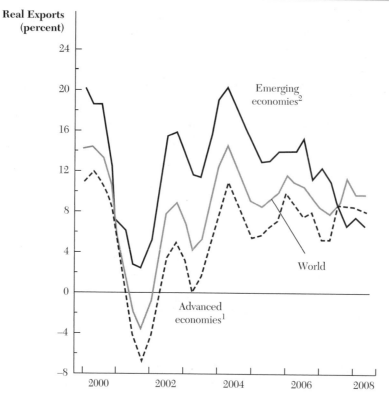

[1]Australia, Canada, Denmark, euro area, Japan, New Zealand, Norway, Sweden, Switzerland, United Kingdom, and United States.

[2]Argentina, Brazil, Bulgaria, Chile, China, Colombia, Czech Republic, Estonia, Hong Kong SAR, Hungary, India, Indonesia, Israel, Korea, Latvia, Lithuania, Malaysia, Mexico, Pakistan, Peru, Philippines, Poland, Romania, Russia, Singapore, Slovak Republic, South Africa, Taiwan Province of China, Thailand, Turkey, Ukraine, and Rep. Bolivariana de Venezuela.

Source: CPB Netherlands Bureau for Economic Policy Analysis for CPB trade volume index; for all others, NTC Economics and Haver Analytics.

Many developing countries have been and continue to be confronted by a huge external debt. The total external debt of developing countries was more than $4.4 trillion in 2008. The debt service on these loans is an enormous burden. Their external debt has put additional pressure on developing countries to increase their export earnings in order to earn the foreign exchange needed to service the external debt. Critics argue that this outflow of scarce foreign exchange hampers governments from spending and investing domestically to produce economic growth.

Since the mid-1980s, private commercial banks in the advanced countries significantly reduced the level of loans to developing nations. This created a net resource transfer (the difference between new loans and debt service) on the order of approximately $30 billion a year flowing out of developing nations to the creditors in the advanced countries. In response, creditors and creditor governments developed initiatives in the early 1990s to reduce the level of debt and debt service without making large new loans. Creditors renegotiated loans at reduced interest

FIGURE 21.3 Current Account Positions (Percent of GDP)

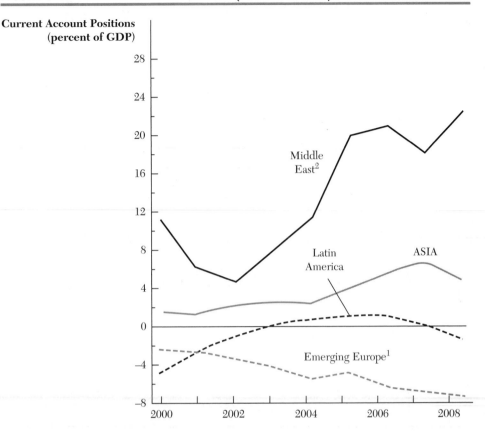

Sources: IMF, *International Financial Statistics;* and IMF staff calculations.

[1] Bulgaria, Croatia, Czech Republic, Estonia, Hungary, Latvia, Lithuania, Poland, Romania, Slovak Republic, and Turkey.

[2] Bahrain, Egypt, I.R. of Iran, Jordan, Kuwait, Lebanon, Libya, Oman, Qatar, Saudi Arabia, Syrian Arab Republic, United Arab Emirates, and Republic of Yemen.

rates or reduced the amount of the original loan. They also devised some creative financial schemes like debt-for-equity swaps, which essentially allow creditor banks to sell a portion of a country's debt to a buyer who purchases the debt on the secondary market at a discount and then uses it as investment capital in the country.

In spite of several well-intended responses on the part of commercial banks, the International Monetary Fund, and the World Bank, the external debt of developing countries still exists at a level that exacts an enormous opportunity cost in terms of the debt service burden. The external debt grew from $1.9 trillion in 1995 to $4.5 trillion in 2008 (see Table 21.5). The debt service payments (interest and amortization) skyrocketed from $175 billion in 1995 to a high of $884 billion in 2008. The irony for developing countries is that between 2001 and 2008 they paid $4.9 trillion in debt service on an external debt of approximately $4.4 trillion, yet they still owe approximately $4.4 trillion. If they had not had this debt, it is reasonable to assume that these countries would have had an additional $4 trillion to spend on pressing social and economic priorities such as

Table 21.5 Summary of External Debt and Debt Service

	2001	2002	2003	2004	2005	2006	2007	2008	2009	2010
				Billions of U.S. dollars						
External debt										
Emerging and developing economies	**2,364.7**	**2,421.0**	**2,631.7**	**2,876.5**	**3,006.4**	**3,321.8**	**4,130.3**	**4,472.3**	**4,440.4**	**4,640.5**
Regional groups										
Africa	269.5	274.3	296.2	311.2	283.4	238.1	265.8	268.0	277.2	294.7
Central and eastern Europe	271.8	312.2	388.1	470.8	514.9	664.7	889.5	1,031.4	980.7	990.5
Commonwealth of Independent States[a]	201.0	212.2	253.0	297.9	360.9	461.8	675.7	735.5	668.2	678.6
Developing Asia	675.0	680.0	712.5	777.2	816.5	896.8	1,022.5	1,128.5	1,222.6	1,323.5
Middle East	173.3	178.4	189.1	215.9	236.2	314.6	441.5	430.6	432.0	459.7
Western Hemisphere	774.0	763.9	792.7	803.6	794.5	745.9	835.4	878.3	859.7	893.5
Analytical groups										
By external financing source										
Net debtor countries of	1,622.6	1,672.5	1,810.3	1,948.5	1,984.9	2,150.0	2,581.7	2,808.9	2,766.9	2,873.8
which, official financing	128.3	128.0	138.7	146.1	132.3	115.9	119.3	123.9	130.4	137.6
Net debtor countries by debt-servicing experience										
Countries with arrears and/or rescheduling during 2003–2007	356.5	350.2	367.6	381.7	396.8	333.0	363.2	374.4	361.9	382.8
Debt-service payments[b]										
Emerging and developing economies	**429.9**	**433.6**	**466.3**	**490.7**	**639.2**	**743.9**	**788.0**	**884.0**	**833.3**	**822.0**
Regional groups										
Africa	26.6	22.0	27.4	29.9	43.0	67.0	30.5	27.8	26.5	28.6
Central and eastern Europe	53.8	59.6	66.0	76.7	104.2	125.8	150.0	184.3	203.8	191.9

Table 21.5 (Continued)

	2001	2002	2003	2004	2005	2006	2007	2008	2009	2010
Commonwealth of Independent States[a]	45.8	55.9	72.7	84.6	119.5	159.6	197.2	268.7	185.6	188.8
Developing Asia	103.3	113.2	103.5	102.3	109.4	122.2	157.5	170.4	181.5	196.3
Middle East	22.3	16.2	20.3	26.6	46.0	40.8	43.4	48.2	43.6	43.2
Western Hemisphere	178.1	166.7	176.3	170.6	217.1	228.5	209.4	184.5	192.3	173.1
Analytical groups										
By external financing source										
Net debtor countries	295.0	292.9	305.7	314.0	404.9	441.3	473.3	494.4	522.6	501.5
of which, official financing	8.8	8.1	7.8	9.6	20.3	14.5	12.3	10.9	11.6	13.8
Net debtor countries by debt-servicing experience										
Countries with arrears and/or rescheduling during 2003–2007	56.4	44.8	54.2	49.4	71.2	63.9	51.0	56.1	58.9	58.7
External debt[c]										
Emerging and developing economies	**128.5**	**121.4**	**109.4**	**92.9**	**77.9**	**71.0**	**74.0**	**65.1**	**86.2**	**84.5**
Debt-service payments										
Emerging and developing economies	**23.4**	**21.7**	**19.4**	**15.8**	**16.6**	**15.9**	**14.1**	**12.9**	**16.2**	**15.0**
Regional groups										
Africa	18.1	14.4	14.2	12.1	13.8	18.2	7.0	5.2	7.3	7.1
Central and eastern Europe	28.8	28.8	25.0	22.4	26.2	26.8	25.6	26.1	35.6	31.8
Commenwealth of Independent States[a]	27.6	31.3	32.4	27.8	30.7	32.8	33.4	33.9	38.7	34.1
Developing Asia	15.0	14.4	10.9	8.3	7.2	6.5	6.9	6.3	8.2	8.7
Middle East	9.0	6.1	6.2	6.2	7.8	5.7	5.3	4.3	5.8	5.1
Western Hemisphere	44.1	41.0	39.7	31.5	33.3	29.5	24.0	18.3	24.9	21.0

(Continued)

Table 21.5 (Continued)

	2001	2002	2003	2004	2005	2006	2007	2008	2009	2010
Analytical groups										
By external financing source										
Net debtor countries	31.6	29.6	26.6	21.9	23.9	21.9	19.8	17.6	22.7	20.6
of which, official financing	15.9	13.7	11.6	11.4	20.2	12.0	8.5	6.2	8.1	8.9
Net debtor countries by debt-servicing experience										
Countries with arrears and/or rescheduling during 2003–2007	53.3	40.4	42.0	31.6	38.6	29.1	19.5	17.4	23.1	21.1

[a] angolia, which is not a member of the Commonwealth of Independent States, is included in this group for reasons of geography and similarities in economic structure.
[b] Debt-service payments refer to actual payments of interest on total debt plus actual amoritization payments on long-term debt. The projections incorporate the impact of exceptional financing items.
[c] Total debt at year-end in percent of exports of goods and services in year indicated.

Source: Data from *World Economic Outlook*, 2009.

health, education, infrastructure, technology, and the environment. In recent years, debt service as a percentage of exports of goods and services has ranged from a high of 23.4 percent in 2001 to a low of 12.8 percent in 2008.

Indeed, since the 1980s many groups have supported debt relief and debt forgiveness as a way for the advanced nations and their commercial banking institutions to relieve the burden of the developing countries' external debt. The pressure to service this external debt becomes even more pronounced in periods of slowing global economic growth, or in periods of financial crisis. Since the 1990s, several countries, including Mexico, Russia, Turkey, Argentina, Brazil, Indonesia, and the Philippines, experienced economic and financial crises that threatened their ability to service their external debts.

Environmental Problems

Population growth provides several strains on the environment. It increases the demand for goods and services. More people mean more wastes. To feed more people, more land must be put into cultivation, and land currently under cultivation must be farmed more efficiently and productively. This requires more water and often more resource inputs, with consequences for human health and the long-term viability of the land itself.

The existence of large numbers of poor people exacerbates environmental problems. In many countries, the pressure to increase nontraditional exports to improve the trade balance and service external debt has resulted in policies that encourage deforestation to permit creation of large cotton and cattle farms. The result is tremendous environmental degradation: not only deforestation, but species extinction, soil depletion and erosion, water contamination, and air pollution.

This issue was one of several addressed at the Earth Summit held in Rio de Janeiro, Brazil, in June 1992. This conference, sponsored by the United Nations, established the link among population growth, poverty, and the environment. It concluded that preservation of the environment and establishment of a framework for sustainable development depend on significantly reducing poverty and population growth in the developing countries. Sustainable development—a goal that had nearly unanimous support at the Earth Summit—is a model of economic growth that respects the integrity of Earth's physical life support system. It means developing a production system that does not degrade or undermine the ability of Earth's life support system to regenerate and cleanse itself. People must use resources in a way that permits renewable resources to renew themselves.

From 1992 to 2009, the global community has been focused on finding ways to achieve *sustainable development*. The quest for development has been largely driven by increasing economic growth. Yet, economic growth by itself does not necessarily translate into development and certainly not development that is sustainable. The concept of sustainability implies that what is required for growth and development can be repeated and continued without inhibiting the process of growth and development or the qualitative dimensions of the growth and development. From an environmental perspective, development and economic growth that is sustainable does not degrade or compromise the quality of human life or the basic biological physical support systems that support life and growth.

This concept also takes into consideration the demographic pressures on limited resources that are both renewable and nonrenewable (fossil fuels). There is also the question of the efficient use of energy resources.

Throughout the 1990s and the first decade of the twenty-first century, the issue of climate change has emerged as one of, if not the most challenging, problems that confronts the human race. It is essentially about the burning of fossil fuels (oil and coal) and the rise in emissions of carbon dioxide into the atmosphere and the impact of this dynamic on the earth's ecological systems, as well as the quality of life for those on the planet and future generations to come. (In the next chapter, we will focus more on this topic.)

As the global community confronts its current economic challenges and struggles to address the very difficult issues related to trade, finance, and development, the emerging market economies have been reluctant to commit themselves to meeting goals and standards related to curbing climate change. They have resisted initiatives (Koyoto, the UN. Intergovernmental Panel on Climate Change, and Copenhagen) because they claim that they do not have the technology or financial resources to do so. Yet, these countries and especially China continue to use production and consumption practices that grow the problem and undermine any success that the advanced economies may make by agreeing to lower their carbon emissions in the years to come. Clearly, the fear of doing anything that may retard economic growth, reduce profits, and cost additional capital is making it difficult to reach a global accommodation.*

Explanations and Solutions for Underdevelopment

As we saw at the beginning of this text, the basic economic problem is essentially one of producing an economic surplus beyond immediate consumption needs. The more efficient and productive a society, the greater the level of economic surplus or savings for investment. And investment promotes growth in the output of goods and services.

Underdevelopment complicates this problem by creating a cycle of poverty that is hard to break. The existence of high levels of poverty builds a base of people with low incomes, most often subsistence incomes that allow for little if any savings. Yet low-income families tend to have more children. The higher birthrates drive population growth, which slows the rate of economic growth. Higher population growth rates also contribute to higher unemployment and underemployment, especially in a slow-growing economy. Productivity is hampered by other consequences of poverty: poor health and nutrition among the population, a low level of savings (which contributes to the low investment level), and a low level of education. The resulting low level of productivity contributes to the low level of income, and the cycle repeats itself.

10. How can the cycle of poverty be broken?

---

*The book *Common Wealth: Economics for a Crowded Planet* (2008) by Jeffrey Sachs, the director of the Earth Institute at Columbia University, explores the contemporary challenge of global poverty and development in the context of the goal of sustainability while addressing the climate crisis.

While there is widespread agreement among economists about what constitutes development and underdevelopment, there is no consensus with regard to what caused this condition to emerge, what perpetuates it, and what should be done to overcome it. Most economists believe solving underdevelopment requires that the low level of savings be offset by savings injections from external sources. These resources must come from the government in the form of direct income transfers or investment in enterprises and **infrastructure** (roads, bridges, airports, seaports, potable water, electricity, education, etc.). The funds for such investments must come from private foreign investment or from borrowing. This capital and the technology that it would bring can act as the primary stimulus for breaking the cycle of poverty and underdevelopment. With regard to more specific solutions, there are three distinct competing perspectives (schools of thought or paradigms): the neoliberal, structuralist, and dependency models.

The Neoliberal Model

According to the **neoliberal model,** developing nations must adopt modern capital and technology to have strong economic growth. Underdevelopment is assumed to be a natural condition characterized by backward and archaic institutions and values. This condition of underdevelopment must give way to progress and modernization characterized by industrialization, the mechanization of agriculture, urbanization, secular values, and political stability.

This model explains underdevelopment as a consequence of geography, culture, lack of capital and technology, and the vicious cycles of unproductive labor and poverty. In this overall context, the model asserts, a developing nation must create dynamic markets in land, labor, and capital. The emergence of dynamic and smoothly functioning markets along with the expansion of free trade are thus the road to progress. Together, the inflow of foreign capital and the transfer of modern technology are the catalysts necessary to provide the stimulus for sustained growth.

The neoliberal view is that only a free and open private market economy can overcome the vicious cycle of underdevelopment. Because foreign (external) capital, emerging financial markets, and technological change are the stimulants for sustained economic growth in this view, it emphasizes the positive role that multinational firms (corporations) and international financial institutions can and need to play in this process. From the perspective of economic policy, the neoliberal model offers the following prescription:

❖ A conservative fiscal policy that shrinks domestic deficits by reducing state spending and increasing taxes

❖ A conservative monetary policy of higher interest rates to reduce inflation

❖ The promotion of free trade and open-market economic policies that invite the free flow of goods, services, and capital. This will often require an adjustment in the currency's exchange rate through an official devaluation or a commitment to free flexible floating exchange rates.

The Structuralist Model

In the late 1960s and early 1970s, many economists advanced a perspective on underdevelopment that modified the traditional view. This group, led by Raul Prebish, a Brazilian economist then with the United Nations Economic Commission on Latin America, argued that the basic economic problem of underdevelopment exists for all countries but must be understood in the proper historical context. For Latin American, Asian, and African countries, their respective states of underdevelopment had to be understood in the context of their historic relationship to the European countries, which conquered them and transformed them into colonies. These countries' economies were therefore shaped by the economic needs of the colonial powers. Only this historical view explains the inequality in the distribution of income and wealth, the concentration in land ownership, the historic dependence on primary export products, the linking of foreign capital with the industrial and finance capital of domestic elites, and the frequent inappropriateness of Keynesian theories and policies to the circumstances of developing nations.

This **structuralist model** did not deny the basic economic analysis of the traditional view but saw domestic political and economic factors as obstacles to development. The structuralists also viewed the international economic and financial system of the 1960s and 1970s as serving the economic interests of the developed nations while reinforcing the dynamics of underdevelopment for the developing nations.

The contemporary proponents of the structuralist view emphasize the importance of a free and open market economy. They support constructive and responsible foreign investment and the transfer of technology from developed countries. Yet they also emphasize the importance of the following measures:

❖ A more genuine and equitable distribution of productive land

❖ A more diversified economy less reliant on primary commodity exports

❖ Government policies that realistically address the problem of poverty and income distribution

❖ An active role for government in the economy

❖ Strong environmental policies

❖ Relief from the burden of external debt

❖ Changes in the international trading and financial system designed to bring about a more equitable integration of developing countries into the global economy

The essence of the structuralist view is that breaking the cycle of underdevelopment requires much more than free and open markets supported by foreign capital and technology.

The Dependency Model

In the 1960s, the **dependency model** challenged the traditional and structural theories by using Marxian analysis to look at the problem of underdevelopment. The dependency model assumed that we must view underdevelopment as a consequence of the historical evolution of capitalism and the integration of developing countries into the expanding sphere of capitalist production globally. This model is based upon a generalized application of a Marxist methodology drawn from philosophy, history, sociology, political science, and economics. The character and structure of a developing country's economic and political system, as well as its class and social stratification system, are explained by its historical experience with colonialism and the subsequent expansion of capitalism.

Such a historical analysis locates the primary dynamic for change in the economic sphere as it represents at any time a historically specific mode of production. This mode of production characterizes the way in which land, labor, and capital are brought together on a domestic as well as global level.

Dependency analysis argues that development can best be understood as a natural product of the process of capitalist development and expansion worldwide. The theory asserts that as capitalism spread from the European countries in the fifteenth century, it exploited the countries in Latin America, Asia, and Africa. The exploitation of labor and natural resources allowed for a transfer of wealth from the now-developing countries to the then-industrializing European countries. The process of capital accumulation systematically required the exploitation and subjugation of the Third World nations. Colonialism was the political and military dimension that enforced this process. Therefore, dependency analysis argues, this process transformed these countries' economies into vehicles that served the primary needs of the advanced countries. The character of this interdependence produced a dependence, in which the economies of less-developed countries were conditioned by the development and expansion of the advanced country's economy.

Proponents of the dependency view focus their analysis on the way a developing country's economy is integrated with the global economy. Dependency theorists examine everything from the banking system to the communications system to the educational system, focusing on the role and behavior of the direct foreign investment of multinational firms and the role and behavior of multilateral institutions such as the International Monetary Fund (IMF) and the World Bank. They argue that these institutions are the instruments and vehicles for the exploitation, domination, and perpetuation of underdevelopment in these countries. They do not deny that some degree of progress, modernization, and economic development result from the spread of capitalism, but they insist that the development is uneven and distorted.

For many years (the 1960s to the 1980s), dependency theorists believed that only a more democratic and socialistically organized society could bring genuine development to these countries by breaking the forms of dependency. The dominating capitalist institutions would need to be replaced. Socialism was seen as one alternative development path. In theory, this was attractive to some, but in practice it proved to be difficult, if not impossible. By the late 1990s, whatever the analytical merit of the dependency view, historic events had spelled, for the time being, the end of socialism in practice in Eastern

Europe and the Soviet Union. Coming off the dismal economic decade of the 1980s, the majority of developing nations entered the 1990s and the early twenty-first century in pursuit of market capitalist development strategies.

MEXICO

Developing countries, confronted with the problems of debt, population, poverty, and the environment, are rapidly adopting variants of the neoliberal model—free and open-market economic strategies for development. Among many countries, Mexico is one of the most dramatic examples of the cyclical character of the experience with the neoliberal strategy. The new Mexican development strategy, which began in 1982 and has been in practice since, involves the following actions:

- ❖ Privatizing state-owned enterprises
- ❖ Opening the economy to foreign investment
- ❖ Opening the economy by eliminating tariff and nontariff trade barriers
- ❖ Stabilizing the economy by reducing inflation and domestic deficits
- ❖ Reducing the level and debt service demands of external debt
- ❖ Entering into free trade agreements with other nations
- ❖ Diversifying exports

The success or failure of this strategy will depend on many internal and external factors. It remains to be seen whether enough capital will ultimately flow to these countries to generate rapid development, if the new market-driven economies are efficient and productive enough to compete on a global scale, and if the new democratic governments can manage to maintain political stability and order as their people wait patiently for the results to spill over to them.

Much of the implementation of the neoliberal model involves the relationship between the IMF and the international commercial banks and the host government. The IMF and commercial banks expect, if not require, governments to implement conservative monetary and fiscal policies in order to provide economic stability (reduce inflation and eliminate budget deficits) and sound economic fundamentals so that capital will flow into the country (and domestic capital will not leave) in order to promote economic growth. In official circles, this kind of economic policy is called "structural adjustment." Many critics of this policy orientation and the IMF's role argue that these policies do not promote growth but induce economic stagnation and reduce the population's standard of living, while serving the vested interests of the domestic financial class and multinational institutions. In some countries, structural adjustment policies have had a major impact on employment and pay, especially for women.

The impact of the free trade policies demanded by the International Monetary Fund and governments such as Mexico that adhere to the neoliberal (structural adjustment) program can be seen in the following article that details the negative consequences of the North American Free Trade Agreement for Mexico.

Why Mexico's Small Corn Farmers Go Hungry

Tina Rosenberg

MEXICO CITY—Macario Hernández's grandfather grew corn in the hills of Puebla, Mexico. His father does the same. Mr. Hernández grows corn, too, but not for much longer. Around his village of Guadalupe Victoria, people farm the way they have for centuries, on tiny plots of land watered only by rain, their plows pulled by burros. Mr. Hernández, a thoughtful man of 30, is battling to bring his family and neighbors out of the Middle Ages. But these days modernity is less his goal than his enemy.

This is because he, like other small farmers in Mexico, competes with American products raised on megafarms that use satellite imagery to mete out fertilizer. These products are so heavily subsidized by the government that many are exported for less than it costs to grow them. According to the Institute for Agriculture and Trade Policy in Minneapolis, American corn sells in Mexico for 25 percent less than its cost. The prices Mr. Hernández and others receive are so low that they lose money with each acre they plant.

In January, campesinos from all over the country marched into Mexico City's central plaza to protest. Thousands of men in jeans and straw hats jammed the Zócalo, alongside horses and tractors. Farmers have staged smaller protests around Mexico for months. The protests have won campesino organizations a series of talks with the government. But they are unlikely to get what they want: a renegotiation of the North American Free Trade Agreement, or NAFTA, protective temporary tariffs and a new policy that seeks to help small farmers instead of trying to force them off the land.

The problems of rural Mexicans are echoed around the world as countries lower their import barriers, required by free trade treaties and the rules of the World Trade Organization. When markets are open, agricultural products flood in from wealthy nations, which subsidize agriculture and allow agribusiness to export crops cheaply. European farmers get 35 percent of their income in government subsidies, American farmers 20 percent. American subsidies are at record levels, and last year, Washington passed a farm bill that included a $40 billion increase in subsidies to large grain and cotton farmers.

It seems paradoxical to argue that cheap food hurts poor people. But three-quarters of the world's poor are rural. When subsidized imports undercut their products, they starve. Agricultural subsidies, which rob developing countries of the ability to export crops, have become the most important dispute at the W.T.O. Wealthy countries do far more harm to poor nations with these subsidies than they do good with foreign aid.

While such subsidies have been deadly for the 18 million Mexicans who live on small farms—nearly a fifth of the country—Mexico's near-complete neglect of the countryside is at fault, too. Mexican officials say openly that they long ago concluded that small agriculture was inefficient, and that the solution for farmers was to find other work. "The government's solution for the problems of the countryside is to get campesinos to stop being campesinos," says Victor Suárez, a leader of a coalition of small farmers.

But the government's determination not to invest in losers is a self-fulfilling prophecy. The small farmers I met in their fields in Puebla want to stop growing corn and move into fruit or organic vegetables. Two years ago Mr. Hernández, who works with a farming cooperative, brought in thousands of peach plants. But only a few farmers could buy them. Farm credit essentially does not exist in Mexico, as the government closed the rural bank, and other bankers do not want to lend to small farmers. "We are trying to get people to re-think and understand that the traditional doesn't work," says Mr. Hernández. "But the lack of capital is deadly."

The government does subsidize producers, at absurdly small levels compared with subsidies in the United States. Corn growers get about $30 an acre. Small programs exist to provide technical help and fertilizer to small producers, but most farmers I met hadn't even heard of them.

Mexico should be helping its corn farmers increase their productivity or move into new crops—especially since few new jobs have been created that could absorb these farmers. Mexicans fleeing the countryside are flocking to Houston and swelling Mexico's cities, already congested with the poor and unemployed. If Washington wants to reduce Mexico's immigration to the United States, ending subsidies for agribusiness would be far more effective than beefing up the border patrol.

Source: "Why Mexico's Small Corn Farmers Go Hungry," first appeared in the *New York Times*, March 3, 2003. Reprinted with permission from Tina Rosenberg.

---

 11. Given this problem, what do you think the appropriate response should be from the U.S. and Mexican governments? Why?

A GLIMPSE OF INDIA

The ongoing spread of global capitalism and its many manifestations in the popular context of globalization has seen India rapidly rise to the world stage. It has a population of over 1 billion people and an economy that has been growing between 8 and 9 percent a year, just a bit behind the phenomenal growth rates that China has posted. China has attracted the majority of the foreign capital flowing to emerging market economies in recent years and has used that money, along with its huge trade surplus, to promote its manufacturing export machine and industrial base. India, on the other hand, has also benefited from a steady and strong flow of foreign capital to build up its technology, computer software, and information services sectors. But, against the backdrop of this very modern and successful slice of the Indian economy, the rest of the economy suffers from the constraints of governmental bureaucracy, poor infrastructure, widespread rural and urban poverty, an unproductive agricultural sector, and weak public educational system. It is a country of many contradictions.

The persistence of deep underdevelopment is juxtaposed with a vibrant modern technology sector. The famed cultural products of Bollywood (*Slum Dog Millionaire* film), the horrific terrorist attack in Mumbai, and the international admiration and respect for the country's microcredit and microfinance anti-poverty organizations are all a testimony to the country's diverse realities.

A special report on India in *The Economist* (Dec. 13, 2008) framed the reality with the title of the report, "An Elephant, Not a Tiger."

The prolific *New York Times* journalist Thomas Friedman has written extensively about the modern and dynamic sectors of the Indian economy and how these sectors have integrated India with the entire global economic and financial system. His books *The Lexus and the Olive Tree* (1999), *The World is Flat* (2005), and *Hot, Flat and Crowded* (2008) document the role that India has played in the globalization dynamic of the past twenty years as the global production system for goods and services has been transformed and integrated.

The global recession of 2008–2009 had a very startling impact on emerging market economies. In the following article, "India, Suddenly Starved for Investment," Vikas Bajaj and Somini Sengupta examine the declining flow of foreign investment. In the second article, "Microbanks Are Getting a Cash Infustion," Carter Dougherty explores the the decision by the World Bank and the German government to inject $600 million into microcredit banks that have been hit hard by the global recession.

India, Suddenly Starved for Investment

Vikas Bajaj and Somini Sengupta

GURGAON, India — Sumit Sapra is a member of that ambitious, impatient generation of young Indians who rode the crest of the global economy. In five years, he changed jobs three times, quadrupling his salary along the way. Even when satisfied with his position, he kept his résumé posted on job sites, in case better offers came along. And he splurged. In three years, he bought three cars, moving up a notch in luxury each time. For weekend jaunts, he bought a motorcycle.

Mr. Sapra's last and best-paying job was at the Indian headquarters of the financial services arm of General Electric, investing western money in Indian energy projects. But last December, foreign money dried up and Mr. Sapra, with a prestigious degree, was laid off.

"Earlier it was money chasing a few projects," Mr. Sapra, 30, said of the change that seemed to come virtually overnight. "Now it's the other way around."

Not long ago, Indian leaders confidently predicted this country would emerge largely unscathed from the global economic crisis. It is now becoming clear that that view was too optimistic, nowhere more so than in this city south of New Delhi that was once the symbol of India's economic boom.

A few short years ago, construction sites here buzzed 24 hours a day, crews working through the night, cramming down food from onsite trucks during breaks in the twilight. Now real estate sites lie fallow. The once-booming art market has slowed to a crawl. And charmed professionals with coveted degrees, like Sumit Sapra, are unemployed or taking pay cuts to hold on to their jobs.

India's phenomenal growth of the last five years was powered in large part by huge injections of cash and investment. Investment accounted for about 39 percent of the country's gross domestic product in fiscal year 2008, up from 25 percent five years ago. At its peak, more than a third of investment came from abroad, according to Credit Suisse. But in the last three months of last year, foreign loans and direct investment fell by nearly a third, to their lowest level in more than two years.

In a recent report, the International Monetary Fund said Indian companies were among the world's most vulnerable, after American firms, because they borrowed aggressively during the boom. Using data from Moody's, the credit rating firm, the I.M.F. estimated in a recent report that defaults among nonfinancial South Asian firms could climb to 20 percent in the coming year, up from an expectation of 4.2 percent a year earlier. (American firms are expected to default on loans at a rate of 23 percent.)

The decline in foreign investment has taken a big toll on sectors like real estate, manufacturing, infrastructure and even art, which was bolstered by demand from globalization's nouveau riche here and abroad. In the last quarter of 2008, the economy's growth rate plummeted to about 5.3 percent, the lowest in five years. While consumer demand, particularly in the countryside, has kept the economy growing, the sudden slowing in the flow of foreign funds will make it harder for the country to grow fast enough to pull hundreds of millions of people out of stifling poverty.

"If India wants to go back to the 8 to 9 percent growth rate, private investment and low cost of capital is essential," said Jahangir Aziz, the chief economist for India at JPMorgan Chase.

Indian policy makers say they believe the country will grow at 6 percent in the coming year, but the I.M.F. forecasts growth of 4.5 percent.

To help fill the gap left by foreign investment, the government is spending more on infrastructure and social programs. The Reserve Bank of India, India's central bank, has slashed its benchmark interest rates, but the cost of private loans has not fallen by as much.

After a wrenching 58 percent drop in the Indian stock market last year, the market is up 42 percent since its March low and some foreign money has started to flow into equities. But economists like Mr. Aziz say the government needs to do a lot more, though few expect bigger interventions until the current elections end and a new government takes power in late May or early June.

In the meantime, activity here in Gurgaon has slowed radically. Just off the highway from New Delhi, a giant hole in the ground sits where the country's largest developer, DLF, had planned to build the nation's biggest mall, aptly named the Mall of India.

DLF officials say that they may reduce the size of the mall and add office space to replace planned retail space.

In the boom, DLF built many of the earliest projects that transformed Gurgaon from a sleepy village into an expansive city that has become home to companies like Ericsson and I.B.M.

DLF turned to foreign lenders and investors like D. E. Shaw, the New York-based investment firm, because they provided money "at lower rates of interest and in larger amounts," said Rajeev Talwar, an executive director at New Delhi-based DLF. "Today, you have no choice but to go to the Indian banks."

But domestic lenders have become more reluctant to extend credit, and the interest rates they offer have made projects unfeasible. Last week, DLF reported that its profits fell 92 percent in the first three months of the year.

A subcontractor, Sunil Kumar Verma, who lays marble floors for builders in Gurgaon, said that business was so bad that half of his 40 workers had returned to their homes in Bihar, a poor eastern state where there was also little work for them.

"All they can do is sit, eat and sleep," Mr. Verma said.

The art market reflects the collapse of the investment boom at the other end of the wealth spectrum.

Over the last years, gallery owners had no need to cultivate buyers. Money was no object. Many artists cranked out works at a furious pace. Not only did veteran collectors snap up the big-ticket items (a painting by M. F. Husain, for instance, or V. S. Gaitonde) but midlevel works in the range of $100,000 drew plenty of buyers, as well.

"There were queues. Shows were sold out prior to opening. We were all on a high," said Arun Vadehra, who owns two galleries devoted to modern and contemporary art in Delhi and a third in London.

In industry, export companies have been hit hard—diamond polishing units and knitwear factories, for instance, are running at a fraction of their capacity.

The job market is another casualty. Not so long ago, as a lot of money chased a small pool of skilled professionals, salaries skyrocketed. Now, it's the other way around, as Mr. Sapra, the former G.E. employee, said.

He has looked for work for several months and only last month heard back from a few potential employers. Like many of his peers, he says he will most likely have to settle for less money than he was making earlier—despite his master's degree from the prestigious Indian Institute of Management.

In the good old days, he invested some of his money in property. Now, he would rather not look at how his assets are doing. He said it would just depress him.

Mr. Sapra is not the only one casting his gaze elsewhere. With the exception of a handful of issues, like food prices, politicians have not spent much time talking about the economy this election season.

Ajay Shah, an economist and columnist, said the next government's challenge would be to reawaken the "animal spirits" of the private sector by removing restrictions on investment, loosening financial regulations and putting money into infrastructure.

But in India's chaotic coalition politics, it is hard enough to predict who will come to power, let alone what they will do once they are there.

Microbanks Are Getting a Cash Infusion

Carter Dougherty

FRANKFURT—The World Bank and the German government said Thursday that they hoped to inject as much as $600 million into microcredit banks, fledgling institutions in developing countries that are being starved of financing as the credit markets have tightened.

The effort highlights how even small banks in poor countries are getting caught in the financial crisis—and it offers them a chance to get public money to replace rapidly diminishing private capital.

"You have some viable projects here where the financing has simply dried up," the World Bank president, Robert B. Zoellick, said from Berlin, where he and the leaders of other economic organizations met with Chancellor Angela Merkel of Germany.

The microcredit investment fund is part of a broader effort to mobilize cash for poorer countries, Mr. Zoellick said. Other funds are focused on infrastructure projects, bank recapitalization and trade finance.

Microcredit institutions, which generally make loans of $100 or less to individuals or small businesses, gained attention in the 1990s as a way to foster private enterprise in poor countries. In 2006, Muhammad Yunus, the founder of the Grameen Bank in Bangladesh, one of the first microbanks, won the Nobel Peace Prize for his work.

Though many banks were seeded with money from Western aid agencies, the process of drawing more investment from private sources was well under way until the credit crisis began.

"In general, there was a lot of momentum from the private sector," said Jack Lowe, president of BlueOrchard Finance, which has been selected to manage the new fund. "But when you have the wind at your back and financial markets are heady, it is easier to raise money."

Under the plan, the World Bank would initially provide $150 million alongside an additional $130 million from the German government. Mr. Zoellick said the bank was soliciting contributions from other countries and agencies, and hoped to mobilize up to $600 million. That would be enough to help 150 to 200 microfinance banks in 40 developing countries.

Like many large commercial banks, many microcredit institutions take deposits from individuals or businesses and lend the cash out. The main difference is that they parcel out tiny loans to finance small businesses. Other microcredit banks function like investment banks, drawing money from wholesale financial markets at one rate of interest and lending it out at a slightly higher rate.

Mr. Zoellick emphasized that the cash being offered was not a recapitalization of microcredit banks after heavy losses.

Microfinance banks are generally solvent, have a strong record of making sensible loans and did not speculate in the complex mortgage-linked securities that have caused so much pain among Western banks. Only 2 to 3 percent of their loans tend to go bad, Mr. Zoellick said.

"It always depends on the institution," he said. "But what we find in general in the microfinance industry is that their problem loan percentage is quite low."

Japan has pledged $2 billion to a separate facility run by the International Finance Corporation, a part of the World Bank, to recapitalize banks in poorer countries.

Conclusion

The early years of the twenty-first century have served to reinforce the seriousness of global poverty and underdevelopment. As we have seen, these problems are growing larger and more complicated. The demographic dynamics and trends provide an enormous challenge. The global public health crisis, led by the HIV/AIDS pandemic that generates on average 3 million more people per year with the virus and about 3 million deaths from the virus, could be helped with a modest financial commitment to support the necessary programs as presented by the United Nations. But with the global war on terrorism and global spending on defense at a level of $900 billion a year, there is a fierce competition for competing resources.

As we will see in the last chapter, the economies of China and India are integrating into the global system at a swift pace. As their economies grow, their demand for fossil fuel energy (petroleum) also is growing and pushing up the demand for and consequently the price of oil. Worldwide, we are seeing intensified pressure not only for fossil fuels but water, food, minerals, timber, and other resources. Indeed, the goal of sustainable development is the new global agenda.

This set of problems and pressures present an incredible challenge for the global community and for global capitalism.

Review Questions

1. What are several of the most common characteristics of a developing country?

2. What is the character and magnitude of global poverty? In what ways is poverty more than an economic problem?

3. What are the five basic categories of economic problems of developing nations? How would you rank them in order of importance?

4. What is the relationship between the problems of economic growth and population? Between population and the environment?

5. What is the basic economic explanation for poverty and underdevelopment in the developing world?

6. Of the three competing views of underdevelopment, which do you find to be the most convincing? Why?

7. By the early 1990s, the governments of developing nations apparently were adopting development strategies with a discernible trend. What was this trend? What do you think are the strengths of this strategy? What do you think are or could be some problems with the strategy?

8. At the Earth Summit in 1992, a consensus emerged on the need for all nations to pursue strategies of sustainable development. What does this mean for developing nations? Advanced nations?

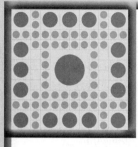

CHAPTER 22

Modern Economic Systems

❖ Introduction

In the twenty-first century global economy, most developed countries utilize a mixed-market capitalist economic system. All developed economies use markets to organize economic activity. Firms compete to provide consumers with the goods they desire at reasonable prices, in the process generating economic growth and jobs. Thus, Adam Smith's ideas are alive and well in the modern world. However, all developed economies also use a substantial amount of government involvement to reduce the problems with market capitalism identified by Karl Marx. Developed countries created labor laws and welfare programs to ease the burden of capitalism that falls on the poor and underprivileged, along with an extensive set of regulations on private sector behavior to prevent the worst excesses of market capitalism. Developed countries also use stabilization policy, based on the ideas of John Maynard Keynes, to smooth out the macroeconomic fluctuations that are characteristic of capitalist economic systems. Thus, modern, developed countries temper market outcomes with government actions.

There are, however, significant variations in the types of mixed-market capitalist systems that exist in the modern world. Some countries, such as the United States, Canada, United Kingdom, Ireland, Australia, and New Zealand, tend to use markets rather than government as the primary tool to organize and direct the economy. These economic systems are called **liberal market economies (LMEs)** because they lean toward the classical liberal (laissez-faire) philosophy of Adam Smith, even though their governments use stabilization policies and limited social welfare programs. Other developed countries, including Germany, France, Italy, the rest of continental Europe, Scandinavian countries, and Japan, use government much more extensively to guarantee the provision of key goods and services and to direct the course of economic activity. These economic systems are called **coordinated market economies (CMEs)** because the *government takes an extensive role in organizing and coordinating the economy, but at their core these economic systems are still market-based. Meanwhile, almost all of the countries that once utilized central planning and espoused a communist or socialist economic philosophy have converted to mixed-market capitalist economies. Russia and China now have vastly different economic systems than they did 25 years ago, and China has been particularly successful in adapting its economic system to be compatible with global capitalism. However, all of these economic systems are facing major environmental challenges in the face of global resource shortages and climate change, and it is likely that there will be major shifts in how economic systems are organized as environmental challenges mount.*

In this chapter, we review the past few decades of the development of economic systems. We will contrast some examples of coordinated market economies with the liberal market economy of the United States, and provide an overview of the economic transitions of the command communist countries to market capitalism. We will also briefly describe China's partial and remarkably successful transition to a hybrid of socialism and mixed-market capitalism. Finally, we examine the effect of market approaches on global environmental issues, and discuss some of the environmental challenges facing modern economic systems.

ECONOMIC SYSTEMS REVISITED: CAPITALISM AND SOCIALISM

Capitalism and socialism were the two predominant models of economic systems in the twentieth century. Capitalism, as we have seen, is characterized by the private ownership of the factors of production. This system relies on markets to allocate scarce resources. The market system allows prices to be determined by the interaction of supply and demand. Under unregulated capitalism, the role of government is limited to the protection of property rights and the provision of public goods, with all other tasks handled by the market system.

Socialism instead relies upon social ownership and the process of planning to make decisions about resource allocation. All major economic decisions are made by government officials, while the scope of the market system is quite limited. Figure 22.1 lays out the basic differences between unregulated capitalism and pure socialism.

These two theoretical economic systems do not exist anywhere in the world today. Modern variants of pure capitalism and pure socialism failed to meet the needs of human societies and were eventually scrapped in favor of the modern, mixed economy.

1. What are the strengths and weaknesses of a pure capitalist system? A pure socialist system?

2. Why do you think neither pure capitalism nor pure socialism worked effectively when they were attempted in the real world?

FIGURE 22.1 Capitalism and Socialism

Capitalism	Socialism
• **Private ownership of the means of production.** Control of the means of production (capital) and the production process by owners of capital or their managerial representatives, with profit as the main objective.	• **Public (social) ownership of the means of production.** Control exercised by government with goals determined by the political process. Primary goal is the welfare of all members of society.
• **A market for labor.** Workers are divorced from ownership and control of the production process. The price of labor (wage) is determined by the supply and demand for labor. Employment is not guaranteed, and a certain level of unemployment always exists (the natural rate of unemployment). The profit motive is used to generate growth and create jobs, and wages and the threat of unemployment are used to motivate workers.	• **Labor outcomes determined by planning decisions.** Workers participate in self-management and/or shared decision making. The price of labor is determined by planners using some market forces along with social goals, including the maintenance of a social wage that meets basic needs. Full employment of human resources is achieved using moral and material incentives, guided by planning.
• **Markets determine the allocation of land and natural resources.**	• **Government determines the allocation of land and natural resources.**
• **Income distribution based on market-determined returns** to owners of factors of production (land, labor, and capital). Inequality preserves incentives.	• **Income distribution based on market forces and government planning,** with significant attention paid to reducing inequality and the exploitation of labor.
• **Markets for all commodities, including basic needs** such as health care, food, housing, and education. People receive basic needs only if they have the income to purchase them.	• **Provision of basic needs to all,** including health care, food, housing, and education, at no charge or at subsidized prices with the goal of maximizing public welfare.

As we saw in Part 1, the Great Depression marked the end of the era of unregulated, laissez-faire capitalism in the United States and most of Europe. While laissez-faire capitalism proved successful at generating rapid economic growth, it was also accompanied by vast inequality, deplorable working conditions, abusive monopoly power, and significant, recurrent crises (recessions and depressions). These factors led to irresistible pressures to reform the system. Following the Great Depression, capitalist countries around the world used a combination of markets and government intervention to stabilize the economy and to correct other market failures. From the 1930s until the 1970s, the size and role of government increased in most of these economies. However, the oil shocks of the 1970s and an increasingly competitive global economy put pressure on the governments to streamline operations and to reduce regulations. From the 1970s through the mid-2000s, most developed countries reduced the amount of government intervention in their economies. With the major financial crisis of 2007–2009, these trends reversed, and many countries began shoring up safety nets for the poor and crafting new forms of government stimulus and intervention. Thus, the developed capitalist economies of the twenty-first century all are characterized by a substantial degree of government involvement, although the degree of government involvement tends to fluctuate with the economic problems of the time.

Just as the Great Depression marked the end of laissez-faire capitalism, the fall of the Soviet Union in 1991 signaled the end of command-style communism as a major variety of economic system. It is important to remember that Marx's vision of communism was very different from the Soviet model. Marx believed that workers should own and democratically control firms and the economy and that there should be no strong central government. Marx's version of communism was never tried on a national scale, although the Mondragon cooperatives in Spain employ more than 80,000 workers operating under a structure very similar to what Marx seemed to envision. Socialism, on the other hand, was an economic system in which the means of producing and distributing goods was owned collectively or by a centralized government that planned and controlled the economy. The Soviet Union and most other communist countries combined the extremely strong central state of a socialist system with collective ownership, communal production, and sometimes worker control of individual enterprises. However, the state was the most powerful entity and determined most economic decisions, giving these countries a strong command structure along with a communal ownership structure—command communism.

The Soviet Union was formed after the Russian Bolshevik Revolution of 1917. The Soviets used a centrally planned government to make all major economic decisions. They organized their economy to extract resources from agriculture and workers in order to invest surpluses in heavy industrialization. This led to rapid industrialization and economic growth in the first part of the twentieth century. However, as the Soviet economy grew and became more complicated, the central planning system proved unable to cope with the complexities. Shortages and surpluses became common, and productivity was stymied by a lack of incentives for workers and farmers, whose incomes were not based on labor productivity but instead were determined by state planners. Meanwhile, the central bureaucracy became more entrenched and resistant to change, the Soviet Union began to fall further behind the United States technologically, and the economy began to crumble under the weight of the vast cost of participating in the Cold War arms race with the United States. After a failed attempt at reform in the 1980s, the Soviet Union and the other members of the Soviet bloc collapsed, at which point individual states embarked on the creation of political democracies and mixed-market capitalist economies. During the same period, China was also moving away from command communism toward a form of market-based socialism/capitalism hybrid. Thus, by the twenty-first century only a few command communist states remained—Cuba and North Korea—while the other former communist countries made the transition to democratic, mixed-market capitalism.

Today, nations continue to attempt to find the right combination of free markets and government policies to achieve stable economic development and the other economic goals that their country prioritizes. But even though the dominant economic system is mixed-market capitalism, a variety of mixed-economies and market-government institutions exist in the world today.

Liberal Market Economies and Coordinated Market Economies

One of the primary delineations that social scientists make regarding modern economic systems is between those economies that lean toward the classical liberalism of Adam Smith and those that lean toward a more substantial role for government intervention. **Liberal market economies** are those in which privately owned firms make the majority of economic decisions in competitive markets based on the forces of supply and demand. Economic relations tend to be legally based (contractual) rather than based on personal relationships, and the government works to establish the appropriate legal environment for markets and to correct market failures, but does not direct economic activity most of the time. Examples of liberal market economies include the United States, United Kingdom, Australia, Canada, and New Zealand. **Coordinated market economies** are those in which private firms make many economic decisions, but the direction of the economy usually involves substantial consultation, coordination, and/or intervention by the government. Firms, labor unions, and government officials frequently work together to make major economic decisions and these groups have long-established relationships that facilitate cooperation and coordination rather than competition. Examples of coordinated market economies include Germany, France, Sweden, the rest of continental Europe, and Japan. Interestingly, both liberal and coordinated market economies have been highly successful in the modern world, indicating that both types of economic systems can be productive, efficient, and internationally competitive.

Table 22.1 shows that, in general, LMEs devote 8.3 percent less of their economic output (GDP) to social programs such as aid to the poor, training and education, social security, and health care. Both LMEs and CMEs are quite wealthy by global standards, and GDP per capita is very similar in LMEs and CMEs. Furthermore, LMEs and CMEs have had very similar rates of growth in GDP per capita since 1970. However, although Ireland had spectacular economic growth in the last three decades, the growth rates in the rest of the LME group all fall below the CME average. Referring back to Table 10.5, we see that income distribution tends to be more unequal in LMEs, and Table 10.9 shows that LMEs tend to have higher rates of child poverty than CMEs. These outcomes—lower levels of child poverty and greater equality—are achieved via the higher taxes that citizens in CMEs pay.

There is also substantial evidence that the culture and institutions of a particular country have a strong influence on which type of economic system evolved in that country. It is no accident that the developed, liberal market economies of the world were all once part of the British Empire. As economist Steven Rosefielde described it, the "Anglo American model" of economic systems is founded on a culture of "individualism, a social contract derived

Table 22.1 Social Expenditures, Real GDP per Capita, and Real GDP per Capita Growth for LMEs and CMEs

	GDP devoted to social expenditures, 2005(%)	Real GDP per capita,[a] 2007(%)	Growth in Real GDP per capita, 1970–2007(%)
Liberal Market Economies			
United States	15.9%	$37,963	109%
Canada	16.5	31,746	103
Ireland	16.7	36,702	347
Australia	17.1	31,343	92
New Zealand	18.5	23,912	60
United Kingdom	21.3	30,149	123
LME Average	**17.7**	**31,969**	**139**
Coordinated Market Economies			
Japan	18.6	28,321	134
Netherlands	20.9	32,609	110
Spain	21.2	24,164	141
Norway	21.6	40,534	183
Italy	25.0	26,553	112
Finland	26.1	31,051	154
Belgium	26.4	30,463	118
Germany	26.7	28,146	112
Denmark	27.1	31,468	100
Austria	27.2	32,152	137
France	29.2	27,312	105
Sweden	29.4	32,615	96
CME Average	**25.0**	**30,449**	**125**

[a]Base year 2000, using purchasing power parity.

Source: OECD, http://stats.oecd.org, 2009.

from the Christian Golden Rule, an obligation to uphold the sanctity of contract law, acquisitiveness, hard work, entrepreneurship, and liberty, complemented with aspects of collectivist state economic governance."[*] The Protestant work ethic, a belief that wealth is a just reward for hard work, the opportunities provided by the vast British Empire and the world's first capitalist economy, along with a society tolerant of a high degree of inequality, provided ingredients for a vibrant, liberal market economic system first in England and then in the other areas of the British Empire. Meanwhile, the harsh climates of Scandinavia tended to result in a society that valued cooperation, moderation, and the collective good in order to ensure survival. And, Scandinavia industrialized after England, which required Scandinavians to work together to overcome the British lead in industrial development. This culture and historical setting evolved into the social democracies of Scandinavia in which firms, workers, and government officials coordinate

---

[*]Steven Rosefielde, *Comparative Economic Systems*, Malden, MA: Blackwell, 2002, p. 82.

activity, and where the world's most generous social safety net ensures that everyone has basic needs met. In Scandinavia, as in other coordinated market economies, we see a blend of individualism and collectivism in which private individuals own and profit from the means of production, subject to strong collectivist controls and obligations.

3. Given its unique culture, could a coordinated market economic system ever work in the United States? Why or why not?

To understand the differences between modern economic systems, it is useful to sketch out in more detail some of the key distinctions that exist by examining how specific countries organize economic activity. We have covered the U.S. economy extensively in this book, so you are already familiar with how the quintessential liberal market economy works. Below, we offer short descriptions of two coordinated market economies, Sweden and Japan, so you can see how coordinated market economies can differ in structure from the liberal market economy of the United States. Subsequently, we discuss the transitions of command communist countries and China to mixed economic systems.

The Swedish Economy

As with almost all modern economies, Sweden relies on market forces and private ownership of the means of production to produce most goods and services and at the same time avoids central planning of the type used in the Soviet Union. Nevertheless, the government intervenes substantially in the economy. For example, Swedes have decided that high-quality education (up to and including the college level), child care, housing, and dental care are basic human rights to which all citizens should have access. Thus, these items are provided to Swedish citizens at no cost or at heavily subsidized rates. Similarly, the Swedish government mandates that all employees receive five weeks of paid vacation (as compared to an unmandated two weeks that most U.S. workers receive) and that parents, including fathers and mothers, receive a combined total of 16 months paid leave to care for new or newly adopted children (as compared with the six weeks of unpaid leave mandated by the U.S. government). These programs are expensive, and to pay for them Sweden has one of the highest tax rates in the world, averaging 53 percent of GDP (see Chapter 12, Table 12.3). However, most Swedes are comfortable paying such a high tax rate because they receive high-quality services and benefits for their taxes.

Sweden also uses partnerships among industry, government, and universities to promote industrial development. The government works to identify key industries and sectors that are ripe for economic development and that will generate high-wage jobs in Sweden. They then partner with private-sector firms, including multinational corporations, to develop industry clusters. The government provides state-of-the-art infrastructure for the industry, the private sector provides the investment funds and market knowledge, and the university system assists with research and development and with training students and workers so they have the perfect skill set for the industry. The government's active labor market program allows workers to go back to school for training in new industries while still receiving a stipend to live on. This encourages workers to move from dying industries into new areas. Sweden's public-private partnerships in research and development and training were particularly successful in the last decade, when Sweden developed into one of the leading European countries in biotechnology and information technology. In essence, Sweden uses education, skills, and public investment to bolster the international competitiveness of its firms.

When comparing the Swedish economic system with the United States, we find that Sweden has a lower level of GDP per capita than the United States, so the average American is wealthier than the average Swede. However, Sweden has higher human development outcomes than the United States because of longer life expectancy, and greater literacy and educational attainment. Another country that has been successful with a different form of coordinated market economy is Japan.

The Japanese Economy

Between 1945–1990, Japan experienced the most rapid rate of sustained economic growth in the world, becoming the world's second-largest economy. Its approach, generating state-stimulated industrial development in high-tech manufacturing, became the blueprint for the economics successes of other newly industrialized Asian countries, including South Korea and Taiwan. Most economists attribute Japan's dramatic rise in manufacturing and exporting prowess to a combination of factors, including high saving and investment rates, the ability to develop and implement technology, a well-educated labor force, as well as government policies that supported the unique institutional structure of Japan's private sector.

The historical influence of Confucianism in Japan has meant a culture in which loyalty to superiors and respect for authority is expected, and there is a general emphasis on loyalty and harmony. These elements of Japanese culture are reflected in interesting ways in their economic system. The Japanese are more disposed to be cooperative and are willing to give up personal, short-term options in favor of long-term commitments. They tend to eschew confrontation and adversarial relations, and are more likely to act in the interests of the larger group or firm instead of acting as individuals. It is not uncommon for Japanese employees at the largest and most successful firms to be guaranteed lifetime employment. In addition, most chief executive officers are chosen from within the ranks of the Japanese firm. These characteristics foster a high degree of loyalty and trust, and facilitate the development of firm-specific skills and training, which has the effect of boosting productivity. And, firms, government agencies, and other institutions often operate as if they were a large family. This enhances social capital and further strengthens productivity and commitment to the organization.

Even firms in Japan are interlocked in a family-like structure. The Japanese economy is dominated by six large corporate groups that are involved in interlocking relations with production, distribution, and finance by way of *keiretsu* arrangements. A production **keiretsu** is a stable, mutually beneficial long-term relationship between a large core firm and its suppliers. It allowed for the emergence of the just-in-time industrial system for which Japan is famous, where suppliers produce and deliver parts required in production precisely when and where they are needed. This eliminates costly inventories, reduces variability, and allows firms to respond quickly to the changing wants of consumers. Most importantly, this system facilitates collaboration and coordination, along with the rapid dissemination of new technologies.

This ownership structure also has important implications for how firms are run. In most large firms in Japan, large banks, insurance companies, and trading partners own 60–70 percent of the stock. In essence, all those doing business with a major firm are also likely to be part of the ownership of a firm, giving economic relationships in Japan a significant degree of closeness. Banks, insurance companies, and trading partners tend to prefer steady returns over a long period of time rather than unsteady, short-term profits, so this characteristic tends to give Japanese firms a very long-term focus, with the goal of steady growth and increasing market share over time.

Compared with Sweden, Japan has a smaller welfare state. Family ties tend to be extremely strong in Japan, and family members are expected to take care of those who fall on hard times. However, Japan's government intervenes considerably in industrial development and is one of the most supportive of the private sector when compared with other developed countries. Japan's approach during its period of rapid industrialization was to target an industry for growth. The Ministry of International Trade and Industry (MITI, now the Ministry of Economy, Trade, and Industry) would select industries based on growth potential, linkages to other sectors (to maximize job growth), and suitability for Japan in terms of being able to fit within Japan's conglomerate structure and technological abilities. MITI would then subsidize the industry, provided it with capital, research and development support, technical assistance, and infrastructure, protect it from international competition via tariffs, and help it form a domestic cartel to secure profits, develop technology, and increase economies of scale. During the period in which Japan was catching up and passing the United States in established industries, such as electronics, steel, and automobile manufacturing, this approach proved amazingly effective and is credited with sparking their extended boom. However, now that Japan has caught up to (and perhaps passed) the United States in many well-established industries, this approach to industrial development is no longer as useful. Revolutionary innovation of the kind necessary to create entirely new industries may require a different set of institutions. Indeed, it is often thought that the United States with its culture of individualism, competition, entrepreneurship, inequality (which includes the possibility of making vast sums of money in new ventures), and independent thinking is particularly well suited to revolutionary innovation, whereas the Japanese culture of cooperation, long-term planning, and greater equality is better suited to incremental innovation over time. It will be interesting to see if these assumptions are valid and if these trends continue into the future.

4. What do you see as the main strengths of liberal market economies? The main weaknesses?

5. What do you see as the main strengths of coordinated market economies? The main weaknesses?

While liberal market economies such as the United States and coordinated market economics such as Sweden and Japan have undergone moderate changes over the last several decades, the most significant changes in economic systems have been occurring in the former communist countries as they have made the transition into different types of market-based economies. When it became clear that command communism was failing economically and politically, these countries embarked on dramatic economic changes as they converted to market capitalist systems. The conversion has gone quite well in some cases, such as China, and less well in other countries, such as Russia. Below, we outline briefly the transition process.

Almost all of the countries that once had a command communist economic system have adopted some form of capitalism since the fall of the Soviet Union in 1989. With the exception of North Korea, Cuba, and a few others, the former communist countries have replaced central planning with market mechanisms, privatized most state-owned enterprises, and liberalized political systems. Russia chose to implement a shock-therapy approach to its transition that sought to implement a market capitalist economy as rapidly as possible. The Russian transition went very poorly and many Russians are worse off economically now than they were under communism. Meanwhile, China has been pursing gradual economic liberalization while maintaining its command political structure for three decades, with a substantial degree of economic success.

Russian Shock Therapy

The basic premise of shock therapy was that market institutions would develop quickly as Russia moved away from communism. Between 1992–1994 Russia moved rapidly to deregulate prices, privatize most state enterprises, and liberalize trade and financial flows. Soviet prices had been extremely distorted under central planning. Soviet planners emphasized economies of scale, so most goods were produced in huge factories by very few producers. When Russia relinquished control of prices, inflation surged as large firms gained control of uncompetitive markets and raised prices. Meanwhile, due to the unstable political environment in Russia, firms took profits out of the country where they could be held more safely. The result was hyperinflation accompanied by plummeting domestic investment.

Privatizing state-owned enterprises—moving from state to private ownership—also proved to be difficult. After decades of communist control, Russia had little entrepreneurial tradition to draw on and its citizens had no experience with financial markets. When Russia gave its citizens vouchers to correspond with their personal share of the nation's state enterprises, most citizens did not understand what these vouchers meant or what value they might have. Most citizens sold their vouchers to large investors for a pittance, and the bulk of the Soviet economy ended up in the hands of a small number of very wealthy and very powerful oligarchs.

Today, Russia concentrates on exporting natural resources and weapons, but very little else is left of the once powerful manufacturing sector. Russian manufacturing was not globally competitive, so when trade barriers were removed rapidly, firms did not have sufficient time to adapt to the market conditions of global capitalism. Russia's GDP declined by more than 50 percent in the first five years after opening its markets. The result was substantial deindustrialization and unemployment. The Russian experience was much worse than that of China, which chose to gradually restructure its economy and open its markets on a limited basis, only after its firms were able to compete on a global scale.

The People's Republic of China

China has one of the longest cultural, political, and economic histories of any country in the world. It was a relatively developed and sophisticated society centuries before Columbus discovered the New World. Yet, as Europe emerged from the Middle Ages and grew into a modern economy, China stood still. By the time the communist revolutionary Mao Tse-tung came to power in 1949 after a peasant-led revolution, China was still basically a feudal agricultural society.

A major thrust of the Chinese Revolution was to reform the agricultural system. This meant taking land from rich landowners and redistributing it to workers. With economic aid and technology from the Soviet Union in the 1950s, China began to transform both the agricultural and industrial sectors of its economy utilizing collective farms and central planning. These efforts met with mixed results between the late 1950s and the mid-1960s, but some growth did occur. Debates over economic strategy and policy centered around work incentives. Proponents of the use of moral incentives argued that the workers' revolutionary consciousness ought to be enough to motivate them to produce for the general welfare. Proponents of material incentives argued that workers' revolutionary consciousness alone would not increase economic output for the general welfare. Wages and bonuses based on productivity would need to be a part of the approach. Those who argued for material incentives also supported the liberalization of the economy and the introduction of market institutions, as opposed to central planning.

Mao chose to emphasize the ideals of the socialist revolution and the primacy of moral incentives. Between 1965 and the mid-1970s, China underwent the Great Proletarian Cultural Revolution under Mao's leadership. Those who disagreed with Mao were denounced and sent from urban areas to work on collective farms in the countryside. Universities were closed, and students were dispersed around the country to spread Mao's ideas. People who resisted the government were arrested and were often tortured and sometimes killed. Meanwhile, the economy stagnated under Mao's repression.

Upon Mao's death in 1976, China's economic system began to change. In 1978, the Chinese Central Committee under the leadership of Deng Xiaoping implemented dramatic reforms that moved China in a more capitalist direction. Deng ended the agricultural commune system, and farmers were then allowed to own land. Farmers were required to sell a certain amount of their crops to the state at a low price, but anything over this quota could be sold in markets for a profit. This policy proved to be an excellent vehicle to allow farmers to adapt to markets over time, while preserving revenues and stability for the state sector. Agricultural productivity surged, and China was able to use the agricultural surplus to invest in new ventures.

The agricultural policies were so successful that China adopted similar policies with respect to other sectors. Many state-owned enterprises became private corporations, and production targets dictated by central planners were replaced by contracts where a small amount of production was sold to the government at a low price but any surplus could be sold in markets. In addition, China allowed towns and villages to create and operate their own businesses. These Town and Village Enterprises (TVEs) were owned by a particular town or village, but they were operated on a capitalist model, free to profit and grow or to sustain losses and go bankrupt, just like capitalist firms. The freedom from central government control allowed TVEs flexibility, and entire communities poured resources into TVEs because they benefited directly from their successes. The result in many cases was rapid economic growth of small businesses and the development of competitive markets.

By the late 1970s, the Chinese economy was much more open. Tourists and those interested in trade and investment opportunities were permitted to travel in China and deal directly with local government officials. Chinese students were permitted to study abroad. A new era had begun.

The Chinese economy continued to grow and expand in the 1980s, with centralized economic plans directing economic activity in the major sectors of the economy, such as heavy industry, but at the same time introducing elements of a market economy in other sectors. The role of the state in the Chinese economy fell significantly. Government spending was 35 percent of GNP in 1978 but only 23 percent of GNP in 1989. Meanwhile, increasing amounts of private ownership promoted entrepreneurship among a wider and wider proportion of the population and set into motion a silent economic revolution that grew rapidly and carried with it pressures to introduce political democracy. This was displayed most vividly in May 1989 when thousands of university students and workers gathered in Tiananmen Square in Beijing to demand greater political freedom. The government responded with force, and many people were killed, arrested, and tortured. World opinion turned against the repressive Chinese government; nonetheless, the democracy movement was driven underground.

China continued to grow rapidly in the 1990s and 2000s as the government maintained its political monopoly while continuing to liberalize its economy. Large free-trade areas called **special economic zones (SEZs)** allowed much of

China to function in an almost entirely capitalist manner while the rest of the economy was protected. Foreign investment flooded into Chinese SEZs as manufacturers sought to take advantage of China's low wages, low taxes, lax regulations and environmental standards, combined with a disciplined and diligent work force. And, the Chinese government fixed the value of its currency, the yuan, below its market value in order to keep Chinese goods inexpensive and further stimulate exports. The Chinese government, awash in cash, snapped up billions of dollars of U.S. government securities, which helped to keep the dollar strong and the yuan weak. As we saw in Chapter 21, in response to the recession following the global financial crisis of 2007–2009, the Chinese government used its vast resources to inject a huge amount of money into its economy, especially in public works and infrastructure, demonstrating that they had learned the lessons of Keynes well.

China's GDP grew at an average annual rate of 9.66 percent between 1977 and 2007, and it transformed from an isolated, regionally based economy to a global economic power and the world's second-largest economy. Yet, despite its amazing economic success over the last three decades, China faces a host of serious problems, including major pollution, deforestation, and other environmental problems, as well as water, raw materials, and energy shortages. And, there is still some simmering unrest regarding the lack of political freedoms. It will be interesting to see if China can continue its economic reforms without addressing its environmental, resource, and political problems in the near future.

Thus, in the last several decades China moved from a command communist, centrally planned economic system to one featuring a much smaller state presence coexisting with a market economy. China's current economic system features largely capitalist economic development within a socialist system in which the state maintains the ability to exercise a very high degree of control, even if it does not always choose to use its power.

6. Why do you think China's gradual approach to its transition from communism to market capitalism was more successful than Russia's shock-therapy approach?

ECONOMIC SYSTEMS, ENERGY, AND THE ENVIRONMENT

An economic system is likely to persist only as long as it continues to meet the needs of society. With looming shortages of water, oil, and other scarce resources and the potentially disastrous economic consequences of global climate change, it seems unlikely that a global capitalist system based on abundant resources and constant growth can continue indefinitely. Will an energy shortage curtail global economic growth? Will an ecological crisis of some sort spell the death knell for modern global capitalism and force economies to change their ways? The next section explores some of the key issues for economic systems with respect to resource and energy use, sustainable development, and the environment.

THE COMING ENERGY REVOLUTION AND THE CHALLENGE OF GLOBAL WARMING AND CLIMATE CHANGE

As the global community confronts the early years of the twenty-first century, there is probably no greater challenge than finding a way to reduce our use and dependence upon nonrenewable fossil fuels. Ending global poverty and bringing about global peace are high on the list, but the immediate and long-term consequences of energy use are at the core of the question of the long-term environmental sustainability of the planet and its people.

Since the beginning of the U.S. war in Iraq, world petroleum prices have increased from $20 per barrel in 2003 to a high of $90 (annual average) in 2008. (Oil prices did hit a daily record high of $148 per barrel in July 2008.) As can be seen in Figures 22.2 and 22.3 and Table 22.2, world oil consumption has been steadily increasing since 1970 from 40 million barrels per day to 85 million barrels per day in 2008. (Projections by the U.S. Energy Information Administration suggest that the world will be using over 110 million barrels per day by 2030.) This raises a number of critical questions: Where will the oil come from? Who will control it? What will it cost? How will the global economic and financial system adapt to this reality?

By the end of 2008, world oil consumption was nearly 85 million barrels a day. The United States was using 20 million barrels a day and needing to import 12 million barrels a day (60 percent of its needs). Needless to say, with oil prices just over $70 per barrel in August of 2009, oil represents a significant share of the trade deficit (current account deficit) for the United States. (As the U.S. dollar weakens, we can observe that oil prices adjust upward.)

FIGURE 22.2 World Oil Consumption, 1970–2008*

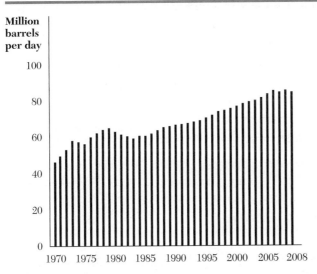

*Prices are for Saudi Arabian light crude, which typically sells at a discount to West Texas Intermediate, adjusted for inflation.

Sources: Energy Information Administration; Rocky Mountain Institute, 2009.

FIGURE 22.3   Oil Prices, 1970–2008

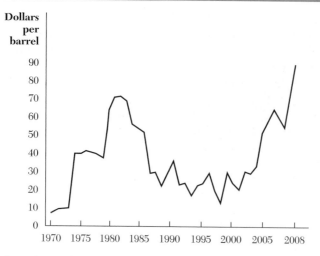

Source: Energy Information Administration; Rocky Mountain Institute, 2009.

Petroleum is a non-renewable fossil fuel that will run out toward the end of this century. More importantly, the supply and demand dynamics will tighten over the next critical decades. There is enormous pressure on the global community to begin a transition toward the serious conservation (reduce use and enhanced efficiency) of nonrenewable energy and the rapid development of renewable energy technologies and sources. Continuing to depend on and use fossil fuels, especially petroleum and coal, will only further accelerate the already serious problem of global warming and global climate change. This problem is not only a resource and environmental problem but a reality that has incredible consequences for the global economic and financial system. See Figures 22.4 and 22.5 for data on U.S. use of fossil fuels and demand for oil from foreign sources.

Table 22.2   Global Oil Demand by Region, 2008
(millions of barrels a day)

	Demand 2008
North America	25.43
Europe	16.30
OECD Pacific	8.63
China	8.00
Other Asia	8.72
Former Soviet Union	3.80
Middle East	5.91
Africa	2.90
Latin America	4.99
World	85.00

Source: International Energy Agency, *Oil Market Report*, 2009.

FIGURE 22.4 U.S. Energy Overview Fossil Fuels

Share of U.S. energy consumption, 2008

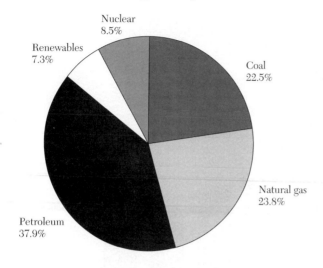

Total consumption: 100 quadrillion BTUs

Source: Energy Information Administration, 2009.

FIGURE 22.5 U.S. Demand for Foreign Oil Imports, 1960–2008

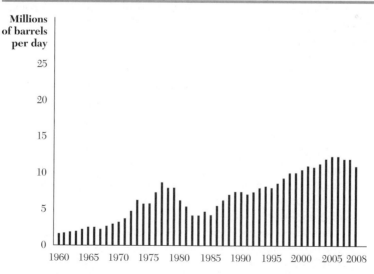

Source: Energy Information Administration, 2009.

FIGURE 22.6 A Chilling Comparison: Greenhouse-Gas Emission (Billion tons of carbon equivalent)

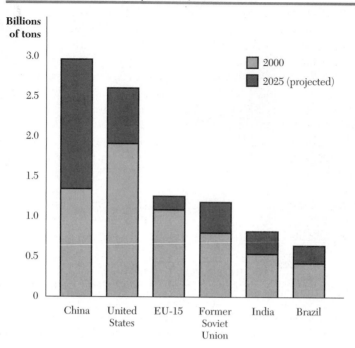

Source: The World Resource Institute, Annual Report, 2006.

As Figure 22.6 makes clear, the World Resources Institute projected 2025 level of contributions to greenhouse-gas emissions (billion of tons of carbon equivalent) will double from the 2000 levels for China. The top six contributors will be China, followed by the United States, the EU-15, the former Soviet Union, India, and Brazil.

In February 2007, the Intergovernmental Panel on Climate Change announced its latest report on the status of Global Warming and Climate Change. The panel predicted temperature rises of 1.1 to 6.4°C (2 to 11.5°F) by 2100. On sea levels, the report predicted rises of 7 to 23 inches by the end of the century. The report said that man-made emissions of greenhouse gases can be blamed for these problems. The study group indicated that it was 90 percent confident in its assessment. This report put to rest the years of scientific debate about whether the problem was real or not and in particular whether it was caused by human use of fossil fuels.

In the following excerpt from Greenpeace's 2006 publication, *Global Energy Revolution: A Blueprint for Solving Global Warming,* we can consider its case for the coming energy revolution and, more importantly, what Greenpeace recommends can be done to accomplish this transition to sustainability.

The Energy [R]evolution

The climate change imperative demands nothing short of an Energy Revolution. At the core of this revolution will be a change in the way that energy is produced, distributed, and consumed. The good news is that America is blessed with some of the best renewable energy resources in the world and after initial success with energy efficiency following the oil crisis in the 1970s, there is still enormous potential for improvement in the United States.

This report shows that we have a choice: we can cut carbon dioxide (CO_2) emissions in the United States nearly 75 percent by 2050 without relying on dangerous nuclear power or expensive new coal technologies. With rapid deployment of energy efficiency and renewable energy we can stop global warming.

Spurred by oil-price volatility and the war in Iraq, the issue of energy security is now at the top of the energy policy agenda. One reason for price increases is that supplies of all fossil fuels—oil, gas, and coal—are becoming scarcer and more expensive to produce. The days of cheap oil and gas are coming to an end. At the same time green energy is booming business in America, and this growth has to continue if we are going to stop global warming. Renewable energy technologies can deliver the energy we need, as this report shows, but only with consistent support based on an understanding that solving global warming is our top energy priority.

The solution to our future energy needs lies in greater use of renewable energy sources for both heat and power. Nuclear power is not the solution. There are multiple threats to people and the environment from its operations. These include the risks and environmental damage from uranium mining, processing, and transport; the risk of nuclear weapons proliferation; the unsolved problem of nuclear waste; and the potential hazard of a serious accident. In addition, uranium, the fuel for nuclear power, is a finite resource. By contrast, the reserves of renewable energy that are technically accessible globally are large enough to provide many times more power than the world currently consumes—forever.

Renewable energy technologies vary widely in their technical and economic maturity, but there is a range of technologies that offer increasingly attractive options. These include wind, biomass, solar, geothermal, ocean, and hydroelectric power. Their common feature is that they produce little or no greenhouse gases, and rely on virtually inexhaustible natural sources for their "fuel." Some of these technologies are already competitive, and their economics will continue to improve as they develop technically. The price of fossil fuels, on the other hand, continues to rise.

At the same time there is enormous potential for reducing our energy consumption, while providing the same level of energy services. This study details a series of energy efficiency measures that together can substantially reduce demand in industry, homes, business, and transportation.

The challenges posed by global warming are great and they require new ways of thinking about energy. At the core of the Energy Revolution will be a change in the way that energy is produced, distributed, and consumed. The five key principles behind this shift are:

1. respecting the natural limits of the environment,

2. implementing renewable solutions, especially through decentralized energy systems,

3. phasing out dirty, unsustainable energy sources,

FIGURE 22.7 U.S.A: Carbon Dioxide Emissions Can Be Reduced
by Nearly Three-Quarters

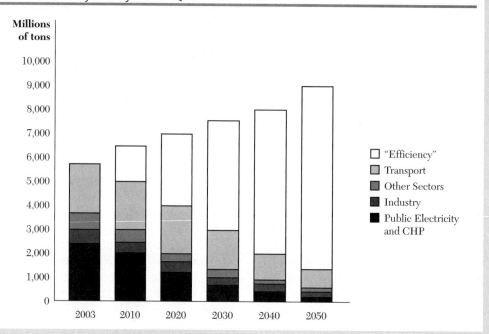

4. decoupling economic growth from the consumption of fossil fuels, and

5. creating greater equity in the use of resources.

Two contrasting scenarios are outlined in this report, the Reference Scenario and the Energy [R]evolution Scenario. The Reference Scenario is based on the reference scenario published by the International Energy Agency (IEA) in World Energy Outlook 2004, and extrapolated forward from 2030. In its report the IEA suggests that global CO_2 emissions will almost double as energy demand grows and most of that demand is met with coal, gas, and oil.

The first goal of the Energy [R]evolution Scenario is to cut global carbon dioxide emissions in half by mid-century. The second objective is to achieve these reductions while

phasing out nuclear energy. This report shows how the United States can achieve these goals. It outlines how the U.S. can more fully exploit the large potential for reducing energy demand through energy efficiency, to ensure we are using our energy resources wisely. At the same time, cost-effective renewable energy sources are accessed for heat, electricity generation, and the production of biofuels.

The Energy [R]evolution Scenario describes a development pathway to transform the present situation into a safe, sustainable energy supply. The key findings of the scenario are as follows:

❖ The electricity sector can pioneer renewable energy development. By 2050, nearly 80 percent of electricity can be produced from renewable energy sources. In the Energy [R]evolution Scenario 34 percent is generated by wind, 18 percent by solar, 14 percent by hydro, and 9 percent biomass. There is a smaller amount of ocean energy and geothermal power, as well as nearly 20 percent fossil generation, 85 percent of which is natural gas.

- Under our Energy [R]evolution Scenario total carbon dioxide emissions are reduced 72 percent without resorting to an increase in dangerous nuclear power or new coal technologies.
- In the heat supply sector, the contribution of renewables will grow to more than 60 percent by 2050. Fossil fuels will be increasingly replaced by more efficient modern technologies, in particular biomass, solar, and geothermal technologies.
- America's oil use can be cut over 50 percent by 2050 with much more efficient cars and trucks potentially including new plug-in hybrids, use of biofuels, and greater reliance on electricity for public transportation.

We have a long way to go. Today in America less than 10 percent of electricity is generated renewably, while the contribution of renewables to heat supply is only 8 percent. More than 95 percent of America's primary energy supply still comes from fossil fuels and CO_2 emissions are projected to increase by more than 50 percent under the Reference Scenario.

The United States faces a significant increase in expenditure on electricity supply under the Reference Scenario. The undiminished growth in demand for electricity, increase in fossil fuel prices, and cost of CO_2 emissions will all result in North America's electricity supply costs rising from $290 billion per year to $750 billion per year in 2050. The Energy [R]evolution Scenario, on the other hand, not only meets global CO_2 reduction targets but also helps to stabilize energy costs and thus relieves the economic pressure on society. Increasing energy efficiency and shifting energy supply to renewable energy resources reduces the net long-term costs for electricity supply by 40 percent compared to the Reference Scenario. In other words, following stringent environmental targets in the energy sector makes not only good environmental sense, but good economic sense, as well.

To make the energy revolution real and to avoid dangerous climate change, Greenpeace recommends that the United States:

- phase out of all subsidies for fossil fuels and nuclear energy,
- set legally binding targets for renewable energy,
- provide defined and stable returns for renewable energy investors,
- guarantee priority access to the grid, and
- institute strong efficiency standards for all appliances, buildings, and vehicles.

Source: From Grynier, *Global Energy Revolution: A Blueprint for Solving Global Warming*, 2006. Greenpeace (http://www.greenpeace.org/usa).

SUSTAINABLE DEVELOPMENT AND THE ENVIRONMENTAL CRISIS

As you have seen throughout this book, an unregulated market economy produces market failure, or negative externalities, when it comes to the physical environment. Even a regulated market system only succeeds at setting a particular level of pollution that is determined to be acceptable (based on an assessment of cost and risk). The pollution and degradation of the environment continue nevertheless. Many critics have argued that preventing current and future environmental degradation requires a new world view that focuses on developing environmentally sustainable ways to produce, consume, distribute, and dispose of goods and services. This argument recognizes the need for global economic growth, but in a way that does not violate or degrade our Earth capital—the physical life-support systems of the planet.

In recent years, many experts have written extensively on the issues of the environment, energy, and sustainability. They have not only focused on these issues specifically but have examined them in the context of a capitalist market economy and the growing global consensus that carbon dioxide emissions from the burning of fossil fuels is driving the long-term problem of climate change.

In his 2004 book, *Red Sky at Morning*, Gustave Speth, the dean of the School of Forestry at Yale University, presented a devastating critique of the failed effort on the part of nations and international institutions to address the mounting global environmental crisis. In this book, he exhaustively identifies and elaborates upon the forces of globalization that are cumulatively bringing about this crisis. His 2008 book, *The Bridge at the Edge of The World: Capitalism, The Environment, and Crossing From Crisis to Sustainability*, advanced his prior critique with a more central focus on the relationship between capitalism and the environment. His conclusion was that the global community needed to find a way to govern and regulate global capitalism to bring about a long-term sustainable system. In 2005, Jonathan Porritt, one of the world's most noted environmentalists, published *Capitalism: As If the World Matters*. His critique of capitalism brought forth many very specific examples of what can and needs to be done especially by corporations and consumers to bring about a sustainable society and economy.

In recent years, the United Nation's Intergovernmental Panel on Climate Change (IPCC) produced updates to its ongoing analysis of the problem of climate change. In 2007, Nicholas Stern's *The Economics of Climate Change* represented the IPCC's most recent analysis of the problem.

Reinforcing the IPCC's conclusions but in a more journalistic and popular form, *New York Times* journalist Thomas L. Friedman published *Hot, Flat, and Crowded* (2008). This book made the case for understanding that climate change was a real threat and needed to be contained. To do so would require nothing less than a global green revolution that had to include China and India. Taking a more academic and even more comprehensive approach was economist Jeffrey D. Sachs, the director of the Earth Institute at Columbia University. His 2008 book, *Common Wealth: Economics for a Crowded Planet*, examined the natural resource aspects of environmental sustainability, the demographic trends and realities putting pressure on the world's limited resources, the development and global poverty challenges, and the relationship between the environmental crisis and economic security. In the last section of this book, Sachs discusses very pragmatic and viable policies for global cooperation.

In 2009, Stern updated his 2007 book with *The Global Deal: Climate Change and the Creation of a New Era of Progress and Prosperity*. This book presents a detailed plan for a global adjustment and transition toward a sustainable future. To further reinforce Stern's analysis, economist Frank Ackerman's 2009 book, *Can We Afford the Future?: The Economics of a Warming World*, added yet another case for moving toward sustainability.

The Stern Report: The Economics of Climate Change

(Summary of the *Executive Summary*)

Climate Change presents a unique challenge for economics: it is the greatest and widest-ranging market failure ever seen.

1. The Benefits of strong, early action on climate change outweigh the costs.

    Uncertainty about the consequences but we can understand the risks. Mitigation must be viewed as an investment. Policy must promote sound market signals, overcome market failures and have equity and risk mitigation at its core. This is the conceptual framework of the Review (report).

    A simple conclusion—the benefits of strong, early action considerably outweigh the costs. Tackling climate change is the pro-growth strategy for the longer term, and it can be done in a way that does not cap the aspirations for growth of rich or poor countries.

2. The scientific evidence points to increasing risks of serious, irreversible impacts from climate change associated with the business as usual (BAU) paths for emissions.

3. The damages from climate change will accelerate as the world gets warmer.

4. The impacts of climate change are not evenly distributed—the poorest countries and people will suffer earliest and the most.

5. Climate change may initially have small positive effects for a few developed counties, but is likely to be very damaging for the much higher temperature Increases expected by mid- to late-century under BAU scenarios.

6. Integrated assessment models provide a tool for estimating the total impact on the economy; our estimates suggest that this is likely to be higher than previously suggested.

7. Emissions have been and continue to be driven by economic growth; yet stabilization of greenhouse-gas concentrations in the atmosphere is feasible and consistent with continued growth.

    Feasibility and costs of stabilization in the range of 450–550 ppm carbon dioxide emissions. Peak in the next 10–20 years, then fall 1–3 percent per year. By 2050, global emissions would need to be around 25 percent below current levels.

8. Achieving these deep cuts in emissions will have a cost. The Review estimates The annual costs of stabilization at 500–550 ppm carbon dioxide emissions to be around 1 percent of GDP by 2050—a level that is significant but manageable.

    Costs incurred but business opportunities as the markets for low-carbon, high-efficiency goods and services expand. GHE (greenhouse emissions) can be cut in four ways:

    Reduce demand,

    Increase efficiency,

    Actions on non-energy emissions (deforestation), and

    Switching to lower-carbon technologies for power, heat, and transport.

Assuming a start point scenario of 2–3 degree warming...the cost of climate change would be equal to a permanent loss of 0–3 percent of global world output; with 5–6 degrees of warming...an average 5–10 percent loss in global GDP with poor countries suffering costs in excess of 10 percent...

The analysis should not only focus on narrow measures of income like GDP. The consequences of climate change for health and for the environment are likely to be severe.

The BAU scenario over the next 200 years...an average reduction in global per capita consumption of at least 5 percent...with environment and health impacts included this increases from

5 percent to 11 percent of global per capita consumption. Total costs rise to about 20 percent…

9. The stabilization of greenhouse gases at levels of 500–550 ppm carbon dioxide emissions will cost on average around 1 percent of annual global GDP by 2050.

10. Looking at broader macroeconomic models confirms these estimates.

11. The transition to a low-carbon economy will bring challenges for competitiveness but also opportunities for growth.

12. Reducing the expected adverse impacts of climate change is therefore both highly desirable and feasible. Net benefits now of over $2.5 trillion…

13. Policy to reduce emissions should be based on three essential elements: carbon pricing, technology policy, and removal of barriers to behavioural change.

14. Establishing a carbon price, through tax, trading or regulation, is an essential foundation for climate-change policy.

15. Policies are required to support the development of a range of low-carbon and high-efficiency technologies on an urgent timescale.

16. The removal of barriers to behavioural change is a third essential element, one that is particularly important in encouraging the take up of opportunities for energy efficiency.

17. Adaptation policy is crucial for dealing with the unavoidable impacts of climate change, but it has been underemphasised in many countries.

18. An effective response to climate change will depend on creating the conditions for international collective action.

19. Creating a broadly similar carbon price signal around the world, and using carbon finance to accelerate action in developing countries, are urgent priorities for international co-operation.

20. Decisions made now on the third phase of the EU ETS provide an opportunity for the scheme to influence and become the nucleus of future global carbon markets.

21. Scaling up flows of carbon finance to developing countries to support effective policies and programmes for reducing emissions would accelerate the transition to a low-carbon economy.

22. Greater International co-operation to accelerate technological innovation and diffusion will reduce the costs of mitigation.

23. Curbing deforestation is a highly cost-effective way of reducing greenhouse gas emission.

24. Adaptation efforts in developing countries must be accelerated and supported, including through international development assistance.

25. Building and sustaining collective action is now an urgent challenge.

26. There is still time to avoid the worst impacts of climate change if strong collective action starts now.

Source: Nicholas Stern, *The Economics of Climate Change,* 2007.

Many experts argue that we have already pushed beyond critical thresholds in our use and degradation of renewable and nonrenewable resources. As the growth of the global population (particularly in developing countries) continues, we can witness many symptoms of damage: early stages of global climate change, or global warming (the greenhouse effect); atmospheric change and ozone depletion; water scarcity; declining water quality; declining per capita grain production; soil erosion; overfishing; overgrazing; air and water pollution; and the loss of species and biodiversity.

FIGURE 22.8 Solar and Earth Capital

Solar and Earth capital consists of the life-support systems provided by the sun and the planet for use by humans and other species. These two forms of capital support and sustain all life and all economies on the Earth.

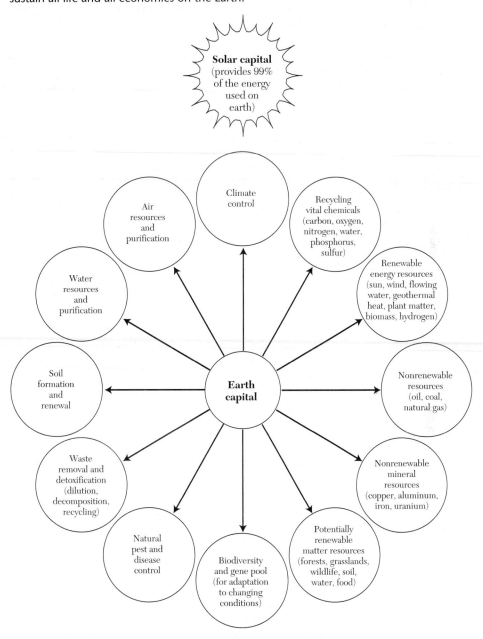

Source: From Miller. *Living in the Environment*, 12E. © 2002 Brooks/Cole, a part of Cengage Learning, Inc. Reproduced by permission. www.cengage.com/permissions.

While particular environmental problems are unique, they typically stem from economic growth fueled by resources that are non renewable, notably petroleum, natural gas, coal, and uranium. Environmental experts believe that the global community is nearing (if it has not already surpassed) many of Earth's physical limits. Their concern is that this kind of industrial economic growth is unsustainable.

This overall perspective is easiest to understand in the context of the following two figures reproduced from a best-selling environmental science textbook, *Living in the Environment*, by G. Tyler Miller. In Figure 22.8, in the center of the diagram is Earth capital, the foundation upon which Earth's life support system is based. Degrading or destroying this foundation undermines the ability to sustain life and the quality of that life. Economic growth that destroys Earth capital is unsustainable. Figure 22.9 identifies the social, political,

FIGURE 22.9 Factors Causing Environmental and Social Problems

Environmental, resource, and social problems are caused by a complex, poorly understood mix of interacting factors, as illustrated by this simplified model.

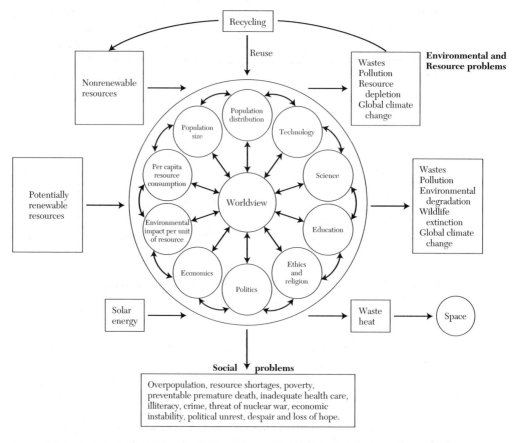

Source: From Miller. *Living In The Environment*, 12E. © 2002 Brooks/Cole, a part of Cengage Learning, Inc. Reproduced by permission. www.cengage.com/permissions.

economic, and environmental problems that derive in part from Earth's environmental and resource problems. Miller takes the position that human beings must adopt a new worldview of sustainability and create the kinds of practices and institutions necessary to preserve Earth's biological and physical integrity.

GLOBAL RESTRUCTURING AND THE FUTURE OF CAPITALISM

In the face of the economic, political, and environmental challenges confronting the global community in a time of rapid change and transformation, it is predictable that there are many competing perspectives on the character of this change and where it will lead in the twenty-first century. Let's examine three distinct perspectives.

Many proponents of the free-market system view this transition, even with its problems, as a necessary adjustment period. The spread of the market system across the world and the global economic and financial integration taking place will lay the foundation for a long period of economic growth for all nations. Their view is that this strong growth will provide the necessary resources to solve many social, economic, health, and environmental problems. This optimistic future anticipates the rapid development of new technologies and the ongoing emergence of political democracy across the globe. This mainstream conservative view sees market capitalism as an economic system that is strong, dynamic, and adaptable.

A more liberal view accepts many of the global changes taking place as necessary and welcome but recognizes that an unrestrained market system will continue to produce undesirable social, political, economic, and environmental outcomes unless the government (or state) plays a more active role in the domestic economy. This view recognizes the need to yield some economic sovereignty at the international level in order to be able to solve many of the economic, financial, and environmental problems that nation-states confront. This view accepts the basic principles of a capitalist market economy but envisions a very different role for the state to play in the future—a role that would involve greater planning, public investment, and a stronger involvement with the private sector.

A more radical view criticizes market capitalist institutions and blames most of the planet's problems on the unrestrained growth and expansion of industrial and finance capital across the global community. This view holds that global capitalism not only exploits labor but destroys the earth as well, producing poverty and inequality, economic insecurity, and uneven growth and development. Proponents of this perspective advocate a more responsive model of socialism than that which was and currently is practiced throughout the world. This view acknowledges the failures and excesses of a bureaucratic and authoritarian (nondemocratic) socialism but envisions a new kind of democratic and market socialism that would bring forward a sustainable model of economic growth. The radical view sees the current dynamics of economic and financial integration as part of a strategic global restructuring of capital-

Pedestrians in the shopping district of Macao, China
(Paul Conklin/PhotoEdit)

ism. This restructuring is a necessary response on the part of capitalists to adapt and maintain their structures of capital accumulation so that the inherent dynamic of capitalism—capital accumulation—can continue unabated while avoiding the system's tendency to move toward economic crisis.

❖ Conclusion

Early in the twenty-first century, we have the opportunity to reflect upon our study of introductory economics. What have we learned that helps us to understand our past, our present, and our future? Will the basic economic questions of today always be the basic economic questions? Will the microeconomic tool kit continue to help us make the kinds of decisions we need to make as educated consumers? Will firms be able to make critical decisions using competitive market microeconomic tools and concepts? Will governments be able to adapt traditional macroeconomic policy to the changing microeconomic, macroeconomic, and international realities of a global system challenged by rapid and unprecedented technological change? Can the economic systems of all nations responsibly manage the environmental, energy, and natural resource challenges of this new century? Can human society conduct its economic affairs peacefully?

Review Questions

1. What are the fundamental differences between capitalism and socialism as economic systems?

2. How do liberal market economies tend to differ from coordinated market economies?

3. During the semester, what variations have you observed in economic structures in liberal market economies (for example, How does the United States differ from the United Kingdom)? What variations in economic structures among coordinated market economies (for example, How does Sweden differ from Japan)?

4. What are the key differences in the economic systems of the United States, Sweden, and Japan? Which of these economies do you think is best poised to deal with globalization and with looming resource and energy shortages? Explain carefully.

5. What are the major differences between the Russian transition to mixed-market capitalism and the Chinese transition? If the government of North Korea were to convert its economy from a command communist one to a market capitalist one, what might it learn about a successful transition based on the experiences of Russia and China?

6. Why does Greenpeace think we need a "Global Energy Revolution"? How might conservatives, liberals and radicals react to their proposals?

7. What is Earth capital? There are two distinct worldviews in terms of the global environment. What are they? What do you understand sustainable economic growth to be?

8. Global capitalism is in transition. What are three distinct views of this transition? Which do you feel is the most accurate? Why?

THINKING CRITICALLY

A CRISIS OF CAPITALISM?

U.S. citizens were painfully aware of the deep and prolonged recession that began in late 2007. Parallels made with the Great Depression exacerbated well-founded fears and pessimism linked to the collapse of real GDP and a 9.5 percent unemployment rate. The story line is familiar—the collapse of the housing bubble, greed coupled with risk management failures of Wall Street, the continued rise in foreclosures, frozen financial and credit markets, the steep decline in household net worth, and the plummet in stocks lowering the value of assets worldwide.

There was hope in the United States that the Obama administration could engineer a comprehensive response to the crisis and set the economy on a more stable and sustainable trajectory and, like Roosevelt, try to save capitalism in another time of severe financial and economic crisis.

But this is not only a U. S. problem. In the larger global economy, IMF data show the spread of the downturn is global with widespread slow or falling economic growth. Even China and India are seeing their projected growth rates cut in half. The International Labour Office estimates that the ranks of the global unemployed will rise to over 50 million this year and the IMF is once again concerned about potential defaults by sovereign debtors and worsening balance of payments deficits for many emerging market countries. The flow of investment capital to these countries is slowing to a trickle at a time when they need it the most. Additionally, public health gains have been reversed as global poverty climbs. The Millennium Development goals and agenda (to reduce global poverty by 50 percent by 2015) are being progressively undermined by slow growth.

In the article that follows, Nobel laureate Amartya Sen addresses the future of capitalism in the context of this global economic crisis. He reexamines the ideas of Adam Smith and John Maynard Keynes as well as other economists in response to these challenges. As you read Sen's article, consider the following questions.

Exercises

1. What might a "new" capitalism entail that the "old" capitalism does not entail? Is thinking about the nature of capitalism useful in light of the recent global financial and economic crisis?

2. Sen thinks that capitalism might not be a term that is "useful" today; that it served a historical role that is now largely obsolete. What lies behind Sen's reasoning? Do you think it is a useful term? What are the characteristics of capitalism? What other characteristics do modern economies have that "the market leaves undone"?

3. In what ways does Sen's description of Adam Smith's writing about capitalism differ from underlying perceptions about today's "free market" capitalism?

4. How does "widespread real mistrust and fear" guide economic decision making in economies recovering from recession? What lessons might we learn from Professor Pigou?

5. What has happened to the U.S. recovery since 2009? The global recovery? Are some nations recovering faster than others? Which ones?

6. How have the emerging market economies fared since 2009? Has global poverty increased, fallen, or remained the same?

7. How do you view the prospect for twenty-first century globalization in light of the worldwide downturn?

8. What might global capitalism look like in the future—following the crisis of 2007–2009?

CAPITALISM BEYOND THE CRISIS

AMARTYA SEN

1.

2008 was a year of crises. First, we had a food crisis, particularly threatening to poor consumers, especially in Africa. Along with that came a record increase in oil prices, threatening all oil-importing countries. Finally, rather suddenly in the fall, came the global economic downturn, and it is now gathering speed at a frightening rate. The year 2009 seems likely to offer a sharp intensification of the downturn, and many economists are anticipating a full-scale depression, perhaps even one as large as in the 1930s. While substantial fortunes have suffered steep declines, the people most affected are those who were already worst off.

The question that arises most forcefully now concerns the nature of capitalism and whether it needs to be changed. Some defenders of unfettered capitalism who resist change are convinced that capitalism is being blamed too much for short-term economic problems—problems they variously attribute to bad governance (for example by the Bush administration) and the bad behavior of some individuals (or what John McCain described during the presidential campaign as "the greed of Wall Street"). Others do, however see truly serious defects in the existing economic arrangements and want to reform them, looking for an alternative approach that is increasingly being called "new capitalism."

The idea of old and new capitalism played an energizing part at a symposium called "New World, New Capitalism" held in Paris in January and hosted by the French president Nicolas Sarkozy and the former British prime minister Tony Blair, both of whom made eloquent presentations on the need for change. So did German Chancellor Angela Merkel, who talked about the old German idea of a "social market"—one restrained by a mixture of consensus-building policies—as a possible blueprint for new capitalism (though Germany has not done much better in the recent crisis than other market economies).

Ideas about changing the organization of society in the long run are clearly needed, quite apart from strategies for dealing with an immediate crisis. I would separate out three questions from the many that can be raised. First, do we really need some kind of "new capitalism" rather than an economic system that is not monolithic, draws on a variety of institutions chosen pragmatically, and is based on social values that we can defend ethically? Should we search for a new capitalism or for a "new world"—to use the other term mentioned at the Paris meeting—that would take a different form?

The second question concerns the kind of economics that is needed today, especially in light of the present economic crisis. How do we assess what is taught and championed among academic economists as a guide to economic policy—including the revival of Keynesian thought in recent months as the crisis has grown fierce? More particularly, what does the present economic crisis tell us about the institutions and priorities to look for? Third, in addition to working our way toward a better assessment of what long-term changes are needed, we have to think—and think fast—about how to get out of the present crisis with as little damage as possible.

2.

What are the special characteristics that make a system indubitably capitalist—old or new? If the present capitalist economic system is to be reformed, what would make the end result a new capitalism, rather than something else? It seems to be generally assumed that relying on markets for economic transactions is a necessary condition for an economy to be identified as capitalist. In a similar way, dependence on the profit motive and on individual rewards based on private ownership are seen as archetypal features of capitalism. However, if these are necessary requirements, are the economic systems we currently have, for example, in Europe and America, genuinely capitalist?

All affluent countries in the world—those in Europe, as well as the U.S., Canada, Japan, Singapore, South Korea, Australia, and others—have, for quite some time now, depended partly on transactions and other payments that occur largely outside markets. These include unemployment benefits, public pensions, other features of social security, and the provision of education, health care, and a variety of other services distributed through nonmarket arrangements. The economic entitlements connected with such services are not based on private ownership and property rights.

Also, the market economy has depended for its own working not only on maximizing profits but also on many other activities, such as maintaining public security and supplying public services—some of which have taken people well beyond an economy driven only by profit. The creditable performance of the so-called capitalist system, when things moved forward, drew on a combination of institutions—publicly funded education, medical care, and mass transportation are just a few of many—that went much beyond relying only on a profit-maximizing market economy and on personal entitlements confined to private ownership.

Underlying this issue is a more basic question: whether capitalism is a term that is of particular use today. The idea of capitalism did in fact have an important role historically, but by now that usefulness may well be fairly exhausted.

For example, the pioneering works of Adam Smith in the eighteenth century showed the usefulness and dynamism of the market economy, and why—and particularly how—that dynamism worked. Smith's investigation provided an illuminating diagnosis of the workings of the market just when that dynamism was powerfully emerging. The contribution that *The Wealth of Nations*, published in 1776, made to the understanding of what came to be called capitalism was monumental. Smith showed how the freeing of trade can very often be extremely helpful in generating economic prosperity through specialization in production and division of labor and in making good use of economies of large scale.

Those lessons remain deeply relevant even today (it is interesting that the impressive and highly sophisticated analytical work on international trade for which Paul Krugman received the latest [2009] Nobel award in economics was closely linked to Smith's far-reaching insights of more than 230 years ago). The economic analyses that followed those early expositions of markets and the use of capital in the eighteenth century have succeeded in solidly establishing the market system in the corpus of mainstream economics.

However, even as the positive contributions of capitalism through market processes were being clarified and explicated, its negative sides were also becoming clear—often to the very same analysts. While a number of socialist critics, most notably Karl Marx, influentially made a case for censuring and ultimately supplanting capitalism, the huge limitations of relying entirely on the market economy and the profit motive were also clear enough even to Adam Smith. Indeed, early advocates of the use of markets, including Smith, did not take the pure market mechanism to be a freestanding performer of excellence, nor did they take the profit motive to be all that is needed.

Even though people seek trade because of self-interest (nothing more than self-interest is needed, as Smith famously put it, in explaining why bakers, brewers, butchers, and consumers seek trade), nevertheless an economy can operate effectively only on the basis of trust among different parties. When business activities, including those of banks and other financial institutions, generate the confidence that they can and will do the things they pledge, then relations among lenders and borrowers can go smoothly in a mutually supportive way. As Adam Smith wrote:

> When the people of any particular country have such confidence in the fortune, probity, and prudence of a particular banker, as to believe that he is always ready to pay upon demand such of his promissory notes as are likely to be at any time presented to him; those notes come to have the same currency as gold and silver money, from the confidence that such money can at any time be had for them.[1]

Smith explained why sometimes this did not happen, and he would not have found anything particularly puzzling, I would suggest, in the difficulties faced today by businesses and banks thanks to the widespread fear and mistrust that is keeping credit markets frozen and preventing a coordinated expansion of credit.

It is also worth mentioning in this context, especially since the "welfare state" emerged long after Smith's own time, that in his various writings, his overwhelming concern—and worry—about the fate of the poor and the disadvantaged are strikingly prominent. The most immediate failure of the market mechanism lies in the things that the market leaves *undone*. Smith's economic analysis went well beyond leaving everything to the invisible hand of the market mechanism. He was not only a defender of the role of the state in providing public services, such as education, and in poverty relief (along with demanding greater freedom for the indigents who received support than the Poor Laws of his day provided), he was also deeply concerned about the inequality and poverty that might survive in an otherwise successful market economy.

Lack of clarity about the distinction between the necessity and sufficiency of the market has been responsible for some misunderstandings of Smith's assessment of the market mechanism by many who would claim to be his followers. For example, Smith's defense of the food market and his criticism of restrictions by the state on the private trade in food grains have often been interpreted as arguing that any state interference would necessarily make hunger and starvation worse.

But Smith's defense of private trade only took the form of disputing the belief that stopping trade in food would reduce the burden of hunger. That does not deny in any way the need for state action to supplement the operations of the market by creating jobs and incomes (e.g., through work programs). If unemployment were to increase sharply thanks to bad economic circumstances or bad public policy, the market would not, on its own, recreate the incomes of those who have lost their jobs. The new unemployed, Smith wrote, "would either starve, or be driven to seek a subsistence either by begging, or by the perpetration perhaps of the greatest enormities," and "want, famine, and mortality would immediately prevail...."[2] Smith rejects interventions that *exclude* the market—but not interventions that include the market while aiming to do those important things that the market may leave undone.

Smith never used the term "capitalism" (at least so far as I have been able to trace), but it would also be hard to carve out from his works any theory arguing for the sufficiency of market forces, or of the need to accept the dominance of

unemployment

capital. He talked about the importance of these broader values that go beyond profits in *The Wealth of Nations*, but it is in his first book, *The Theory of Moral Sentiments*, which was published exactly a quarter of a millennium ago in 1759, that he extensively investigated the strong need for actions based on values that go well beyond profit seeking. While he wrote that "prudence" was "of all the virtues that which is most useful to the individual," Adam Smith went on to argue that "humanity, justice, generosity, and public spirit, are the qualities most useful to others."[3]

Smith viewed markets and capital as doing good work within their own sphere, but first, they required support from other institutions—including public services such as schools—and values other than pure profit seeking, and second, they needed restraint and correction by still other institutions—e.g., well-devised financial regulations and state assistance to the poor—for preventing instability, inequity, and injustice. If we were to look for a new approach to the organization of economic activity that included a pragmatic choice of a variety of public services and well-considered regulations, we would be following rather than departing from the agenda of reform that Smith outlined as he both defended and criticized capitalism.

3.

Historically, capitalism did not emerge until new systems of law and economic practice protected property rights and made an economy based on ownership workable. Commercial exchange could not effectively take place until business morality made contractual behavior sustainable and inexpensive—not requiring constant suing of defaulting contractors, for example. Investment in productive businesses could not flourish until the higher rewards from corruption had been moderated. Profit-oriented capitalism has always drawn on support from other institutional values.

The moral and legal obligations and responsibilities associated with transactions have in recent years become much harder to trace, thanks to the rapid development of secondary markets involving derivatives and other financial instruments. A subprime lender who misleads a borrower into taking unwise risks can now pass off the financial assets to third parties—who are remote from the original transaction. Accountability has been badly undermined, and the need for supervision and regulation has become much stronger.

And yet the supervisory role of government in the United States in particular has been, over the same period, sharply curtailed, fed by an increasing belief in the self-regulatory nature of the market economy. Precisely as the need for state surveillance grew, the needed supervision shrank. There was, as a result, a disaster waiting to happen, which did eventually happen last year, and this has certainly contributed a great deal to the financial crisis that is plaguing the world today. The insufficient regulation of financial activities has implications not only for illegitimate practices, but also for a tendency toward overspeculation that, as Adam Smith argued, tends to grip many human beings in their breathless search for profits.

Smith called the promoters of excessive risk in search of profits "prodigals and projectors"—which is quite a good description of issuers of subprime mortgages over the past few years. Discussing laws against usury, for example, Smith wanted state regulation to protect citizens from the "prodigals and projectors" who promoted unsound loans:

> A great part of the capital of the country would thus be kept out of the hands which were most likely to make a profitable and advantageous use of it, and thrown into those which were most likely to waste and destroy it.[4]

The implicit faith in the ability of the market economy to correct itself, which is largely responsible for the removal of established regulations in the United States, tended to ignore the activities of prodigals and projectors in a way that would have shocked Adam Smith.

The present economic crisis is partly generated by a huge overestimation of the wisdom of market processes, and the crisis is now being exacerbated by anxiety and lack of trust in the financial market and in businesses in general—responses that have been evident in the market reactions to the sequence of stimulus plans, including the $787 billion plan signed into law in February by the new Obama administration. As it happens, these problems were already identified in the eighteenth century by Smith, even though they have been neglected by those who have been in authority in recent years, especially in the United States, and who have been busy citing Adam Smith in support of the unfettered market.

4.

While Adam Smith has recently been much quoted, even if not much read, there has been a huge revival, even more recently, of John Maynard Keynes. Certainly, the cumulative downturn that we are observing right now, which is edging us closer to a depression, has clear Keynesian features; the reduced incomes of one group of persons has led to reduced purchases by them, in turn causing a further reduction in the income of others.

However, Keynes can be our savior only to a very partial extent, and there is a need to look beyond him in understanding the present crisis. One economist whose current relevance has been far less recognized is Keynes's rival Arthur Cecil Pigou, who, like Keynes, was also in Cambridge, indeed also in Kings College, in Keynes's time. Pigou was much more concerned than Keynes with economic psychology and the ways it could influence business cycles and sharpen and harden an economic recession that could take us toward a depression (as indeed we are seeing now). Pigou attributed economic fluctuations partly to "psychological causes" consisting of

> variations in the tone of mind of persons whose action controls industry, emerging in errors of undue optimism or undue pessimism in their business forecasts.[5]

It is hard to ignore the fact that today, in addition to the Keynesian effects of mutually reinforced decline, we are strongly in the presence of "errors of...undue pessimism." Pigou focused particularly on the need to unfreeze the credit market when the economy is in the grip of excessive pessimism:

> Hence, other things being equal, the actual occurrence of business failures will be more or less widespread, according [to whether] bankers' loans, in the face of crisis of demands, are less or more readily obtainable.[6]

Despite huge injections of fresh liquidity into the American and European economies, largely from the government, the banks and financial institutions have until now remained unwilling to unfreeze the credit market. Other businesses also continue to fail, partly in response to already diminished demand (the Keynesian "multiplier" process), but also in response to fear of even less demand in the future, in a climate of general gloom (the Pigovian process of infectious pessimism).

One of the problems that the Obama administration has to deal with is that the real crisis, arising from financial mismanagement and other transgressions, has become many times magnified by a psychological collapse. The measures that are being discussed right now in Washington and elsewhere to regenerate the credit market include bailouts—with firm requirements that subsidized financial institutions actually lend—government purchase of toxic assets, insurance against failure to repay loans, and bank nationalization. (The last proposal scares many conservatives just as private control of the public money given to the banks worries people concerned about accountability.) As the weak response of the market to the administration's measures so far suggests, each of these policies would have to be assessed partly for their impact on the psychology of businesses and consumers, particularly in America.

5.

The contrast between Pigou and Keynes is relevant for another reason as well. While Keynes was very involved with the question of how to increase aggregate income, he was relatively less engaged in analyzing problems of unequal distribution of wealth and of social welfare. In contrast, Pigou not only wrote the classic study of welfare economics, but he also pioneered the measurement of economic inequality as a major indicator for economic assessment and policy.[7] Since the suffering of the most deprived people in each economy—and in the world—demands the most urgent attention, the role of supportive cooperation between business and government cannot stop only with mutually coordinated expansion of an economy. There is a critical need for paying special attention to the underdogs of society in planning a response to the current crisis, and in going beyond measures to produce general economic expansion. Families threatened with unemployment, with lack of medical care, and with social as well as economic deprivation have been hit particularly hard. The limitations of Keynesian economics to address their problems demand much greater recognition.

A third way in which Keynes needs to be supplemented concerns his relative neglect of social services—indeed even Otto von Bismarck had more to say on this subject than Keynes. That the market economy can be particularly bad in delivering public goods (such as education and health care) has been discussed by some of the leading economists of our time, including Paul Samuelson and Kenneth Arrow. (Pigou too contributed to this subject with his emphasis on the "external effects" of market transactions, where the gains and losses are not confined only to the direct buyers or sellers.) This is, of course, a long-term issue, but it is worth noting in addition that the bite of a downturn can be much fiercer when health care in particular is not guaranteed for all.

For example, in the absence of a national health service, every lost job can produce a larger exclusion from essential health care, because of loss of income or loss of employment-related private health insurance. The United States has a 7.6 percent rate of unemployment now, which is beginning to cause huge deprivation. It is worth asking how the European countries, including France, Italy, and Spain, that lived with much higher levels of unemployment for decades, managed to avoid a total collapse of their quality of life. The answer is partly the way the European welfare state operates, with much stronger unemployment insurance than in America and, even more importantly, with basic medical services provided to all by the state.

The failure of the market mechanism to provide health care for all has been flagrant, most noticeably in the United States, but also in the sharp halt in the progress of health and longevity in China following its abolition of universal health coverage in 1979. Before the economic reforms of that year, every Chinese citizen had guaranteed health care provided by the state or the cooperatives, even if at a rather basic level. When China removed its counterproductive system of agricultural collectives and communes and industrial units managed by bureaucracies, it thereby made the rate of growth of gross domestic product go up faster than anywhere else in the world. But at the same time, led by its new faith in the market economy, China also abolished the system of universal health care; and, after the reforms of 1979, health insurance had to be bought by individuals (except in some relatively rare cases in which the state or some big firms provide them to their employees and dependents). With this change, China's rapid progress in longevity sharply slowed down.

This was problem enough when China's aggregate income was growing extremely fast, but it is bound to become a much bigger problem when the Chinese economy decelerates sharply, as it is currently doing. The Chinese government is now trying hard to gradually reintroduce health insurance for all, and the Unites States government under Obama is also committed to making health coverage universal. In both China and the United States the rectifications have far to go, but they should be central elements in tackling the economic crisis, as well as in achieving long-term transformation of the two societies.

6.

The revival of Keynes has much to contribute both to economic analysis and to policy, but the net has to be cast much wider. Even though Keynes is often seen as a kind of a "rebel" figure in contemporary economics, the fact is that he came close to being the guru of a new capitalism, who focused on trying to stabilize the fluctuations of the market economy (and then again with relatively little attention to the psychological causes of business fluctuations). Even though Smith and Pigou have the reputation of being rather conservative economists, many of the deep insights about the importance of nonmarket institutions and nonprofit values came from them, rather than from Keynes and his followers.

A crisis not only presents an immediate challenge that has to be faced. It also provides an opportunity to address long-term problems when people are willing to reconsider established conventions. This is why the present crisis also makes it important to face the neglected long-term issues like conservation of the environment and national health care, as well as the need for public transport, which has been very badly neglected in the last few decades and is also so far sidelined—as I write this article—even in the initial policies announced by the Obama administration. Economic affordability is, of course, an issue, but as the example of the Indian state of Kerala shows, it is possible to have state-guaranteed health care for all at relatively little cost. Since the Chinese dropped universal health insurance in 1979, Kerala—which continues to have it—has very substantially overtaken China in average life expectancy and in indicators such as infant mortality, despite having a much lower level of per capita income. So there are opportunities for poor countries as well.

But the largest challenges face the United States, which already has the highest level of per capita expenditure on health among all countries in the world, but still has a relatively low achievement in health and has more than forty million people with no guarantee of health care. Part of the problem here is one of public attitude and understanding. Hugely distorted perceptions of how a national health service works need to be corrected through public discussion. For example, it is common to assume that no one has a choice of doctors in a European national health service, which is not at all the case.

There is, however, also a need for better understanding of the options that exist. In U.S. discussions of health reform, there has been an overconcentration on the Canadian system—a system of public health care that makes it very hard to have private medical care—whereas in Western Europe the national health services provide care for all but also allow, in addition to state coverage, private practice and private health insurance, for those who have the money and want to spend it this way. It is not clear just why the rich who can freely spend money on yachts and other luxury goods should not be allowed to spend it on MRIs or CT scans instead. If we take our cue from Adam Smith's arguments for a diversity of institutions, and for accommodating a variety of motivations, there are practical measures we can take that would make a huge difference to the world in which we live.

The present economic crises do not, I would argue, call for a "new capitalism," but they do demand a new understanding of older ideas, such as those of Smith and, nearer our time, of Pigou, many of which have been sadly neglected. What is also needed is a clearheaded perception of how different institutions actually work, and of how a variety of organizations—from the market to the institutions of the state—can go beyond short-term solutions and contribute to producing a more decent economic world.

Notes

[1] Adam Smith, *An Inquiry into the Nature and Causes of the Wealth of Nations,* edited by R. H. Campbell and A. S. Skinner (Clarendon Press, 1976), I, II. ii. 28, p. 292.

[2] Smith, *The Wealth of Nations,* I, I. viii. 26, p. 91.

[3] Adam Smith, *The Theory of Moral Sentiments,* edited by D. D. Raphael and A. L. Macfie (Clarendon Press, 1976), pp.189–190.

[4] Smith, *The Wealth of Nations,* I, II. iv. 15, p. 357.

[5] A. C. Pigou, *Industrial Fluctuations* (London: Macmillan, 1929), p. 73.

[6] Pigou, *Industrial Fluctuations,* p. 96.

[7] A. C. Pigou, *The Economics of Welfare* (London: Macmillan, 1920). Current works on economic inequality, including the major contributions of A. B. Atkinson, have been to a considerable extent inspired by Pigou's pioneering initiative: see Atkinson, *Social Justice and Public Policy* (MIT Press, 1983).

Glossary

Absolute advantage In international trade, a condition in which one nation can produce more of a particular commodity with the same amount of resources as another nation uses for producing that commodity.

Aggregate demand The total quantity of goods and services demanded by households, businesses, government, and the international sector at various prices.

Aggregate supply The total quantity of goods and services producers are willing to supply at varying price levels.

Alienation The condition resulting from the separation of the worker from the means of production. Alienation from the worker's point of view results from no control over the product, no control of the means of producing it, and an antagonistic relationship of workers and owners.

Antitrust policy Laws that attempt to limit the degree of monopoly in the economy and to promote competition. In the United States, the passage, interpretation, and enforcement of antitrust laws have involved varying degrees of emphasis on market performance, market conduct, and market structure. See *Sherman Antitrust Act.*

Appreciation of currency The relative strengthening of a currency in a flexible exchange rate system. The appreciated currency rises in cost and value relative to the depreciated currency.

Assumption A proposition that is accepted as true. Economists use simplifying assumptions in building economic models.

Average cost Total cost divided by the number of production units.

Average fixed cost Total fixed cost divided by total units of output.

Average propensity to consume (APC) Total consumption divided by total disposable income. This is the average consumption income ratio.

Average propensity to save (APS) Total saving divided by total disposable income.

Average revenue Total revenue divided by total output.

Average variable cost (AVC) Total variable cost divided by total output.

Balance of payments A summary record of a country's transactions that typically involves payments and receipt of foreign exchange. Credit items and debit items must balance, since each good that a country buys or sells must be paid for in one way or another.

Balance of trade The difference between the value of exports and the value of imports of visible items (goods and services).

Barriers to entry Obstacles to a firm's entry into new industries or markets. These obstacles may be political (such as tariffs or trade restrictions), economic (economies of scale or limited resources, especially in oligopolies), or legal (patents, copyrights, or monopoly).

Board of Governors A seven-member group members are appointed by the U.S. president and approved by the Congress to head the Federal Reserve. The board coordinates and regulates the nation's money supply. See *Federal Reserve System.*

Breakeven point (1) In national income accounting, the amount of income corresponding to consumption of the entire income. There is no saving or dissaving. (2) For an individual business, the amount of revenue corresponding to a production level at which revenues exactly equal costs. There are no profits or losses.

Bretton Woods Agreement (1944) The international agreement that formed the basis for today's international financial organizations. After World War II, the Allied nations agreed that international financial affairs would be overseen by the International Monetary Fund. GATT and the World Bank were also outcomes of Bretton Woods.

Budget deficit   The amount by which government expenditures exceed government revenues during the accounting period.

Built-in stabilizers   Automatic, nondiscretionary forms of fiscal policy that compensate for particular trends of aggregate changes in national income.

Business cycle   Recurrent ups and downs of business activity, shown in a host of business indicators. Expansion and contraction phases are both thought to have certain cumulative features. They may also contain the seeds of the turning points at the cycle's peak and trough.

Capital   A factor of production, along with labor and land; the stock of a society's produced means of production, including factories, buildings, machines, tools, and inventories of goods in stock.

Capital account   Unilateral and capital transfers in balance-of-payments, accounting; capital transfers of nonproduced, nonfinancial assets.

Capitalism   An economic system in which the basic resources and capital goods of the society are privately owned. Decisions are usually made by individual units, which may be relatively small (pure competition) or quite large (monopoly/oligopoly). Decisions tend to be based on profitability in the case of businesses, or, in the case of individuals, on economic self-interest.

Cartel   An organization of producers designed to limit or eliminate competition among its members, usually by agreeing to restrict output in an effort to achieve noncompetitive prices. An example is OPEC.

Central Bank   A Federal Reserve Board operation that serves the nation's banks. Besides its major responsibility—control of the money supply—it conducts some restriction, regulation, and investigation of the banking industry.

Ceteris paribus   Literally, "other things being equal"; a term used in economics to indicate that all variables except the ones specified are assumed not to change.

Change in demand   A shift in the demand curve due to a change in one of the determinants of demand.

Change in supply   A shift in the supply curve due to a change in one of the determinants of supply.

Class   In an economic sense, a group of people defined in terms of their relationship to production. For example, under capitalism, one class of people (proletariat) works the means of production, and another class (capitalists, bourgeoisie) owns the means of production. This concept was used largely by Karl Marx.

Classical economics   A school of economics that usually refers to the doctrines of the British Classical School of the late eighteenth and early nineteenth centuries, especially those of Adam Smith and followers. They emphasized competition, free trade, and minimal state intervention in the economy.

Classical liberalism   A doctrine stressing the importance of rationality, property rights, individual freedom, and laissez-faire.

Collusion   Agreements to avoid competition or to set prices.

Commodity   Marketable item produced to satisfy wants. Commodities may be either tangible goods or intangible services. Marx considered labor under the wage contract a commodity because it orders wage contracts and responds to supply-and-demand conditions.

Communism   An economic system characterized by socialization of labor, centralization of the ownership of the means of production, centralized coordination of production, centralization of credit policy through a central bank, and reduction of alienation and exploitation of the worker.

Comparative advantage   In international trade, a country's productive advantage with respect to a particular commodity, based on its ability to give up fewer other commodities to produce a unit of the commodity than another country would have to give up.

This relative cost of production is most significant in determining mutually beneficial patterns of trade among nations.

Competition Theoretically, competition exists in a perfect and an imperfect form; the former is known as perfect competition, the latter as monopoly, oligopoly, and monopolistic competition.

Concentration ratio The percentage of total sales in an industry that is accounted for by a specific number of firms.

Conglomerate merger Companies in unrelated industries merge.

Conservative economist An economist who advocates classical theory, classical liberalism, and classical economics (i.e., that government should intervene only when necessary, and then only minimally).

Consumer Price Index (CPI) A government statistic that measures inflation in terms of the weighted average composite of goods and services commonly consumed by average families.

Consumer sovereignty The doctrine that the market follows the dictates of consumers, and is driven solely by consumer tastes and preferences. Producers respond to consumer demand.

Consumption Expenditures by households and individuals on consumer goods.

Coordinated market economies Economies in which the government is involved in most major economic decisions, either directing, coordinating, or consulting with economic actors. Private firms still make many economic decisions, but labor unions and government officials also get input into most major economic decisions, and these groups have long-established relationships that facilitate cooperation and coordination.

Corporation A form of business organization with a legal existence separate from that of the owners, in which ownership and financial responsibility are divided, limited, and shared among any number of individual and institutional shareholders.

Cost-push inflation A general increase in prices associated with increases in the cost of production. Categorized as supply inflation.

Creative destruction The process of the transformation of industries due to extraordinary innovations in which the most innovative actors tend to succeed while non-innovating establishments are destroyed.

Crowding out Loss of funding as a result of the competition between economic units for the use of limited funds. The term usually refers to the federal budget deficit and the continued borrowing of the U.S. Treasury. Funds used to finance government spending deprive businesses of necessary capital, thus crowding out investment.

Currency Any recognized material accepted as national money; almost always paper or coin.

Current accounts In balance-of-payments accounting, the accounts that summarize the flow of goods and services between one nation and the rest of the world.

Cyclical (budget) deficit The part of the federal deficit that fluctuates with the state of the economy. It increases when there is a downturn of the business cycle.

Cyclical unemployment Measure of unemployment due to decreased demand during the troughs of business cycles, when output is curtailed. Workers who are cyclically unemployed are expected to be reinstated as the cycle moves upward.

Deficit spending Government spending when net government revenues are less than net government expenditures.

Demand (1) Quantity demanded. (2) The whole relationship of the quantity demanded to variables that determine it, such as tastes, income, population, and price. (3) The demand curve.

Demand curve A hypothetical construction depicting how many units of a particular commodity consumers would be willing to buy over a period of time at all possible prices, assuming that the prices of other commodities, money incomes of consumers, and other factors are unchanged.

Demand deposits Checking accounts in commercial banks. These deposits can be turned into currency "on demand," i.e., by writing a check. Demand deposits are a main form of money in the United States.

Demand, law of A principle concerning the relationship between price and quantity demanded: All other things constant, the lower the price, the higher the quantity demanded. In other words, price and quantity demanded are inversely related.

Demand-pull inflation A general increase in prices arising from increasing excess demand for a given level of output.

Dependency model A model that assumes that underdevelopment is a consequence of the historical evolution of capitalism and the integration of developing countries into the expanding sphere of capitalist production globally.

Depreciation (1) Loss of value in capital equipment due to use or obsolescence. (2) The loss of value in any valuable good or commodity due to use or market forces (such as currency exchange rates).

Depression A prolonged downswing of economic activity exemplified by mass unemployment, a level of national income well below the potential level, and great excess capacity. A depression is more severe and longer lasting than a recession. The economic breakdown of the industrialized world in the 1930s was called the Great Depression. See *Recession*.

Derived demand Demand of a good for use in the production of goods and services.

Devaluation A downward revision in the value at which a country's currency is pegged in terms of a foreign currency.

Dialectics The study of the contradictions within the essence of things; an exchange of a thesis and anti-thesis that results in a synthesis; the struggle of opposing forces in the economy that, according to Karl Marx, drives economic change.

Discount rate Interest rate charged on loans from the Federal Reserve Bank to its member banks. The rate is pegged to the fed funds rate.

Discretionary fiscal policy A fiscal policy designed to respond to a particular situation in the macroeconomy. These policies are implemented to achieve specific goals, usually high output, high employment, and stable prices.

Diseconomies of scale The phenomenon of disproportional increasing costs as a firm's long-run productive capacity grows. Simply put, the growth of production costs in an expanding firm outstrips the growth in production.

Disintermediation Resource allocation, particularly investment, by a firm that excludes intermediary institutions such as savings and loan institutions, banks, or brokerage firms.

Disposable personal income Amount of personal income remaining after payment of various federal, state, and local taxes and other nontax payments.

Dissaving Deficit or negative spending; that is, borrowing or drawing down other financial assets in order to consume.

Distribution (of income) The division of the total product of a society among its members. The distribution is sometimes described by a classification according to income size or by a classification including factor payments.

Division of labor Subdivision of a productive process into its component parts, which are then handled by specially skilled or trained laborers. Adam Smith believed it was a major source of increased productivity over time.

Dumping Sale by an exporting nation of its product at a lower price in an importing country than in its own country. Dumping tends to ruin the importer's domestic industry while strengthening the exporter's market share.

Economic dependence The relationship of unequal interdependence, endured by the less advanced countries with the developed countries. Theoretically, a country is in a state of economic dependence if the expansion of its economy depends on that of another country. See *Imperialism*.

Economic development Progressive changes in a society's ability to meet its economic tasks of production and distribution. Development is characterized by increasing output and the growth of economic institutions, relationships, and methods that facilitate society's ability to generate economic growth.

Economic growth Increase in productive capabilities beyond the necessary elements of survival. Expansion creates more jobs, goods, and income.

Economic planning The planning of investment, consumption, and similar decisions by one or more bodies. Several variants (among which are corporate planning, command planning, and indicative planning) demonstrate variety in what is to be planned and who does the planning.

Economic profits A return to capital above "normal profit"; profit remaining after opportunity costs have been taken into account.

Economic system The "mode of life" of a society; the manner in which people organize themselves for production and distribution.

Economic theory A theory of economics or resource allocation. Examples are Marxist, classical, and Keynesian theory. See *Theory*.

Economics The study of the allocation of resources, the production of goods and services, and their distribution in societies.

Economies of scale The phenomenon of decreasing average costs in large-scale production (usually oligopolistic production). The growth of production in an expanding firm outstrips the growth in costs.

Efficiency In economics, allocation of scarce resources to best meet the needs and wants of society.

Elasticity A function that describes the sensitivity of demand or supply of a product to changes in its price. Elasticity equals the percentage change in quantity demanded (supplied) divided by the percentage change in price.

Employment Act of 1946 U.S. federal law that created a Council of Economic Advisers to advise the president on the state of the economy and on how best to achieve the goal of full employment.

Enclosure movement In England during the Middle Ages, a series of parliamentary acts by which the feudal nobility fenced off or enclosed lands formerly used for communal grazing, destroying feudal ties and creating a large, new "landless" labor force.

Entrepreneur In the classical liberal sense, an innovator and owner of the means of production. In the modern corporate world, an entrepreneur is often considered a businessperson.

Equation of exchange The quantity theory of money, expressed as $MV = PQ$, where M is the money stock, V is velocity of money, P is price level, and Q is real national income. It is a tautology, because V is defined as PQ/M.

Equilibrium A state of balance in which there are no endogenous pressures for change. A market equilibrium is said to exist at the price where the quantity demanded equals the quantity supplied.

Exchange rate The price of a nation's currency in terms of another nation's currency.

Exhaustive spending Governmental purchases of goods and services.

Exports Any unit of production that leaves the country where it was produced for sale in another country.

Externalities Costs of productive activity that the firm is not obliged to bear. The costs are borne by the public as social costs of production. Also known as third-party effect. Externalities may be detrimental (external costs) or beneficial (external benefits).

Factor of production Any implement or agent whose services are used in the production of economic goods and services. Three basic factors are land, labor, and capital.

Fed funds rate The interest rate that banks charge when they lend reserves to other banks for short periods of time; the Federal Reserve currently targets the fed funds rate and uses policy tools to achieve the stated target.

Federal Reserve System (Fed) An independent agency of the federal government and instrumental in determining monetary policy. Its main tools are altering reserve requirements and conducting open-market purchases and sales of governmental securities. See *Discount rate; Monetary policy; Reserve requirements; Open Market Operations.*

Feudalism The economic system that preceded capitalism. Relations of class were between lord and serf. Feudalism existed in a society in which tradition and ceremony played the major roles.

Financial account In balance-of-payments accounting, all financial flows in and out of a country.

Financial intermediaries Institutions such as banks, savings and loans, insurance companies, mutual funds, pension funds, and finance companies that borrow funds from people with savings and then make loans to others (borrowers).

Financial intermediation Use of financial institutions to deposit or acquire funds from the public. Such institutions pool numerous funds and then provide them to businesses, governments, or individuals.

Firm Unit that makes decisions regarding the employment of factors of production and production of goods and services.

Fiscal policy Governmental policy concerned with the tax and expenditure activities of the federal government, including the size of public spending and the balancing or unbalancing of the federal budget. This policy is designed to promote certain macroeconomic objectives—usually full employment, stable prices, economic growth, and balance-of-payments equilibrium.

Fixed exchange rate A rate at which a currency is fixed (set) to establish its price relative either to a universal exchange (gold) or to another currency.

Floating exchange rate A currency exchange rate that rises or falls in response to the forces of international supply and demand. See *Exchange rate.*

Forces of production All of the necessary elements—tools, machines, factories, means of transportation, labor, science, technology, skills, knowledge, etc.—required to produce goods and services.

Fractional reserve system A banking system under which commercial banks are required to maintain reserves equal to a prescribed percentage of their demand or other deposits. See *Reserve requirement.*

Free trade A situation in which all commodities can be freely imported and exported without special taxes or restrictions being levied because of their status as imports or exports.

Frictional unemployment Loss of jobs caused by temporary mismatching of laborers with jobs due to differences between the needs of business and skills of labor.

Full employment A condition under which those who wish to work at the prevailing wage are able to find work. In the United States, full employment is defined as 4 percent unemployment.

General Agreement on Tariffs and Trade (GATT) An association of countries that "sets and regulates the code of international trade conduct and promotes free trade as part of the Bretton Woods System."

Gini coefficient A measure of inequality in income distribution derived from the Lorenz curve. To calculate it for a population, find the difference in area between a 45° line and the population's Lorenz curve, and divide the difference by the entire area below the 45° line.

Glut An excess of production over the amount purchased. This usually leads to a decline in production and possibly a recession.

Gross domestic product (GDP) The market value of all final goods and services produced in an accounting period by factors of production located within a country.

Gross national product (GNP) The market value of all final goods and services produced in an accounting period by factors of production owned by citizens of that country.

Hidden unemployment Workers who are unemployed or underemployed but are not counted in official unemployment statistics. Includes discouraged workers who are unemployed but have given up looking for a job, and workers who are working part-time but would like more hours of work.

Historical materialism Developed by Karl Marx, an in-depth historical study of material relations of people. The basis of social and economic change resides in class relations of people. The base of a society is its mode of production, and all class struggle emanates out of the relations of people to the mode of production. The superstructure, which is determined by the base, includes the philosophy, religion, ideology, etc., of the specific epoch.

Horizontal merger The combination of two companies in the same industry.

Imperialism One country's economic, social, political, and cultural dominance over another country. Imperialism, as developed by Lenin, Sweezy, Baran, Magdoff, and many others, is a historical problem and directly related to the growth and development of capitalism.

Imports Goods brought into a country for sale, having been produced elsewhere.

Income elasticity of demand The percentage change in quantity demanded divided by the percentage change in income. It measures how much the demand for a product changes when income changes.

Income flow The path that income follows in the economy. Businesses pay rents, wages, interest, and profits to households, which in turn spend their incomes to continue the flow.

Income velocity of money The rate of turnover of money in the economy. From the equation of exchange, velocity is GDP divided by the money supply. See *Equation of exchange*.

Incomes policy A governmental policy designed to limit inflation by instituting direct and indirect controls over prices, wages, profits, and other types of income.

Index number A weighted average of a given variable with a specified base number, usually 100.

Indirect business taxes Taxes imposed on the production and sale of goods. Examples include sales tax, excise tax, custom duties, and property taxes.

Industry The collective group of producers of a single good or service or closely related goods or services.

Inefficiency in production A condition in a noncompetitive market in which output is not at minimum average cost.

Inefficiency in resource allocation A condition in a noncompetitive market in which the good's price does not equal marginal cost.

Infant industry An industry that has recently been established in a country and has not yet had time to exploit possible economies of scale and other efficiencies. Such industries provide one of the traditional arguments for tariff protection.

Inflation A general rise in the average level of all prices in an economy as defined by some index (Consumer Price Index, wholesale price index, or GDP price deflator).

Infrastructure Necessary supports for development, such as transportation routes and social services.

Innovation A change for the better in technology or production. A change is considered "better" if it involves higher efficiency and/or lower production costs.

Institutional economics An approach to studying the economy that focuses on understanding the role and evolution of human-made institutions in shaping the economy and economic behavior.

Institutionalist Economists practicing institutional economics.

Interest (1) The price of borrowing money. (2) The rate of return to owners of financial capital.

Interest rate The amount of interest expressed as a percentage of the initial sum.

International Monetary Fund (IMF) International organization founded with the goal of encouraging trade by establishing an orderly procedure for stabilizing foreign exchange rates and for altering those rates in the case of fundamental balance-of-payments disequilibrium.

International trade Buying and selling of goods and services across national borders. The country that sells is the exporter, and the country that buys is the importer.

Inventories Stocks of goods kept on hand to meet orders from other producers and customers.

Investment An addition to a firm's or society's stock of capital (machines, buildings, inventories, etc.) in a certain period of time.

"Invisible hand" Term coined by Adam Smith to suggest that individuals who are motivated only by private (not social) interest will nevertheless be guided invisibly by the market to actions and decisions beneficial to the welfare of society.

Kanban The "just-in-time" system in which services and supplies are produced and delivered only when needed.

Keiretsu A production relation between a large core firm and its subsidiaries that allows for a stable, mutually beneficial long-term relationship.

Keynesian economics Theory characterized by its emphasis on macroeconomic problems, the special role of aggregate expenditure in determining national income, and the possibility of unemployment equilibrium; its attempt to synthesize real and monetary analysis; and its argument for a greater government involvement in the economy.

Keynesian multiplier (*k*) The number of dollars by which a $1 increase in spending (*C*, *I*, *G*) will raise the equilibrium level of national income. Represented as *k*, it can be expressed mathematically in relation to the marginal propensity to consume (MPC) or the marginal propensity to save (MPS):

$$k = \frac{1}{1 - \text{MPC}} \quad k = \frac{1}{\text{MPS}}$$

Labor The physical and mental contributions of humans to the production process. Collectively, labor refers to all workers.

Labor force participation rate Percentage of actual civilians participating in the labor force compared with the total number of civilians of working age.

Labor theory of value Theory held by Marx (and Smith in differing form) that the value of a commodity is proportional to the labor embodied in its production.

Laissez-faire A doctrine that the state should largely leave the economy to its own devices. Associated with Adam Smith.

Land A means of production that includes raw materials and the land upon which productive activity takes place (i.e., factory, farm).

Law of diminishing returns Principle that in the production of any commodity, as more units of a variable factor of production are added to a fixed quantity of other factors of production, the amount that each additional unit of the variable factor adds to the total product will eventually begin to diminish.

Law of specialization The tendency for productivity to increase when laborers specialize in one particular task.

Liberal economist An economist who accepts capitalism and advocates government intervention when market failures occur.

Liberal market economies Economies in which privately owned firms make the majority of economic decisions in competitive markets based on the forces of supply and demand. Economic relations tend to be legally based, and the government works to establish the appropriate legal environment for markets and to correct market failures, but does not direct economic activity most of the time.

Liquidity The ease with which an asset can be converted into cash. Considerations in measuring liquidity include the time necessary to acquire cash, the cost of conversion, and the predictability of the asset's value.

Liquidity preference Demand for money as a function of the interest rate; the willingness to hold money on hand.

Liquidity trap In Keynesian theory, the point in the economy when all economic agents desire to keep each additional dollar on hand. To them, the existing interest rate does not warrant the acquisition of bonds. The demand for money is thus perfectly elastic or horizontal, and monetary policy is completely ineffective in stimulating aggregate expenditures.

Long run Any extended period, usually longer than three to five years. For a firm, the time necessary to effect changes in "fixed" resources. Economists view the long run as the period in which equilibrium is reached.

Lorenz curve Graphs the extent of income inequality by charting the cumulative percentage of income against the cumulative percentage of families.

Macroeconomics The branch of economics concerned with large economic aggregates such as GDP, total employment, overall price level, and how these aggregates are determined.

Malthus, Thomas Economist who developed a theory that population tends to grow at a geometric rate while food supplies can, at best, grow at an arithmetic rate. Thus, in Malthus's eyes, extreme poverty, famine, plague, and war would continually beset humanity.

Marginal cost (MC) The change in total cost resulting from raising the rate of production by one unit.

Marginal factor cost The cost of an additional resource or factor of production (which in competition equals the price of the resource).

Marginal physical product (of labor) The additional output realized when one more unit of a variable input is used, assuming all other input levels are held constant.

Marginal propensity to consume (MPC) The change in consumption divided by the change in income ($MPC = \Delta C / \Delta Y$).

Marginal propensity to save (MPS) The change in saving divided by the change in income that brought it about ($MPS = \Delta S / \Delta Y$).

Marginal revenue (MR) The change in a firm's total revenue arising from the sale of one additional unit.

Marginal revenue = marginal cost In microeconomics, the point at which profits are maximized for a firm.

Marginal revenue product The additional revenue realized when one more unit of a variable input is used, assuming all other input levels are held constant.

Market (1) An area over which buyers and sellers negotiate the exchange of a well-defined commodity. (2) From the point of view of a household, the firms from which it can buy a well-defined product. (3) From the point of view of the firm, the buyers to whom it can sell a well-defined product.

Market economy An economy functioning largely through market forces (supply, demand, etc.).

Market failure The inability of the market to produce an efficient (or acceptable) result.

Market power A condition in which the firm can exercise control over the price of a good or service because the firm supplies the total quantity.

Marxian economics School of economics aimed at understanding the class system (or private property system); the methods of production and commodity exchange under capitalism.

Materialism In Marxian economics, the notion that production of goods and services for survival is the essential human activity in all societies. This activity colors and structures all other aspects of life.

Medium of exchange The function of money as intermediary. Since money is accepted in payment for goods and services and is valued for the goods and services it buys, money is a medium of exchange.

Mercantilism A characteristic European economic doctrine in the sixteenth to seventeenth centuries, emphasizing the role of money and trade in economic life and the desirability of active state intervention in the economy.

Microeconomics Branch of economics that deals with the interrelationships of individual businesses, firms, industries, consumers, laborers, and other factors of production that make up the economy. Focuses on markets.

Mixed economy An economy in which there are substantial public and private sectors, in which private enterprise and the market are significant determining factors, but in which the state also takes on certain basic economic responsibilities (e.g., full employment and business regulation). See *Capitalism*.

Mode of production In Marxian economics, the major economic structure, or base, of society, composed of the forces of production and the relations of production.

Monetary aggregates Various measures of the money supply used by the Federal Reserve System and include M_1 and M_2.

Monetary policy Governmental policy concerned with the supply of money and credit in the economy and the rate of interest. This policy is designed to promote certain macroeconomic objectives, usually full employment, stable prices, economic growth, stable exchange rates, or balance-of-payments equilibrium.

Money Anything that is generally accepted in payment for goods and services and in the repayment of debts.

Monopolistic competition A market structure in which each firm is relatively small, but each has a monopoly on its particular version of the product in question. Competition in such a framework includes advertising, easy entry product differentiation, limited price control, and other forms of non-price competition.

Monopoly A market structure in which there is a single seller of a commodity or service that has no close substitutes.

Monopoly capitalism An economy that marks the dominance of imperfect competition; productive forces or factors are extremely concentrated, and markets are imperfect. See *Capitalism*.

Multinational corporation A corporation that operates within more than one country.

Multiplier See *Keynesian multiplier; Transfer multiplier.*

National debt The net accumulation of federal budget deficits; the total indebtedness of the federal government.

National income The total income of factors of production in the current productive period.

Neoliberal model A model that assumes that developing nations must adopt modern capital and technology to have strong economic growth.

Net national product (NNP) Total output of final goods and services produced in an economy in a given period of time, including net rather than gross investment. NNP = GDP − depreciation or capital consumption allowances.

Newly Industrializing Countries (NIC) A group of countries (Hong Kong, Taiwan, Singapore, Malaysia, the Philippines, South Korea, Brazil, Mexico, and Argentina) that have allowed foreign firms to set up operations favorably and have generated sizable export capabilities.

Oligopoly A market structure in which a few large firms dominate the industry. Some of these industries produce an undifferentiated product, others a differentiated product. In either case, a special feature of oligopoly is that the firms recognize their interdependence.

Open-market operations Federal Reserve purchases and sales of government securities on the open market. These activities are an important instrument of monetary policy because sales of government securities reduce the money supply, while purchases increase it. See *Federal Reserve System*.

Opportunity cost   The cost of an economic good as measured in terms of the alternative goods one must forgo to secure it.

Organization of Petroleum Exporting Countries (OPEC)   Organization of oil-producing nations, largely in the Middle East, that have joined together for the purpose of controlling the production, export, and price of petroleum.

Orthodox economics   The mainstream approach to economic theory, which emphasizes the rational, calculating nature of human behavior and seeks to model that behavior quantitatively and scientifically.

Paradigms   A set of assumptions, concepts, values, practices, and so forth that inform a specific discipline (e.g. orthodox economics, Marxian economics, or institutional economics) during a particular period of time.

Paradox of thrift   Economic principle, identified by Keynes, that an increase in the desire to save decreases output, even though investment may also increase.

Peak (of business cycle)   The height of the business cycle; characterized by greatest economic activity and followed by contracting economic activity.

Per capita income   Total national income divided by total population.

Perfect competition   The market structure characterized by large numbers of small firms producing and selling a homogeneous product in a competitive market with easy entry and exit.

Petrodollars   Dollars and currency in the form of monetary reserves controlled by the oil-exporting (largely OPEC) nations, accumulated by selling petroleum.

Phillips curve   Graph showing the relationship between inflation and unemployment.

Political business cycle   Distortion of the basic business cycle caused by the actions and policies of politicians bidding for reelection. Usually a four-year cycle in sequence with presidential elections.

Political economy   Social science dealing with political policies and economic processes, their interrelationships, and their mutual influence on social institutions.

Possessions   Personal items people own and use, including home, farm, or tools. Private property, in contrast, reflects ownership of impersonal property used by the owner only to collect rent on land, interest, and profits on capital; it is used (worked) by others.

Postindustrial society   A society that has encountered the processes of industrialization and has gone beyond industrialization in terms of benefits accruing to the people. Some people consider the United States a postindustrial society.

Praxis   Practical activity with an added twist, i.e., the dialectical interrelation of thought and practice. The term was used by the young Hegelians and especially Marx.

Precautionary demand for money   Holding money in order to cover unexpected or temporary expenses or losses of income.

Present value   The value today of a sum to be received or paid in the future, adjusted by a prevailing or assumed interest rate.

Price   An amount of money that guides resource allocation and reflects the value of a good or service. Prices are transmitted by markets through which producers make decisions about what factors of production to use, and consumers decide what to consume.

Price ceiling   A legally set, maximum price (price control), designed to keep prices in a particular market below the equilibrium price.

Price elasticity of demand   The sensitivity of demand for a product to changes in its price.

Price elasticity of supply   The sensitivity of supply of a product to changes in its price.

Price index   See *Consumer Price Index; Index number.*

Price leadership   The practice of a single firm in an industry announcing a price change and other firms following suit.

Price stability   Price policy that aims to counter wide fluctuations in aggregate price levels. During a period of high inflation, for example, governments seeking price stability adopt anti-inflationary measures such as credit withdrawal, higher interest rates, and decreased government spending (or increased taxes).

Price wars Progressive price cutting to increase sales.

Primitive accumulation A way of accumulating wealth that fuels class conflict. In particular, the early formation of capital that accompanied the development of capitalism, often characterized by piracy and plunder.

Product differentiation Business strategy in which substitute products retain some distinctive difference. Means of differentiating products include brand names, coloring, packaging, or advertising.

Production possibilities curve Graph that illustrates scarcity and opportunity cost by showing that whenever society chooses to have more of one type of good, it must sacrifice some of another type of good.

Productivity (of labor) The output produced per unit of input (output per hour of work).

Profits Excess of revenues over costs. Normal profits are equal to the opportunity costs of management. Economic profits are the profits above the normal profit. Theoretically, in pure competition, economic profits equal zero in the long run. However, in imperfect market structures, they do not.

Progressive income tax Tax that claims an ever-increasing percentage of income as the income level rises.

Property Tangible or intangible possession that may be used to produce some product or aid in the selling of the product. Certain legal rights are attached to this "private property."

Property rights In capitalism, where productive property is privately owned, owners' rights to control the use of these productive resources. See *Possessions*.

Protectionism Policy that institutes high tariffs on incoming goods, so as to preserve domestic industry. Protectionism was prevalent during mercantilism. See *Infant industry; Tariff*.

Public debt The amount of outstanding federal debt held by individuals, corporations, and nonfederal government agencies.

Public goods Goods or resources that benefit the general public and are not necessarily directly paid for by all those who use them. Examples are street signs and public schools.

Public sector Local, state, and federal governmental offices, organizations, and institutions.

Putting-out system Labor system in which an owner would give workers the necessary materials and pay the worker to make a finished product. Replaced the handicraft type of industry and marked the emergence of private capital.

Quantity demanded The specific number of units of a product in the economy that is desired by economic agents at a given price level.

Quantity supplied The specific number of units of a product in the economy that is provided by producers at a given price level.

Quantity theory of money Theory that the quantity of money in the economy largely determines the level of prices. Stated as $MV = PQ$, where M is the quantity of money, V is the income velocity of money, P is the price level, and Q is real national income. The theory postulates that V is largely determined by institutional factors and Q is determined by factor supplies and technology; hence changes in M will be reflected in proportionate changes in P.

Quotas Limits on the quantities of goods imported or exported.

Radical economists Economists who are critical of classical and neoclassical theory and view economic problems as resulting directly from the capitalist system itself. Thus, the only serious relief to these problems is a change of economic system.

Rational expectations An economics-based theory about the nature of economic agents, stating that all agents are rational, logical, and aware of what is best for them and what the consequences of decisions and developments in the economy will mean for their well-being. Agents will act logically to take advantage of changes in the economy and enhance their position.

Real wages Wages measured from a specific point; wages that reflect the rate of inflation. If a worker's wage level increases 10 percent and inflation increases 10 percent in the same period of time, then we say that the real wage remains the same. Usually contrasted with money wages, which in the example would reflect only the 10 percent increase in the worker's wage.

Recession A slowing down of economic activity, resulting in an increase in unemployment and in excess industrial capacity. Less severe than a depression. Sometimes defined in the United States in terms of a decline in GDP for two or more successive quarters of a year.

Regulation Q Federal regulation placing a ceiling on interest rates payable by banks on deposits. This regulation has been phased out.

Relations of production The relationships among people in the production process, especially the class structure (for example, slave/slaveowner, serf/lord, laborer/capitalist).

Rent (1) Payment for the services of a factor of production. (2) Payment for the use of land.

Reserve army (industrial) A term developed by Marx to describe the functioning of capitalism in which worker strength was greatly decreased, in proportion to the amount of unemployment.

Reserve currency A currency that is accepted in settlement of international exchanges.

Reserve requirement In banking, the fraction of public deposits that a bank holds in reserves.

Ricardo, David One of the reformers of classical liberalism, developed by Adam Smith. Ricardo's analysis was based on an economy composed of many small enterprises.

Savings All income received by households and not spent on the consumption of goods and services.

Say's law The doctrine (named after J. B. Say) that "supply creates its own demand."

The production of one good adds to both aggregate supply and aggregate demand. In this nonmonetary world, depression and mass unemployment are not possible.

Scarcity Inability of a society to produce or secure enough goods to satisfy all the wants, needs, and desires people have for these goods.

Seasonal unemployment Joblessness created by changing seasonal conditions or demand.

Services Duties (or work) for others that do not necessarily render a good but are nevertheless worth payment.

Sherman Antitrust Act A major U.S. antitrust law passed in 1890 prohibiting "every contract, combination in the form of trust or otherwise or conspiracy, in restraint of trade or commerce," and prescribing penalties for monopoly.

Shortage Disequilibrium situation wherein quantity demanded exceeds quantity supplied. In such a situation, price will tend to rise until it reaches an equilibrium level (where quantity supplied equals quantity demanded).

Short-run For a firm, the period in which some inputs are fixed.

Smith, Adam Economist who in 1776 published *The Wealth of Nations*, noting the foundation of a new individualist philosophy, classical liberalism.

Socialism An economic system in which property and the distribution of wealth are subject to control by the community.

Special Drawing Rights (SDRs) A bookkeeping device created by the International Monetary Fund to increase international liquidity. SDRs may be drawn by each country in proportion to its original fund contribution.

Special Enterprise Zones (SEZs) Areas in China, mostly in Southern China in coastal cities, where foreign companies are able to invest and operate freely as if they were in a capitalist market economy.

Specialization (of labor) Methods of production in which individual workers specialize in particular tasks rather than making everything for themselves.

Speculative demand for money   Function that describes the amount of assets held by households and firms in the form of money, relative to the interest rate.

Stagflation   Term coined in the 1970s to describe the coexistence of unemployment (stagnation) and inflation afflicting the United States and other countries.

Standard of deferred payment   Acceptability as future payment; a characteristic of money.

Stock   Shares of ownership in a corporation. May be common stock and/or preferred stock.

Store of value   An asset that holds value into the future. Money has this characteristic.

Structural (budget) deficit   The federal budget deficit which remains if the economy is at full employment.

Structural unemployment   Type of permanent unemployment that stems from shifting demand and/or technological changes requiring new skills for workers. Disparities in geographic locations of workers and jobs also contribute to this phenomenon.

Structuralist model   A model that assumes that domestic political and economic factors affect development.

Superstructure   Society's ideals, institutions, and ideologies, including laws, politics, culture, ethics, religions, morals, and philosophy that, according to Marx, support the economic base of society and the existing mode of production.

Supply   The amount of goods or services produced and available for purchase.

Supply curve   The set of all points representing the amount of goods or services that will be offered at different price levels.

Supply shock   Events that are unexpected and that limit the aggregate supply of goods and services.

Supply, law of   Economic principle that says the lower the price, the lower the quantity supplied, all other things being constant. Price and quantity supplied are positively related.

Surplus   A state of disequilibrium wherein quantity supplied exceeds quantity demanded. Price will tend to fall until it reaches an equilibrium (where quantity supplied equals quantity demanded).

Surplus value   In Marxian terms, the amount by which the value of a worker's output exceeds his or her wage. Hence, a source of profit for the capitalist.

Tariff   A tax applied to imports.

Terms of trade   The prices of a country's exports in relation to its imports. Any improvement in a country's terms of trade means a relative increase in its export prices, while a deterioration in its terms of trade indicates a relative increase in its import prices.

Theory   A cogently expressed group of related propositions declared as principles for explanation of a set of phenomena.

Total cost   The cost of all factors of production involved in producing one good.

Total fixed costs   The sum of all costs that do not change with varying output (in the short run). A firm incurs these costs regardless of production levels.

Total revenue   The amount of funds credited to the firm for sales of its output; price multiplied by units sold.

Total variable costs   The sum of all costs that fluctuate in relation to the activity of the firm and the productive process. The two major variable costs are labor and resources.

Transactions demand for money   Function that indicates the amount of money balances that individuals desire for purchasing purposes. Considered relatively constant, given a level of income and consumption pattern.

Transfer multiplier   The ratio that relates the change in the equilibrium level of income to a change in government transfer payments.

Transfer payments   Government payments to individuals that are not compensation for currently productive activity.

Trough (of business cycle)   The low point of the business cycle, representing the slowest level of business activity. Following this low point, the cycle begins an upward swing.

Unemployed A person sixteen years of age or older who is not working and is available for work and has made an effort to find work during the previous four weeks.

Unemployment A condition wherein workers who are ordinarily part of the labor force are unable to find work at prevailing wages. May take any of five specific forms: (1) Frictional unemployment arises from workers changing jobs, etc.; all labor markets have this kind. (2) Seasonal unemployment results from changing seasonal demand and supply for labor. (3) Structural unemployment results from changing or shifting product demand; i.e., it is a function of geographic and job skill mobility. (4) Cyclical unemployment arises from changes in demand of labor during the business cycle. (5) Hidden unemployment consists of frustrated potential workers who have given up looking for a job.

Unemployment rate The number of people unemployed expressed as a percentage of the total number of people in the labor force.

Unit of account A measure of value or the standard way of quoting prices and keeping accounts in an economy.

Value added Strictly, the value of a final product less the cost of production.

Variable costs Costs that fluctuate due to the activity of the firm and the productive process. The two major variable costs are labor and resources.

Vertical merger Companies in different stages of an industry merge.

Wage and price controls Mandatory regulation of wages and prices by the government in order to contain inflation. The U.S. government applied such controls to certain segments of the economy with varying force from 1971 to 1974.

Wages The price paid for units of labor or service supplied in the market per unit of time.

World Bank A bank that assists poor countries by lending or by insuring private loans to finance development projects. Officially the International Bank for Reconstruction and Development (IBRD) established after World War II to promote postwar reconstruction and development of underdeveloped countries.

Photo Credits

Chapter 1, p. 5: AP Wide World Photos; p. 13: SuperStock, Inc.

Chapter 2, p. 23: CALIVIN AND HOBBES © 1990 Watterson. Reprinted with permission of UNIVERSAL PRESS SYNDICATE. All rights reserved.

Chapter 3, p. 37: Corbis- NY.

Chapter 4, p. 53: © 1974 by Noah's Ark, Inc. (for Ramparts Magazine). Reprinted by permission of Bruce W. Stilson.

Chapter 7, p. 107: David Young- Wolff/PhotoEdit Inc.; p. 115: The Terry Wild Studio, Inc.

Chapter 8, p. 153: Michael Newman/PhotoEdit Inc.

Chapter 9, p. 180: Mary Kate Denny/PhotoEdit Inc.

Chapter 10, p. 215: © 2004 by Nicole Hollander.

Chapter 11, p. 232: CORBIS- NY.

Chapter 12, p. 260: Bonnie Kamin/PhotoEdit Inc.; p. 274: Cartoon by Matt Wuerker "Affirmative Action" from "Field Guide to the U.S. Economy: A Compact and Irreverent Guide to Economic Life in America" by Jonathan Teller-Eisberg, Nancy Folbre, James Heintz with the Center for Popular Economics. Reprinted with permission. All rights reserved. The Cartoonist Group.

Chapter 13, p. 285: TOLES © 1993 The New Republic. Reprinted with permission of UNIVERSAL PRESS SYNDICATE. All rights reserved.

Chapter 14, p. 322: © Hulton Deutsch Collection/CORBIS All Rights Reserved.

Chapter 16, p. 407: Toles © 2009 The Washington Post. Reprinted with permission of Universal Uclick. All right reserved.

Chapter 18, p. 461: Toles © 2009 The Washington Post. Reprinted with permission of Universal Uclick. All right reserved.

Chapter 20, p. 508: Eddie Stanger/PhotoEdit Inc.

Chapter 21, p. 527: Mark Richards/PhotoEdit Inc.

Chapter 22, p. 577: Paul Conklin/PhotoEdit Inc.

Name Index

He Zuefeng, 529
Hegel, Georg Wilhelm Friedrich, 51
Heilbroner, Robert, 20
    The Making of Economic Society, 20
Hernandez, Macario, 542–543
Hood, Robin, 28
Henry VIII, 25–26
Houghton, Walter E., 66
    The Victorian Frame of Mind, 66
Hoyt, Katherine, 491
Hufbauer, Gary Clyde, 489
Hume, David, 34
Hunt, E.K, 10, 21
    Property and Prophets, 10
Husain, M.F., 546
Hutcheson, Francis, 34

Jacobs, Andrew, 527, 529
Jackson, Thomas Penfield, 266
Jefferson, Thomas, 247
Johnson, Lyndon, 275
Jordan, Michael, 239

Katz, Lawrence, 459–460, 462
Keen, Maurice, 26
    The Outlaws of Medieval Legend, 26
Kennedy, John F., 269
Kerry, John, 13
Keynes, John Maynard, 2, 11, 60, 62, 64, 70–72,
    79–81, 314, 321–347, 376–377, 413, 425,
    454, 551, 579, 585–588
    The End of Laissez–Faire, 94
    The General Theory of Employment, Interest, and
        Money, 339, 348, 368, 399–400, 418
Khrushchev, Nikita, 449, 451–453
King Harold, 26
King Henry VIII, 25–26
King John, 26
Kirk, Ron, 488
Kollar-Kotelly, Colleen, 266
Kondratieff, Nikolai, 85
Kristof, Nicholas D., 519–520
Krober, Annette, 520
Kroc, Ray, 180
Krugman, Paul, 13, 582
    The Great Unraveling: Losing Our Way in the
        New Century, 13
Kuhn, Thomas, 9
    The Structure of Scientific Revolutions, 9

Landler, Mark, 511, 515
Lardy, Nicholas R., 515
Lee, Thea, 491
Leonhardt, David, 449–450, 453
Locke, John, 34

Long Feng, 528
Lowe, Jack, 548

Macfie, A.L., 589
Malthus, Thomas, 2, 44, 455
    Principles of Political Economy, 44
Mao Tse-tung, 561–562
Mao Zedong, 528
Marshall, Alfred, 2, 7, 9
    Principles of Economics, 7
Marx, Karl, 2, 11, 17–19, 32, 46, 48–63, 74, 80–83,
    88, 322, 551, 554, 582
    Capital, 48, 50, 51, 58
    The Communist Manifesto, 48, 50, 55, 58–59
    Critique of Political Economy, 53
    The Economic and Philosophic Manuscripts of 1844, 55
    The German Ideology, 17, 40, 50, 72
    The Grundrisse, 55
McCain, John, 12, 580
McCloskey, Deidre, 321
McNally, David, 25
    Political Economy and the Rise of Capitalism, 25
Meany, George, 494
Mellon, Andrew, 320, 322
Mill, John Stuart, 2, 48, 313
    Principles of Political Economy, 48
Miller, G. Tyler, 574–576
Morgan, J.P., 68

Nader, Ralph, 14
Newton, Isaac, 84
Nixon, Richard M., 401, 513
Nordhaus, William, 440

Obama, Barack, 13, 79, 100, 275–276, 403, 449,
    453, 455–458, 461–462, 489, 495, 514, 579,
    586–588
O'Connor, Sandra Day, 267
O'Neill, June, 458
Orszag, Peter, 458

Parkin, Michael, 429
Parks, James, 490
Paulson, Henry M., 522
Perot, Ross, 490
Phelps, Edmund, 436
Phillips, A.W., 435
Pigou, Arthur Cecil, 580, 585–589
Pitt, Brad, 211
Plender, John, 49
Polanyi, Karl, 35, 45
    The Great Transformation, 35, 45
Porritt, Jonathan, 571
Pollin, Robert, 14

Subject Index

International trade, 466–474
  and developing countries, 529–530
  issues, 487–493
  modern theory of, 475–487
International Working Men's Association, 50
Investment, 96, 329–330
  changes in the multiplier and, 339–341
  two-sector model and, 336–339
  defined, 337
  foreign, 344
  as an injection, 339–340
  interest rates and, 337
  planned and actual, 338–339
Invisible hand, 39, 41–42, 44–45, 82, 133, 159–160
Involuntary part–time workers, 318,
        See Unemployment
Iraq War, 362

Japan, 493, 558–560

Keiretsu, 559
Key currency, See Reserve currency
Keynesian cross, 338
Keynesian economics, 10–13, 321–345
  multiplier analysis, 324–328, 339–341
  resurgence of, 323
  role of injections, 327
  role of leakages, 326
Keynesian liquidity trap, 394–395
Keynesian model, 330–345
  equilibrium wage, 424
  fixed wage, 424
Keynesian Revolution, 321
Keynesian theory,
  consumption expenditure in, 324
  fundamental psychological law, 331
  liquidity trap, 394–395
  money and, 391–395
  multiplier and, 324–328
Keynesian multiplier, 324–341, 392
Knights of Labor, 231
Korean War, 99

Labor, 19, See also Workers
  early development of labor force, 31
  influence of labor incomes, 210–211
  in Quantity Theory of Money, 315–316
  in radical analysis of capitalism, 13
Laborers, 40
Labor market, 234–235, 422
Labor theory of value, 55
  Marx's use of, 55
Labor unions, 7, 236–241
  and corporations in the 21st century, 241–242
  economic effects of, 234–238
  growth of, 235–236

history of, 231–234
  problems with, 231
  future of, 238
Lags,
  action lag, 399
  implementation, 356
  inside lag, 399
  in fiscal policy, 356
  legislative, 356
  in monetary policy, 399
  outside lag, 399
  reaction lag, 356
  recognition lag, 356, 399
Laissez–faire, 33, 44–45, 322, 553
  definition of, 33
  and financial crisis, 78–79
  flowering of, 64–65
  and free trade, 68
  Keynesian critique of, 70–72
  socialist critique of, 48–62
  in the United States, 68–70
  in the Victorian Age, 66
Land, 19
Landowners (landlords), 40
Law of diminishing returns, 83–84,
        137–140
Law of specialization, 137–140
Leakages, 326, 329–330
  in the money creation process, 389
Liberal economics, 12
  and changes in the global
        community, 576
  elements of, 12–13
  and government regulation, 247
Liberal market economies, 551, 555–556
Limited liability, 222
Liquidity, 377
Liquidity preference, 377
Liquidity trap, 377–378, 394–395
Long run, 136
Long term capital management, 402
Lorenz curve, 206–208

Maastricht Treaty, 487
Macroeconomic goals, 287–300
Macroeconomic policy, 295–296
Macroeconomics, 285
  defined, 285, 287
  goals of, 287–300
  tools of, 301
Magna Carta, 26
Manor, 21
  decline of, 25–26
Marginal cost, 148, See Cost
  pricing, 263–264
Marginal external benefit, 256